PHILIPPINE DUCHESNE
PIONEER ON THE AMERICAN FRONTIER
(1769 - 1852)

COMPLETE WORKS

PHILIPPINE DUCHESNE
PIONEER ON THE AMERICAN FRONTIER
(1769 - 1852)

COMPLETE WORKS

VOLUME 1

Edited by
Marie France Carreel, RSCJ, and Carolyn Osiek, RSCJ

Translated and Edited by Frances Gimber, RSCJ

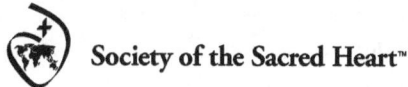

©2019 Brepols Publishers, Turnhout, Belgium 2017.
All rights reserved. No part of this publication may be reproduced, stored in a retrieval system, or transmitted, in any form or by any means, electronic, mechanical, photocopying, recording, or otherwise without the prior permission of the publisher.

ISBN: 978-0-9971329-4-6 (Volume 1)
Printed in the U.S.

Society of the Sacred Heart
www.rscjinternational.org

TABLE OF CONTENTS

Acknowledgements	1
Preface to the English Edition	3
General Introduction	7

VOLUME ONE

CHAPTER I	1769-1818—Before the Great Departure	35
	Introduction	37
	Duchesne Family Tree	45
	Jouve and Perier Family Trees	46
	Letters	47
	Account 1: Story of Sainte-Marie d'En-Haut (SSM)	47
	Journal 1: Journal of the House of Grenoble 1804-1813 (JG)	83
	Journal 2: Journal of the House of the Religious of the Sacred Heart in Paris 1815-1817 (JP)	255
CHAPTER II	1818-1821—The First Foundations	291
	Introduction	293
	Letters	303
CHAPTER III	1822-1828—In Full Activity	557
	Introduction	559
	Letters	567

ACKNOWLEDGEMENTS

Our gratitude goes first of all to Clare Pratt and Kathleen Conan, former superiors general of the Society of the Sacred Heart, who confided to us the publication of the whole collection of the writings of Saint Philippine Duchesne. It also goes to Anne Leonard, general archivist in 1998; by drawing attention to the importance of these texts for our spirituality, she opened the way for our research.

We especially thank the following archivists for their collaboration: Margaret Phelan, general archivist, Federica Palombo and Alice Usai, Society of the Sacred Heart, Rome; Maryvonne Duclaux, Society of the Sacred Heart, France; Robert Bonfils, SJ, Jesuit Archives, France; David Miros, Jesuit Archives, Central-South Province, Saint Louis, Missouri; Father Veissier and Brigitte Tandonnet, Archives of the Archdiocese of Bordeaux; Father Edmond Coffin and Frédérique Corporon, Diocesan Archives of Grenoble; Marie Françoise Bois Delatte, Municipal Library of Grenoble; Anne Boulenc, Municipal Archives of Grenoble; Rena Schergen, Archdiocesan Archives, Saint Louis, Missouri; and Andrew H. Rea, Vincentian Library, DePaul University, Chicago.

Our gratitude also extends to Marc Estrangin, direct descendant of Amelie Duchesne de Mauduit, sister of Philippine, who was so often called upon for verification of biographical notes, and whose welcome in the familial home at Grâne is always available. We also thank Henry de Pazzis for having shared with us his research on the Duchesne-Perier family.

This work appears at the anniversary of the arrival of the first Religious of the Sacred Heart in the United States. We are grateful to Mr. Luc Jocqué of Brepols Publishers for his collaboration and for having given us support and encouragement all along the last months of preparation of the original French edition.

Marie-France Carreel, RSCJ
Carolyn Osiek, RSCJ

PREFACE TO THE ENGLISH EDITION

BIOGRAPHIES OF PHILIPPINE DUCHESNE

Because there are already several biographies of Rose Philippine Duchesne, this publication does not give extensive biographical information. Two shorter and more popular biographies were written in English in the early and middle twentieth century: Marjory Erskine, RSCJ, *Mother Philippine Duchesne* (Longmans Green, New York, 1926) and M. K. Richardson, *Redskin Trail* (Burns Oates, London, 1952). T. Gavan Duffy wrote his memorable and still-quoted pamphlet, *Heart of Oak* (Saint Louis, 1940) at the time of Mother Duchesne's beatification. But it was the important study published in 1957 by Louise Callan, RSCJ, that remains the definitive biography today.[1] When she was preparing to write this excellent biography, Mother Callan was not allowed access to the whole collection of letters; she was denied access especially to any in which Philippine expressed criticism of those in authority. In later years, all of Philippine's correspondence was made available for research.

Later, Catherine M. Mooney published an important biographical study from a different perspective: *Philippine Duchesne: A Woman with the Poor* (Paulist Press, 1990; reprint Wipf and Stock, 2007). For a recent brief sketch of Philippine's life and significance, see Carolyn Osiek, RSCJ, *Saint Rose Philippine Duchesne: A Heart on Fire across Frontiers* (Society of the Sacred Heart, 2017).

Declared Venerable on December 9, 1909, by Pius X, Rose Philippine Duchesne was beatified on May 12, 1940, by Pope Pius XII, and canonized on July 3, 1988, by Pope John Paul II. In 1981, in view of her canonization on July 3, 1988, Jeanne de Charry, RSCJ, undertook the publication, in four volumes, of the correspondence between Madeleine

---

[1] L. Callan, *Philippine Duchesne, Frontier Missionary of the Sacred Heart*, Westminster, Maryland: Newman Press, 1957. In 1964, a shortened version was published under the same title, translated into several languages: Spanish by M.T. Guevara, RSCJ, in 1964; French by Jacqueline Erulin in 1989; Polish by Maria Zeranska in 2008; and Korean by Maria Cecilia Amarante, RSCJ, in 2013.

Sophie Barat and Philippine Duchesne.[2] This collection includes 146 letters of Philippine, spanning the years 1806 to 1852. In 2001, Chantal Paisant, who specializes in French missionary writings, edited *Les Années pionnières, Lettres et Journaux des premières missionnaires du Sacré-Cœur aux États-Unis (1818-1823)*, collecting for this period Philippine Duchesne's letters to Sophie Barat, to her family and to priests, as well as writings of six of the first Religious of the Sacred Heart in America.[3] This volume remains untranslated into English.

Translation

It is common in translation projects to speak of two complementary but differing principles guiding the work of translation: formal correspondence, whereby effort is made to remain as close as possible to the original text while rendering it comprehensible in the new language; and dynamic equivalence, whereby more latitude is allowed and more freedom is taken to conform to the fluency of the new language, all the while conveying the meaning of the original.

This complete English edition of the writings of Rose Philippine Duchesne seeks to render as faithfully as possible the sense of her own style and ways of thinking, while at the same time producing a text that reveals the person of the writer. Effort has been made toward consistency of spelling with regard to proper names, even though there are often differences in the original texts.

The word for Native Americans has been rendered throughout as "Indian." In the early years, the most common term used was *les Sauvages*, which does not have the negative connotations in French that "savages" has in English. Already in the early years in America, however, Philippine began to use the expression *les Indiens*, which was probably a direct borrowing from English in use among the white inhabitants of Missouri.

The common way to refer to persons of African descent in the letters is *un Nègre*, in feminine form, *une Négresse*, occasionally *les noirs*. While these terms are no longer in use today, they have been maintained here for accuracy. Unless the context indicates, there is no way to be certain that the reference is to a free or enslaved person.

---

2 J. de Charry, ed., *Correspondence, Saint Madeleine Sophie Barat - Saint Philippine Duchesne*. 4 volumes, Translated by B. Hogg, J. Sweetman, A. O'Leary, M. Coke, Rome, 1988, 1989, 1992, 2000.

3 Ch. Paisant, *Les Années pionnières. Lettres et Journaux des premières missionnaires du Sacré-Cœur aux États-Unis (1818-1823)*, Cerf, Paris, 2001.

The translations that appear here have sometimes drawn on several earlier sources: those already done by Louise Callan in her biography, the translators of Jeanne de Charry's edition of the correspondence between Madeleine Sophie Barat and Philippine Duchesne, the M.A. thesis of Anne Webster, RSCJ,[4] and anonymous transcriptions and translations of Philippine Duchesne's letters in the Callan collection of the USC archives. At other times, the translations are original to this publication.

Frances Gimber, RSCJ, and Carolyn Osiek, RSCJ

---

4   *The Correspondence between Bishop Joseph Rosati and Philippine Duchesne*, translated and annotated. Saint Louis University, 1950.

GENERAL INTRODUCTION

In 1856, the superior general of the Society of the Sacred Heart, Madeleine Sophie Barat,[5] wrote in these terms to Amelie Jouve,[6] superior in Grand Coteau, Louisiana:

> Do not forget to collect everything relating to your aunt Philippine; *I would very much like to have her life written and published before the good God makes an end of me; it would be an immense consolation for me to leave behind this edifying life.* Therefore, do all in your power, daughter, to obtain these precious documents; later there will be no one to render this service for us; it is already quite late....[7]

Without delay,[8] Amelie Jouve undertook the work and drafted a notice entitled *"Life of our holy Mother Duchesne,"* which was neither printed nor published.[9]

The present work, *"Philippine Duchesne, Pioneer on the American Frontier. Complete Works,"* fulfills that appeal to her memory. Several written works have preceded it, but they have used the body of her writings only in the measure in which they were known at the time. In

---

5   Madeleine Sophie Barat (1779-1865), founder and first superior general of the Society of the Sacred Heart of Jesus, was canonized on May 24, 1925, by Pius XI. For a biography of Mother Barat, see A. Cahier, *Vie de la Vénérable Mère Barat*, Tomes I-II, Soye et Fils, Paris, 1884; M. Luirard, *Madeleine-Sophie Barat (1779-1865), Une éducatrice au cœur du monde, au cœur de Dieu*, Nouvelle Cité, Montrouge, 1999; Phil Kilroy, *Madeleine Sophie Barat, A Life 1779-1865*, Cork University, 2000.

6   Amelie Jouve, RSCJ (1799-1880), entered the novitiate in 1821 in Paris, made her first vows in 1823 and her profession in 1829. In 1847, she left for America and visited her aunt in Saint Charles, before going to Saint-Vincent, Canada. She was named superior in 1848, visitatrix and vicar of the West in 1855, and superior at Grand Coteau in 1860. Having returned to France in 1879, she was vicar in Orléans, where she died on January 18, 1880.

7   Excerpt of a letter addressed to Mother Amelie Jouve, Vicar of America, Paris, April 27, 1856, AGSC, C-VII 2 Duchesne-life, Box 2, *Blessed Philippine Duchesne, Personal documents*. The passage in italics was underlined by Mother Barat.

8   In 1857, Mother Jouve collected "notes and details that were to serve for the publication of the life of her venerable aunt." Unsigned testimony, Selma, Alabama, April 26. AGSC C-VII 2. Duchesne-life, Box 3, *Testimony to her life and virtues, given by old pupils and secular friends*.

9   Amelie Jouve, *Life of our holy Mother Duchesne*, AGSC C-VII 2 Duchesne-life, Box 3.

1878, Father Louis Baunard wrote *l'Histoire de Madame Duchesne*.[10] In 1913, there were still unknown documents or documents of uncertain attribution, according to the attestation of the superior general, Janet Erskine Stuart:

> I the undersigned, attest that to my knowledge there do not exist in the archives of the motherhouse or in our different houses writings attributed to Venerable Mother Duchesne besides the following, already examined in view of her cause: 1°) *Journal* attributed to the Venerable, at Saint Charles; 2°) Her letters; 3°) Manuscript of Mother Amelie Jouve on her sojourn in America; 4°) Manuscript written by the Venerable, in which is told the story of Sainte-Marie, *Story of Sainte-Marie d'En-Haut*.[11]

In 1957, Mother Louise Callan published *Philippine Duchesne, Frontier Missionary of the Sacred Heart*.[12] When she was preparing to write this excellent biography, access to the whole collection of letters was not authorized, fifty of them being considered part of the "secret archives of the motherhouse, reserved to the superior general." After the Second Vatican Council, changes in mentality and in governance allowed them to be consulted. One of these was the letter of June 5, 1846, which lifted the long and trying silence between Philippine Duchesne and Sophie Barat.[13]

Declared Venerable on December 9, 1909, by Pius X, Philippine Duchesne was beatified on May 12, 1940, by Pius XII. In 1981, in view

---

10   Louis Baunard, *Histoire de Madame Duchesne, Religieuse de la Société du Sacré-Cœur de Jésus et Fondatrice des premières maisons de cette Société en Amérique*, Poussielgue, Paris, 1878. *The Life of Mother Duchesne, Religious of the Society of the Sacred Heart and Foundress of the First Houses of that Society in America*, translated by Lady Georgiana Fullerton, Roehampton, 1879. As if to underline its importance, the introduction specifies: "This history complements that of Mother Barat." The date of the death of Mrs. Rose Euphrosine Duchesne, Philippine's mother, is given there as 1793, not 1797. This erroneous date was repeated in other works and/or archival classifications.

11   Mount Anville, Dundrum, Dublin, June 22, 1913. AGSC C-VII 2) Duchesne-life, Box 3.

12   Louise Callan, *Philippine Duchesne, Frontier Missionary of the Sacred Heart*, Newman Press, Westminster Maryland, 1957. In 1964, a shortened version was published under the same title, translated into several languages. J. Érulin produced the French translation: Louise Callan, *Philippine Duchesne 1769-1852. Une femme, une pionnière, une sainte*, Ed. G. de Bussac, Clermont-Ferrand, 1989.

13   Although it is not possible to state the cause with certainty, it seems that this silence came about as the result of the suppression of the altar dedicated to Saint Francis Regis at Saint Ferdinand, and of the announcement of the closing of the house in Saint Charles. The manner in which Mother Galitzine had the decrees of the General Council of 1839 applied did not please Mother Duchesne, who expressed her disapproval thus: "I consider the visit of Mother Galitzine a scourge. Clothed with every power, she acted so as to wound the bishops, people both within and without; and the poor sisters like sheep let themselves be directed as if she had been the superior general herself." Letter September 10, 1847 to Mother Barat.

of her canonization, which took place on July 3, 1988, Sister Jeanne de Charry undertook the publication, in four volumes, of the correspondence between Madeleine Sophie Barat and Philippine Duchesne.[14] While the first volume contains only two letters from Philippine, written in 1806, the three others present 144, sent from Bordeaux and from America, from 1818 to 1852. In 2001, Chantal Paisant, who specializes in missionary writings, edited *Les Années pionnières, Lettres et Journaux des premières missionnaires du Sacré-Cœur aux États-Unis (1818-1823)*, collecting for this period Philippine Duchesne's letters to Sophie Barat, to her family and to priests, as well as writings of the first Religious of the Sacred Heart in America.[15]

These three publications—of Louise Callan, Jeanne de Charry and Chantal Paisant—offer a good number of the writings of Saint Philippine Duchesne. However, more than two thirds of the extant documents are not included. "To collect everything written by Philippine" has been our purpose, therefore, in order to determine how this uncommon personality is, today as yesterday, a woman for our times. The chronological presentation of the documents allows us to follow the episodes and events of the life of this missionary as they unfold.

Correspondence over a Lifetime

This epistolary work is composed of seven chapters. Chapter I is entitled "Before the Great Departure, 1797-1818." It can be seen as a kind of diptych—call and sending. It opens with the *Story of Sainte-Marie d'En-Haut*, the monastery where the meeting of Madeleine Sophie Barat and Philippine Duchesne took place.[16] The letters, the *Journal of Grenoble* and the *Journal of Paris* locate Philippine's family roots and her network of relationships. The reader discovers here her invincible desire to be sent far beyond the frontier to make the love of the Heart of Jesus known. One can also see the expansion of the newly founded Society of the Sacred Heart of Jesus and form an idea of the political and ecclesial context of France at the time. In 1818, five religious were sent

---

14 Jeanne de Charry, ed., *Correspondence, Saint Madeleine Sophie Barat - Saint Philippine Duchesne*. 4 volumes. Rome: Pontifical Gregorian University, 1979-1981. Translated by B. Hogg, J. Sweetman, A. O'Leary, M. Coke, Rome: Society of the Sacred Heart, 1988, 1989, 1992, 2000.
15 Chantal Paisant, *Les Années pionnières. Lettres et Journaux des premières missionnaires du Sacré-Cœur aux États-Unis (1818-1823)*, Cerf, Paris, 2001.
16 Anne Davidson, RSCJ, evoked this meeting beautifully and adroitly in her icon "The Meeting of Two Saints," Academy of the Sacred Heart, Saint Charles, Missouri.

to Louisiana, at the request of Bishop Dubourg:[17] Philippine Duchesne, Octavie Berthold,[18] Eugenie Audé,[19] Catherine Lamarre[20] and Marguerite Manteau.[21] They left Bordeaux on March 19 to embark on the *Rebecca*, at Royan, on March 22, 1818.

Chapter II, "1818-1821—The First Foundations," lets us follow the crossing of the Atlantic and the journey up the Mississippi, travel in the vast territory of Louisiana, to identify there the chief actors in evangelization and the difficulties the religious had to face to establish themselves in Upper Louisiana. Their foundation was initially foreseen for Saint Louis, but Bishop Dubourg sent them to Saint Charles, "the most remote

17   Louis Guillaume Dubourg (1766-1833) was born at Cap-Français, Saint-Domingue (today Cap-Haïtien, Haiti), studied in Bordeaux, and was ordained priest in 1790, in Paris. He sought refuge afterwards in Spain and embarked for Baltimore in 1794. Named president of Georgetown College by Bishop Carroll in 1796, he founded Saint Mary's College in Baltimore in 1798. He was ordained bishop of Louisiana in September 1815. While in Paris (1816-1817), he asked Mother Barat to send him some religious to teach catechism to indigenous girls. He returned to France in 1826, where he was named bishop, then archbishop of Besançon in 1833.

18   Octavie Celestine Berthold, RSCJ (1787-1833), was born on September 2, 1787, in Geneva, Switzerland, into a highly educated Calvinist family. In 1809, she left for Grenoble to be a teacher there. She converted to Catholicism and entered at Sainte-Marie d'En-Haut in 1814. She finished her novitiate in Paris, made her first vows on February 5, 1817, and her profession February 2, 1818, just before her departure for America. At first she was assistant and class mistress (1818-1827); then she became superior of the house at Saint Ferdinand (1827-1829). In 1830, she left for Saint Louis. Stricken with cancer of the face, she died on September 16, 1833, after eight years of suffering. Cf. Letter of Philippine to Sophie Barat, September 17, 1833; letter 1 to Eugenie Audé, end of 1833; *Vies des Religieuses du Sacré-Cœur en Amérique, État du Missouri et de la Louisiane* (VR), AGSC C-VII 2) c Duchesne-Writings about the history of the Society, Box 1.

19   Eugenie Audé, RSCJ (1795-1842), was born on January 1, 1795, at Moutiers, Savoy, entered at the Sacred Heart in Grenoble on November 25, 1815, and made her first vows on June 12, 1817, in Paris. She asked to go to Louisiana and made her profession on February 8, 1818, the very morning of the departure. In America, after having been at Saint Charles (1818-1819), then at Florissant (1819-1821), in August 1821, she founded with Mary Layton the house of Grand Coteau. In 1822, they were joined by Anna Xavier Murphy, who came from France, and Marguerite Manteau and Mary Ann Summers from Florissant. In 1825, at the request of Father Delacroix, she made another foundation at Saint Michael. In 1834, a cholera epidemic struck six religious. Eugenie cared for them and assisted at their deaths, all while attending to the needs of the boarding school. Her health was severely shaken. Named assistant general for America in 1834, she visited all the American houses, returned to France and remained there for health reasons. She founded the house in Marseille. In 1838, she was sent as superior to the Trinità dei Monti in Rome, where she died on March 6, 1842.

20   Catherine Lamarre, RSCJ, coadjutrix sister, was born in 1779, and made her profession in 1816 in Amiens. At the end of January 1818, she went to join Mother Duchesne in Paris, in order to be part of the founding community of the American houses. After Saint Charles (1818-1819), she was in Florissant from 1819 to 1827, then at City House, Saint Louis, until 1841, when she went back to Florissant. She died in 1845.

21   Marguerite Manteau, RSCJ, coadjutrix sister, was born in 1779. She entered the novitiate in Poitiers on October 17, 1807, and was sent to Niort, July 22, 1813. In February 1818, she joined Mother Duchesne in Poitiers. After having been in Saint Charles in 1818, and in Florissant in 1819, she left in 1823 for Grand Coteau, where she remained until her death in 1845.

village in the United States, on the Missouri, which is frequented only by those who trade with the Indians."²² He did not entrust them with the education of Indian girls but with that of Americans. The following year the community moved to Florissant, far from any city. In such a limited horizon, Philippine could not find advisers. Communications with the motherhouse in Paris became very difficult, for Bishop Dubourg had placed them far from the Mississippi, the only route linking them with a port of embarkation for France. Thus during the first year, the religious received no mail from Europe. In this New World, Philippine Duchesne's network of relationships found itself suddenly reduced alarmingly. Two years later the foundation of Grand Coteau, in Lower Louisiana, would be more favorable because of proximity to New Orleans. Two religious, Eugenie Audé and Mary Layton,²³ the first postulant who had entered in August 1820, were sent there in August 1821. Two others were meant to join them, but their departure from France was delayed, and they arrived in New Orleans only on February 2, 1822. Anna Murphy²⁴ went directly to Grand Coteau, while Lucile Mathevon²⁵ went to Saint Louis with Bishop Dubourg.

Chapter III, "1822-1828—At the height of activity," presents the development of the foundations in Lower Louisiana (Saint Michael in 1825, La Fourche in 1828) and in Missouri (Saint Louis in 1827, Saint Charles in 1828). In June 1823, two events in Missouri modified the ecclesial environment. The first was the arrival at Florissant of thirteen Jesuits, accompanied by three Negro slave couples. The second event was the installation of the Sisters of Loretto at the Barrens.²⁶ The bishop entrusted

22   Letter to Mother Barat, October 8, 1818.
23   Mary Layton, RSCJ, was born in Kentucky in 1802, and went with her family to the Barrens, in Perryville, Missouri. She entered the novitiate in Florissant on August 19, 1820; still a novice she left with Eugenie Audé to found the house at Grand Coteau, Louisiana, in 1821. She made her first vows there on June 6, 1822. She was not the first to enter the Society of the Sacred Heart in America, but she was the first to have remained. Subsequently she lived at City House, Saint Louis, and in 1845, at Saint Mary's Mission, Kansas, where she stayed until her death in 1876.
24   Anna Xavier Murphy, RSCJ, was born on July 27, 1793, in Cork, Ireland, a close relative of the bishop of that city. She entered the novitiate in Paris in May 1820. She made her first vows on November 6, 1821, with the goal of going to America. She arrived in New Orleans on February 2, 1822, left for Grand Coteau, and made her profession on May 14, 1822. She was superior there from 1825 until her death in 1836.
25   Lucile Mathevon, RSCJ (1793-1876), was a pupil at the Sacred Heart in Grenoble; her missionary vocation developed through contact with Philippine. She entered the novitiate in 1813 and made her profession in 1818 at Sainte-Marie d'En-Haut. She left for America in November 1821 and arrived at Florissant in April 1822. In 1828, with Mary Ann O'Connor, she reopened the house in Saint Charles. In 1841, she was the superior of the mission to the Potawatomi, transferred later to Saint Marys, Kansas. She remained there until her death, March 11, 1876.
26   The Sisters of Loretto at the Foot of the Cross were founded in 1812 in Kentucky by a Flemish priest, Father Charles Nerinckx.

them with small communities to serve the poor, which Philippine also wanted to foster.[27] The boarding school for little Indian girls was inaugurated at Florissant on April 6, 1825. A second foundation in Lower Louisiana was proposed for Saint Michael; Eugenie Audé went ahead with it before she had Mother Duchesne's consent, thinking she had been encouraged by Mother Barat, who sent her official authorization only on April 7, 1825, and named Philippine superior of all the American houses. The house at Saint Michael opened on October 31, 1825. The one in Saint Louis followed in May 1827, thanks to a donation from a wealthy landowner, Mr. John Mullanphy,[28] on condition of receiving twenty orphaned girls. The arrival of four religious from France, in September 1827, allowed the reopening of the house in Saint Charles in October 1828; Helene Dutour[29] was sent to La Fourche as superior of the convent left to the Society of the Sacred Heart by the Sisters of Loretto.

Chapter IV, "1829-1833—New growth and conflicts," shows the development of the houses in Missouri and Louisiana, as well as some new difficulties. Tensions and rivalries arose among the three superiors in Louisiana. Mother Dutour sought to bring the level of the studies in her school up to that of the other two schools instead of maintaining the program of a boarding school for middle class children, like the one in Saint Charles. Upon Mother Barat's express request, Philippine went to Saint Michael, at the end of the year 1829, in order to meet with the three superiors to try to find solutions to the ongoing problems. But she did not claim her authority and nothing was settled. Helene Dutour's enormous expenses led to the closing of the house in La Fourche in 1832. In addition, criticisms of Philippine's manner of governing were sent to the motherhouse by Eugenie Audé and some religious who had arrived recently in Missouri. Bishop Rosati[30] intervened then with

---

27 See Letter to Mother Barat, May 20, 1823.
28 John Mullanphy (1758-1833) was born in County Fremanagh, Ireland. In 1792, he emigrated to Philadelphia with his wife, Elizabeth Browne Mullanphy; he went to Baltimore, then to Frankfort, Kentucky, before settling in Saint Louis in 1804. A brilliant businessman, he was also a benefactor of social services including the "City House" of the Society of the Sacred Heart (1827) and the first hospital in the city, under the direction of the Sisters of Charity (1828). His son Bryan Mullanphy became mayor of Saint Louis in 1847. His daughters, Jane Mullanphy Chambers (1799-1891) and Anne Mullanphy Biddle (1800-1846), and their children were close to the Sacred Heart, either as pupils or parents and benefactors.
29 Helene Dutour, RSCJ (1787-1849), originally from Savoy, entered the novitiate in Grenoble on December 30, 1813, and made her profession on May 29, 1818. She left for America in 1827 and was the superior at La Fourche (1828-1831). She died in Natchitoches, January 1, 1849.
30 Joseph Rosati (1789-1843), a Lazarist from Naples, arrived in Baltimore with his confrere Félix de Andreis, on July 26, 1816. With him he founded the seminary of Saint Mary at the Barrens, near Saint Louis. In 1823, he became coadjutor bishop with Bishop Dubourg, then residing in New Orleans, and in 1826, bishop of the newly erected diocese of Saint Louis. He was a valuable support for Philippine Duchesne; he opposed the strong criticisms sent to

Mother Barat in order to maintain Philippine Duchesne in her role as superior of the American houses. The year 1833 was noteworthy for the death of Octavie Berthold—one of Philippine's companions from the beginning—and for the closing of the house of Sainte-Marie d'En-Haut in Grenoble. In 1834, Eugenie Audé was named assistant general for the houses of the Sacred Heart in America.

Chapter V, "1834-1839—Return to Florissant," presents the period when Philippine was replaced in Saint Louis by Mother Catherine Thiéfry[31] and was living in Florissant. She wrote regularly to Mother Audé, who was on a visit to France, to keep her *au courant* of the situation in the American houses, and she begged her insistently to come back. But it was Mother Elisabeth Galitzine[32] who was sent to America as visitatrix in charge of making sure the much disputed decrees of the General Council of 1839 were being obeyed. Philippine asked then to be superior no longer: she left Florissant to go to Saint Louis. Bishop Rosati returned to Europe soon after for health reasons.

Chapter VI, "1840-June 1842—The dream comes true," is the climax in Philippine Duchesne's missionary life. The call to teach the Indian girls of America that she received in 1806 became a reality in 1841. With the

---

Mother Barat asking that she be removed as superior of the American houses. Health reasons required him to leave America in September 1840. In 1841, he was named Apostolic Delegate to Haiti. He died in Rome in 1843, when he went there to give an account of his mission. Felix de Andreis, CM, born in 1778 in Demonte, in the Piedmont, was ordained priest in 1801, and was professor of Theology in Rome at Monte Citorio. He left from Bordeaux for Louisiana on June 13, 1816, with Fathers Acquaroni, Carretti, Ferrari, and Rosati, and founded Saint Mary's Seminary in the Barrens. He was master of novices, first Lazarist provincial in America, and also became vicar general of Bishop Dubourg. In December 1819, he gave a retreat to the religious at the farm. He died in Saint Louis in 1820.

31 Catherine Thiéfry, RSCJ, was born in Belgium in 1792; she made profession in 1825. In 1830 she was superior at Florissant, then mistress of novices in Saint Louis in 1834. She left later for New York (1841), then Sugar Creek (1842), and Natchitoches (1848), where she died in 1867.

32 Elisabeth Galitzine, RSCJ (1795-1843), was born on February 22, 1795, in Saint Petersburg, into a princely family of the Orthodox Church. She converted to Catholicism in 1815. Directed by Father Rozaven, SJ, she entered the Sacred Heart in Metz in 1826, and made her novitiate at Conflans, near Paris. She made her first vows on December 29, 1828, at the Trinità dei Monti, in Rome, and her profession on February 2, 1832. Returning to France, she was named secretary general in 1833. At the General Council of 1839, she was the principal author of the decrees so soon disputed. Elected assistant general, charged with visiting the houses in America, she arrived there on August 31, 1840, and relieved Philippine of her role as superior. She visited the houses, went to New York to prepare for a foundation there, then went to the Potawatomi mission. She moved the novitiate from Saint Ferdinand to McSherrystown, Pennsylvania, planned the foundation of Saint-Jacques de l'Achigan, near Montreal, and returned to France on April 19, 1842. She was back in New York as visitatrix, on July 25, 1843; she stopped at McSherrystown and Saint Louis and went to Saint Michael to spend the winter. She died there of yellow fever on December 8, 1843. Cf. Ch. Paisant, "Élisabeth Galitzine, Russe convertie, première provinciale d'Amérique des religieuses du Sacré-Cœur," in *Histoires et Missions chrétiennes N°21*, Éd. Karthala, Paris, Mars 2012, p. 141-171.

support of her superior general and the Jesuits of Missouri, Philippine reached the mission at Sugar Creek. But her presence there was short: her health and her inability to learn the language of the Potawatomi obliged her to return to Saint Charles.

Chapter VII, "June 1842-1852—When the grain of wheat falls to the ground," covers the last stage of her life: a life of prayer, of meetings with pupils or alumnae, making church linen or work for the Indian missions. In 1846, she intervened unsuccessfully with Mother Barat to avoid the closing of the house in Florissant. Her correspondence became less frequent. In 1847, she received a visit from her niece, Mother Amelie Jouve, en route to Canada. A final visit, on the eve of her death, was that of Anna du Rousier, who was sent to visit the North American houses before going to make the first Sacred Heart foundation in Chile.[33]

Historical Interest

The publication of these letters aims at making the life of Saint Philippine Duchesne accessible by means of her writings. It allows Religious of the Sacred Heart of Jesus to take possession of this constitutive treasure of their spirituality and to facilitate translation into different languages.[34] This heritage is also part of the patrimony of those who are members of the great family of the Sacred Heart: alumnae and alumni, associates, friends, co-workers, and base communities.

To the spiritual value of these texts is added a historical interest. The publication is addressed also particularly to historians. It represents an important contribution to the history of French Catholicism in the nineteenth century and to that of the beginnings of the American church. Researchers can consider it a "logbook," however modest, of the progressive establishment of the Catholic Church amid populations already evangelized by Protestants or still devoted to the gods of the native peoples.

---

33 Anna Pélagie du Rousier, RSCJ (1806-1880), made her religious profession on June 10, 1831. She was mistress general of the boarding school in Turin, then superior of the house and mistress of novices; she went to Paris in 1848, and there headed the boarding school at the Hôtel Biron. In 1851, she was named visitatrix of the fifteen houses of North America. On August 5, 1853, she left New York to go to found the first house of the Sacred Heart in Santiago, Chile. See M. de Canecaude, *La Vie voyageuse et missionnaire de la Révérende Mère Anna du Rousier, religieuse du Sacré-Cœur, 1806-1880*, Beauchesne, Paris, 1932; M. F. Carreel, "Plein Cap pour Santiago, avec Anna du Rousier, RSCJ, (1853)," in Ch. Paisant, ed., *La mission au féminin*, Brepols, Turnhout, 2009, pp. 287-342; Alexandrine de La Taille, *Educar a la francesa: Anna du Rousier y el impacto del Sagrado Corazón en la mujer chilena* (1806-1880), Ediciones Universidad Católica de Chile, Santiago, 2012.

34 The 2000 Religious of the Sacred Heart, living in forty-one countries and five continents, speak fifty-nine official or local languages.

For American readers these documents constitute a valuable source of the history of Missouri and the missionary church on the American frontier during the first half of the nineteenth century. Along the way, they provide an answer to questions that certain researchers are posing today, among others: why so many women in Europe in the nineteenth century wanted to be missionaries, to cross continents and frontiers? While some French historians, like Claude Langlois and Élisabeth Dufourcq, have formulated answers to this type of question, their assessment may have to be reformulated through contact with Philippine Duchesne, an outstanding figure.

As Sarah A. Curtis emphasizes, the study of women missionaries did not belong, even recently, to "the three great sources of historical literature: religious history, colonial history and women's history."[35] Yet the letters of missionaries represent a wealth of information that only they can bring. Such is the case of Saint Philippine Duchesne's writings, as much by their number as by the variety of the persons addressed.

Epistolary Style

Many of Philippine's letters to Religious of the Sacred Heart, her family and friends were preserved. Others were lost in the mail, or disappeared because of shipwreck on the Mississippi or during the Atlantic crossing. Even so, the present corpus, numbering 656 letters, along with several accounts and journals, is sufficiently large to enable us to appreciate the quality of the writing and the variety of style.

The function of the letter is obvious: to create a space of freedom of spirit between persons beyond the constraints of daily routine and distance. Thus, conventual cloister seems to be lifted and proximity restored. As Patrick Goujon observes, "Correspondence nourishes the social bond as much as it records it."[36] That is apparent in the different bodies of letters: to the family, to religious, to pupils and to churchmen. The same is true in the journals, in which some information comes from other Sacred Heart houses or from correspondents living abroad.

The level of language and its tonality vary according to the person being addressed and the purpose of the missive; that goes without saying. The style is more or less direct; the expression more or less restrained. Differences are visible in the letters addressed to former pupils

---

35 S. A. Curtis, ed., *L'autre visage de la mission : les femmes*, "À la découverte de la femme missionnaire," *Histoire et Missions chrétiennes N° 16*, Paris: Karthala, 2010, pp. 5-18. See also idem, *Civilizing Habits: Women Missionaries and the Revival of French Empire*, Oxford/New York: Oxford University Press, 2010, pp. 23-97.

36 P. Goujon, *Prendre part à l'intransmissible*, ed. Jérôme Million, Grenoble, 2008, pp. 47-61.

or to the family and those that concern matters of government. The reader, like a traveler, can thus discover aspects of Philippine Duchesne's personality, according to changes in decor, perspectives, actors, and human and ecclesial issues.

From the time of the arrival on American soil, the educator gives in to her desire to share her first discoveries about the New World. The letters sent to the pupils of Grenoble and Paris offer unedited descriptions, sometimes panoramic, at other times, close-up. The one of June 3, 1818, very well constructed, is an example. She speaks at first about "these Indians for the love of whom we had made such a long journey," of her surprise at seeing them so despised, treated "like animals" in this luxurious city of New Orleans. She describes the dress of the slaves and the wealth of their masters. She takes pleasure in giving a dynamic description of nature. In this way the quality of her observations made at entering the Gulf of Mexico, at the mouth of the Mississippi and in the course of the navigation up to Saint Louis, allows the reader to feel transported with the current, to slide from one landscape to another, from decor to faces.

Affection is simply expressed at the beginning and end of the letter, as if the picture she is painting is framed by her tender feelings:

> Your names carried on my heart and in my heart are always present to me. I will never forget you; at the same time I attest to the fact that there is joy in leaving all for God who gave all for us. (…) In a word, I end by telling you that I have you all in my heart and try to place mine in the Heart of Jesus.

Her attachment to the members of her family was unadorned, and affection shows in each of her letters. Writing to her niece Euphrosine Jouve,[37] she does not hide her emotion at the thought of her imminent departure:

---

37 Adele Euphrosine (Aloysia) Jouve, RSCJ, was born on March 25, 1796, in Lyon, the third child of Mr. and Mrs. Jouve; she was a boarder at Sainte-Marie d'En-Haut until 1809. On November 21, 1810, she made a vow of virginity, entered as a postulant on November 9, 1814, and became a novice on December 24th. However, in keeping with her mother's wishes, she did not receive the habit until Easter 1815. She made her first vows on November 21, 1816, and her final vows on November 21, 1817. In the course of that year, 1817, she developed a mortal illness that little by little left her body covered with sores. Nevertheless with courage and competence she carried out the functions of sub-assistant, sub-mistress of novices, councilor and secretary (August 1818 to the end of 1819). The following year, in spite of her growing infirmity, she became assistant and admonitrix, replacing the superior for four months. She died on January 21, 1821. Some conversions took place near her tomb; twelve days after her burial her body was discovered to be incorrupt. *Vie de Madame Euphrosine Aloysia Jouve, religieuse du Sacré-Cœur*, notice written by Ph. Duchesne, Archives USC, after that in the General Archives, entitled *Vie de la Mère Aloysia Jouve, Religieuse du Sacré-Cœur, morte en odeur de sainteté le 21 janvier 1821*. AGSC C VII 2 Aloysia Jouve.

Having confided myself and all close to me to the divine Hearts of Jesus and Mary, I know neither what you are doing nor where you are; I hope you are always under the hand of God and ready to do his will. I submit in advance to his entire will; nevertheless I have felt that I am holding on to you still; even in my sleep, it seemed to me that you were calling me, urging me, saying that I would never be on time! I seemed to run, but believing myself near you, waking up showed me that I was hundreds of leagues far away and I renewed my sacrifice.[38]

The liveliness of her pen reflects that of her thought. Sometimes the tone is solemn, as in the account of her vocation, where the reference to her vow "to consecrate myself to the religious instruction of infidels according to obedience" has a note of gravity.[39] Sometimes it is dramatic, as in her narration of the crossing of the Atlantic: "The ship tossing violently in an angry sea gives the impression of the confusion of the last day. The sky seems to roll up rapidly behind the mountains of water, dragging the stars with it. The sea, nearly black in the storm, constantly gapes wide, disclosing bottomless depths; the waves sweep over the deck as the ship rolls and pitches."[40] Then the tone becomes playful, even teasing, in the letters to Father Louis Barat,[41] and enthusiastic in the one to Father Joseph Varin when she is dreaming of going toward the Pacific Northwest of the United States even as far as Korea and Japan.[42] It achieves an unexpected depth when she grasps the form

---

38 Letter 4 to Euphrosine Jouve, March 2, 1818.
39 Letter 3 to Mother Barat, January or February 1818.
40 Letter 8 to Mother Barat, May 16, 1818.
41 Louis Barat, SJ (1768-1845), was his sister Madeleine Sophie's tutor. A deacon and regent at Collège Saint-Jacques in Joigny, he retracted his oath of allegiance to the Civil Constitution of the Clergy, and fled to Paris where he was imprisoned. Liberated in January 1795, he was ordained priest clandestinely on September 19, 1795. He entered the Fathers of the Faith in 1800. He became superior of the college of Saint-Galmier, afterwards went to Belley, then to the college of Argentière. He gave retreats at Sainte-Marie d'En-Haut, in Grenoble; it was then that he and Philippine Duchesne became friends. In 1807, the Fathers of the Faith were assigned to their diocese. Louis exercised his ministry in Joigny, Migennes, and Troyes where he became superior of the seminary in 1811. Sent away for his opposition to Gallicanism, he was under house arrest in Bordeaux from 1812 to 1814. He entered the Society of Jesus in 1814. He was prefect of studies at the college and seminary of Bordeaux. In October 1821, he left for Paris, where he became a doctor of theology and professor in the scholasticate. He died on June 21, 1845.
42 Joseph Désiré Varin d'Ainvelle, SJ (1769-1850), born February 7, 1769, in Besançon, entered the Seminary of Saint-Sulpice in Paris in 1784, and left it in 1789 to join the counterrevolutionary army. In 1794, in Holland he joined the Society of the Sacred Heart, whose founder, Léonor de Tournély, planned to establish a society of women. Ordained priest on March 12, 1796, in Augsburg, Father Varin succeeded Father de Tournély as superior, and with Madeleine Sophie Barat, brought about in 1800 the foundation of the new women's institute, which in 1815 took the name of the Society of the Sacred Heart of Jesus. After having been its superior,

of martyrdom to which the mission calls her "never reaching those little Indians," the object of all her desires.⁴³ This moment is comparable to the plot of a novel; the design of the mission takes shape there: that of the grain of wheat falling into the ground of America.

The mention of certain moments in Philippine's life takes one to the accounts: first of all, in the *Story of Sainte-Marie d'En-Haut*, an account written at the request of Mother Barat; later in some letters addressed to former pupils of Grenoble, in which the missionary refers to the beginnings and then the progressive advancement of the work. The *Sommaire historique des fondations*, sent in 1843 to Mother Margaret Murphy,⁴⁴ comes out of the same vein.

The progressive change in tone of the letters, from 1818 to 1833, denotes passage from a certain lightness and intrepidity to seriousness that sometimes deepens into sadness and self-doubt. The writing bears the stamp of painful events. That is how the chronology of *Events of Interest (1818-1834)*⁴⁵ stops at the closing of Sainte-Marie d'En-Haut, after which Philippine asserts that she no longer feels able to undertake anything, the acquisition of and the repairs to the convent having cost her family so much.⁴⁶ The letters addressed to her cousin and friend, Mrs. Savoye de Rollin,⁴⁷ reveal her great preoccupations. It was from her that Philippine learned about political developments in France and the rest of Europe. As Amelie Jouve noted: "Nothing will alter the holy friendship that unites these two souls so well suited to appreciate each other. In moments of distress, Mother Duchesne turned to her friend whose purse like her heart was always open to her."⁴⁸

---

with Mother Barat and Father Druilhet, SJ, he drafted Constitutions. He entered the Society of Jesus in 1814 and became assistant to Father de Clorivière, then superior of the residence on the rue des Postes (1818-1821; 1825-1829). He opened the college in Dole in 1823, and afterward returned to Paris, rue de Sèvres, where he died on April 19, 1850. See Phil Kilroy, *Madeleine Sophie Barat, A Life 1779-1865*, Cerf, Paris, 2004, pp. 62-84.

43 Letter 5 to Father Barat, November 21, 1818; letter 9 to Mrs. de Rollin, 1819.
44 Original autograph, AGSC C-VII 2-c) Duchesne-writings History of Society, Box 1. Postmark: St. Charles, August 1843.
45 Original autograph. AGSH C-VII 2-c) Duchesne-writings History of Society, Box 1, *Lettres intéressantes depuis 1818 jusqu'à 1836*, p. 102.
46 Letter 30 to Mrs. de Rollin, January 13, 1834.
47 Elisabeth Josephine Perier (1770-1850) married Jacques-Fortunat Savoye de Rollin in 1788 and followed him in his different missions as prefect; she was distinguished by her charity and, at the siege of Antwerp in 1814, by her courage in ministering to the wounded whom she accompanied in field hospitals and clinics. After the death of her husband in 1823, she bought the property of the orphanage directed by Rosalie de La Grée, those of the Good Shepherd (at the sum of 70,000 F) and founded the Society of the Ladies of the Work of Providence for the education of poor young girls in Grenoble.
48 AGSC C-VII, 2 d) Duchesne-life, box 3. Notes given by Reverend Mother Aloysia Jouve, vicar of Central France, niece of the venerable Mother Duchesne.

In 1846, her suffering intensified faced with the imminent closing of the house of Saint Ferdinand, "the sweet shelter dedicated to Saint Regis, La Louvesc of America."[49] Her insistence took the form of a complaint: "Forgive this long letter. I have counted on your kindness; if I am refused, I will submit; but I will never be consoled; the wound is too deep."[50] As for her last letters to her brother Hippolyte Duchesne[51] and to her sister Mrs. Jouve,[52] she emphasizes "the tender friendship that has always connected us"[53] and the sorrow of seeing her sister left in solitude.

In December 1851, some months before her death, Philippine Duchesne recalled the spiritual experience of April 4, 1806:[54] this reference serves by way of conlusion in the ensemble of her writings. Her life, given in response to the call received forty-five years before, spent on American soil for thirty-three years, was about to come to an end.

The diversity of those addressed in this correspondence allows us to grasp the resources and the vulnerability of this upper class woman, as harp strings sound different harmonies. The quality of the writing masks neither the allusions to Counter-Reformation theology nor the ideological boundaries of this pioneer. But beyond this cultural conditioning, her dynamism and her unshakable confidence in the action of the Risen Christ offer the reader a surge of hope.

---

49   John Francis Regis, S.J. (1597-1640), entered the novitiate of the Jesuits in 1616 and was ordained a priest in 1630. He dreamed of going as a missionary to Canada, but he was sent to minister to the rural poor of Ardèche and Cévennes, in Velais and Vivarais, regions that were devastated by the religious wars. At the invitation of the bishop of Vienne, he went to celebrate Christmas there in 1640, but on December 31, he died of pneumonia at La Louvesc, where his body is venerated. He was canonized in 1737. Called Apostle of Velais, he was one of the greatest Jesuit missionaries. His picture still exists in the church in Grâne.
50   Letter 138 to Mother Barat, June 5, 1846. Letter 139, September 10, 1847.
51   Antoine Louis Hippolyte Duchesne (1781-1854), Philippine's brother, was born February 27, 1781, in Grenoble. He married Coralie Durand on November 14, 1814. He was general advocate at the court of Grenoble, deputy of the Isère during the Hundred Days (March to July 1815) and from 1835 to 1837. As a member of the liberal party, he demanded the resignation of Napoleon I after the defeat at Waterloo, opposed the proclamation of Napoleon II, and supported the ministers of the July Monarchy (1830-1848). In 1819, at Grâne, he was responsible for the building of a 3900 meter lengthening of the dike to prevent the floods that were destroying crops and dwellings. An inscription engraved on the first stone read: "By curbing the Drôme, he enriched the country." He died on September 9, 1854, at Saint-Ismier.
52   Charlotte Euphrosine Duchesne (1772-1857), married Jean Joseph Jouve (1752-1834), manufacturer and businessman in 1794. They had eleven children, of whom four daughters became religious (three at the Sacred Heart: Amelie, Euphrosine, and Constance) and one son, Henri, a Jesuit.
53   Letter 2 to Hippolyte Duchesne, August 29, 1852; Letter 85 to Mrs. Jouve, August 17, 1852.
54   Letter 2 to Mother Brangier, December 19, 1851.

A Spiritual Profile

To use Mother Barat's word, how was the life of Philippine Duchesne *"edifying?"* If to edify through encountering her life means to awaken a desire for growth, to develop oneself on a solid base, the life presented here can contribute to that. The collection of the writings does not reveal a spirituality that was proper to her. All the same, a profile can be drawn against the horizon of devotion to the Sacred Heart.

The account of the spiritual experience of Holy Thursday 1806 opens the location of the future mission: the New World.[55] Then it indicates the source of the invincible courage of which Philippine gave proof: the living water flowing from the open side of Christ:

> All night long I was on the new continent, and I traveled in such good company. First, I carefully collected all the blood of Jesus from the Garden, the Pretorium and Calvary; I took possession of him in the Blessed Sacrament, and holding it close, I carried my treasure everywhere to spread it without fear of its being exhausted.[56]

After that vision, Philippine Duchesne had to wait twelve years to go to announce the love and compassion of the Heart of Jesus to young Indians who did not yet know him. She arrived in New Orleans on May 29, 1818, and in Missouri at the end of August. Soon, in "this field, the object of so many longings,"[57] she became herself the "grain of wheat." In a letter to her friend Josephine, she states this truth:

> We are the grain perishing in the earth. At the moment, we could hardly return it at all, but we are full of confidence, all of us inspired to perseverance in the hope that it will bear fruit someday. It is not important to taste it in this life, as long as God is served.[58]

---

55 The account of this vision is much more concise than that of the "prophetic dream" of Marie of the Incarnation, but the expressions and the images are analogous: the ardor of crossing vast countries so that Christ may be known, loved and adored there. See *Le Témoignage de Marie de l'Incarnation, Ursuline de Tours et du Québec*, première partie, Neuvième état d'oraison, I-IV, Ed. Beauchesne, Paris, 1932, pp. 183-196. Marie Guyart (1599-1672), known by the name of Marie of the Incarnation, was an Ursuline of Tours, France, and of Quebec, Canada. Married in 1616, widowed in 1619, she raised her son, then entered the Ursulines of Tours. In 1639, with two other Ursulines, she went to found a monastery in Quebec for the education of Amerindian girls. She was canonized on April 2, 2014.
56 Letter 2 to Mother Barat, April 4, 1806.
57 Letter 1 to Mother Bigeu, May 30, 1818.
58 Letter 12 to Mrs. de Rollin, February 18, 1821.

The biblical metaphor of the grain of wheat fallen into the ground denotes a movement of incarnation in American soil. As for the brief description that accompanies it, it reveals Philippine's spiritual attitude: a radical sense of poverty lived in profound confidence in God.

"It matters little…" Philippine ratifies what was asked of her: to give way to the reality and the unknown of the fruitfulness to come, in abandonment to Providence. Thus she lived what the Constitutions proposed to her: "…unite themselves to the interior dispositions of the Heart of their Divine Spouse, Who, although Master of all riches of Heaven and of earth, lived in the most complete destitution of all things." Here is found the Berullian understanding of interior abnegation that unites one to the self-annihilation of Christ in the Incarnation.[59]

From her arrival in Saint Louis, a rude trial prepared her for this form of acceptance: Bishop Dubourg let her know that her mission was not to be with the Indians, as had been agreed to in Paris, but with American girls. To Father Barat, to whom she made known the bishop's change of plan, she confided in these terms:[60]

> The bishop shows us his position and that of the first Ursuline Sisters, and tells us to love our abjection now, that the fruits will come in the future. In his presence I was like a rock pounded by hammers. I proceed with closed eyes. Providence will open the way if he wishes.

Her abandonment to the action of Christ, with a clear awareness of the adversities, would characterize her for her whole life. It was expressed again at the time of the bank failure and the devaluation of the currency:

> God permitted that when we arrived in Saint Louis, money was plentiful, land and houses at excessive prices. It seemed better to build where we are. This was not my opinion but it was necessary to follow that of others and to borrow in order to finish it. Now that the failure of all the banks has made disappear the bills that were almost the only kind of money used here, we could have land and houses for nothing in Saint Louis. Instead, we have to pay back what was borrowed at a time when money is worth ten times more. These are unexpected events against which human prudence can do nothing. But Providence is there and we count on it so much that

---

59 P. de Bérulle, *Opuscule CXXXII*, col. 1165, c 914, Ed. Migne. Quoted in the *Dictionnaire de Spiritualité*, R. Daeschler, *Anéantissement, I.*, « L'anéantissement actif », pp. 560-561.
60 Letter 3 to Father Barat, August 29, 1818.

we remain firmly at our post. We are so persuaded that God placed us here himself, that no one regrets it.[61]

For this woman whose missionary intrepidity was accompanied by a real capacity for initiative, such abandon necessitated a profound interior freedom, received from the One whom she preferred in all things. The secret of her intense activity, of her active compassion towards the sick, of her kindness to the pupils and the novices was, in effect, her union with the "interior dispositions of the Heart of Jesus."[62]

In 1847, during a visit to the Religious of the Sacred Heart in Brussels, Father De Smet[63] traced anew the spiritual profile of our missionary, five years before her death. Céline de Groote transmitted his testimony thus:

> He told us that Mother Duchesne has climbed all the rungs on the ladder to holiness, and he said that he has never seen a soul more ardent in love for Our Lord, that in his opinion she could be a rival to Saint Teresa, that he had never met a soul who was poorer in her personal life, that she was a latter-day Saint Francis of Assisi; even more apostolic at winning souls than Saint Francis Xavier. She had communicated to him her zeal for the conversion of infidels.

The three comparisons are significant. According to the first, Philippine Duchesne was "an ardent soul" in the style of Saint Teresa of Avila. The vision of her missionary vocation in America, the night of Holy Thursday 1806, indicated in effect the type of prayer to which the Lord called her. The references to the Song of Songs that appear in the first exchange of letters with Sophie Barat reveal it in turn: from the "Beloved" she expected everything, received everything in order to offer it to him in return. That is why she was as valiant as Saint Teresa.

Her limitless generosity was never exhausted, whether regarding the pupils or the Jesuit scholastics or the young superiors in Louisiana, to whom she sent reinforcements to the detriment of the Missouri houses. Mrs. Ella M. La Motte, an old pupil, recalls it in concrete terms:

---

61 Letter 12 to Mrs. de Rollin, February 18, 1821.
62 The expression "unite and conform oneself to the interior dispositions of the Heart of Jesus" occurs very often in the Constitutions of the Society of the Sacred Heart of Jesus.
63 Pierre Jean De Smet, SJ (1801-1873), was born in Belgium; he was a celebrated missionary to the Indians of the Northwest. Having arrived in America in 1821, he made his novitiate with other young Jesuits in Maryland. He left for Missouri in 1823, was ordained priest in 1827 and immediately began his long missionary journeys. The Indians had so much confidence in him that he was often their travel companion and interpreter with the government. After returning to Saint Louis, he became treasurer of Saint Louis University. In 1838, he left to found a mission to the Potawatomi. He often visited Philippine and took care of her Indian pupils.

Her face was strong and tender. She had a great love of the little children and kept them near her as much as possible; and while at that time she spoke very little and in very bad English, all the girls adored being with her. Even though times were hard and provisions were often scarce, she took care that the pupils had the best possible, and every Sunday they had a special treat. She took the girls into her office where each one could choose from the pantry whatever she wanted. Her gentleness on these occasions was enormous.[64]

She used to pray for long hours during the night. Several old pupils of Grenoble told this story: seeing Mother Duchesne in prayer in the chapel in the same position, evening and morning, after Compline they placed small scraps of paper on the hem of her veil. When they arrived the next morning, the bits of paper were still there....

The testimony of Mother Monzert suggests one of the fruits of this gift of prayer:

This venerated Mother seemed to have an intuitive knowledge of facts and events. On the occasion of my departure from Saint Charles, strict orders had been given not to say anything about it to Mother Duchesne. But the morning of my departure, she came to me, embraced me affectionately as a farewell without saying a word; it was the time of greater silence. Her eyes were filled with tears as she made her way to the chapel.[65]

Beyond the triteness of these anecdotes, can be seen what animated the life of this missionary: through contemplation, to unite herself to Christ to make known his liberating love, always being offered. The Potawatomi Indians were not mistaken in calling her "the woman who is always praying."

Father De Smet's second comparison concerns her understanding of poverty. According to him, Philippine was "another Saint Francis of Assisi." Mrs. Thatcher testifies as follows:

---

64 AGSC C-VII 2 d) Duchesne-life, Box 3, Testimony to her life and virtues, given by old pupils and secular friends. Testimony of Mrs. Ella M. La Motte.
65 AGSC C-VII 2 d) Duchesne-life, Box 3, Testimony to her life and virtues, given by RSCJ. Testimony of Mother Monzert. Marie-Rose Monzert, RSCJ, born in 1828 in Berne, Switzerland, arrived in Saint Louis, Missouri, with her family in 1830. She entered at the Sacred Heart in Saint Louis in 1847, and made her first vows in 1849. As an aspirant at Saint Charles, she was in charge of caring for Philippine after her return from Sugar Creek. She made her religious profession in 1876, and died on December 8, 1903, in Saint Charles.

> I have seen her working in the garden, shucking the corn, pulling up the cabbages, and I have seen her chapped hands, bleeding because of the rough work. I noticed particularly that when she was working that way, she had a gentle, peaceful expression on her face, as if her thoughts were in heaven.

What follows is a vivid description: "Her skirt resembled patchwork, and her shoes: I have never seen any like them, and I never shall again. If ever a religious practiced poverty, it was she!"[66]

The joy of the *poverello* went along with that simplicity of life and was communicated to the boarding school; Mrs. Thatcher attests:

> I have never seen a more joyous, a holier school than hers. And when we moved to 'The City House' in Saint Louis, we were astonished to find there a worldly spirit, so different from that of our happy house in Florissant.

The witness of Mrs. Lamotte serves to confirm it: "She was a noble and brilliant woman but with the simplicity of the child who followed her along the rows of potatoes in the vegetable garden."

For a long time, Philippine wanted "only to render service to Our Lord and to be rich only in Him."[67] In her last years that impulse was very strong and expressed itself in the form of little gifts for the Indian missions: "It is the gift of a poor person," she said to Father De Smet, "to the poor, the real friends of Jesus Christ."[68]

The third comparison has bearing on her missionary zeal. For the apostle of the Rocky Mountains,[69] only Saint Francis Xavier was "more apostolic." In the account of her vocation, Philippine Duchesne recalls the attraction and influence of Jesuit missionaries, in particular of the apostle of India and Japan: "How many times did I not say in my impatience: '*Great Saint, why do you not call me, and I would answer you.*' He is the saint I love."

Upon the arrival of the Religious of the Sacred Heart in New Orleans, the Ursulines' doctor predicted the rapid development of Upper Louisiana "converted in a few years to another France as to climate,

---

66 AGSC C-VII 2 d) Duchesne-life, Box 3, *Testimony to her life and virtues, given by old pupils and secular friends*. Testimony of Ann B. Thatcher, Ferguson Mo., July 18th 1892, a former pupil of Florissant (1838-1840), born Ann Biddle Chambers. She was the granddaughter of John Mullanphy, donor of the property in Saint Louis.
67 Letter 1 to Mother Barat, March 1806.
68 Letter 3 to Father De Smet, April 29, 1849.
69 P.-J. De Smet, *Missions de l'Oregon et voyages dans les montagnes Rocheuses en 1845 et 1846*, Poussielgue-Rusand, Paris, 1848.

fertility, commerce and civilization."⁷⁰ Philippine began then to dream of going farther West, to Korea and Japan, to undertake there other missionary foundations.

At the same time, she did not hesitate to rebuke Sister Catherine Lamarre who refused to work with the Ursulines' slaves. She reminded her that the education of blacks was exactly the reason they had come, that they had the same soul as she, were redeemed by the same blood of Jesus Christ and were members of the same church; and that if she did not wish to be around them, she could go back to France in the ship that was about to depart.⁷¹ But a deep disappointment awaited her in Saint Louis: not only did she have to give up her initial plan to educate Indians, but also she had to conform to the practice of racial segregation that forbade the admission of girls "of color" to the boarding school, the free school and the novitiate.

This form of exclusion must have been the subject of a difficult spiritual combat in which her family's frame of reference could have affected her here and there. In effect, while her education had given her the cultural and ecclesial assumptions of the *Ancien Régime*, she had also been endowed with intellectual openness and a new sense of social justice. In her family circle she had been acquainted with Joseph-Marie de Gérando,⁷² a precursor of French ethnology, who with Camille Jordan⁷³ contributed to the development of instruction to the children of

---

70   Letter to Father Varin, June 4, 1818.
71   Letter 10 to Mother Barat, June 7, 1818.
72   Joseph Marie de Gérando (1772-1842) studied with the Oratorians in Lyon with the Jordan and Perier boys. Engaged in the federalist movement in Lyon that was fighting against the troops of the National Convention, he emigrated to Italy in 1793. Having returned to France in 1795, he earned first prize in the contest of the *Institut de France*, of which he was elected a member in 1804. The author of one of the earliest guides to ethnographic inquiry, he established the principles of participant observation of primitive peoples and defined ethnology as a science. In 1802, with Camille Jordan and Mathieu de Montmorency, he founded the Society for the encouragement of industrial education of people. He published the *Cours Normal* for student teachers (1815) and a report on schools for girls (1816). Co-founder of the first savings bank (1818), he created the *École des Chartes* (1821). Named a Peer of France (1837), he is the author of famous works, known across the Atlantic: the *Traité de la Bienfaisance publique* (1839) summarizes the direction of his philosophic and political action.
73   Camille Jordan (1771-1821), was a cousin and childhood friend of Philippine, and a student with Joseph de Gérando, in Lyon. An adversary of the Revolution, he participated in the insurrection in Lyon in 1793; he fled to Switzerland, then to England, and returned to France in 1796. As a deputy from the Rhône on the Council of the Five Hundred in 1797, he defended freedom of worship and opposed the deportation of priests. Thanks to the intervention of J. de Gérando, he escaped deportation, 19 Fructidor An V (September 4, 1797), fled to Basle, then to Tübingen and Weimar, where he met his friends Mounier, Gœthe, Schiller, and Herder. Back in France in February 1800, he was welcomed by J. de Gérando, often visited Chateaubriand and the *salons* of Mᵐᵉ de Staël and Mᵐᵉ de Récamier where he exercised real influence. In 1805, he married Louise Philippine (called Julie) Magnieunin (1785-1860). In August 1815 he was named president of the electoral college of Lyon and elected deputy

factory workers. As for her father, he had promoted a law for the public instruction of the poor before the assembly of the Tribunal.

It is understandable that one whose fervor could have rivaled that of Saint Teresa, imitated Saint Francis of Assisi and had been a disciple of Saint Francis Xavier, would have taken offense at the dishonest commerce of the fur traders, characterized as the "real savages," because they contributed to making the Indians dependent on alcohol, a subtle form of slavery. Her indignation was so strong because it was for them that she had come to America.

A Historical Distance

The cultural shock experienced by this pioneer invites us to put in perspective the European and American contexts, both marked by ethnocentric currents with contrasting values. In certain letters or accounts, imaginations clash. Philippine Duchesne's first evaluations reveal French humanist categories. The fact that her opinions are expressed confidentially—to the superior general or to her friends—does not extenuate them but rather reveals the cultural background that governs them. According to Dominique Deslandres, the latter is common to missionaries who "simply cannot believe in a better way of living than their own. It melts away all their certitudes."[74]

Upon her arrival in New Orleans, Philippine Duchesne was shocked by the atmosphere of racism, astonished that "only black persons are in service in this country," that whites refuse to do this kind of work under a pretext of equality among people of the same race. She asked therefore that coadjutrix sisters be sent to do the gardening and the housework. It was costly for this woman of the upper middle class of Grenoble to discover behaviors far removed from the values of Sacred Heart families in France. Even though she was able to leave those she loved, tear herself away from her native land, her "mountain," and cross the ocean, she had not broken with her background, her culture and her frame of reference. She rose up against an American life style that went against the aims that motivated her coming to the New World. The vivacity of her pen crossed the boundaries of social restraint.

---

from Ain from 1816 to 1818. He died in Paris, May 19, 1821; he was buried in Père-Lachaise Cemetery.

74 D. Deslandres, *Croire et faire croire: Les missions françaises au XVIIe siècle*, « Le phénomène missionnaire à l'aube des temps modernes », Fayard, Paris, 2003, pp. 31-33.

All the same, just as her father was a man on the threshold between the *Ancien Régime* and modernity,[75] in the same way Philippine's frame of reference came from both the past and the present. As Sarah A. Curtis notes, her concepts were "rooted in the *Ancien Régime* as well as in the new religious dynamism that had succeeded the destruction of the Catholic Church by the Revolution."[76] Maybe certain difficulties in governing found their cause here. While her decision to adapt the Sacred Heart plan of studies indicates an accommodation to American culture, her resistance to easing up on cloister came from an attachment to a former way of religious life that did not facilitate visits or dealings with the parents.

Like most Catholics of her time, Philippine Duchesne considered Protestants "heretics." This prejudice runs the risk of surprising, even shocking today. It comes from Counter-Reformation theology. Her conception of sufferings and of the judgment of God is that of the seventeenth and eighteenth centuries,[77] when the theological horizon was characterized by a dolorism inherited from the Augustinian doctrine of original sin, reinforced by Jansenism. Her interpretation of the calamities that occurred in Saint Louis in 1849 (terrible fires followed by cholera and dysentery) is a striking example. They were seen as "chastisements God sent because of the want of observance of his laws."[78] This way of interpreting some human dramas was common in Europe at the time.[79]

---

75 Pierre François Duchesne, son of Antoine Duchesne and Marie Louise Enfantin, was born in Romans on October 6, 1743; he studied law at Orange and practiced law in Grenoble. He married Rose Euphrosine Perier on September 28, 1766. In 1781, he founded the public library in that city and was the director. Esteemed for his independence of mind and the honesty of his pleadings before the court, he was president of the Bar of the *Parlement* of Grenoble in 1788. In the face of the excesses of the Revolution, he retired from public life (1789-1797). In May 1797 he was elected deputy from the Drôme in the Council of the Five Hundred, then secretary; he became a member of the Tribunal (December 25, 1799), and president of it in June 1800. He was the only other one besides Carnot to vote against the consulate for life demanded by Bonaparte in 1802. Returned to the Bar of Grenoble, he was elected as a candidate for the Senate, but the Emperor refused to name him. He died in Grenoble, March 29, 1814.

76 Sarah A. Curtis, "Traverser les frontières: Philippine Duchesne et les Sœurs du Sacré-Cœur dans le Missouri des années 1820 aux années 1840," *Missionnaires catholiques français aux États-Unis, 1791-1920, Histoire et Missions chrétiennes N°17*, ed. Tangi Villerbu. *Histoires et Missions chrétiennes* No. 17. Paris: Karthala, March 2011, p. 59.

77 Ph. Duchesne and J. Savoye de Rollin were boarders at Sainte-Marie d'En-Haut. From their formation, they kept the same image of God. The author of Josephine's obituary refers to it thus: "Her heart, so pure and so Christian, could not defend itself at the last moment against fear of the judgments of God." Albert du Boÿs, *Notice nécrologique de Mme Savoye de Rollin*, Bibliothèque municipale de Grenoble, 0. 14568.

78 Letter 82 to Mrs. Jouve, September 12, 1849.

79 Ph. Boutry, P.-A. Fabre et D. Julia, eds., *Rendre ses vœux, Les identités pèlerines dans l'Europe moderne (XVIe-XVIIIe siècle)*, « Promesses, dons et mécénat. Le pèlerinage noble au Portugal entre salut et représentation, XVe-XVIIIe siècles », École des hautes études en sciences sociales, Paris, 2000, pp. 341-362.

Certain practices are in danger of being misunderstood if they are not situated in the context of the epoch: for example, the vow to Saint Francis Regis, made on June 16, 1817.[80] Carrying it out *ipso facto* created the obligation of honoring the promise, for the meaning of the particular vow was that of a religious debt. According to Alain Boureau, the medieval vow began with Augustine, for whom from the emission of a vow, the person is bound. It is no longer permitted for the person to act otherwise; the person has become a debtor of the vow *(voti reus)*.[81] The *Decretum* of Gratian (1150) adds a juridical content: one becomes "debtor of a vow by the obligation that follows from it." Apparently, it is to this signification that Philippine refers when she asks to have Masses said at La Louvesc, to honor the picture of Saint Francis Regis and the altar erected in his honor at Saint Ferdinand.

The historical distance of these concepts and convictions implies, therefore, crossing frontiers and discovering two somewhat unfamiliar cultural spaces, that of nineteenth century European missionaries and that of the New World in the process of coming into being. To situate them in dialogue with our own culture permits a meeting with this missionary who, in 1818, went to pitch her tent at the edge of Indian tribes and the American Congress.

This work with which we are occupied is being published on the occasion of the 200 years since the arrival of Philippine Duchesne and her companions in North America: an occasion to recall the memory of one who was recognized by the state government in Jefferson City, in 1918, as the premier pioneer woman of Missouri.[82]

---

80 Original autograph. Blessed Philippine Duchesne, Personal documents-birth-baptism. Some letters and notes. AGSC C-VII 2) d) Duchesne-life-Box 2. This vow involved four obligations: to have a novena of Masses said at La Louvesc at the time of the embarkation for Louisiana; to be employed in the instruction of Indian girls according to the desire of Saint Regis; to erect an altar in his honor; and to dedicate the house to him and to celebrate his feast. For complete text, see chapter IV.

81 Alain Boureau, *Le désir dicté, Histoire du vœu religieux dans l'Occident médiéval*, « Lettre 127 adressée à Armentarius et Paulina en 411 », Les Belles Lettres, Coll. Histoire, Paris, 2014, pp. 22-24.

82 AGSC C-VII 2 d) Duchesne-life, Box 3. *'ET EXALTAVIT HUMILES'! Homage rendered by the State of Missouri to Venerable Mother Philippine Duchesne, April 9, 1918:* "Two large bronze plaques, one with an allegorical representation of types, the other engraved with the names of the chosen, were set up at the *Jefferson Memorial*, a superb historical museum. (…) The first place was assigned to Rose Philippine Duchesne, Religious of the Sacred Heart; when the question was asked: "Who should be placed at the head of the list of our famous women?" That was the unanimous vote of the committee of 200 members, men and women, almost all Protestants."

The Work of Editing

Two Religious of the Sacred Heart, one from each of the countries where Saint Philippine Duchesne lived, have prepared this edition. They share the same conviction: the spirituality of the Religious of the Sacred Heart is made of different "veins" and tonalities. For this reason, it is important to make known even more the life of this saint who did not hesitate to cross frontiers to proclaim the Gospel. Today her missionary figure can make sense in our globalized world.

Marie France Carreel, doctor in Educational Sciences from the Université Lumière Lyon 2, has given workshops in France and abroad on the specific educational character of the Society of the Sacred Heart of Jesus. She has published her thesis and several articles and has contributed to the publication of anthologies of missionary texts. She has taught philosophy of education in *Licence de Sciences de l'Éducation* at the *Institut catholique Saint-Jean* and at the *Centre de Formation des Professeurs d'École de l'Enseignement Catholique*, in Marseille, and philosophical anthropology at the interdiocesan Seminary of Avignon.

Carolyn Osiek was professor of New Testament at Catholic Theological Union in Chicago, then at Texas Christian University in Fort Worth for thirty-two years. Former president of the Catholic Biblical Association of America and of the Society of Biblical Literature, she is the author or editor of ten books and numerous articles. Since her retirement in 2009, she has been archivist of the Province of the United States-Canada of the Society of the Sacred Heart. Her contact with Saint Philippine Duchesne began at the age of eight when she was enrolled at the Academy of the Sacred Heart in Saint Charles, Missouri, the first school founded by Mother Duchesne and the house in which she died.

The publication in French by Éditions Brepols is the fruit of their close collaboration during the entire editing process. Marie-France Carreel, a Frenchwoman, established the list of documents and transcribed the texts. Carolyn Osiek, an American, was in charge of the preparation of the chapters and of the process of editing. Together they composed the notes, Marie-France Carreel having the responsibility of the French documentation and Carolyn Osiek, that of the United States.

Archival Sources

Together the writings include 656 letters, narratives, one of which is the *Story of Sainte-Marie d'En-Haut* (1801-1813), three house journals and a few chronologies of the foundations of the Society of the Sacred

Heart of Jesus or the life of Mother Duchesne.[83] The letters form several series: 146 to Madeleine Sophie Barat, superior general; 150 to other Religious of the Sacred Heart (including her three nieces); 143 to her family; 196 to priests, of which 148 to Bishop Rosati; and 21 to pupils and other lay persons. Except for one letter in English, all the writings are in French. Most of them are located in the General Archives of the Society of the Sacred Heart of Jesus in Rome;[84] a few are found in the Archives of the Province of USA-Canada (USC).

RULES OF TRANSCRIPTION

While certain letters have been typed, most of the documents are in manuscript, whether they are originals or copies. Philippine Duchesne sometimes wrote on a scrap from an envelope, on very thin paper, with very pale ink that had been thawed. Reading such manuscripts is therefore laborious; they had to be deciphered patiently.

The following rules were observed in the transcription: complete reproduction of the text with slight modernization of punctuation and grammatical agreement to facilitate reading and comprehension; and restitution of proper names, the spelling of which was not settled in the nineteenth century. When the reference is to a priest, the name is preceded by Father in all letters and journals, even though the French usually does not distinguish a priest from other gentlemen. Likewise religious are called Mother or Sister even though the French often refers to choir religious as Madame. Words and phrases underlined in the manuscript are italicized; words added are in brackets. In the letters, the recommendation to Saint Anthony of Padua was more or less abbreviated; we have respected these variations that form part of the epistolary style.

Some of the biographical notes are brief or incomplete; in the General Archives of the Society of the Sacred Heart of Jesus, no register of vows exists before 1820, and there is no *Catalogue* for the period between 1801 and 1840. Moreover, the *Annual Letters* often relate only the last days of the life of the dead person, and some house journals have been lost; such is the case for the house in Grenoble for the period 1822

---

83 *Journal of Grenoble* (JG); *Journal of Paris* (JP); *Journal of the Society in America* (JSA), also called the Journal of Missouri, composed in Saint Charles, Florissant and Saint Louis.

84 In the General Archives there are three collections: *Cantiques, Vie des Saints* and *Prières*, written by Mother Duchesne. They have not been included in this edition, because most of the texts seem to have been copied from another source. The same is true for *La Vie d'Aloysia Jouve*, composition based on the text of Therese Maillucheau; even so it is interesting because of omissions or additions that indicate the independence of mind of Phillippine Duchesne.

to 1830. Failing a trustworthy official document like a birth certificate or act of vows, it was necessary to consult not only existing catalogues but also the *Annual Letters* and the *List of Deceased* to verify dates. The same was true for the names of persons. *For every entry in the index, the note containing a biographical sketch is in italics and bold.*

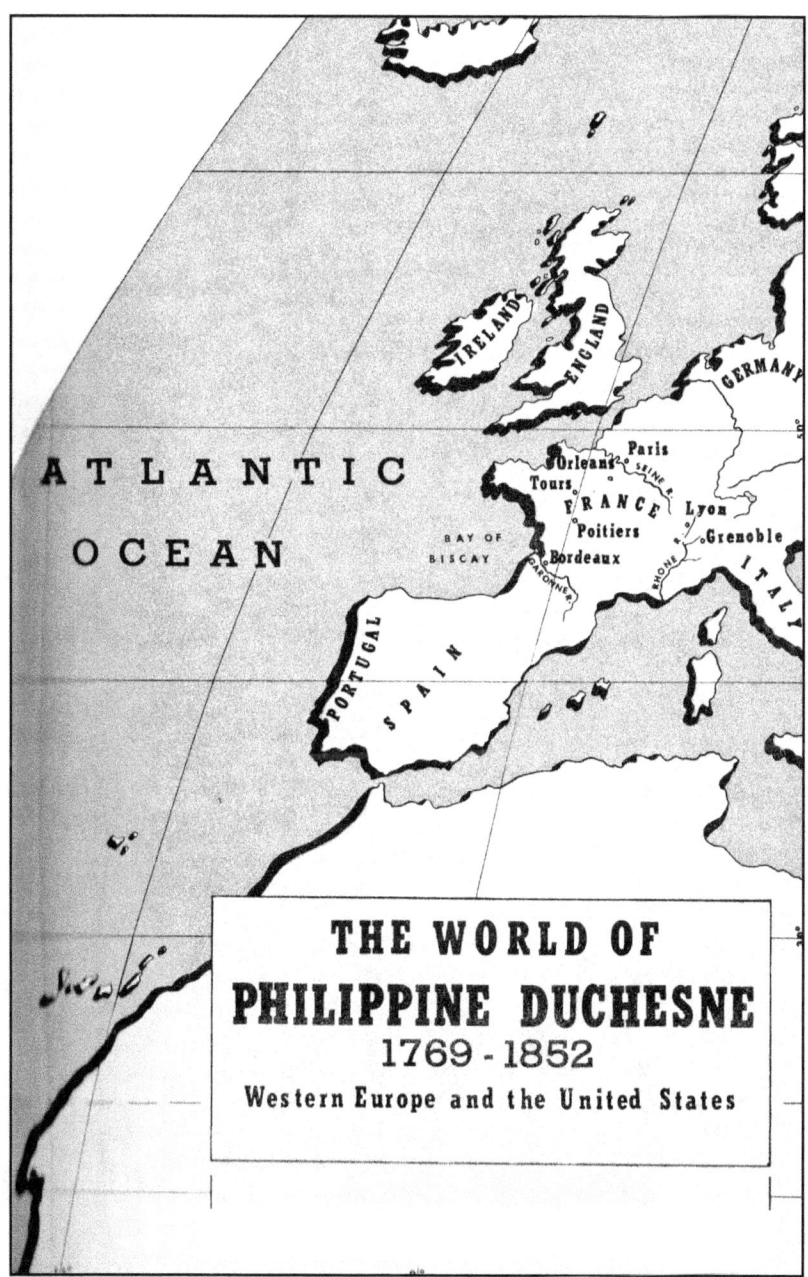

CHAPTER I

1769-1818

BEFORE THE GREAT DEPARTURE

INTRODUCTION

A Country, a Family, a Culture

Before 1790, the Province of Dauphiny corresponded to the present *départements* of Drôme, Hautes-Alpes and Isère, to the principality of Orange and part of the Rhône.[1] In the eighteenth century, it experienced a period of economic growth from which the bourgeoisie profited: fabric in Voiron,[2] gloves and sheets in Romans, woven and knitted silks in Vizille and the Rhône. Intellectual life was vigorous there, especially in Grenoble, where a public library was opened, certain members of which, scientists, philosophers, and politicians, have remained famous.[3] The geographic situation of that province and its history, crossed by the terrible wars of religion, forged the character of the inhabitants whose tenacity, depth, keenness and calm became legendary.

It was in this land that Rose Philippine Duchesne was born on August 29, 1769, in Grenoble, the second child of Pierre-François Duchesne,[4] a lawyer in the *Parlement* of Grenoble, and Rose-Euphrosine Perier.[5] The Duchesne family lived in the same building as Claude and

---

1   In the eleventh century, Dauphiny was a state, a subdivision of the German Holy Roman Empire. In 1349, it was annexed by the Kingdom of France, forming the portion of the eldest son of the king of France who from birth had the title of Dauphin. In 1790, it was divided into *départements*.
2   Jacques II Perier (1702-1782) was the father of Mrs. Duchesne, Philippine's mother. Consul of Grenoble, founder and director of the cloth factory of Voiron, stockholder in the Company of the Indies, he owned numerous properties in France, in particular in Dauphiny and Provence.
3   Among them were: Déodat Gratet de Dolomieu, geologist; Jacques Vaucanson, inventor of robots and knitting machines; Gabriel Bonnot de Mably and Étienne Bonnot de Condillac, philosophers; Jean-Joseph Mounier and Antoine Barnave. Pierre-François Duchesne founded this public library in 1781.
4   Coat of arms of the Duchesne family: in silver, with green oak, background shaded, gold acorns, and a red enameled star on either side. See Dr. Ulysse Chevalier, *Armorial historique de Romans*.
5   Rose-Euphrosine Perier, born June 4, 1748, married Pierre-François Duchesne (1743-1814) in 1765. They had eight children, two of whom died at an early age. Two daughters became religious: Philippine in the Society of the Sacred Heart of Jesus and Melanie in the Visitation at Romans.

Marie-Charlotte Perier,[6] at 4 Grande Rue, near the *Parlement* square and the collegiate Church of Saint André.

These two families of an upper middle class of men of finance and of the law generously provided a brilliant education for their children. Philippine and her cousin Josephine Perier were entrusted at first to a governess, Miss Sophie, then to the Visitandines, at Sainte-Marie d'En-Haut, a convent built on Mount Chalmont, situated in the midst of Mount Rachais, on the right bank of the Isère.[7] Upon return to their family, they benefited from some courses of Abbe Raillane, tutor of the Perier boys and their cousin Camille Jordan. After returning to the family, Philippine studied foreign languages and experienced life in the world. At the age of 17, she refused the marriage her parents proposed and announced her firm intention of becoming a Visitandine. In January 1788, she entered the novitiate at Sainte-Marie d'En-Haut.

A Political Situation on the Edge of an Abyss

At the end of the nineteenth century the French monarchy was confronted with a serious political, economic, and financial crisis, as attempts at reform had not been carried far enough. The people, indignant at the persistence of privilege for the upper classes, would not put up with the deteriorating living conditions. On August 21, 1787, the province of Dauphiny was the first to demand the session of the Estates General. The decisive turning point took place in the year 1788.

By means of the edicts of May 8, 1788, Lamoignon, the Keeper of the Seals, and Loménie de Brienne, Controller of Finance, reduced the powers of the provincial *parlements*. The opposition then won the whole country. The *Parlement* of Dauphiny—or *Parlement* of Grenoble—was a sovereign court of justice that fought against despotism and struggled for the defense of the liberty of Dauphiny. The magistrates of Grenoble refused to enact Brienne's edicts. In the face of their stubborn resistance, the governor insisted that they leave the city and withdraw to their country houses. The whole body of lawyers, directed by Pierre-François Duchesne, left the city. But the alarm sounded, the townspeople arrived, and the whole population rose up against their departure.[8] A riot followed; projectiles were thrown from the roofs on the troops of the Royal Marine. As the retaliation had caused the death of two persons

---

6   Claude Perier (1742-1801), Philippine's uncle, married Marie-Charlotte Pascal (1749-1821) in 1767. A banker and industrialist, he became the owner of the château of Vizille in 1780. In 1800 he participated in the creation of the Bank of France; he composed its statutes and served as one of its regents. Mr. and Mrs. Claude Perier had twelve children.
7   This monastery had been founded by Saint Jane de Chantal, on April 8, 1618.
8   In Grenoble, a fortified city of 20,000 inhabitants, lawyers, prosecutors, bailiffs, clerks, litigants and public service writers lived off the presence of their *parlement*.

and the wounding of others, the governor withdrew the order to the magistrates to depart. So ended the "Day of the Tiles," June 7, 1788.

Following this event, a first meeting of the Estates General of Dauphiny took place on July 21, 1788, at the *château* of Vizille. The second was held at Romans on September 9 the same year. Mr. Duchesne chose not to attend but rather to be present for his daughter's reception of the habit on September 10, 1788. A year later, foreseeing the antimonarchical and revolutionary drift of the government, under the baton of Antoine Barnave,[9] Mr. Duchesne withdrew from government and did not authorize his daughter to make vows in the Visitation order, though he allowed her to remain as a novice.

In fact, the Constituent Assembly did not long delay in decreeing drastic measures: October 29, 1789, suspension of religious vows; November 2, 1789, nationalization of the properties of the Church and of the clergy; on December 21, the domains belonging to the crown were declared property of the nation; February 13, 1790, prohibition of monastic vows; sequestration of the properties of immigrants, confraternities (with the exception of the Freemasons); in 1792 the same regulation for religious schools and on March 8, 1793, for schools and colleges of cities, parishes and religious communities.

As a measure of prudence, Philippine's parents withdrew her from the convent before the nuns were all obliged to leave. In fact, in September 1792, the community of Sainte-Marie d'En-Haut was forced to disperse.[10] A good number of émigrés fled to Savoy, to Switzerland and Italy. Others were arrested and imprisoned. In the prisons of Grenoble they arrived in the hundreds. Philippine and her cousin Josephine joined the Ladies of Mercy[11] to visit those men and women in their different places of detention.

---

9   Antoine-Pierre Barnave was born in Grenoble on October 22, 1761. Spearhead of the radical revolution, he opposed Mounier (1758-1806) who wanted an English style constitution with two houses and a king who had the right of veto. He was afterwards arrested, imprisoned first at Sainte-Marie d'En-Haut in Grenoble, then in Paris, where he was guillotined November 29, 1793.
10 On the eve of the Revolution, the convent was home to twenty-nine choir nuns, six lay sisters and five out sisters. "1792 saw the departure of the religious. Objects of value were sent to the Treasury in Lyon and the books to the Library of Grenoble. The convent was turned into a house of detention for suspicious persons and was quickly overpopulated, but in 1794 at the end of the terror, it was emptied. In 1797, it became a poorhouse. The buildings not cared for began to fall to ruin." Paul Dreyfus, *Histoire du Dauphiné*, Hachette, 1976, p. 278.
11 "Confraternity founded in Grenoble in 1633 by Father Bernard d'Anglès, 3rd superior of the Jesuits of that city. These admirable women visited imprisoned priests, brought them medicine, assisted them with alms at the time when detainees suffered from hunger in state prisons, accompanied as far as the scaffold those condemned to death and collected their blood." J. Pra, *Revue du livre* d'Anne-Marie de Franclieu, *La persécution religieuse dans le département de l'Isère*. Tome III, Tournai, Imprimerie Notre-Dame des Prés, 1906, pp. 422-423.

Return to Sainte-Marie d'En-Haut

After the Terror, Philippine went back to Grâne (Drôme), to the country estate acquired by Mr. Duchesne. She was there in June 1797 when her father left to take his seat on the Council of the Five Hundred in Paris,[12] and when her mother breathed her last on June 30, 1797. Two letters from Philippine, addressed to her sister Amelie de Mauduit,[13] date from the end of the same year. The first was written from Romans,[14] the second from Grenoble. In 1800, Philippine made a pilgrimage to the tomb of Saint Francis Regis at La Louvesc.

On December 10, 1801, through the intervention of her cousin, Mr. Savoye de Rollin,[15] and her uncle, Mr. Claude Perier, she obtained possession of Sainte-Marie d'En-Haut and went there to settle on December 14.[16] Mother de Murinais,[17] former superior, joined her in March 1802, accompanied by some other nuns. But this attempt at reopening was of short duration: the former Visitandines left in August 1802. They feared a new expulsion; the decree legalizing the reopening of the boarding school of Sainte-Marie d'En-Haut had not yet been obtained.

Arrival of Mother Barat

Philippine then received support from the vicars general of Grenoble, Fathers Brochier and Rivet,[18] who were in charge of administering the

---

12   The Directory (1795-1799) succeeded the Convention. It was characterized by violent opposition between the party of the left and the royalists, and by enormous financial difficulties. This situation led to the *coup d'État* of Napoleon Bonaparte, who took power on November 9, 1799, had himself named First Consul, and demanded in May 1802 to be Consul for life. The vote of the Tribunal and the legislative body was positive, but Mr. Duchesne voted against it and gave his resignation influenced by the president of the Tribunal.
13   Amelie Duchesne (1771-1837), Philippine's younger sister, was married on October 24, 1786, to Joseph-Constans de Mauduit, chevalier du Plessis (1760-1850), Officer of Infantry.
14   This letter is the first writing, chronologically, preserved in the General Archives of the Society of the Sacred Heart of Jesus.
15   Jacques-Fortunat Savoye de Rollin, baron of the Empire, was then the substitute of the imperial Prosecutor General.
16   See the account of these events in *l'Histoire de Sainte-Marie d'En-Haut*.
17   Until August 1792, Mother Anne Felicity d'Auberjon de Murinais was superior of Sainte-Marie d'En-Haut, where there were twenty-nine choir religious, six lay sisters and five extern sisters. She was afterwards imprisoned there.
18   Jean-François Brochier, born June 25, 1733, was vicar general of Grenoble and chaplain of the Church of Saint-André. He died August 9, 1822. Father Rivet was vicar general of Grenoble and secretary of Cardinal Caprara (1733-1810), legate of the Holy See. He negotiated with the Fathers of the Faith for the merger of Sainte-Marie d'En-Haut and the house in Amiens; he was chaplain and confessor of the community from 1804 until his death in 1826.

diocese in the absence of the bishop, Henri-Charles du Lau.[19] In 1803, Father Rivet directed his sister, a former Carmelite,[20] towards Sainte-Marie d'En-Haut. Father Brochier drew up a rule for the community, which he called "Daughters of the Propagation of the Faith." Philippine made simple vows in it on March 3, 1803.

The following year at the suggestion of Father Rivet and through Father Roger as intermediary,[21] the religious asked to join the nascent congregation, which subsequently took the name of "Society of the Sacred Heart of Jesus,"[22] and whose first house was in Amiens. Father Roger visited the community and returned there with Father Varin on July 31, 1804. He thought "it was necessary to send Mother Barat there immediately for the formation of the house."

On December 13, 1804, Sophie Barat arrived in Grenoble. After a year of novitiate under her direction, Philippine made her perpetual profession on November 21, 1805. Her missionary vocation was not long in taking shape. On April 4, 1806, during a night of adoration, she understood in a vision that she would go to teach the Native Americans in the New World.

The Documents from the Period

This first chapter, "Before the Great Departure," is composed of the *Story of Sainte-Marie d'En-Haut*, some journals of the houses of Grenoble and Paris, and 91 letters: 62 to her family, 22 to religious, three to the community of Sainte-Marie d'En-Haut, three to some lay persons and one to the pupils of Grenoble.

---

19 Henri Charles du Lau d'Allemans (1747-1802) was ordained bishop of Grenoble in April 1789 by the archbishop of Rouen. He was then retained in Paris by his uncle Jean-Marie du Lau d'Allemans, archbishop of Arles. After the vote on the Civil Constitution of the Clergy in 1790, he went into exile in Piedmont, then in Switzerland and Austria, governing his diocese through his vicars general as intermediaries. He died in Austria in 1802.

20 Marie Rivet (1768-1841), RSCJ, sister of Father Rivet and a Carmelite novice before the Revolution, joined Philippine Duchesne on October 31, 1802. Named superior of the community in 1803, she asked to be part of the future Society of the Sacred Heart. In 1818, she would be sent to Chambéry, and would live there until her death.

21 Pierre Aimé Roger (1763-1839), SJ, born at Coutances (Manche), ordained in 1788, entered the Society of the Fathers of the Sacred Heart in Augsburg; he returned to France with Father Varin in 1800. He was one of the witnesses of the consecration of Sophie Barat on November 21, 1800, in Paris. In 1804, he was living in Lyon with Father Barat; he joined the Society of Jesus in 1814.

22 Until 1815, the official name was: "Ladies of Christian Instruction." That of the Sacred Heart was forbidden, as it evoked either the Vendean revolt of 1793 or the Society of the Heart of Jesus of Father de Clorivière, proscribed in 1804 by Portalis, minister of worship.

The *Story of Sainte-Marie d'En-Haut* (SSM) relates the events preceding the arrival of Mother Barat. The *Journal of the House of Grenoble* (JG) preserves the memory of the events that took place after the foundation. It shows how news circulated from one house to another and the interest shown in all the information coming from relatives or friends. The opening of other houses (Ghent, Cuignières, Poitiers, Niort) did not fail to be mentioned; the same was true for political and religious events. The length of the descriptions indicates the importance given to the events; for example, the pope's stay in Grenoble, on his way to Fontainebleau:[23] a number of details are mentioned except the presence of Philippine at the interview with Pius VII.[24]

Most of the letters from this period are addressed to her sister, Mrs. Jouve. They outline the family network and indicate the difficulties and the joys. The mutual attachment of the two sisters is evident: Euphrosine asks for more letters; Philippine opens herself to the troubles of this beloved sister; she encourages her and exhorts her. Political events are alluded to. In March 1814, at the time of the French counter-offensive that pushed the Austrians back to Geneva,[25] Philippine answers thus to Mrs. Jouve's request to have her daughters return to Lyon:

> I thought about the departure of your children at the same time as others were asking shelter from us, and it will take place, if it is possible, but without a carriage, without horses and maybe with closed doors. I do not know whether this plan can be carried out.

It seems she was well informed about the advance of military operations around Lyon, for she specifies:

> Now a proclamation by the general has appeared exhorting self-defense, and it is said that the enemy is near. They are trying to make him understand

---

23   On November 21, 1806, Napoleon had decreed a continental blockade on England; Pius VII refused it. The emperor's reaction was not long in coming: the Papal States were reduced to the Patrimony of Saint Peter (1806-1818); Rome was placed under military occupation (February 2, 1808); the Papal States were annexed to the Empire (May 17, 1809); Pius VII and Cardinal Pacca were imprisoned at Savona (1809-1812), and Pius VII was transferred to Fontainebleau (1812-1814).

24   See: *Notes de la Mère de Vidaud sur la Vénérée Mère Duchesne*. N° 7; *Notes données par la Révérende Mère Aloysia Jouve, vicaire du Centre, nièce de la Vénérable Mère Duchesne*. C-VII, 2 d) Duchesne-life, box 3.

25   The allies of the Empire had refused to maintain the blockade of England, demanded by Napoleon. On December 15, 1813, the armies of the coalition (Austrians, Prussians, Russians, United Kingdom, Sweden and several German states) attacked France. On the Rhône Front (referred to in Philippine's letter to her sister), the Austrians took Geneva on December 30, 1813, then occupied Mâcon, Annecy and Chambéry.

that without troops and only a few of the national guard it is impossible to resist.[26]

The letter of April 18, 1814, indicates that their sister, Mrs. Amelie de Mauduit, has been "held back by snow from God and the troops who are barring the other route." Consequently, "the burial [of their father] was simple, given the circumstances and the risk of ringing the bells that day; it was March 29."

After the abdication of Napoleon on April 6, 1814, Louis XVIII, Louis XVI's brother, ascended the throne. The Bourbon dynasty had returned; it was the Restoration.[27] A year later, in October 1815, Philippine Duchesne was called to Paris to participate in the General Council that gave the name of Society of the Sacred Heart of Jesus to the new congregation composed of five houses[28] and adopted its Constitutions. Philippine was named secretary general and would remain in that office until her departure for America.

By virtue of that office she composed the *Journal of the House of Paris* until December 1817. The precision and conciseness of the writing make of this text a page in the history of the beginnings of the Society of the Sacred Heart. Philippine recalls at first the attempt of Father Sambucy de Saint-Estève,[29] in Mother Barat's absence,[30] to claim for himself the power and title of the founder of the first community in Amiens. She then shows how this attempt at usurpation was undone and underlines one of the main points of divergence, the aim of the institute: "The first design of our founders was to dedicate us especially

---

26 In fact, Marshall Augereau, charged with defending Lyon and taking back Geneva, evacuated the city of Lyon during the night of March 21 to 22, 1814, in order to prevent its destruction; and he fell back to Valence.
27 On the occasion of the Hundred Days, Napoleon tried to regain his power (March 20-June 22, 1815), but his defeat at Waterloo, June 18, led to his abdication on June 22 in Paris.
28 These five houses were in: Amiens, Grenoble, Cuignières, Poitiers, and Niort. The house in Ghent, founded in 1808, left the Society of the Sacred Heart in 1814, on account of problems provoked by Saint-Estève. It would ask for reincorporation in 1832.
29 Louis Sambucy de Saint-Estève (1771-1847), studied with Father Varin at the seminary of Saint-Sulpice in Paris and joined the Fathers of the Faith at the college in Amiens as professor and spiritual father. Father Varin named him confessor of the religious in 1803, without realizing that, in his absence, Sambucy would try to usurp the position of superior general. A congregational crisis followed, which was resolved only at the general council of 1815 and by reception of the papal brief of July 1816, denouncing the wiles of him who, disguised under the name of Stephanelli, wanted to intimidate and annex the Society of the Sacred Heart to the house of Saint-Denys in Rome.
30 See on this subject: J. de Charry, *History of the Constitutions of the Society of the Sacred Heart, Second Part, Vol. I. Historical Account*, "Introduction: The Association of the Ladies of Christian Instruction on November 1, 1815 – The question of the Constitutions," Translated by B. Hogg, RSCJ, Pontifical Gregorian University, Rome, 1977, pp. 37-42.

to the Sacred Heart of Jesus; therefore those who wished to follow this primary vocation had to have a rule in which everything was brought to bear on loving and glorifying the Sacred Heart." Then she narrates the proceedings of the General Council of 1815.

After these pages that recall to mind "the birth or rather the strengthening of our Society, which has always desired to be able to congratulate itself on belonging in name and in fact to the Sacred Heart of Jesus," she mentions the reception given to the Constitutions in each of the communities by the local bishop. The new foundations are described: in Beauvais, March 19, 1816; in Paris, rue des Postes, March 27, 1816. The latter is introduced as motherhouse, place of welcome, of transition and sending of the religious, the number of whom was growing rapidly. A general novitiate was opened. Octavie Berthold arrived there from Grenoble on April 19, 1816; Eugenie Audé, on July 15. They would form part of the first community sent to America two years later.

On October 21, 1816, a first allusion was made to this project:

> After a conversation he had with Bishop Dubourg of New Orleans, Father Barat gives us hope that our Society will be able to be established in his diocese for the instruction of little girls, a work that is all the more important as this poor country lacks every kind of resource.

May 16, 1817, is declared "noteworthy and dear." Bishop Dubourg came for a third visit to Mother Barat, "who promised him six religious for the next spring." A last mention was made in December 1817: Father Martial, vicar general of Louisiana, "came to Paris for business concerning the mission and to discuss with our mother general the departure of the little colony that she has destined for that country."[31]

On February 8, 1818, Philippine Duchesne, Eugenie Audé, Octavie Berthold and Catherine Lamarre left the community on the rue des Postes in Paris. They met Marguerite Manteau in Poitiers. When they arrived in Bordeaux, they were welcomed at the convent of the Dames Vincent, where they waited a month for their departure, which took place on March 19. From Bordeaux, they went to Royan, where on March 22 they embarked aboard the sailing ship *Rebecca*.

---

31 Bertrand Martial, born in Bordeaux in 1770, accompanied the five religious from Bordeaux to New Orleans, where he exercised his ministry for several years. He was vicar general for Bishop Dubourg, traveled with him as far as Saint Louis, and afterwards was chaplain to the Ursulines in New Orleans, where he died in 1832.

INTRODUCTION

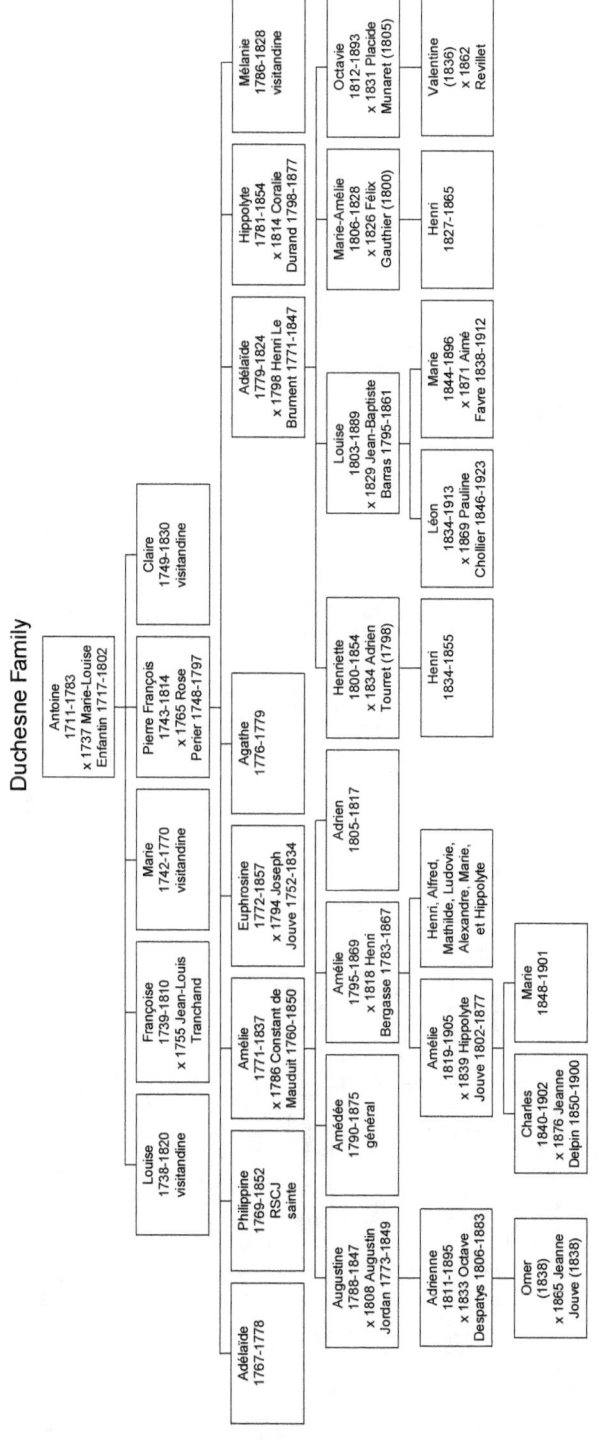

Duchesne Family

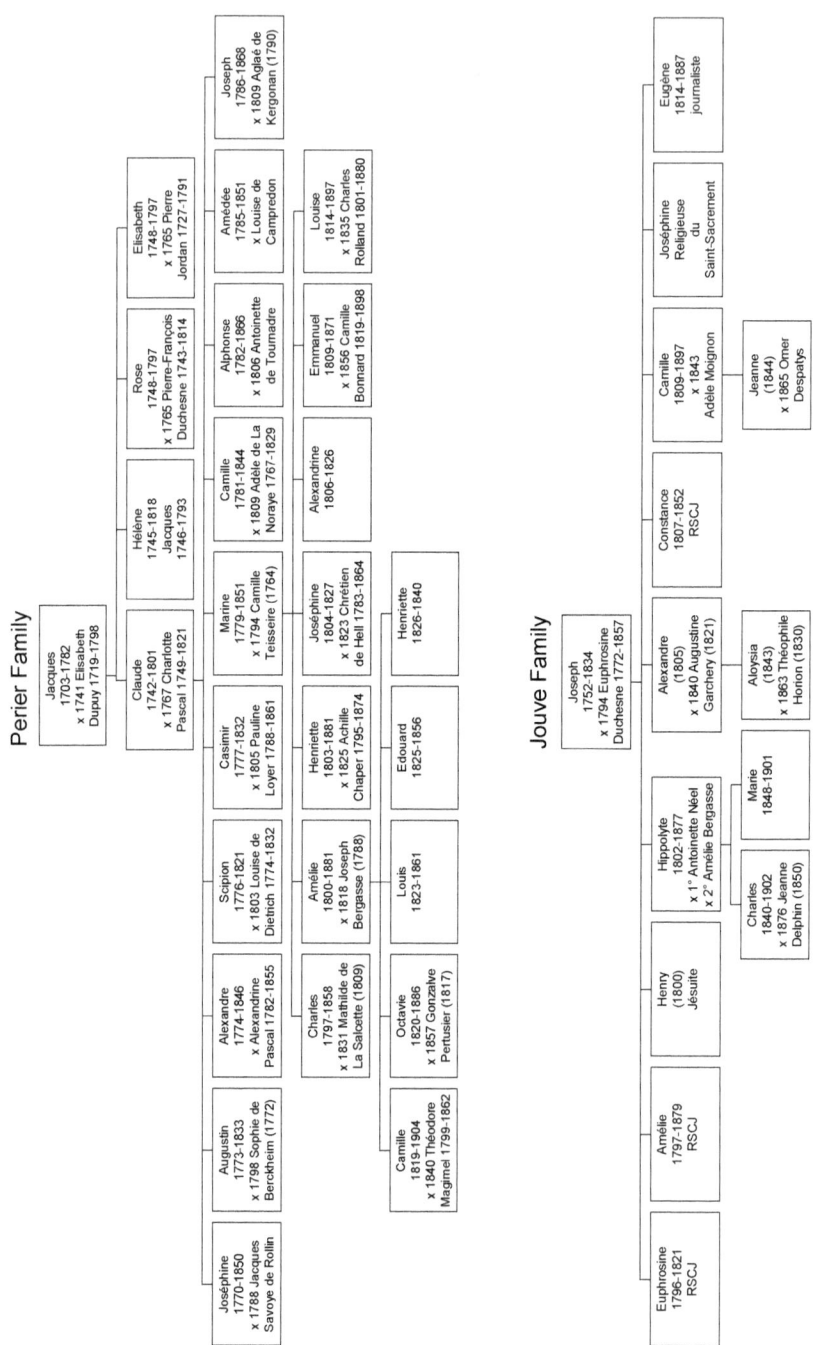

LETTERS

Account 1: Story of Sainte-Marie d'En Haut[32]

To the greater glory of God

Story of Sainte-Marie d'En-Haut (in Grenoble)
By Mother Duchesne

I see finally *on the holy mountain the feet of those who bring good news and show the truly good.*[33] I thank divine Providence a thousand times for having destined me to prepare the dwelling where so many souls will come to receive the word of God and carry its fruits far in the world. Happier still, if unworthy to join the holy group[34] who battle under Jesus Christ, I am nevertheless admitted out of sheer mercy, so that I too can attempt to seize souls away from their common enemy in order to give them to our noble master.

The decree[35] that obliged all religious women [in France] to return to secular life obliged me to go back to my family. My heart was never attached to this sort of life, and it was a land of exile for me, a foreign land; and Sion, my true country, remained the goal of my desires and of my costliest endeavors. The dwelling for which I longed was the

---

32 An archivist added on the cover page: History of Sainte-Marie d'En-Haut, which became on December 13, 1804, the second house of the Society (Grenoble), by Mother Philippine Duchesne.
33 Isa 52:7.
34 The future Society of the Sacred Heart, to which was attached the community of "Daughters of the Propagation of the Faith."
35 By the decree of August 4, 1792, the Legislative Assembly ordered the closing of all the religious houses of France. The Visitandines left Sainte-Marie d'En-Haut. The convent then became a prison, where very soon 140 persons (nobles, bourgeois, refractory priests, religious, and artisans) were confined. This included Fathers Ravenaz and Guillabert who were guillotined June 24, 1794, at Place Grenette. From the end of the Reign of Terror (July 27, 1794) until 1797, priests and monks of the Grande Chartreuse were incarcerated there. Then Sainte-Marie d'En-Haut was transformed into a shelter for beggars. The buildings continued to deteriorate.

sanctuary of religious life. Although I was very lovingly inclined toward the cloister in which I had received my vocation—and never for an instant did I feel a repugnance toward it—still, from the time of our dispersal several orders in different countries attracted my thoughts and became the object of my prayers that I might know the will of God in my regard. Several times I changed my mind about the place and the order, but never did I lose sight of my high ambition.

I lived two years in a town[36] of the Drôme, which was near the tomb of Saint Francis Regis. I had often heard one of my companions in the convent relate stories of the marvels worked by this saint, and there was a picture of him and one of Saint Francis Xavier in the church in the town, where we prayed during the stormiest days of the revolution, but without Mass there. The popular devotion of the countryside to this great Saint Francis Regis revived mine, and I constantly invoked his aid.

In that neighborhood they always spoke of him as the *Holy Father*. Every house had a picture of him and a copy of his life. Nearly everyone who was given to piety made a visit to his tomb, and many even went every year. I went there in spirit frequently, but my family objected to the trip of twelve or fourteen leagues, and I had to defer that pleasure. In this same neighborhood, however, I had the privilege of making the acquaintance of two former Jesuits, whom I consulted at different times about my vocation and who strengthened me in my resolve. One of them had been confessor to the Bishop of Grenoble, Bishop du Lau,[37] who had said to him, "If I return to my diocese, you will come to establish a Jesuit house." The death in exile of this truly venerable man deprived him of this happiness to witness to his faith in Jesus Christ.

The time of trial, but not of indecision, seemed an eternity to me; and if, reflecting on its length, I wondered at times whether God meant me to remain in the world, he saw to it at once that some passage of the Gospel referring to detachment from one's family came to my attention and revived my courage. The separation from my father, who went to Paris,[38] and the death of my mother, which occurred shortly after that, set

---

36 On May 31, 1792, Philippine's father purchased the château and land of Mr. Paul-César Eléonor Chabrières de la Roche, at Grâne, for the amount of 141,200 *livres*. The family moved in in September.

37 Bishop du Lau did not die in exile, but Philippine did not yet know it. He was assassinated in Paris on September 2, 1792.

38 On April 9, 1797, Mr. Pierre-François Duchesne was elected by the departmental assembly to the Council of Five Hundred (the legislative body). He went to Paris in May 1797 and in 1798 was named secretary of the Council of Five Hundred. He made many proposals and reports, accessible in the National Library of France or in the Municipal Library of Research and Information of Grenoble; several are in favor of the education of poor children. Philippine's mother, Mrs. Rose-Euphrosine Duchesne, née Perier, died June 30, 1797.

me at liberty to leave home and return to Grenoble in order to associate myself with some women who wished to live under a religious rule.

One of the Jesuits whom I had known was still living. As soon as he learned of my decision, he wrote to me, saying *that I had taken a step for which God would hold me accountable*. At the same time he told me that public worship would soon be restored in France, according to a prediction of the Venerable Benedict Labre[39] to a religious of Le Puy, when he passed through on his way to Italy. In another letter, he urged me to go to La Louvesc and wanted me to see him on the way, because he had then a shelter along the route of this holy pilgrimage. I wanted it keenly because my position was most difficult. I had not found anyone with whom to join, and I took advantage of a journey to Romans[40] to go all the way to the tomb of my patron. I was accompanied by one of my grandmother's servants, who was very devoted to this saint because he owed his restoration of health to him, having been cured through his intercession of a melancholy that made him despair of life itself. It was May 3, feast of the Holy Cross, 1800. I learned afterwards that the Jesuit who had urged me to make the trip a long time ago had died that very day. I did not know then where he was. As I had only two days for my trip to La Louvesc and back to Romans, I saw neither him nor the holy Archbishop d'Aviau[41] of Vienne, who in imitation of the

---

39 Saint Benedict Joseph Labre (1748-1783) led the life of a mendicant and pilgrim, going from sanctuary to sanctuary. This way he traversed Vivarais in Ardèche on his way on several pilgrimages to Rome, where he settled in 1778. He was canonized in 1881 by Leo XIII.

40 Her paternal grandmother, Marie Louise Duchesne, née Enfantin, lived at Romans. Cf. Letter 1 to Mrs. de Mauduit. Philippine's grandmother, Marie Louise Enfantin, born April 15, 1717, married Antoine Duchesne (1711-1783) on January 15, 1737. She died on October 7, 1802. Marie Louise Duchesne had eleven children, six of whom died at an early age. Her son Pierre-François (1743-1814) was Philippine's father. Three daughters were Visitandines: Marie Louise, in religion, Sister Françoise Melanie (1738-1820); Marie (1742-1770) and Claire, Sister Claire Euphrosine (1749-1830). Another daughter, Françoise (1739-1810) married Jean Louis Tranchant in 1755; she was the mother of Marie Julie Tranchant, Visitandine of Romans.

41 Bishop Charles François d'Aviau du Bois de Sanzay (1736-1826) was a brilliant student with the Jesuits at La Flèche and at the Royal College of Poitiers. He entered the Sulpician seminary at Angers in 1753, was ordained priest in 1760, then archbishop of Vienne (Isère) in January 1790. In February the government enacted the law abolishing religious vows and monasteries and in July promulgated the Civil Constitution of the Clergy. Bishop d'Aviau opposed it and was attacked by the revolutionaries. In 1791 he was accused of disruption of public order and of treason. His episcopal palace was attacked and the churches of his diocese pillaged or closed. The decree against refractory priests (November 29, 1791) caused him to go into exile from 1792 to 1797. When he returned to France, he was hunted down as an enemy of the Constitution of Year III and was obliged to hide and change residence often. Beginning in 1799, he tried to rebuild the institutions destroyed by the Revolution. In 1802 he was named archbishop of Bordeaux. A French noble, officer of the Legion of Honor, commander of the Royal Order of the Holy Spirit, he lived in simplicity, charitable to all, poor and rich, Jews and Catholics. He was declared "blessed" by Pius XI in 1926.

apostolic life of the saint of Velais had hidden near his tomb during the worst persecution. They said he was still there.

I did not go to La Louvesc in search of sensible consolation, and I did not experience any, though I had expected to. Everything about the place had an air of desolation resulting from the devastation of the church. Mass could not be offered in the sanctuary, as one altar was smashed to pieces; several figures of angels, which had supported [the relic of] the saint, were broken; and one could have gathered up handfuls of dust on his altar. The Mass was offered in a miserable barn, and I could not receive Communion on account of the crowd; but I had this happiness after the crowd had withdrawn. I left the shrine completely gripped by a desire to devote myself to the instruction of the poor in imitation of Saint Regis.

Arriving again in Grenoble, where good schools for little girls were not lacking, I took charge of a few little boys who were entirely neglected and were living like animals. I dwell with pleasure on them, for they were a real trial to my patience, and I really think that in a way we owe to them the house we now possess. It was difficult to get hold of even 3 or 4 of them, but a few good meals and the promise of some clothes at last induced them to come for an hour a day. They brought along some of their playmates, so in this way I got together about 15 or 20 boys, fairly well intentioned but so unbearably indolent and so noisy that they enraged everyone in the house against me. Their eagerness to greet me in the streets was also an embarrassment; it seemed as if I was acquainted with all the street-urchins in the town. They pointed me out to their parents, several of whom got after me because I had told the boys not to work on Sundays. Really, if devotion to Saint Francis Regis had not sustained me, I would many a time have abandoned my apostolate. I had, however, some consolations: several of these boys, who had never even heard of the Blessed Trinity, learned the entire catechism, their prayers and some hymns, and taught all this to their parents. They all went to confession, and several made their First Communion.

I got them to pray that God would enlighten me as to my vocation, and indeed the hour of his mercy was drawing near. On Pentecost Sunday 1801, I went for a walk up to Sainte-Marie, where I had lived 2 years as a pupil and 4 and a half years in the trials of the novitiate. I was with some former Carmelites, and I talked of almost nothing but my love for that house and my desire to return there. I grew so enthusiastic in the conversation that I seemed already to see the place peopled with Visitation nuns and the Carmelites installed in the former chaplain's house.

The feast of Saint Francis Regis was drawing near, and I felt an increase of confidence in him. Both before and after the feast I made novenas in his honor to know the will of God in my regard. It occurred to me one day that my return to Sainte-Marie would be quite possible if it were reconverted into a religious institution, and I felt inspired to make a vow in honor of Saint Regis in order to obtain that grace. I asked the permission of my confessor and worded my promise this way:

1. If within a year I am back at Sainte-Marie in a manner in keeping with my desires, I will send someone to La Louvesc to have a novena of Masses offered at the tomb of Saint Regis and also a novena of prayers;
2. I will receive Communion on the feast of Saint Francis Regis every year and fast on the eve in his honor; and if I cannot do this, I will ask someone else to do so;
3. I will arrange an oratory in the convent in honor of Saint Regis;
4. I will instruct or have instructed twelve poor people in religion.

With my intentions placed in such good hands, I felt new courage and I began to take action. I consulted, or had others consult, the administrators of the diocese as to the proper course to take in order to get possession of Sainte-Marie. They all thought it very desirable to do so, but they did not agree as to the wisdom of trying just then or on the means that would succeed best. One of the vicars general was Father Brochier, a man of wide experience and animated by the spirit of God. I set great store by his approbation, foreseeing even then that many people would disapprove of our enterprise and that it was wise to have the support of highly respected authorities. I was not then acquainted with Father Brochier, so I asked my confessor to consult him for me. Since he [Father Brochier] was not in favor of my purchasing the monastery, and as it was after all my own project, I wrote to him, hoping to influence his decision. I told him in detail my motives and my hopes and all that the vivacity of my desires put into my mind. My letter was long; so was his answer. It began with the words, *Digitus Dei est hic*, "The finger of God is here;" but he insisted that it was not wise to purchase the place yet, that the money could be better employed in other ways, and that to all appearances *that house would be given back to us some day*, but that we should try to get possession of it by some other means. I held to buying it, and I ended by going to see Father Brochier myself in order to obtain his consent, but he held firmly to his opinion.

It was not enough to act with the consent of my ecclesiastical superiors. I could not overlook the former superior of the house on whom I was building my hope for the new establishment, so I went to the country place where she was living, in order to find out her intentions. She seemed quite pleased with the prospect of returning to her convent. I went a second time, and she wrote a letter in concert with the former confessor of Sainte-Marie to Mr. Dubouchage,[42] who was then holding the position of prefect of Grenoble, to ask his help in this enterprise. I carried the letter myself and received his verbal answer to the effect that the time was not yet opportune for making such a request of the government and that we had better wait. This was also the opinion of Father Rey,[43] one of the vicars general, who advised me to wait at least two months. I waited longer than that, for my father came home from Paris and asked me to spend the vacation with him, and I did so. We went to Romans, and there I had the consolation of spending a few days in a convent of the Visitation, which one of my aunts, a former religious of that monastery, had just rented in order to gather together her sisters and establish a boarding school. We had conceived exactly the same idea at the very same time; but she had no need of contradictions, as I had, and in a short time her house was reorganized and the rule was in full vigor.

During that vacation with my father, I confided my hopes to him, and I enlisted the prayers of all the pious souls I knew and joined with several at Romans in forty days' prayer for this intention. On the last day I was free to return to my holy cloister. No sooner was I back in Grenoble than Mrs. de Rollin, my cousin and most loyal friend, begged her husband[44] to petition the prefect[45] to let us have Sainte-Marie; and he promised to rent it to us on favorable terms, though at a rather high price. We had to address a petition to him, which I expected to have signed by the superior of the house and the religious who would contribute to the establishment. Divine Providence allowed it to happen that the authorities were slow in drawing up that petition;

---

42 Mr. Joseph Dubouchage was the maternal great-uncle of Mother Louise de Vidaud, who was born February 13, 1801, entered the Sacred Heart in 1818, and made final profession December 11, 1825.
43 Father Rey, then vicar general, was to be named superior of the community by Bishop Simon, November 20, 1805.
44 Jacques-Fortunat Savoye de Rollin, Baron of the Empire, was then Deputy Imperial Prosecutor General.
45 Gabriel Joseph Xavier Ricard de Séalt, lawyer in Saint-Maximin, was Prefect of the Isère from March 2, 1800, to his death in 1802. He was replaced by Joseph Fourier, polytechnician, mathematician, physician, and member of the Academy of Sciences, who remained in that office until 1815.

and when at last they brought it to me, it was worded in the singular. The anxiety that the delay had caused me, the need of secrecy to avoid a raise in the price, the distance of Mother de Murinais, the superior, the complaints of some of her religious who had got wind of my visit to Mr. Dubouchage, all were reasons that determined me to sign the petition myself in order to take advantage of the efforts of the people who were actively interested in our project. The house was made over to me on December 10 [1801]. The prefect seemed to have enjoyed my happiness. I was to pay 800 francs in rent yearly and to be responsible for the repairs, which were rather extensive.

My first impulse on leaving the prefecture was to go and thank God for his goodness at the bedside of a poor sick man whom I visited almost every day and in whose room I had often invoked Saint Francis Regis, both for him and for my own intentions. He seemed to forget his suffering in the joy that my news gave him. I told him first because he represented Jesus Christ, my good Master, by his sufferings. From there I went to the home of Sister [Cecile] Faucherand, who had shown the most enthusiasm about a reunion; but the agitation that was apparent in her whole person made me foresee her lack of perseverance. From her house I wrote to Mother de Murinais, offering to send a carriage for her and never dreaming that she would make the least delay in taking possession of her house. She answered coldly that she congratulated me on the success of *my project*, and that she could not leave her present home without consulting her nephew, who was supporting her. I called again that same day on all the vicars general, and they congratulated me and said I had certainly been inspired in my action.

Then I went home and began to pack my things and dispose of what I would not need. I remained indoors in order to avoid meeting the people who were displeased with me. All the former religious of the house were. They said I was rash in going to live in a building that was falling in ruins and from which I might be expelled again. They accused me of acting without consulting anyone and of sacrificing all to my own selfishness. "Has she the means with which to support the religious who have lost all their revenues? We do not want to starve to death. We have made a vow of poverty, but not of begging our living. We will not return to our convent until we can be sure of the same security as we had before." All these remarks were made with ill-temper and repeated in the same spirit, so I considered it useless to make any advances toward these women, as they were angered by the least suggestion of a return. It was enough for my peace of mind that the door was now open to them and that both the ecclesiastical and the religious superiors had been consulted.

Father Rivet, whom I knew but slightly then, came to congratulate me, inspired by his zeal for the glory of God. His visit gave me great joy, for he knew about the signing of the Concordat[46] and encouraged me with the thought that I was not too far ahead of time in this work.

On December 14, 1801, I returned to the house of the Lord. It would have been a consolation to have done so the previous day, anniversary of the death of Saint de Chantal, but I could not manage it. All the little boys of my catechism class carried my bundles with remarkable alacrity in spite of the rain that poured all day. Not one of them stole a thing. I thought my only companion would be a poor girl of twelve whom I had instructed in religion, for Sister Faucherand had written me that she had had a slight hemorrhage and thought it only charity to wait until Easter in order to give her sisters time to make up their minds. I replied that I was not going to put off for a single hour my return to that holy place for which I longed so earnestly, and that it was time to show the world that it had lied in daring to say that we had been kept in the cloister as victims of force and that we were glad to be back in secular life. I hastened to leave my apartment. Late in the evening, in a storm of wind and rain, I reached Sainte-Marie in the wake of my baggage, which the caretaker had put in safety. I was not as badly drenched as my poor little boys. Water streamed from their clothes, but every face beamed with pleasure, an indication, I took it, of our Lord's approval.

Sister Faucherand, realizing my determination to carry out my plan, stirred up her own courage and reached the house some hours sooner than I. In spite of my happiness at having a companion, I was a bit put out, for I had to sleep in the room with her to quiet her fears. My dearest wish had been to spend that night in the august sanctuary where for so many years the name of the Lord had not been hallowed. I wanted to have the whole night for prayer, enjoying God's favors and giving him my humble thanks.

The building was without lock and key, but I was not afraid; for I realized that as God had been my guide, so he would be my protector until I had had time to assure us of safety. I got to work on this at once, and my days were spent either with the workmen doing the repairs,

---

46   On July 15, 1801, the negotiations between the French government and the Holy See resulted in the Concordat, published on April 10, 1802. The Catholic religion was recognized as that of the majority of the French, but not of the state, which nevertheless would name the bishops to whom the pope gave the canonical appointment (like the preceding Concordat of Bologna in 1516).

or cooking meals for the community of two, or sweeping parts of the house that had not been cleaned for nearly 10 years, or shoveling out snow and mopping up water, or trying to repair the window panes—the most thankless task of all, for the paste froze immediately as I put it on, would not stick and gave me plenty of occasions to exercise my patience. With the exception of this one task, all the labor in the house was a pleasure for me. I experienced all the consolations that Saint Teresa had when sweeping her monastery. Never had the keenest worldly pleasure given me such satisfaction. We went to pray in the church, where three windows and a door were missing. The cold was intense, but we did not feel it, and neither one of us took cold.

Finally we had the first Mass offered in the church, with the outer door closed. As no priest could come for Mass on Christmas day, we went to assist at midnight Mass in the city, accompanied by a young girl who had been with us only a few days and a workman who had formerly been a brother at the Grande Chartreuse and who was always a kind friend of the house. We had made habits for ourselves, and they were blessed before Mass. We took them afterwards as a present from the Infant Jesus, and I had mine on two days later when we had a visit from the Archbishop of Corinth,[47] and Bishop Caselli, both of whom are cardinals today. They had finished their work on the Concordat. Mrs. de Rollin, who was acquainted with the Archbishop of Corinth, had told him about my returning to Sainte-Marie, and he had had the kindness to ask Bonaparte to allow us to have the place rent free, but no reply had been forthcoming, and his interest in us had not produced the desired effect. It was Father Rivet who had procured for us the honor of this visit. I thought it would help to lessen the ill-feeling; but, quite the contrary, it increased it, and it seemed sure that the superior herself [Mother de Murinais] would not come. Realizing now that if I was going to get companions at all, they would have to come from different orders or be seculars contemplating religious life, I came to the conclusion that there should be a rule we might propose to newcomers. The Visitandine Rule of Sainte-Marie could not be observed strictly just then, but many parts of it could be put into practice. I gave a copy to Father Brochier, begging him to indicate the articles of the Rule that should be observed and those that might be modified for the present.

---

47   Joseph Spina (1756-1828), ordained priest in 1796, bishop in 1798, named titular archbishop of Corinth and cardinal in 1801 by Pius VII, and archbishop of Genoa in 1802. He was part of the delegation charged with negotiating an accord between France and the Holy See in 1801. In 1823, he participated in the conclave that elected Pope Clement XII.

He consented to do this and composed a rule very wisely planned, which kept the interior spirit of Sainte-Marie: seclusion, detachment, obedience, all things in common, but was outwardly less strict. He wished a superior to be elected for a year as soon as there were four in the group; then a superior elected for three years, according to the rule, as soon as there were twelve of us and we could be more certain in our choice. This rule was signed by all the vicars general except one, the former spiritual father of the convent, whom we had not asked to take up that position again because of his advanced age. Another of these priests insisted on adding this article: "Places must be reserved in the house for the religious to whom it belonged formerly." That was the dearest wish of my heart, and I persuaded Father Brochier to agree to it.

This rule, from which I had hoped such great things, produced the worst effect. The religious criticized it loudly, especially the article on all things being held in common, which they found simply impossible. They had no scruple about retaining the ownership of their belongings, yet they raised an outcry about the overthrow of the former Rule because the order of day was not exactly as it had been before, and the election was slightly different. "Our former superior is alive," they said; "why speak of electing another?" They did not consider the fact that there was no question of a superior for the religious who were still dispersed, but only for those who would come to the convent, which must have a head. Another article of the rule answered their objections, as it expressly stated that as soon as circumstances allowed, all the proposed changes would give way to strict observance of the former Rule. But they wanted to complain and found a topic in the two discourses that Fathers Brochier and Rivet gave in our church on the feast of Saint Francis de Sales, the first at Mass, the second after Vespers. They both said that soon *the daughters of this great saint, finding their dwelling, will come together eagerly*. But the nuns said, "Why make us take on obligations that we do not have? The return to our house is impossible now, and without complete stability restored, we will not return. The bishop must be in place, the concordat established, the government must authorize us and assure us that we receive our support." The majority did not come to celebrate the feast with us but went instead to a private oratory, and after Mass assembled *to protest against what they called the measures taken by Madame Duchesne*. They then acquainted some of the vicars general with that protest.

I was in complete ignorance of what was going on, and I enjoyed the greatest consolation on that feast of Saint Francis de Sales. Several priests of high standing came to offer the Mass for us with the joyous enthusiasm that holy souls experience at the sight of a work begun that may bring glory to God. The public entrance of the church was still closed, but the people came in crowds through the interior of the monastery, and our church was the first in Grenoble in which Catholic worship reappeared in all its splendor after the Revolution.

Some days later, I learned that I was considered an intruder. I said this jokingly to my companion, who had been joined by a young girl and an extern sister. Her mind was somewhat unbalanced, and in former days she had had some mental lapses. Her return to the monastery recalled these to her in a painful way. She imagined that they feared her, that she was an obstacle to the return of her sisters, that they surely had better ideas than I, that they were saints and could not err, and that it was really ridiculous that a novice had all of this in her head, that she could not change the superior, and that it was indeed true that I was a usurper. She went to reveal her difficulties to her former superior, who then hesitatingly tried to find out if she would succeed in attracting her daughters back, or if she should stay away to acquiesce to the wish of the majority, who feared this change. I do not know what she said to Sister Faucherand, but her contrary spirit was so habitual, her sleep so disturbed that I did not doubt from the first day that she would lose her head and that she would perhaps try to strike me in a doorway, which had happened at other times toward others. When I was singing with her in choir, I noticed the change in her face; but relying on the one who had brought me into contact with her, I thought that I would not be tested beyond my strength.

My conjectures were confirmed, but also my hope that I was not mistaken. She lost her mind for a time, but I had nothing to suffer as a result, except from her withdrawal. One morning, feeling ill, she told me she needed a change of environment; she left the house and did not return to live with me again. I felt this keenly, all the more because it presaged further departures. The enemy had so disturbed the young girl who had come recently that she cried all day and longed for the time when I would find another companion; then she could depart without leaving me entirely alone. The extern sister did not hide from me the fact that her courage was failing, too, and she would stay but a short time. I went through some very bitter hours in view of all this, though I still counted a little on Mother de Murinais. She had told everyone that I had done nothing in the matter of recovering possession of the house without her consent and that she intended to keep her word and return to the monastery. Many people even told her that it was a point of honor for her to do so, especially since her letter to Mr. Dubouchage [prefect of Grenoble] was generally known. The former confessor of the house was of that opinion. He was her director, and I chose him, too, thinking that since the house was to be re-established, this was a point of rule for me.

A secular lady, backed by some who feared the return of Mother de Murinais, came to see me one day and urged me insistently to write to her not to come, that I would not regret it, given the opposition that her family and her religious daughters were forming. I was told that I would endanger her life by this change of residence. I firmly refused to write such a letter, considering it contrary to the good of the institution and to general edification. It would, moreover, confirm the suspicions of those who said I wanted to dominate everything.

Finally she decided to come during Passion Week with a young nun who laid down the condition that she would have no employment but the care of the superior's health. She also brought with her two lay sisters, one of whom was about 80 years of age, as was also Mother de Murinais. I had been joined a few days before by a new companion, an Ursuline nun, who really wanted only to be a boarder. The young girl had left at once. At this time Father Rivet gave a retreat in our church. It was very well attended, though the public entrance was still closed. We made bold to open it on Holy Thursday, and it has remained open ever since, as has also that of the hospital, which was opened even before ours.

It was a great joy for me to lead into our choir, in the presence of so many people, the venerable mother for whom I had waited so long. It was a triumph. I had reasoned that her arrival would produce a very good effect on outsiders, would please my family, who really suffered because of my solitary position and the heavy burden of the house and would edify the public who were gossiping about the indifference of religious who did not take advantage of the cloister opened to them. I hoped, too, that a boarding school would be established. I limited my hopes to that when Mother arrived. Certainly things were better than before, but they in no way came up to my expectations of a religious institution. We had only Office in choir and meditation; there was no silence, no religious practice, no reading at meals, no *Benedicite* and grace in common, no cloister, no uniformity of dress, nothing. There was not even question of introducing these gradually. They all said they were just making a trial of it, for they had not made up their minds to persevere even in so easy a manner of life. What each one brought with her showed that; they had left their belongings elsewhere and had brought just about enough for a month in the country. In the depths of my heart I experienced much bitter anguish, realizing what all this augured for the near future. But while all this was in no way satisfactory, I was more distressed by the illness of the superior, which seemed to justify the predictions that a change of residence at her age would be fatal; and indeed they were already blaming me for her death. She recovered. I thought God intended to spare me, but he was really preparing me for a still greater affliction.

Two religious who had some pupils offered to join us, and Mother accepted them. In a conversation in which I took part and in which I insisted on the necessity of uniformity of dress, they said that *I wanted everything my way and did as I pleased, but that they also would do whatever they pleased*. The superior was present, but she had not a word to say. I withdrew, and I said afterwards to the confessor that I had wept bitterly when I realized with what intentions they had come, and that there was no hope that the government of the house would be firm enough to enforce the mildest rule, verging really on disorder. He shook his head and replied "that I had not wept enough, that I had but begun to weep, and that I must realize that it was enough for me to propose a thing to have it rejected, but that I must arm myself with courage." So the household was composed of a superior who, in order to attract subjects, accepted all types of characters, or rather yielded to each one, several religious who were doing each as she pleased, and some young girls who were boarding pupils.

When the superior first came, I asked her what employment she assigned to me. She replied that I was to remain in charge of the repair work being done on the building, the sacristy, the portry, and of one pupil. Mother wanted to be treasurer herself and direct our household, along with that of her sister, who had remained at their country home and did not want that burden. This meant that we would have our accounts in common with a completely separate house, and we considered this an impossible arrangement. I had, moreover, told the superior that I would at the first opportunity give her an account of what I possessed and turn over to her my purse. But her illness made me postpone these explanations; afterwards I considered it more harmful than useful to do so. Since everyone was keeping what she had, I would only cause trouble without improving conditions generally. I even had in my possession 3000 francs, which a very generous person wished to give us, if the establishment succeeded. I asked the benefactor to lend us the money in the meantime and gave a receipt, with the consent of the superior. That money was to be used for repairs on the building, and the work was urgently needed.

I realized that wills were unstable. Often there was such coldness toward me. I foresaw the breakup of the community. I did not want to have the least thing with which to reproach myself for having contributed to this, but everything tended that way. While not being involved, I always consulted the superior for major expenses, though they still fell back on me. I asked her permission to go out and for everything I thought belonged to good order. But other than that, there was no other communication than that of friendship that she always showed me, although less than before. I brought to her the children that others brought to me, and with her approval I became close to several by the care I gave them, so that if there were to be a separation, I could keep some public image and not be alone again. She soon regretted that approval upon the complaint of other religious that she had promised them the direction of the boarding school. But since she only spoke to me, without requiring that I relinquish them, I kept them. These religious had the confessor tell me that *if I kept the children, they would leave, too*. That did not frighten me. I would have seen it as an advantage. So they did not want any communication between their children and mine, which produced a very bad effect. I alerted Father Brochier, who asked the superior to bring them together for recreations, and that was done afterwards but with many complaints. It was pointed out to these women, and they realized it themselves, that discipline was absolutely necessary in the house, so they got together, both outside the convent and inside, to compose a rule, never having accepted that of Father Brochier. The superior showed me a copy, though they had asked her not to do so. I made a copy of it and showed it to Fathers Rey and Brochier, as it contained the vaguest kind of statements, which gave not the slightest hope of making for a stable union. There was no single purpose, no holding possessions in common, no cloister; one could come and go at will. They both advised me to keep out of the way as much as possible and to contribute to the upkeep of the house only as much as each of the others did, and said that as a result they might all move out and a better order of things might be established later on.

I followed their advice. I said to the superior that I did not think there could be order when everyone had money and worked for herself. I warned her that I would not make any commitment to an association of that kind. When there was a financial reckoning, I contributed my part like the others, but not more. Before that, I only created unhappy people and did not bring about anything good. I would now hold myself completely to one side. Either there would be one purse into which everyone put what she had, abandoning herself to Providence, or everyone should contribute to the repairs and other expenses.

A few days later I learned that they were planning to leave but did not want me to know it. One of the sisters who was loyal to me came to tell me what she had learned. I hastened to throw myself at the feet of Mother de Murinais in an effort to keep her; but as I could not do so without acting against my conscience by saying the same to two others who were trying to get her to leave, she held firmly to her resolution. The same sister came to tell me *that I could get her to stay by promising to do all that she required and by turning everything over to her*. I found these conditions too hard. That complete self-surrender would have been a joy to me, had I made it to anyone who was determined to observe a rule—no matter of what order. But what I saw around me every day convinced me that I would be making a useless sacrifice, so I added nothing further to my entreaties to the superior.

On the feast of Saint de Chantal I probed the depths of my soul to determine whether some passion, some selfish interest, some resentment kept me from taking the steps necessary to prevent the scandal of a rupture in the community. It seemed to me I could say I would in all sincerity submit myself entirely even to the person who had made me suffer most, if only she willed to enforce the strict observance of the rule, and I begged Saint de Chantal to be judge between me and her daughters. That thought occupied me all during the High Mass, and I offered myself to God, being willing even to leave Sainte-Marie if I was the obstacle to the good that could be accomplished there. But I knew that if I left the cloister, not a single person would remain, and so I resigned myself to being practically alone again. That very day I learned secretly that they were leaving me in just four days, on August 26. And at just this very moment of bitterness God sent me a great consolation. Father Rivet, who knew how matters stood in the house, suggested the possibility of some of the *Dilette* coming there. At the first mention I was strongly attracted to that recently founded order; and had it not been for my agreement with the government and my desire to prove to the world, in the very face of the collapse of our efforts, that the yoke of Jesus Christ was my happiness in spite of so much trouble, I would have asked to go to Rome at once.

There are several circumstances I consider remarkable in all these events. All the former religious of the Visitation came for a reunion at Sainte-Marie on July 2, the feast day of the order. I found the spirit so different from what I had formerly known and the will to return so undecided, that alone and prostrate before the Blessed Sacrament with the utmost agony of soul I said to him that on that very feast of the Visitation I must make the sacrifice of the order. That agony was so intense it brought on a hemorrhage. When my handkerchief was saturated with blood, I could not remain in the church, and I had to leave our Lord all alone, though the house was filled with his spouses. It was, moreover, on the feast of Saint de Chantal [August 12] that I learned that the date of the departure was set. Furthermore, on the anniversary of her death, December 13, the vestments that had been made for the celebration of her canonization were carried off to be sold. The 26th, the date fixed for the departure of Mother and her daughters, was the anniversary of the dedication of our church; and it was being abandoned by the very people for whom it had been blessed. On the eve, Mother de Murinais sent for me to tell me they were leaving the next morning. She was quite calm and spoke kindly to me. I have since thought that God took from her all regret in order that I might act more freely in a greater enterprise. I replied to Mother by tears rather than words, and I expressed the hope of seeing her return; but she offered me not the least encouragement on that score, saying that she was too old for such undertakings and that they called for youth and courage like mine.

On the 27th [of August] I found myself left with a select few: an Ursuline nun, Sister Giraud,[48] then a boarding student, who had come to the school on the feast of Saint Aloysius Gonzaga, a fact to which I called her attention that very day as an exceedingly good sign, and one lay sister, a former novitiate companion of mine,[49] who got her sister to come and help her with the work, and 6 to 8 pupils. I was crushed. I was a subject of scandal. Gossip had it that I had driven away the religious, that I would not yield in anything, that no one could bear to live with me, that Fathers Brochier and Rivet with their high-flown ideas were the only ones who took my part. The latter came to see me on that day of greatest affliction and pointed out to me that on just such a day Saint Teresa had begun her reform and that the whole city had risen up

---

48   Emilie Giraud, RSCJ (1783-1856), born June 11, 1783, arrived at Sainte-Marie d'En-Haut as a boarder on June 13, 1802, and entered the community of the Daughters of the Propagation of the Faith the following October 31. She was joined by Marie Balastron on November 13, 1802. Emilie and Virginia were part of the first group of novices admitted by Sophie Barat, Virginia on December 13, 1804, Emilie on January 1, 1805. They made their profession November 21, 1805. Sent to Poitiers in 1818, Emilie Giraud went as superior to Niort and later to Lille, where she died on August 27, 1856.

49   In September 1792, before their expulsion, the lay sisters were: Marie Betoux, Therese Bonnoi, Colombe Chabert, Suzanne Emery, Louise-Françoise Blanc and Marianne Girard. Philippine's companion was thus one of them.

against her. I cannot say how much that conversation consoled me. He also wrote at once to Father Roger to inform him that the house was now free, if he could only induce Father Varin to send some religious. But that grace had to be merited by a long delay.

Meanwhile God consoled me very much by the coming of Mother Rivet. After making a retreat with us, she decided to join our group and came on the feast of All Saints. Just before Christmas we were joined by Miss Balastron.[50] As there were now four of us (the Ursuline still wanted to remain free), we begged Fathers Brochier and Rivet to form us into a little society, as there was no prospect that the ladies whom we were awaiting would come soon. Father Rivet had offered to take charge of the direction of the house, and so I had no further contact with the former chaplain who, I learned, had been appointed to the care of a large parish. I let him know, moreover, that as we hoped to join the *Dilette*, the Fathers of the Faith would naturally become our spiritual directors.

I think these priests were not entirely convinced that I had a fear of being placed in authority; and as they knew I was not fit for such a position, they cast aside all my suggestions of association and union [with the *Dilette*]. It was useless for me to protest that we were not practicing any more virtue in the new order of things. They paid no attention to me. Worn out with these delays, I went at last to Father Brochier and got him to agree that we could have Mother Rivet for superior. He gave his approval and told me only to wait.

Then in a few days the bishop[51] was asked that Father Brochier be our ecclesiastical superior. He made some changes in his first rule, gave us temporarily the name of *Daughters of the Propagation of the Faith*, and on March 3, 1803, received our simple vows of chastity and obedience at the moment of Communion, after having preached a very touching exhortation. After Mass, Mother Rivet was named superior and I had the tremendous consolation of seeing at last in that holy house a form of religious life and the practices customary in communities. We had never given up the recitation of Office, even when we were only two.

---

50 Marie Balastron, RSCJ (1783-1862), born near Grenoble, arrived November 13, 1802. She was admitted to the novitiate in 1804, making first vows in Grenoble on November 21, 1805, with six others, including Philippine. She was the recipient of 45 letters from Madeleine Sophie, and died March 25, 1862, in Marseille. She may have had a younger sister ("the younger Miss/Sister Balastron") named Virginia, to whom Philippine refers in *JG* August 4, 1816. There is no other record of her. Hortense Balastron, RSCJ (1819-1873), was Marie's niece.

51 Claude Simon (1744-1825), born in Semur-en-Auxois, was named bishop of Grenoble October 7, 1802, succeeding Henri-Charles du Lau d'Allemans.

Our boarding school increased to 16 or 18, and we spent several months in that uniform and peaceful life. Father Rivet obtained for us plenary indulgences for the feast of Saint Ignatius, Saint Xavier and Saint Francis Regis, whose feast we celebrated very solemnly with a sermon by Father Rivet.

Our peace was disturbed at times by the fear that the house would be taken for a seminary or for the hospital of Bicêtre. Kind relatives who had secured the good will of the prefect toward us also parried the blows and even succeeded in saving me from paying a single sou of rent for the house.

Although we were quite happy together, we always aspired to join a larger religious society in which we could do more for God. So when Father Rivet was going to Belley[52] to make a retreat, we begged him to plead with Father Varin to admit us into the order of the *Ladies of the Faith* and to send us one of those religious as superior. Father Varin instructed Father Roger to come to Grenoble to examine the people and the houses, and he gave us hope of a speedy accomplishment of our desires. *His heart, however, was really closed against us; something repelled him*, and his attitude influenced Father Varin, who wrote to Mother Rivet that he could not yet reach a decision about us. So we were as far as ever from realizing our hopes. We even believed that they were entirely lost and that we would have to turn to the Visitation to increase our numbers and enlarge the work of the institution. Among the Visitandines in Grenoble I could see no one who desired or who was really able to direct the house. My mind and heart turned spontaneously toward my former mistress of novices, Mother de Bayane, sister of the Cardinal,[53] who was then living in Naples, where she had sought refuge in a house of her order after having been driven successively from those in Milan and Rome. Her virtues had made such a profound impression on me that she was always present to me in our Lord, but she would have to be induced by some means to return to her native land. I got the bishop to extend her an invitation to this effect; but she did not accept, giving as her reasons her age and the fact that the Cardinal Bishop of Naples would not consent to her departure unless she were returning

---

52 Belley is a small town located in the district of l'Ain, in the region of Rhône-Alpes, 80 kms. from Grenoble.
53 Alphonse Hubert Guillaume, Duke de Latier de Bayane (1739-1818), born at Valence in Dauphiny, was made cardinal by Pius VII, whose legate he was (1808). Promoted as Count of the Empire and senator (1813) by Napoleon, he nevertheless voted for the deposition of the Emperor (1814) and was named a peer of France by Louis XVIII (1814).

to a strictly cloistered monastery, of which we could not assure him. After the refusal of my good mistress of novices, I applied to her sister [Marie-Eulalie] in Milan and to another religious of eminent virtue who was with her. Their answer was the same as that of Mother de Bayane in Naples. So I had not the slightest doubt that despite all my efforts to restore this house to the Religious of the Visitation, it was God himself who had taken it from them, intending it for a different destiny.

As soon as I gave up my correspondence with Naples and Milan, the Holy Spirit made Father Varin understand *that he is opposed to delay*, and that a decision in our regard must be given, since the humble Saint Francis Regis, who had become our protector, deserved that for love of him one should not despise what was small and weak. After that inspiration, Father Varin sent us word that he was coming to celebrate the feast of Saint Ignatius with us. He arrived the evening before with Father Roger. After Mass the next morning, they went through the whole house. I took my place directly behind Father Varin so I could hear all he might say and note any least sign he might give of satisfaction or disapproval. But there is no way of knowing the thoughts of these people who are so completely self-controlled, and I who am not like that began to be not a little irritated. When he came to the chapel of the Sacred Heart of Jesus, he said: "Ah, here we see what makes religious life at the Visitation so appealing." That was not what I wanted at all. Father Roger gave me no more satisfaction. When I asked him why they had made this trip, he said, "We came to see Father Rivet." I thought to myself that for people who were so detached from earthly things, this was yielding too much to friendship.

That evening at Benediction, the Holy Spirit inspired Father Varin with a decision completely in our favor, but he did not tell us. But when Father Roger suggested that I should note the fact that we had celebrated the feast of Saint Ignatius together, Father Varin said that he would accept that augury. They were leaving the following day, and it seemed to me that the only outcome of the visit would be to confirm the statements of those who accused me of never desiring the return of the Visitation and of being the one and only cause of the departure of the religious. This opinion was already being strengthened because some inkling of our desires had got out, especially since the first visit of Father Roger.

Finally the next day came. Mother Rivet and I went again to see the two priests after Mass. Father Varin spoke to me again of *holy indifference and of the slowness* with which the works of God are accomplished. I think I answered him that, on the contrary, Holy Scripture represents him as *racing with giant strides*,⁵⁴ and I followed this up with the statement that had Saint Francis Xavier acted with such deliberation before undertaking good works, he would never have accomplished them nor covered so much ground in so few years. Father Varin laughed at my vehemence and agreed that *he must not delay and that he must send Mother Barat to found a convent for us as soon as possible.* This consoling promise lifted at last from my heart that heavy mountain of uncertainty that had weighed me down for so long. That day was a day of happiness. In the afternoon I had a private interview with Father Varin that was very helpful; and on the following day, before leaving, he assured us that we could depend on his promises. He urged us to pray for the health of our future mother, and we did so frequently with all our hearts.

He had been back in Lyon only a few days when I began to think he had forgotten us. So I wrote to him to express once more the intensity of my desires, and in order not to give offense I hinted that this was ordinarily regarded as a sign of vocation. I was getting impatient for a response when I received a letter from one of my aunts in Romans informing me that by a decree of the Emperor she and her companions were again in possession of their former house and recognized as Visitandine teachers. Her letter caused me both joy and anxiety. On the one hand, she encouraged me in the hope that I might one day share the same good fortune; on the other hand, I knew very well that once the decree was made public, it might arouse the religious who up to this time had held back through fear of opposition; and then I would be obliged to give refusals both painful and hard to explain on many counts or to witness the collapse of the project we had formed on the feast of Saint Ignatius.

August 15, 1804

At our request Father Rivet wrote to Father Varin, who was still in Lyon, to ask what line of conduct we should follow in these circumstances. Father Varin answered him and also sent me the following reply:

> Father Rivet has assuredly shared with you my answer to his letter putting before me the reasons for taking action with the government in favor of your house. Tomorrow I leave for Paris, where I hope to receive shortly the information I asked Father Rivet to procure. I do not need to tell you that I shall use all interest and zeal in cooperating with the plans of Providence

---

54   Ps 19 (18):6. Philippine was reading it from the Vulgate: *In sole posuit tabernaculum suum et ipse tamquam sponsus procedens de thalamo suo exultavit ut gigas ad currendam viam suam,* (Vulgate: Ps 18:6).

for your house. *I would sooner forget my right hand than the project about which we came to an agreement.*[55] I shall write to you at the end of my journey and tell you when we shall be able to carry out that agreement. I shall hasten matters, inasmuch as they depend on me. Help me by your prayers in the delicate business I have on hand. I also count on the prayers of Mother Rivet and your other companions. Every day I offer you and them in the Holy Sacrifice of the Mass.

September 11, 1804

Having arrived in Amiens, Father Varin wrote to Mother Rivet to tell her that Mother Barat, our dear mother, would come to Grenoble sometime during October to make the foundation. Time passes very slowly when one is eager for things to happen, and before that letter reached us, I had written to our father complaining of his silence. He replied:

> I am astonished that you have not received my letter from Amiens. I repeat the assurance that I gave you, that Mother Barat will leave early in October to fulfill the promise I made you. She will take two of her young companions with her. They will be accompanied by an ecclesiastic who, I assure you, is worthy of all your confidence. It is a great sacrifice for me to let him leave me, but I shall be repaid by the services he will render to your house, and I shall do my best to see for myself how things are going just as soon as possible.
>
> I read with great satisfaction the details you gave me about the first steps you have taken to obtain a favor similar to that secured by the Ladies of Romans. Follow the plan you submitted to me and give me news of its progress. When the moment comes, I shall do my part to help you.

We had indeed taken the first steps to secure the ownership of the house. Mr. and Mrs. de Rollin, my cousins, to whom I already owed in part the first success in my undertaking, and likewise Mr. Perier, father of Mrs. de Rollin, were all in Grenoble just then. They consented to plead my cause, as well as Mr. Perier. He agreed to use his influence with the prefect of the *département* of the Isère to secure an annotated recommendation at the end of our petition, which would greatly strengthen it, and also a recommendation from the municipal authorities. The bishop refused to add his name because he did not want to make requests for anyone just as he was trying to get possession of a building for his seminary and meeting with little success.

55   Ps 137:5.

That petition, in which we asked not only for ownership of the property but also recognition as teachers of girls of the well-to-do classes and of children of the poor whom we would instruct gratis, was addressed to Mr. de Gérando in Paris who, as friend of quite a few members of my family and with unflagging energy, carried on and completed our business. Mrs. de Rollin and my father also recommended it to Mr. Dedelay d'Agier,[56] a senator and avowed protector of the Ursulines of Romans. He himself outlined the course we should follow and from the first assured us of success.

While we were busy with all this, two religious of the Visitation, but not of the community to which I had belonged, came in the name of their superior and twenty of their companions to propose to act in common with us to get government approval and possession of our house. I was deeply disturbed by this proposal. I had to give a refusal that was hard on members of a religious order to which I had belonged, and they seemed to have no other hope for a re-establishment than our house. While those who had belonged to my community and had at one time been kind to me did not put in an appearance, I felt that my refusal reflected on them and seemed to repay with ingratitude and injustice all the kindness I had received. I was glad I did not have to make a decision, and I told them in a sympathetic way, but without hesitation, that we could not act in common, explaining that, since they had seemed to refuse a reunion previously, I could now do nothing except in concert with those who desired to unite their interests with ours, and that I was already a dependent member.

That statement caused exactly the result I had anticipated. All the old reproaches were hurled at me; I was again called a *usurper*. My heart carried this pain, and I knew it was part of the price I must pay for the happiness to which I aspired. But what was not my suffering when from a letter of Father Varin I was led to suspect that he had forgotten his promises and was leaving us without hope in a situation that was most painful in regard both to the public and to the religious who had just asked to reunite with us. He had seen the articles of the decree concerning the Ladies of Romans; he disapproved of several of them, and he wished us to break off negotiations. I wrote at once, begging him to consider the fact that, at a time when so many religious were

---

56 Claude Pierre Dedelay d'Agier (1750-1827), writer and politician, was mayor of Romans-sur-Isère (January 1788-February 1790) and had voted for the suppression of monastic orders and all religious orders in February 1790. A representative under different governments (*Constituante, Directoire, Consulat*, First Empire and Restoration), he favored the coup d'état of Bonaparte and was member of the Senate in 1800.

roused to activity, if we did not continue with our petition, it was to be feared that we would have to give up the house itself to those who might receive approbation ahead of us, for although through delicacy they had not demanded it, it might be offered to them [by the authorities].

October 6, 1804

At the time Father Varin was not very impressed with my reasons and replied that, "although (he) sympathized with the motives that made me desire to press the negotiations and considered them serious, the inconveniences that might result were also grave, and if we took our time, we might obtain more favorable conditions." So he wanted to see the end result of these negotiations before he decided on the journey of Mother Barat. He added:

> Do not worry if the journey of your friend is postponed. I am concerned about it and so is she, but the greater good seems to require a little further delay. I am writing to her today, saying how much your house deserves her consideration. Let us pray to the Lord for the perfect accomplishment of his plans. Please send me at once a letter for Mr. de Gérando, authorizing me to confer with him about the affair you have entrusted to him.

I did not delay in sending him a letter in which I begged Mr. Gérando to do nothing about our petition without Father Varin's consent, but to try to overcome the repugnance he felt toward pushing the matter. My letter to Father Varin himself was very pleading. My heart held on in the fear that so much delay might result in a break with him and an end to his agreement with us, and that my own position in regard to the religious in the city would be more and more difficult. It began to look as if I had only wished to put them off and that my ties with another group were mere pretexts. I had, moreover, nothing to offer as proof to the parents of the children placed in our care or to the people who were looking after our interests and who saw no one arrive. It looked as if we had put up a pretense in order to gain confidence and to reject the religious and several very worthy people who had asked to lodge in our house.

Father Varin answered on October 19, insisting on further delay and stressing in particular Mother Barat's repugnance for the articles to which he himself had raised objections. That was one of the most painful periods I and Mother Rivet ever endured. Two years and a half seemed already a very long time, and we were in continual fear about the future, yet there seemed no possibility of organizing our life any other way, unless we were forced to give up hope of finding a place in that holy society, which was the object of our most ardent desires.

At last the time of testing passed, and here is Father Varin's letter, written on October 25, which revived our courage. I omit nothing of it because it brought such consolation:

> Madame, I wrote to you a few days ago and my letter—since it left still some uncertainty at least about the departure of those whom you so greatly desire—my letter, I say, could not have given you full satisfaction. *I do so want to give you some consolation* that I am not waiting for your answer before telling you something positive. Every day I feel urged to fulfill your expectation. I see by Madame Barat's last letter that she too shares these sentiments of mine, in spite of the repugnance she has to the articles about which I wrote to you. Your perseverance and that of your companions in the project of reunion, which we decided upon, is a sign to me that the dear Lord will bless its execution. I shall leave on Monday for Amiens, and I hope in a very short time to announce to you the day on which your friends will set out for Grenoble. Remember, I did not deceive you when I assured you that I took your interests as much to heart as if they were my own and that your religious family will be as dear to me as my own. Today I saw Mr. de Gérando[57] and handed him your letter. I had delayed doing so because he was away in the country. Seeing he was making a longer stay than I had anticipated, I went to see him. He told me that your affair had met with no obstacle and that yesterday the petition had been granted, save for a final ratification, which should be obtained in the next week. My representations to Mr. de Gérando came too late. There was nothing more to hold back, since the case had been won. He told me he wrote to you yesterday and promised to let me know as soon as the ratification is given.
>
> For the rest, I think I should tell you that if I desired a delay in the presentation of your petition, I had excellent reasons that you will know eventually. Now that the thing is done, let us believe that the good God will gain glory from it. *Write to me.* I shall not be long at Amiens. From there, however, I hope to send you the date of departure of your friends. I commend myself to the prayers of all. In my own prayers I make no distinction between you and those who are most dear to me. Let us not belong to ourselves but to Jesus Christ.

---

57 When Father Varin met him, J.-M. de Gérando had just been named general secretary of the Minister of the Interior (the Count of Champagny); he would remain in that post for seventeen years.

Two days later I received another letter from our kind father in which he said:

> You should have received by now a letter from me, which would have relieved the anxieties caused by previous ones. I leave for Amiens the day after tomorrow, and my first word to Mother Barat will be about her departure for Grenoble.

From the time I was twelve years and some months old, when God bestowed upon me the grace of a religious vocation, I believe I never let pass a single day without praying to him to enlighten me about it and make me faithful to it. At first I put it under the protection of the Blessed Virgin, and the *Memorare* was my favorite and continual prayer to her. The many favors I received through the intercession of Saint Francis Regis had inclined me to pray more directly to him. But during my retreat I read how the Carmelites of Saint-Denis, at a time when their monastery was about to be closed, were saved by the entrance of Madame Louise into their community as a result of a novena to the Blessed Virgin. Full of confidence in her loving protection, I realized that I had somewhat neglected this mother of mercy. I begged her pardon, addressing her as mediatrix of all graces, and I begged her to obtain for us an end to our painful uncertainty. I asked Mother Rivet to have the entire household make a novena of fasts, Communions and prayers in honor of Our Lady. It was on the last days of that novena that we received the assurance of at last being admitted into the Society [of the Ladies of the Faith] and of ownership of the house.

This last piece of news came to me through Mr. Perier, to whom Mr. de Gérando wrote three lines: "My good friend, I write to you from the office of Portalis[58] to tell you with all speed that Madame Duchesne's petition has been fully and completely granted." But this statement was not really true. In the change of ministry[59] a great number of papers had got lost, ours among them; and had it not been for the vigilance

---

58 Jean Étienne Portalis (1746-1807) was an attorney in the *Parlement* of Aix in 1765. Imprisoned during the Reign of Terror, freed July 27, 1794, elected representative to the *Conseil des Anciens* over which he presided in 1796, he pleaded for suppression of the laws against *émigrés* and non-juring priests. Condemned to exile as a royalist, he had to flee to Germany, returning to France after Bonaparte's coup d'état, 18 Brumaire (November 9, 1799). Named a Councilor of State in September 1800, he was the principal author of the Civil Code. Charged with implementation of the Concordat made with Pius VII in July 1801, he was named Director of Ecclesiastical Affairs in October 1801 and Minister of Religious Affairs in July 1804.
59 It concerned the creation of the Ministry of Religious Affairs in July 1804. Between 1801 and 1804, there was no one in the government in charge of religious affairs.

of Mrs. de Rollin, we would have remained for a long time under a pleasant illusion. But she sent me word that we would have to begin negotiations all over again and send a new petition. At any other time, this news would have crushed me, but Father Varin's letters had brought such joy to my soul that I really felt the weight of my happiness needed some counterbalance. I had in the depths of my heart the hope that the house was assured to us by the will of Heaven.

I answered Father Varin's letters with an outpouring of gratitude, telling him that even in the midst of the most crushing trials I had not mistrusted the paternal kindness, of which his recent letters had given a still more consoling proof. He replied on November 10:

> I received your letter of the 2nd. I congratulate you on having so generously resisted the sad impression my first letter might have made on you and for having trusted *the sentiments of which I have given you assurance.* I am eager to share your letter with Mother Barat. I can assure you that she is *yours* and is as intimately *united* to you and your companions in mind and heart as to her own; she makes no distinction. Her companions on their side are already so closely identified with you that they seem to forget all the heartaches Mother Barat's absence will cause them and to think only of the mutual joy that will result from this union. Mother Rivet should have received yesterday a letter from Mother Barat and one from me announcing the departure on the 22nd of this month, and certainly it will take place that day. I shall look forward with pleasure to the coming of spring, when I shall witness for myself the progress of your community in the service of God.
>
> Unite yourself very especially with the family of Mother Barat on the 21st of this month; that day is extremely dear to them, for it is the birthday [of their religious life]. Some here will have a new birthday[60] that day. It will be spent in a holy joy, which the thought of the morrow's sacrifice will increase rather than lessen.

Here is the letter of our Mother Barat to Mother Rivet after the journey had been decided. It was in answer to one Mother Rivet had sent in the name of us all, expressing the joy we felt to be able to be soon under her direction:

Amiens, November 2, 1804

---

60   Among them were Rosalie Debrosse and Catherine Maillard, who would go to Grenoble with Mother Barat.

Madame, I received your letter of September 19, which expressed your sentiments in the name of all your companions in a way that fills me with joy because it shows me souls so well disposed and therefore ready to fulfil the designs of a loving Providence. Your dispositions make me regret keenly that God has chosen me to cultivate them; so many others would have been able to help you with far greater success than I ever can, or than I would ever dare to hope for, did I not trust entirely in God. But plants that grow in rich and fertile soil need less skill and care on the part of the gardener. Undoubtedly that is why the Lord has chosen me, poor, worthless, lacking all human means. But this is what fills me with consolation and assures me in advance that the Lord will bless you, and that by your prayers you will obtain for me the graces that are so necessary if I am to help you accomplish his designs. What a consolation it is for me to find souls who will to love our good God and make him loved by others, souls ready to sacrifice all for his glory! How fortunate you are to have been called to such a sublime vocation! And happier still to be determined to spare nothing in order to make yourselves worthy of this grace.

I am very eager to be with you and to assure you personally of the great affection and interest I bear you. My two young companions desire as ardently as I to express to you their sentiments of affection for you and to thank you for the opportunity you have procured for them of laboring in more than one place to spread the knowledge of him whom alone they love.

Our departure is set for the 22nd of this month. It was impossible to arrange it sooner. The change of building[61] did not permit us to leave the house earlier. I send you and your companions affectionate greetings and beg a place in your prayers. We do the same for you here. Since we are soon to form but one community, we should already be very united in the Lord.

That letter from Mother Barat was enclosed in one from Father Varin to Mother Rivet expressing the same kindly interest. On November 27 he wrote to me to tell me of the departure of Mother Barat:

The friend for whom you have waited so long," he told me, "set out with her two young companions on the day fixed, the 22nd of this month. She stopped two days in Paris and is today at Joigny, between Sens and

---

61 The religious at Amiens left rue Neuve to move to rue de L'Oratoire, in the old environs of the school of the Fathers of the Faith, from then on at Saint-Acheul.

Auxerre, where she will spend a week with her family. She will be in Lyon on the feast of the [Immaculate] Conception and will remain there three or four days to see some persons who may very soon become members of your house. She is going to write to Mother Rivet from both Joigny and Lyon.

She and I were both expecting to hear from you and your companions in answer to the letter we wrote on November 2.

I am sharing your joy in the near arrival of your friends. God will draw His glory from a reunion that has him alone for its purpose. I already experience real *consolation* in joining you in spirit, and I shall actually be with you in a few months. Let us hope all things from the generosity of our Lord, and let us be persuaded that the more we hope, the more we shall obtain. Let us open our hearts wide that he may be lavish in his mercies. I shall go to Paris in 8 or 10 days. Address your reply to me there. Your companions have become very dear to me in our Lord. Count on my entire devotedness.

November 27

It seemed to me that Father Varin had promised me to come to see us before spring, and I expressed to him the disappointment the delay caused me that would cast doubt on the organization of our community. He had the extreme kindness to answer me on this as follows:

> I wrote to you this morning, and this afternoon I received your letter of the 19th. I shall not repeat what I said about the arrival of Mother Sophie Barat, leaving on the 22nd with two companions, in Joigny today, at Lyon on December 8, and some days later with you. But I add that I could not have promised to accompany these ladies, for you realize as well as I that at the time it is impossible for me to do so.
>
> If, however, by a false calculation you counted on my coming sooner, I shall try by serious consideration to fit my schedule to your calendar. I told you this morning I greatly desire it. Yes, I can say truly that your soul and the souls of your companions are very dear to me because I have realized that nothing will hinder them from belonging entirely to God.
>
> I understand your desire not to be bound to earth even by a thread. Strengthen that desire more and more. Keep on expecting me, and do not be put out with me if I am obliged to defer the day for which you are longing and on which I shall see for myself the progress you have made. I am....

That is the last [letter] I received from Father Varin before Mother Barat's arrival amongst us, which took place on December 13 of that same year, 1804. That day, blessed and never to be forgotten, was—I speak according to my own heart—the First Vespers of another day of grace for me, December 14, 1801, on which I returned to this blessed house to work here at my own sanctification and for the salvation of souls. It is pointless to speak of the joy of that day; it belongs to our Lord who gave us this inestimable grace, and it is to him that we will speak of it with sentiments of humble gratitude.

The community was then composed of the four persons of whom I have already spoken, along with Miss Second, who had joined us during the previous summer; two widows who resided with us; an Ursuline religious on the same footing, that is, following exteriorly the same spiritual exercises as we but not bound to dependence or to our rule as far as personal conduct was concerned; there were also 20 boarding pupils[62] and five girls helping with domestic work. The other Ursuline, my former companion, had left us two months before.

Besides our individual employments, all helped in the boarding school except Miss Second and the Ursuline, who conducted the free school for the poor of Jesus Christ.

For more than two years Father Rivet had helped us with the boarding school and said Mass for us daily with untiring zeal. He increased the solemnity of our liturgical feasts by inviting many priests to take part in them and to preach, and twice the bishop honored us with his presence: 1) the feast day of Saint Francis de Sales, 1803, when he presided in pontifical style and 2) the day of the Visitation, 1804, when he gave Confirmation the second time to some boarders in our church.

The moment has arrived to be silent; I must obey and say with deep feeling:

"I will sing forever the mercies of the Lord."[63]

Domine memorabor justitiae tuae soluis.[64]

Since then, the decree of the Emperor in our favor has come. It assures us possession of the house and recognizes us as an educational institution. It is dated from the Palace of the Tuileries, 6 Pluviose, year 13 (January 25, 1805).

---

62 Among them was Euphrosine Jouve, Philippine's niece, having arrived September 3, 1804.
63 Ps 88:1.
64 "I will take up only your justice," formerly the Communion antiphon, 16th Sunday after Pentecost.

Events

1. Journey to La Louvesc .... May 3, 1800
2. Walk to Sainte-Marie in which my soul
   was given over to the desire and hope to
   return to this house .... Pentecost, 1801
3. Vow to Saint Francis Regis to obtain it .... July 25, 1801
4. The house is allocated by a lease .... December 10, 1801
5. I returned .... December 14, 1801
6. The Religious of the Visitation left .... August 26, 1802
7. Formation of our association under the title
   of Daughters of the Propagation of the Faith .... March 3, 1803
8. Visit of Father Varin .... July 31, 1804
9. Arrival of Mother Barat .... December 13, 1804

Letter 1   L. 1 to her sister, Mrs. de Mauduit[65]

November 21 [1797][66]

My dear Friend,

I am still at Romans. It is not at all as easy to leave as I thought it would be; I have let slip several opportunities, not wishing to leave our dear grandmother alone; and now I have no means of getting away. Julie is already very astonished at my delay and seems put out with me for postponing my visit, but I do not have wings to fly to her.[67] Grandmother has expressed herself in no uncertain terms regarding my departure; it will make her quite happy. I had a pretty lively scene with her as a result of some representations I tried to make to her. I did not succeed at all in calming her wrath against either her tenants or the domestics. From the conversation I gained only my own dismissal, and that in very pointed language.

---

65 Amelie Duchesne (1771-1837), youngest sister of Philippine, married Joseph Constans de Mauduit, Chevalier du Plessis (1760-1850), an infantry officer.

66 Copy: *Cahier, Lettres de la Mère Duchesne à sa famille*, p. 8-9, *Lettres dactylographiées*, C-VII 2) c Duchesne to her family and lay people. Box 5. It is difficult to determine the dates of the first two letters; they are situated, in any case, between 1797 and 1800, for Mrs. Duchesne, Philippine's mother, died June 30, 1797. In *The Story of Sainte-Marie d'En-Haut*, Philippine dates her pilgrimage to La Louvesc on "May 3, feast of the Holy Cross, 1800."

67 Marie Julie Tranchant, her cousin, lived in Saint-Marcellin, where the Visitandines from Romans had taken refuge.

In seeing the changes the years have wrought in our grandmothers, I cannot help reflecting sadly. Their blood flows in our veins, and already we feel in ourselves flashes of their fiery impatience. Let us try to control ourselves now in the first stages of this defect, which increases with age and may become incorrigible, lest the years make us scourges of our households and the torment of our families. Let us try not to be too exacting with others, but rather to pass over in silence those thousand little annoyances that tend to embitter us. For we know that no one is perfect in this life and that we must put up with other people's failings.

Every day I marvel at Rose [the servant]. No matter how indignant she gets, she never says more than "Poor woman, she makes me feel sorry for her."[68] She's a lamb, a treasure of patience and peace in the face of suffering on all sides. I encourage her in this patience and have made her promise not to leave the household. No one else would hold on, unless out of *an easy, hidden self-interest*.

Letter 2   L. 2 to Mrs. de Mauduit, at Crest[69]

[End of 1797 or beginning of 1798][70]

You already know, my good Friend, of my arrival in Grenoble; you must have understood the reason for my journey. Certainly I never would have had the courage to undertake it for a few days' pleasure here. Do not accuse me of deception on my part towards you, my first friend. If in leaving the place where you were staying, I did not tell you of my ultimate intentions, then subject to a thousand uncertainties and to the duty I might have felt obliged to shoulder at Romans, I had no fixed plan at the time. I simply left to Providence the care of lighting my path and showing me God's will. It was easier, too, in leaving my beloved sisters, not to consider the possibility of a long absence.

The reception I got from grandmother and the dismissal she gave me were the first reasons for putting my project into action. Far from being angry at her reception, I regard it as a real favor, for it wards

---

68 Philippine quotes her in dialect: *Quella poura femme, fa compassion*.
69 Copies: *Cahier, Lettres de la Mère Duchesne à sa famille*, pp. 4-7, *Lettres dactylographiées*. C-VII 2) c: Duchesne to her family and lay people, Box 5. Added: "This letter carries a subscript: To *Citizen* Mauduit."
70 The content of this letter indicates that it was written after the death of Mrs. Duchesne (June 1797), after Philippine's spiritual retreat at Saint-Marcellin (not made before November 21) and before the wedding of her sister Adelaide (May 1798). Therefore it must be dated between December 1797 and April 1798.

off the reproaches Papa might have made to me for refusing to carry out his wishes, since she herself refused to have me around. Besides, with three daughters[71] near her, all quite as free as I am, and two good domestics, there was not the least anxiety about the way in which she would be cared for.

My old desires were rekindled by the reflections that occupied my leisure time, and when I visited Saint-Marcellin, I really had no intention of remaining there. In the retreat I made there, I tried to rid myself of all over eagerness in desire, of all attachment to my own views and of all merely human sentiments. Alas! How could human sentiments have a part in a resolution that forced me to overcome those very sentiments, to rise above nature in order to follow a higher, stronger attraction? Rid of myself, I said, I searched to know the divine will, and I made up my mind.

Few persons understand what I am talking about, and few will refrain from blaming me! I forgive them in advance; I excuse their intentions as I beg them to excuse mine if they cannot praise them. My father especially, whom religion cannot aid, will always be prejudiced against me; and I will carry even to the grave, the sorrow of causing him pain; it will come to disturb all my pleasures and spread bitterness on my sweetest joys. The view of his present situation has often put a stop to my desires, but higher views have always dominated. No, I said to myself, I do not arrange the events that cause pain or console; I have no power over the heart to bring calm. In uniting myself to the One who directs all events and consoles all hearts, I can do more for my father than by seeking to please him by my attentions and faithful companionship. Yes, I have often asked that all the pain of this separation may fall on me, that I may feel it in its full force, and that I may win for my family happiness, cordial union and constant peace.

Could Papa complain as long as you remain with him? You were his daughter; now you have almost taken our mother's place by managing the household; he loves your children as his own, and they increase his family circle and promise long years of joy. Take care of yourself for his sake, and for your husband, for your sisters and their children; you are the head of the family; you must make it your duty to care for your health and preserve it for them. Moderate your work, let others do it; things will go less well, but you will be calmer and in better health. What is the temporal interest for which we must make sacrifices?

---

71 The two Visitandines and Mrs. Françoise Tranchant.

Adelaide,[72] of an age to govern a household, is certainly able to second you; dear Adelaide will pardon me as you will, if I leave you more trouble. My intention was never to abandon you without compensation. You will be fair-minded enough to believe that only one motive has always guided me; my plan was formed when I had no property at all. Even after a great misfortune[73] brought me an inheritance, I thought only of enjoying it by giving it up, reserving for myself only heavenly hopes. Formerly I foresaw without imprudence a means of existence; now that things have changed, my plan cannot be the same; it seems impossible for me to follow my desire, as I cannot find any religious congregation. But I want this letter to bear witness against me if ever self-interest comes between us, and I am not ready to make the most advantageous arrangement for you.

I have found a companion older than I and free as I am; she has a small income, which with her work is enough for her to live on and to support a very good young woman who has been in her service for ten years and whom we shall keep. We are just about to rent an apartment; as it is necessary to make a down payment immediately, I will need some money. It would please me very much if you could send me about 300 F without depriving yourself. I intend to write to Papa to ask him to allow me to take the most necessary furniture from what he has in storage. As he had the intention of selling, that may enter into his arrangements; we are getting someone to give an estimate. If our lodging allows for placing what remains, that would dispense with the need of furniture rental. My companion already has many household effects.

Plead my cause with father quickly, I beg you; do not let him worry lest events should bring failure to our business; it is so limited that we do not run any risk; we shall not undertake anything that could be dangerous, only some good works. We will live hidden lives; that is our wish, so do not speak about me at all or of what I am doing; our welfare demands that.

Grandmother is very well.

I embrace you and my sisters tenderly.

Philippine

---

72 Adelaide Helene Duchesne (1779-1824), fifth child of the family, was born April 16, 1779, and married Henry Lebrument (1771-1847), a banker in Lyon, May 1, 1798.
73 The death of her mother, June 30, 1797.

Letter 3   **L. 1 to her sister, Mrs. Jouve**

February 14, 1802[74]

How you have consoled me, my good Friend, in letting me know that your children were out of danger. Two days ago I received a letter from Melanie[75] that hardly left me any hope for your Euphrosine's[76] life. I was worried about it all the time and was on the point of writing you a letter of condolence when yours arrived announcing that God had heard the voice of your tears and spared Euphrosine. Tell your husband how keenly I have shared his anxieties and how I now share his joy. My eagerness to write to you makes me put off my response to Melanie, for I am so busy, I cannot write to her also today. So please give her my best love and to Mrs. Jordan[77] also. Is Camille still in Lyon?

Have you received a box I sent to Adelaide [Lebrument] and also a small package for her in care of Mrs. Datret? Let me know of the fate of these two things, and try to send me my black scarf right away.

I am so sorry about the loss of the Lebrument suit and also sad about yours. Tell me the outcome.

You are very kind to take an interest in the difficulties inseparable from an undertaking such as ours. What I feel most keenly is the opposition from some persons from whom I expected gratitude. I have had people talk about me in different ways; but as I have not acted through worldly motives, I am not upset by blame or elated by praise. I want that to come from God alone and from the indescribable joy of finding myself once more in God's house. I have received expressions of lively interest from many people. The archbishop of Corinth [Bishop Joseph Spina] has entered a petition to have us exempt from paying rent; he has had no response, and I have been prudent enough not to hasten the first payment. Maybe you know that he came to see us; don't say anything about his petition. As for repairs needed, they are very extensive; but Providence, always so generous to us, has inspired

---

74 Certified copy conformed to the original, Paris, November 18, 1895. Vicar general: R. Bureau, v.g. Seal of the archbishopric of Paris. Other copies: *Cahier, Lettres de la Mère Duchesne à sa famille*, pp. 1-3; *Lettres dactylographiées*. C-VII 2) c Duchesne to her family and lay people, Box 5
75 Melanie Duchesne (1786-1828), Philippine's youngest sister, lived in Grâne; she would become a Visitandine at Romans.
76 Adele Euphrosine (Aloysia) Jouve, RSCJ, was attacked at the age of five by a contagious illness, of which the person caring for her died.
77 Sylvie Jordan, née Gueymar de Roquebeau (1774-1837), married Alexandre Pierre Jordan (1768-1824), January 26, 1798.

some zealous people to contribute, and if we succeed I know several others who will donate. My confidence grows when I reflect on the charity already shown me, for it reminds me of old times; it is a mistake to say that charity has grown cold among the faithful, for I have seen them with tears in their eyes offer me money with as much eagerness as others might show when begging in case of urgent need. In return may God be willing to bless our undertaking.

We are still only four;[78] but at Easter I expect Mother de Murinais and several religious who have reserved their rooms. We are making good use of our garden and hope to profit by what we raise. The church is lovely; Mass is still celebrated behind closed doors; we had six Masses on the feast of Saint Francis de Sales and two sermons, one given by Father Brochier, who is greatly interested in our work and is a counselor for both spiritual and temporal matters.[79]

Goodbye, good and dear Friend,

Philippine

Aunt Lagrange is recovering.[80]

[On the reverse:]
To Mrs. Jouve
rue de la Convention, 22
Lyon

---

78 They were Philippine Duchesne, an Ursuline nun, Emilie Giraud and a lay sister, a former Visitandine novice.
79 Father Brochier was vicar general of the diocese of Grenoble.
80 Louise Marie Lagrange, née Léger, married François Perier, called Perier-Lagrange (1729-1805), Philippine's great-uncle, an entrepreneur who made a fortune in the textile industry in Voiron; he was a counsellor to the king.

JOURNAL 1

Journal of the House of Grenoble

Called Sainte-Marie d'En-Haut
From its Foundation, December 13, 1804, to December 27, 1813[81]

(Handwritten manuscript of Mother Duchesne) 1804-1813

December 13, 1804

The arrival of Mother Barat and her companions[82] was the beginning of a better situation for us. We could go forward blindly under her direction, and we could combine with the pure happiness of living in dependence on her that of seeing built the solid edifice that we hoped to see come about for the glory of God, and which we had prepared for with such burning desires. She was accompanied here by Father Roger, named by Father Varin to be our superior, and by Father Coidy,[83] who was destined for the formation of our consciences. We had first thought that our entrance into this new and holy way of life would be marked by a retreat, but Father Roger thought it better that beforehand we have the time to get to know one another and deferred it until after the feast of the Kings. He returned to Lyon after naming Mother Barat superior.

The feast of Christmas was drawing near, so the contemplation of Jesus in the crib was our natural focus during the time when we were to review in ourselves all the virtues of his infancy. Mother Barat presented him to us ceaselessly with all his attractiveness. At each recreation, she placed him in our midst to teach us to make him the object of our predilection, as she did. Sometimes we had to offer him what would most satisfy devotion that was too natural and sensitive; sometimes what was too pleasing or convenient; sometimes an attachment or a too tender

---

81 Original autograph, 85 pages, C-VII 2-c) Duchesne-writings History of Society, Box 1. Copy: A-II 1) d) Box 3, December 13, 1804-December 27, 1813. An archivist added on a cover page: precious document, original text on the events of the Society. Paris Archives, Motherhouse.
82 Sophie Barat arrived in Grenoble with Rosalie Debrosse and Catherine Maillard. Rosalie Debrosse, RSCJ (1785-1854), born November 22, 1785, took the habit April 8, 1803, at Amiens. She made her first vows with Catherine de Charbonnel and Marie du Terrail, November 21, 1804. She died October 31, 1854, at Charleville. Catherine Maillard, RSCJ (1784-1854), coadjutrix, made her first vows August 16, 1817, in Paris, and her profession March 21, 1829. In 1819, she was sent to the foundation of Lyon and in June 1830, to Beauvais. She died on October 13, 1854, at Charleville.
83 Father Coidy would later be assistant treasurer of the minor seminary of L'Argentière, then vicar general of the diocese of Lyon.

friendship. Jesus received from the hands of our superior the sacrifices to which we were giving birth. We would lay them down before her so that this outpouring of our souls in hers would gain for us the regard of this perfect model of dependence and religious detachment. After stirring us up to bring our presents to the crib, she rejoiced at the inconveniences of the house, the snow that came through in several places and caused a bitter cold.

1805

Father Roger finally arrived to put us into retreat. He began it on January 11. The [spiritual] exercises were held in the novitiate chapel, located exactly above the main altar of the church. During the whole time, we had permission to have Mass and the Blessed Sacrament. We were relieved of all external occupations in order to be more focused on interior reform. During the ten days, Sisters Debrosse and Maillard conducted the boarding school.

The retreat was done according to the method of Saint Ignatius, with three meditations and one consideration each day. Father Roger gave us a preparation for half an hour before beginning to speak, often with much unction and strength, then left us to our reflections for an hour. The other exercises were two periods of reading, half an hour of adoration before the Blessed Sacrament, Office and the rosary. Here is the order of the meditations:

1st day
The three meditations were on the end of humanity and the consideration on the qualities and virtues that the servants of Jesus Christ should have.
2nd day
The first two meditations on sin, the third on hell, and the consideration on confession.
3rd day
The first meditation on death, the second on judgment, and the third was an invitation to choose between the cause of Jesus Christ and that of the Devil. The consideration was on the imitation of Jesus Christ.
4th day
The first meditation on the mercy of God, the second on the beneficence of God, and the third on penitence. The consideration was on the use of time.
5th day
The first meditation on the benefits of the religious vocation, the second on the humility of the Incarnation of Jesus Christ, and the third on the poverty of Jesus Christ in his birth. The consideration on interior life.

6th day
First meditation on the humility and mortification of Jesus Christ in his circumcision, the second on the sacrifice of Jesus Christ in his presentation, and the third on the hidden life of Christ. The consideration on detachment and the spiritual life.
7th day
First meditation on the two standards; the second, examen and consideration of the three sick people who want to be healed, representing the different intentions of sinners who want to be converted. The third meditation on the degrees of humility. The consideration and examen on vocation.
8th day
First meditation on the public life of Jesus Christ, and his zeal for the salvation of souls; the second on the gentleness of Jesus Christ, and third on the institution of the holy Eucharist. The consideration on the nature of true zeal.
9th day
First meditation: Jesus in the Garden of Olives.
[The rest is lost.]

Our reverend mother had yielded to our insistence and admitted us into the novitiate even before the beginning of the retreat, so that the last day of the year [1804] was for us the beginning of our birth into the new life that we were embracing. The novitiate was composed of all our little Society: our mother was the mistress, and the two young companions whom she had brought continued the exercises, having anticipated the usual time of making vows in order to come to Grenoble; along with them, we five took our first steps.

1805

A new companion came to join us on January 21, the second to last day of our retreat. It was our sister Claudine Chenevier, who came to help as a coadjutrix. She spent some time in the house without following all our exercises and followed them soon after, having made a private retreat.

On the first days of February we received the imperial decree that has already been spoken of in the first part of this account,[84] which was written after its reception.[85] Since I have been directed to include events

---

84 The *Story of Sainte-Marie d'En-Haut* and the *Journal of the House of Grenoble* were thus considered to be a single account, drawn up at the request of Sophie Barat.
85 Sainte-Marie d'En-Haut (nationalized since 1792) was turned over to Mother Duchesne by auction on December 10, 1801. The imperial decree of January 25, 1805, authorizes them

that I had left out, believing that I was to present to our mother only the situation before her arrival, I will have to repeat here. The prefect [Joseph Fourier], to whom I went to present the copy of the decree, congratulated me cordially, applauded our efforts and promised us his continuous benevolence, the good effects of which we have already experienced.

Bishop Claude Simon

The bishop also promised us his. So God, who is always good and easy to serve, facilitated our abandonment to his service by offering such firm support.

Soon after, we gave new thanks to this dear Master for the gift he gave us in our Sisters Piongaud[86] and Deshayes.[87] The first was mistress of the boarding school at Lyon. Her success in education seemed to destine her for a larger field; and Father Roger, knowing her attraction for the religious life, had her realize two goods to accomplish in coming to this house, where she entered on February 14, 1805, for a difficult time that made her first period here painful, but she ended by loving it.

February 20, 1805

Mother Deshayes arrived the 20th of the same month. She was one of the first who formed the house of Amiens, where she was mistress general of the boarding school and of the poor school. She did not feel like a stranger in a house where she found the superior of Amiens, two of her sisters and new ones completely disposed favorably toward her. Nevertheless, she remained without employment for a while along with Miss Piongaud. The work of sacristan and infirmarian had been given to Sister Rivet, that of portress to Sister Balastron, and that of vestiaire to Sister Giraud, who was also in charge of the junior boarders. Sister Debrosse had the second class. I was destined for the first and to see to

---

    free of charge to be a house of education of girls, on the condition of having a free school for the poor girls of the city and the region. The convent thus remained property of the state, which repossessed it in 1833.

86 Marie Jeanne Piongaud, RSCJ (1772-1820), entered at Sainte-Marie d'En-Haut on February 14, 1805, and left in August with Henriette Grosier for the foundation of Belley. She then went to Poitiers, where she died on May 19, 1820.

87 Geneviève Deshayes, RSCJ (1767-1849), entered at Amiens in October 1801 and was named assistant and mistress general in November 1804. On February 20, 1805, she arrived in Grenoble to be superior there (1805-1813), afterwards went to Cuignières, then to Beauvais as assistant. She was named mistress of novices in Paris in 1818, but was replaced in October 1820 by Sophie Barat and returned to Amiens. She then went to Marmoutier, where she died on July 1, 1849. She is the author of *Notes sur les commencements de la Société*, Tours, 1845, A-II 1 a).

supplies for the house. Sister Maillard was most often surveillante of the children, and Sister Second had class in the poor school every day from 9:00 in the morning to 11:00 and from 2:00 in the afternoon until 4:00.

Here was the order of day from the beginning of our novitiate:

Rising at 5:00, meditation from 5:15 to 6:15; Office at 7:15 followed by Mass and breakfast; classes with the boarders from 9:00 to 10:00; dinner at noon followed by recreation until 1:30, when we prayed Vespers and the Rosary. At 4:00 our young sisters had classes to form them for education. At 5:00 there were classes for the boarders until 6:30; at 7:15, Matins; at 7:45 supper followed by recreation; at 9:00, prayer; examen and retire at 9:45.

This schedule was subject to change, as will be said in what follows.

On Wednesdays and Saturdays, there were no classes for the children, nor on Sundays. But on Sundays and Wednesdays, everyone assembled in the novitiate for the conference at 5:00. There was also one on two other days of the week to deal with issues about the boarding school.

Our mother went to Lyon in mid-Lent. Father Varin had to go there at the time of the Pope's visit and for the organization of the college that the Fathers of the Faith were going to begin at L'Argentière, having received the house from the government as well as the Charterhouse of Lyon for use for liturgy and to give retreats. He did not arrive in Lyon on the day he had set, which made our mother stay there longer. She returned only on the Monday after the first Sunday after Easter and brought us as our twelfth companion Sister Henriette Girard,[88] whom Father Varin had known for a long time and whom he had promised to be received among his daughters. Mother Barat had not left Lyon without having made the effort to procure the blessing of our Holy Father Pius VII. He gave it to her for herself and for her daughters and blessed with his own hands the two houses of Amiens and Grenoble. We came back to life at her return to this latter city with an alacrity that is easy to imagine. There was no self-seeking spirit of triumph over those who

---

88 Henriette Girard, RSCJ (1761-1828), originally from Lyon, sheltered and hid Bishop d'Aviau during the Reign of Terror. She was the first postulant of the Sacred Heart at Sainte-Marie d'En-Haut. She entered April 22, 1805, and made her vows on November 21, 1805. She accompanied Sophie Barat to the foundation of Poitiers in July 1806, and in June 1809, she went to Amiens. She was a member of the General Council of 1815 and remained at the motherhouse. She was there at the departure of Philippine and, after her, kept the Journal of the Paris house (December 25, 1817-Februrary 27, 1819). She then went to Amiens, where she died. She wrote two notebooks on the beginnings of the Society, titled: *Notes de la Mère Girard sur la maison d'Amiens I*; *Notes de la Mère Girard sur les fondations de Poitiers, Niort, Sainte-Pezenne, Cuignières, Beauvais, Paris, Quimper, La Ferrandière II*, A-II 1 a).

said that she would not return and that she had carelessly abandoned this house because it was impossible to maintain.

People still could not stop talking about this house. Without repeating the old judgments that were held against the first persons who had lived there and which surfaced again, the shameful jealousy, the malevolence, the impiety dared to attack the pure virtue of the courageous ones who had left the center of tranquility and happiness to take on the difficulties of a new foundation because they envisioned there the glory of God and his will. They had the indignity of calling them penitents, to cast doubt on their good faith. They found mysterious a way of life completely hidden in God with Jesus Christ and concluded that they were suspect.

Many people did not go that far, but set themselves to criticize the firmness applied to prevent useless admissions, to want only subjects who were young and able to bend to the rule, to remove customs of the ancient monasteries that could no longer go with the crucial times in which we are today. Finally, they denied their abilities, laughed at their youth and especially that of our mother, as if the gifts of God were given only at a certain age and that his spirit depended on our humanity. When I saw her always acting according to the inspiration of God who guided her, when I compared the unction of her word with the bitterness of those who attacked her, I had no trouble distinguishing between passion and the virtue that seeks only God; and attaching myself to her, I laughed at the stirring up of passion that could for a time stop the work of God but did not know how to destroy it. They made great efforts to take from us some of our dear companions, especially Miss Girard, for in Lyon as in Grenoble, they energetically criticized our union.

Soon after the arrival of our mother, one of the lay ladies left us. This exit stirred up again the judgment of our unsociability, even though she contributed nothing to this, but on the contrary spoke favorably of the community and gave no other reason for her change than her bad health. But still it had the effect of hindering the growth of the boarding school. Without ignoring this slowing of the work of God, we know, when we seek only him, to bless him for having tied our hands, since it is he who stops us and not the fear of wearing ourselves out for him. God rewarded us by the abundance of graces that he bestowed on our little flock.

May 1805

On the first of May, two Fathers of the Faith arrived in Grenoble: Father Lambert[89] and Father Gloriot.[90] They came for the celebration of the Jubilee,[91] which had the most admirable success. On the same day, they came up to Sainte-Marie, where we loved to see those who worked in the apostolate. They found our children gathered in the novitiate, singing the praises of the Mother of God on that day that began *the month of Mary*. This was the occasion for Father Lambert to inspire in them a tender devotion toward the mother of goodness, and this holy preacher, distinguished in all of Europe, took pleasure as did his master to be among children and instruct them. They went several times to the cathedral to hear him, as well as Father Gloriot, but these two also came several times to our mountain to make a few streams of their solid and appealing eloquence flow. Father Lambert preached at Mass on the feast of Pentecost. He did the same for the First Communion of our children on the feast of the Sacred Heart of Jesus, and, after having instructed them on the way to receive the Lord Jesus well, he himself placed him on their innocent lips. Father Gloriot showed us in the afternoon true devotion to the Heart of Jesus Christ in all its expanse and excellence. He preached again on the feast of the Visitation.

It was on this feast that our holy bishop, invited by the missionaries, came to spend the day with us. After dinner, he kindly distributed the prizes to the children who merited them. He crowned seven and gave the first ribbons of merit to those of the boarders to whom their companions had awarded them as prize for their good conduct. This day made remarkable by the pleasant reunion of the persons to whom we owe the most, by this first distribution of prizes, was made even more so by the gift of the Holy Spirit that the first communicants received that day in Confirmation. When the bishop had withdrawn, Father Lambert spoke in the midst of the children about their happiness, invited them never to extinguish in their souls the spirit of fire and love and departed blessing them and us.

The following Sunday, with the young people of the congregation assembled, we heard him speak against human respect. Several times

---

89 Father Lambert gave missions in several French cities, including Grenoble and Poitiers. In 1806, he played an important role in the foundation of the house of Poitiers. In 1815, he was canon of the cathedral.
90 Charles Gloriot, SJ (1768-1844), was one of the first companions of Father de Tournély in the Society of the Fathers of the Sacred Heart. He was present at the inauguration of the novitiate of Poitiers on September 8, 1806. He entered the Company of Jesus after its restoration in 1814 and died at Avignon on February 2, 1844.
91 The Jubilee of 1805 celebrated the return of freedom of religion in France.

again in familiar conversation, he inspired us either to the practice of virtue or to the desire for heaven. His benevolence did not stop there; when preparing to leave Grenoble, he asked our bishop to transport the one he was bringing them, whom they had merited by their important services, thus changing the face of a sinful city and bringing those who had closed their hearts for 30 to 50 years to appreciate the word of God. Father Lambert had already brought us the bishop for the feast of Saint Francis Regis, our dear and zealous protector. In these two visits, we did not know which to admire more, the goodness of the pastor who visits his flock, or Father Lambert's ability to draw him in by seeming himself to act as pastor.

After the distribution of prizes, our boarders returned to their ordinary exercises. Our mother, however, changed something in their order of day and put the class after dinner at 3 o'clock. The same teachers were continued.

Mother Deshayes, who was already librarian, was mistress general of the poor school, whose pupils were divided into two classes: the older ones confided to Sister Girard, while the little ones continued with Sister Second as teacher. Sister Piongaud was instructor in penmanship and drawing. But that was not for long, as her departure was soon decided, as we will tell after saying a word about the last meeting with Father Lambert. He thought of us up to the last moment. On the feast of Saint Ignatius, he brought us permission from the bishop to have Benediction every Sunday and on all the principal feasts of the Church and of our order. We had asked for this grace to no avail, and we owed it to the just recognition of all that the bishop owed to Father Lambert, who could not even obtain it himself except after many requests.

He preached the same day at the Mass of the holy founder. His zeal did not stop there, but again after the Mass, he gathered us together and spoke to us informally about the pleasure that he had in seeing in us a contentment so pure and so visible that it shone out at first sight. He exhorted us to put ourselves above worldly judgments; he showed us the advantages of the common life that we had embraced, and he congratulated us on being mad in the eyes of the world as he himself was mad; but at the same time, he expanded on that divine folly, the folly of the cross that makes us as pleasing to Jesus Christ as despicable in the eyes of the world. He left the same morning to go to a country place near Lyon to rest from the tiring work of the mission. Father Gloriot also left with him.

Father Varin did not delay in coming to fill in the gap left by the absence of these good missionaries. He arrived during the octave of

Saint Ignatius and spent 4 days in Grenoble. He visited the house, he examined the changes made since his last visit, and he was witness to the delightful gaiety that reigned in our exchanges. He could only wish for us the continuation of our happiness, and he exhorted us to make ourselves worthy. His business and his health, which was not very good, prevented him from speaking to us as much as we would have wanted; but he testified to his satisfaction at seeing us all on the way where God had placed us to cooperate in his work. He seemed like a father in the midst of his children and always left us more imbued with his continual goodness.

August 1805

From this time period, it was decided that Mother Piongaud would go to Belley in a new house. She was wanted to establish order in a numerous boarding school that the Fathers of the Faith had run up to that point. For a long time, Madame de Luiset, a canoness who had begun a house of education in Belley, wanted to be assisted and even replaced by the sisters of our Society. Her request was finally heard: Mother Piongaud left several days after her father to be mistress general. Mother Grosier,[92] who was destined to be superior of this first house where order reigned, but especially humility and charity, came ahead of time to spend some time in our midst.

September 7, 1805

It was not long before we were visited by some men of God, and this was not one of the least of the advantages of our situation of being with them in a community of prayer and of receiving their instruction. Father Barat, brother of our mother, came to Grenoble. We were even more astonished at his high virtue than at the depth of his learning and had a little difficulty approaching him; but charity knows how to bend,

---

92 Henriette Grosier, RSCJ (1774-1842), born in Beauvais on December 24, 1774, was assisting her aunt, Miss Devaux, at Amiens when the boarding school became the first house of the future Society of the Sacred Heart, October 15, 1801. She made her first vows on November 21, 1801, her profession May 29, 1803, and was mistress of novices after the departure of Sophie Barat for Grenoble. She went to found a house in Belley in the autumn of 1805. When that effort failed, she went to Poitiers, where she was named superior in May 1808. She left from 1816 to 1818 to replace Marie Prevost at Amiens and, in 1824, to carry out with Angelique Lavauden the foundation of the house in Metz at the request of Bishop Jauffret. She was assistant general from 1815 to 1827 and admonitrix to the superior general. From 1832, she was responsible for the houses of the West of France. She was not able to attend the general council of 1839; she wanted to participate in that of 1842, which was to be held at Lyon, but she was seriously ill and had to stop in Paris, where she died on July 28. The 171 letters of Sophie Barat reveal Sophie's deep friendship with the one she sometimes called "my Henriette."

and soon we could not have been more desirous of profiting from the five days that he stayed here. These brief moments were put to good use; especially when he gave us three solid and touching exhortations.

The first was on the confidence in the will of God that he drew from these words of the Blessed Virgin: *"May it be done to me according to your word."*[93] He presented it to us as always lovable, whether it wounds or strengthens, always connected to our perfection about which, in order to enter into its intentions, we should not slacken in working along the way of the most difficult sufferings and humiliations. He presented the lover of Jesus as so avid to conform herself to his example that she no longer wants to live without the piercing sword that afflicts the soul, and without that holy melancholy, daughter of an ardent love that has no taste for any earthly thing because she finds there only obstacles to her union with the beloved. He noted these ardent souls: Saint Teresa of Avila and Saint Magdalene de' Pazzi,[94] who could not exist without suffering.

The second exhortation was on zeal for the salvation of souls; and to stir it up in us, he presented to us the devil as more devoted, more persevering for the loss of souls than we are to save them. It was a terrible consideration, quite capable of moving a soul indifferent to the salvation of one's brothers and sisters; but while exhorting us to work for it, he warned us at the same time to do it first for ourselves, and he showed that it was necessary, and how to do it.

In the third exhortation, he represented to us *wisdom* abiding in heaven and *fear* abiding on earth, where we cannot help trembling in view of our faults and the justice of God. But since that way of apprehension is too difficult for our nature, he taught us how to advance in the way of heaven by the help of *devotion* that renders us fervent in God's service. Devotion or rather its exercises can be different according to our state, and it is *learning* that will show us those that are appropriate for us. But how can we embrace them when they contradict our inclinations and attitudes, without the gift of *strength* that enables us to overcome all the obstacles opposed to our salvation? And he showed us the effects of this gift in so many saints who were conquerors of souls and who made of their bodies victims always ready for immolation. *Strength* can go too far; it can pull us off track when we do not know how to discern the spirit that leads us. So *learning* and *counsel* are

---

93   Luke 1:38.
94   Mary Magdalene de' Pazzi (1566-1607), of Florentine origin, was a Carmelite mystic whose spirituality and writings had a strong influence in Europe. She was canonized by Pope Clement IX on April 22, 1669.

necessary. It was the desire for that learning that made Saint Augustine say: *"May I know you, Lord, and may I know myself. May I know you in order to love you and may I know myself in order to hate myself. May I know you in order to tend toward you; may I know myself in order to leave myself."*[95] But the *counsel* that directs *learning* and *strength* belong chiefly to the directors of souls. Finally, *intelligence* makes us know that there is no happiness except in God and in heaven where he lives. This sixth gift makes us wish for heaven where we will be united to eternal wisdom and where we have a taste only for heaven. Father Barat, leaving us in such good dispositions, left us the same morning, promising to remember us before God.

September 1805

A few days after his departure, on September 23 we held the solemn distribution of prizes, preceded by three days of retreat. The distribution was done by Father Royer, Sulpician and director of the seminary of Saint Irenaeus in Lyon.[96] Fathers de la Gré, pastor of the cathedral, Rambaud the elder and Rivet assisted him. The next morning, Father Royer again was good enough to come to say Mass for our children, to receive at the foot of the altar the crowns[97] and prizes that they came to offer at the Mass, and to speak to them about the ceremony of the previous day to animate some to reach out for the reward since God offered it to them, and to moderate the joy of others by teaching them to value only the glory of heaven and the crown of immortality.

November 13, 1805

After the distribution of prizes, our mother made her retreat, after which our Sister Grosier, destined to be the first superior at Belley, arrived with Sister Felicity [Lefèvre],[98] her companion. They were both supposed to stay in our house until after the retreat that began on November 13, a feast dear to us since it is that of one of the most famous novices of the

---

95   This quotation does not correspond to Saint Augustine's text on self-knowledge; it comes rather from Augustinianism.
96   Father Royer was pastor of the church of Saint André at Grenoble until February 1805, when he was named director of the seminary of Saint Irenaeus at Lyon, at the request of Cardinal Fesch.
97   When a prize or honorable mention was granted to a student, she was given a book and a crown. The offering of prizes and crowns, made during the Mass that followed, was an act as important for the recipients as for the community.
98   Felicity Lefèvre, a novice who came from Amiens with Henriette Grosier in October 1805, was destined for the foundation at Belley, but her obedience changed. She accompanied Sophie Barat to Amiens on November 23, returned to Grenoble with her in May 1808, and left the Society of the Sacred Heart in August 1808.

Company [of Jesus], Saint Stanislaus Kostka.[99] Father Varin and Father Roger had arrived two days before to give the retreat themselves. Other than those of the house whose names have already been given, there were also Miss Crouzas,[100] Miss [Jeannette] Rivet and Miss Messoria,[101] all three of whom had come to share our lot. The last one was obliged by her mother to leave again for a while. The first two entered the novitiate the next day after the retreat. Before and since then, Sisters Marie Bonnet and Marie Borin[102] entered with us as coadjutrices.

The retreat was in common for every one of the house except our mother, one other for the care of the boarding school, the boarders and the service girls. Father Varin gave the opening on the feast of Saint Stanislaus in the interior chapel of the house, where we had the bishop's permission to have Mass said and have the Blessed Sacrament kept during the retreat. It was he who gave the consideration at four o'clock every day. He expanded on the end, the spirit and the advantages of our Society; he spoke of recollection, interior spirit, poverty, obedience, the education of youth, on devotion to the Sacred Heart of Jesus and on the way to act so as not to lose the fruit of the retreat. The three meditations were given each day by Father Roger.

Meanwhile, in the house everyone sought to create in her heart a worthy abode for the Holy Spirit and invoked him every day to inspire for our good fathers the rules that we should follow. They used every moment not dedicated to the retreat to revise and abridge them. In a few days, they were finished and presented to the bishop by our mother and one of her daughters, the eve of the Presentation. He approved them verbally, unable to do anything else, and gave his blessing to them and all of us in the person of our mother. At the same time he designated for our superior Father Rey, who had long experience of religious houses. We were astonished not to hear named for this role Father Brochier, who could thus no longer help us except by his advice and his prayers; for to crown his labors, his zeal and his fidelity, God

---

99 Stanislaus Kostka (1550-1568), a Polish Jesuit novice, died soon after beginning his novitiate in Rome. His radiant joy and spirit of service were attractive to all. He was canonized on December 31, 1726, by Benedict XIII, and his feast is November 13. He is the patron of novices in Ignatian congregations.
100 Christine de Crouzas, RSCJ (1771-1828), from Savoy, left Sainte-Marie d'En-Haut in August 1807, to enter the Visitation at Chambéry, but returned to the Sacred Heart on June 23, 1809. She died in Grenoble on March 2, 1828.
101 Caroline Messoria, RSCJ (1783-1838), entered at Sainte-Marie d'En-Haut in November 1805, and went to Poitiers in August 1818, then to Bordeaux in 1819. She died on January 27, 1838.
102 They did not stay: Marie Bonnet returned to her family, and Marie Borin went to the Visitation at Romans.

afflicted him in his vision and hearing in such a way that he could no longer be occupied for his glory in this way.

November 21, 1805

God, who watches over the welfare of the house, enabled us to find in Father Rey an enlightenment and interest that made us very grateful for his goodness. He wanted to assist at the ceremony of our vows, which took place on the evening of the feast of the Presentation in the inside chapel. Fathers Rambaud and Rivet were also there with our two fathers. Father Varin gave the address before the ceremony and took these words as his text: *"This day will be celebrated among you."* He compared it to our baptism and our First Communion and showed that the state of infancy had hindered us from profiting from them or being aware of their importance, but now this time we had the means to purify ourselves by our sacrifice as if in a new baptism and that Jesus Christ was going to take full possession of our souls.

The evening before, he laid out for us the extent of our obligations with regard to the four vows that we were going to make and the modifications that the vow of poverty would require. Each one made them after the address; kneeling before the altar upon which the Blessed Sacrament was exposed and in the hands of our mother, who was standing to the right side of the altar; she placed the formula that she had just said, signed with her signature. This formula contained the vows of poverty, chastity, obedience, and to dedicate oneself to the education of youth. Our mother and the senior professed had begun by renewing their vows; they were Sisters Grosier, Deshayes and Debrosse. Those who had the happiness to make their first commitment were, in this order, Sisters [Marie] Rivet the elder, Duchesne, Girard, Giraud, Balastron, Second and Maillard. Our other sisters remained novices.

The retreat continued until Sunday, when in the morning Father Varin gave the discourse on gratitude for the conclusion of the retreat. His text was taken from the words of Tobiah to his father: *"Father, what will we give him for all the benefits he has given us?"*[103] In the evening, he gathered us all to propose to us a sacrifice that he recommended us to make during Benediction, without telling us yet what it was. After Benediction, he told us what it was: Mother Barat was going to leave us for a while, and to make up for it she would leave us Mother Deshayes. She had to go to Amiens on Society business. Her departure was very soon and it took place the following Friday.

---

103 Tob 12:2-3. Philippine added in a note: *"To the angel who had guided him."*

December 11, 1805

She had for traveling companion Sister Felicity, who was no longer destined for Belley where Sister Grosier went alone soon after and arrived on December 11. On the 13th of the same month, we kept with lively gratitude the anniversary of the happy day when our mother and her two companions arrived in this house.

We soon learned with great consolation that Mother Barat's journey had all the success that we could have desired. She obtained for Belley from the superiors in Lyon the same approbation that we had from our bishop, and this house did not delay in prospering under the care of Mother Grosier. From the beginning, she had sixteen very fervent daughters and more than 50 boarders.

But our mother's consolations were even greater at Amiens.[104] She found there her first companions growing in fervor and regularity and a flourishing house that was already creating in several cities the desire to have a similar one. Father Varin and Father Roger were also in Amiens near Christmas in order to review all our rules with Mother Barat, to obtain their approbation from the bishop of Amiens, Bishop de Mandolx,[105] and to proceed to the election of the superior general of our new Society.

January 18, 1806

On January 18, 1806, our Mother Barat was designated by a plurality of votes of the senior professed to continue the responsibility, the functions of which she was already carrying out.

Mother Barat arrived in Amiens on December 14, 1805, and Father Varin on December 24, 1805. They held a general conference to revise the rules and regulations, and they compiled the Constitutions.

On January 18, 1806, Mother Barat was elected superior general according to the stipulations of the Constitutions, in the presence of Father Varin [superior] general
of Father Roger, his assistant
of Father Sambucy, confessor of the house
the secretary: Mother Ducis[106]

---

104 Philippine was not aware of the difficulties in the house in Amiens, where Father Sambucy de Saint-Estève and Mother Baudemont tried to seize power. Mother Barat was neither wanted nor welcomed. Her election as superior general was by a majority of a single vote.

105 Jean François de Mandolx (1744), vicar general in Marseille, had emigrated to Italy and Germany during the Revolution. In February 1803, he was named bishop of La Rochelle, then of Amiens in 1805. In June 1811, he attended the Council of Paris convoked by Napoleon, while Pius VII was a prisoner in Savoy, and supported the prerogatives of the pope against the emperor's attempts at usurpation.

106 Henriette Ducis, RSCJ (1774-1844), niece of the poet Ducis, entered at Amiens in 1804 and

Mothers Ducis and Desmarquest[107] were commissioned by Father Varin to review the notes on suffrages.

On January 19, 1806, the professed made their vows in the hands of the new general, Mother Barat, with these words:

Formula of Vows

I (first and last name), humbly prostrate at the feet of the Holy Trinity, and in the presence of the Blessed Virgin, Mother of God, of the whole heavenly court, of the apostles Saints Peter and Paul, and of all the saints, promise to Almighty God and to you, very Reverend Mother (name) who hold for me the place of God, and to all those who will succeed you, perpetual *poverty, chastity and obedience*, and in conformity to that obedience, to consecrate myself to the education of youth according to the end and rules of the Institute: all understood with the meaning with which it was explained.

At.... (city)...in the church of the house of the Institute.

This... (day of the month of the year).

General explanation of the vow formula

Made on November 21, 1805, and for the first time, in the house at Grenoble.

1. The vows are perpetual, but it is a constitutional rule that the Society always reserves the right to exclude someone for very grave reasons, and in this case, she is released from her vows.

> made her first vows July 31, 1805. During the crisis of 1806-1814, she took the side of Father de Saint-Estève, but accepted the decisions of the General Council of 1815. She was secretary general from 1820 to 1833, then superior of the house at Conflans. For health reasons she returned to Amiens, where she died September 4, 1844.
>
> 107 Felicity Desmarquest, RSCJ (1780-1869), born at Guillaucourt (Somme) August 13, 1780, entered September 19, 1804, in Amiens and made her vows on July 31, 1805. In 1808, she was superior at Cuignières, near Saint-Just-en-Chaussée (Oise), a house destined to serve as refuge in time of persecution, transferred to Beauvais in February 1816. She was elected councilor general in 1815, then assistant general and admonitrix in 1827. She was at the same time mistress of novices and responsible for first-year aspirants in Paris (1822-1830). In August 1830, she went with the novitiate to Middes, Switzerland, founded the houses of Turin, of Santa Rufina in Rome (1831), of Conflans (1833), and of Quimper (1835). In July 1835, replaced by Eulalie de Bouchaud in the general novitiate in Paris, she left for the Trinità dei Monti in Rome. On her return to Paris, she was superior of the house at Conflans, where she stayed until 1854, and responsible for the probanists (1843-1863), while also making visits of houses. But in 1863, she was struck with a paralysis of the lower extremities and released from her responsibility as assistant general in 1864. She died on March 11, 1869.

2. In the present circumstances, one makes the vows with this understanding that, if she finds herself in the above case, the authority is left to the ordinary confessor of the house to dispense from the vows, according to the determination of the superior assisted by her council.

Specific Explanation on the Vows

1. Obedience does not oblige under pain of mortal or venial sin, except in the case in which the superior commands in virtue of obedience or when the thing is already evil in itself.
2. In the present circumstances, one makes the vow of poverty in such a manner as to keep the right to possess and to make all the civil dispositions in the same way as she did in the world, but she does not exercise this right except according to the advice of the superior.
3. The vow to consecrate oneself to the education of youth is so subordinated to obedience that even if one's whole life is occupied with other functions by the same obedience, she would have fulfilled the vow no less meritoriously than if she had been employed in the education of youth.

Note for Amiens only: The vows are null and no longer exist in the case when one is interrogated by incompetent authority for what concerns the internal forum. Exceptions are the pope and the bishop of the diocese.

It was also decided what would be the name that we would bear, and we chose that of *Daughters of the Sacred Heart of Jesus*, the name that Father *de Tournély*, who first undertook to restore the order of the Jesuits, wanted to give to his first associates, who for the most part were united with the Jesuits of Russia since their re-establishment by the Pope. At that time Father de Tournély, of whom Father Varin was one of the first disciples and is now his successor in the overall charge of the Society of missionaries, had resolved to form a society of women who would carry that beloved name. His wishes, not accomplished during his lifetime, were carried out by unanimous desire of everyone who participated in the choice of the name; and already at Amiens, the cachet of the house was the Sacred Heart of Jesus.

We welcomed the news of our new name with great joy, and even more on learning that divine Providence was preparing a new house for us in Ghent.[108] We did not know the details of this project until after the return of our mother, which did not happen until May 1806. She no longer found here Miss Marie Borin, who returned to the Visitation at Romans, nor Marie Bonnet, who returned to the world, since her vocation did not seem sure. But she found all her other daughters and Miss Messoria, who had come to join us on Wednesday, not yet sure that she would be able to stay with us.

Our mother general returned from Amiens with Sister Felicity [Lefèvre] and had taken with her along the way Miss de Cassini,[109] who, 15 days prior, had set out to become a religious at La Trappe in Switzerland, and Miss Gouttenoire de Montbrison, who, three weeks earlier, had been forced to leave in order to convince her family of her vocation, which seemed to irritate them a great deal.

June 13, 1806

On June 13, feast of the Sacred Heart this year, we all renewed our vows in the inside chapel at eleven in the morning, in the hands of our venerable Mother Barat, who renewed hers first, promising to God alone; then, repeating word for word the formula said by Mother Deshayes, we promised obedience to our mother general. Her naming to this important position of superior general no longer allowed her to be in charge of the running of this house. Thus, from two days after her arrival, she named Mother Deshayes for us as local superior, no longer as interim and temporary.

June 16 was also a notable day for this house. It was the feast of Saint Francis Regis, our generous patron, whom we tried to celebrate as best we could.

The next day our superior general shared with us several letters from Father Varin, from Amiens, and especially one from Father de Sambucy,

---

108 The foundation was made in May 1808, in the ancient abbey of Dooreseele in Ghent, then in French territory.

109 Cécile de Cassini (1777-1867) was the daughter of Jean-Dominique de Cassini (1748-1845), astronomer, director of the Observatory of Paris, and member of the Academy of Sciences, having contributed to the development of the metric system and the reorganization of France into *départements*. In 1803, Cecile entered the house at Amiens and left in 1806 for an unsuccessful attempt at La Trappe. In 1825 and 1826, she accompanied Mothers Bigeu and Lavauden to Rome. In 1858, more than 81 years old, she made a new try at the Sacred Heart. She died in 1867 at Orleans, without having made a definitive commitment. She most likely participated in the elaboration of problems in astronomic geography, proposed in the *Exercises of 1805*, the solution to which required a high-level of formation. Cf. M-F Carreel, *Sophie Barat, Un projet éducatif pour aujourd'hui*, Ed. Don Bosco, Paris, 2003, pp. 205-206.

who governs the house at Amiens and who was charged to go to confer with the bishop of Ghent[110] for the foundation that he wanted to make. Our mother designated me to transcribe his letter. Here it is:

May 10, 1806
Reverend Father,

I left without telling anyone the day after the First Communion of the students in the house of the religious. I went first to Roulers as I had already indicated to you. From the first conversation with the good and very dear Leblanc,[111] I told him: "*Salutem ex inimicis nostris et de manu omnium qui oderunt nos.*"[112] I added: "God wants you to make expiation for all the evil you have said and done against women." "It is true," he told me, "I think so, too." He showed me all kinds of interest and promised me with admirable grace to procure for me acquaintances from one side or another for the work of God, for here are the facts:

At his last trip to Ghent, the bishop, after showing him much kindness, told him that he would like to have a boarding school for girls similar to the one in Amiens. Our good Leblanc, snared as in a net, responded gladly and was ready to break out in a laugh; but fearing that the bishop would think him mad, told him: "Bishop, I am laughing because, wanting never to get mixed up with women, I find myself nonplussed[113] by your excellency. Nevertheless, I ask you to permit me to bring to negotiate this business one of ours who is in a better position to do it." It was all agreed upon on condition that I come quickly.

After Father Leblanc's order, I left as soon as possible for Roulers, at the expense of Mother Baudemont,[114] as you well know, after having

---

110 Étienne de Fallot de Baumont de Beaupré (1750-1835), bishop of Vaison in 1786 and exiled in Italy (1790-1801), was named bishop of Ghent (1802-1807), then of Plaisance. At the Council of Paris in 1811, he was one of the prelates in favor of the emperor. Repudiated by Cardinal Pacca, he was deposed from his episcopal see. Bishop Maurice de Broglie (1766-1821) succeeded him in Ghent in 1807 and remained there until his death.
111 Charles Leblanc (1774-1851) entered the Society of the Fathers of the Sacred Heart in 1794 and returned to France in 1801. He was superior of the community of Fathers of the Faith in Paris during the visit of Father Varin to Rome (July-August 1802). In 1804 in Amiens, he gave instructions to the boarders at rue de l'Oratoire. Supported by Miss de Peñaranda, whose spiritual director he was, he founded the college at Roulers near Ghent in 1805.
112 "Saved from the hand of our enemies from all who hate us." Luke 1:71.
113 The word is "*angarié*" from old French of Poitiers meaning: to be burdened or constrained. Father de Saint-Estève was deliberately using fancy language.
114 Anne Baudemont (1764-1834), previously a Poor Clare, visited Father Jean-Nicolas Loriquet imprisoned at Reims. She entered the community in Amiens with her friend Miss Capy in April 1802, and was named superior at the departure of Mother Barat for Grenoble in November 1804. Under the influence of Father Sambucy de Saint-Estève, she tried to usurp the position of superior general. Sent to Poitiers in September 1814, she sowed seeds of trouble there,

recommended it all to the prayers of one or other, who, however, did not know what this was all about. With this safeguard, I left full of confidence, and that was not in vain. They told me at Roulers that the bishop was impatient about this project, that he would push me to begin immediately, and that it would be difficult to extricate myself from this step, in spite of all the good reasons that I had to oppose it. But the good God foresaw all the difficulties.

Two days after my arrival at Roulers, I went to Bruges to see Mr. Caïtan, Miss de Peñaranda,[115] and a good Flemish cook who wanted to join Miss de Peñaranda, and finally I embarked on the canal for Ghent, where I arrived about 4 or 5 o'clock. I went first to greet the bishop, who kept, lodged and fed me. Scarcely arrived at his house, I had to talk about the main topic of conversation until 7:30 in the evening. I was very happy with all the answers I gave him; he held me in great affection and filled me with kindness, to the point of wanting himself to show me to my room and to carry my torch in spite of all my remonstrances and objections. The next day, after having said Mass and had breakfast at the episcopal residence, we again dealt with the business and agreed on all points. I told him that this project could not happen earlier than in six months and maybe more because of the lack of personnel. He agreed. I told him about your projects regarding Miss de Peñaranda. He was very happy and regards it as indispensable to have in leadership here someone who speaks Flemish. (She cannot come to Amiens for a month.)

After everything was agreed on both sides, he told me: "Go with my secretary to see *the rich residence* (a house so named because of its ancient opulence). There are still 22 Benedictine religious," he was told. "It doesn't matter," he responded. "We are going to go visit this house from the basement to the attic. Imagine a beautiful building in a square around a cloister, a charming church with organ, two large gardens, a canal, quiet parlors, and separate buildings for the poor school, etc." We gave an account of the visit. "That is not enough," he told me. "*In Ghent there is a very beautiful convent of Carmelites. Go there too to become acquainted with the places.*" I obeyed and went there, accompanied by the secretary. I saw first a small entry into the church of Saint Thomas Aquinas, that is, a church in front, a courtyard in front of the church, and

had to leave, and in October 1815, she went to the Roman monastery of Saint-Denys.
115   Marie Antoinette de Peñaranda, RSCJ (1779-1830), born in Bruges, Belgium, student in the house in Amiens, entered the novitiate in 1806 and made her first vows February 5, 1807. On May 26, 1808, she founded the house at Dooreseele (Ghent), but in 1814, she separated from the Society of the Sacred Heart because of the Gallican tendencies promulgated by the National Council of Paris in 1811. In 1822, she asked to be reintegrated and made her profession January 27, 1823, and went to be superior in Beauvais. In 1827, she was sent to the foundation of the house in Lille, where she died in February 1830.

a portal similar to that of Saint Thomas Aquinas. I entered the church and found the loveliest church in Ghent with two wings, two lateral altars, and an organ. The convent is one of the most modern in Ghent and one of the best built. It is a square building around two cloisters, about 60 cells, and enough place for 200 boarders; besides, basements, superb attics, an immense garden, separate building at the back for the schools, retreats, etc. One difficulty remained: it is occupied by 22 Carmelite fathers and could cost 120,000 francs. Not at all: before we left the house, the Carmelite who had acquired it said to the secretary that the house belonged to him alone, that he rented the apartments for profit for the Carmelite fathers, that he had already put it in his will that he would bequeath the convent to the hospices and that if he could find religious persons who were consecrated to the education of young people, he would willingly give them preference, because he had it at heart that this good project would return to the Church. He asked only for what would furnish a living for his brothers. We reported this to the bishop who, blessing Providence, took the responsibility to negotiate the business and to deal with the city of Ghent, which earnestly desires a girls' boarding school, and he hopes for everything in time, with Divine Providence.

I again take up my travel journal, undoubtedly late, but this feast day (Ascension) has doubled our objects of concern. The bishop, after having told me that he would move heaven and earth for the Carmelite house, added: "*And I will give you the first 8000 francs for expenses.*" Now it is worth noticing, said Father Leblanc, that when he promises something, he doubles it. Besides, he told Father Leblanc that he would find for these religious 30,000 francs against 30 sols for him. In truth, Father Leblanc hoped to find mountains of gold, and he was disappointed in his hopes, which amused the bishop because, he says, he is quite used to what Father Leblanc will see by experience, that in general people are not as generous in this country as he had persuaded himself. A few good souls, though rare, give to the bishop especially by bequest; the others are like everywhere else. Corruption is very widespread, especially in Bruges and Ghent. I have had some examples of it, and the bishop gave me tangible proof. That is also why the bishop attaches so much value to education, especially of future priests. There is a substratum of religion in that country, so that when cultivated it produces those like Wrints, like Peñaranda, but how many others are not like them at all! There is so much laxity among them that he can hardly cite one priest who will not permit his penitents to combine religion with comedy and balls, two things against which he fulminates as a man of God, so that he said in passing that he wants neither master of *dance* nor master of *comportment*.

The most delicate point is the one I am going to explain to you. He told me: I cannot discuss with Father Leblanc the subject of these religious since he does not want to get involved, so I can discuss it only with you, and if you do not want to agree to my request, I will have recourse to good Father Varin. Here is the issue. He said: "I want this establishment of these religious, but I want them here only if they have passed through the training at Amiens, and I want it to be one of yours who comes to install them, so that I am sure that it is your spirit that will reign there. Otherwise I have no one," he said, turning toward his secretary, "not you, Father Van Scanwerberge, right? Is it not true, then, that if it is not one of these fathers, it will not have a good outcome?" Father Van Scanwerberge answered that it was true. "So you must come, at least for the first month and every three months as extraordinary confessor, to see how everything is going."

After the latitude that Father Leblanc had given me, I was thinking that taking two weeks in October and every other month when there is not a feast and at the Ember Days[116] when I am aided by Father Tranel with the religious and where I could be aided by Father Leblanc in the neighborhood, it would be possible to satisfy the bishop. Without promising anything, I left him with the possibility. "For the rest," he said, "I count on good Father Varin to obtain everything, and when he gives you the order, you will stay with me." I answered: "Bishop, it is not our custom. Perhaps it would be better if I stayed at the seminary." I had a thought *alta mente repostum*.[117] "You are right," he said. "Your stay at the seminary will be more useful. First, you can get to know all my 70 students; you will choose which ones you think would be good for you and send them to Father Varin to send them wherever he wants. 2) You will choose and train a confessor for your religious and a secretary for me. 3) Finally, you will communicate to the others your vivacity and energy of the South. Good, very good." He was very good to me and wrote to Father Leblanc that he loved me as much as he. We got along together marvelously, and out of respect for him, Father Leblanc will go ahead with everything so that I will be free to follow this work. Provided that he does not pay for the travel and that I do not sign anything on his account; provided that he relates only to me and not with the women and that I am the only

---

116 At the beginning of the four seasons of the year, there was in the Catholic liturgical calendar a week called "the Ember Days," in which Wednesday, Friday and Saturday were days of fast. They were situated after the first Sunday of Lent, after Pentecost, the feast of the Holy Cross (September 14), and the third Sunday of Advent. The religious had at these times an "extraordinary confessor," other than the usual one assigned to them.
117 "Deeply stored in the mind" (Virgil, *Aeneid* 1.26).

one belonging to him who is involved in this, he will be charming both for the project at first and to me, too. He surprised me by all these good things already.

This letter from Father de Sambucy hopes only for a foundation in Ghent. Our mother general received soon after one from Father Varin that determined that of Poitiers to follow; it had been prepared by a mission that Fathers Lambert and Gloriot had given there. Miss Chobelet[118] had bought the old house of Les Feuillants, prepared it, and was there then with a companion [Josephine Bigeu],[119] two serving girls and two little boarders. She had a respectable revenue and, what is more, enjoyed an excellent reputation, which she had acquired by distinguished merit.

July 10, 1806

Mother Barat, who should begin this establishment herself, did not delay preparations for her departure. It happened on July 10, 1806. She chose from among all of us to accompany her Mother Girard[120] from Lyon. They both stopped together for two days in Lyon and happily took up their route to Poitiers. There they found the two missionaries who gave them during that first period every spiritual support. Mother Barat was soon presented to the bishop [Bishop Dominique de Pradt] who gave her the warmest welcome, granted her everything she asked for the foundation, and even wanted, in open consultation, to have her word that she would make Poitiers her residence. She refused this

---

118 Gabrielle Lydie Charlotte Chobelet du Bois-Boucher, RSCJ (1765-1832), was born at Soullans (Vendée) on December 24, 1764. In 1793, she had been imprisoned in Poitiers. When she left prison, she opened with her sister Reine a boarding school for young girls at Les Feuillants. Named treasurer at the foundation of this fourth house of the Sacred Heart, she made her vows on November 21, 1807. She died at Les Feuillants on November 15, 1832.

119 Marie Anne Josephine Bigeu, RSCJ (1779-1827), was born January 1, 1779, in Poitiers. In 1796, she entered the community of the Chobelet ladies who had a boarding school for girls at rue des Feuillants. In 1806, Sophie Barat received her with Lydie Chobelet in the fourth house of her new order. Josephine made her profession November 1, 1807, and was named mistress general, mistress of novices, and assistant (1807-1812). In December 1812, she left for Grenoble as mistress of novices and became superior in 1813. She was elected assistant general in 1815, and was mistress of novices in Paris (1816-1818) in a rented house in rue de l'Arbalète, near rue des Postes. She then went to Bordeaux to meet Mother Vincent and engaged in the foundation of Quimper (1817), then was superior at Chambéry (1818-1821), Bordeaux (1821-1823), and Turin (1823-1825). Charged with negotiations with the Holy See about approbation of the Constitutions, she lived in Rome from 1825 to 1826. On April 6, 1827, she was reelected assistant general, but she died on December 19.

120 Henriette Girard was forty-four years old. Her age could thus make her serve as a "respectable" companion for Mother Barat, who was then the object of lively criticism, in part because of her youth.

request and wrote to us afterwards that she told him that Grenoble was her house. The bishop, not getting everything he wanted, got from her at least that she would stay in his city during the winter.

So Poitiers was the fourth house of our little Society. Ghent and Bordeaux would be the fifth and sixth. Mother Barat went to that city to inspect the property and to see several young people who had been long interested in religious life.

The archbishop of Bordeaux was at that time Bishop d'Aviau, previously archbishop of Vienne in Dauphiny, well known for his holiness, his zeal and apostolic simplicity. He very much wanted one of our houses in his diocese; but since he did not have a house ready, our mother general put off the foundation until the following spring and left filled with the blessings of the holy bishop, with 8 young women between the ages of 18 and 36 years old, who, not yet finding what they wanted in Bordeaux, went to Poitiers and soon entered the novitiate.[121]

During this time, God began to multiply a Society that had nothing for its end but his greater glory, to which he gave to each one the substance of desire to devote herself completely by her prayers, her good works, and even by paying for herself. A young woman shared with us two letters written from Macao, the port of an island of China, which gave details about the missions of Tonkin and Cochinchina. This letter was from Father Isoard, a priest of our diocese and apostolic missionary in those lands. He complained of the small number of workers who came to these lands ready to produce fruit if they were cultivated. Father Enfantin[122] also had interesting details on the subject of China.

121 They were: Elisabeth Maillucheau, Anne-Charlotte (Brigitte) Berniard, Jeanne (Gertrude) Lamolière, Louise Macquet Olivié, Marie (Marinette) Guiégnet, Angela*, X. (La Croix) Roger, and Perpetua Mougette. The last three returned to their family for reasons either of business or health. Archives of France, *Journal de Poitiers 1806-1808*, text given by M.-T. Virnot, RSCJ. Anne-Charlotte (Brigitte) Berniard, RSCJ, entered the novitiate in August 1806 and made her profession July 9, 1809. Jeanne (Gertrude) Lamolière, RSCJ, born at Saint André de Cubzac in 1769, made her profession in 1809 and died May 17, 1818, in Poitiers. Louise Macquet Olivié, RSCJ, born in Bordeaux, died February 27, 1811. Marie (Marinette) Guiégnet, RSCJ coadjutrix, born in Bordeaux, was professed in March 1808 and died December 24, 1808. Therese (Elisabeth) Maillucheau, RSCJ (1777-1857), was born January 1, 1777, at Saint André de Cubzac, near Bordeaux, and tried to found a religious community. Through the mediation of Father Enfantin, Mother Barat accepted these women in Poitiers. Therese was professed November 21, 1807, and was named superior of the community. In September 1808 she left for Grenoble as mistress of novices and mistress general of the boarding school. Returning to Poitiers in November 1809, she was sent to Ghent (1810-1814), then again to Grenoble as superior (1814-1822), to Quimper (1822-1837), to Nantes (1838-1845), and to Bourges (1846-1850). Health problems forced her to retire to La Ferrandière and Marmoutier, where she died on July 28, 1857.
122 Louis-Barthélémy Enfantin (1776-1854), born in the Drôme, a distant cousin of Philippine, whose paternal grandmother was born Marie-Louise Enfantin, entered the clandestine seminary organized by Bishop d'Aviau, and was ordained priest in September 1800. As a Father

Finally, on September 21 the superior of Saint Irenaeus in Lyon wrote to the director of that seminary (Father Royer), then at Grenoble, that they had received news that the emperor of China had been baptized and that Propaganda was asking for a strong missionary thrust for that country. Several in the house were saying then: "Could I not do something good in China? Oh, what happiness to leave everything to labor without human interest for the glory of God!"

September 22, 1806

The next day, September 22, the bishop came to distribute the prizes. He was accompanied by this first vicar general, Father Bouchard; Father Rey, our superior; Father Royer, director of Saint Irenaeus Seminary; Father Rambaud, our confessor, and four other ecclesiastics. He continued to show interest in us as well as our students, who then numbered 26.

On the evening before, Father Royer had prepared them for this ceremony by an informal discourse; and the next day, he came to say the Mass of thanksgiving, to receive from the students the offering of their crowns and to speak with them about the way to sanctify their studies and to profit from them.

On October 18, we saw the return to us of Miss de Cassini, former novice of Amiens who had not persevered. Our Mother Barat had brought her with her in May in order to make it easy for her to go to the women's convent at La Trappe at Reidra near Fribourg in Switzerland. Since her health could not hold up under the rigorous rule of that house, she came here to recover for a while, then to go wherever God would call her.

The same day, Father Barat, brother of our reverend mother, arrived as extraordinary confessor. Everyone profited by making to him a thorough review of their conscience, and a number of the boarders did so as well. It was a renewal in the house. He did not stop with confessions; every day he gave a conference taken almost entirely from these words: "*I am from God, I am made for God. He is my end, to which I should tend.*" From this he deduced the great truths of creation: the end of humanity, the enormity of mortal and venial sin, death, judgment, hell; then he took the opportunity to review for us our principal obligations: obedience, poverty, chastity, love of the cross and love of God, by which he ended the retreat. The whole house profited from the conferences.

---

of the Faith on mission in Bordeaux, he founded in 1806, at the request of the archbishop, the house of the "Ladies of Christian Instruction" where Elisabeth (Therese) Maillucheau and the seven religious mentioned above entered. His parish missions in Bordeaux and Valence were very successful.

Only eight people made the entire retreat; the majority were waiting for the one before vows. Father Barat left on the 27th.

During this retreat Sister Magdeleine Méran entered for the second rank [as a coadjutrix sister]. This was October 23. She was later put into the third rank.[123]

On November 25, our two Sisters Espié and de Gap, cousins, entered, one for the second rank, and the younger for the third. The first one left six weeks later. On the 29th of the same month Miss de Lestrange, sister of the Abbot of La Trappe, entered with a servant girl; they remained in the house only until December 12. The distinguished Abbot of La Trappe passed by here on November 1 and kept silence about his sister, which left one to suppose that he doubted that she would fit. He returned later and showed no regret about the dismissal of his sister, considering only the holy will of God.

November 21, 1806

Our Mother Barat had promised that we would have one of the missionaries for the vow retreat. Father Varin himself promised to be here; but he could not fulfill his promise, so our Mother Deshayes led the retreat herself for all the persons of the house who had not made it with Father Barat. The renewal of vows was made in her hands, before the altar in the retreat room where the Blessed Sacrament was. None of the fathers came for this ceremony, nor for extraordinary confessions all through winter and spring.

At the end of the same month of November, Miss Lambert, who had come as a boarder for six months, was admitted to the number of those interested in entering. On February 11, 1807, Miss Felicity Ribau[124] was admitted to the house. On March 11, Miss Maujot[125] was also received. They all began their novitiate the following Easter.

This was the first time that six of our students made their First Communion and that they all renewed it after a retreat of eight days, during which several gave touching consolation to their mistress by the ardor of their desires and their fervor.

---

123 The third rank is probably that of "domestic servant given to the house," without a religious commitment. Philippine makes such an allusion about Felicity Lefèvre on August 1, 1808.
124 Felicity Ribau, RSCJ (1789-1823), entered at Grenoble on February 11, 1807, made her profession November 21, 1809, and went to Poitiers on March 1, 1816. She was mistress of studies and mistress general. She died September 15, 1823, at Chambéry.
125 Claudine Maujot, RSCJ, called Benoît (1774-1839), was received as a choir novice at Grenoble on December 28, 1818. At her request, she became a coadjutrix novice in July 1819. Her departure for America was discouraged by Philippine, cf. letter 262, December 27, 1825. She died on August 1, 1839, in Bordeaux.

March 10, 1807

Soon after, we received the news that the Emperor, by a decree of March 10, 1807, approved our Society for France and the colonies, under the name of Society of the *Ladies or Sisters of Christian Instruction*. The request was made to him by Father Jauffret,[126] bishop of Metz, in the name of Her Highness the mother of the Emperor, and of the bishop of Amiens. The houses already established were in Amiens, Grenoble, Belley, Poitiers and Ghent. This new sign of God's protection stirred up our fervent gratitude, to which we testified by Communions of thanksgiving and a novena in honor of Saint Francis Regis.

At the same time or a little later, we received permission to establish in our church the Confraternity of the Sacred Heart of Jesus,[127] whose feast we already celebrated solemnly and for which we had indulgences. The very day of this feast, this year on June 5, all our sisters and our students were recorded in the register along with many secular persons.

The 16th, feast of Saint Francis Regis, was celebrated as best we could with all the solemnities of great feasts, a High Mass and several Low Masses. The panegyric of the saint was preached by Father Lacoste, an Oratorian.

The 21st, Saint Aloysius Gonzaga, was celebrated as solemnly as it could be among us.[128]

We now made the Visitation only a second-class feast, and Saint Ignatius was celebrated more in the heart than externally; only we made it a solemn day; the students followed their regular daily order.

August 2, 1807

On August 2, we received the visit of Father Enfantin, a missionary distinguished by his virtue, his zeal and his success in the ministry. He let us hope that someday we could have a ministry in foreign lands; he stoked the ardor of several to go there when obedience would indicate

---

126 Gaspard-André Jauffret (1759-1823) had been a seminarian in Aix-en-Provence with Joseph Fesch, uncle of Napoleon. As vicar general in Lyon, he administered the diocese while Cardinal Fesch was on embassy in Rome (1803-1804). He was named bishop of Metz in July 1806.

127 A lay association whose end is to make known devotion to the Sacred Heart and live it. It was erected by ecclesiastical authority in churches of religious, cathedrals and parishes. The first was established at Coutances in 1688, then others from 1729 in Canada and Rome by Father de Gallifet. Under the influence of Saint Margaret Mary Alacoque from Paray-le-Monial, their expansion was rapid: in 1773, there were one thousand ninety. Slowed in their impetus during the French Revolution, they recovered new life from 1801 on.

128 Aloysius Gonzaga, SJ (1568-1591), left the court of King Philip II of Spain to enter the Jesuit novitiate in Rome in November 1585. He made his first vows two years later. After caring for those ill from the plague, he died on June 21, 1591. He was canonized on April 26, 1726, by Benedict XIII. His feast is June 21.

to them. Even though he stayed only 24 hours, he gave us two sermons and heard the confessions of many sisters. He was accompanied by his brother who is also destined for apostolic work.

August 8, 1807

After this visit, we did not count on being favored so soon with that of our Father Varin. He happily surprised us on August 8, and this is the third time that Saint Ignatius has sent him near the time of his feast. He completed our joy by promising in an inspired tone that our care for young souls would not be limited to these lands but—perhaps soon—we would be established in the colonies. He preached four times, twice to the boarders on the happiness of serving God in one's youth and how to do it, and twice only to us.

The first was on the happiness of our vocation: 1) because our state distances us from many dangers and provides for us many means of sanctification; 2) because on the contrary, in the world one encounters more dangers with fewer means to avoid them. Then he entered into detail about the advantages that we enjoy: the care and charity of a superior to take hold of us and guide us, the example of our sisters, prayer, reading, separation from distracting things, the presence of God, etc. He then exhorted us not to be too attached to particular attractions or inspirations that seem good to us, when they depart from the spirit of community and obedience.

The second discourse was on: "I have chosen you so that you will go out, that you will bear fruit, and that your fruit will remain."[129] The three divisions were: 1) the foundation of our vocation: the call of God and not our own ideas ("I have chosen you"); therefore to understand our vocation, it is not enough to relish it, to persevere; it is also necessary that superiors who hold the place of God approve of it. 2) The spirit of our vocation ("I have chosen you"): humility, since only God can give it. Second, gratitude because he has given it with no merit on our part. 3) The end of our vocation ("so that you will go forth and bear fruit"). Zeal for the salvation of souls demands a full commitment, being ready to leave a superior who has formed us, sisters whom we love, and a house that pleases us for the least sign of obedience to go to the most disagreeable place with unknown persons.

The consolation that the visit of Father Varin brought was troubled at the end by the withdrawal of perpetual adoration that Mother Barat had permitted us to try while we waited for her consent. Since winter,

---

129 John 15:16.

we had been doing it during the day, and since the feast of Saint Mary Magdalene, we had begun doing it at night. She based her refusal on such plausible reasons, especially to bring us into the uniformity that should reign in all the houses, that we could only praise her intentions in causing us such a big sacrifice.

He saw during his stay the two last arrivals: Miss Mercier from Lyon and Marguerite Foussala,[130] whom we had had since August 4. The first stayed only a few days in the house and returned to Lyon; the second entered the novitiate, from which in the middle of October, Miss Lambert left to go to a secular school, and Miss Crouzas found a place in Chambéry in a new house of the Visitation.

November 1807

The decision for both of them to leave was made during their retreat, which they made with the community under the guidance of Father Barat, who came to spend a month here, heard the confessions of all in the house, and gave two retreats, one of ten days for the religious and the other of nine for the students who numbered 26 or 28. In both, he gave three conferences or meditations daily.

Confirmation, November 3, 1807

The students' retreat ended with a solemn general Communion and the next day with the First Communion of a young student whom Father Barat found so well disposed that he admitted her to this favor, which was given to her six days after the feast of All Saints and after November 3, the day when ten students received Confirmation at the hands of our bishop.

Father Barat, who left only two days earlier, had heard their confessions and prepared them by instructions right up to the time he departed.

During the conferences for their retreat, the most striking points were:
1. On the recollection that he wanted them to acquire by watching over the three powers of the soul, over the appetite, the imagination and over every one of our senses. Without this attention to oneself, he thought it impossible.
2. On chastity. He made known the impossibility of keeping this virtue without humility, which is chastity of spirit, subject of the conference on the vigil, without prayer and without flight from all the pleasures where our good angel cannot accompany us.

---

130 Marguerite Foussala, RSCJ coadjutrix, was formed in Grenoble. On September 18, 1819, she went to replace her sister Veronique in Chambéry.

3. On the Blessed Virgin, who he said was represented by the Ark of the Covenant containing the Tables of the Law, a prefiguring of Jesus Christ our legislator; the rod of Aaron, figure of Jesus Christ the great high priest; and the manna, figure of Jesus Christ our nourishment. He exalted her greatness, her privilege, her virtues, and showed her as the principal link in the chain that unites us to Jesus Christ.

The most striking considerations of the retreat for the religious were:

1. On recollection, the same subject as for the students' retreat.
2. On fidelity to the rules. He spoke forcefully to underline the necessity; he said that Saint Ignatius despaired of seeing women keep them; that our brothers groaned to see us so far from their full observance; that if they asked him how they found us, he could only answer: *pray for them, you know them.* That it was not because they were so *great* that we did not keep them, but because they were so *little*, while in the meantime venerable old men, who grew old in the ministry, wept with bitterness over their least infractions and accused themselves with the most profound humility. That God never permitted an unworthy person to finish his days in the Society [of Jesus], that there were two demons who cried out to him without ceasing: *get out, get out*, that he ended by asking to leave and that no one ever insisted on keeping him. That Saint Ignatius had said that he would receive candidates with pleasure, but that when they did not fit, he watched them go with even more pleasure.
3. On penitence. He highlighted the advantages and said that one would never arrive at sanctity without corporal mortification; that one should not go at it in a measured way, nor fear to give blood for Jesus Christ. That Saint Ignatius had not prescribed any corporal mortification in his rule, not to spare ourselves, but so that one would never stop in the belief of having satisfied what one should do. That in the realm of penitence, we should not cede even to the most austere orders.
4. On obedience. He highlighted the advantages, showed it as the fundamental virtue of the institute, noted the different degrees, and spent time especially on obedience of judgment, saying that we should be in the hand of our superiors like sticks that they can use as they wish and then reject at will and without resistance. And that, when one has not obeyed, God himself *will avenge the superiors.*
5. In the last conference that he gave on the rules, he said that if one was not disposed to reveal to one's superior one's soul and all of one's thoughts, one must *leave*; that if one was not disposed to

renounce knowledge of the things of the world, one must *leave*. That one must not think about the persons one loved except at the moment of holy Communion to pray for them for a moment; that if one lost a companion, one must not think of that person until the next day after Communion; that it would be unfortunate to be four years in a house in fear of getting attached to it, and that one would not be where one should be until one is dead to all.

Renewal, November 21, 1807

On November 21, the senior professed renewed their vows in the retreat room. Misses Doelle Vainade and Brunel[131] arrived at this time to join us.

A few days later, Mother Grosier arrived, returning from Belley, where the house was going to close. She brought with her our Sisters des Granges from the house of Belley and du Terrail[132] from that of Amiens, which she had left to assist Mother Grosier at Belley, and a little boarder. They were followed a few days later by Sister Piongaud, who had left us more than two years ago to go to Belley, and Sisters Furnou[133] and Boulard,[134] the latter a coadjutrix sister of the same house, and again, a boarder.

Later, Sister Louise from the same house also came, but she stayed only until the departure of Mother Grosier, who took her back to Lyon, thinking that she was not called to be among us.

Departure of Mother Grosier, February 9, 1808

The departure of Mother Grosier took place on February 9, 1808, on the occasion of a projected foundation in Niort, where she had to go after having stayed in Lyon on business and in Poitiers to confer with Mother Barat and the others who will be in the same establishment.

In Lyon, she saw her last two daughters from Belley, Sisters Grolet and Françoise Duchêne,[135] the last a coadjutrix sister, whom she sent to

---

131 Antoinette Brunel, RSCJ (1786-1816), was born at Montbrison (Loire), and died December 17, 1816, in Grenoble.
132 Marie du Terrail, RSCJ (1771-1813), entered at Amiens in October 1803 and made vows November 21, 1804. In 1805, she accompanied Henriette Grosier to the foundation of Belley. In November 1807, she returned to Grenoble to be mistress general of the day school. She died November 30, 1813.
133 Antoinette-Therese Furnou, RSCJ coadjutrix (1741-1849), was born October 12, 1781, received the habit November 19, 1805, and made vows February 26, 1816. She died at Aix-en-Provence.
134 Felicity Boulard, RSCJ coadjutrix (1787-1866), was born October 25, 1787, received the habit September 14, 1806, made her profession May 1, 1814, and died at La Ferrandière (Lyon).
135 Françoise Duchêne, RSCJ coadjutrix (1781-1851), was born January 19, 1781, received the habit March 30, 1804, and left Grenoble to go to Lyon on November 28, 1819. She died at

this house, where they arrived on February 24, 1808. They learned in Lyon that the Fathers [of the Faith] of the houses of Roanne, L'Argentière and Belley, dispersed by order of the government in November 1807,[136] have been partially placed: Father Lambert as canon in Bordeaux, Father Cabarat[137] as canon in Lyon, Father Bonard as superior at Fourvière, and the others in other places as pastors or vicars. Father Roger had just given a very consoling mission at Saint Just in Lyon.

Departure of Sister Grolet, May 6, 1808

At the beginning of May, we had a terrible affliction: our Sister Grolet, proficient in all kinds of good qualities, with a most recollected appearance, was struck with an illness that affected her reason. Our mother knew that she had previously been so afflicted, and judging that with such an illness she could not fulfill our obligations, she notified her mother that she was going to send her home and had her leave without telling the reason for her trip, in order to control her reactions. On May 6, 1808, she was thus separated from us. She was accompanied by Sister Benoît, a novice like her, who for a long time was supposed to be sent home for reasons of health and a penchant to melancholy. Since during this trip she was going to visit her family, our mother prevailed upon the latter to take her, since it would not be appropriate for us to do so. She wanted in this way to remove the bitterness of her departure. In spite of this letter, she returned, hoping to have this decision changed; not succeeding, she left again two or three days after her arrival, very sad.

This trial was followed by a few moments of consolation in the two-day visit of Father Royer, during which in two exhortations, he revived our fervor for the practice of our duties.

Miss Vainade also returned to her family during this month, for health reasons; soon after, her two companions, Sisters Dall and Brunel, entered the novitiate.

The latter was employed with the poor school, where Sister du Terrail was mistress general; under her, the schedule of the poor school changed. In order to improve this class most interesting to the Society, our mother determined to keep them all day. They come at nine in the

---

Chambéry.

136 The success of the colleges of the Fathers of the Faith annoyed Napoleon, who was not very favorable to a renewal of religious fervor and wanted to hold a monopoly on education. The decree of Messidor (June 22, 1804) promulgated the dissolution of the Fathers of the Faith, but its application was effective only in October 1807 by administrative order.

137 Before becoming a Father of the Faith, Father Cabarat was canon and vicar general in Tours. From 1805 to 1807, he was rector of the college of Roanne. Welcomed in Lyon by Cardinal Fesch, he resumed his functions as canon and vicar general.

morning and stay until six in summer; during all this time, they are under the eye of the teachers and do not run outside. They are divided into four classes: two of the older ones and two of the little ones. We give them notes, merit points, prizes and medallions, just like the boarders. Their big feast is July 19, feast of Saint Vincent de Paul, which they spent all day in the house. On the day of their First Communion, all the time that they are not in the church, they spend in the house, where the leading boarding school students make it their duty to welcome them. This practice, advantageous for the poor of Jesus Christ, has attracted a greater number. On July 1, they were almost seventy. They could no longer stay in their first rooms that were now too small, so it was arranged to build two very large ones where they can be at least 150. In August, they were almost 100.

August 1, 1808

In the first days of August 1808, Felicity Lefèvre, who had come twice from Amiens, the first time with Mother Grosier, the second with Mother Barat, was not deemed suitable for religious life; and since she did not want to stay as a *donnée*,[138] she left to return to her mother.

On the 8th of the same month Sisters Piongaud, des Granges, Messoria and Xavier Boulard left for Poitiers. They were asked for to replace those of our sisters of that house, among whom was Sister Emilie Giraud, who had gone to Niort. The superior was Mother Geoffroy[139] and their third companion was Sister Bernard,[140] who was the core of this establishment. She had begun at Niort the only school that existed there for boys and for girls. She worked with the girls and a good sister associated with her was engaged with the boys with such success that several are already the foundation of a good seminary.

Miss Bernard had great desire for the religious life and so informed the vicar general and especially Fathers Lambert and Enfantin when they gave a mission in Niort. They did not want her to leave Niort permanently, where she had done so much good; but they counselled

---

138 As a domestic servant belonging to the congregation, without membership as a religious and without a real salary.
139 Suzanne Geoffroy, RSCJ (1761-1845), born May 1, 1761, near Poitiers, entered the novitiate at Les Feuillants October 15, 1807. Eight months later, she was sent as superior to the foundation of Niort and made her vows in 1809. In 1826, she went to Lyon, where she died May 13, 1845.
140 Henriette Bernard, RSCJ (1767-1830), was born March 15, 1767, and at the age of 17 made a vow to always do the thing she believed to be most perfect. At Niort after the French Revolution, she was engaged in the instruction of poor children. She entered the novitiate in Poitiers in November 1806, made vows November 21, 1807, and contributed to the foundation of the house at Niort in 1808. She then went to Bordeaux, where she died October 6, 1830.

her to leave the care of her school to her sisters, to come to do her novitiate in Poitiers; and afterwards she would come with others from that house to develop an establishment for Christian instruction. This was agreed upon with Mother Barat, who went to Niort, and soon the plan was executed.

Friday, July 1, 1808, was the beginning of this establishment that reproduced the poverty of the first dwelling of Jesus on earth. They were only three, including Mother Barat, who had left Sister Emilie still in Poitiers, and they did not have enough beds for all, or furniture to decorate their largest room. The little altar was set up in a place not intended for this use; the backdrop of the main altar was a little image of the Sacred Heart, under whose protection this poor house began. Everything was borrowed in order to offer the Holy Sacrifice, except for one chasuble that had come along, given by the house of Grenoble.

In this refuge, everything breathed poverty but also joy, peace, and an inexpressible interior relish. Mother Geoffroy rose first the next day to render homage to the Sacred Heart, whose perfect devotee she is. A dove came through the window to settle near her; it did not leave the house all day, let itself be captured, and left in the evening without ever returning, which was taken as a good omen. The founder of the boarding school was the niece of Mother Therese [Maillucheau]; Sister [Henriette] Bernard also sent one. So on October 1, this was the whole boarding school of this house: there are 72 poor students, 3 choir religious, 2 observers, a coadjutrix sister and a little portress. So as not to abandon the work with the boys, the elderly sister companion of Sister Bernard is carrying it on in another house, and the little society just beginning supplies its needs. Mother Barat was not long in this new foundation; she called Sister Emilie [Giraud] there, made Mother Grosier superior at Poitiers, and left herself for Amiens with Mother Therese. During her travel, we had, on August 10, Father Enfantin, who gave us several conferences and saw most of the sisters individually.

The carriage that took our sisters to Poitiers brought us back from Roanne Miss Bonabaud,[141] who wanted to join us, and two boarders, one of whom is the niece of Mother Barat; she replaced in the boarding school Miss Laetitia, who was sent to Poitiers. And Miss Bonabaud took the place of Miss Brunel with the poor; she left at the same time as Sister Piongaud to recover her health in her family. Sister Meyran was also sent back to hers. On September 14 and 23, Lacroix and Jean François, two brothers from Roanne, were attached to the house, one as sacristan and steward, the other as carpenter.

---

141 Sister Bonabaud died in 1849 at Annonay.

For a long time we were hoping to see Mother Barat again. Finally, we were told that we would have her for some time with Mother Therese, whom she was giving us as mistress of novices. Mother Therese arrived a few days ahead with Sister Gabrielle, whom our Mother was bringing to be one of her daughters. It was September 23, 1808, when Mother Therese Maillucheau entered the house and began her work. Mother Barat arrived the next Tuesday, September 24, with Sister Benoît,[142] who had obtained permission from her to reenter. Our joy was full in that happy moment, and we resolved to profit better from her stay than we had in the past.

September 29, 1808

The distribution of prizes had been delayed because of her absence; the bishop came to distribute them on the twenty-ninth with several ecclesiastics. They were more solemn than usual; and in the evening, when the ceremony was finished, we gathered to celebrate the feast of our mother, who is called Sophie. Since she has been in our midst, she speaks to us only of the one she loves uniquely and of what is for his glory. It is from her that we learned of the establishment at Niort. Here are some details about that of Cuignières [commune of Saint-Just-en Chaussée, Oise], established at some distance from Amiens in the country. It began during Lent of 1808; Mother Desmarquest is the superior. There are already a number of fervent novices, eight boarders, and a number of poor students. Regularity, peace and joy reign there along with holy poverty from which they derive their happiness.

The house in Poitiers has also had weak beginnings. Here are a few remarks: Misses Chobelet and Bigeu had bought the house of Les Feuillants and were advised by Father Lambert, while giving a mission in Poitiers, to call on Mother Barat. She went there with Sister Girard during July 1806, and after having stayed for a few days, she went to Bordeaux to see the candidates that Father Enfantin had prepared for her and who were living under the guidance of Mother Therese, the most experienced in religious practice. Mother Barat returned to Poitiers with them, added to them several observers from Poitiers, opened the novitiate and began the regular establishment on September 8 of the same year, 1808.

---

142 Gabrielle Benoît, RSCJ coadjutrix, born January 23, 1770, entered September 8, 1807, left in May 1808, and reentered September 24. She made her profession September 7, 1816, and died in Poitiers in 1848.

October 24, 1808

Our Reverend Mother Barat had brought with her Mother Therese Maillucheau to form the novices. Already in the world, she had formed some companions whom she instructed in virtue, and in Poitiers she had filled in for Mother Barat during a month's absence with great success. Since then, she had been assistant and so was not new in the exercise of leadership positions in this house. Now she had that of mistress of novices, who made up the greater number of the community, and of mistress general of the boarding school, which was composed of about 60 students. She was besides councilor and admonitrix to Mother Deshayes. However important her responsibilities were, she carried them with ease, aided by Our Lord to whom she was united by a continuous presence, by long prayer, sometimes of six hours, and by daily Communion. Her conferences to the novices and her retreat meditations to the students revealed this union with Jesus Christ and inspired in souls a tender love for him. Recreations with both the novices and the students also brought out her tender devotion and her goodness to all. She began her residence here by a two-week retreat; this was followed by First Communion of eight students. It took place on November 13, 1808, feast of Saint Stanislaus Kostka, a day that ran concurrently this year with the feast of the dedication of churches. On the next day, the fourteenth, the bishop came to give to the first communicants and several others the sacrament of Confirmation. These two moving ceremonies were followed by the general retreat for the house and the renewal of vows for the professed on the 21st, feast of the Presentation.

November 21, 1808

The departure of our reverend mother general happened before First Communion. She had come intending to spend the winter here, but pressing business obliged her to go promptly to Amiens during the First Communion retreat. On December 15, Miss de Portes,[143] and a few days later the younger Miss Balastron, entered the house; and on January 29, 1809, feast of Saint Francis de Sales, Miss Lavauden[144]

---

143 Louise (Laure) de Portes d'Amblérien, RSCJ (1782-1868), born in Grenoble, had fled to Germany with her family during the French Revolution. She entered the novitiate in Grenoble in 1808, made her profession June 27, 1813, then went to Paris to be surveillante of the novitiate. In 1819, she succeeded Catherine de Charbonnel as superior at La Ferrandière (Lyon), and in 1823, she founded the house in Turin with Angelique Lavauden. She was then superior at Amiens, Autun, Marseille, Layrac and Niort. In 1862, she went for a rest to Montfleury (Grenoble), where she died September 22, 1868.

144 Angelique Lavauden, RSCJ (1787-1872), entered at Sainte-Marie d'En-Haut in 1809 and made her profession June 27, 1813. In 1818, she went to Chambéry with Josephine Bigeu, succeeded

was also received, and after a few months, they began their novitiate together with a good woman, Marie Richaud, who was not kept because her age and health were obstacles to her admission. This last one had been sent during *Advent* by Father Enfantin, who had come to preach in Grenoble. He did not have the astonishing success that he had had elsewhere, either because a mission with more frequent discourses works better, or because the weak spirit of worldly people could not deal with his simplicity. Several fortunate, more enlightened people saw in him an apostle and made use of him to advance towards perfection.

He came to visit us often during that time; every Wednesday was devoted to us; he saw into the conscience of each sister and many of the students. His main conferences were on penitence, hell, and the Sacred Heart; or at least, those were the most striking. Several times, it seemed in his conversations that God made him know the state of the house, for better or for worse. One time among others, he said in an intense way: "*God is unhappy; if this does not change, I will not return; and when I promised that to God, he was somewhat appeased.*" Several days later, he said: "*Everything is all right.*" He left the first days of January and gave a number of missions in the countryside, fruitfully everywhere; but the most abundant fruit was borne at Valence, where he preached Lent. This city is not very religious; churches are always deserted. One sees only the priests and two or three workers during the day. On Sundays, people disperse without bothering with Mass, the rich even more easily. The sacraments were completely abandoned. It was appropriate and in the designs of God that religion should shine out again, in a place watered by the labors of Saint Francis Regis, by the one who declared himself the faithful imitator and promoter of his devotion.

All [the city of] Valence went to hear Father Enfantin. It was noticed that the prefect was perhaps the only person held back by the spirit of the world. This good father rested from his labor by day only by hearing confessions late into the night. In this city and at Romans, where he went almost immediately to give a mission, preaching four times a day, he brought more than 14,000 people to the sacraments, among whom were sinners who had not been to confession for 40 years. They spoke of him in no other way than as a saint, and he gave the lie to the proverb "*No one is a prophet in his own country,*" since he was born very near Romans. His reputation spread in all that region so much that he was wanted everywhere for missions, which he stopped doing in Advent, at

---

her as superior in 1820, and accompanied her to Rome (1825-1826). She was then superior in several houses and died at Montfleury on January 10, 1872.

Die and at Crest. When on June 16, he decided to go to La Louvesc to make a retreat and renew his apostolic spirit, his arrival in the flesh was announced as a worthy imitator of the [holy] patron celebrated there. They say that he heard about it and immediately fled.

1809

This year, 1809, the house was composed of 100 people, of whom a great number were weak, but not a single ounce of meat entered the house during Lent.

May 14, 1809

We had the fortune to see this good father again on May 14, still exhausted from the missions at Valence and Romans, unable to speak and forbidden by his superiors to work for a while, which deprived us often of hearing and seeing him. He stayed in Grenoble for a few days.

The health of Mother Therese gave us some concern during the winter, and our mother made a vow to Saint Francis Regis that if by Easter we were free of our most serious worries about her, someone would go in the name of the house to have a novena [of Masses] made at La Louvesc. Jean François, who was attached to the house, made this pilgrimage the week after Easter, and his companion Lacroix went on the saint's feast day to fulfill the second vow for the recovery of Mother Deshayes, who for the whole month of May was in a weakened state that made us fear everything for her health. We also owe him thanks for the recovery of our children, even though they were less visibly protected than in the past. During the journey of Jean François, the cook used a cauldron with verdigris to serve the soup, and they were poisoned; fifteen or sixteen began to vomit in a terrifying way, but prayer and care had their effect. By evening, only 4 or 5 were still sick, but one of them had such a nervous reaction that we feared for her reason and her life.[145] The doctor who came at midnight reassured us; and after eight days, she had completely recovered.

At this time our mother's health was upset; viper tea, and even more, Saint Francis Regis brought her back to her usual state. But the hand of God did not cease to weigh on the boarding school until winter: long but not dangerous fevers and a thousand other indispositions were continual. Saint Francis Regis our protector was several times deaf to our requests but was more favorable to the house in Poitiers. Mother Grosier

---

145 This was Euphrosine Jouve. In her funerary notice, added to the part edited by Therese Maillucheau from her own memories, Philippine specifies that her niece was served last. She thus ate from the bottom of the container, where the verdigris had accumulated.

was there in a very suffering and even dangerous state; as soon as our mother made a vow to send someone to La Louvesc, she got better in such a way that it seemed a miracle. It was for the fulfillment of this last vow that Jean François made the third journey to La Louvesc during the octave of the Nativity of the Blessed Virgin, one of the principal feasts of that devotional place.

June 9, 1809

The First Communion of ten students was held on May 22, second feast of Pentecost.[146]

And several of our sisters were admitted to make their vows on the feast of the Sacred Heart, June 9.

June 22, 1809

The prizes of June 22 were distributed by Messrs. Duchesne and Perier, the latter who more than anyone contributed to the temporal negotiation of our business, getting the government to give us several years' rent that we owed, and working to get the house and land given to us for the establishment [of education of girls]. That favor was also solicited for a time [at the end of autumn, 1802] by Mr. and Mrs. de Rollin.

That gesture of gratitude and the quality of the prefect of Romans in [the person of] Mr. de Rollin made them grant possession of the house on July 14, 1809. Also present was Mr. de Montmorency of the illustrious family of the Constables [de Lesdiguières], whose devotion and zeal made him curious to know an establishment that would be useful to society. They were also accompanied by Mr. Augustin[147] and Mr. Scipion[148] Perier. After having heard Mass, breakfasted in the house,

---

146 Monday after Pentecost.
147 Augustin Charles Perier (1773-1833), childhood friend of Philippine, was one of the first students of the *École polytechnique* (1794) and of the *École des Mines,* from which he graduated as a geographic engineer in 1797. In May 1798 he married Louise Henriette (called Eglantine) de Berckheim (1772-1863); he contributed to the foundation of the *Banque Perier,* in Paris; he was general councilor of the Isère, in charge of his father's business affairs in Dauphiny while the father was living in Paris; afterwards, he was president of the commercial court of Grenoble. Representative of the *département* of the Rhône during the Hundred Days (1815), he was then deputy of the Isère (1827-1831) and peer of France (1832). Deceased December 2, 1833, at the château of Frémigny, in Bourray-sur-Juine (Ile de France), he was buried in Père-Lachaise Cemetery in Paris.
148 Antoine Scipion Perier (1776-1821) married Louise Charlotte Sophie de Dietrich (1774-1832) in Strasbourg in 1802. He founded the *Banque Perier, Flory et Cie* with his brother Casimir; he was a regent of the *Banque de France* (1818-1821). Owner of the foundry of Chaillot, of cotton and woolen looms, and of two sugar refineries, he was a member of the General Council of Manufacturers and of the Conservatory of Arts and Crafts. In 1819, he was named to the Superior Council of Commerce, administrator of the Mining Company d'Anzin, of the Royal Insurance Company, and director of the Savings Bank and contingency fund.

and toured it, they went to see our students of the highest class. They gave greetings prepared for Mr. and Mrs. de Rollin and recited verses. After many congratulations on the happiness that we enjoyed and on the success of our establishment, these gentlemen and Mrs. de Rollin withdrew and never ceased to speak favorably about the house.

Our Sister de Crouzas, who had left a year and a half ago, reentered on June 23. Miss Camoin, who had entered during the year, had also left for a little while during the year because of health. She was replaced by Miss Choppin[149] from Villefranche who entered July 15; Miss Testour de Menis who entered August 16; and Miss Moulin[150] who entered September 1 and was sent to Lyon by the fathers whom we know. Miss Boisson[151] who entered September 23, was also from Villefranche. Since then, we also received Miss Pout from Grenoble on October 9, and Miss Gallien also from Grenoble on November 4. Two coadjutrix sisters who entered at the same time left soon after during the first days of November, since they did not have a vocation. One of them was called Flavie Durand, from Pont-de-Beauvoisin, and the other Françoise Maurice, also living in Pont-de-Beauvoisin. Marguerite, a girl not admitted to the Society but received in the house since September 1802, was also sent home a few days later, since our mother wants sisters only for domestic service. For the same reason, the other secular girl we had kept was dismissed after Easter.

July 20, 1809

The most interesting event of the whole year was the visit of the pope to Grenoble, which secured many favors for our house. Pius VII, then on the chair of Saint Peter in very difficult times, was taken from Rome at night by order of the Emperor of France, Napoleon, with no time to take anything with him nor the liberty of bringing anyone to accompany him. By an act of Providence and without an express intention of the emperor that the captain who conducted the pope could interpret, he was brought to Grenoble, after having made the long journey from Rome almost without stopping, and without seeing

---

149 Clotilde Choppin, RSCJ coadjutrix (1787-1855), was born November 20, 1787, entered the novitiate in Grenoble, received the habit December 27, 1809, and arrived March 1, 1816, at Niort, where she made her profession June 21, 1816. She died in Toulouse, September 18, 1855.

150 Marie Moulin, RSCJ (1781-1839), entered the novitiate in 1809 in Grenoble, made her first vows February 2, 1816, and her profession, November 1, 1820. On September 14, 1830, she went to Lille, where she died February 1, 1839.

151 Benoîte Boisson, RSCJ coadjutrix (1787-1837), entered at Grenoble September 23, 1809, left in August, 1812 for health reasons, returned December 2, and made her first vows June 27, 1813. She died at La Ferrandière (Lyon) on August 18, 1835.

a cardinal who was a prisoner like himself,[152] lodged separately. He arrived on July 20, 1809, at four in the afternoon.

Since he was to lodge at the prefecture, across from our windows on the other side of the Isère, we could see his carriage surrounded by gendarmes, his very small group in poor coaches, consisting of his chamberlain, the prelate Doria, a chaplain, a surgeon, chamber valets, and a cook. We saw the cardinal, separated and sent to another lodging. The next day, we had the good fortune to loan a missal and cruets for the pope's Mass. Mrs. de Vaulserre,[153] who still lived in this house, could see him from afar and obtained permission from the captain to return the next day and bring our mother [Deshayes]. So she went at the time of Mass but it had already been said. She did not have her usual clothes, but she was dressed in black taffeta like a widow.

The pope asked permission by name to see Mrs. de Vaulserre, who had lodged Pius VI when he came through Grenoble. When they saw our mother, they thought she was Mrs. de Vaulserre. By this happy misunderstanding, the pope gave her the best welcome and several times gave her his ring and his feet to kiss. Meanwhile, our mother identified herself as someone else and asked the pope for his blessings for her spiritual mother, her sisters, and more than 400 children. Then he seemed to be suffering, either from compassion for religious persons in these unhappy times, or because he feared to be compromised by this visit, because no priest or religious had entry to the prefecture while he was lodged there, unless by specific identification; but the mistake could have happened only during the first days. The bishop was away doing an ordination in Lyon. He hurried to return, but was never able to get permission to see the pope. They wrote to Cardinal Fesch to learn how to approach the situation. His answer seemed favorable, but just as we thought the Holy Father was free, the malefactors hurried his departure.

Returning to the visit of our Mother Deshayes, God so disposed the heart of the captain in her favor and that of Mrs. de Vaulserre, that when she asked him to show our house, identified as a boarding school, to the Holy Father as he walked, so that he could bless it, the captain answered: "But why do you not bring them here? I do not want the young ladies to be mixed in with the crowd of those who want to

---

152 Bartolomeo Pacca (1756-1844), cardinal in 1801, secretary of state (1808-1814), was imprisoned by order of Napoleon in the fortress of Fenestrelle (Piedmont). Pius VII was then under house arrest in Savona. He was later transferred to Fontainebleau, where Cardinal Pacca joined him in 1812.
153 Marie Louise Angelique de Vaulserre (1759-1812), the widow of Mr. de Brénier, lived at Sainte-Marie d'En-Haut, without being part of the community; she rendered many services.

see the Holy Father if they could see him in a private apartment. I will take charge of their entry tomorrow at 10:00 a.m., and they will have a separate room." After the thanks that such a favor deserved, we prepared for the next day's visit. She was sent home, according to the captain's advice, at four in the afternoon.

The students to the number of sixty, dressed in white, bare-headed with a black veil around their neck, went in order to the prefecture, accompanied by our mother, Mrs. de Vaulserre, and Sister Ribau. Since the captain was out, they were received rather badly by the other officers and employees at the prefecture. They had to leave and go to a church to await the captain's return. He carried out his cooperation all the way, making the crowd stand aside and saying in a loud voice: "*Only the boarders will enter.*" When all the students were arranged, he had the pope come in, and he went to each one of them, putting his hand on her head and having her kiss his ring.[154] The captain asked him if the sight of modest youth was moving to him, he said with goodness *that it pleased him. He blessed them* paternally. They withdrew, several of them not daring to look at him. They had formed a semi-circle on their knees around him.

The others of the house who could not go to him received his blessing at the windows every evening, because the pope gave it to the immense crowd who wanted to see him and to have him bless pictures, crosses, rosaries, etc. His walk was fixed at six in the evening until seven or seven-thirty. While he made it—it was in the City Garden—all the balustrades were closed; one could see him only through windows and neighboring gardens or around barrels. In spite of our distance and the angle of the Mountain,[155] we could make him out well, and we noticed him looking at our house and seeming to set it apart for a special blessing. Undoubtedly the captain had not forgotten his recommendation, or the shape of our house indicated a religious establishment; or he had the curiosity to be informed about it.

The laundry woman of the prefecture was also ours and brought us a surplice of the Holy Father. We had the consolation to repair the lace and the sewing, and to change the taffeta that lined the bottom

---

154 According to an undated document, "all the students of Sainte-Marie d'en Haut, on whose head the hand of Pius VII rested with deliberation, eleven of them, became religious, nine at the Sacred Heart: Euphrosine Jouve, Amelie Jouve, Olympie Rombau, Louise de Vidaud, Josephine de Coriolis, Julie Dusaussoy, Olympe de Causans, Caroline Lebrument, Louise de Rambert," C-VII 2) c Duchesne-Varia, Box 9, Env. 3, approbation-reports, *Note sur les élèves de Sainte-Marie d'en haut, bénies par le pape Pie VII, et religieuses ensuite.*

155 The convent of Sainte-Marie d'En-Haut is built on the flank of Mount Rachais, on the plateau of Chalemont.

of the sleeve. We kept the old pieces like precious relics, because we could say that he touched these pieces, since he had not abandoned this vestment since Rome. Nearly every day, at the time of Mass, our mother sent over articles to be blessed: our uniform medals, our crucifix, crosses, rosaries, pictures and flowers. On July 31, there was a full basket. The pope spread them out on a table for everyone to see, and he knew that it came from us.

August 2, 1809

On this day the rumor circulated that he was going to be free, that the emperor had not heard that he was oppressed; but the next day, feast of Saint Peter in Chains, August 1, we learned that he had been obliged to leave at three in the morning, not having been forewarned except by a few minutes. His people had been told after nine in the evening and in spite of their efforts, they could not make up all the packages or bring back his linens that had been in the laundry. In the disorder of this departure, the pope preserved a perfect calm, spoke with goodness to everyone, and praised the welcome he had received in Grenoble. He was the same along the route all the way to Savoy, where he is now, but the excitement broke out especially at Avignon, where they cried out, "*Long live the pope!*" and at Nice.

In Grenoble, especially on Sunday, the crowd at the City Garden was immense. They came from every side, from Lyon, from Romans, etc. One lady arrived here with her children from farther away than Geneva to see him, but he had gone that same night. The same thing happened to the Abbot of La Trappe, whom we had during that day with one of his religious.

Father Enfantin and Father Caillat,[156] from the same Society of the Fathers of the Faith, were more fortunate and saw him in the City Garden but without being able to approach him or speak to him. Father Caillat, who was with us at the time that they brought us the Holy Father's surplice, put it on devoutly and shared with us our little theft. Father Enfantin left the same night as the pope.

This favor of the blessing of the representative of Jesus Christ repeated so many times was followed by another that made its fruit increase. Father Royer, director of the seminary of Saint Irenaeus in Lyon, gave the boarding school a retreat of several days with unusual zeal and devotion.

---

156 Jean-Baptiste Caillat, SJ (1765-1853), born in Trévoux (Ain), entered the Society of the Fathers of the Faith in Austria. He was sent to Rome, then in France, and was professor at the college of Amiens until 1807. In 1825, he entered the Jesuit novitiate, and died in Aix-en-Provence.

In spite of so many graces, our mother, not very happy with the boarding school, delayed the prizes for six weeks, and there was no trimester in September.

September 21, 1809

This month we had the visit of Father Barat. He stayed seventeen days, hearing confessions and giving a sermon each day for the spiritual renewal of the Institute that he found weakened, as well as fervor in the boarding school. These discourses communicated the pain he experienced; he said *that the wrath of God floated over the house, that we were fortunate that it broke out in the afflictions and illnesses that hit the boarding school,* and he began a renewal. We awaited it with fervent prayers made for this intention and by the special help of the Holy Spirit that was given to 9 students on the second of October, feast of the Holy Guardian Angels, by our bishop in our church. He was assisted in this ceremony by Father Rey, vicar general and our superior.

November 10, 1809

The same evening, our Mother Therese began a retreat that would end her mission among us. She emerged from it only on the feast of Saint Theresa to receive the bouquet from the students and novices for her retreat. It was Mother Barat's intention to send her back to the house in Poitiers. She did not again take up her duties but continued her retreat until the day of her departure, November 10. In all, [this retreat] was about six weeks. She spent them in the greatest isolation, sometimes passing fifteen or sixteen hours in prayer, bearing very perceptible crosses not only with patience but even with ardor, never denying what we often heard her say: *"I am tired of not suffering, I would like to be despised! Testimonies of affection are a burden to me. Whoever does not want to suffer does not love. Life is extremely bitter for me. Who will cut the thread of my days?"* We hope that the expected renewal will follow the ardent wishes that she addressed to heaven for the sanctification of the people in the house.

Father Loriquet,[157] asked by Mother Barat to come to Grenoble to give his advice about the studies and order of the boarding school,

---

157 Jean-Nicolas Loriquet, SJ (1767-1845), entered the Fathers of the Faith in 1801 and was professor and prefect of studies at the college of Amiens in 1803. He gave courses in pedagogy to the religious of the future Society of the Sacred Heart and was the editor of the *Provisional Plan of Studies of the House of Amiens* (1804), revised before the departure of Sophie Barat for Grenoble. At the General Council of 1820, he presided at the sessions for revision of the plan of studies and the rule of the boarding school, texts that he then recommended to other feminine congregations.

spent 48 hours completely given to that task. The conferences for the students were nearly continual, and stopped the dismissal of several whose conduct was disturbing their companions.

It was he, when going to Paris, who took charge of taking our Mother Therese who was to find Mother Barat there at the home of Mrs. de Gramont.[158] She left without seeing the students and most of the sisters, whose regret could have sparked her attention but not diminished her courage. For several days, the perspective of God alone had raised her above human weakness. In Paris she had a great sacrifice to make: to see for only two days Mother Barat, who wanted to hasten her journey here and have her profit from a convenient opportunity for Poitiers. She arrived quickly and was received there with great joy.

The prizes that had been so delayed were finally held. The exercises begun before the arrival of Father Loriquet continued, and the bishop came to do the distribution of prizes on November 15.

The renovation of vows was not done in common on the feast of the Presentation; it was deferred until the arrival of Mother Barat. It took place on Saturday, December second, and brought us a young novice from Poitiers called Eulalie de Saint André; she is replacing Sister Balastron the younger, who left a month ago to restore her health.

December 12, 1809

Mother Barat did not speak to us in common or make any changes in the house. She wanted to see everything first. Today, December 12, she entered into retreat all day to offer the first moments of her thirty-first [year], where she now is. Tomorrow, December 13, is the anniversary of a day that is just as happy, the one on which she arrived in Grenoble five years ago to form the establishment.

Nothing important happened in the months of December and January. We learned only about the change of house of Mother Therese, whom our mother general sent to Ghent to help in a house that was afflicted by the loss of Father de Peñaranda, brother of the superior, her

---

158 Gabrielle Charlotte Marie Eugenie de Boisgelin de Gramont d'Aster, RSCJ (1766-1836), born April 17, 1766, in Brittany, was Lady in Waiting to Queen Marie-Antoinette. In 1789, she fled with her family to Italy, then to England where, after the death of her husband in 1795, she opened a boarding school for young English girls. In 1802, she devoted herself to God by a vow of chastity. When she returned to France, she rented an apartment in the house of the Sisters of Saint Thomas of Villanova, rue de Sèvres, in Paris. After her daughters Eugenie (1806) and Antoinette (1811), she was received (1813) into the novitiate in Amiens and made her first vows April 17, 1814. A year later, Louis XVIII asked her in vain to return to the court. She refused and made her profession March 1, 1816. Named assistant and mistress general in Amiens, she left in 1817 to found the house at Quimper, and in 1821 that of Le Mans, where she died January 16, 1836.

confidant, her friend, and the support of the new house by his lessons and exhortations. He was from the house of the fathers at Roanne, and everyone agreed that he was the living image of Saint Aloysius Gonzaga. Mother Therese was named mistress of novices in Ghent.

April 15, 1810

Father Barat came to see our reverend mother and devote his care to the boarding students during the first days of April. He heard all their confessions and gave absolution to all after they had been disposed by retreats that took place continually during his stay. In the evening, he gave the whole house an instruction for an hour and a half, the text of which was always taken from the first commandment and served to prepare five young students for First Communion. He had them do it on Palm Sunday, and left the same day, less unhappy with the house than in October, full of zeal and concern for the salvation of the students, who now number 64.

Mother Barat chose several of our sisters for the houses of Poitiers and Niort. The departure, planned for the second Monday after Easter, was put off until a new date would be decided on.

May 12, 1810

Father Enfantin, who visited us in October and January, came again on May 12, said Mass, and in the evening gave an exhortation that was strong and touching, as it were inspired, on obedience. He recalled that of soldiers given a mortal order who did not recoil from it. He spoke of the pain that follows the difficulties one causes to a superior, and the consequences of disobedience, especially in an age and in a way that makes the example contagious. He insisted on happiness, the promptness with which one should obey without distinguishing superiors. He came the next day, but not finding things the way he wanted, he left without hearing confessions or giving a new exhortation. Nevertheless, everyone at his discourse gave signs of bitter sorrow at their faults.

May 17-21

Our Sister Gaby died as the result of a cold;[159] she is the first to die in our house and the first in the Society who was assisted in her last moment by our mother general. Her death was very edifying. She made her vows, but secretly; she was not intended for the Society and was

---

159 This general term [*catarrhe*] could mean a severe inflammation of the lungs, or infection of the nasal passages or throat.

going to be sent away; she asked God rather to die. Three days later, she fell ill. She gave continual signs of joy in her illness, awaiting her end.

June 8, 1810
Reverend Mother Barat left us on June 8 with the promise to return, but the general business that affects the good of the Society leaves us fearing a long absence.

16-20
The feast of Saint Francis Regis was celebrated solemnly; Father la Corte preached a panegyric on the saint. Since the feast coincided with the Ember Days, we celebrated the feast only on the 20th.

29
The feast of the Sacred Heart occurred on the 29th, feast of Saint Peter, so was deferred to Sunday. The octave was as solemn as that of the Blessed Sacrament, which was exposed every day.

July 16
The feast of Saint Vincent de Paul; we distributed the prizes to the little poor children.

July 25
Miss Berthé[160] entered for admission as a coadjutrix sister.

August
On August 3, Reverend Mother Barat returned from her journey during which she was able to confer with Father Joseph [Varin], since they met at the Baths at Vichy. The rest of the time she spent partly at the home of Mr. de Saint-Palgue in the country and in Lyon, and she saw numerous young people, as many there as at Roanne, who wanted religious life and desired to benefit from her advice.

August 14 and 15, the Abbot of La Trappe was at Grenoble and as usual asked for hospitality from us. He had previously come through on June 14.

July 31
The feast of Saint Ignatius was preceded by a novena of fasting and Communion and perpetual adoration. On the day itself, the Blessed

---

160 Marie Berthé, RSCJ coadjutrix (1786-1851), was born October 1, 1786, and took the habit July 10, 1810, in Grenoble. In 1816, she went to help Philippine set up the house on rue des Postes in Paris. She made her profession on July 6, 1816, and died January 13, 1851, at Poitiers.

Sacrament was exposed in our interior chapel; and in the evening it was brought in solemn procession through our dormitories and cloisters all the way to the church.

August 15

The feast of the Blessed Virgin was celebrated as solemnly as possible. The students renewed their public consecration in the church.

August 21

The feast of Saint Chantal was celebrated in the church with the same ceremonies as in previous years; Father Rivet preached. At Benediction in the evening were the prior of the Carmelites of Florence and a Carthusian, both chased out of Italy in the revolution that they had just experienced. The [father] general of the latter was recently in Grenoble for the same reason.

September 1

Father Barat arrived as extraordinary confessor and to give a retreat. From the first day, he preached on the dispositions for hearing the word of God and on the different kinds of vanity: reputation, health, wealth, beauty, etc.

September 20

Prizes were distributed today by the bishop accompanied by several ecclesiastics. The two medallions were not merited this time, nor the prize of honor.

Father Barat, who had been away, returned from Chambéry on the 29th. He was here at the same time as Father Loriquet, who made his retreat; he reviewed all the rules of the boarding school and made necessary notes for the reform of several articles. His retreat ran concurrently with that of the students, during which Father Barat gave three discourses, besides the instruction of the little ones, to whom he gave constant attention all during his stay. For those outside the retreat, there was always a discourse in the evening at six-thirty and two on Sunday. Besides his instruction for the whole house, he gave us some in private about the explanation of the rules, observance of the vows, and especially All Saints' Day, the day chosen for renewal of vows, preceded by a conference about this sacred act. The general instructions[161] were at first about sin and the terrible punishment of it in the afterlife, all based

---

161 General instruction was a conference given to the students each week on a spiritual or moral subject.

on striking examples of conversion and final impenitence caused by sins hidden and not confessed. He followed with all the dispositions necessary for confession; then he talked about the holy Eucharist as sacrifice and sacrament, about the happiness of the saints, and about purgatory [during] the whole octave of the dead. Finally, to prepare us for the feast of the Presentation, he commented on all the litanies of the Blessed Virgin. On the feast of the Holy Rosary, the discourse was already on the prerogatives of Mary and on devotion to the Rosary.

These different subjects were developed in more than one hundred discourses, repeated to the little ones, which doubles the number; and if one adds the approximately 20 given to us privately, we were nourished by the word of God in more than 120 instructions, and part of the boarding school by 220.

November 19

This day was very painful for the house; it took away Mother Barat for a long time. She left with Mother Debrosse and Eulalie to go to Amiens and from there to Ghent or Poitiers. Her brother met her in Lyon and left here the 21st, feast of the Presentation.

Sister Lavauden the younger[162] entered the novitiate November 13, feast of Saint Stanislaus, and Miss Clement from Saint Marcellin entered the house on November 15.

During December, several students left for various kinds of discontent, of which these are the main ones: bad notes in review of conduct, difficulty for parents to see the students, their bad conduct, the little work that they do, and cost. So the boarding school that had gone up to 69 was reduced to 58. All the students went to midnight Mass.

1811
January 2, 1811

On the second, we wanted to celebrate the feast of reverend mother, who was getting better from her illness of six weeks.

20, 1st Communion

On the 20th of the same month, feast of the Holy Name of Jesus, five students had the happiness to make their First Communion with solemnity in our church, and we had the consolation to see them keep the benefits.

---

162 Adelaide Lavauden, RSCJ (1789-1869), born September 30, 1789, entered June 4, 1810, in Grenoble, made her profession June 21, 1816, and went to Chambéry on November 28, 1819. She died December 18, 1869, at Montpellier.

On March 28, we had the pleasure of seeing Father Enfantin, who stayed until April 22. At the time of his arrival, we were preparing 6 students for First Communion. He gave them the retreat conferences in spite of a fever that had tormented him for several months. One could scarcely see a retreat that bore so much fruit in the boarding school, which was truly rid of several who were intractable and less pious, so it was diminished to nearly 15. The discourse on the passion of Jesus Christ that he preached on the evening of Good Friday for 2 and ½ hours without losing anyone, even among the youngest students, made a deep impression; near the end, his voice was drowned out by their sincere tears.

April 14, 1st Communion

First Communion took place April 14, on the holy feast of Easter.

On the 22nd, Father Enfantin left for Romans without being healed. He heard almost no confessions this time.

May 2, Confirmation

On May 2, the bishop gave Confirmation to 16 students.

On the 29th of the same month, Sister Espié, who had been here since November 22, 1807, but had not made vows, left for health reasons.

On April 19, Sister Brunel returned; she had been away for three years because of health.

Sister Balastron the younger, who had left because of health in October 1809, returned.

On June 21, feast of the Sacred Heart of Jesus, we had the happiness to renew our vows.

On July 3 we had the distribution of prizes for the trimester, rescheduled this time because this year there had been only two trimester distributions, that of February 27 and this one.

August 15, 1811

On the feast of the Assumption of the Blessed Virgin, five of our students had the happiness to make their First Communion. One of them was in bed, very ill of a malignant cerebral fever for which she had already received Extreme Unction. She died on the 17th, the first of all of the students in the house, and was buried on the 18th.

When we told Reverend Mother Barat about this death, we spoke with her about a new request for the foundation in Genoa. In the absence of his eminence the cardinal archbishop, the prefect and the mayor asked the mother of one of our students, Mrs. Costa, if we would ever want to go there, and it was his intention to ask for a house from the minister.

In the same letter, we sent her a copy of a letter from Mothers [Marie Eulalie] de Bayane and de la Playne, Religious of the Visitation at Milan, who offered to us to go to Brescia, where the authorities had set aside a superb house for an educational establishment.

A third offer was made in Digne, *département* of the Lower Alps, where a lady wants to turn over her goods and where three girls want to enter. It was Father Augier, director of the seminary in that city, who came expressly to make the proposition.

Reverend mother answered by neither accepting nor refusing anything for the moment, nevertheless proposing to open one of these houses in the spring.

29

She left us to keep an eye on Agatha Giroud, a young shepherdess who is thought to be favored with extraordinary graces. She entered at the end of August, the 29th.

August 21

The 21st of the same month, six Trappist religious, who came from Bordeaux where they had gone to go to America but had not been able to leave France, asked shelter from us. We were not able to receive them because of doubt about the reason that motivated them. Several days later, the prior of the men's house near Briançon said Mass in our church. He told us that all of their houses, of both men and women, had been destroyed all over the French Empire. The resignation of these good religious is perfect; they even sang High Mass on the day of their departure.

September 3

On September 3, Father Rambaud, our worthy confessor and his brothers, keepers of the body of a saint belonging to the Carthusians, brought it to us in the hope of being able to keep it permanently. It was placed in our interior chapel. It is a martyr taken from the cemetery of Calixtus in Rome. He is called Alexander.

6

On the 6th Miss [Jeannette] Rivet left for Amiens, where she will redo her novitiate.

24

Prizes could not be distributed on September 22 this year, because the day was not convenient for those who should be there. They were given on the 24th. Father Bouchard, first vicar general, distributed the prizes in the absence of the bishop who has not returned from the council.[163] The father superior of the seminary accompanied him. Father Bouchard spoke to the children after the ceremony in a manner both unctuous and helpful.

October 15

On the 15th a young girl named Bérard entered, who did not work out. At the same time, our sacristan Jean Lacroix entered the seminary. He was replaced by Philibert Foussala, brother of Jean François Foussala,[164] who began service in the house on September 19.

The months of October, November and December were consecrated to the retreats given in bands, to whom our mother, whose health was much stronger, gave the exercises. With them came two persons from outside, desirous to know about our way of life: Miss de Saint Ferréol and Miss Forest, from Chatte, near Saint-Marcellin, where she has been educating girls for a long time.

During her retreat, Father Enfantin came from Grenoble. During his stay of 48 hours, he visited us and promised to return, but God disposed otherwise. The bishop of Valence soon named him canon with honors at his cathedral, and in that capacity, he preached. Someone then took the occasion to denounce him as contravening a decree that prohibits missionaries from preaching, and he was exiled to Nîmes, where he was very happy to suffer for Jesus Christ. When he received that order, he came through the place with a laughing and calm attitude, seeming to want more difficulties to suffer for God. The bishop of Valence asked for him again and gave as a reason that he had preached as canon and by his order.

December 31

The celebration of Christmas was followed by [spiritual] exercises for the boarding school, followed by the distribution of prizes on December 31. The cold made us change the intended destination of the eight days

---

163 Napoleon convoked the National Council of Paris (June-August 1811) with the aim of being able to create bishops without recourse to the pope. The majority of the prelates upheld the prerogatives of Pius VII.
164 Before their dispersion in November 1807, they were brothers at the college of the Fathers of the Faith at Roanne.

of [vacation of] the trimester; we worked for the poor and rejoiced on the occasion of the feast of our mother. On the eve and the day itself, there were plays and edifying conversations in the boarding school and the novitiate, where they represented the obedient soul, the right disposition of will, and the birth of Our Lord.

1812
January

We received the visit of our bishop who gave us all sorts of signs of benevolence, and whom we have not seen since his return from Paris.

At the same time, we also received a letter from Milan asking again for the foundation in Brescia. The city authority was not dissuaded by the year's delay asked for, nor the difference of languages. To facilitate it, he intends to prepare several subjects, keep a very beautiful house surrounded by gardens, and offer 14,000 Italian francs for the first expenses. These proposals were sent to Mother Barat, from whom he asked for some information about our Plan of Studies.

We do not need that to believe that God protects us at the same time that he tests us. We were worried about a request from the mayor to visit our house, and in Lyon there was rumor that we were finished, and that was said even farther afield. But we knew that the mayor had no hostile intention but simply wanted to fulfill a formality as one in charge of national buildings in the name of the city, without authority to change their purpose.

January 17

Since January 1, illness has also come to visit us. A mucous fever attacked Mrs. de Vaulserre, our distinguished friend and inseparable guest. Eight days later, Sister Clement, a novice, had a throat discharge. Two days later, Reverend Mother feared a cold and fever that was happily halted. On January 17, a student who had been sick since before Christmas with a cold and fever left; she had recovered, but remained in a state of listlessness that necessitated a stay in her family.

The illness of Sister Clement ended happily. But the student, who left after a long period of weakness, died at home with her parents. The house and physician were accused of not recognizing the illness, and they said that the child died as a result of the constraints and the heart seizures that she had. We were also blamed about another older student about whom they said that we did not sufficiently care for her health and the delicacy of her temperament; they said she was condemned by the physicians. Another left because of pains in the side that got worse; another for humors in the blood that made her hands disgusting; another for a severe whooping cough with chest pains; another for a problem in a finger bone that it was necessary to amputate.

The number of sick people who stayed in the infirmary for the whole winter was considerable. They were the whooping coughs, bad colds, pains, problems in the side, obstructions, and fever. A child of 12 years was very ill with a throat discharge; happily, she recovered.

February 12, 1812

But Mrs. de Vaulserre died on Ash Wednesday, February 12. She gave constant edification until the end. The virtue for which she is most remembered is a great zeal for the salvation of souls, which made her make considerable monetary sacrifices to obtain it. This same zeal led her to take charge of a class of 20 to 30 poor girls whom she loved as her very own and whom she instructed perfectly; she took on, besides, the responsibility to speak to the parents of all our day students, a quite necessary thing to do to promote the good with them. The second virtue that shone in Mrs. de Vaulserre is *humility*: she called herself the house dog, and considered the others, even the coadjutrix sisters, as far above her; she always took the last place and spoke to everyone with an admirably lowly manner in a person who was distinguished in spirit, birth and education.

Part of her furniture stayed at the house; her heir is her sister, Mrs. de Marette. She also left us a sum of money for Masses for her for a year, which gave us the happiness of having two every day.

April 10, 1812

Soon after her death, Sister Pout took her place in the infirmary; she had a tumor on the lip that she had had removed in order to enter with us. The second year, the same tumor appeared on her nose and penetrated deeply inside. A cauterization and antiscorbutic treatments did not prevent the tumor turning from her nose to settle in the throat. The physicians declared her to be attacked with scrofulous and scorbutic consumption. The malignancy grew rapidly and brought her to the tomb on April 10. The virtues that distinguished her are perfect obedience and regularity; no one saw her commit a fault. This purity of conscience gave her calm resignation to death and perfect peace.

May 3, 1812

Illness continues in the boarding school; the most worrisome are the continual choking coughs of several of the weakest ones. These poor children have placed their confidence in Saint Alexander, the translation of whose relics took place on the first Sunday of May, which was May 3 [feast of the Holy Cross], and after the ceremony, several were no longer sick.

The body was placed on the small altar of the church. The feast that we have permission to have is set for the first Sunday of May, and every year like this one, we can leave the sarcophagus open, exposed for the veneration of the faithful. We continue all month the novena that we have begun in his honor, and we do not doubt his protection over us.

May 17, 1812

Nevertheless, our infirmary is not emptied, and we have there a child who has recovered from a throat discharge; and another, who appeared to recover from a double tertian fever that lasted four months, has just been attacked by the illness called Saint Vitus' Dance.[165] Her shoulders jump constantly; baths and other calming treatments do nothing to soothe her; she has no appetite and does not sleep. We were obliged to send her to her family for a while; she recovered only on the way.

May 24

These days we have had the great consolation of seeing *Mother Barat* again amongst us, with the hope of keeping her for a long time. She came partly to supply the requested establishments, but everything else remains in silence for now.

June 5

On June 5, seven students made their First Communion from the hands of our bishop, who also confirmed two of them. The day concurred with the feast of the Sacred Heart of Jesus, the day marked by the renewal of vows, which because of this ceremony was delayed to the feast of Saint Francis Regis, which is usually celebrated solemnly. And we had besides the consolation of seeing the depiction of this holy protector in our church, done for this intention in the house itself.

On the 25th, the trimester prizes were given.

At this time we learned that our Holy Father the pope had been transferred very secretly from Savoy, place of his detention, to the castle of Fontainebleau near Paris, where it is said that they are preparing the

---

165 An infectious childhood nervous disease with involuntary movements, called Sydenham's chorea, from the name of the seventeenth century English physician, Thomas Sydenham, who diagnosed the symptoms. The name "Saint Guy's Dance" (or in English, Saint Vitus' dance), dates from the ninth century, the result of miraculous cures attributed to Saint Guy, then considered the patron of epileptics.

archiepiscopal palace for him. No one can speak with him without the approval of those who guard him.

July 9, 1812

It is also at this time that we learned of the arrest of Father de Sambucy, benefactor and confessor of the house at Amiens, and the order to send away his confreres from the seminaries and colleges where they had positions. This order forced Father Gloriot to leave Besançon, and since August 4 he has been in Grenoble where he gave the mission with Father Lambert.

August 7

On the 6th, the superior general of the *Daughters of Wisdom* came with her companion and Father Bossard, superior of the seminary, to visit the house. She is in Grenoble to start a foundation of her religious, who are nurses, at the general hospital. They are on the way and she will return to Aix-en-Provence, from where she came, when she has set them up. Her houses at Aix have changed since her visit here, where she has established her residence.

September 22, 1812

On September 22, the bishop did the distribution of prizes for the trimester, accompanied by the vicars general, Fathers Bouchard and Chabannier, and several other priests.

October 2

On October 2, Mother Barat went to Besançon to see our revered founder [Father Varin] and confer with him about various items of Society business, especially about the means to bring all the houses into unity. That of Amiens received a revision of the constitutions from Father de Sambucy, which they hold in high esteem and have put them into practice contrary to the wishes of the other houses and the approval of those who advise our mother general, who fears a rupture now. But all affirm the wish to continue to live in obedience to her.

This house has not been without worry because of the dismissal from the Society of Miss Jeannette Rivet to Amiens and from Amiens. Her family is offended and have set many people against us and even threatened to denounce us to the government. After a long time of patience, our mother succeeded in getting our superiors to make the complainers cease and to get the family to desist from its efforts to have Miss Rivet return; she had not been received definitively.

November 13

Our mother returned on November 13. She found the time too short to prepare the novices to make their vows. Several had left in recent months, both novices and observers: Miss Damirans on August 25, Miss Crémant on September 7, Miss Testout on October 6, Miss Therese Perier on December 18, and Miss Chapuy, observer, on the 8th, having also stayed only eight days in December. Sister Boisson, who had left in August because of her health, returned on the 2nd. She contented herself with a renewal on the part of the senior professed on the feast of the Presentation; and the newly professed along with the novices admitted to vows made the eight-day retreat before the feast of Saint John the Evangelist, the day on which the renewal ceremony took place for both the senior and young professed, and profession for Sisters Crouzas, the younger Lavauden, Moulin, Choppin, and the elder Chauvin [Bertille]. The last made her vows as coadjutrix, and all for one year only. The same day, Miss Victoire Roland was admitted to the novitiate as coadjutrix; she had been in the house since June 23.

We had the consolation to see the arrival, on December 23, of Mother Bigeu, mistress general, mistress of novices, and assistant in Poitiers, with Miss Chatain,[166] an observer to become a coadjutrix sister.

January, 1813
The 10th

The ordination of Father de Janson,[167] who renounced the advantages of fortune to give himself to God, attracted him to Grenoble, and we had a retreat of eight days from him for the whole boarding school, which was fruitful for the students and for those of our sisters who had not made the vow retreat. It served as preparation for the Confirmation of eleven boarders and the First Communion of another. This ceremony took place on January 10. Father de Janson preached twice that day

---

166   Marie Chatain, RSCJ coadjutrix (1790-1863), born May 2, 1790, was received into the novitiate June 21, 1812, and made her profession November 21, 1818. For many years she cared for the physically handicapped at the Rue de Varenne until the closure of that work in 1850. She was then infirmarian in Poitiers. She died at Orléans on May 20, 1863.
167   Charles de Forbin-Janson (1785-1844), official at the State Council in Paris, renounced an administrative career for the priesthood. Ordained in Chambéry in 1811, he was named superior of the seminary (1811-1812), then vicar at Saint-Sulpice (1812-1814) in Paris, retreat preacher in France (1814-1824), and bishop of Nancy in 1824. With Jean-Baptiste Rauzan, he began in 1814 the Congregation of the Fathers of Mercy and founded a community at Spring Hill near New Orleans in 1839. In 1840, he was present at the Council of Baltimore, was named vicar general of the diocese of Montreal, and preached in 1841 the first retreat for the clergy in Quebec. When he returned to France in 1842, he founded the Holy Childhood movement.

and again two days later, with a zeal and unction that brought tears when he left.

Several days later, we received the repeated invitation of the civil authority of Brescia to go to his city and found a boarding school for which he intends a very beautiful house. The purpose of his letter was to learn the requirements of each person and the expenses of travel. Our mother answered with the detachment that should characterize us. Mother Eugenie de Bayane, supporter of the Visitation in Italy, who had been much protected by the emperors, was the first broker of this negotiation and has just died without its being interrupted.

24

On the 24th, Mrs. de Lesgalier, aunt of one of our students, repeated a similar invitation for Nîmes, where she wants to sell a beautiful house and contribute to the work and success of a boarding school. The same invitation came the same day from Archbishop d'Aviau of Bordeaux, urged by our mother general's brother, who lives there.

February 22

A new letter from Brescia from the new civil authority, who wants to accomplish the work begun by his predecessor and who will take charge of everything in its regard. He announced at the same time that the person responsible to lead the little colony will arrive in Grenoble during Holy Week.

April 4

A letter from Mrs. de Playne from Milan and from the civil authority in Brescia that says that as his envoy was about to depart, the government showed him a law of the land that prohibits entry to any founder without attestation from one's own country and who does not know Italian. He asks an urgent answer from the prefect and mayor of Grenoble, to whom they wrote from Brescia to this end in January.

These attestations took a long time to obtain because of military occupation and sending them to the ministry. They were sent only in May or June.

May 26

Misses Chavy and Teillard[168] entered.

---

168 Marie Teillard, RSCJ (1792-1816), born in 1792 at Rive-de-Gier (Loire), made her vows before her death on January 10, 1816.

June 16

Celebration of the feast of Saint Regis. There was exposition of the Blessed Sacrament, sermon, High Mass, and nine others. We celebrated it as a major feast, but the students worked.

June 25

The feast of the Sacred Heart was kept with the same solemnities, but the students did not work.

June 27

Today Sisters de Portes and Lavauden the elder made their final vows; Sisters Brunel, Boisson, Forest and Bertet made them for a year; Sister Fonsala[169] renewed them a one year, and the older ones made the usual renovation. The whole ceremony was done in the internal chapel. It was delayed until Sunday instead of the feast day in order to wait for Father de Janson, who gave the retreat conferences and that of the renovation. Sister Chatain was received as a novice.

July 2

Today there was a celebration in the church, which was full at the evening Benediction because of the indulgence. There were three Low Masses in the morning, but we worked. Agatha Gauthier[170] entered on June 24, 1813, to be a coadjutrix sister.

9

Departure of Sister Josephine Dullo after six years of residence. She was conducted to Gap by Miss Espié, another novice who left here and who has started a boarding school that she wishes to unite with the Society.

---

169 Marie Fonsala, RSCJ coadjutrix (1786-1838), entered in Grenoble in 1807 and went to Chambéry and then Turin. With Angelique Lavauden, she accompanied Mother Bigeu to Rome in 1825. She died at the Trinità dei Monti, Rome.

170 Agatha Gauthier, RSCJ coadjutrix (1788-1870), was born September 21, 1788, at Pont-de-Beauvoisin (Isère). Received in Grenoble June 24, 1813, she entered the novitiate February 2, 1814, and left for the foundation at Quimper, where she made her profession August 15, 1818. An excellent gardener, she then went to Paris, Besançon, Annonay and Lyon, where she died May 25, 1870. She wanted ardently to go to America. She kept until her death an undated letter of Philippine: "My very dear Sister Agatha, I received your note, and though it would give me great pleasure, that of seeing you with Mother Lucile would have been even greater. You would have passed from little Louisiana to the big one, but our common Louisiana is the Heart of Jesus, where we always find each other if we are gentle and humble. I remember all your work in Grenoble; you would be at a disadvantage here. Perhaps that is what attracts you, but obedience gives you tranquility since it is the expression of the will of God. I am yours for all of life in the Heart of Jesus. Signed: Philippine." C-I, d 2, *Lettres Annuelles, 1870-1871.*

13
Departure of Jean François, who returned to his country.

14
Entrance of Miss Lucille Mathevon as a choir religious.

26
Entrance of Miss Butri to be a coadjutrix sister.

29
Entrance of Miss Nanette to be a coadjutrix sister.

30
Entrance of the elder Miss Forest[171] to be a coadjutrix sister. Her second entrance was October 9.

August
2
Entrance of Miss Parisot[172] to be a choir religious.

15
This day of the death of the Blessed Virgin was doubly precious for us, since several of our children made their First Communion; they are: Miss de Bondard the younger, two sisters Isoard, Blanc, Dusaussoy,[173] and Calhetin. Father Rivet, our chaplain, did the ceremony and all the conferences. He also preached on the 21st, feast of Saint Jane de Chantal, and the High Mass was sung by the father director of the seminary of Lyon.

September
19 and 22
On the 22nd we had the ceremony of the general distribution of prizes by the bishop. The 19th, he had already come to give Confirmation to those who had already made their First Communion, except Miss de Bondard, and besides, to Misses de Vidaud the elder[174] and de Jonquière.

---

171 Therese Forest, born in 1786, died in 1815.
172 Françoise-Jeanne Parisot, RSCJ (1785-1857), born September 2, 1785, entered the novitiate November 1, 1813, and made her profession May 29, 1818. She died at Montpellier on March 7, 1857.
173 Julie Dusaussoy, RSCJ (1800-1842), was one of the four nieces of Mother Barat who became Religious of the Sacred Heart. She entered the novitiate in Grenoble, then went to Lyon still as a novice, on November 28, 1819. On April 2, 1830, she accompanied Mother Angelique Lavauden to Avignon. She died at Conflans, then the novitiate house, on October 21, 1842.
174 Louise de Vidaud, RSCJ (1801-1879), born February 13, 1801, was a boarder at Sainte-Marie

September 25, 1813

On the 25th of the same month, Mother Barat left with Mother Deshayes to go to see Father Varin. After a short stay of about six weeks, they both took the road to Paris, having decided that the term of superiors would be three years. On November 9, Mother Barat wrote to the community that she was giving us as superior Mother Josephine Bigeu, a professed of the house of Poitiers, who had entered that house December 24, 1812, and was already in charge of the novitiate. Mother Deshayes went to the house at Cuignières, with Mother Barat accompanying her before returning to Paris, where she continues to be occupied with the business of the Society to determine several things that are not yet well settled.

October 10, 1813

Miss Dutour entered the house to be a choir religious.

November 1, 1813

Miss Henriette Lebrument, who was not ready to make her First Communion on the feast of the Assumption, having been withdrawn, made it today, the feast of All Saints.

13

We celebrated the feast of Saint Stanislaus Kostka in the retreat chapel.

2

On the feast of the Presentation, Sister Fonsala made her final vows. All the professed renewed theirs, and Misses Parisol and Chavy entered the novitiate; Miss Mathevon was already there.

30

On the 30th, feast of Saint Andrew, we lost our sister Marie du Terrail, professed religious of Amiens, of an illness of exhaustion, caused by the extreme fatigue with which she gave herself for a long time to the instruction of the students, the poor, and the persons from outside who needed it. Her distinctive virtue is zeal for the salvation of souls. Her death was very edifying.

---

d'En-Haut with her sister Zoe. She entered the novitiate in 1818 and made her final vows on December 11, 1825. She died in Orleans.

December
8

On the 8th, we celebrated the feast of the Immaculate Conception in the retreat chapel.

25

We had three midnight Masses and a great number of communicants.

27

We celebrated the feast of Saint John the Evangelist in the retreat chapel.

The same day, we were given the alarm about the approach of the Austrian and Bavarian army that they say has arrived in Geneva. But the news was false, and we are still uncertain how things will turn out.

Letter 4   **L. 2 to Mrs. Jouve**

November 1804[175]

I am sending you, my good Friend, your daughter's first essay, which she took great pleasure in writing for you. She is very well, although she has a slight cold; her school work goes well in spite of her liveliness that makes long study times a little hard; I can recognize her at a distance by the animation of her little body. Aunt Perier[176] came to see her and took her out on Sunday. Aunt Lagrange also wanted her on Thursday, but it was too soon after the first outing.

Would you believe, good friend, that the news of the success of our petition was false. A letter yesterday from Mr. de Rollin told me that all of his efforts failed in such a way that the case cannot be reopened.[177]

---

175 Copies: *Cahier, Lettres de la Mère Duchesne à sa famille*, pp. 23-24; *Lettres dactylographiées*. C-VII 2) c Duchesne to her family and lay people, Box 5. An archivist had dated this letter 1806 or 1808. But Euphrosine entered the boarding school at Sainte-Marie d'En-Haut on September 3, 1804; her first written work, therefore, is earlier than 1806. The loss of the documents relating to the authorization of the boarding school happened at the end of October or the beginning of November 1804, in the Ministry of the Interior. The letter is therefore from November 1804.
176 Marie-Charlotte Pascal (1749-1821) in 1767 married Claude Perier (1742-1801). The Perier family lived in the same building as Philippine Duchesne's family, N° 4, Grand-Rue, in Grenoble.
177 On October 25, 1804, Father Varin met Joseph de Gérando, the general secretary of the Interior Ministry who assured him of "the complete success" of Mother Duchesne's request. Cf. *Story of Sainte-Marie d'En-Haut*. But a little while afterwards, the document was lost. The process was then renewed and the imperial decree only reached them the following year, dated 6 *Pluviôse An XIII* (January 25, 1805).

We must begin our pursuits all over again as on the first day. I am quite tired of all this, and I regret the trouble I am causing my kind relatives. I am keeping the whole business an inviolable secret so that we will not be prevented from trying again; don't speak about it to anyone.

Goodbye, dear Sister, I consider myself happy to have here a sign of your tender love; in her I seem to see you again.

Philippine

Letter 5   **L. 3 to Mrs. Jouve**

December 14, 1804[178]

What a joy it was, my good Friend, to recognize your writing on one of the letters handed to me a few days ago. Yours was a proof that you had recovered; I was waiting for that news with keen impatience. Before telling Euphrosine, I wanted to test her feelings, so I asked her what news would give her the greatest joy in the world; she answered immediately that it would be her mother's cure. The high color and the troubled look in her eyes assured me that the wish came straight from her heart. She added that she had said the rosary many times for you.

She is not writing to you today, as the school schedule is somewhat upset by the arrival of three religious who came from Amiens with Father Roger, who accompanied them from Lyon.[179] It looks as if we have been most fortunate in getting them here. One of them [Mother Barat] is to be our superior; she has charmed all the boarders by her gentle manner.

I embrace you affectionately,

Philippine

---

178 Copies: *Cahier, Lettres de la Mère Duchesne à sa famille*, p. 29; *Lettres dactylographiées*. C-VII 2) c Duchesne to her family and lay people, Box 5.

179 It was Mother Barat with Rosalie Debrosse and Catherine Maillard.

Letter 6   **L. 4 to Mrs. Jouve**

March 22, 1805[180]

My hopes of seeing you in Lyon are vanishing, my good friend. As the trip is not necessary, it probably will not take place. It was judged necessary for the religious who will give you this letter; urgent business obliges her to leave us for about ten days. She will not stay with you, as you so kindly offered; because she is alone and unaccustomed to walking great distances, she would be too far from the center of her business. I did not think it wise to send Euphrosine with her for so short a time. I planned to give her the pleasure of seeing you only if I were going to share it. I do not have to tell you how much I should have enjoyed seeing you in the midst of your dear family, of whom I still know only one lovely member; but you realize, my good Friend, that my vocation requires a commitment to sacrifice and to the privation of natural joys; and at this moment I am exchanging the joy of embracing you for that of keeping my promises and proving to God that his yoke is always lovable, for there is joy in sacrificing for anyone we love.

I have not said anything to Euphrosine about the possibility of the pleasure of going to Lyon; she is writing to you. You will have more satisfactory details about her from Mother Barat who will take my letter to you. She loves her very much.

Here is your daughter's letter—an embarrassment to her and to me! Remember me to your husband and to our cousins.

All yours.

Good Father Pison died two days ago.[181]

---

180 Copies: *Cahier, Lettres de la Mère Duchesne à sa famille*, pp. 34-35; *Lettres dactylographiées*. C-VII 2) c Duchesne to her family and lay people, Box 5.
181 In 1791, Jean-Baptiste Pison (1725-1805), vicar general of Grenoble, canon of the Church of Saint-André, was governing the diocese in the absence de Bishop du Lau. But the correspondence with his bishop earned him condemnation and imprisonment in Grenoble at the *Conciergerie*. Exiled afterwards for several months, he returned to Briançon on March 7, 1793, and was incarcerated in Grenoble, at Sainte-Marie d'En-Haut, until *25 Messidor An II* (July 13, 1794). As metropolitan commissioner, he welcomed Claude Simon, the bishop named by Bonaparte, on October 6, 1802. He died on March 19, 1805.

Letter 7   **L. 5 to Mrs. Jouve**

Grenoble, September 17 [1805][182]

You are experiencing a great void, dear Friend, in being separated from a daughter you love so dearly, and I feel the same in missing you. The sweet habit of seeing you for several days makes me feel all the more the pain of being separated from you almost all the time. Although you warned me that you would probably not be able to write to me upon your arrival, I will be anxious until you tell me that you had a safe arrival.

Upon arriving in Lyon you will have learned that Adelaide has had her baby.[183] Her husband has just told me of the birth of their fifth daughter; he is resigned to it. Yours is one of my joys here and provides recreation in the midst of more serious occupations; at catechism lessons she speaks almost as much as I do, corrects those who make mistakes and forestalls their answers. Like a well-informed person, she explains matters with assurance, using correct terms. She sends her love to you as well as to her father and sisters.

Goodbye, dear Sister, far from you, I see with joy your image in your daughter and cherish her doubly.

Letter 8   **L. 6 to Mrs. Jouve at Crest**

February 14 [1806][184]

My good Friend,

Mrs. de Butet is here with the Ladies of Mornays, but I have not seen her at all; we avoid receiving visitors; besides, maybe she would rather I were a Visitandine.

Through our little Italian, I have had news of Mother Eulalie de

---

182 Copies: *Cahier, Lettres de la Mère Duchesne à sa famille*, p. 14; *Lettres dactylographiées*. C-VII 2) c Duchesne to her family and lay people, Box 5.
183 Adelaide Lebrument, Philippine's sister, had five daughters: Caroline (1799-1854), Henriette (1800-1854), Eugenie (1802-1857), Marine (1803-1861) and Delphine (1805-1833) who had just been born.
184 Copies: *Cahier, Lettres de la Mère Duchesne à sa famille*, p. 3; *Lettres dactylographiées*. C-VII 2) c Duchesne to her family and lay people, Box 5.

Bayane,[185] who received a visit from the king and queen of Naples. Besides gracious assurances of protection, she obtained from them a beautiful convent and land enough to produce good crops; she and her community have been in want of food for several years.

Miss de Saint-Laurent made her First Communion, and Miss de la Bareyre is preparing for hers. Father Lacoste gives religious instruction to our students twice a week.

My regards to father and every good wish to the happy company. All yours,

Philippine

Find out, I beg you, whether Duchesne has withdrawn my income[186] and deposited it at the address I gave him.

Letter 9   L. 1 to Mother Barat

[March 1806][187]

Long live Jesus!

Reverend Mother,

I was longing to tell you of my joy and gratitude towards divine goodness, when I received your letter. So now I may give free rein to my dearest hopes! You do not take away from me the hope of fulfilling my wishes one day; I can direct my desires and prayers to the countries where I would be able to render some service to Our Lord and to be rich only in him. What a powerful goad to work at self-reform is the fear of being unworthy of my high destiny! With what respect mixed with tenderness would I hear these delightful words: "I send you…among

---

185 Eulalie de Bayane was the sister of Eugenie de Bayane, Philippine's mistress of novices at Sainte-Marie d'En-Haut. Their brother, Cardinal Alphonse-Hubert de Latier de Bayane (1739-1818), legate of Pius VII in Paris in 1809, was responsible for significant negotiations at Savona and Fontainebleau.
186 In 1797, after the death of her mother, Philippine had given over to her brother, Antoine Louis Hippolyte, and sisters the estate she inherited from her mother in exchange for an annual income, which provided her with a modest livelihood and thus freed her from material preoccupations.
187 Original autograph, C-VII 2) c Duchesne to Barat, Box 2. Cf. *Saint Madeleine-Sophie Barat-Saint Philippine Duchesne, Correspondence*, Text presented by J. de Charry, I, L. 10, tr. B. Hogg, pp. 30-34.

wolves,"[188] if only you could add "as a lamb." With what emotion would I take your venerable hand and place it on my head to be blessed with these words: *Ab illo benedicaris in cujus honore cremaberis!*[189]

I am often in spirit at the moment of decision and still more in the places where I was intending to go. But would you believe this if you did not know me as I am? I am no better than when you left us, maybe less good; the more I feel myself strong for the future, the more I realize my present cowardice. It is a long time since I have spent such a dreary Lent; I am unspiritual, unmortified, totally centered on myself.

I have had a letter from my cousin in Bordeaux [L.-B. Enfantin], the one you spoke to about me. I don't know if you did so in veiled terms, but he writes to me as if he does not know what I am preoccupied about. I lost no time in clarifying the matter, for I was in a hurry to be in correspondence with him; the more so that I imagine he may be the person God wishes to use to further my only ambition. This letter from my cousin was opened by our good mother who thought it was for her.[190] She understood nothing of what it was about. I was already reproaching myself for not having told her about my hopes, and I told her about them then.

I am longing to know what you will have to say on the subject, and I hasten to kneel before you in spirit to hear. I had to be resigned when I saw in the letter to her from V.[191] that I must wait until the end of May. Is that what you promised us so solemnly? I don't so much fear the bouquet of absinthe you foretold for me,[192] as these repeated delays. I would need you to make me wait for (the occasion of) a visit in your little office; I will have to sacrifice my eagerness.

Our mother must have told you: the business of our first two years of renting is finished in the most advantageous way possible: I was pleased about it even more because it seemed to me that I could say *nunc dimittis* even better now that I am totally unnecessary where I am.[193] I hope that you will write before Holy Thursday and that you will

---

188 Mt 10:16; Lk 10:3.
189 "May you be blessed by him in whose honor you will be consumed." Liturgical blessing of incense.
190 Mother Deshayes, superior, could have confused the name "Duchesne" with "Deshayes."
191 The reference is probably to Father Varin.
192 In her letter of January 20, 1806, Sophie Barat speaks to her of the "bouquet of myrrh" *(Song 1:13)* that will become "like an apple tree among the trees of the wood" *(Song 2:3).*
193 Ph. Duchesne was lease-holder of Sainte-Marie d'En-Haut, which had been awarded to her on December 10, 1801, when the convent, a national property since the expulsion of the Visitandines in 1792, had been put up for auction. On January 26, 1805 *(6 Pluviôse An 13)*, an imperial decree legally recognized the Institution of Sainte-Marie d'En-Haut. Thanks to a new intervention of her family, Philippine obtained the right to use the house without having to pay rent for the past years. Cf. *Journal de Grenoble*, manuscript, p. 24.

lift that cruel prohibition of never spending the whole night. Please, I need that in order to speak at leisure to our good Master.

If we have the money, I would also be in favor of renovating, simply, of course, the cells along the terrace; that could be done during May. Your recommendations concerning economy are faithfully observed; I am inclined that way and necessity supports the inclination. How much stronger when obedience imposes both as a duty!

After many trials this winter, it has seemed to me to be most in the spirit of poverty, without prejudice to suitability and to needs, to make the bread, as we did when you came here, for supper, *goûter* and lunch and to buy bread from the baker for the other meals. It is certain that it costs more to make white bread. That was the former custom in this house, based on experience. In this whole region in all large houses there are two [kinds of] bread; that satisfies all tastes and stomachs and is less costly. It would not suffice to have only homemade bread; we would appear extravagant to have only bakery bread. However if bakery bread proves to be cheaper, as I said, we can change. If you could make a decision about this matter before Easter, we would begin then to do what you would like.

Our children are fairly well. They send you their humble respect and were very happy with the lines addressed to them in your last letter. I hope my good Felicity [Le Fèvre] does not forget me; I remember her always with great interest.

My regards, if you please, to Mother Baudemont and her daughters. I am your very unworthy,

Ph.D.

God alone.

Letter 10   **L. 2 to Mother Barat**

[April 4, 1806][194]

My good Reverend Mother,

What happiness your letter gave me and how much good it did my soul. I needed it to soften my heart; for three weeks my heart had been as hard as a rock; but when I read your words, it melted like wax before the fire. My eyes were no longer dry, and my heart was filled with

---

194 Original autograph, C-VII 2) c Duchesne to Barat, Box 2. Cf. J. de Charry, I, L. 12; Hogg, pp. 37-39.

sweet joy that I seemed to taste all night, for the letter arrived before the night watch of Holy Thursday.

O blessed night, when I believed a second time that my prayer was heard! I am convinced of it, dear Mother, because of the pure joy I taste and the firm confidence I have. Oh, if only I might go before the year is out! I have almost persuaded myself that I shall. All night long I was on the new continent, and I traveled in such good company. First, I carefully collected all the blood of Jesus from the Garden, the Pretorium, and Calvary; I took possession of him in the Blessed Sacrament, and holding it close, I carried my treasure everywhere to spread it without fear of its being exhausted. Saint Francis Xavier helped me to make this priceless seed bear fruit, and from his place before the throne of God he prayed that new lands might be opened to the light of truth. Saint Francis Regis was the travelers' pilot, with many other saints eager for God's glory. All went well, and no sorrow, not even holy sorrow, could find place in my heart; for it seemed to me that the merits of Jesus were about to be applied in a wholly new manner. The twelve hours of the night passed very quickly and without fatigue, even though I knelt the whole time. The evening before I had felt I could not hold out for an hour.

I had all my sacrifices to offer: a mother—and what a mother!—sisters, relatives, my mountain; and then I found myself alone with Jesus alone, with dark, uncouth children, and I was happier in the midst of my little court than all the princes of the world. Good Mother, when you say to me: "*Ecce, ego mitto te,*"[195] I shall quickly answer, "*Vadam.*"[196] It is good that I must wait a while for the pleasure of talking to you about all this. There would be too much enjoyment in such an outlet. Besides, I would not like to have nuns knocking at the door at every instant wanting to speak to their mother; I should want her all to myself.[197]

I am going to try to be sad for the rest of Good Friday, but I cannot rouse that sentiment: my hope has risen so high.

I am very respectfully at your feet, your humble and submissive daughter,

Phil. D.

Good Friday morning

---

195 "I send you." Ex 3:10
196 "I shall go." Ex 3:13.
197 Philippine wants to have a long visit uninterrupted by importunate knocking.

Letter 11   **L. 7 to Mrs. Jouve in Lyon**

[1807][198]

My good Sister,

Mrs. de Vaulserre offered to have me put a few lines in her letter to you; I profit from the opportunity with great pleasure. The letter will be brought to you by Father Roger, who has overwhelmed us with kindness and spiritual nourishment during his stay.

A few delights of this kind are necessary in order to survive life's privations; having Melanie[199] so far away is a great one for me. She is so happy to be at Romans that her relatives are consoled. Yesterday I received a letter from her in which she seemed in transports of joy; she will have Miss Chièse as a novitiate companion.

Goodbye, I embrace you tenderly and am all yours.

Letter 12   **L. 8 to Mrs. Jouve**

[1807][200]

My dear Friend,

By now you should be reassured about your husband. I was happily surprised to see him, and the time we spent together seemed very short; I received him in the parlor because since Mrs. Lebrument was here,[201] we have become stricter about cloister, and we do not have to make any mystery about it since we received our decree. I should have been very proud to show him our terrace at sunset, and I feel he would have been enthusiastic about it. Your daughters were wild with joy at seeing him; happily he was not too demonstrative and did not make over Euphrosine too much; she is already well aware of her own merits; but in any case, she is better; her manner is calmer; she is more affable

---

198 Copies: *Cahier, Lettres de la Mère Duchesne à sa famille*, p. 9; *Lettres dactylographiées*. C-VII 2) c Duchesne to her family and lay people, Box 5.
199 Melanie Duchesne (1786-1828) had just entered the Visitation at Romans; she took the name of Sister Marie Xavier.
200 Copies: *Cahier, Lettres de la Mère Duchesne à sa famille*, pp. 10-11; *Lettres dactylographiées*. C-VII 2) c Duchesne to her family and lay people, Box 5.
201 Philippine's sister, Adelaide Lebrument, had come into the interior of the house when she visited her children, but the rule changed afterwards.

and devoted. If this continues, she will be allowed to make her First Communion on the feast of the Assumption of the Blessed Virgin.[202] As to the trip you want her to take, that is not possible; we are refusing it to everyone. She can be godmother to the baby by proxy.[203]

You gave me the day of the baptism of your daughters but not the year; please note this for us.

Your husband generously offered me some money; but as we shall have to purchase many things in Lyon, it would be more convenient for us, if you agree, to be able to draw on you there for the money.

I did not know of Melanie's [Duchesne] illness until your husband spoke of it. Mrs. de Mauduit did not seem so anxious about it. It seems that Melanie's sight is impaired; if she becomes blind, God has given her a double grace in calling her to religious life. They love her very much in her convent.

Goodbye, good Friend, believe in my constant affection.

Letter 13   **L. 9 to Mrs. Jouve**

Grenoble, April 9, 1807[204]

To satisfy your desires, my good Sister, we are allowing Euphrosine to go home for ten days, two weeks at most. I am a bit unhappy about it, for she is the first pupil for whom this exemption from the rule has been made, and others will take advantage of it or will complain. However costly it is for the parents, I cannot change the rule or find fault with it, realizing as I do that the children are noticeably more content and studious when their heads are not full of outings and trips. Last year's trip was certainly detrimental to your daughter, as far as docility is concerned. I beg you, ward off the undesirable effects of her father's

---

202 Euphrosine could have made it on September 8, 1808, but she refused this honor because her companions were judged insufficiently prepared by the superior and the mistress general.

203 The reference was to the baptism of Constance Jouve, RSCJ (1807-1852). She entered the novitiate in Paris on August 22, 1829, but the revolution in France in 1830 obliged Madeleine Sophie Barat to move the novitiate to Middes in Switzerland. From there Constance was sent to the house in Turin, where she made her first vows on August 22, 1831, and her final profession on October 30, 1836. After being mistress general in Turin, she became superior at Pignerol, then at Chambéry, where she combined the duties of superior and mistress general. She was struck with a pulmonary illness in September 1851; she was so highly esteemed that the vicar general of the diocese and Archbishop Alexis Billiet both came to visit her. Reverend Mother Prevost also went to see her in May 1852. She died June 15, 1852.

204 Copies: *Cahier, Lettres de la Mère Duchesne à sa famille*, pp. 12-13; *Lettres dactylographiées*. C-VII 2) c Duchesne to her family and lay people, Box 5.

excessive praise. I know how well founded this may be, for Euphrosine is quite advanced for her age and full of ambition; but of what use is fruitless knowledge without the more desirable traits of modesty, piety, and docility? On these three points she has a long way to go.

After giving you this little sermon, it is only fair to tell you that I am so glad that you and your daughter will have this happy time together and that I really helped to secure it by pointing out how sad you would be at a refusal.

I am losing dear Adelaide [Lebrument] this evening; how happy I was to see her again with her lovely little family; it is evident that she has them well in hand. They sing the praises of your little Amelie [Jouve]; I send her my love without knowing her, and I am glad that you have such a dear and good companion at home.

Your daughter is taking home with her a chronology to study. She should also read the history of the emperors in order to keep up with her class. You will find in her cases two heads she has sketched, two geography maps and her latest church history exercise.

Our other nieces are well and send you their regards. Give me news of Jordan,[205] and tell him how concerned I am about his health. Good wishes, too, to Camille [Jordan] from me.

I love you tenderly,

Philippine

Letter 14   L. to Miss Julie Pinet[206]

25th [1807]

My dear Julie,

You should have received a letter from me in return for the one you wrote me for my feast. Your dear mother passed through here in such haste on her way home from Lyon that she did give us time to fulfill your desires. On her first stop she told us, to our regret, that you would not return to us with Adele. God willed it, so we must not complain

---

205 It is difficult to know whether she is referring to Alexandre (1768-1824) or to Augustin Jordan (1773-1847).
206 Exact copy of the original, which is in possession of Mrs. Dromard (Jules), in Besançon. Signed: L. de Jalleyrangs, canon, chancellor of the archdiocese of Besançon, January 22, 1902. C-VII 2) c Duchesne to her family and lay people, Box 5. Note: the letter has the postmark of Grenoble.

about that sacrifice. I am very anxious to have Adele well prepared for her First Communion. For her, more than for others, this will either strengthen her character or leave her a slave to her defects. Then pray, exhort, urge, that this act be accomplished in a worthy manner. But preach by the example of your fervor rather than by words. That is the very best sermon.

As to a method for tutoring your sister in grammar—you know how we teach it. It needs constant repetition and the use of good models and the dictionary, along with aptitude and application. The last two factors are indispensable.

Chauvert's death is distressing and a very great sorrow. You realize that such blows prove the inconstancy of fortune and worldly happiness and force us to look to the future life and to convince ourselves of the need of making good use of the present.

I have had no details about Jenny's death. Sophie is so stunned by this loss, and still more by the loss of her mother, that she is, as it were, in a stupor. For more than a month she did not write at all, then in so confused a fashion as to tell us nothing, except that for the present she is alone with Rosalie and that her younger sisters are at the academy in Chambéry, near their guardian. Rosalie is quite broken-hearted. Tell Lesbros to pray for that grief-stricken family that is so dear to her and to serve God with fervor, since we carry to the future life only the merits of such service.

Jouve has just been godmother to a little sister.[207]

The family has moved out of the city to live in the Chartreux district, which gave her a great deal of work. They told her a tale about your being married and taking a trip to Lyon. It was the result of confusing you with Lambert.

I have had news from Lise. She inquired about you, for her friendship with you is very cordial…

I see very little of Durand. The Fourrats may have called on you or passed very near you. They are in Montpellier, but I have not had letters from them.

Pray for Mother Deshayes who is very suffering. She has great affection for you and so have all in this household, and I share their sentiments sincerely.

Love to Adele and Lesbros.

My respects to Mrs. Pinet.

---

[207] Euphrosine, godmother of Constance (1807-1852), who would become a Religious of the Sacred Heart.

Your friend

Philippine

[On the reverse:]
To Miss
Miss Julie Pinet
House of her mother
At Veynes
Hautes-Alpes

Letter 15   **L. 10 to Mrs. Jouve**

[1807][208]

I see you are impatient to know when the children's First Communion will take place. It has been delayed for all of them. I hope it will be before Christmas, between All Saints and the feast of the Immaculate Conception. Euphrosine is preparing for it rather coldly;[209] still I think she will merit this privilege; her character simply lacks the effusiveness of demonstrative souls. She will serve God generously, but she will not enjoy much sensible fervor. She still shows the stiffness[210] in her behavior that makes her seem proud and disdainful, not responsive and helpful. She needs the help of religion for her reform; she is not one from whom you can expect much now in the way of helpfulness; she needs further conviction and more experience of the trials of life to learn how to be compassionate.

So in spite of the fact that you seem to want her at home, I think

---

208 Copies: *Cahier, Lettres de la Mère Duchesne à sa famille*, pp. 22-23; *Lettres dactylographiées*. C-VII 2) c Duchesne to her family and lay people, Box 5.
209 On October 21 she wrote to her mother: "First Communion (...) that I have wanted so much is set for the feast of All Saints or two or three days later. I will have the happiness of receiving Confirmation at the same time. *Letters of Euphrosine Jouve to her Mother*, C VII 2 Aloysia Jouve. After First Communion, she said to her father: "I had this happiness on the third Sunday of November, the day of the dedication of churches. (...) I hope that you will leave me here until the next prize day. I am well aware of the pleasure you would have to see me again, and I would have it infinitely, but I also know that I need to ground myself in the good principles that I have received." November 27, *idem*. She wrote this in her retreat notes: "Lord, I thank you for the grace you have given me during this retreat, to make me know my [religious] vocation; grant me, O Jesus, the grace to be faithful. Yes, my God, I want to belong only to you alone and to bind myself uniquely to you." She chose Saint Aloysius Gonzaga as protector. *Life of Mother Aloysia Jouve, RSCJ*, C VII 2 Aloysia Jouve.
210 Philippine uses an old French word, *roideur*, which means lack of flexibility, firmness that does not bend.

she needs another year here very badly. If you are too hard pressed by the boarding fees for the two girls (besides all the incidental expenses), go back to what I begged you to do in the beginning: stop worrying. You will have to pay only for Amelie while Euphrosine stays with us.

She is not doing as well in drawing as she could because of restlessness and lack of patience; in everything else she succeeds perfectly. Amelie is very good, except for a little stubbornness when corrected for a fault.

I saw Augustin Jordan; he promised to give you my love anew. I must leave you.

Philippine

Letter 16   L. 11 to Mrs. Jouve

Long live Jesus!

Grenoble, November 19, 1807[211]

Believe me, my good Sister, it is as hard for me to have to write briefly as it is for you to receive letters that give you insufficient details about your daughters; but forgive me on account of how busy I am. I have charge in part of 38 children and of ordering meals for sixty people. There are days when I should have quite enough to do if I only answered the door and read the children's mail, and even so I must teach my classes and secure time for my spiritual duties. I would like Euphrosine to be able to supply details for which I have no time, but it is as impossible for her to write at any length as it is for others to express their ideas briefly. She has a brief, concise way of expressing herself; she is laconic without sentimentality, although she is intensely affectionate, but she will never excel in showing it.

She has not been confirmed; she was not judged sufficiently devoted and gentle; however, I find that she has grown a little. At least she has faith, and I find her better disposed to do what she is asked. As she is equal to everything, nothing dismays her. As to politeness, let us not speak of it. You can imagine that refusal of Confirmation, even after she had received absolution in preparation, humiliated her deeply; and she is in no hurry to tell you about it. She has argued that in refusing her this

---

211 Copies: *Cahier, Lettres de la Mère Duchesne à sa famille*, pp. 15-17; *Lettres dactylographiées*. C-VII 2) c Duchesne to her family and lay people, Box 5.

source of help, we have taken away all means of resisting temptation. She is making much progress in her studies and just now is learning some Latin and Italian (but not more than I know, as you may guess); however, I hope that by herself she may be able to surpass the little that I have learned, will be able to say her prayers in Latin and read easy Italian (speaking is something else). Far from all that being difficult for her, she takes to it with enthusiasm and in general loves study. She needs only a more lively piety, modesty and gentleness, but that is essential.

Amelie has become very negligent in the care of her belongings, but she is notable for piety and kindness as well as for study. She has composed and written a rule of piety for herself and her little companions; you can guess what it is like. Both of them are very well, and I will watch out for chilblains, as you asked. They will both have need of a dress; please permit me to have them made. Euphrosine is already in the process [of sewing them] under the direction of one of our religious who is a very good dressmaker.

Caroline and Henriette [Lebrument] are very well. They are very promising children, but just now they are willful little things; they are improving.

The event you wrote me about is certainly of importance to religion. Those who are feeling its full rigor will bear it with perfect resignation, I am sure, even with deep peace.

I embrace you tenderly as well as your daughters and our nieces,

Philippine

A thousand greetings to your husband and a reminder of my business matter.

Letter 17   L. 12 to Mrs. Jouve

[1807][212]

My good Sister,

Mrs. de Vaulserre's personal maid, before coming here, is going to Lyon to see her son, whom her former mistress is supporting at L'Argentière. I am taking advantage of the opportunity to send you some

---

212 Copies: *Cahier, Lettres de la Mère Duchesne à sa famille*, pp. 11-12; *Lettres dactylographiées*. C-VII 2) c Duchesne to her family and lay people, Box 5.

of your daughter's drawings and her first geographic map, with which I am very happy.[213] It bodes well for the future; tell me what you think of it as well as of her summary of the *Iliad*.

I will profit by the freedom you gave me to have a dress made for your daughter when she will need it; it will be soon. As for the knitted skirt, she will make it very well herself; she is very clever at needlework when she sets her mind to it, but you know how lively she is.

You complain about the brevity of my letters, and I am aware that it is impossible for me to reform on this point, as I have so few free moments. I can tell you in one line that I am more and more content with what has befallen me; my companions are, too. I am very well and see time rapidly flowing by.

Letter 18   **L. 13 to Mrs. Jouve**

December 2, 1807[214]

My dear Friend,

In spite of my promptness and good intentions, I was able to have Amelie [Jouve] only on Sunday evening. Camille and Augustine [Jordan] did not want to give her up and our *commissionnaire*, very obedient and little used to resisting, came quite peacefully to say: "I could not bring her." Mrs. Teisseire[215] brought her in the evening. She had heard that she would be in class with her cousins, a lower class. That, joined to the bitter memory of you, made her cry very much in leaving her cousins. To console her, I tried to find out what class she wanted to be in, and to please her she was put in the second class where she is very content. Henriette [Lebrument], at least, and Amelie Teisseire will join her there soon. We will pay great attention to her diet and still more to prepare your daughter for her First Communion.

---

213 "I am applying myself to my drawing and the teacher is pleased with me. By the first opportunity I must send you some of my sketches of heads. I hope they will please you. I have begun to learn Latin and Italian. I like it very much. I am going to try as hard as I can to give pleasure to my good parents and to make up to them for the trouble I have given them." L. 3, Grenoble, November 28, 1807, *Letters of Euphrosine Jouve to her mother*, C VII 2 Aloysia Jouve.
214 Copies: *Cahier, Lettres de la Mère Duchesne à sa famille*, pp. 17-18; *Lettres dactylographiées*. C-VII 2) c Duchesne to her family and lay people, Box 5.
215 Mrs. Hyacinthe Teisseire, née Adelaide Helene (called Marine) Perier (1779-1851), married Camille Hyacinthe Teisseire (1764-1842, industrialist and politician, in 1794. Her daughter Amelie was born in 1800.

I am astonished at Mrs...'s behavior. How can she say that she withdrew her daughter? She would surely have left her with us; she was kept only so that she could make her First Communion and Confirmation; and we sent her away, as we were not able to keep for a long time the daughter of a person whose story we had learned and from whom we could not accept money with integrity. This child cost us a great deal; we can only pray for her; there are too many obstacles to her return. When we had discovered the secret, we made every effort to keep it, as much for the others as for ourselves.

All yours, I embrace your children,

Philippine

Letter 19 **L. 14 to Mrs. Jouve, at Grâne by way of Crest**

Grenoble, May 2 [1808][216]

I waited until today, my good Friend, to send Amelie's letter so as not to add weight to the one you must have received from Euphrosine through Mother Deshayes, along with the report cards. My second reason was that Euphrosine had an attack of fever the very day she wrote, and I wanted to know how it would develop before telling you about it, for we have had some cases of scarlet fever. Fortunately Euphrosine's illness lasted only a day. She had energy enough to learn and act a part in a little play given on my feast; she did very well and so did her sister who is quite hoarse today from singing too much. The prize Euphrosine received and her first *accessit* to the ribbon of merit have gone to her head, and she again assumed her haughty and impetuous manner; she has recognized this weakness and has been on a good path for two weeks. For 3 or 4 weeks she has been 1st in her class, but she works very little.

I learn with pleasure the good news of dear Augustine [de Mauduit];[217]

---

216 Copies: *Cahier, Lettres de la Mère Duchesne à sa famille*, pp. 19-20; *Lettres dactylographiées*. C-VII 2) c Duchesne to her family and lay people, Box 5.
217 Augustine de Mauduit du Plessis (1787-1847) married Augustin Jordan (1773-1849), on November 4, 1808. He was a diplomat, attached successively to the Embassy of France in Vienna (1802-1811), secretary general of the prefecture of Les Bouches-du-Rhône (1811-1814), first secretary of Bishop Cortois de Pressigny, bishop of Saint-Malo and ambassador of France to the Holy See in Rome, and director of ecclesiastic affairs at the Ministry of the Interior (1819-1822). Augustin Jordan, son of Marie Elisabeth Jordan, née Perier, was Philippine's cousin.

our Aunt Gueymar[218] came to see me yesterday. We spoke little of all the unhappiness. I would not have been able to change her attitude; she is a striking example that one can be very unhappy with all the advantages of a fortune and that our happiness is in ourselves rather than in exterior pleasures. She is always worried, and that makes those suffer who want only her happiness.

I answered Mrs. de Mauduit on the subject of the 75 F that she does not owe me at all; when she wants an official receipt, she will send me a model.

I embrace you and your daughter and send my respects to Father,
Philippine Duchesne

Mother Therese [Maillucheau] sends you a thousand affectionate messages. All yours.

Letter 20   L. 15 to Mrs. Jouve, in Lyon

Grenoble, August 10, 1808[219]

I received, my good Sister, your letter sent by Mrs. Teisseire containing the receipt from Mr. Rusand. I would have answered sooner, but it was not possible. I thought that Euphrosine had told you in her letter that her First Communion had been put off; it was for everyone, and I don't know at this moment when it will take place; I can't tell you anything about it.

As for the other part of your letter in which you criticize our severity concerning outings, if you are basing your criticism on what I said to our sister about her daughter, that must not influence you. Young Amelie is a perfect child; her piety has nothing rigid or annoying about it; we are enemies quite as much as you are of devotion that prevents fulfilling one's duties towards one's parents. Was it too great devotion that caused Augustine's disagreement with her mother? On the contrary, it is since she has had more devotion that our sister is more content.

You do not have to be afraid of a devotional program for your Euphrosine; she is too lively ever to become rigid, and she is too

---

218   Mrs. Gueymar, née Helene Perier (1745-1818), daughter of Jacques Perier (1703-1782) and of Marie Elisabeth Dupuy (1719-1798), married Alexandre Gueymar de Salière, a lawyer in the Parliament of Dauphiny, magistrate and vice-president of the Court of Appeals in Grenoble. She was one of the sisters of Philippine's mother.
219   Copies: *Cahier, Lettres de la Mère Duchesne à sa famille*, pp. 20-22; *Lettres dactylographiées*. C-VII 2) c Duchesne to her family and lay people, Box 5.

good-hearted to forget what she owes you and her father. Her devotion is not increasing, at least exteriorly, but she has faith; that is why you noticed fervor in her letter to her father. Maybe it is her impetuosity and her character little given to tenderness that cause us not to perceive sensible fervor. Her character is also still inflexible, and in disputes she never yields. However, in general she is better and loves to render service; that pleases me greatly because I imagine that when she is with you, it will make her happy to console you. Amelie is very good, but she shows a little temperament from time to time; the report card will tell you the rest.

I embrace you tenderly; greetings to your husband,

Philippine Duchesne

Letter 21   L. 16 to Mrs. Jouve, in Lyon

Grenoble, December 26, 1808[220]

...Euphrosine is gaining ground in character and piety but not much yet in politeness and consideration; she consults only her own inclination in those areas, with little regard for respect and duty. She is always among the first in studies and very skillful at needlework, even though she does not do much because of her classwork and her teachers. Drawing has been neglected a little because of holidays, the teacher's absence and her retreat in preparation for her First Communion.

Amelie will also be very skillful, but a little less inclined to study than Euphrosine.

I am still very busy; that is why I have to shorten my letters and assure you briefly but with all the affection possible that I am yours devotedly,

Philippine

---

220 Copies: *Cahier, Lettres de la Mère Duchesne à sa famille*, pp. 24-25; *Lettres dactylographiées*. C-VII 2) c Duchesne to her family and lay people, Box 5.

Letter 22   **L. 17 to Mrs. Jouve, in Lyon**

[1809][221]

My dear Friend,

It is a pleasure to add some lines to your daughter's letter, not to praise her sentiments, as you know them well, but her heart. She is really beginning to realize all she owes you. You know she has appeared to be wanting in feeling, but this, I believe, has come from a lack of reflection so common at her age, rather than from any unpardonable hardness of heart towards her good parents. She now speaks more often of you both with an expression of gratitude, and one day she said she would gladly spend her life in a dungeon, provided she was with you. But this increase in affection does not lessen her love for Sainte-Marie. She seems to like it here.

So does Amelie. That little air of melancholy is pure imagination, the effect of a prejudice against us because we are opposed to the ways of the world or maybe the result of her own personal appearance, so attractive and gracious. I have questioned her and have had others do so, among them her mistresses and companions, and she has always replied that she is very happy and has no desire to leave school. I would not be surprised, however, if she cries sometimes at the thought of her parents, for she is very sensitive. One day she came to me in tears to say: "Aunt, I have been wanting for a long time to ask you for a Communion for my sister because she is very unhappy." She is not lively like Euphrosine, and they do not get along very well. She still wants drawing but it has not yet begun; I am waiting for some other pupils at the end of the month. The teacher is very good; he teaches at the *Lycée* and at three of the best boarding schools. We hope that ours will increase the numbers that have induced him to come to us on favorable terms.

A tender goodbye,

Philippine

---

221 Copies: *Cahier, Lettres de la Mère Duchesne à sa famille*, pp. 25-26; *Lettres dactylographiées*. C-VII 2) c Duchesne to her family and lay people, Box 5.

Letter 23 L. 18 to Mrs. Jouve

Grenoble, February 6 [1809][222]

I was very sorry to see your change of plans for Euphrosine; I wanted her to remain here until September; that would be almost the end of the year you wished to give her after her First Communion, from which she has profited well. I am afraid those fruits of virtue will never ripen if she finds herself right away in a life of excitement that may flatter her vanity, and in which she will lose the habit of those things that at this moment are contributing to her improvement in character and piety. If it is the fees that put you off, you may ignore them, as I have already offered.

You have been misinformed by those who said that you would see your daughters only in the parlor; you could have stayed with us, even though the custom is that people come in only for retreats and in case of sickness. Even had you stayed with our aunt, we would have made arrangements for you to be able to see them to your satisfaction. Don't let that reason put you off, I beg of you, if you are still giving us the hope of a visit.

Your daughters are very well.

I embrace you and write in haste, not having been able to do so earlier,

Philippine

Letter 24 L. 19 to Mrs. Jouve in Lyon

May 28, 1809[223]

Dear Mama,

I am very happy to see the end of the month arrive because that is usually when I have the joy of coming to spend time with you. My heart finds so much sweetness and delight that it seems only an instant with Mama and Papa, with my brothers and sisters, hearing them and speaking to them; I wish these precious moments would last forever. I

---

222 Copies: *Cahier, Lettres de la Mère Duchesne à sa famille*, pp. 31-32; *Lettres dactylographiées*. C-VII 2) c Duchesne to her family and lay people, Box 5.
223 Philippine wrote this short letter following the one of Euphrosine. Letter 8, *Letters of Euphrosine Jouve to her mother*, C VII 2 Aloysia Jouve.

would also like you to answer more often, for you don't know how dear your letters are to me; they are my only consolation in being separated from you, my good Mama.

Do not forget me, I beg, with my good Papa and Tatau [Mrs. de Mauduit]. Let them know of the tender respect I have for them and the desire I have to see and embrace them.

As for Amelie [de Mauduit], I beg you to tell her for me that I always think of her and that she is always dear to me in the Lord. I hope she will write to me as soon as she can.

All the young ladies, especially her classmates, want to see her and be remembered to her.

I embrace Hippolyte, Alexandre and Constance.[224] My love for them and for my other brothers is unchangeable; it can neither grow stronger nor diminish. Amelie and I are very well.

I have the honor, dear Mama, to send you feelings of the most respectful tenderness.

Your very humble and obedient daughter,

Euphrosine Jouve

[Philippine writes following Euphrosine's letter]

I am afraid, my good Friend, that your daughters' report cards caused you some anxiety about Euphrosine's health. It is perfect at present. I would have told you sooner about her illness if I had not thought it best to have her examined before raising any painful fears about her. Some baths and sedatives have sufficed to cure dear Euphrosine. Her conduct has been better this month; her studies go well. Needlework progresses slowly, but believe that I do not push her there. There must be nothing too tiring that could cause new irritation to her nerves. The departure of one of her companions, a blue ribbon student, obtained the ribbon for her, as she had the second *accessit* [next in order] at the last distribution. It is a much sought-after honor in the boarding school, but no one is jealous of her.

Amelie [Jouve] is always very good, but not in the highest rank. A note from Mrs. de Mauduit yesterday told me that you had returned home and how charming your family is.

Do not be put out if your daughters did not write to their father in your absence; it is partly my fault and partly the elder Jouve's.

---

224 Hippolyte (1802-1877), Alexandre (1805-*) and Constance (1807-1852), Euphrosine's brothers and sister.

The bell for Office is ringing; I leave you with an embrace,

Philippine

Letter 25   **L. 20 to Mrs. Jouve, in Lyon**

Grenoble, August 15, 1809[225]

I received your letter, my dear Friend, and waited for Adelaide's departure and a good opportunity to answer. You can imagine what a joy it was to see my sister after an absence of two years, and how I enjoyed seeing her happiness in being able to embrace her children whom she loves so much. She arrived Friday evening and stayed here with her two little girls [Caroline and Henriette Lebrument]; she spent Tuesday and Wednesday at Vizille and left Thursday after dinner. The news she gave me of Augustine [Jordan] was both consoling and disappointing. The main thing is that she is doing well and that both she and her baby are safe. Please give her and her husband my regards and tell them how happy I am for them.

Camille [Jordan] was kind enough to come to see me yesterday and give me news of you. The visit was so pleasant. He repeated what I have so often heard about the zeal, piety and talents of his brother Noël[226] and the remarkable merits of *Father Rozan*. Do take advantage of his presence in your neighborhood. I want Euphrosine to learn to appreciate him and to stand firm when she leaves school. She is so well grounded that I am hopeful, but she has not improved much in thoughtfulness, kindness and politeness. I hope we will easily find an opportunity for her for the end of September.

You will have learned all the details of the Pope's stay here, of his journey to Nice and the extraordinary welcome they gave him, especially in that city. This involuntary visit of the Pope has had the effect of a mission everywhere; there were more confessions and demonstrations of faith wherever he went. God has drawn good out of evil. The long experience we have had of his goodness makes us hope that he will withhold the arm of his justice and not punish us to the end. We are very grateful to you for your solicitude about us, but we are remaining calm, living from day to day; we are children of Providence. God has

---

225 Copies: *Cahier, Lettres de la Mère Duchesne à sa famille,* pp. 27-28; *Lettres dactylographiées.* C-VII 2) c Duchesne to her family and lay people, Box 5.
226 Antoine-Noël Jordan (1778-1843) was a priest.

given an increase to this house without visible means; if he destroys it, he is the master; we live in safety.

Your daughters will send you their news during the week.

I embrace you tenderly; greetings to your husband,

Philippine

Letter 26   L. 1 to Mother A. Michel[227]

Long live Jesus!

Grenoble, August 17, 1809[228]

How pleased I was, my dear Sister, to have been favored with one of your letters; if I had followed my inclinations, I would have been the first to express my esteem and affection for you. The bonds that unite us are so pleasing that they draw us close, and it often seems to me that the dear house in Ghent was founded in common with our own. It would have been very agreeable for us to really transport your house to ours during the Holy Father's stay here. It was for only twelve days; but when we figure that we were in the farthest place in France, we cannot bless God enough for such a privilege. He came to France one other time,[229] but the present circumstances make the blessings he is bestowing on his children still more precious.

Our mother [Deshayes] and our pupils went as far as his apartment and received his blessings with expressions of the most touching kindness, and he said that the meeting with young children was most pleasant. God had so touched the heart of the colonel who accompanied him that he hurried to let our young people enter, and he moved aside all the persons who tried to mingle with ours in order to enter along with them.

You were not forgotten in this precious situation, and our mother included everyone in the blessing she received. We have had it in her person, but every evening we were able to have it again from afar; for as our house dominates the place where he walked, he was seen without difficulty when he moved through the grounds to bless the immense number of people who wanted to see him but who could not enter as the garden gates were closed.

---

227 Adrienne Michel, RSCJ, born on July 24, 1789, took the habit on July 26, 1806, and made her vows on September 8, 1809, in Grenoble. She died September 7, 1858.
228 Original autograph, C-I-A, 1, G-Box-17, *Vol. 102*, p. 1.
229 For the coronation of the Emperor Napoleon Bonaparte in Paris, December 2, 1804.

People admired his constancy and his extreme gentleness. He had with him only one prelate, his nephew and chamberlain [Doria], a chaplain, a doctor and a few servants. A cardinal who came with him was put in a separate place and at the moment of departure was made to take a different route. The Pope is to be in the surroundings of Nice at eight o'clock and the cardinal [Bartolomeo Pacca], in a fortress in Piedmont, Fenestrelle.[230] We have had the privilege of making a surplice for the Holy Father and of lending some things for the chapel, which have been returned to us.

I would like, dear Sister, not to put an end to this conversation, which pleases me so much; but we have so many things to do, and today we will profit by heavenly favors and the good will of a Sulpician father in a retreat for the whole house. I will remember you particularly.

With the most tender and constant sentiments, I am in the divine Heart of Jesus, your humble servant.

Philippine Duchesne

I beg you to offer my respects to Reverend Mother de Peñaranda.

[On the reverse:]
To Mother
Mother Michel
House of Christian Instruction
In Ghent

Letter 27   L. 21 to Mrs. Jouve

[1809][231]

My dear Sister,

I am so grateful to your husband for giving me the news that you have had your baby[232] and also of the godparents chosen. I thought Augustine [Jordan] was at Grâne. Euphrosine will not be able to take part

---

230 Cardinal Pacca, pro-secretary of state of Pius VII, was imprisoned in that fortress, from July 1809 to January 1813.
231 Copies: *Cahier, Lettres de la Mère Duchesne à sa famille*, pp. 32-33; *Lettres dactylographiées.* C-VII 2) c Duchesne to her family and lay people, Box 5.
232 The reference is to the birth of Camille Jouve (1809-1897). Euphrosine returned to her parents' home on November 15, 1809.

in the prizes, as they have been postponed for six weeks. I do not yet know of a good opportunity for her. I hope she will contribute to your happiness, lessen your work, and thereby repay the care we have always taken of her, which has been lavished on her with earnest affection.

Amelie will suffer because of her departure. Although her character is gentler than that of her older sister, I doubt that she would be more helpful to you, as she is indolent and not very generous in trying to overcome this defect. I hope that after she makes her First Communion, and especially after she is confirmed, she will develop more energy. Strength certainly is needed to face life in the world and to stand by right principles, especially in our times, when people have lost all taste for the true joys of mind and heart. Vice is clever at disguising itself; it would be more easily avoided if it showed its real ugliness. I am glad that Euphrosine is called to a quiet, laborious life.

I embrace you tenderly.

Loving messages to Augustine [Jordan] and to your husbands.

Ph. Duchesne

Letter 28   **L. 22 to Mrs. Jouve**

Grenoble, January 10, 1810[233]

I received your letter, my very good Friend, containing your New Year's wishes. I had hoped to be ahead of you this time, but my position here forces me to set aside my own personal pleasures in order to fulfill duties and obligations much less pleasant, but such that they must come first, since they touch upon the common good.

I trust your heart completely, knowing that it will always welcome the outpourings of my own, since the friendship that unites us is without distrust and without reserve. Being powerless to give you all I wish for you, I beg God to bless you and your children very particularly, so that the seeds we are sowing in their hearts may bear fruit in his good time and so give you much consolation, just reward for all the care you have given and still give them. Euphrosine is too strong a character ever to waver in her principles: she does not have the art of pleasing, but that is so dangerous that I do not desire it for her. If she is faithful to her duty, that is the main thing; with less personal attractiveness on her part, you

---

233 Copies: *Cahier, Lettres de la Mère Duchesne à sa famille*, pp. 30-31; *Lettres dactylographiées*. C-VII 2) c Duchesne to her family and lay people, Box 5.

will have more peace. We must be content with what contents God; he did not make all the good people lovable; nevertheless, he loves them and does not change them. I am just giving you a word of warning, for I fear that you count very much on little attentions and courtesies from your daughter. She is simply not observant; one has to suggest things to her and not to expect from her both the little joys of life and the great hopes of eternity. When one has the essential, one must be content; children are brought into this world only to be prepared for the next. I prefer Euphrosine, stiff and positive in character, to Amelie, who is too soft and lazy; she does not work to develop her character, dreading the least effort. Euphrosine is meant for great things; Amelie will only ornament a household and not without shadows, for she is rather temperamental.

Philippine

Letter 29   L. 23 to Mrs. Jouve

Grenoble, December 2, 1810[234]

...I have heard praises of Euphrosine that touched my heart. They came from a missionary who went to Nantua; he spoke very favorably of her to Mr. Lebrument. If it is her confessor, I will be less pleased; for paternal affection weakens judgment, and a father like him can speak only of the good. I would be more pleased to hear from you that you are happy with her and that you hope for the same success for our Henry.[235]

I will pray to God to bless your choice, your desires, and your zeal for the welfare of your children.

I embrace your three daughters and ask to be remembered to your husband.

I embrace you tenderly,

Philippine

---

234 Copies: *Cahier, Lettres de la Mère Duchesne à sa famille*, p. 34; *Lettres dactylographiées*. C-VII 2) c Duchesne to her family and lay people, Box 5.
235 Henri (Henry) Jouve, SJ, born February 11, 1801, in Lyon, entered the Jesuit novitiate in May 1821, after his conversion following the death of Euphrosine (Aloysia). He studied theology in Rome, where he was ordained a priest on February 24, 1831. He exercised several ministries, often changing houses: Chambéry, Lyon, Vals near Le Puy, Dôle, Avignon, Grenoble, Toulouse, Lyons, Saint-Etienne, Avignon, Marseille, Castres; he rarely remained more than a year in the same city. He died in Lyon, August 25, 1878. He was Philippine's godson.

Letter 30   **L. 24 to Mrs. Jouve**

Grenoble, January 1 [1811][236]

I have not had news of your arrival in Lyon, my good Friend, but I like to think that your trip was a happy one and above all that your child did not suffer from tiring travel.

You are very kind to send me good wishes; one of the best would be that God renders me helpful to my good relatives and that your daughter fulfills my desire to see her worthy of you and the support of the laborious life that you are destined to lead for a long time yet. Nothing can be added to her intelligence, but I pray that God grants her the goodness and flexibility that make for happiness in our own life and in the social circle in which we find ourselves.

I had a letter from Paris that appears to have been left in Lyon by Mr. de Mauduit. I am impatiently awaiting the news of his arrival in Grâne and of the way in which he will take up his country life again. I always keep that house in mind; it holds so many dear things, when I know that my friends are suffering without being able to help them.

Goodbye, very lovingly,

Philippine

Letter 31   **L. 25 to Mrs. Jouve in Lyon**

24th [1811][237]

Your letter caused great sorrow, my dear Friend, to me and to all who know our dear Euphrosine, especially Mother Deshayes. She immediately had the whole house begin a novena to pray for our sick one. I hope for her cure; she will be still more fervent after having been ill. And you, you will thank twice over the giver of every good gift: he is making you aware at this moment that children are only lent to you, that they belong to him.

I am asking him to strengthen you at this painful moment; I understand and, even more, share completely in your suffering.

All yours,

Philippine

---

[236] Copies: *Cahier, Lettres de la Mère Duchesne à sa famille*, p. 38; *Lettres dactylographiées*. C-VII 2) c Duchesne to her family and lay people, Box 5.

[237] Copies: *Cahier, Lettres de la Mère Duchesne à sa famille*, pp. 59-60; *Lettres dactylographiées*. C-VII 2) c Duchesne to her family and lay people, Box 5.

Letter 32   **L. 26 to Mrs. Jouve**

Grenoble, May 22 [1811][238]

I was waiting for your daughter's letter, my good Friend, to enclose mine with it; but she has sent hers without saying anything to me, so mine is delayed; I am annoyed at having to send it by post. Joseph Abranchand, who will take care of it, has not entirely reassured me about dear Euphrosine. How I share your anxiety and would like to ease your sorrow!

At least I try to do so by bringing it to God with all the fervor that the sincerest love and interest can inspire. Mother Therese shares it and presses me for news of your daughter. I know that Mother Barat has seen her; but according to my cousin, she is not yet in a condition to feel anything except pain.

When you were so near to losing her, did you not think of offering her to God, even in this world, since human means were powerless to save her? Euphrosine has never confided in me, but I have reason to think she has some idea of the convent. One day she let fall this remark: "Someone spoke of chastity; *that is the virtue I love above all others.*" Without letting her realize it, you can find out whether I am right in this idea and sound her out regarding courage. Who knows whether some interior struggle may be the cause of this illness.

Amelie is all right without being fervent. I am as eager as you to see her obtain her great desire; however, its fulfillment has been postponed a few days at the earnest request of Mr. de la Valette whose daughter is dying in Avignon. His son-in-law, Mr. de Vidaud, cannot leave [his wife] for some days; but he wants to be present at the First Communion of his own daughter here.

Tell Camille [Jordan] how much I shared his anxiety and now share his joy at his wife's recovery and her mother's. I believe that you have already thanked Mrs. Jordan for all the care she gave our [name missing] who is now perfectly well.

Amelie has neither whooping cough nor a sore throat. Her leg is better, but she still has to limit her walking.

I leave you in a great hurry. Every good wish to your husband and to Euphrosine.

Philippine

---

238 Copies: *Cahier, Lettres de la Mère Duchesne à sa famille*, pp. 45-46; *Lettres dactylographiées.* C-VII 2) c Duchesne to her family and lay people, Box 5.

Letter 33   **L. 2 to Mother A. Michel**

For Mother Adrienne

Long live Jesus! January 2, 1812[239]

My very dear Friend in Jesus Christ,

The cold at my fingertips prevents me from writing well, but not from feeling how kind you are to send me news of yourself and of my dear Therese.

As I had not spoken of your letters, communicating freely with my friend, I did not know how to answer you and would not have been able to without permission. My very kind mother has taken charge of sending you this little word of thanks for your remembrance and for your New Year's wishes. You are foreseeing crosses; but in our way of looking at things, the more abundant the harvest, the more we will be blessed. I have gone through the trial you fear; I have tasted all its bitterness, and God willing, I have not lost out on the reward! You will be more generous if you find yourself in such a situation, although I do not know what it will be. Whatever the will of God, let us be quiet and await in silence what he prepares.

If you do me the favor of writing to me again, do not stress your affection. As I believe I am required to show my letters, it would not be a good idea for our relationship to appear to be based too much on human love but on the love of Jesus alone. That will be purer and will give a truer opinion of the effect of his zeal on your soul that repeats so often and with such relish, "Jesus alone, O beautiful heaven!" It is there that we hope to be united in a friendship that will know no reversal…

I am your unworthy sister in the Sacred Heart,

Philippine

---

[239] Letter copied by Adrienne Michel, C-I-A, 1, G-Box-17, *Vol. 102*, p. 10.

Letter 34   **L. 3 to Mother A. Michel**

For Mother Adrienne
July 30, 1812[240]

My dear Sister,

Having served as secretary to your dear mother [Barat], I cannot see a blank page at the end of her letter and not give in to the temptation to tell you of my constant union in the heart of our Spouse. He does not forbid us to meet to remember him; thus we can also see each other and love in the hearts of Magdalene and Teresa, so united to his. I have not added any other title: the most august, the noblest is that of spouse, beloved and lovers of the all-powerful king. The dear mother's feast went off without incident; we postponed the joyous feast of Saint Sophie, saving for her our pious tears, and there was reason to shed them.

Yesterday I had news from Mother Therese; I answered her today. She is consoling her mother as much as I am afflicting her; do not imitate me in this, but that is useless advice.

Esperance wrote for the feast of Saint Mary Magdalene; there was a message for me; I was touched less by the pious sentiments she expressed about which I had some worries, according to your last letter.

I beg you to remember me to the sisters who are too kind to forget the neediest of their friends. Victoire and Florence are names I love to hear from the mouth of their mother; her stay here transports me to Ghent and I love to speak of it. We need a few pleasant sights among so many others that cause pain; we must wish for the one and not get attached to the others.

Mother is less well than when she arrived. She sleeps very little and her eyes are very tired; she is obliged to make use of a secretary, which will diminish their enjoyment.

Do not forget, my dear and beloved Sister, the weakest of yours,

Philippine

If I may, I dare to ask you to offer my respects to your reverend mother [de Peñaranda].

---

240 Letter copied by Adrienne Michel with this comment: "These letters [3 and 4] from Mother Duchesne are loving and interesting." C-I-A, 1, G-Box-17, *Vol. 102*, p. 17.

Letter 35   **L. to Mrs. Ruelle**

Grenoble, December 6, 1812[241]

Madam and very dear Friend,

I should much prefer the pleasure of seeing you; but since divine Providence has upset your plans and my enjoyment of them, I am glad I can still chat by letter with one of our dearest friends, whose friendship we hope to keep always. I have prayed most fervently that the divine Will may be accomplished in you and that you may be happy; and I seem to have been answered, judging by your good dispositions and your happiness. And I shall think this true always, even when suffering comes to you; for what state of life is without it? Is any life completely free from suffering? We must struggle here in order to reign there. We must bear up bravely if we are to be soldiers of a Leader who entered into glory only by enduring the Cross. Your own future crosses will seem slight if you hold on to these thoughts; or at least instead of surprising you, they will give you the assurance that when God gives you a share in the chalice of his Son, he will also give you a share in his Kingdom.

You asked my advice, and you see I begin with that, for I am convinced that a young married woman, on whom everything has smiled, may think at the time of her wedding that that condition of things will last a long time. She does not yet foresee the suffering that comes with bearing and rearing children or the loss or diminishment of fortune. Now I do not want you to be surprised by anything, but rather always disposed to regard happiness and home duties as God's design for you, without wavering in his service, without neglecting to pray regularly, to frequent the sacraments, and to avoid too great pleasure-seeking. You will have satisfying friendship in the company of Mrs. Gautier and Mrs. Callandre. Remember me to them cordially, and tell them we do not forget them.

Mother Barat, who is still with us, and Mother Deshayes both wish to be remembered to you. I have had news of Mothers Debrosse, Piongaud and Emilie [Giraud], who has been ill but is better now.

I have no news of Walter.

Jouve and Mauduit are in good health and good conduct. Desplagnes

---

241 Copy conformed to the original, which is in the possession of Mrs. Dromard (Jules), in Besançon. Signed: L. de Jalleyrangs, canon, chancellor of the archdiocese, Besançon, January 22, 1902. C-VII 2) c Duchesne to her family and lay people, Box 5. Note: the letter has the stamp of Grenoble: 37.

is coming back to school, having begged this from her guardian. We also expect Henriette and another niece of Mother Barat.

I still teach the same class, but I never forget the pupils I had in former years. Tell them all this for me and believe me, your very devoted friend.

Philippine

My regards to your dear mother.
Greetings to Miss Espié.

[On the reverse:]
To Mrs. Ruelle
At Gap
Département of Hautes-Alpes

Letter 36   **L. 4 to Mother A. Michel**

Mother Adrienne

[End of 1812] [242]

My very dear Sister,

Reverend Mother told me that you would like me to speak to you about the methods I use for rhetoric and logic. I am neither rhetorician nor logician; those names scare me; I have no other rhetoric than that of the heart and no other logic than the reason God has given me, which I use so badly. Concepts succeed badly with me; I do not remember them, and I believe that I have no advice to give others than to read very good authors, to be in the company of persons who speak well and pleasantly. Without these aids, rules are of little use; with these aids one can educate oneself well. It is like language that is learned better by use than through books.

I have seen people who have had a course in rhetoric whose style is elegant to the nth degree, whereas others (Mother Therese in particular)

---

242 Letter copied by Adrienne Michel with this comment: "I was asking for an *Arithmetic*, maybe a *Manual of Rhetoric and Logic*; Mother Duchesne answered me negatively. Today the studies of our young religious leave nothing to be desired in this area." C-I-A, 1, G-Box-17, Vol. 102, p. 17. The letter is not dated, but must be placed between July 30, 1812, and February 1813 (third and fifth letter).

are often eloquent, without artifice and without rules. It is the heart that supplies what is necessary to persuade, and right reason, what is needed to convince. I know nothing else and am even incapable of knowing anything else. Methods are not in my field, I admit it.

The bell for class is ringing to humiliate me…

I am ending without signing[243]

Letter 37   L. 5 to Mother A. Michel

For Mother Adrienne

Long live Jesus!

February 9, [1813][244]

My very dear Sister,

An opportunity is coming up. I did not need this occurrence to remind me that it is a very long time since I have written to you. Nevertheless, the bonds of our union are always strong: the same thoughts, the same hopes, the same state, a common mother, a friend whom we share without any division. Not even that much is needed in the world to form relationships that are said to be solid. How then shall we describe ours? They will have to be eternal and holy. They will be holy in order to merit being eternal, and again holy because of the center from which they come, the very holy and sanctifying Heart of Jesus.

I hope to have some interesting details about one of these lovers of Jesus whom you know and love. Her niece, who learned that I share your feelings and who has returned to her own country, wrote to me for the 1st time and told me right away that she is learning on the spot

---

243 Mother Barat adds at the bottom of the letter: "A word, daughter. Mother Philippine has just completed the History of France and a geography; these are her fields, but what you are asking her for is the exact opposite. If we had copyists, we would be able to send you a few notebooks; Mother de Charbonnel has some on this topic; ask her for them. Your poetic essay is flattering to your mothers!"

244 C-I-A, 1, G-Box-17, *Vol. 102*, p. 18, Letter copied by Adrienne Michel with this comment: "Mother Duchesne in this letter announced Mother Therese's return to Grenoble. Mother Bigeu had governed this house for a while after the departure of Mother Deshayes. Mother Therese replaced this reverend mother, who is so valuable for this new society and so needed by our reverend mother, who is carrying the weight of all the houses by herself."

many edifying and remarkable things about her aunt, about which she will inform me in writing. When I receive this precious collection, I will send it to you, if you will promise that if you have interesting information on similar subjects, I shall share it. Never have I needed more to be helped by these good examples.

Mother Sophie [Barat] has a slight cold at the moment. She has called her dear Mother Bigeu to be with her. Earlier she was very close to Mother Therese, but since her trip to the North, she is much less communicative, being strongly united to Jesus in darkness and silence, in which she is happy to plunge. Mother Bigeu's departure will force her, it seems, to reappear somewhat, as the house has need of her assistance.

I recommend to your devotion and zeal several establishments being proposed, which need the sanction of heaven. What happiness for us to see retreats multiply, where God finds hearts that serve him!

I beg you to give me news of Miss…

I am with the tenderest affection, your unworthy sister,

Philippine

Letter 38   L. 27 to Mrs. Jouve in Lyon

[1813][245]

My dear Friend,

I have learned from different people who have seen you that you have gotten thin and seem to be pregnant; I do not doubt that for you this is a new cross; for as much as we love the children Providence sends us, we fear as much for those coming; it is right and natural to dread the sufferings and inconveniences of a large family. I sincerely sympathize with you and would lighten your burden in every way possible. Here is a thought I have had: I can arrange my business affairs so as to increase my income a little. Then from spring on, I can take care of the fees for Constance, should you wish to send her to us, or Amelie's, if you think Constance is too young to leave you.

You know with what eagerness my superiors and I make this offer; we realize that a mother who feeds and manages such a large household

---

245 Copies: *Cahier, Lettres de la Mère Duchesne à sa famille*, pp. 39-40; *Lettres dactylographiées.* C-VII 2) c Duchesne to her family and lay people, Box 5.

must have very little time left for the many lessons necessary for boys and girls of different ages. We are only sorry that your little boys cannot also become part of our family.

Philippine

Letter 39   **L. 28 to Mrs. Jouve**

Grenoble, May 25 [1813][246]

Yesterday I received a letter and a package from Mrs. [Adelaide] Lebrument; but as I wrote to her not so long ago, I prefer to devote these few free moments to you. My heart must tell you how much I share in all your sufferings. I trust that God, who is giving you little rest in this life, will make up generously to you in the next.

Mrs. Lebrument consoles me by telling me how good your children are, how much less troublesome to you. I hope that the one you are carrying, who will perhaps be the last, may be a Joseph or a Saint Bernard. God blesses large families; and when he does great things, it is ordinarily one of the youngest whom he chooses, because his way is the reverse of ours: he chooses the weak to confound the strong. If you are carrying a saint at this moment, you will be amply rewarded for the additional hardships.[247]

Yesterday I had the pleasant surprise of a visit from father. I found him still young in appearance; but I noticed that his legs are becoming stiff, and it is difficult for him to go down stairs. I cannot believe he is growing old. His kindness makes me wish he would never die, but unhappily there is no earthly joy untroubled by the thought of separations or of death!

I have no time to write to your daughters; I have received their letters; give them and your husband many affectionate messages from me.

All yours,

Philippine

---

246 Copies: *Cahier, Lettres de la Mère Duchesne à sa famille*, pp. 40-41; *Lettres dactylographiées*. C-VII 2) c Duchesne to her family and lay people, Box 5.

247 Eugene (1814-1887) would actually be her last child.

Letter 40   **L. 29 to Mrs. Jouve**

November 24 [1813][248]

My very dear Sister,

I wrote to you by Adelaide and have not had any news from her since she left. I was hoping you would answer me about Constance, whom I asked you to send us in Henriette's place. It seems from your silence that this plan does not please you, given your daughter's age; surely she is well cared for at home and better off there than elsewhere. But realizing that you are so burdened with cares, I wanted to come to your aid as a devoted sister and, if possible, to do even more for you.

For a long time I have been suspecting the secret yearnings of your eldest daughter, although she hid them from me. This was the subject of a suggestion I made to you when she was so ill, a suggestion that I was told caused you much pain. Yet what I merely guessed at then is a reality today. Euphrosine wishes to leave you, not for a human husband and an earthly home, but to give herself to God who has given her everything. Only recently did she confide her desire to me. Knowing her love for Mother Deshayes, I told her that she would no longer be at the head of this house; however, that did not alter her desire to enter here. She has but one obstacle to overcome: her love for you and the great pain she feels in speaking to you about it.

I promised to do so first, knowing that I am speaking to a loving mother but still more to a Christian who is accustomed to heroic acts of resignation. I do not preach to you; I am letting grace plead, grace that is active in the generous hearts of both mother and child. If the uncertainty of political conditions frightens you, you must realize that we place the condition that we remain free in case of catastrophe. Besides, there are *(word missing)* and how many events in the future can assure more stability; anyway, is there stability in anything under the sun?

Forgive me if my forthrightness wounds you; but accustomed to see God as the only end of all things, I did not believe it would offend you to suggest him as the one end for which your beloved daughter was created.

I must stop hurriedly and embrace you tenderly.

---

248 Copies: *Cahier, Lettres de la Mère Duchesne à sa famille*, pp. 36-37; *Lettres dactylographiées.* C-VII 2) c Duchesne to her family and lay people, Box 5.

Letter 41   **L. 30 to Mrs. Jouve in Lyon**

Grenoble, January 2 [1814][249]

My very good Sister,

Through the sorrow that appears in your letter, I see the same virtue that shone out in the one you wrote me when it seemed as if God were taking your daughter from you in a much harder way than he is asking today. I marveled at the fullness of your resignation in that sacrifice, though I am not a mother. God seems eager to increase your merits by facing you with this sacrifice a second time and so doubling your reward.

I will not dwell on the words of a father who was so keenly afflicted in his children, friends, goods and personal health: "The Lord gave; the Lord took away; blessed be his holy name. If we have received good things from him, shall we not also receive bad things?"[250] If a loving mother was offered the most attractive prince in the world as a fiancé for her daughter, but one who would take her far away, the mother would forget the pain of separation and think only of the illustrious alliance and speak of it with joy.

Why is Jesus Christ the only one to whom it is so terrible to give oneself; where is our faith then? Where is the fruit of our experience? X.'s marriage was approved of; did he provide many advantages to her, to her family, to society; will she have lovely, happy children? One blamed X. for the decision she made: did she heap criticism on her father because of the effects of his troubles? She is happy; she makes herself useful in society. Your daughter would be able to do much more than she and offer your sacrifice to God; as a reward there would be blessings for her and for her family; there are many examples. You speak of her health, but that broke under the strain of hiding from you her great desire; and if God gave you the strength to be glad to give your daughter, you would very soon see her health restored. Upon leaving here, she already had a crisis of nerves that I thought resulted from excessive emotion. Still, while I plead for her, I put myself in your place, as far as natural sentiments are concerned; and I feel what a weight of sorrow such a plan must cause you in the case of the daughter from whom you could expect so much help.

249 Copies: *Cahier, Lettres de la Mère Duchesne à sa famille*, pp. 71-74; *Lettres dactylographiées*. C-VII 2) c Duchesne to her family and lay people, Box 5.
250 Job 1:21.

You may be sure, nevertheless, that this trial comes straight from God. Euphrosine is not the kind of person who lets herself be influenced; she makes her own judgments. God himself gave her a vocation; she kept it secret. If I surmised it, it was the effect of my observations of her character and the tastes I perceived in her, which, if she placed no obstacle to the inspiration of grace, had to lead her to the cloister, to independence from a husband and to a mission to help souls. Do you believe she has made a poor choice in preferring Jesus Christ to any man? The riches of heaven to those of earth? Occupations that raise us upward to those that fasten us to earth? There is nothing low, nothing merely human in Euphrosine's views. There is no outside force urging her on; her desires have come from God who makes us realize that God governs hearts as he wills. Is she not fortunate to have been found worthier than others to be united to him, to have been given such a privilege?

Far from being displeased with you, I share your suffering while at the same time rejoicing in a vocation whose cost I realize. I hope that when you and your husband are calmer, you will consider that your children belong to God before they belong to you. You would have given him Henry, or so your husband told me, and he wants Euphrosine. Don't earthly sovereigns take your children without consulting you? The mystery of the necessity of suffering in this world is hard to understand, but it is inevitable.

I embrace you tenderly,

Philippine

Letter 42   **L. 31 to Mrs. Jouve**

At the home of their father, Mr. Duchesne, in Grenoble

March 2, 1814[251]

The news I have received today of my father's state of health grieves me; I think that one of us had better spend the night at his bedside. You were there last night; Amelie [de Mauduit] is ill; so it is my turn. I can do it, as mother has consented. If you foresee that he is going to have a bad night or that he should receive the last sacraments, please have

---

251 Copies: *Cahier, Lettres de la Mère Duchesne à sa famille*, p. 42; *Lettres dactylographiées*. C-VII 2) c Duchesne to her family and lay people, Box 5.

someone come to get me before 8:30; for this evening, I will have no companion available. Let me know if the priest visited him this morning, and don't put off the sacramental helps of the Church; that is our chief duty now, that and saying a few words about God from time to time. Even the most devout sick people have need of that help; for pain absorbs them, and the devil goes about in search of his prey.

All yours

Philippine

Letter 43   L. 32 to Mrs. Jouve

April 18 [1814][252]

I do not want to keep you waiting any longer for news; I will tell you that our brother leaves for Paris next week and will give you all the details you can wish for: that my sister was detained by snow sent from God and the troops barred the other route, so she left only today. She and I were together at father's side when he died; his agony was long and painful; for several days he did not speak; his body no longer functioned; he was a prey to fears. We had extreme unction given to him and a 2nd and 3rd absolution with a plenary indulgence. The funeral was very simple in view of the conditions here and the prohibition against the ringing of bells that day;[253] it was the 29th of March. I trust he is with God.

Now that everything is quiet again, I repeat my request for Constance. I think that Mr. Durand, who is coming to see his daughters, would gladly bring her; he is a very kind gentleman; no one expressed more sincere sympathy to me than he at the time of father's death.

If you are generous enough to let Euphrosine come with Constance, you will have the merit of mothers who willingly offer their children to God; but I leave it to God to inspire you in this matter. I will write you a longer letter by way of my brother.

---

252 Copies: *Cahier, Lettres de la Mère Duchesne à sa famille*, pp. 44-45; *Lettres dactylographiées*. C-VII 2) c Duchesne to her family and lay people, Box 5.

253 After the defeat at Leipzig (October 1813), the campaign for France took place. From January to March 1814, the forces of the coalition reached Dauphiny and the Isère, fighting those of Napoleon.

Letter 44   **L. 33 to Mrs. Jouve, in Lyon**

[1814][254]

My dear Friend,

I received your letter and I am annoyed that you are refusing to send us Constance. If you withdraw Amelie in spring, I fear she will only give you more work to do because of her character, which is often self-indulgent, peevish, and intractable. Her piety is undeveloped; and it is very difficult to influence her, as she does not give anyone an opening and sets a standard for herself that is very comfortable.

There is very little to say about her studies because of her great facility; but she does her work carelessly, as you can see by her writing and spelling, though she could do much better. She would like to neglect everything for reading, which is very easy for her. I have been obliged to limit her reading and to forbid her teachers to give her as many books as she asks for, for I have seen the bad effects of an immoderate taste for reading. Nothing dries up the unction of piety as this does. This will take the place of a report.

All yours,

Philippine

Letter 45   **L. 34 to Mrs. Jouve in Lyon**

July 4 [1814][255]

My very dear Friend,

I received your letter and I believed it to be of no use, for at that moment, there was talk only of peace terms and arrangements. Now a proclamation of the general [Augereau] has appeared, exhorting us to defend ourselves; and it is said that the enemy is at hand.[256] They

---

254 Copies: *Cahier, Lettres de la Mère Duchesne à sa famille*, p. 43; *Lettres dactylographiées*. C-VII 2) c Duchesne to her family and lay people, Box 5.
255 Copies: *Cahier, Lettres de la Mère Duchesne à sa famille*, p. 47; *Lettres dactylographiées*. C-VII 2) c Duchesne to her family and lay people, Box 5.
256 On April 6, 1814, Napoleon abdicated. General Augereau launched a final battle to protect Lyon from the Austrian invasion, but it was in vain. On April 16, he ordered his soldiers to adopt the white cockade of the Bourbons, denouncing Napoleon as a tyrant. In Grenoble, reactions were different: in June and July, the garrison opposed resumption of royal power, causing demonstrations.

are trying to make him understand that without troops and with only a few of the national guard, it is impossible to resist; and we believe that we are not in a position to obtain favorable conditions. Nevertheless, I thought about having your children leave at the same time that others were asking for shelter; and their departure will take place if it is at all possible; but without a carriage, horses and maybe closed gates, I do not know if the plan can be carried out, and even with a carriage, what accompaniment for the children! Your trip would be equally useless, for you would not be able to get through. But be as calm as I believe I can be; in a little while you will have news of us, in Lyon or in Valence.

Letter 46   L. 35 to Mrs. Jouve in Lyon

Grenoble, November [1814][257]

My dear Friend,

The pleasure of seeing Euphrosine has not kept me from realizing and sharing the pain you have felt in giving her up. We can only trust that it is all for the greater glory of God and that the Master who repays a hundredfold will shower his graces upon you and on your whole family. Euphrosine still seems rather strained; she says she is happy, and I believe her character is free from pretense. I had been told that she had got over her stiff manner, but she has not. I notice it particularly with people she knows only slightly. This defect is hidden by so many other good qualities that I feel she is a very promising candidate. Her sister Constance is very happy; she looks at her lovingly all the time and is kept on her best behavior always.

The wedding took place today, and since then I have seen your husband only for a moment to hear about it.[258] I very much fear that on one side God did not have reason to be content in the matter of religious duties. I had hinted at this in letters but I got no reply, so I do not know the result of my efforts. We can only trust that the future may bring an improvement.

Mother Bigeu sends you her regards. She knew that Euphrosine had told you that she did not want her to go to the wedding; she simply

---

257 Copies: *Cahier, Lettres de la Mère Duchesne à sa famille*, pp. 63-64; *Lettres dactylographiées.* C-VII 2) c Duchesne to her family and lay people, Box 5. This letter was written a few days after Euphrosine Jouve entered as a postulant, November 9, 1814.
258 The wedding was that of Hippolyte Duchesne and Coralie Durand, November 14, 1814.

said she thought it better for her not to go, and besides, Euphrosine was not invited. My brother had told me two days before, concerning Miss Coralie Durand, that the young ladies were not being invited to the wedding. Your daughter will have told you all about her visits.

All yours.

Letter 47   L. 36 to Mrs. Jouve in Lyon

Grenoble, November 25, 1814[259]

Never worry about my feelings for you, my good Sister; although I attributed your silence to heart-suffering rather than to your many occupations, I was really neither surprised nor annoyed. For while as a religious, I marvel at the work of grace in your daughter and the faith that gave you courage enough to consent to the separation, as sister and friend I share your suffering and beg God to pour healing balm on the wound he has created by a sacrifice that will be a source of grace for your whole family.

I knew when Euphrosine left school that many people thought she would not persevere, but that was because of the cordial manner I urged her to cultivate with our kind relatives. I had been distressed by the stiff and abrupt way she acted with Mrs. de Rollin. I begged her to improve, not only for her own sake but for the honor of religious life. So many people believe that a nun cannot be her open and affable self with her family. Besides, Euphrosine is getting along well; she has a lively manner; she wanted to keep her plans secret, but everyone knew, thanks to [Hippolyte] Duchesne and Mr. Durand.[260] That added to the gossip that spread the rumor that she was either hesitating because she did not wish to explain herself, or that she was too fitted for the world to give herself to God.

All this gossip made no impression on me; and I find Euphrosine, just as I expected, firm in her resolve but without that enthusiasm that is often merely emotional rather than the effect of grace. As to her tender love for you, have no doubt of it. She may have had strength and courage enough to hide it from you; but the tears she has shed over your letters, which could not be simulated, show the depth of her affection

---

259 Copies: *Cahier, Lettres de la Mère Duchesne à sa famille*, pp. 48-51; *Lettres dactylographiées*. C-VII 2) c Duchesne to her family and lay people, Box 5.
260 Most probably Mr. Durand, Hippolyte Duchesne's father-in-law.

for her beloved mother. As for her singing in the carriage, I neither saw nor heard that, but there are so many mean interpretations!

Do believe that neither Father Fauvet[261] nor any of us made up that vocation. But I surmised it a long time ago, as you yourself could have understood from the letter I wrote you when she recovered from that dangerous illness. She never gave me the slightest confidence in the matter, but judging from things she said and preferences she expressed when she was a pupil here, I drew this conclusion; for God always gives a natural inclination toward the things for which he destines a soul. She had great strength of character; she would have to have this in order to leave such good parents. She had no attraction for married life. She said several times: "The virtue I like to hear most about is virginity." At times when she was giving herself to teaching the poor, she aspired to suffer martyrdom. One day I gave as an exercise a speech of exhortation to martyrdom: she did it with such precision, such noble, elevated language that I saw very well that there was something beyond natural wit in her composition and that her soul aspired to more than the human. More than two years after she went home, when persecution was rife, she smiled at the thought of having an opportunity to prove her faith. She wrote me a letter that filled me with consolation and assured me that when peace returned, a religious vocation could no longer be astonishing. If you never heard her speak of her vocation, don't be surprised. When the desires of one's heart call for separation from one's family, it is not easy to speak of them. The heart suffers, knowing it must cause suffering. Remove then from your mind all bitter thoughts; bless God who asked of you a gift that pleases him, that places before him an offering and thanksgiving that he has the right to ask of you. Imitate in a small way what so many generous mothers have done for God: the mother of Samuel, who had only one son who lived in the temple; Joachim and Anne, who had only one daughter, who also lived in the temple, etc.

Will you not have the courage to change your decision about not allowing her to take the religious habit for a long time? That would prevent her being employed actively and of being with us when the habit is required. She will not be any more bound to us by wearing the habit, and with us the time of probation is longer than at the Visitation. Tell us your wish in this matter.

I was happy with Caroline; my sister left this morning; I learned it through my brother and sister-in-law who are leaving here and seem very happy.

---

261 Father Fauvet, a Carthusian missionary in Lyon, was Euphrosine's confessor.

Your daughters are well.
All yours,

> Philippine

Letter 48 **L. 37 to Mrs. Jouve in Lyon**

> Grenoble, [end of December 1814][262]

My dear Friend, I received the letter and must rejoice with you that among many troubles the ones you particularly dreaded have been turned away. As a Christian mother who is full of faith, you are witnessing to your gratitude to God by a sacrifice that is hard for your heart but will be for your daughter's happiness. It is not to a man that you are giving her; it is to God, and can one call lost what will always be found in him and that he will give back one day with interest?

Euphrosine felt all that you are doing for her and her generosity does not keep her from the tenderest feelings towards you. She had grown a great deal with you; I hope God will give the same grace to those of your children who are still causing you sorrow.

Remember the prayers of Monica and her happiness in Augustine. I wish you a similar happiness, and I will learn with much consolation that my godson and Amelie will give you joy. Constance is a subject of great hope, but less docile than she was; she is well.

I am all yours,

> Philippine

Letter 49 **L. 38 to Mrs. Jouve in Lyon**

> Paris, November 2, 1815[263]

My good Sister,

Through your care and that of my kind brother I made the trip without inconvenience. I left my first traveling companions with transports of delight, those of the boat with great joy, and those of the stage

---

262 Copies: *Cahier, Lettres de la Mère Duchesne à sa famille*, pp. 62-63; *Lettres dactylographiées*. C-VII 2) c Duchesne to her family and lay people, Box 5. Euphrosine entered the novitiate on December 25.

263 Copies: *Cahier, Lettres de la Mère Duchesne à sa famille*, pp. 60-62; *Lettres dactylographiées*. C-VII 2) c Duchesne to her family and lay people, Box 5.

coach without regret. The officer of the engineer corps was the best of the lot; people with education respect the outward conventions at least. Here I am then in Paris, I am sorry to say; with what difficulty the taste for solitude adjusts itself to the noise and bustle of great cities! The soul finds itself under tyranny.

Do not hold against dear Euphrosine the happiness she is tasting. The joys of the spirit are as far above other pleasures as heaven is above earth. You have done more for her in giving your consent to her reception of the habit than if you had made her a queen. I was worn out by my first ventures into the world during my stay with you; I made the acquaintance of your dear family, and I enjoyed for an instant the pleasure of seeing you again.

I do not know when that will happen again, but I would not want to give you so much trouble; it pained me to see how much inconvenience I caused you. I think I left a small combination knife and corkscrew with you; please keep it for me. Mother Bigeu sends you greetings; she has not yet received the package; I beg my nephew to ask about it again and find out where we can go to have it picked up. If it has not left yet, the address is: rue de Sèvres, Maison des Dames de Saint Thomas. Mother Barat's health is better as is Mother Bigeu's; Mother Deshayes is very well.

I am all yours,

Philippine

P.S. Mr. de Rollin came to see me before your arrival; a thousand affectionate messages to your kind husband and your children. The food you provided lasted until we reached here, and your shawl gave the cold no chance to penetrate; I did not take it off the whole day. May I keep it until my return? Without it I would have suffered.

Letter 50   **L. 39 to Mrs. Jouve in Lyon**

December 14 [1815][264]

My dear Friend,

At the moment of renewing my vows in the hope of doing so with peace and security under a stable government, I want to regulate my

---

264 Copies: *Cahier, Lettres de la Mère Duchesne à sa famille*, pp. 51-54; *Lettres dactylographiées*. C-VII 2) c Duchesne to her family and lay people, Box 5.

temporal affairs in such a way as to have no anxiety of conscience. It would have been a great satisfaction for me in breaking completely with the world to have left my dear sisters in easier circumstances; but divine Providence, which does all things well, wanting to detach them from goods that are nothing but vanity, has taken them from you and permitted that I who have so few needs am not able, out of consideration for those associated with me, to strip myself entirely of my possessions.

I have only arranged everything in such a way that if no unforeseen misfortune happens, Constance and Josephine can complete their education at Sainte-Marie during my lifetime. And wishing to give my godson a little mark of affection, I am going to ask my brother to send you a note for a thousand francs; it will be addressed to your husband without his knowing its purpose, which you will take care of hiding from him as well as from Henry. It is best that way so that no one will talk about it.

If, against all probability, Aunt Gueymar were to die without a will, I will make no claim against her estate; and my portion will go to you. It may surprise you that I foresee such a case; but what I mean is that I am renouncing the right to this inheritance, and if according to the law, the case should occur, my three sisters would represent me.

I received the letter of exchange that your husband sent me and have cashed it. I beg you to tell him so and to thank him for his attentions.

If any money is left over after our purchases have been made, he could put it into a little sealed packet that he would be kind enough to give to the Misses Fonsala to give to the first one of our nuns who passes through Lyon. I do not know yet whether it will be Mother Bigeu or myself or whether we will stop, given the season and the bad weather. What detains us and may continue to do so is the foundation of a house in Paris. It cannot be made just now in these bad times, but it is necessary to find a house, and that has not yet been done.

In any case, don't write to me here before I write to you myself.

I am all yours and I embrace the children,

Philippine Duchesne

I commend myself to the prayers of your good pastors.
Special messages for Amelie.
If I do not see you before New Year's Day, my best wishes for the New Year.

Letter 51 **L. 1 to the Religious of Sainte-Marie d'En-Haut**

SS. C. J. et M.

Paris, January 8 [1816][265]

My dearest Sisters,

As I am not going to see you again, I should pause at the beginning of this letter to think seriously of the meaning of these words that are to be placed at the beginning of all our letters now: *Sacratissimi Cordi Jesu et Mariae*. All we do is for the divine Heart, and it is in the Heart of Jesus that we bring all to a close. So we cannot withdraw from the Heart of Jesus, either in beginning or ending our actions; and even if we are entirely separated from one another, we declare that we shall always be united closely in this lovable center of all our affections, the divine Heart of Jesus.

I received your New Year's wishes with gratitude; and if I waited for the departure of our mother to respond, I did not fail to say how much I appreciated them, for I spoke of them to God in prayer the very moment I received them, and in his presence I formed special wishes for your perfection. I rejoiced in the hope that God will be glorified in that house, which is so dear to me and in which I have often taken too keen a personal interest. But God watches over it far better than I can; you know this very well, and so you must live in peace under the sheltering care of divine Providence. You will receive a mark of God's goodness in the return of your good mother. Her two companions have given convincing proof of their attachment to the Society and their aptitude for the work of the boarding school in Ghent; they are going to be a new blessing from God.

It is really not my fault that our absence has been prolonged, for I am very tired of our worldly life. All the beauties of Saint-Sulpice are of less value to me than the quiet of our own chapels. I long for the day when we can secure a little corner for lodgings in our own convent and no longer see the streets of Paris. Our mother will tell you that in the street [rue des Postes] where our house will be there are several religious houses, as there are in the location where we are now. The

---

265 Original autograph, C-VII 2) c Duchesne to RSCJ and Children, Box 4. Copy, C-VII 2) c Duchesne-Writings about the history of the Society, Box 1, *Extract from the Journal of the House of Grenoble, from its foundation in 1804 to the year 1830*, pp. 144-147.

Faubourg Saint-Germain is the section of religious establishments and the pious quarter of Paris. I see many people at Mass and Communion but few at confession; the eve of the Feast of the Kings when I went to the parish church in the evening, I saw no one at the confessional.

I am so glad to know that you are staying well. As for colds, it seems that a good way to avoid them is to go out often in the fresh air. We have had to go out in all kinds of weather, and none of us has had a cold. Mother Bigeu, however, had a sore throat and fever for a few days and afterwards was in that weak and languid condition that we sometimes noticed in Grenoble. She said to me as a result: "You see, my state of health is not the fault of the house."

Our mother will have many interesting things to tell you; those that will rouse your curiosity the most with reason will be those concerning our holy rules, and actually nothing is more satisfying to us than to be able to know our obligations well and then be more faithful to them. Let us ask God's pardon for the past and make all things new again in ourselves. When you have enjoyed all these details, you will be able to pay attention to less elevated subjects that also have to do with the service of God. You will learn that his arm is never shortened, that there are still saints. There is a woman[266] in Munster who has been living in continual contemplation for 7 years without taking any nourishment except a few drops of liquid; she has the stigmata on her body and the wounds of the Crown of Thorns on her head; every Friday these wounds bleed abundantly. I am told that authorities, both religious and civil, have verified these facts.

One of the fathers [Jesuits] has just exorcised a possessed girl near Amiens; the demon often put her to sleep to prevent her going to confession and refused to respond to questioning; but not being able to withstand the suffering caused by conjuring him in the name of the Sacred Heart of Jesus or the Immaculate Conception or holy confession, he finally told how he had entered into this girl, that he was from the 7th legion, that of Juda, and that his name was "dissolute," that he would leave during the first days of January. It was only possible to have some power over him by putting a blessed hair shirt on the girl. So, have ever greater devotion to the Sacred Heart, to the Immaculate Conception, to confession and to penance.

---

266 Anna Katharina Emmerich (1774-1824), born September 8, 1774, at Coesfeld, near Munster, entered the Augustinians of Dülmen in 1802. A mystic, she had visions and the stigmata of the passion of Christ. At her bedside the poet Clemens Brentano noted these visions and transcribed them. She is said to have cured a religious of tuberculosis of the lungs and larynx. She was beatified by John-Paul II, October 3, 2004.

If our mother tells you the story of Father Giraud, who was the head of religious instruction at Saint-Sulpice last year, you will learn something quite extraordinary.

Pray very much for me, dear Sisters, and believe that I am all yours in the divine Heart of Jesus.

Philippine

[On the reverse:]
To the Mothers
of the Society of the Sacred Heart of Jesus
At Sainte-Marie
Grenoble

Letter 52   L. 1 to Mother Maillucheau

SS. C. J. et M.

February 26 [1816]
[Paris at Saint Thomas of Villanova][267]

My dearest Mother,

I received your letter and I have shared deeply your sufferings and those that will arise with the responsibility of being superior. But at the same time God has consoled you by the courage and virtue that your dear daughters have shown in circumstances that are painful to their grateful hearts.

Euphrosine's letter gave joy to all to whom I read it. The second ceremony, in which she had a greater part, consoled me very much.

I am sending on to you a little account of the planting of religion in Korea that I ask you to distribute at Sainte-Marie. Please give one to Father d'Hyères for the seminary and send the other to the seminary in Chambéry.... Fathers Rambaud and Rivet may also be glad to read it. Please be kind enough to give news of Father Rambaud.

Nothing new for us or for me. We are still at Saint Thomas and do not know when we shall leave.

I am all yours in the Sacred Hearts of Jesus and Mary.

Philippine

---

267 Original autograph, C-VII 2) c Duchesne to RSCJ and Children, Box 4.

I beg you, Mother, to have those promises kept at Sainte-Marie and be very exact in saying the prayer to Saint Regis, or substitute something else if that promise is not carried out.

[On the reverse:]
To Mother
Mother Therese
at Sainte-Marie [d'En-Haut]

Letter 53   **L. 40 to Mrs. Jouve, in Lyon**

Paris, Holy Saturday 1816[268]

My good Friend,

With the hope of having an opportunity of sending you a letter, I am hastening to write it today to tell you that if you have any commissions for me, there will be some young people from Grenoble at the home of the Misses Fonsala en route here. They could take charge of them.

Euphrosine's tendency to brevity in letters makes her overlook the fact that you love us too much not to want details about us. I am going to give you some: we now bear the name of Religious of the Sacred Heart; our habit consists of a thin veil over a white cap fastened under the chin; the veil is white for the novices, black for the others; a black dress, cut *à la vierge*,[269] a black pelerine, a silver cross, a gold ring. The work of the institute is the education of young women and of the poor, and providing the means of making retreats for lay people.

The general novitiate is in Paris; there are three to six months of postulancy in different houses, after which the novice goes to Paris

---

268 Copies: *Cahier, Lettres de la Mère Duchesne à sa famille*, p. 55; *Lettres dactylographiées*. C-VII 2) c Duchesne to her family and lay people, Box 5.

269 The capitulants chose a simple dress that was in style between 1815 and 1825: the dress cut in the style called "*à la vierge*" was worn with a white bonnet with a fluted frill. J. de Charry describes it this way: "Henceforth this costume for both the choir-sisters and the coadjutrix sisters was fixed: black woolen dress, with a pelerine for the choir-sisters and a shawl for the others, a white cap and a black veil for the professed and the aspirants, or temporary professed, a white one for the novices; the medal of profession was replaced by a cross. (....) with the Heart of Jesus in relief and the initials of the inscription: *Cor unum et anima una in Corde Jesu.*" *Histoire des Constitutions de la Société du Sacré-Cœur*, Seconde partie, *Les Constitutions définitives et leur approbation par le Saint-Siège*, Vol. 1 *Exposé historique*, Rome, 1979, p. 75; *History of the Constitutions of the Society of the Sacred Heart*, Second Part, *The Definitive Constitutions and Their Approbation by the Holy See*, Vol. 1 *Historical Account*. Translated by Barbara Hogg, RSCJ. Rome, 1979, p. 68.

for two years; she then makes vows for five years and is employed in different houses; after five years if she perseveres, she makes perpetual vows. There is no fixed dowry; it depends on the means of each one: the ample resources of some make up for the penury of others. You know that I have provided for Euphrosine, and I would have been happy to do more; but we are without income and our houses have greater expenses than other religious houses because of the retreats, so all is used up!

I am very happy that Henry is well established; a thousand messages to him and Amelie and their brothers, still more especially for your husband.

I am all yours in the Heart of Jesus,

Philippine

Letter 54   L. 41 to Mrs. Jouve in Lyon

Paris June 1, 1816[270]

My dearest Sister,

I received your letter, not by way of the young ladies from Grenoble who could still offer you an opportunity to write to me since they have not yet passed through, but by another means. I believe, like you, that we should not count very much on Mr. Rusand; what is entrusted to him meets with many delays.

You gave me much pleasure in writing about Bishop Dubourg; I also heard his praises from Augustin. We hoped he would come to Paris, but troubles arising in his diocese have perhaps delayed his journey; however, I am told that the United States government wants to reach an understanding with the pope and that the faith is making progress in that part of America; at Georgetown in Maryland, there is a wonderful Jesuit college, and a house of the Visitation, no doubt the 1st in the New World. Father Neale is the Catholic bishop of that city.[271]

Since you wish to know exactly all about the financial arrangements of those entering with us, here is our plan: 1) Nothing is settled for the dowry. It is arranged according to the means of the parents and the

---

270 Copies: *Cahier, Lettres de la Mère Duchesne à sa famille*, pp. 56-59; *Lettres dactylographiées.* C-VII 2) c Duchesne to her family and lay people, Box 5.
271 Leonard Neale, SJ (1746-1817), was ordained a priest in 1773. He was bishop of Baltimore 1815-1817.

usefulness that may be expected of the subject, her health, etc. 2) The novitiate is two years and is preceded by a three months' trial; after these two years and three months, the novice makes her first vows for five years, and after five years her perpetual vows; that is profession. It is only then that the person loses the right to inherit or bequeath, and even that will not be obligatory until after the approbation of the Holy See, which can take a long time to obtain, since everything in Rome is done with great deliberation. There are already several parents who have said that they preferred to give a dowry; and consequently the person renounced everything that might come to her. But I suppose that if a daughter leaves religious life, it would take state laws, as before, to impede her going back on her action; at least so it seems to me.

The arrangement I have made for myself is to give me ease of conscience regarding poverty; I was not obliged to make it until the solemn approbation we desire but do not hope for very soon; many societies, even men's, have been asking for it for a long time without obtaining it. It requires lengthy examination; in earlier days princes took an interest in such solicitations; we are in different times.

When I made over to Euphrosine the life annuity of 450 francs, it was with a view to relieving you of a financial burden that might have been difficult for you in these hard times. You have until her profession, five years from now, to consider what arrangement you will make with regard to her rights. At that point I hope we shall be in a more stable condition. In the old orders they still profit from the permission they received from the pope and from state law to inherit even with the vow of poverty.

Our house is still coming to birth; we will gather there on the 21st, which will be, I hope, the day of our installation and solemn blessing of our chapel, which is not yet finished. We are in a quiet section of the city, surrounded by gardens, near a supply of fresh water, in the most elevated part of Paris, near Saint Étienne-du-Mont, formerly Sainte-Geneviève. At her tomb and in all the other places of devotion, I have not failed to pray for you, your husband and all your children, especially for Henry, my dear godchild, and your three daughters who are mine by affection and interest.

I am your totally devoted sister,

Philippine Duchesne

Letter 55   Letter 42 to Mrs. Jouve in Lyon

SS. C. J. et Marie

June 15, 1816[272]

My dearest Sister,

I am taking advantage of an opportunity for Lyon to give you some news of myself. It is a very long time since I have written you because I have had injuries to the fingers of my right hand since before the departure of my brother and sister-in-law, to whom I gave messages for you verbally, since I could not write.

I am happy to write today to tell you of my loving thought of you, to ask about your health and your husband's and to inquire about the family, especially the piety of the children, which is, I am sure, the measure of your earthly happiness. Above all how are Amelie and my godson?

Is Providence as good to you as it is to us? It is always good, but sometimes the justice of God prevails, and it is in this sense that I understand the word *good*. So, are you suffering from all the troubles of the times, or are you enjoying special attention from Providence? I am concerned also about Mrs. Lebrument and Euphrosine; my brother told me some sad things regarding... *(The paper is torn and about eight lines are missing)*... without anything having happened for a few days.

Goodbye, a thousand messages to your husband and to my dear Amelie,

Philippine

June 15

[On the reverse:]
To Mrs. Jouve
Rue Royale, Maison Monicaule
In Lyon

---

272 Original autograph, C-VII 2) c Duchesne to her family and lay people, Box 5.

Letter 56   **L. 1 to Euphrosine Jouve**

SS. C. J. et M.

[June 1816][273]

My dear Euphrosine or Sister Aloysia,

My letter will reach you only after the feast of the Sacred Heart; I do not know if you will have had the happiness you were awaiting; for when I presented your request, our mother wanted to give herself time to think about it, and she left without giving me an answer. Whatever happens, you are sure that the will of God is being done and we must bless it, whether it consoles us or causes us to suffer. We all have trials at this moment, and the Heart of Jesus lets us experience what our title requires of us: consecration to the sufferings that pierce that Heart.

It was not without emotion that I thought about you celebrating the feast of Saint Francis Regis without me. Do not fail to tell me how it was solemnized at Sainte-Marie and whether you keep up your devotion to him; you have real need of his continual protection.

As the 16th fell on a Sunday when we did not work, I told myself that no one would see me here that day. Actually I came back only for dinner. First I had 5 Masses said in honor of Saint Regis by the fathers at the Visitation monastery. At 9 o'clock I went to Sainte-Geneviève, where the procession of the Blessed Sacrament was just coming out of the church. There I assisted at 4 more Masses, the last being solemn high after the procession re-entered the church and ending at 1:30. Immediately after dinner I went to the [Church of the] Blessed Sacrament, where Father Varin preached, and I finished my day at Sainte-Geneviève, where, after the Office, there was another procession of the Blessed Sacrament inside the church. There were two repositories, so in all I had six benedictions, for here benediction is given both before exposing the Blessed Sacrament and when replacing it. But it is never taken down so that when it is to be exposed one has the blessing only at the beginning of exposition, and it is not replaced after Mass, even the most solemn ones.

I leave you now to go to take up my station in a church where the good God is quite alone and where one can call him at certain times the *unknown God*.

---

273 Original autograph and copy: C-VII 2) c Duchesne to RSCJ and Children, Box 4. In June 1816, Aloysia was a novice at Sainte-Marie d'En-Haut, in Grenoble, and Philippine, secretary general in Paris.

I am all yours in the depths of the Sacred Heart,

Philippine

Mr. Caron received the letter from Grenoble; he gave me a lovely picture.

Give my greetings to all our sisters and the students, especially my class and yours.

Do not fail to welcome Mrs. de Rollin very warmly; she does all kinds of favors for us.

Letter 57   L. to Mr. Roussel[274]

Sir,

In asking you to withdraw the note of two thousand five hundred francs, I had the intention of repaying the advances that you had the kindness of making and the last six months' rent of our house until April 1, eighteen-seventeen.[275] Mother Bigeu has sent you from Grenoble fifteen hundred francs by a letter of exchange for the first six months; I have the honor of sending you seven hundred fifty francs and beg you to consider us paid for the year.

I have the honor to be with gratitude, Sir, your devoted servant,

Philippine Duchesne

July 12 [1816]

[On the reverse:]
To Mister
Mr. Roussel
Paris

---

274 Original autograph, C-VII 2) c Duchesne to her family and lay people, Box 5.

275 April 1, 1817. For administrative documents, it was customary to write out the date and the sum.

Letter 58   L. 2 to Mother Maillucheau

SS. C. J. et M.

July 27 [1816][276]

My good Mother,

Our Mother Barat, who is leaving just now for Amiens where she will spend ten days and install Mother Grosier as superior, has asked me to send on to you two excerpts from letters from Father Soyer who wrote to Rome to find out the truth about the letter of Father Stephanelli. Here they are:

> I received yesterday a brief from his Holiness in response to a letter I had the honor to write to him about your affairs during the crisis. The sovereign pontiff praises the steps taken to find out the truth from him. This brief confirms what the bishop of Saint-Malo had said and discusses the lies that have been published in newspapers concerning the house of Saint-Denys in Rome. His Holiness's secretary added a personal letter to the brief asking me to acknowledge receipt of the brief and to give news of the state of your houses. These are historic documents for your order. If you would like copies of these and of my letter to the Holy Father, I will send them to you.
>
> I received a brief from the pope in response to my letter of December 15 (brief of June 15, 1816). His Holiness confirms what you have done me the honor of writing to me and what I have learned from the bishop of Saint-Malo. The supposed Father Stephanelli is only an imposter. *Immerito fides data est falsis et exageratis quabusdam publicarum ephemeridum relationibus, circa domum ad S. Dionisii, puellis educandis in hâc urbe.*[277] Words of the response of his Holiness, which would surely not please Mr. de Sambucy. There is still nothing definite about the house of Saint-Denys.

Father Soyer has taken care to instruct Poitiers and Niort about the brief; our mother will do the same for Beauvais and Amiens. It is only right that I who believed the letter from Father Stephanelli, with however

---

276 Original autograph, C-VII 2) c Duchesne to RSCJ and Children, Box 4.
277 "It was wrong to put any faith in the false and exaggerated news concerning the house of Saint-Denys, destined for the education of young girls in this city...." Cf. J. de Charry, *Histoire des Constitutions de la Société du Sacré-Cœur, La Formation de l'Institut*, I, pp. 717-765; *History of the Constitutions of the Society of the Sacred Heart, The Formation of the Institute*, I, pp. 387-405.

some doubt and suspicion, should be the one to come to tell you of its falsity. I ask you to tell Fathers Rambaud and Rivet about it, as both knew about this intrigue against our Society.

Fathers Joseph [Varin] and Roger made their vows on the feast of Saint Vincent de Paul. The former, who has been keeping a great distance from us, not being willing to set foot inside here, finally came to give the habit to two novices. In his sermon, it seemed that he had received a great increase of grace in making his sacrifice, for he was penetrated with the spirit of God and the unction of the Heart of Jesus. He greeted us from the altar for the first time with this beautiful name, and many were weeping. He has gone through harsh and cruel trials and will be even better disposed to exercise a responsibility, of which he is already so worthy.

If the packet of our three travelers has not yet left, please add to it a good length of serge *de Mende* at about 42 or 43 *sols*, unfinished. It would not be good to send it by itself as it would be damaged en route, and our mother does not wish to send it *accelérit*, as the cost is prohibitive.

I wrote to several of the pupils yesterday; I would willingly continue today, but I have time only for you.

It seems that we will change something for the *(word erased)* of the office; I will let you know in time; but what is decided is that it is necessary to send the names and the date of death of our deceased sisters, with some notes about their birth, life etc. to put in a common book for the whole Society.

It was also decided that three days a month the sisters may stay in bed an hour longer, and those days they are dispensed from morning meditation without the obligation of making it up. However, our mother thinks it well that they are allowed a half hour in free time.

I am all yours in the Sacred Heart of Jesus and Mary,

Philippine

My respects to Fathers Rivet and Rambaud.

[On the reverse:]
To Mother
Mother Therese Maillucheau
Superior of the Religious of the Sacred Heart
at Sainte-Marie [d'En-Haut]
In Grenoble

Letter 59   **L. 2 to Euphrosine Jouve**

SS. C. J. et M.

August 4, feast of Saint Dominic[278]
For Aloysia [1816]

My dear Aloysia,

I am very late in congratulating you on your happiness, and I hope you are going to wear the external sign of the black veil because there are not to be any novices in the individual houses. Here you are beyond childhood in the spiritual life, and I hope you will bear the fruits of a strong, generous soul. Doubtless you have read the life of Saint Ignatius; nothing is better suited to revive courage and make one love one's vocation. Father Joseph [Varin] is a good representative; he had entirely broken with us, like the saint with Dame Roser.[279] Finally, he has appeared two or three times on the horizon, but sparingly.

We had Father de Janson's Mass on July 31, but he did not want to preach; he had astonishing success in Nantes with Father de Rosen. They have to go to Bordeaux and have spoken of an invitation from the bishop for Grenoble.

Friday benediction was given by the superior of the [Paris] Foreign Missions. He had just received a letter from China in which he was given details of the martyrdom of the last bishop of the country[280] who was there for 40 years and whom he knew. This man was arrested in May 1805 but was rather free though detained, well housed, well thought of, well treated by the mandarins who respected him; he was always driven in a coach to the courts. Finally, on September 14, 1815, he was condemned to death by the viceroy of the province of Szechuan.

---

278 Original autograph, C-VII 2) c Duchesne to RSCJ and Children, Box 4.
279 Isabelle Roser, born into a noble family of Barcelona, a friend of Saint Ignatius, was widowed in 1541, left for Rome with two companions in 1543, and obtained from Pope Paul III permission to place herself "under obedience" to Saint Ignatius. On December 25, 1545, the three women pronounced their vows in the Society of Jesus, to which Isabelle bequeathed all her fortune. Rumors of legal difficulties arose. On October 1, 1546, the religious left the Society, and in 1547, Ignatius obtained from the pope the right to be free forever to refuse to have communities of women under his obedience. Ignatius had written that there was no woman in the world to whom he owed more, probably on account of her unfailing financial support during his years of study, perhaps at Alcalá and Salamanca, and certainly in Paris (John Padberg, SJ).
280 Jean-Gabriel Taurin Dufresse (1750-1815), member of the Foreign Missionaries of Paris, titular bishop of Thabraca and apostolic vicar of Sechuan, China, was arrested May 18, 1815, taken to Chengdu (province of Sichuan), condemned and decapitated on September 14, 1815. He was beatified on May 27, 1900, and canonized on October 1, 2000. His feast is September 14.

However, he went to torture on foot in perfect calm, which aroused the admiration of the crowd of idolaters who came to see him decapitated. There were 30 Christians dragged from prison and threatened with death if they did not renounce the faith. Immediately they threw themselves at the feet of their bishop to ask for absolution and his blessing. The bishop gave absolution and was immediately decapitated. The threat of death was not carried out against the other Christians, but they were led back into prison, and the persecution continued. The head of the holy bishop was exposed, and above it were written his name, title, and the cause of death. Pictures of his head with the same inscription were made and sent everywhere. This good superior wants his establishment in Pondicherry given to the Jesuits, who would be able to send priests from several countries; they would be better accepted than those of the Foreign Missions who are all French, as the English dominate this country.

Mr. Lainé,[281] the minister [of the interior] asked the superior of the Missionaries of the Holy Spirit for priests to send into Senegal, which they wished to attach to France through religion. Though this superior had no organized group of his priests who had formerly had missions in Senegal, Cayenne, and Louisiana, they still would like him to send Jesuits as it were in his name. We are located alongside the former house of [the Society of] the Holy Spirit,[282] which is now the Normal School.

We have 12 novices, 3 postulants and several who are waiting; 24 in all and 4 boarders.

Good-bye, all yours,

Philippine

Much love to all the children; have them pray for the missions.

---

281   Joseph-Henri-Joachim, viscount Lainé (1768-835), was president of the Chamber of Deputies from 1814 to 1816, minister of the interior from 1816 to 1818, member of the French Academy and a peer of France.
282   The Society of the Holy Spirit was founded by Claude-François Poullart des Places, in Paris, May 28, 1703, for the evangelization of the poor. In 1816, the Holy Spirit Seminary was given charge of the training of the clergy of the French colonies. In 1848, it joined with the Congregation of the Holy Heart of Mary, founded by Francis Libermann, in Amiens, in 1841. Their members are known as Missionaries of the Holy Spirit or Spiritans.

Letter 60   **L. 43 to Mrs. Jouve in Lyon**

Paris, August 4, 1816[283]

My dear Sister,

I have been told that the Abbot of La Trappe is leaving for Lyon; I am taking advantage of the opportunity to write to you and to acknowledge your letters of June 11 and July 9. I would have answered them, but the arrival of our religious from several places, the arrangement of the house, and our religious ceremonies have taken up all my time. We are finally in community with our good God in our house.[284] Father d'Astros,[285] the vicar general, who was detained for a long time by Bonaparte, and Father Perreau,[286] one of the chaplains to the king and also a confessor of the faith, did the ceremony of blessing of our chapel. It had been desired at first to make it an elaborate affair; but in the end, the simplicity that I do so love, still more since the calamities, was decided upon. So I was very happy with the whole thing.

You are curious to know my position in this house; it is the same as at Sainte-Marie. Mother Bigeu is mistress of novices in our general novitiate, and Mother de Gramont[287] is mistress general of the boarding school, which is still being set up, as we have very few children, but we need patience.

I know that Augustin Jordan is surprised at the slow progress of our establishment and that he does not like the variety and multiplicity of religious houses. I have tried personally and without success to alter his opinion and many others that characterize men of the world and that grieve me, revealing as they do how seculars judge their fathers in the faith and meddle in ecclesiastical affairs. As to us, does he think

---

283 Copies: *Cahier; Lettres de la Mère Duchesne à sa famille*, pp. 66-68; *Lettres dactylographiées*. C-VII 2) c Duchesne to her family and lay people, Box 5.
284 This letter was written at the time of the installation of the first house of the Sacred Heart in Paris, 40 rue des Postes.
285 Bishop Paul d'Astros (1772-1851), superior of the house in Paris, was later named bishop of Saint Flour (1819), Bayonne (1820), archbishop of Toulouse (1830) and cardinal (1850).
286 Reverend Pierre Perreau (1766-1837) was ecclesiastical superior general of the Society of the Sacred Heart, delegated by Cardinal de Talleyrand-Périgord, archbishop of Paris.
287 Eugenie de Gramont, RSCJ (1788-1846), was born September 17, 1788, entered November 1, 1806, in Amiens, made her vows October 21, 1807, and was assistant to Mother Baudemont, then mistress of novices. Elected a general councilor in 1815, she was mistress general of the boarding school in Paris until 1830. The Parisian revolts obliged her to take the students to Montet (Switzerland). Upon their return, she was superior at the Hôtel Biron (1831-1846). In 1839, she opposed the decisions of the general council. She died in Paris, December 19, 1846.

such a complex foundation can be made and developed favorably in three months! We took possession of the house only on April 1, and the community was assembled the first of July. Has he succeeded in all his enterprises on schedule? Let him refrain from criticizing us: we must see that our work strikes deep roots of humility and patience, so that it may enjoy success without danger.

I continue to hear many praises of Euphrosine; Constance is more easily handled by Mother de Crouzas, her class mistress. I am very distressed that Henry's health does not improve; it would be better for him to ease up on study than to become too exhausted.

Goodbye, all yours *in Corde Jesu*,

Philippine

Letter 61   L. 3 to Mrs. de Mauduit at Crest

August 8 [1816][288]

My good Friend,

I am taking advantage of an answer I have to make to Mr. Jouve to spare you the cost of a letter. I had hardly finished writing to you than yours arrived; I repeat that I limit myself to 10,000 francs and find that to your advantage, since the income you give me represents an investment of 15,000 francs at eight percent per year. Our Society is not accustomed to act strictly, and my heart prefers the interests of my family to my own; it has always been my wish to be able to renounce my own goods.

We are in the situation of being in need ourselves; it is surprising that our Paris foundation, set up in such troubled times, is not suffering from them. The action of Providence that I saw in the establishment of Sainte-Marie gives me confidence that if you put your interests in God's hands, he will take care of you. I carried the weight of that house for several years; and there, where we spent 9 or 10,000 francs, the notary, Mr. Renandon, said: "I know about these things: you have spent 50,000 francs, I am sure." How many unhappy families have existed that way by a miracle of God's goodness. And while sharing and feeling the depth of your troubles, I would like you to carry heroism to the point of seeing

---

[288] Copies: *Cahier, Lettres de la Mère Duchesne à sa famille*, pp. 69-71; *Lettres dactylographiées*. C-VII 2) c Duchesne to her family and lay people, Box 5.

your resources diminish in silence, as so many saints have done. God who does not allow himself to be outdone in generosity would bless your harvests of every kind. Weary as you are of administering it, could you not turn it over to Amelie[289] and follow in the world that attraction to retirement about which you spoke to me in one of your letters; but above all, my good friend, suffer in silence following the example of our Lord Jesus Christ.

I too sigh for the moment when I shall be free of temporal cares; the soul loses much in their midst, and Clement XIV was right to say "Among earthly cares, one's heart becomes earthly."

Adrien's[290] state makes me very sad; dedicate him to Saint Regis; Euphrosine is terribly ill. How these poor mothers' hearts have to suffer! I share your feelings for your children, and I am so sorry that you do not tell me whether Amelie is some consolation to you. Seek it purely in the humble, gentle Heart of Jesus Christ, and you will find it firm and lasting.

I received the 600 francs note, which constitutes an advance on the 10,000 francs. Miss de Saint-Pern,[291] whom you knew by another name, wants to be remembered to you. She is a great example of detachment; she has furnished the house at Quimper, and among us she is like a humble servant, asking to help in the kitchen, being content with everything. She is admirable in her humility.

Goodbye, my good Sister. The proposals accepted, you will carry them out in due time.

I am all yours,

Philippine

Letter 62   L. 3 to Mother Maillucheau

SS. C. J. et M.

August [1816][292]

My dearest Mother,

---

289 Her daughter, Amelie de Mauduit du Plessis (1795-1869), married Henry Bergasse (1783-1867) on September 10, 1818.
290 Adrien was her fourth and last child (1805-1817).
291 Anne Marie de Saint-Pern, RSCJ, born January 31, 1768, in Quimper, was received as a postulant on August 15, 1817, in Paris, at the age of 49. She became gravely ill, returned to Quimper, and made her profession September 8. She died January 6, 1819.
292 Original autograph, C-VII 2) c Duchesne to RSCJ and Children, Box 4.

Your illness has pained me very much; besides feeling your suffering state, I cannot be indifferent to the harm your absence does to your community, where I always am in spirit. I have prayed so much for you as well as for the first communicants. I was happy with the letter from Marine[293] and hope she will persevere in good behavior and give good example to her sister. I learned that you had the kindness to ask for her, and I suspect that my sister will accept your proposal gratefully.

I owe you thanks for the attention you have given in sending me my notebooks, caps and chemises. As for the notebooks, I am missing a large one of modern history, but if it is difficult to find, don't trouble yourself; I will let it go until it surfaces by itself. About the caps and chemises, I recognize the care of the kind *vestiaires*, and I thank them for it; but as they must love my soul more than my body, I beg them to forget the body so as to care for the soul by leaving it some privations and aiding it by their prayers.

Mother Bigeu has sent you a letter from Rome, which must have pleased you. I don't know if it is she or Father Joseph's [Varin] leaving the novitiate, but it is less difficult to give in to the wishes of his daughters. Besides the clothing day, he preached to them on the feast of the Blessed Virgin, said Mass and did so again today. He procured for us daily Mass by one of his brothers; they have arranged to give us two Masses on Sunday. He also obtained a very good confessor from another society.

Finally, God is giving us many graces at this moment of our gathering. Our mother draws them down by her prayers, for she is in retreat in Amiens. Before going in, she took the whole community to the chapel of Our Lady and confided them especially to her, as well as Mother Grosier who seems to be getting on very well in her new house. Three postulants have entered in a month and 4 or 5 boarders.

Mother [de Gramont] d'Aster is very edifying by her humility and Mother [Eugenie] de Gramont here; she does not appear more important than the last of the novices; at table she takes the least desirable food, busies herself with the laundry and with the *b, a, ba* of the little children. In effect, she is undoubtedly one of the most distinguished subjects in the Society.

Mother Desmarquest also draws down many blessings by her humility. Enthusiasm for her establishment at Beauvais continues, but she puts others forward, above all Mother Deshayes, and believes herself very unworthy of the place she holds. However, Father de Clausel, the vicar

---

293 Her niece, Marine Lebrument (1803-1861).

general, who has marvelous insight, calls her an *excellent superior* and goes to see her almost every day. Father de Beauregard writes that the house in Poitiers is also going extremely well; the sacrifice they made of Mother Grosier has given renewed courage and contributed to the practice of solid virtue.

We are expecting Mother's [Barat] return for several *prises d'habit*, notably that of Miss Fontaine,[294] a wealthy, modest young person, well-educated, who said a generous goodbye to the world. She was from the parish in the Île Saint-Louis; and that island seems to be favored by God; it is like a holy city in the middle of a corrupt one. However, our postulant was known and distinguished for her virtue; everyone misses her. Zoe is most comical; she is the only one heard at recreation; silence is often shattered, but she is still content, especially now that her confessor is no longer giving her the catechism.

Goodbye, my good Mother, continue to pray for me and believe me all yours in the Sacred Heart of Jesus,

Philippine

August 18, 1816

Loving greetings to all your daughters, especially Mothers Victoire [Paranque][295] and Adrienne [Michel].

[On the reverse:]
To Mother
Mother Therese
Superior of the Religious of the Sacred Heart at Sainte-Marie
Grenoble

---

294 Aglae Fontaine, RSCJ (1791-1854), born January 31, 1791, entered the novitiate September 6, 1816, made her profession January 18, 1819, and went to La Ferrandière (Lyon). She was superior at Autun (1831-1846) and Bourges (1846-1854). She went for a rest to La Neuville-les-Amiens, where she died April 20, 1854.

295 Victoire Paranque, RSCJ (1782-1838), was born in Beauvais, entered in Amiens in 1806, and pronounced her vows on October 21, 1807. She went soon after to Doorseele (Ghent) as assistant and mistress general, and remained there until 1814, when that house separated from the Society. She returned to Amiens, then to Grenoble in 1816, then was superior of the foundation at Autun (1822), then at Grenoble (1823-1833) and at Aix (1834-1837). She returned to Paris in 1837 and died the next year.

Letter 63 **L. 2 to the Religious of Sainte-Marie d'En-Haut**

SS. C. J. et M.

Paris, January 5, 1817[296]

My dearest Mothers and Sisters,

Our reverend mother general has received a letter enclosing three envelopes, one for Mother Bigeu, one for me and one for Mother Barat. I noticed that she found the order reversed; and she was disappointed that the seal and different postage stamps deprived her of the pleasure of reading your whole letter. She wasn't any less eager to answer you, but the responsibility of the whole Society, of a brand new house, of a novitiate, and her health, which suffers from pains and toothache, do not allow her to write all her letters. She keeps confidential and business letters for herself. She handed over yours to me, and I have great pleasure in answering it because I can spend more time with you while obeying her.

We have another grievance against you: it is that you are too brief in giving details that may interest us; you have said only a word in passing about the vows of our two young sisters:[297] however, everyone is interested in such a ceremony: Did the bishop come? Who preached? Were the children impressed by it? Likewise at the *prise d'habit*.

As for me, I like to tell my sisters all that I can relate to them; so I will begin by giving you news of the outside and then come to our own news.

Mother Bigeu has returned from Bordeaux after making her retreat there under Father Barat; she did not settle the business for which she went there. God does not want it for the moment. She found the house at Niort flourishing, but several have weak health, especially Mother Caroline [Messoria], and there is a great shortage of priests. Sainte-Pezenne, an orphanage, is asking for help. So is Poitiers, where the boarding school has more than 80 pupils. Sister Ribaud is not too well there. From Poitiers Mother Bigeu went to Quimper, ordered by our mother at the request of the bishop, who was very sick during her stay and [Sister Catherine] Maillard has "a loose handle;"[298] she had to leave

---

296 Original autograph, C-VII 2) c Duchesne to RSCJ and Children, Box 4.
297 Euphrosine (Aloysia) Jouve and Olympie Rombau made their vows on November 21, 1816, in Grenoble.
298 Philippine uses a colloquial expression that means, not solid, in bad health.

there and will be here in a week, unless there is a change of plan. There is much that is good there and many obstacles, as in all works for God.

In Amiens, Mother Grosier who has been very sick is getting a little better. Mother Deshayes was laid low for three weeks by an indisposition that usually affects her for a week each month; this time it was more serious. They have so much work to do that they had to employ the novices.

To go back to Brittany: it is a very good part of the country. Father Joseph [Varin] traveled there lately with his father to see one of their houses at Auray. In one city, where some missionaries were saying Mass, the church was full in an instant; the brothers, eight of them, gave a mission at Saint-Brieuc, Fathers Thomas and Caillat among others; they had amazing success: 30 confessors were not enough, and when it was not possible to enter the church through the door, people jumped in through the windows. It was noted that everywhere the missions had the greatest success.

Father Legris Duval, the king's preacher for Lent, was very effective at the court on one of the feasts when he preached. I heard him once at Saint Thomas for a profession and I was charmed.

We are having a good share of the Word of God these days; besides the retreat of almost three weeks, the priest preached again at the *prise d'habit* of Miss Harant on the feast of the Immaculate Conception [of the Virgin Mary], etc., and he is beginning a series of instructions every week to the novices on the rules [of the Society of the Sacred Heart]. You can see what advantage we have; that is lacking in a novitiate in an individual house.

Father Joseph, upon return from his journey, greeted us with an instruction on the holy Child Jesus and stressed particularly this thought that we ought to have when meditating on Jesus in the crib: *Here is my Victim*; and he invited us very movingly to be *his victims*. On the feast of Saint John, he preached on these words: *See what charity the Son of God had*,[299] and after pointing out all that Jesus Christ had done for us in the mystery of the Incarnation, he urged us again to be his victims and to say on every occasion in peace and recollection: *Ita Pater, yes Father*.[300] There is an act of devotion: *yes, Father*; there is an act of meekness, of humility, of obedience, to everything: *yes, Father*. Finally the last hour will come, he will say: *Come, my beloved*, and the soul will answer: *yes, Father*. That was the end of the sermon. Then on New

---

299 1 Jn 3:1.
300 Mt 11:26; Mk 14:36.

Year's Day he came again to greet us and preached on these words *"Gloria in Excelsis,"* and spoke of the great glory the Son rendered to his Father in the Incarnation; he invited us to unite ourselves to him by trying to glorify him as we can. And on these other words: "and peace to men of good will,"[301] he stressed again the necessity of being entirely submissive to the will of God, to obedience, etc.

My good Sisters, these are great graces. Pray for all of us, and for me in particular, that we do not waste them, but that we do the will of God in everything.

It is in union with the Sacred Hearts that I am your unworthy sister,
Philippine

Mother Adrienne [Michel] should place in the Mass ceremonial for Saturday that on the 1st Saturday of the month, instead of the Litany of the Blessed Virgin, we say the Litany of the Heart of Mary.

[On the reverse:]
To the Mothers and Sisters
of the Sacred Heart of Jesus
at Sainte-Marie d'En-Haut
Grenoble

Letter 64 **L. 44 to Mrs. Jouve in Lyon**

Paris, January 9 [1817][302]

My dearest Sister,

I am most grateful to your husband for the service he has rendered us, and to you for your remembrance and for the good wishes you express for my happiness. I shall always find it in the accomplishment of God's will in my regard, so a change of residence will make no difference. When I came to Paris, I neither expected nor desired to remain here. I prefer the simplicity of small towns. Wherever I may be, I shall always find a way to give you news of myself and receive news from you, but as yet nothing has been decided; I am waiting to tell you later what is going to happen.

---

301 Lk 2:14.
302 Copies: *Cahier, Lettres de la Mère Duchesne à sa famille,* pp. 74-75; *Lettres dactylographiées.* C-VII 2) c Duchesne to her family and lay people, Box 5.

If you wish to give me a welcome New Year's present, please have a Mass offered for me at Fourvière. Euphrosine wrote me that she is drinking ass's milk for the 5th month, which tells me that she is not free of the lung trouble. God is sending us a great trial in her illness. The more I reflect on conditions in our little Paris house that can no longer contain us, the more I realize that she is better off in Grenoble. *Fiat* in everything.

Believe, good Sister, in my inviolable attachment,

Philippine

Letter 65   **L. 45 to Mrs. Jouve in Lyon**

July 3, 1817[303]

My dear Friend,

I wrote to you two days ago about the news that we had from Grenoble according to principles that are dear to me; today I see from your letter that mine gave you pain, and I am very sorry. I made known your wish to our superior general who, understanding the desire of your tender love, wanted to reconcile your wishes with our obligations and Euphrosine's desire not to leave Sainte-Marie. Finally, her wisdom has found a way to harmonize these three. She told me that there is a certain latitude still as to our going out to take the [thermal] waters and that your request in this situation presents fewer inconveniences and is made in a very urgent case. Thus, my dear Sister, she grants you permission to take your daughter to consult the doctors you choose, but when they have reached a diagnosis and prescribed the treatment that you take her back at once. She is writing to Grenoble today to indicate her intention to Mother Therese and to reassure Euphrosine. So you may go to get her, unless our prayers have obtained the health of this dear niece or sister before you depart.

We are interceding with Heaven, especially Saint Regis, with an express wish for the return to health that we believe must be for the glory of God one day. I have hope of being heard, and I share sincerely in all your motherly anxiety.

---

303 Copies: *Cahier, Lettres de la Mère Duchesne à sa famille*, pp. 64-66; *Lettres dactylographiées*. C-VII 2) c Duchesne to her family and lay people, Box 5.

We learned that the affairs of the Church of France are concluded and signed in Rome on June 11.[304] Bishop de Pressigny[305] is archbishop of Besançon and the grand almoner [Cardinal de Talleyrand-Périgord] is archbishop of Paris.

Goodbye, all yours, many affectionate messages to your husband and children,

Philippine

P.S. Mother Bigeu has been at our house at Quimper. Mother Deshayes is in Beauvais in a house that is very prosperous; there are almost 80 boarders and 300 in the poor school. Our mother general, who is here, is the only one to whom I could address your message. She shares your sorrow; she says it would be like a holiday to enjoy all the good things they say about Euphrosine in Grenoble.
Good-bye.

Letter 66   L. 4 to Mrs. de Mauduit, at Crest

[July 1817][306]

My dearest Friend,

As the last letter I wrote you was delayed in Lyon, I grew anxious about your silence; and either to relieve my own anxiety or because I thought that Mr. de Mauduit was as interested as you in the proposal I made to you, I wrote to him directly to get news of you and to repeat my offer. He answered that you had talked about it and that he agreed to the reimbursement of 10,000 francs, but that he did not have that sum available. It is up to you to decide now, and I cannot help thinking it would be to your advantage to accept, for if I live an ordinary lifetime, it will cost you far more. To make things easier for you, here is my last proposal: you would give me the 10,000 francs now by promissory note, and we will cancel the 6 months' arrears due me. This will be an

---

304 The reference is to the Concordat signed on June 11, 1817, between the Holy See and the Kingdom of France. But this concordat was not validated, and the Concordat of 1801 remained in effect until the law of separation of December 9, 1905.
305 Gabriel Cortois de Pressigny (1745-1823) was born in Dijon and was bishop of Saint-Malo (1786-1801). Named archbishop of Besançon in 1817, he remained there until his death, May 2, 1823.
306 Copies: *Cahier, Lettres de la Mère Duchesne à sa famille*, pp. 76-78; *Lettres dactylographiées*. C-VII 2) c Duchesne to her family and lay people, Box 5.

easement that you can make use of for Amelie. When you send me the promissory note, I would burn our written agreement or put it in the hands of a third person. You could ask Scipion [Perier] to keep your copies, for they are too bulky for the post.

As to the observations you were willing to offer me, I understand their usefulness, but they carry no weight with me. I have never regretted the money I put into Sainte-Marie; and if I had not done so, would I have been able to provide for the service to Adelaide [Lebrument]?[307]

I know several of our religious who are the only resource for their brothers and sisters for the education of their children who are too numerous for the parents to pay their fees. When one wants to do good, it is best not to count the cost, and God will repay with interest.

I am convinced that I shall never be in want: Providence is admirable in caring for us and provided for our unusual needs during those unhappy years when there was even danger of starving to death. And if I must experience privations, I shall be happy to practice my vow of poverty.

I hope that by casting your anxieties into the heart of God it will be the same for you and your children; it must be because you were pleasing to God that you were tried by suffering, by temporal losses; but he will never let you be overwhelmed, for he will give you strength at the moment when you believe yourself to be plunged into sorrow; he will lift you up and give you peace. I pray much for you and yours. Adrien's poor health grieves me; you would like to make him a priest; perhaps God will make him an angel; but no, pray the good doctor, Saint Fr. Regis, and he will cure this beloved child.

They write me from Grenoble that Euphrosine's condition is still the same. How little we can count on health! Hers seemed so flourishing! Several vows have been made at [Our Lady of] Fourvière, to Saint Regis for her cure, and God seems deaf.

The founder of our house at Quimper, Miss de Saint-Pern, a cousin of Miss du Verger, is going to take the habit in a few days here in Paris, where she has just arrived. She has spoken much of you and of Augustine [Jordan]; she is herself a model of detachment and of virtue.

---

307 For the education of her seven daughters at Sainte-Marie d'En-Haut.

Letter 67   L. 5 to Mrs. de Mauduit, at Crest

Paris, August 17, 1817[308]

My dear Friend,

...[309] Father Enfantin preached a sermon on the Blessed Virgin this evening (August 16) that took him only half an hour to prepare but that I prefer to all those I have ever heard. He has truly natural eloquence and God blesses his ministry; his simple manner is no obstacle to his influence with pious and refined persons. And it gives fresh luster to his virtue that praise does not affect.

Remember me to my brother, to Miss de Mauduit and to Amelie.
All yours,

Philippine

Letter 68   L. 1 to her cousin Mrs. de Rollin in Grenoble

SS. C. J. M.

August 29, 1817[310]
No. 1

My dearest Cousin,

I am taking advantage of an opportunity to write to you. I also have a special reason for writing to you, but I am not ashamed to speak of special interest since it is not personal but regards the service of God and interests of the neighbor; since your departure,[311] my desires for America have not lessened, and God seems to lend himself to my wishes. I saw the bishop of Louisiana on the eve of his departure; he must be in America by now. Our mother promised him six of us, and I am of

---

308 Copies: *Cahier, Lettres de la Mère Duchesne à sa famille*, p. 39; *Lettres dactylographiées*. C-VII 2) c Duchesne to her family and lay people, Box 5.

309 An archivist's note: "This fragment is evidently from 1817. In what Father H. Jouve has crossed out, there is a reference to the *prise d'habit* of Miss de Saint-Pern."

310 *Copies of letters of Philippine Duchesne to Mrs. de Rollin and a few others*, No. 1; *Cahier, Lettres à Mme de Rollin*, pp. 1-2; *Lettres dactylographiées*. C-VII 2) c Duchesne to her family and lay people, Box 5.

311 Josephine Savoye de Rollin left Paris to return to Grenoble with her husband, deputy and president of the electoral college of the Isère (1815-1823).

the number, next spring. We have, therefore, a sacristy to get ready; and the vicar general [Bertrand Martial], who remained in Bordeaux as agent for the mission, wrote to our mother to ask her to procure fabric: muslin, linen, braid, and all that can be used for the liturgy to impress the Indians whom we wish to attract by the pomp of the ceremonies. You are so sympathetic to bodily misery that I am convinced that you will be more so to the conversion of souls on which depends their eternity. You had told me one day that in Grenoble you had several things that could be useful to us; look for them, good friend, or beg them. God will bless you. But don't speak of me in all this; I am so unworthy of this inspiring work that I am always afraid it is going to get away from me. Not a word then about me; but speak in general of the needs of a diocese of 400 leagues where there are no wealthy people.

You learned from my cousin that we have withdrawn a part of the sum you had on deposit, and you know its destination.

One must never make fun of holy people, and those who laughed at the preacher who gave the eight o'clock sermon would be very surprised at the number of conversions that followed his sermons.

Remember me, please, to Mr. de Rollin, to my aunt, my cousins, especially Mrs. Teisseire whom I never forget.

I am your wholly devoted cousin in the Heart of Jesus,

Philippine

Letter 69   L. 3 to Mother Barat

[January or February 1818][312]

Dear Reverend Mother,

I have often had occasion to speak to you about my vocation to instruct Indians or idolaters; however, the different indications on which my hopes to have God on my side were based seemed very weak, so to speak, and did not have the same force as if they were united in one whole. Therefore, after a Communion, I decided to leave it to you, since I understood how apprehensive you must have been about entrusting this all-important work to me: a work we were to undertake at such a

---

312 Original autograph, C-VII 2) c Duchesne to Barat, Box 2. Before leaving Paris, Philippine had entrusted this letter to Father Perreau. Cf. J. de Charry, II, I, L. 83; Hogg, pp. 7-16; *Philippine Duchesne et ses compagnes, Les Années pionnières, 1818-1823, Textes présentés par* Chantal Paisant, Cerf, Paris, 2001, pp. 62-68.

great distance from those who had passed on their spirit [the Jesuits] to us and also too far from you who have caught that spirit, so as to impart it to all your daughters.

But if it was God who showed me my vocation, if it was also God who opens the way to accomplish it, there is reason to hope that he will sustain his work by the feeblest means and unworthy persons who are incapable of succeeding.

My first longing to become a missionary came from conversations with a good Jesuit father who had been a missionary in Louisiana and told us stories of the Indians. I was only eight or ten years old, but nevertheless I considered these missionaries blessed; I envied their work without astonishment at the dangers, for at the same time I was reading the lives of the martyrs with lively interest. The good Jesuit father was the extraordinary confessor for the house where I was a boarder; I went to confession to him several times, and I liked his simple, friendly manner, a manner he had adopted with the Indians.

Since that time the names of Propaganda,[313] of the Foreign Missions, of priests destined for them, of religious who were making foundations abroad have made my heart tremble.

It was the desire to exercise some kind of apostolate that made me choose the Visitation, where young people were educated, [in preference] to the Carmelites whom I loved very much, when I entered religion at the age of eighteen and a half.

My community was imbued with the spirit of the Jesuits; we prided ourselves that our constitutions were drawn from theirs; the library was enriched with almost all their works because at the moment of the suppression,[314] three Jesuits were left in the chaplaincy. At their death they had bequeathed their library to the house. During the two years of my novitiate I read nothing except Rodriguez[315] without getting tired of it. In order to have some stories to tell at the gathering after Vespers, I related, one after the other, the lives of almost all the Jesuit saints. The life of Saint Francis Xavier was the one that impressed me the most: the gesture of the Socotorans stretching out their arms to him on the shore, his enthusiasm in the garden of Goa, the tears of consolation that flowed in the islands of Mauros,[316] so frightful in themselves; the cries of "More, still more," when it was a question of work, and finally

---

313 The Roman Congregation for the Propagation of the Faith.
314 The suppression of the Society of Jesus took place in France in 1764 and by the pope in 1773.
315 *Treatise on Christian Perfection* by Alphonsus Rodriguez (1526-1616), a Spanish Jesuit.
316 Probably Morotaï, an island in the archipelago of the Moluccas, Indonesia.

his touching appeals to colleges in Europe begging for missionaries. In my impatience I often turned to him saying, "Great Saint, why do you not call me and I would answer you." He is my favorite saint.

My devotion to Saint Francis Regis was born at the same time as a result of a conversation with a religious who had taken him for her patron. I often prayed before his relic (it was one of his teeth). His work was closer to what I could do because it was more obscure, and for love of him I have instructed some poor people. When the Revolution chased us out of our convents in 1792, I found in my father's house some [books of] Hours that contained the prayer of Saint Francis Xavier for the conversion of infidels. For the last 24 years I have said this prayer almost every day for missionaries as well as prayers of the early saints of the Society of Jesus.

I said the prayers before the altar of these two saints in our parish in the country, where their names were added to the Litanies. In the neighborhood of La Louvesc almost all the houses had pictures of Saint Regis, who is known as the *holy father*. At the same time, I made the acquaintance of two former Jesuits; one of them was my confessor on occasion; he urged me to go to La Louvesc; I went on the very day of the death of the holy Jesuit and was relieved of my great sorrow; he surely brought before God my desire to return to religious life. For when I had left my family and returned to Grenoble to associate myself if possible with some former religious, he wrote: "You have taken a step which God will credit to your account;" and he announced the return of religion in France, according to the predictions of Venerable Benedict Labre, who was passing through the Vivarais on his way to Rome. The Jesuit told me this four years before the Concordat.

I was drawn to pray to Saint Francis Regis; and in the hope that he would act on my behalf, I made a vow in his honor, binding myself to keep it if I returned to Sainte-Marie within the year. I took several steps, and all went so well that in six months instead of a year I was back at Sainte-Marie. The vicar general [Father Brochier], who was governing the diocese and whom I was consulting about how to proceed, answered my first letter: *Digitus Dei est hic!*[317] He supported me in the many setbacks I had to go through, as well as another holy priest, a hospital chaplain, who had established devotion to the Sacred Heart there and who never failed to make the solemn novena to Saint Francis Xavier every year.

Since my admission to the Society, I have spoken still more of the foreign missions but in general terms, rather of esteem for them than

---

317 The finger of God is here. Ex 8, 15.

of the possibility. Finally, on January 10, 1806, while making my meditation in the children's dormitory on the detachment of the Magi, I was seized with the idea of imitating them. I saw my strong attachment to the house that had cost me so many tears fall away, and I made up my mind to offer myself for the instruction of idolaters in China or some other country. I wrote to you, Reverend Mother, on the 27th of the month to tell you of this desire, and you answered, "That is what I have been expecting of you." I made the same request of Father Varin, and he answered, "If it is given to me to enter into the Heart of God, I see written there in capital letters that you are destined to bring God honor in distant lands." I still have a copy of your letter, but Father Varin's and Father Brochier's, in which he said *Digitus Dei est hic*, were destroyed by order of one of my confessors.

Father Varin came to Grenoble shortly afterward and reminded me of my letter; I asked him to promise me to be the first to leave for heathen countries; he said, "I promise you." I answered, "Well then, Father, bless me for this work." He did so with arm outstretched farther than usual.

My desires increased when after several years of trials, contradictions and faults, I saw this process as a necessary means of expiation for me and a safeguard for my conscience; I also wanted to avoid occasions of sin, and this desire along with that of saving souls made me pray most ardently. During the two nights of Holy Thursday in 1806 and 1808, I believed I had been heard, as I seemed to hear a person in a low voice in or near me say, "Why do you doubt?" and on the feast of the Assumption, "It will be." It was almost certain that on the great feasts and feasts of apostles my desire would flare up even more after Communion when I found myself in tears. I said to myself: where does this come from? I have read nothing, said nothing, heard nothing that could recall these ideas, and then I realized that it was the feast of an apostle.

When I had to fight this desire the most, I avoided reading anything that might foster it. I tried not to build my hopes on any pecuniary means I possessed; but everything was useless, and one day after Communion, I decided to write to the vicar general in Rome [Father Jean Perelli] to consult the pope to see whether I ought to follow or stifle my desires. You know the fate of my letter. When afterwards I was called to Paris, I was disappointed because I thought you wanted to take away all my hope of succeeding, although I wanted the pope to decide that I should think of it no longer and thus obtain the tranquility that results from indifference. But also during the journey I had moments of consolation thinking that God would make use of a sojourn in Paris to undertake the negotiation with Bishop Dubourg that I had deemed possible. I resolved to make a novena of Communions in Our Lady's chapel at Saint-Sulpice before making my request.

During this novena I prayed to her most earnestly there for indifference, as well as before her statue at Saint Thomas,[318] at Montmartre, in the Carmelite church and the church of the Foreign Missions. But then balance deserted me; and I was prepared to brave all human respect, all blame, every coldness so that nothing would be lacking on my part to achieve the success I desired. When I saw Father Varin so opposed, I went to Saint-Sulpice in a state of anguish and said to Our Lady: "You have deceived me then; the more I prayed, the more my desire for the missions grew, and nevertheless, you see how my wishes are thwarted." I had not finished speaking when I heard in the depths of my heart: "Daughter, it is because you have not prayed as you should." I understood that I had counted too much on my own efforts and that if I was to succeed, I should hand over everything to my superior. I was calmer then; I renewed my desires to Our Lady, and she made me a promise for my future.

In order to have merit from this moment on, I asked Father Varin to allow me to make a vow to consecrate myself to instruction of infidels according to obedience, but on my part to refuse nothing to further this work. He said yes, and I made the vow a few minutes later fearing that he might change his mind. It is that vow that now prevents me from refusing an office that I consider beyond me.

The feast of Saint Francis Xavier I went to Mass at the Foreign Missions church; these words of the epistle: "How will they know the truth if no one instructs them, and how will they be instructed if no one is sent to them?"[319] pierced my soul; I was in floods of tears in spite of myself; I did not know where to hide. In order to avoid the same thing happening again, I made up my mind not to return to this church in the afternoon; but I don't know how it happened, I found myself locked out of the house, and I was drawn to the place where the relic of Saint Francis Xavier was. I was very close to it and to the Blessed Sacrament, which was brought to his chapel. My hopes were high during the whole of his novena, which I made carefully to know the will of God.

---

318 During the General Chapter of 1815, the Religious of the Sacred Heart stayed with the Sisters of Saint Thomas of Villanova, where the Black Virgin of Paris, "Our Lady of Deliverance," is venerated. During the novena, Philippine went also to pray in other churches located in the 6e, 7e, 20e *arrondissements* of Paris: at Saint-Pierre de Montmartre, where Saint Ignatius and his first companions had made their first vows, August 15, 1534; in the Carmelite church, rue Madame, where the massacre of one hundred twenty priests had taken place on September 2, 1792; at the *Missions Etrangères de Paris*, rue du Bac; at the Church of Saint-Sulpice.
319 Rom 10:14.

I forgot to tell you, my good Mother, about an incident that happened at Grenoble during the time when there were efforts to take Sainte-Marie from us and when Fathers de Janson and Enfantin believed we should give back that house; my heart was broken. Finally I resolved to let it go, to see the dear establishment destroyed and to laugh at my expenditures; I went to make my spiritual reading in Deuteronomy near the lost well. My eye fell on different passages that touched me very much, especially this one: *Cumque introduxerit te dominus Deus tuus in terram et dederit tibi domos plenas cunctorum opum, quas non exstruxisti, cisternas quas non fodisti, vineta et oliveta quae non plantasti.... Ne...elevetur cor tuum.... Et cibavit te manna in solitudine.*[320] These words sent a torrent of consolation into my soul. I was assured that God was confirming the gift I had made of Sainte-Marie; and not finding any explanation of *oliveta*, I interpreted it as new gifts full of spiritual sweetness in the plans for the mission that filled my mind. Oh! Dear Mother, *oliveta* is explained for me by the consolation I now feel at seeing my vows accomplished, and naturally by the excellence of the fruits of Louisiana, as my good Jesuit says. I must no longer meditate on anything but: *ne...elevetur...cor tuum*. In my high calling, it is well to say, *Non nobis*,[321] adding all the same, *Non fecit taliter omni nationi... fecit mihi magna*.[322]

You do know that one day I found in our church in Grenoble two pictures of Our Lady (the Immaculate Conception and Our Lady of Sorrows); they were very ugly and dirty, but I remembered that Father Enfantin owed his conversion to having kept something similar, so I felt drawn to honor them in order to obtain going to foreign lands. A little while later, I found another one of Saint Francis Regis, so ugly and dirty that my first impulse was to burn it; but then again overwhelmed by my preoccupation for the missions, I was filled with love for the saint, and I made a promise to preserve this picture for love of him and to have him honored by the Indians if he obtained for me the grace to go to instruct them. I am taking this dear picture to keep my promise; I regard it as a shield, and the vow I made to consecrate the house in Saint Louis to him is what is hastening and facilitating my happiness.

---

320 When the Lord your God has brought you into the land [that he swore to your ancestors ... to give you], a land with ... houses filled with all sorts of goods that you did not fill, hewn cisterns that you did not hew, vineyards and olive groves that you did not plant," Deut 6:10-11; "Do not exalt yourself ... he fed you in the wilderness with manna ..." Deut 8:14-16.
321 "Not unto us ..." Ps 115 (113 b).
322 "He has not dealt thus with any other nation" Ps 147:20; "He has done great things for me" Lk 1:49.

I told you also that a few days before Bishop Dubourg's visit, I saw him in a dream telling me to be calm; I was mystified, as I had not thought of it the day before; I waited that day but he came only two or three days afterwards. The feast of the Ascension [May 5, 1817], my desires flared up from morning onward at these words that gripped me as I entered the choir: "Go, teach all nations." They caused almost continual emotion, a bitterness sweeter than all pleasure; I wished to attempt to meet new demands, but I said, "I have exhausted everything; it is up to you, my God, to act." Bishop Dubourg came the next day, but what was my astonishment and delight when speaking to the novices, he said that he had been singularly struck the evening before by these words: "Go, teach all nations." I understood that God had given us both the same thoughts to fulfill a similar vocation.

It remains only to tell you that I have had a pain in my side for fifteen years, which has sometimes been so severe that I have thought about a blistering poultice to relieve it; it disappeared suddenly upon learning that Father Barat had begun to talk with the bishop of Louisiana; that I had communicated that day for him and his missionaries without knowing it; that the vow to consecrate the foundation in Louisiana to Saint Francis Regis was hardly made; and that Father Barat wrote to me urging me to choose him as its patron.

How good God is, Mother.

[Additional page]

SS. C. J. et M.

Very Reverend Mother,

The paper came to an end and kept me from adding that I value above all else the grace of belonging to the Society of the Sacred Heart of Jesus and that of being able to contribute towards its expansion. No other position in the world could outweigh this heartfelt choice of belonging; at this moment, I am fully aware of all I owe to the Society, and I will try to live up to it and make the spirit of the rules of our Society appreciated. To renew often this holy commitment that, thank God, binds one to the Society even at a great distance will be my consolation.

Now all that remains is to prove to myself that my attraction for the Carthusians[323] was not inconsistent with that for the missions. But my

---

323 The Grande Chartreuse (Isère, France) is the motherhouse of the Carthusian order, founded in 1084 by Saint Bruno (1040-1101).

main concern was the return of the Carthusians rather than our going to them. Furthermore, I never dreamed of setting out when sea voyages were impossible. I was in fact pleading for the return of the Carthusians rather than our installation there. Perhaps God wanted me to unite my desires with those of the Carthusians. It seems to me that he had given me a presentiment of something I could not then understand, but which forced me to ask. Since they returned, despite all my efforts I have been able to remember only the first words of Saint Bruno's prayer, which I had said for many years. Therefore I do not say it anymore.

Permit me, my good Mother, to ask your pardon once again for all the pain I have caused you. Perhaps God has provided me with a way of expiation by giving me that same office that you have carried out for me; my greatest happiness will be to form daughters worthy of you; if I fail to do this I would rather die.

I am with respect, good Mother, your very humble servant,

Philippine Duchesne

[On the reverse:]
To Mother
Mother Barat
Superior General of the Religious of the Sacred Heart
Paris

Letter 70   **L. 3 to the Religious of Sainte-Marie d'En-Haut**

SS. C. J. et M.

Paris, at Saint Thomas [1818][324]

Dearest Mothers and Sisters,

When I look into my own soul, I cannot find any reason for expecting you to remember me. I know full well that I deserve to be forgotten, and I really ought to desire this very thing. For if you remember me, you must inevitably recall all the faults I committed, faults that were prejudicial to an institution for which I would willingly give my life, faults I repent of most sincerely.

But when I think about the charity that is the bond of union in our

---

324 Original autograph, C-VII 2) c Duchesne to RSCJ and Children, Box 4.

holy Society, I am not surprised at your thoughtfulness; and I beg you to add to it pardon for all my past faults and prayers that I may avoid such conduct in the future.

You must be as merciful to me as God himself is. Ordinarily he gives one outstanding grace to a soul, and this one becomes the source of many others. For me that signal grace was my return to Sainte-Marie and my blessed membership in the privileged Society of the Sacred Heart; it was far beyond anything I could have hoped for! And still, in spite of the fact that I have profited so poorly from so much instruction on solid perfection, so many sermons, examples of sublime virtue on the part of those I know, God in his goodness is opening to me a new career that calls forth all my gratitude and overwhelms me with confusion when I think of it! Already many bishops have praised our voyage overseas and have given it their blessing from afar. Among them was our worthy and pious superior, Bishop d'Astros, appointed bishop of Orange, to whom our mother was kind enough to present me along with Octavie, my future companion; he was very encouraging.

But what need we both have of your continual prayers; one infidelity can stop the flow of grace, and we commit them constantly. Our happiness is promised us; graces are offered to us, but we have not yet obtained them. How many reasons for fear and vigilance! I hope you will not cease praying to Our Lady and Saint Regis for this great work. I have shed many tears for America before the Blessed Virgin who obtained for Saint Francis de Sales freedom from his temptation; the statue is now at Saint Thomas [of Villanova] where I spent several months. I believe I owe her shrine a great deal as well as the one at Montmartre. Invoke them especially, I beg you.

How our zeal should be inflamed; it is true that God seems to refuse our going to Poland; but we are asked for in Spain, Normandy, Lorraine, Languedoc, etc. The bishop just appointed to Fez preached here on Christmas Day and the bishop of Verdun, on the feast of the Immaculate Conception [of the Virgin Mary].

I am all yours in the Sacred Heart,

Philippine

Letter 71   **L. 2 to Mrs. de Rollin,**
                      Rue Saint-Honoré N° 352, Paris

No. 2
[January] 24, 1818[325]

My very good Cousin,

    Since I last had the pleasure of seeing you, I have had a visit from Cousin Augustin and his charming family. He offered me the money that Mr. de Mauduit had asked him to make over to me, and I asked him to remain my banker; but the next day I learned that our departure would be advanced and all the money we shall take with us must be in Bordeaux the 10th or 11th of February. So I would like to ask you to give me what remains and Augustin and my cousins Scipion and Casimir[326] to return to me what they owe through letters of exchange on Bordeaux for the dates indicated.

    My brother sent me a note for 7000 francs, which I am not in a hurry to cash until there is need, but I would not like the several sums to be decreased by the exchange rate or through delay; those who are coming with me are bringing nothing except their good will. The bishop warned us not to count on him; the cost of the voyage and the necessity of providing a dwelling will use up all the money. That is what is forcing me to collect as much as possible; money is to be desired only if it is to be usefully spent. I await your reply regarding my notes.

    All yours,

                                                             Philippine

Tell Augustin about my plans, but do not let it reach my sisters.

---

325 *Copies of letters of Philippine Duchesne to Mrs. de Rollin and a few others*, No. 2; *Cahier, Lettres à Mme de Rollin*, pp. 2-3; *Lettres dactylographiées*. C-VII 2) c Duchesne to her family and lay people, Box 5.

326 Augustin, Scipion and Casimir Perier are Josephine Savoye de Rollin's brothers. Casimir Pierre Perier (1777-1832), served in the army of Italy in 1798 and was promoted to adjunct to the general staff of the Military Engineers Corps. Upon the death of his father in 1801, he found himself at the head of a vast fortune; he left the army and became one of the major shareholders of the mining company d'Anzin. On October 13, 1805, he married Pauline Loyer (1788-1861). A liberal opponent of Charles X during the Restoration and regent of the *Banque de France* (1822-1832), deputy of the Seine (1817-1827), then of l'Aube (1827-1832), he was named president of the Chamber of Deputies on August 6, 1830, then president of the Council and minister of the Interior of the government of Louis Philippe, March 13, 1831. He succumbed to the cholera epidemic on May 16, 1832, and was buried in Père Lachaise Cemetery, where a mausoleum for him was constructed in 1837, surmounted by his statue and decorated with three bas-reliefs representing Eloquence, Justice and Strength.

Letter 72   L. 3 to Mrs. de Rollin
Rue Saint-Honoré, Hôtel de Mayence, Paris[327]

SS. C. J. M.

No. 3
Recommended to St. A. de Padua

My dearest Friend,

Taking advantage of your offer, I am sending you all our notes. There is one with my Perier cousins that is not due yet, but I am hoping they will be willing to advance payment, since we are taking no interest on sums payable for several months.

I could not make out a receipt for what my cousin Augustin Perier is to give me from Mrs. de Mauduit because I could not remember the exact amount; I will send it as soon as I have the information. For all these sums, I beg my cousins to give me a bill of exchange for 600 francs to repay Mr. Jouve and all the rest in bills of exchange on Bordeaux, payable the 12th or the 13th of February and made out to me, if my cousins cannot give me enough to complete payment without inconvenience. I have heard of a banker in Paris who handles our business and to whom we could appeal confidentially.

I have already told you that it is useless to solicit help from the minister of the Merchant Marine, unless he would retract the refusal he already gave. Our arrangements must be made with the captain of the vessel on which we are to sail, and you know that once the agreement is made we must pay. Nearly all our money will be eaten up en route, but God who has willed this work will sustain it. As it is part of his plan, however, that we should help ourselves by every possible means, I recommend this work to you and beg you to contribute to it as long as you live. You will have the consolation of helping in the salvation of souls who would be lost if they were not given spiritual food and sometimes material food to attract them. You will do so, less for the friendship that unites us, the bonds of which are so dear to me, than for the blood of Jesus Christ that is often ineffectual because of our lack of zeal in helping enterprises aimed at winning souls.

Let me know at once if you can do something about the black vestment; there is no time to have it dyed. I believe I have already asked you

---

327 *Copies of letters of Philippine Duchesne to Mrs. de Rollin and a few others*, No. 3; *Cahier, Lettres à Mme de Rollin*, p. 4-6; *Lettres dactylographiées*. C C-VII 2) c Duchesne to her family and lay people, Box 5.

to inform my cousins, especially Augustin and Camille [Jordan][328] about what is happening to me. But I stress the fact that my sisters should not be told before I write to them myself.

Tell Mrs. Teisseire also that the departure is advanced. If you have an opportunity for Valence, I beg you to send to Mrs. de Mauduit the notarized statement I am sending you that shows that she no longer owes me anything by virtue of what she has already paid.

Good bye, my good Cousin, my affection for you will endure always and in every place. I am in the Sacred Heart,

Philippine Duchesne

January 28, 1818
1 bill of exchange 2000
2 of 1500..3000
3 of 1000..2000 *(sic)*
1 of Messrs. Perier..2000
1 from M. Maillucheau ....1212, 10 c.
What Aug. Perier has for Mrs. de Mauduit,
from Mrs. de Rollin...5000

**Letter 73   L. 4 to Mrs. de Rollin
to Mrs. Teisseire, c/o Mrs. Bergasse[329]
to be forwarded, please, to Mrs. de Rollin in Paris[330]**

SS. C. J. M.

No. 4
Monday [end of January] 1818

My dearest Friend,

My two trips to the police commissioner made me realize more keenly than ever how much I am obliged to you for all the long trips you have been making to render service to me in this continually bad

---

328 During their childhood, Josephine and Philippine shared many activities (lessons, reading, games) with Augustin Perier and Camille Jordan.
329 Mrs. Teisseire was her cousin, née Marine Perier. Mrs. Bergasse is Amelie (1800-1881), daughter of Mrs. Teisseire, who married Joseph Bergasse (1788-1861) January 20, 1818, in Paris.
330 *Copies of letters of Philippine Duchesne to Mrs. de Rollin and a few others,* No. 4; *Cahier, Lettres à Mme de Rollin,* pp. 6-7; *Lettres dactylographiées.* C-VII 2) c Duchesne to her family and lay people, Box 5.

weather. I owed you my return to Sainte-Marie, and I feel that I owe you everything just now.

I thought there would be three of us to go to the commissioner, but our sister from Amiens will arrive here only on Thursday; there will not be sufficient time to secure her passport here, so she will have to join the two in Bordeaux. They tell me that the consuls in Bayonne and Bordeaux continually issue passports for Spain; this will be the solution if we do not obtain here assured permission to leave the Kingdom, which I beg you to procure. I think that if it will be necessary to go to the prefecture of the police, we could manage without the help of my kind relatives, who might be inconvenienced. Let me know this evening or tomorrow morning, or even send me our papers. You could entrust them to Mr. Ricolet, the grocer, who lives in the same building as Mrs. Bergasse, to have them sent to us.

Tell me whether you did not suffer greatly from the cold yesterday. I did not pay attention to the fact that you did not have proper covering, and you, you take such good care of me.

I am all yours,

Philippine

Loving greetings to Mrs. Teisseire and her daughters.

Letter 74　　　　L. 5 to Mrs. de Rollin

No. 5

Religious of the Sacred Heart, rue des Postes N° 40[331]

Request for three passports for three religious who are going from Paris to Bordeaux, where they will embark for New Orleans:

Mothers	Octavie Berthold	age	28
	Catherine Lamarre		38
	Philippine Duchesne		48

Request that permission be delivered to the Prefect of Bordeaux to grant passports to religious who are also to embark for New Orleans:

---

331 *Copies of letters of Philippine Duchesne to Mrs. de Rollin and a few others*, No. 5; *Cahier, Lettres à Mme de Rollin*, p. 8. C-VII 2) c Duchesne to her family and lay people, Box 5.

Mothers	Eugenie Audé	age	26
	Marguerite Manteau		38

Name of the vessel: The *Rebecca*.

Letter 75 **L. 6 to Mrs. de Rollin**

No. 6[332]

Reminder of the promise of a letter of recommendation to the ambassador of France to the United States for Mother Philippine Duchesne and four other religious of the Society of the Sacred Heart who, at the request of the bishop of Louisiana, are going to his diocese to open a house for the instruction of young ladies and of poor children.

Letter 76 **L. 46 to Mrs. Jouve, Lyon**

Paris, February 1 [1818][333]

My dearest Sister,

I am speaking to you about Mother Bigeu, for the foundation about which I have spoken to you will probably be made soon, but I will not be in Paris then. I am leaving perhaps within a week. Bordeaux will be my first stopping place, and if God places no obstacles, Louisiana will be the last. I have had the opportunity here to meet Bishop Dubourg, who is the bishop of Louisiana; for a long time I have wanted to confide in him my desires to instruct infidels, desires long opposed by my superiors and confessors, but finally Providence has arranged everything for the accomplishment of these desires. Bishop Dubourg has shown me much kindness, and we will live in the same city with him. It was agreed that six of us would leave in the month of May; but the earlier departure of a ship, whose captain is well known, the departure of one of the vicars general and other missionaries has made us leave sooner than expected. Unless there are obstacles, I shall leave France this month.

---

332 *Copies of letters of Philippine Duchesne to Mrs. de Rollin and a few others*, No. 6; *Cahier, Lettres à Mme de Rollin*, p. 8. C-VII 2) c Duchesne to her family and lay people, Box 5.

333 Copies: *Cahier, Lettres de la Mère Duchesne à sa famille*, pp. 83-84; *Lettres dactylographiées*. C-VII 2) c Duchesne to her family and lay people, Box 5.

But in leaving I shall carry with me my affections, my memories of my kind sisters and their children. You will pray for me, as I will for you; and at the moment when I am leaving everything to work for the salvation of a few souls, I pray most earnestly that you will cling to the *one thing necessary*; tell Henry and my Amelie the same thing; I have no time to write to them. One does not make such a move without having a great deal to do.

I am and will always be totally yours in the Sacred Heart of Jesus,
Philippine Duchesne

P.S. Many tender greetings to my brother-in-law. All in the Perier family are well; the wedding is over. Good Mother Barat understands that after Constance, Josephine will take her place in Grenoble. The latest news of Euphrosine has not made me happy; she shows perfect virtue and resignation; be quite sure that she is being cared for with affection and receiving all kinds of little attentions. God is allowing that they have no success; we must see only his will.

Letter 77   L. 6 to Mrs. de Mauduit at Crest

[February 1818][334]

My dearest Friend,

I have received from Cousin Augustin [Perier] the sum of 1514 francs, for which I enclose the receipt. I have given Mrs. de Rollin the contract made between us, and she will hand it over to you at the first opportunity.[335]

I see her rather often; the wedding is over and everyone is happy. I also see Mrs. Teisseire who is kindness personified.

I have confided to these two dear cousins the project that I am now going to tell you about. For a long time, a very strong and definite attraction has drawn me to the teaching of infidels. I thought even of going to China, but that was not practicable because women cannot appear in public there. God has listened to my prayers and has let me find nearer home and at less cost the happiness for which I have been waiting. In Paris I met the bishop of Louisiana, and it is in his diocese

---

334 Copies: *Cahier, Lettres de la Mère Duchesne à sa famille*, pp. 78-80; *Lettres dactylographiées*. C-VII 2) c Duchesne to her family and lay people, Box 5.

335 The financial agreements mentioned in Letter No. 4 to Mrs. de Mauduit, July 1817.

that I am going to work at teaching Indians and with some companions to open a house of our Society. The departure was set for May 1, but other missionaries are going this month on a well-known ship with a good captain, so it has been decided that we shall go also. I am leaving Paris on Monday; we will be only five this time, but in September there will be another group.

I hope you will give me news of yourself. I ask you to send me a supply of seeds of all the kinds you have, labeled with the time for sowing indicated. The ground is so fertile in the place where we will be living that cattle are hidden in the high prairie grasses. If you can send this little shipment overland, address it to *Mr. Caseaux, c/o Mr. Johnston, façade des Chartreux à Bordeaux, for the bishop of Louisiana*; inside the packet, put a letter saying it is for me.

Believe me, my much loved Sister, that we will always be united; you, your daughters, your husband, your son[336] will be continually in my prayers. Tell Amelie [de Mauduit] to remember her first fervor and never to forget the one thing necessary.

Goodbye, my dearest Sister, have a Mass said at Saint Regis,

Philippine

Letter 78   L. 4 to Mother Maillucheau

SS. C. J. et M.

[Paris, February 4, 1818.
On the point of departing for Louisiana][337]

My good Mother,

I received your letter with gratitude for the zeal in seeing to sending our effects and the constant interest you show me; actually your greatest joy is, justly without doubt, to see devotion to the Sacred Heart being carried across the sea. It has done marvelous things in China; pray that the same will be true in Louisiana.

God is showing himself clearly; everyone is now congratulating me and blessing the undertaking; several are saying, "I envy your lot."

---

336 Amédée de Mauduit du Plessis (1790-1875) would be a general, commandant of the *département* of the Ain, officer of the Legion of Honor and knight of Saint-Louis. His brother Adrien died in 1817 at the age of twelve.

337 Original autograph, C-VII 2) c Duchesne to RSCJ and Children, Box 4. Copy: C-VII 2) c Duchesne-Varia, Box 9, *Cahier Y, Lettres de la Mère Duchesne*, pp. 1-4.

It is truly to be desired; Octavie has gained much by the departure, for it has allowed her to make her final vows just one year after the first. Eugenie Audé will perhaps be favored also; she arrived this evening, even though no one thought it possible that she could be here on Sunday. It seems that God made her fly. She left everyone weak and suffering in Quimper; they are asking for help.

In your last letter you told me to give our mother 50 francs from the 400 that you sent beyond the required amount for the *dixième*, but you are mistaken: it is short by 60 francs.[338] Since the new houses cannot yet send the *dixième*, the expenses to which it is applied exceed the sum. The foundation we are going to attempt will cost this house a great deal, but everyone has interest in it; it has revived Mother Bigeu, who is better or at least appears to be so, for she has said nothing about her health.

Our mother has been very suffering, not sleeping. I don't know if Octavie prayed, but the night before her profession our mother slept straight through the night and could get up and be at the ceremony, presided over by Father Varin.

Mother Grosier has gone to be superior again in Poitiers; she took with her Mother Brigitte who had accompanied Mother de Charbonnel,[339] who is now back in her place as treasurer general. I have handed over to her all the accounts.[340] I have permission to go to Montmartre tomorrow with Octavie; we will go to the church of the Foreign Missions to hear Mass at the altar of Saint Xavier.

Only 540 francs were sent for Mother de Crouzas instead of 600.

Mr. Jouve told me he had paid for the last semester; I had him pay our debt; he owes 450 per year for his daughter, on January 1 and July 1. If you have already sent …

(The last page is missing.)

---

338 The *dixième* is the sum based on the income from the pupils that each house sends to the motherhouse.
339 Catherine Emilie de Charbonnel, RSCJ (1774-1854), entered the house of Amiens November 15, 1803, made her vows November 21, 1804, and replaced Sophie Barat as teacher of the higher classes. In 1810, she went to Poitiers as director of studies. From 1815 until her death, she fulfilled the offices of assistant general and treasurer general. According to the Journal of Paris, Philippine assisted her in Paris from 1816 to 1818: "Mother Barat, seeing that the absence of Mother Duchesne would leave a large hole in the house, brought from Poitiers Mother de Charbonnel, superior at Poitiers, to take up the position of treasurer general that Mother Duchesne performed in her absence." *JP*. 1818, written by Henriette Girard.
340 Philippine had assumed the charge of general treasurer during Mother de Charbonnel's absence from Paris.

Letter 79   L. 3 to Euphrosine Jouve

SS. C. J. et M.

[February 1818][341]

I am leaving Paris, my good Aloysia, and soon I shall be leaving France. We shall meet in heaven at least, if on earth we do not have this consolation. Offer your sufferings for us and pray for us.

Today we made a pilgrimage with Octavie [Berthold] to obtain new protectors. We visited Our Lady at Saint-Sulpice and the statue of Our Lady of Saint Francis de Sales. We also went to the church of the Foreign Missions to hear Mass at the altar of Saint Francis Xavier, and we had Communion from the hand of a bishop from China. From there we went to Montmartre.

Our mother is better.

I learn that you are suffering; let your ills be your prayer for me and for our abandoned children. I will offer for you the eloquent prayers of the poor. Envy my happiness and enjoy your own. God wills to separate us; he will reunite us in his Heart.

Goodbye, dear, good Sister.

Philippine

A thousand messages to mothers, sisters and the pupils.
I have told my sisters and my brother about my departure.

[On the reverse:]
for Euphrosine Jouve
Sainte-Marie d'En-Haut

Letter 80   L. 4 to Mother Barat
(following Octavie Berthold's letter)

[From Octavie Berthold]

February 13, 1818[342]

The mission to Louisiana, among all the miracles it has wrought, has made one of the most striking: it is that Reverend Mother Duchesne

---

341 Original autograph and copy: C-VII 2) c Duchesne to RSCJ and Children, Box 4.
342 Original autograph, C-VII 2) c Duchesne to Barat, Box 2. Copy: *Cahier Y*, C-VII 2) c Writings, List-Varia, Box 9, *Letters of Mother Duchesne*, pp. 4-8.

gives us her blessing and embraces us when we wish. She takes even too much care of us; but we think, Sister Eugenie and I, that it is our responsibility to watch over her health. Have the kindness, my good Mother, to tell her to obey us on this point; she does so much that she is going to ruin her constitution. Her desires grow by the day.

We are amusing ourselves together in advance: saying, (what) if they chase us out of Louisiana as adventurers and if we are sent back to France like packets of dirty linen that are thrown into the bottom of the vessel. We are laughing about everything, so much so that if something untoward happens[343] we will not be surprised.

February 14

Here I am at the end of my paper, but I must speak to you about our holy Sister Marguerite who asked me to offer you *(word missing)* and her gratitude for the mission you have allowed her. She has been with us since Poitiers where we met her.

We went to introduce ourselves to the archbishop of Bordeaux, Archbishop d'Aviau. We were presented by Father Boyer,[344] the superior of the house, who looked intently at all three of us, but at Sister Eugenie and me in an extraordinary manner. After examining our appearance for almost a quarter of an hour, he said to the archbishop: "I have scrutinized these souls at depth, and I perceive nothing but inalterable calm." "And joy," added our mother. He spoke to us with extreme kindness, and the archbishop gave us a fatherly blessing. Father Barat came this morning to hear our confessions; he is so good; I was expecting nothing less from the reverend brother of the one to whom my heart turns so often.

Receive, Reverend Mother, my apologies and my gratitude, and believe me always your child.

Octavie

I ask your pardon for having written so badly in the first part of my letter, but I was so cold that I could not hold my pen.

---

343 Cf. Antoine Boissieu, SJ, *The Holy Gospel of Jesus Christ, explained in Meditations for each day of the year*, ch. 2: "Thus, no matter what happens to distress me, in whatever state you wish me to be, I wish to say everywhere with David, *in Domino confido*, I trust completely in the Lord," Librairie Jacquenod et Rusand, Lyon, 1786, p. 210.

344 Father Joseph Boyer (1762-1819), born in Rodez in 1781, accompanied his bishop, Jérôme Marie Champion de Cicé, named to the archbishopric of Bordeaux. Director of the Seminary of Saint-Raphaël in 1789, he refused to take the oath of the Civil Constitution of the Clergy. In 1791, he founded the community of the *"Dames Vincent"* or "Sisters of Notre-Dame," of which he was superior. After Archbishop de Cicé was exiled, he became administrator of the diocese (1794-1802), then vicar general of Archbishop d'Aviau.

[On the reverse, a letter of Philippine:]

My very dear Mother,

My heart was less sore yesterday. Good Father Barat came to see us and we went to confession, all five of us; I had great need of it. As the departure will not take place until sometime between the 20th and the 25th, we are going to make a little retreat under his direction. Our voyage will be longer and more expensive than we thought at first. It would have been impossible for women to travel by the route Bishop Dubourg took; he suffered a great deal and passed through routes known only to animals, besides the cost of 4000 francs per person.

Yesterday we saw the archbishop of Bordeaux and Father Boyer who gave us the best welcome and wants to come to see us. Father Vincent,[345] who was with him, for what reason I don't know, did not want to see us lodging with Mother Vincent.

Mr. Dubourg (the bishop's brother) is waiting for me. I am at your feet,

Philippine

[On the reverse:]
To Mother
Mother Barat Superior of the
Religious of the Sacred Heart
Rue des Postes n° 40
Paris

Letter 81   **To the Boarders of Sainte-Marie d'En-Haut**

SS. C. J. et M.

Bordeaux, February 15, 1818[346]
To the young ladies of the boarding school of Sainte-Marie d'En-Haut

---

345 It seems likely that this is Father Pierre Vincent, born in Bordeaux December 16, 1779. Named parish priest of Saint-Laurent (Médoc), March 10, 1817, he remained there until his death in 1850.
346 Original autograph and copy, C-VII 2) c Duchesne to RSCJ and Children, Box 4. Another copy: C-VII 2) c Writings, Duchesne-Varia, Box 9, *Lettres de la Mère Duchesne, Cahier Y*, pp. 12-16.

My very good Friends and dear Children,

At this moment when I am leaving everything, almost as if I were going to die, since it is almost certain that I shall never see you again on this earth, as well as so many mothers, sisters, relatives and friends, I believe I am authorized to ask a great deal of God with the same confidence that Saint Peter had when he said to Jesus Christ: "We have left everything for you; what will be our reward?" Ah! That reward that I beg for from him is the great, the ineffable consolation of learning that you are all fervent in his love, that he has you doing good works and that by that you are tending to the solid piety whose happy result will be enjoyment of God in this world through grace and in the next in the state of glory. Yes, across the immense space that is soon going to separate us, my heart will still seek you and form wishes for your happiness.

If I can contribute to it by having the interesting young people who will become the flock of Jesus Christ pray for you, I will not neglect so strong a means that my heart dictates. When I see myself in the midst of a troop of simple, innocent souls, I will say: "Let us pray for these children whom I have left and whose dear memory has added so much to the cost of my sacrifice; let us pray for our first benefactors; they do not know you and already they are praying for your conversion and contributing to procuring it by the gifts they destined for you. Nothing uncouth or merely human has sullied their offering; they would not know the teachers and friends who would distribute them and would acknowledge them. They have done everything for God, for the salvation of your souls." How much then will they be urged to pray for you!

I hope to give you details of our establishment in the New World, if God places no obstacle. I ought to have left today with my four companions, but there is a few days' delay. It gives me time to write to you and to get you to promise to continue to set aside things that can be rewards and means of attracting the little Indians we will be instructing. I hope to see them in two or three months; our voyage by New Orleans will be much longer than by Baltimore but less dangerous. We will go up the Mississippi on steamboats that are built like small vessels with rooms in which there are beds. We will be there twenty to twenty-five days. These boats are driven by steam.

In the uncertainty we have of success and of the results of our voyage, pray very much for us.

I am in the Sacred Heart yours devotedly,

Philippine Duchesne

Letter 82   L. 5 to Mother Maillucheau

SS. C. J. et M.

[Bordeaux, about February 15, 1818][347]

My very good Mother,

I have been touched by the sensitivity of your last letters, no less by the mercy of God in my regard; even so I am in a hurry to board the ship that will take me to the goal of my desires. I can leave any time, or there can be a delay; that depends on the weather.

I leave in France many cherished objects; I will hold them dear forever by the strongest bonds; they seem to tighten even more when, through a benefit I owe to the Society, I will have the joy of contributing to its spread in new lands and to the flourishing of the devotion to his Heart. You were wishing for the same lot for yourself; God is employing you usefully where you are, and as for me who could not do anything here, he is trying to have me do something elsewhere, like persons who are changed from one house to another in order to have them profit from different trials. Ask that I may not still be unfaithful.

My companions keep up their courage and are the envy of many, even to Father Boyer, the vicar general; he said he would like to go if he were younger. He is showing us much kindness, as is Archbishop d'Aviau, whom we have been to see and who has visited us. Today again we have been to his Mass, which he said for us.

The fathers are true to form; Father Debrosse[348] is willing to take charge of receiving and sending our letters when there are ship movements. You may, therefore, send them to him, by opportunity especially, but do not give this address to anyone else for fear of imprudence or indiscretion. The two trunks, the small suitcase and the vine plants have arrived; the charge is about 170 francs. Please, I beg you, in sending the painting do not use the address I gave you, but this one: to *Mrs. Fournier, c/o Mrs. Caseaux, rue de l'église, près de Saint-Surin, N° 7.*

---

347 Original autograph and copy: C-VII 2) c Duchesne to RSCJ and Children, Box 4.
348 Robert Debrosse (1768-1848), SJ, born at Châtel-Chéhéry (Ardennes), March 23, 1768. Imprisoned under the Reign of Terror, he was ordained a priest in Liège, in 1798. Affiliated to the Fathers of the Faith, and close to the Jesuits who were suppressed in France, he was, in 1803, superior of the college of Belley, where Lamartine was a pupil. He entered the Society of Jesus when it was re-established in 1814; he was superior in Bordeaux, then at Sainte-Anne d'Auray, Billom, Paray-le-Monial and Laval. He was the uncle of Rosalie Debrosse, who arrived with Mother Barat in Grenoble on December 13, 1804. He died in Laval on February 18, 1848.

Father Debrosse is too far from the port, but small packages may be sent to him by opportunity. His address is the minor seminary. I was hoping to have another letter from Father Rambaud, to whom I wrote from Paris; I waited for it in vain. Please tell him that and recommend me to his prayers.

I am filled with gratitude for all the prayers you have had said for me; you will have all the merit of our mission and we, all the danger to soul and body.

Mr. Marange has had the kindness to give us wine for the journey; I owe that attention to you. After several days of waiting, I finally was able to embrace Mrs. Marange and Miss Emeline; they are the souls of kindness; I have never had a warmer welcome. Elisa was not able to come but wrote me a charming letter, and they are going to give us preserves and apples, the best fruit for satisfying thirst.

In so much attentiveness given with such heart, I have easily recognized the heart of my Mother Therese. We must see each other again. I am with deep respect, good Mother, your old daughter and always sister and friend.

Philippine

Letter 83 L. 7 to Mmes Bergasse, Teisseire and de Rollin, Place Saint-Sulpice, Paris

SS. C. J. M.

No. 7
1818[349]

My dearest Cousins,

It would have been a great satisfaction for me to have written to you just as soon as we reached Bordeaux to try to express my undying love for you and all the gratitude I feel. How much these sentiments have increased during the past weeks, if increase were possible, seeing all the trouble you have gone to for me, all the important services you have rendered, all your tender solicitude. When my thoughts revert to what I am leaving in France, I put them aside, being intimately convinced that I have desired only one thing, that is, to answer God's call and abandon

---

349 *Copies of letters of Philippine Duchesne to Mrs. de Rollin and a few others,* No. 7; *Cahier, Lettres à Mme de Rollin,* pp. 9-11; *Lettres dactylographiées.* C-VII 2) c Duchesne to her family and lay people, Box 5.

myself to his Providence; so the voyage and the trials ahead will never be as great as the help I may confidently expect from him.

So far our journey has been pleasant. As the ship is not yet ready to sail, we are making a few days of retreat. I have gone out only to call on the archbishop and the sister of my future bishop. She has made the voyage we are undertaking six times, so she knows exactly what we need. As she is very zealous about her brother's mission, she has taken charge of the arrangement of our berths, and with her brother she is directing our embarkation.

I have learned from them that the *piastre* is very costly now, being much sought after for trade with India; they are drawing only a few for us and converting our bills of exchange into other papers on Baltimore and New Orleans. They assure us that navigation on the Mississippi becomes easier every day. There are always about a dozen steamboats traveling up and down, and they are almost as large and commodious as an ocean-going vessel. They have informed the Ursulines in New Orleans of our arrival, and we shall lodge with them or with relatives of our bishop.

The letters to the Consul of France will be very necessary for us to be able to get our effects through customs promptly and for a protection in this country where we will be so far from any support. I have just received the two new letters of recommendation to the ambassador and the consul, and I put aside the first one to the ambassador for fear of a mistake.

For this last attention on the part of Mrs. de Rollin, I can add only that she has already deserved my life-long gratitude, so in piling up so many kindnesses on our behalf, she is accumulating for herself an inexhaustible treasure of pure joys in this life and of the merits of charity in the next.

The letters from my sisters are a weight on my heart that I pray God to lighten, as I beg him to alleviate the hardships in their lives. But the cross is for everyone and only those who know how to carry it are happy.

Remember me, I beg you, to all my kind relatives and especially to my dear Amelie [Jouve] and Henriette [Lebrument].

The ship leaves Bordeaux Tuesday to go as far as Pauillac, but I don't know what day we will go aboard. It cannot be long now.

I am with deepest and closest affection all yours,
Philippine Duchesne

February 17 [1818]

My companions send you their deep respects. Not remembering Mrs. de Rollin's address, I ask pardon of Mrs. Bergasse for the liberty I have taken.

Letter 84   L. 7 to Mrs. de Mauduit, Crest

Bordeaux, February 18, 1818[350]

My dearest Sister,

The bishop of Louisiana, in care of whom you addressed your letter to me, is in his diocese; and I am still in Bordeaux, where the ship in which we are to travel is leaving in only a few days.

I knew your heart well enough to be sure that my departure would cause you sorrow, but I was also sure enough of your courage and faith and the judgment you would pass on my motives, which have overcome the opposition of my superiors. I knew also in advance that my decision would not alter in the least the loving union with you that has been the joy of my life and that now is adding to the cost of my sacrifice. No, to expose oneself to dangers is nothing in comparison to giving up a tender and holy friendship; but, no, it will endure, grow stronger and increase just because of the detachment; and God who is always generous will give us graces that will make its value infinite. My prayers will be with you always, and if God blesses my efforts, you and your family will have a large share in the work of our inspiring mission. God has been drawing me to it for many years and has granted me the grace after many prayers. The guidance of divine Providence is so admirable in the manner of their accomplishment that all holy souls see the finger of God in it.

The bishop of Louisiana has shown me a fatherly interest, and I find myself at ease with him as if I had known him all my life. He thought it best to go ahead of us to prepare the way, and he has promised to look after our interests as if they were his own. We five will leave with his vicar general, another ecclesiastic and a nephew of our bishop who knows New Orleans, where we will go at first. We will be able to continue to study English with him; it is so necessary, although we must still speak French.

We are lodged here with a fervent community of religious, and in New Orleans we hope to be with the Ursulines. The same ship that took

---

350 Copies: *Cahier, Lettres de la Mère Duchesne à sa famille*, pp. 87-90; *Lettres dactylographiées*. C-VII 2) c Duchesne to her family and lay people, Box 5.

nine of them last year is the one we are taking; they made the crossing in thirty-five days and had Mass almost every day. In September it will leave with more of our nuns if we have need of recruits. In any case, don't think any more about the seeds for which I asked you; all I could want arrived from Grenoble.

Mesdames de Rollin, Perier and Teisseire, as well as Augustin [Perier] and Camille [Jordan] have shown me every possible mark of affection. They have obtained letters of introduction to the consuls of France and to the ambassador to the United States, where our mission is situated. The vicar general [Father Martial] and the bishop's brother and sister have arranged everything regarding our embarkation; we are taking advantage of the delay for a retreat; the departure date is not yet certain and cannot be predicted because of the winds, but I will write to Mrs. Jouve at the last minute, who like you has written me the most affectionate letter.

The first missionaries from Rome are dead, three or four of them, victims of their zeal during an epidemic. We shall live in the same place as a holy Roman Lazarist, named Father d'Andreis [sic]; he may be our confessor. He will be in charge of a seminary and consequently will remain at the same post. The trip up the Mississippi has been made much easier by the invention of steamboats, which are run by steam from a continually burning fire. They offer the same space and conveniences as sailing vessels.

I am so grateful to you for the Mass at Saint Regis; nothing could have made me happier.

Goodbye, then, my good Sister, our friendship is too strong to be weakened by distance; I will always love you tenderly, my beloved Sister, and your husband and his sister and your children. Remember me to all of them and have them pray for me; I will do so for you constantly in the generous Heart of Jesus Christ.

Philippine

I have been to see the archbishop of Bordeaux; I ought to be a saint: I have been so much in the company of saints.

Letter 85   L. 5 to Mother Barat

Reverend Mother Barat
SS. C. J. et M.

[Bordeaux] February 18, 1818[351]

---

351 Original autograph, C-VII 2) c Duchesne to Barat, Box 2. Cf. J. de Charry, II 1, L. 87; Hogg,

My very good Mother,

We are in retreat; I have seen no one about the embarkation, and I know no more about the date fixed for our departure than I did in my last letter; have the kindness to answer by return mail; I have the hope of receiving your letter. You should have had several from me, and Mother Bigeu, an answer, I beg you, on the subject of day pupils, whether we can admit them,[352] and permission for the Office of the Dead every six months.

At last I have received your letter and those of my sisters. How grateful we are for this proof of your maternal love. Mother Bigeu's remembrance of each one was equally pleasing. I have delivered her letter to Father Barat; we see him nearly every day, and he hears our confessions on alternate days, but is unable to give us talks. He says that by evening he is exhausted; he has so much to do. However, this week he gave two instructions to some very fervent Carmelites who have just established their convent nearby. Father Wrints is giving them a retreat. I was struck by the emaciated appearance of this good father (Father Wrints). He is a skeleton surmounted by a head on fire, so much so that one fears he has a serious malady of the nose, at least that is how he strikes me. Father Jennesseaux has only passed through; he has departed for Forcalquier.[353]

I have been to Mrs. Fournier's house, Bishop Dubourg's sister, who had arranged for rooms for us and hired a servant and someone to look after our meals; all near the *Réunion*,[354] where she wanted us to go. But I cannot do this because of the retreat. She has also taken charge of our beds aboard ship and speaks now of comforts, namely nourishing things to take with us for the needs of our bodies.

As for wine, Mr. Marange has kindly taken charge of it.[355] Yesterday Father Boyer paid us a long visit; he is showing much interest in us and predicts great consolations. He is to give us some relics. I don't know if it is he who would be the most opposed to the merger;[356] I

---

pp. 23-28; Ch. Paisant, pp. 80-84.
352 The admission of day pupils to the boarding schools was refused then. This rule was abrogated very soon.
353 Nicolas Jennesseaux (1769-1842), SJ, former Father of the Faith, was rector of the College of Amiens. Having entered the Society of Jesus in 1814, he was then rector of the minor seminary of Forcalquier (Basses Alpes, today Alpes de Haute-Provence).
354 The "*Réunion* of the Sacred Heart of Jesus" was a religious house in Bordeaux, not to be confused with the "Dames Vincent" who gave hospitality to Philippine and her companions.
355 A relative of Mother Therese Maillucheau who lived in Saint-André de Cubzac, north of Bordeaux.
356 Here the reference is to the union of the "Dames Vincent" with the Society of the Sacred Heart, which would take place July 20, 1825.

suspect rather that it is Mother Vincent who clings to her own customs, I believe, more Jesuit than we. If the government changed, she would also be anxious about the fate of her mother, sisters, brothers and niece. She and her sisters, who are most edifying, could not be more attentive and charitable to us.

But all this kindness that surrounds me is neither you nor my sisters, and although it sustains my strength and even the ardor of my desires, even so I find myself upon arriving here in a state of anguish, of hardness, of darkness that made me dwell, when entering the church of Saint Andrew, on the words, *O bona Crux, diu desiderata et jam concupiscenti animae praeparata.*[357] My sisters, too, have had their moments of weakness, which I observed and supported doubly, while perceiving the many lacks that render the goodness of God in choosing us all the more astonishing.

Your brother gives a good push forward to any of us who lag on the way to perfection.

I always fear Octavie's self-love and heedlessness. Hardly were we two blocks from the place where we had left everything, when our hearts should have been absorbed by great thoughts, she took out of her pocket her English notebook to display it before me and those gentlemen; I made her close it and a few tears flowed. I shall be more firm with Eugenie who does not yet have what is needed for this work; she read me with great satisfaction an account she had written about our trip; it was childish and full of light-hearted banter. I asked her if that was the style of our fathers, and told her that you had disapproved of Olympie's[358] account, etc. She rewrote her letter on her own, but she did not read it to me.

We had agreed that during the retreat we would have one recreation in the evening. Catherine felt the need of talking in the morning and took recreation with one and then two of the others; some unseemly things were said, but she felt so bad that she came to tell me about it. I am afraid that Marguerite has never been truly tested and that she has been too highly praised. But all these faults are less serious than mine. I wish I could reassure you about myself so as to diminish your anxieties. But how would I do that?

---

357 "O good cross, how I have longed for you. Finally, here you are, offered to my heart's desire." Ancient litany for the feast of Saint Andrew, November 30, Second Vespers, Antiphon of the *Magnificat.*
358 Olympie Rombau (1797-1874), RSCJ, accompanied Mother Bigeu on the foundation of Quimper in 1817. Philippine is probably alluding to the style of the *Journal de voyage* composed by Olympie on that occasion.

Octavie was saying that we were too well received everywhere, that we had no crosses. She was more afraid of mosquitoes attacking us on the river than of anything else.

I would like to write to our good Fathers Joseph [Varin] and Perreau. Meanwhile a thousand respects.

My precautions to avoid letters from my family have been useless; friendship is inventive, and I needed this little extra cross. I have not yet written to Mrs. de Rollin, and I am distressed about it, but as your brother did not think I ought to go to the prefect, I don't know how to tell her that I have not made use of her letters;[359] later I shall arrange that better. I must tell her that I was waiting until the retreat was over, and we were ready to depart.

For the information of travelers, it is necessary to be more and more convinced that it is better to take care of arrangements oneself. I arrived at the stagecoach too late to avoid the weighing of all our small packages, which had been sent by cart and arrived before we did. Everything was put immediately in the imperial,[360] even the basket of food, which I had difficulty getting back. And how could I be assured of the correctness of the weight? I was expecting to pay 80 francs for the bundle and the chest; we were allowed only 50 kilos gratis, and we paid, besides our seats, more than 200 francs,[361] at a rate of 11 sols per pound. This is why it is so unsatisfactory to go by stagecoach; all complaints are useless; they just seized the paper from Paris. Besides the outrageous price, there is the question of distances; you get out before the Garonne, and everything that you cannot carry with you is put onto a cart and taken to an office very far away. It is delivered only several hours later.

We went on foot to Mother Vincent's house; she had sent a sister to meet us. We would have suffered from the cold and were afraid of rain, had we waited for a cab. I did not lose sight of our two porters, who jumped onto the boat in spite of us and left their ropes so as not to lose our packages. I did not trust them at all. But in the end everything arrived, even the trunks from Grenoble. I am going to find out the cost of shipping from Paris; at present I don't know anything about it.

---

359 Once again, Mrs. Josephine Savoye de Rollin used her connections to facilitate the realization of Philippine's plans. From 1815, her husband was deputy from the Isère, after having been prefect of the Eure, of the Lower Seine and of Deux-Nèthes (Province of Antwerp, Belgium, today) from 1805 to 1814.
360 The upper level of the stagecoach.
361 This sum seems exorbitant, for the wages of a workman were from 1 to 5 francs per day at this time. Philippine had to have recourse to her family to pay such costs.

We have eaten at an inn only once; the horrible looks and unpleasant smiles at Octavie gave me pause, and a bad supper for four of us cost 15 francs. At the next stop soup and an omelet cost us 12 francs; they had asked 15 but ungraciously reduced the price. Where we have not had to sleep, we have taken only coffee with milk, which has satisfied us completely, and some little things from the basket served for dinner. We supped very well at Barbézieux for 6 francs for five persons and the tip. We had no difficulty waiting until noon the next day. Our basket arrived in Bordeaux still full, for it had been so well provided; it is true that in Poitiers they replenished it. We are all well. However, Father Barat makes Octavie eat in the morning; he takes great care of her.

Your second letter [of February 13, 1818] has just been given to us and fills us with joy.

I am at your feet for my whole life, your submissive daughter.

Philippine

Letter 86   **L. 6 to Mother Barat**

SS. C. J. et M.

[Bordeaux] February 20, 1818[362]

My good Reverend Mother,

I have just received the packet of letters of introduction and am writing immediately to Mrs. de Rollin. As I know her and was very sure that she would not forget me, I waited for them to arrive to write to her. She has every right to my trust.

We find here in Mrs. Fournier an equally zealous and active woman; she has made the voyage we are undertaking six times and knows everything about it; only I find her a little over cautious. My bent would be to have as little as Saint Francis Xavier, whose poverty I envy, and to leave our health to Saint Francis Regis. But you do not want us to neglect human means; they are all provided for, and I am very sure of doing the will of God in obeying you and following the advice of your brother, our good father to whom I am submitting everything, and he enters into all the details (even about sugar). I have laughed with him about Mrs. Fournier's list of comforts; it will be sent to you by some

---

362 Original autograph, C-VII 2) c Duchesne to Barat, Box 2. Cf. J. de Charry, II 1, L. 88; Hogg, pp. 28-30; Ch. Paisant, pp. 84-85.

opportunity in order to calm your motherly anxiety. I have greater need for calm about your health; you tell me nothing specific about it. Your letters are always balm to our spirits; they are going to form the second volume of my collection and will be all the more necessary to me on account of the enormous distance that is going to separate us.

We are all steadfast; however God has begun the trials. The retreat was very difficult; I am hard as a rock; my head is full and pressured. One cannot imagine the wearisome details of a voyage such as ours; there is no end to it. Our baggage, sent on Saturday before Quinquagesima [January 31], has not yet arrived. We wrote to Mr. Menglar. Mother Vincent's care of us is unflagging; nevertheless, we feel that we are a burden and a source of trouble. All this increases our desire to leave. She relies on Providence, all the while telling us that no one gives her anything, that bread cost her more than 3000 francs this year, and the pupils paid 3000 francs less. I admire her virtue and her daughters'; she has six novices and four postulants of good dispositions; only one is for domestic service [lay sister]. Seven of them make night adoration; they sleep in the same dormitory near the tribune where they make an hour's adoration in turn; as a result no one is afraid, and each has to go only a few steps to wake the next person; they replace one another every hour. Life is austere; truffles at almost every meal and fish, rice and peas; but they are in good health, except Mother Vincent who coughs and does not take care of herself. I have already made great progress in changing my diet, as I had never eaten seafood before.

I am at your feet, good Mother, your unworthy daughter.

Philippine

My companions are well; only Octavie has her stomach trouble and so does not fast. I beg our mothers and sisters to receive our affectionate remembrances in Our Lord.

[On the reverse:]
To Mother
Mother Barat
Rue des Postes n° 40
Paris

Letter 87   **L. 7 to Mother Barat**

SS. C. J. et M.

[Bordeaux, February 28, 1818][363]

Very Reverend Mother,

    I have just received your fourth letter, which enclosed several from Grenoble. The kindness that moves you to write by every opportunity shows me that your heart understands how much mine needs this consolation. I often seek to know how things are with you and to imagine your troubles so as to share them. I realize how much I have need of more instruction from you.

    I am uncertain about Communions. Father Barat told them, "Do whatever you are told;" and most of them expect to receive almost every day. Eugenie, in particular; she has not made a difference for the novena after her vows, which she made conscientiously; but at present and in the future it seems to me there should be a limit; she is the one who holds herself aloof; the others are candid and simple. Seeing her as the one most suited for serious responsibilities, I am troubled to see her strong sense of independence. Even though I said nothing to your brother, he himself said to me, "Be firm with that one; you must be both firm and motherly." Octavie is better, both in body and soul; her father [Louis Barat] takes care of both and had me buy some wine against scurvy for the trip. The other two are fine as to the soul, but somewhat less so materially. Mother Geoffroy did not tell me that Marguerite had had a rather unpleasant illness. She has bad body odor, which may be troublesome for the children. Catherine has had a cauterization.

    Bishop Dubourg's nephew has come to suggest that we go aboard ship on Thursday when it leaves Bordeaux. I waited to answer until I had consulted Fathers Barat and Martial, for if it is going to be several days in Pauillac[364] where it stops, it would be better to join it by boat. In any case, you will have a letter that day telling you the answer.

    All our effects from Paris and Grenoble have arrived, but the costs are enormous; our travelling companion [X. Evremond-Harissart][365] paid

---

363 Original autograph, C-VII 2) c Duchesne to Barat, Box 2. Postmark: Bordeaux, February 28, 1818. Cf. J. de Charry, II, 1, L. 89; Hogg, pp. 30-34; Ch. Paisant, pp. 86-88.

364 A port located on the left bank of the estuary of the Gironde. The religious were going to join the ship at Royan, the port on the right bank of the estuary.

365 Born in Paris May 15, 1792, Xavier Evremond-Harissart later was called Xavier Evremond. Ordained by Bishop Dubourg in Missouri, he entered the Jesuits in 1831 in Bardstown. He worked in Kentucky as a teacher of astronomy and geography and in several other ministries.

300 francs for his baggage of one trunk and three cases by stagecoach or cart. I don't know the exact price for us, but I expect to pay about 900 francs; I have not seen the invoices, which are still with Mr. Caseaux. Another time it would be better to arrange things ourselves, including the cost. From Grenoble to Paris, express shipping is 15 francs per hundred and that cost us 25; the difference is enormous. In the future maybe we should buy as much as we can in the port of embarkation. It is too bad that we could not embark from Le Havre, as Mrs. de Rollin advised. Father Debrosse told me that in the future he wants to make all the purchases of books, that is to say, be our agent. He will have Masses said for us on the day we depart. He has lent us Jean François to make many purchases for us: trunks for the cabins, umbrella, alarm clock, etc., our beds including a mattress, pillow, two blankets, and a mosquito net costing 144 francs each. If we stay here a long time, there will be more and more ideas for things to buy; I am tired of it and more anxious to depart in the measure that we are depleting our purse, and we are here at Mother Vincent's expense. She was saying again yesterday that she was living from day to day. We are very well off, but that is not what we should be looking for. She, her sisters and Father Boyer are overwhelming us with kindness.

The holy archbishop [d'Aviau], at 82 years, did not hesitate to pay us a visit. I missed him, as I was at the prefecture when he came, at Father Martial's advice, to make several requests. I did not find the prefect; I wrote to him to assure him that we are grateful for the eagerness he has shown to be helpful to us based on the recommendation of Mrs. de Drel and others; I don't know if she is the one to whom we owe the 150 francs that Father Debrosse gave us. I am thanking her or the Misses de la Myre;[366] that is what I suspect. Miss de Saluce's aunt wants to come to see us tomorrow.

Our places on the ship will cost 900 francs each. The food will be of good quality; there are live chickens, milk they have learned to preserve by a secret formula, etc. Mr. Marange has offered a supply of wine; your brother sent it to Father Martial who told him that it should be in a barrel; I have not seen it, however. Mrs. Marange and Miss Emeline were to come today, but bad weather deterred them.

Propaganda is replacing Bishop Dubourg's missionaries who have died, and a wealthy person is giving a large sum for their voyage. All praise Bishop Dubourg and his priests with one voice. Father Barat

---

He returned to France in 1844 and died in Paris on April 13, 1859.
366 Relative of Cecile de Cassini (1777-1867) whose uncle, Bishop de la Myre of Le Mans, favored the foundation of a house of the Sacred Heart there in 1821.

admires Father Martial especially, as well as a young ecclesiastic whom he wishes to send; the problem is money for the voyage. I see that is lacking for our companion from Paris, and Father Martial cannot get paid; his pupils are leaving him since he is going away. I find him very much changed, and he admitted that he was ailing. In spite of so many troubles, I beg you not to send us anything at all until I ask you; it is agreed with your brother; I want to see how we can manage. For intermediary, we can have the fathers in Washington, which I have learned is the same city as Georgetown; only a river separates them.

I am still like a sister with Mother Vincent, but I am also still persuaded that she does not desire a merger. She has spoken to me about her sufferings with Mother Julie,[367] has repeated several times that she was *a worrier*, that she had deprived them of their rule without giving them another, that she took away adoration, which caused Mother Vincent to weep, etc. It seems that Mother Vincent did not like Maillard.[368] "I had one like that; I sent her away after twelve years," she said. I answered that she was much better. She said also that the archbishop was not willing that her house depend on a house in another diocese.

A thousand messages to all our sisters.

I am at your feet.

Philippine

[On the reverse:]
To Mother
Mother Barat
Superior of the Religious of the Sacred Heart
Rue des Postes n° 40
Paris

Letter 88 **L. 47 to Mrs. Jouve in Lyon**

Bordeaux, March 1, 1818[369]

My good Sister,

As my departure has been delayed, I received your letter in Bordeaux;

---

367 Saint Julie Billiart (1751-1816), founder of the Sisters of Notre-Dame de Namur. At the request of the Dames Vincent who desired to join her congregation, she went to Bordeaux in 1807; but there was a misunderstanding, and the Dames Vincent took back their autonomy in 1811.
368 Catherine Maillard seems to have made a trial of her vocation with the Dames Vincent, before entering the Sacred Heart.
369 Copies: *Cahier, Lettres de la Mère Duchesne à sa famille*, pp. 90-91; *Lettres dactylographiées*. C-VII 2) c Duchesne to her family and lay people, Box 5.

we will leave from here tomorrow perhaps, weather permitting. I was quite convinced of your feelings towards me, and the idea of the sacrifice of such good sisters forms a large part of the total sacrifice I am making to God in order to fulfill his designs. If he accepts and blesses our work, I will dare to ask him in return for the most abundant blessings for you and your family, to whom I remain deeply united, and I will maintain those bonds by sending you news of us. I have already written to Mrs. de Mauduit, and I beg you to share this letter with Mrs. Lebrument.

There are five of us leaving, all members of our Society, a house of which we are going to establish in the diocese of Bishop Dubourg in Saint Louis or Louisbourg in Upper Louisiana. We are going by way of New Orleans, where we are to stay with the Ursuline nuns, who have had a house there for a long time. Here we are staying with a very edifying community. I went to visit the archbishop once, and another time he said Mass for us in our chapel. I hope that so many saints who are praying for us will make it possible for us to be holy one day. That is the only reward I ask in return for this separation, for which only God can compensate.

Goodbye, dearest of sisters. I will never forget you.

Philippine

Everything confirms for me that we will have one of the holiest bishops; he is compared with Saint Francis de Sales; everyone praises him. Remember me to my brother-in-law and your children.

Letter 89   L. 6 to Mother Maillucheau

SS. C. J. et M.

March 2 [1818][370]

My good Mother,

I still had time to receive your letter; it came the same day that I wrote to you telling you that I had seen Mrs. Marange and Miss Emeline, the letter that contained some songs. This one today is my last from France. The ship went down today to Pauillac, where we will join it in two days. Father Martial, the vicar general, will be the only priest aboard; and if he is ill, and already he is not too well, we will be deprived of

---

370 Original autograph and copy: C-VII 2) c Duchesne to RSCJ and Children, Box 4. Copy: C-VII 2) c Duchesne-Varia, Box 9, *Cahier Y, Lettres de la Mère Duchesne*, pp. 38-40.

holy Mass. But how can I be downcast since you are so generous with your prayers and your help, all of which stir up all my gratitude? My heart will never cease to thank you.

As to the hope of seeing you again, I count on it very little. You are doing good in France, and if Aloysia [Euphrosine Jouve] must do so elsewhere, it will be necessary for her to leave you. Maybe God is awaiting this sacrifice in advance before curing her of her languor, making use of her for his glory and making up to you by other conquests, for she has truly been the most remarkable of your daughters.

How I thank you for your care of her and your charity for the Lebrument girls. My sister is in admiration of it and sees that only Christian charity can do what friendship alone would shirk from. Again this morning, I saw your kind sister and your lovable niece. It is necessary to have patience, but I hope that God who is working in her will attach her to himself one day. I leave overwhelmed with their kindness, imbued with yours that only the Heart of Jesus can recognize. The picture you sent to Paris will leave by another ship; that will involve a delay of more than a month.

A thousand messages from me to all my sisters and children.

Philippine

[On the reverse:]
To Mother
Mother Therese Maillucheau
Superior at Sainte-Marie d'En-Haut
Grenoble

Letter 90   **L. 4 to Euphrosine Jouve**

For Aloysia

Bordeaux, [March 2] 1818[371]

My dear Sister,

Having confided myself and all close to me to the divine Hearts of Jesus and Mary, I know neither what you are doing nor where you are; I hope you are always under the hand of God and ready to do his

---

371 Original autograph and copy: C-VII 2) c Duchesne to RSCJ and Children, Box 4. Letter inserted in the one to Therese Maillucheau.

will. I submit in advance to his entire will; nevertheless I have felt that I am holding on to you still; even in my sleep, it seemed to me that you were calling me, urging me, saying that I would never be on time! I seemed to run, but believing myself near you, waking up showed me that I was hundreds of leagues far away, and I renewed my sacrifice. Almost the same thing happened regarding my aunts at Romans. Give me news of them and tell them mine.

I forgot to tell Mother Therese that the transportation costs are so enormous they are often greater than the worth of what is being sent; and I expect that, lacking the huge sums needed to redeem them, things could be lost. I ask her therefore not to send us anything before receiving letters that I will write when I am better informed about conditions.

Remember me to your dear parents, to Constance, to the Lebrument girls. Have the names of my nieces added to my letter to the boarders, which will come from Paris.

All yours in the Heart of Jesus.

Ask Mrs. de Mauduit to have a novena of Masses said for me at La Louvesc, an obligation of my vow.

If my brother withdraws my income, he may need it for a commission I am giving to Mr. Jouve. I ask you, therefore, to find out if it is necessary to add to the bill of exchange of the religious in New Orleans.

When you see my brother, my sister-in-law and the Teisseire family, do not forget to remember me to them.

A thousand messages to my sisters. If they have not received my letters, copy the journal for your mother.

All 4 are well and happy.

I am all yours in the Sacred Heart.

Philippine

[On the reverse:]
To Mother
Mother Therese Maillucheau
Superior at Sainte-Marie d'En-Haut
Grenoble
Département of the Isère

Letter 91 **L. 8 to Mrs. de Rollin**
             Rue Saint Honoré, Paris

March 5 [1818][372]

SS. C. J. M.

My good Cousin,

The delay of our embarkation gives me again the sweet consolation of expressing my gratitude to you.

I have already written a letter to both you and Mrs. Teisseire, and I hope it has reached you. I have not yet been to the prefect's office; I could not meet either him or Mr. Rubichon and their wives, but they have all expressed their desire to assist us after the kind introductions you obtained for me. The relatives of our bishop here have taken charge of all of our business, which is quite complicated; it never ends. The vicar general with whom we are traveling is gaining merit by going with us; that increases his concerns. It will serve for my perfection, for I suffer when I see that I am causing trouble; it is only my kind cousin who has the gift of taking away all the weight of gratitude and leaving only the sweetness.

The prefect is giving us a letter to the consul in New Orleans and has written me an extremely kind letter.

If on our way to the ship I can go up to see Mr. Rubichon, I will offer him my thanks for his good will, which we have not had to put to the test, except for being paid.

Everything augurs for a happy voyage. A multitude of prayers is rising to heaven for us; the holy archbishop of Paris has said Mass for us. I leave tranquil about what will happen; if things end in misfortune, God will have intended another good than what we envisage in his will, which we must bless in everything.

Goodbye then, my good Cousin, accept the sincere and tender expression of my eternal devotedness.

Philippine Duchesne

---

372 *Copies of letters of Philippine Duchesne to Mrs. de Rollin and a few others,* No. 8; *Cahier, Lettres à Mme de Rollin*, pp. 11-13; *Lettres dactylographiées.* C-VII 2) c Duchesne to her family and lay people, Box 5.

A thousand affectionate remembrances to Mesdames Teisseire, Perier, their nice daughters and my cousins.
My regrets to my aunt.
I am not leaving today; contrary winds prevent it.

JOURNAL 2

Journal of the House of the Religious of the Sacred Heart in Paris[373]

September 1815

The storms, the final persecutions of Bonaparte's reign and the extraordinary revolution that arrived before the end of the first year of the reign of Louis XVIII in France prevented the completion of the work of our Society. There was need for a brief meeting to regulate many points of observance that differed considerably in the diverse houses.

Since the separation of [the house of] Ghent, which wanted to be more in conformity with the spirit of the Jesuits, there remained only five houses of our Society: 1) Amiens, where they observed exactly the rule redacted by Father de Sambucy; 2) Grenoble, the second house; 3) Poitier; 4) Niort; 5) Cuignières. In these four houses, there was nothing in common with Amiens except what was practiced from the beginning of the Society, and we had refused to adopt Father de Sambucy's rules until there would be a meeting that represented the whole Society, which would choose or reject what seemed best in Our Lord.

Nevertheless, these delays gave concern to several; and Father de Sambucy, who was quite sure that his work would be selected, sought to have it approved by the Holy See. He was then in Rome and was secretary to Bishop Pressigny of Saint-Malo and ambassador of France to His Holiness. He sought besides to establish in Rome itself a house that would follow this rule; and in order to found it, he obtained the location at Saint-Denys, which belonged to the French. He solicited for Mothers Copina and de Sambucy, religious of the house at Amiens, the necessary permissions to be released from their obedience to Mother Barat, to leave their house and go to that of Saint-Denys to unite with religious of several different orders under the name of *United Ursulines*.

The pope's permission for the establishment of this house in Rome was given too quickly for an approbation that constitutes a religious order. As a result, after a letter came from Father Stephanelli of the Roman College, who was devoted to Father de Sambucy, which he wrote to our mother general with copies sent to all our houses, we were divided in opinion. Some blamed the behavior of Father de Sambucy—who

---

[373] Archives of the Society of the Sacred Heart, Province of France, B 06.115 l.

rejected our superior general in order to establish one in Rome—and wanted to remain united, all the while assuming that the approbation of the rules of Father de Sambucy was the true one. Others, mostly those from Amiens who had been formed to a love and practice of his rules by their confessor, Father de Sambucy, and Mother Copina, their mistress of novices, did not want any other rules than theirs and believed they had the pope on their side.

Since on either side, we wanted only to go toward the greatest good and seek the glory of God, it was not possible to remain very long in error.

Our mother general, in response to the letter and threats of Father Stephanelli if we did not conform ourselves to the Roman house, asked to see the bull, the rescript and the approved rule. Father Soyer, vicar general of Poitiers and superior of our house in that city, did the same. From several sides and in different ways, we made the same request.

While we awaited the result, our mother general, who had been ill for five months in Amiens, from where she had seen Mothers Copina and de Sambucy leave, arrived in Cuignières, and from there in Paris to consult with Father Varin, our founder. Mother Bigeu, superior at Grenoble, went there at the same time to learn about the state of our situation; she left for Grenoble on September 20.

It was then appropriate to delay no longer this meeting that was so desired and that was carried out immediately by having the superiors and one professed from each house come to Paris. All had arrived by November 1, feast of All Saints. Soon we learned that the house in Rome, begun October 9, was not seen as the center of an approved order, but a simple establishment that had no other attention from the pope than what bishops give to communities founded in their diocese.

We were enlightened in this regard:
1. By the silence met by the request for the decree of approbation.
2. By the reports of different people come from Rome.
3. By the letters written from Rome to the superior of Poitiers and to others.
4. By a response from Father Stephanelli himself to a letter written from Grenoble, of which a copy was also sent to all the houses, in which, instead of being able to bring satisfaction about the approbation of the rules, he spoke only about a rescript for the opening of the house and an indult from the Holy Father for the religious of other orders who would like to enter the new house in Rome.

The mothers assembled here saw with the persons they consulted:
1. That the pope had not at all approved the rules of Father de Sambucy, and even less required that all the houses of our Society embrace them.
2. That since the first inspiration of our founders was to devote ourselves especially to the Sacred Heart of Jesus, those who wanted to follow this original vocation should have a rule in which everything aimed to love and glorify the Sacred Heart.
3. Besides the fact that this essential point was lacking in the rule of Father de Sambucy, he had also changed the original plan of government that we had seen practiced.

The Constitutions that were supposed to be given to us were just finished, thanks to the zeal and care of Father Varin. Before beginning to read them at our assembly, we gathered in the oratory of Father de Clorivière, Jesuit.[374] He gave us all a discourse on the advantages of the devotion to which we were about to make a special profession. This was the first session of the general council of the assembly of ten religious who had come from five houses of the Society. It was held the.... *[date not given]*

In the following sessions, Father Varin came himself, accompanied by Father Dollet, to do the reading of the Constitutions and Rules. At the same time, he made remarks that everyone's experience made necessary, and he followed them with many corrections, changes or additions. Together it formed a collection composed of:
1. The general plan of the Institute.
2. The Constitutions.
3. The rules of those who form the government of the Society with the superior general.
4. The other particular rules.
5. The common rules.
6. The rules of modesty.
7. The letter of Saint Ignatius on obedience, just as he wrote it, but translated.

---

374 Pierre-Joseph Picot de Clorivière, SJ (1735-1820), entered the Society of Jesus in 1756. When the Jesuits were expelled from France (1764), he left for Liège (Belgium), was ordained priest in 1763. After a stay in England, he returned to Belgium for the formation of young Jesuits in exile, then went back to France as a secular priest. In 1790, he founded the Society of the Sacred Heart of Jesus (or Priests of the Heart of Jesus) and the Society of the Heart of Mary (or Daughters of the Heart of Mary), both groups of religious living in the world. He was imprisoned from 1804 to 1809; afterward he prepared for the re-establishment of the Society of Jesus in France, of which he was given official charge in 1814. He was named superior and master of novices until 1816, when he asked to be relieved of his offices for health reasons. He died at Montrouge.

8. The ceremonial.
9. The consecration to the Sacred Heart of Jesus, proper to the Society.
10. The different deliberations of the assembly about dress,[375] food, the way to be called, to write letters, to seal them, to mark linens, trousseaux, etc.

When everything was settled, we had the election for those who would form the council of Mother Barat, superior general, and then the renovation of vows. They were preceded by a novena to the Sacred Heart of Jesus and to the Blessed Virgin, in the chapel of the Religious of Saint Thomas of Villanova and before the miraculous statue of the Blessed Virgin, taken from the church of Notre Dame des Grès, who obtained for Saint Francis de Sales calm and peace after his furious temptation to despair. The Sacred Heart of Jesus also has an altar in this chapel. These objects of our dearest devotion and the circumstances of our gathering and our assemblies in the house of these religious should prevent us from ever forgetting them.

December 15, 1815

The election of the assistants general and the other religious as members of the council took place on the day of the octave of the [feast of the Immaculate] Conception, December 15, in the presence of Father Perreau, secretary of the grand chaplain of France, who was willing to accept the responsibility as our superior general, and who took his place.

After the invocation of the Holy Spirit by the *Veni Creator*, we proceeded to the elections by secret ballot, and the three assistants were: the first, Mother Bigeu, superior of Grenoble; the second, Mother de Charbonnel, assistant at Poitiers; the third, Mother Grosier, superior at Poitiers. In the same way, we held the election of the three other members of the general council and elected them in this order: Mother Desmarquest, superior at Beauvais; Mother Geoffroy, superior at Niort; and Mother Eugenie de Gramont, assistant at Amiens.

On the evening of the same day, our mother general gave a conference on the renewal of vows that we would make the next day. We had

---

375 Philippine later at different times mentions the change of religious dress, different in each house. After the General Council of 1815, "Henceforth this costume for both the choir-sisters and the coadjutrix sisters was fixed: black woolen dress, with a pelerine for the choir sisters and a shawl for the others, a white coif and a black veil for professed and aspirants—or temporary professed—a white one for novices; the medal of profession was replaced by a cross (...) It will bear the Heart of Jesus in relief and the initials of the inscription: *Cor unum et anima una in Corde Jesu.*" Jeanne de Charry, *History of the Constitutions of the Society of the Sacred Heart*, part two, *The Definitive Constitutions and their Approbation by the Holy See*, vol. 1 *Historical Account*, Rome, 1979, p. 68.

accusations and pardon, and we disposed ourselves by recollection for the consecration to take place the next day.

It was done in the little chapel of the Recollect Religious[376] on rue de Grenelle, who happily left it free for our ceremony.

December 16

Therefore, December 16, 1815, was the time of our birth, or rather, the affirmation of our Society, which had always wanted to be glorified by belonging to the name and meaning of the Sacred Heart of Jesus.

Father Perreau celebrated Mass in this oratory and gave a touching exhortation with regard to the ceremony, and each one, with candle in hand, made her renovation before Communion. This day was spent in holy joy.

December 17, 1815

The next day, December 17, we held the other elections required by the Constitutions to assist the superior general in government or to work with her. Mother Bigeu, already first assistant, was elected general admonitrix; Mother de Charbonnel, second assistant, was elected treasurer general; and Mother Duchesne was elected secretary general.

One of the things that had most preoccupied the assembly was the formation of the general novitiate and the choice of a house in Paris in which to bring it together. We considered the simple location that had belonged previously to the Religious of Saint Michael,[377] who are now in the house of the Visitation on rue Saint Jacques. This house, located on rue des Postes, N° 40, does not have a large enough space, but it is necessary in these unhappy times not to increase expenses too much.

With all the items that had occupied the attention of the assembly completed, our mother general permitted the superiors to return to their houses. Mothers Grosier and de Charbonnel from Poitiers, and Mothers Geoffroy and [Emilie] Giraud from Niort left Tuesday, December 19. As soon as they arrived, Mother Grosier asked Father Soyer, their superior, who for a while was of the same opinion as Father de Sambucy, to come to see her to give the approbation of the bishops to our rules. At first he seemed very satisfied, as did Father de Beauregard, confessor of the community. The whole house was joyful, but the episcopal

---

376 The Religious of the Rule of Saint Clare, known by the name of Recollects, were established in Paris in 1637.
377 The Sisters of the Good Shepherd, or of Saint Michael, took their name from a famous statue of Saint Michael in their chapel. From 1724 they were at Clos des Poteries (Gallo-Roman pottery of Mount Saint Genevieve), but their convent was closed in 1792. They returned in 1806, on rue Saint Jacques.

approbation, far from increasing it, began to trouble it by its restrictions and observations on the authority of the superior general, the wishes of the superior general, on the renunciation of goods at profession, and on the admission of other priests, which seemed to exclude the fathers who had established us from any relationship with the house.

Niort, being in the same diocese, has the same arrangement for the establishment of the regulations.

December 20, 1815

On December 20, Mother Desmarquest, superior at Cuignières, left to go there with Mother Deshayes. The house, which is too small, will be leased to the Sisters of the Third Order of La Trappe, and our religious will take possession in Beauvais of the house of the minor seminary, which has been moved elsewhere. They are going there at the invitation of both ecclesiastical and secular authority. The mayor is taking charge of the rent of their house, at 2,400 francs, and of the repairs.

January 8, 1816

Mother Bigeu also left for Grenoble on January 8, and brought with her two of our mothers who had come from Ghent at the time of the separation of this community from our Society. One of them, Mother Victoire Paranque, had been assistant and mistress general there; the second, Mother Adrienne Michel, had been mistress of studies. Their arrival to our sisters in Grenoble spread happiness there at the reading of the holy rules, which were welcomed with enthusiasm.

January 16, 1816

Mother Barat wanted to go to Amiens to consolidate the work of our union under the same rule and was preceded on Tuesday, January 16, by Mother de Gramont and her sister.[378]

January 20

On the 20th, a Saturday, she herself left with Sister de la Croix and stopped one day at Beauvais. She carried to Amiens, along with the book of the Constitutions and Rules, the act by which all the members of the assembly of our Society accepted them and promised to observe

---

378 Antoinette de Gramont, RSCJ (1789-1844), boarding student in Amiens, entered the novitiate in 1811. She made her profession November 21, 1816, in Paris. In 1829, she went to Le Mans as mistress general, assisted her mother at the time of her death and replaced her as superior. Severely ill in November 1842, she went to rest in Paris in January 1843. She died in April 1844.

them, unless our Holy Father the pope decreed otherwise. Everyone signed the act at the assembly of the general council, and here are the names of those who constituted it:

Mother *Barat*, superior general
Mother *Bigeu*, superior of Grenoble, 1st assistant general
Mother de *Charbonnel*, assistant of Poitiers, 2nd assistant general
Mother *Grosier*, superior of Poitiers, 3rd assistant general
Mother *Desmarquest*, superior of Cuignières, 4th councilor
Mother *Geoffroy*, superior of Niort, 5th councilor
Mother de *Gramont*, assistant of Amiens, 6th councilor
Mother *Giraud*, mistress of the boarding school of Niort
Mother *Deshayes*, former superior of Grenoble
Mother *Girard*, professed of Amiens
Mother *Duchesne*, assistant of Grenoble

February 2

The house of Grenoble was the first to see our holy rules in vigor, since they found in their Bishop Simon the best of intentions to give it his approbation. He came himself on February 2, feast of the Purification, to receive the first vows that were made publicly in our Society. He gave the appropriate discourse for the ceremony, greatly praising the devotion that we make our principal end and that has as aim the love and glory of the Sacred Heart of Jesus. On this happy day, seventeen were vowed to Jesus Christ, some for five years, the others for always. Those who were already professed renewed their vows in the hands of their bishop, and all from that time have worn the new dress.

February 15

On the 15th of the same month, four novices who had gone for more than a year without wearing the veil that had not been adopted, received it; and four postulants the same day took the habit and veil, in the way indicated in the ceremonial.

February 15

The new members in Amiens were not less happy. Bishop [de Mandolx] of that city gave complete approbation to our rules and Constitutions by a decree that he wanted added to the documents to give them all the force that episcopal authority can give. On the 12th, our mother general went to bring him the submission of all his daughters to his decree, and he showed great joy.

February 19, 1816

On the nineteenth of February, Father d'Astros, the one of the vicars general of Paris to whom Father Varin and Mother Barat had made their first request to allow our Society in Paris, agreed to assume direction of the efforts with the civil authority, to present our application to the prefect to get his agreement, and to fulfill the other formalities with Mr. [André Joseph] Jourdan,[379] the minister in charge of these kinds of things.

Father de la Myre,[380] another vicar general, also promised both his protection and his services for our establishment in Paris.

At the same time, Mr. de Gramont[381] was working to get us to choose the establishment destined for the daughters of the Knights of Saint Louis.[382] Our mother general and our mothers and Sisters de Gramont responded to the first proposals that will perhaps be more accepted by certain people who want to be treated preferentially.

March

When these proposals were better explained, our mother general and her council realized that the work of the daughters of Saint Louis could not be appropriate for us, first, because it would be a burden that the house could not sustain, since the tuition would be at too low a price; second, because they would exercise a surveillance on the operation of our establishment that would hinder our procedure.

March 1, 1816

We received the news that on the first Friday of March, feast of the Five Wounds of Our Lord, the impressive ceremony of vows was held at the same time in Amiens and Poitiers, as well as the change of dress. Father Fournier, vicar general and superior of our sisters in Amiens, gave the discourse and presided at the ceremony there, and Father Soyer,

---

379 André Joseph Jourdan, born in Aubagne, fought for freedom of religion when he was deputy from Bouches-du-Rhône to the Council of Five Hundred in 1795. Destined for deportation, he fled to Spain. Councilor of State in 1815, he was named Minister of Religious Affairs with the responsibilities of the former Minister of Cult.

380 Bishop Claude de la Myre Mory (1765-1830) was the uncle of Cecile de Cassini. He was vicar general of Paris, bishop of Troyes in 1817, and was named bishop of Le Mans on March 19, 1820, where he favored the foundation of a house of the Sacred Heart (1821).

381 Probably Colonel Antoine de Gramont d'Aster (1787-1825), an ultra-royalist. He received the cross of the Royal Military Order of Saint Louis in 1817.

382 This Order was a military institution of honorary membership, reserved for Catholic career officers who had served for more than ten years and were distinguished for courage and worthiness. It was suppressed by a decree of the Convention, October 15, 1793. Louis XVIII restored it on September 28, 1814.

at Poitiers. The same day, our Sisters Ribau and Choppin arrived there, the first destined for Poitiers and the second for Niort, where she went immediately. They had come from Grenoble with Mother Bigeu and stayed in Paris for Quinquagesima Sunday[383] and the two following days.

The return of Mother Bigeu was hurried so that she could see to the repairs on our house, which were delayed and were not going on without difficulties. This also necessitated an appearance by our mother general, who came from Amiens and stayed in Paris from the 11th to the 15th, when she left for Beauvais for the foundation of our establishment in that city on the feast of Saint Joseph, as well as the ceremony of vows and the change of dress. Mother Bigeu accompanied her, and Mother de Gramont went to Amiens, where our Sisters de la Croix, Dainval,[384] and Marie, coadjutrix, had already arrived from Beauvais. Sister Desiree Girard[385] made her 1st vows and all the others renewed theirs. Father de Clausel, vicar general of the bishop of Amiens for Beauvais,[386] gave the discourse and the ceremony at which the first ladies of the city assisted, as well as the mayor and his wife who bear a special interest in this house. The mayor added that, to what he had already done for the establishment, from that day he would no longer pay the rent for the house, but would buy it in the name of the city in order to leave the property to our sisters.

From Beauvais our mother general left with Mother de Gramont for Amiens, and Mother Bigeu arrived here on the 28th and went down to rue des Postes.

March 27, 1816

Because the day before, March 27, we had begun to set foot in our new house and had moved from the apartment at the Religious of Saint Thomas, Mother Duchesne with Sisters Maillard and Berthé went there to sleep the same day. The situation has not made it possible to have the Blessed Sacrament, so they and Mother Bigeu went to seek spiritual resources in neighboring churches, especially that of the Religious of

---

383 The Sunday before the first Sunday of Lent, which is the fiftieth day before Easter.
384 Aimee d'Ainval, RSCJ (1788-1857), born in Montvivier, entered the Sacred Heart in 1812 at Amiens. She made her profession on September 19, 1816, in Beauvais. She was secretary to Mother Henriette Coppens, assistant general at the motherhouse in Paris.
385 Desiree Girard, RSCJ, born January 18, 1792, entered the novitiate June 30, 1811, and made her profession May 25, 1818. She died September 9, 1853, at Jette Saint Pierre, Belgium.
386 Suppressed by the Concordat of 1801, the diocese of Beauvais would be reestablished only in 1823. In 1815, the diocese of Amiens included the *départements* of the Seine and the Oise. There was, therefore, a vicar general in each *département*.

the Visitation, rue des Postes, and the Religious of Saint Thomas at the Child Jesus, which used to be an orphanage.

April 11, 1816

The number did not grow to four until Holy Thursday with the entrance of Miss Marie Frederique Ledo Thévenin,[387] who wants to enter the Society of the Sacred Heart. She is from Besançon and spent part of her life in Portugal.

April 15

This is the day when we are able to take possession of the whole house, which will facilitate bringing together the sisters who will enter the establishment.

19

On Friday 19th, our Sisters Parisot, who made her five-year vows, and Octavie Berthold, a novice, arrived from Grenoble. The latter stayed in Paris to finish her novitiate; as for Sister Parisot, she left the following Monday for Beauvais, where she would be much needed because of the growth of the boarding school and of the poor school, which has up to 200 children.

April 29, 1816

On April 29, our mother general arrived from Amiens and Beauvais. She wanted to leave two days later to visit the houses of Poitiers and Niort, but she was kept here by illness. She told us when she arrived that the holy ceremony of vows and the change of dress would take place at Niort on May 3, feast of the Finding of the Holy Cross, the first Friday of the month, and the second anniversary of the return of the King.

May 3, 1816

Several days later, we learned from Mother Geoffroy that, from that day on, they—she and her daughters—were united in the dress of the Society.

---

387 Frederique Thévenin, RSCJ (1784-1860), worked in Portugal and was the first postulant in the novitiate of Paris, entering April 16, 1816, a little before the arrival of Octavie Berthold, a novice who came from Grenoble. She took the habit July 25, 1816, made her profession June 6, 1823, and went to Autun, then to Besançon. She died in Marseille.

9

The ninth was the day of the arrival of Sister Magdeleine Raison,[388] one of the oldest coadjutrices in the Society.

13

Our mother, feeling better, left with Mother Bigeu for Poitiers and Niort. Two days later, Sister Magdeleine Raison accompanied her nieces to Beauvais and stayed there in the absence of the mother to help the sisters of the house of Beauvais, whom the Lord blessed by sending them an abundance of work. The boarding school is growing; the day schools have many, and besides these two interesting works, popular instructions on Sundays are added. There are three: one for older people, one for girls, and one for children. The place is barely big enough to contain the numbers of people who come.

19

The news brought by Mother Bigeu announces the joy with which our mother general was received at Poitiers and her perfect agreement with Father Soyer, superior of the house and vicar general.

24

The next letters told of a light indisposition of our mother general and her departure for Niort.

June

The whole month of June was spent by her visiting this house and going to Bordeaux, where there was hope of forming a union of our Society with the house of Miss Vincent. This house of Miss Vincent follows nearly the same rules as we do and has the same goal of the instruction of young people. Having returned to Paris from Bordeaux, our mother was again held back by an indisposition that prevented her being in Paris on June 21, feast of Saint Aloysius Gonzaga, this year on the same day as that of the Sacred Heart of Jesus, the day on which it would have been very significant to install the novitiate house. Everything was already ready for this day, but God did not permit us to have this joy.

During the final moments of her stay in Poitiers, our mother general placed as superior there Mother de Charbonnel, who had been named treasurer general by the assembly of the council. She designated Mother

---

388 Magdaleine Raison, RSCJ coadjutrix, died in Paris on March 3, 1837.

Grosier, who governed the house of Poitiers, to be superior of that of Amiens, which, since the departure of Mother Barat, did not have a named superior, with the assistant, Mother de Gramont, filling in.

June 30, 1816

With this change and Mother Barat's recovery, there was no longer any obstacle to her return, and she arrived in Paris with Mothers Bigeu and Grosier on June 30. There she found our chapel completed and the house [rue des Postes] ready to receive the novices and boarding students.

July 4

Miss Aglae Fontaine will be the first observer to be received there. She was formed by Father Ronsin, responsible for the congregation of young people, who often exercised his ministry with the religious of the Congregation of Our Lady, where that young lady had withdrawn for a while to gain clarity about her vocation during a retreat. She entered on July 4.

July 15, 1816

Since her arrival, our mother has been occupied with the blessing of the chapel. After several delays, it was done on July 15. At first we wanted pomp in this ceremony, but later, Father Perreau and our mother general decided to keep it simple. Father d'Astros, vicar general, did this blessing assisted by Father Perreau and Father Coulon. Fathers d'Astros and Perreau said the Mass. We all received Communion at the first one and were only nine, including three sisters and two observers, Misses Aglae Fontaine and Frederique Thévenin, who have been with us since Holy Thursday this year, each in the dress appropriate to her position, and it was the first day on which it was worn in the house in Paris.

We also dressed in white two young children, the foundation of the boarding school. They are daughters of immigrants, born in Canada and formed to the language and customs of the English. There were besides at this consecration of our chapel five or six pious ladies who returned in the evening for solemn Benediction. We were made more numerous by the arrival of several of our sisters from Grenoble: Mother de Portes, named submistress of novices, Sisters Hippolyte Lavaudan, Roustaing and [Eugenie] Audé, choir novices, [Marie] Chabert,[389] coadjutrix novice, Catherine Berne and Genevieve Bonjour, coadjutrix observers.

---

389 Marie Chabert, RSCJ (1796-1817), born in Grenoble, made her vows July 18, 1817, and died October 31, 1817, in Paris.

July 16

The next day, Mother Eugenie de Gramont also arrived from Amiens with four choir novices: Sisters Laloux,[390] Gillot,[391] Hinard, and [Adele] Lefevre;[392] and Miss Chevalier, choir observer.

The first two days were spent getting settled and getting to know one another. There were no rules except Mass and Office, which had been recited since the day of the consecration of the chapel, when the Blessed Sacrament came to be with us.

July 19

On the 19th, work assignments were fixed and the rule put into full observance. This day, feast of Saint Vincent de Paul, is the birth of our general novitiate.

July 25

On the 25th, Sisters Antoinette Chevalier and Thévenin took the holy habit; it was given them by Father Varin who had hardly appeared among us. He gave a very moving discourse about religious duty and the happiness to be especially devoted to the Sacred Heart.

July 2

Departure of our mother for Amiens.

July 31

We celebrated as solemnly as possible the feast of Saint Ignatius, but without sermon. Father de Janson, known for his detachment from the world, his piety and success in the missions, said the community Mass. He has been joined for several years with Father Rauzan, the famous missionary, and a number of other priests to give missions. He obtained from the King Mount Valerien, where Father de Lestrange, abbot of La Trappe, had already begun to restore the Stations of the Cross that still continue.

---

390 Aldegonde Julie Laloux died in the course of her novitiate at the age of 26 years, May 3, 1815, in Amiens.
391 Angelique Gillot, RSCJ (1793-1824), entered in Amiens and made her novitiate and profession in Paris. She went to Beauvais to be teacher, surveillante and mistress of health. She then went to Niort, where she died February 3, 1824.
392 Adele Lefebre, RSCJ (1792-1867) born February 14, 1792, entered the novitiate at Amiens July 16, 1815, and made her profession March 19, 1822. She lived the last six years of her life at Saint Ferréol, where she died September 3, 1867.

August 1

August 1 will be forever memorable for this house and for the Society. This is the date of the letter of Father Perreau to our mother general, to share with her the letter of Father Soyer, vicar general of Poitiers, that contained the brief from His Holiness, addressed to the vicars general of Poitiers, since the episcopal seat was vacant, in response to the questions put to him with regard to his intentions for our Society. We did not know what to do with the letter of Father Stephanelli, who wanted us to join with the house of Saint Denys in Rome. The pope praises the vicars general for their submission to the Holy See, and declares that he had no intention to join us to the house of Saint Denys, which has no solemn approbation. Finally, it declares the letter of Father Stephanelli to be false and without any merit.

The cardinal responsible for the expedition of the brief also asks for information on the number and quality of our establishments. A copy of the same brief was sent by Cardinal Fontana to Mother de Montjoie, superior of the Visitation, who had been asked to write to him with information on the same subject. Our mother sent to each house a copy of the brief, which was disseminated everywhere with joy and gratitude to God who thus seals our union.

August 4

Several days later, Mother Virginia Balastron,[393] professed religious of Grenoble, and Sister Josephine Meneyroux,[394] a novice of 19 months, arrived in this house, the first to help in the work of the community and the second to continue her novitiate.

August 15

For the Assumption, a feast very dear to the Society because of the consecration to Mary that it renews on that day, we had several Masses; that of the community was said by Father Varin who, after his thanksgiving, gave us a moving discourse on the Blessed Virgin. The one after dinner was said by a missionary of Father Rauzan.

---

393 Virginia Balastron may be the "younger" Balastron to whom Philippine refers several times in 1808-1811. There is no further record of her.

394 Rosalie (Josephine) Meneyroux, entered at Sainte-Marie d'En-Haut on November 21, 1814, went to Paris August 4, 1816, and returned to Grenoble for health reasons January 7, 1817. She returned to the novitiate in Paris on December 21, 1817, and made her first vows in 1820, then went to rest at her father's house. With the approval and support of Father Barat, she left Bordeaux for America in 1821. She arrived in New Orleans December 24, 1821, and at Grand Coteau in February 1822. Bishop Dubourg and Eugenie Audé were shocked by her behavior. In May, she returned to France and then left the Society of the Sacred Heart.

On the last days of the month, we had the consolation of seeing our mother general arrive; she had been in Amiens to place as superior Mother Grosier, previous superior in Poitiers and a professed of Amiens. On the way back, she had stopped in Beauvais and was away for nearly a month. She intended to go right away to Grenoble, the only one of her houses that she had not visited since the meeting of mothers in Paris, but that trip was delayed.

August 31

On the last day of August, our mother received two postulants: Miss Pauline Pain[395] from Roanne in Lyonnais, and Florence, who had been in service in Paris. The 1st was destined as choir religious and the 2nd for a domestic role. A third observer destined for domestic service is Marie Beureau, also from Roanne.

September 8

All the feasts of the Blessed Virgin should be dear to us. That of the Nativity was celebrated with devotion, and this devotion was inspired by Father de Grivel,[396] professed in Russia and now rector. He shows a particular beneficence toward our Society. He is followed in this by Father Fontaine, a senior professed, who spent the time of the Revolution in England, where he told us about the existence, in a sort of desert, of a beautiful Jesuit college. These two good Fathers have several times seen us and preached the word of God to the community.

September 6

Two days before the 6th of the month, which was the first Friday, Sisters Aglae Fontaine, Genevieve Bonjour and Catherine Berne took the veil, and Sister Angelique [Marie] Berthé made her final vows as a coadjutrix sister. Father Ronsin did the ceremony and gave the discourse.

September 17

On the 17th Miss Elisabeth Kerulvay entered as a choir postulant; she

---

395 Pauline Pain, born in 1798 in Paris, lived with her grandfather in Roanne. She made a vow of virginity when very young. She entered the novitiate October 20, 1816, and was employed in the infirmary. She died October 27, 1817, in the course of an epidemic.

396 Fidèle de Grivel, SJ (1769-1842), entered the Society of the Fathers of the Sacred Heart in 1794, and joined the Company of Jesus in 1803 in Russia. After the expulsion of the Jesuits from Saint Petersburg in 1815, he went to England and in 1831, to the United States, to be superior and master of novices. He died at Georgetown, where he was a professor in the college. He is the author of *Breve ragguaglio dei principi e progressi della Società del Cuore di Gesù*.

is from Lorient in Brittany and has been a teacher in a private house, on account of reversals of fortune.

October 10

The novitiate grew on October 10 with two choir novices: Miss Kerulvay and Pauline Pain. Father Grivel did the ceremony and gave the discourse. The evening before, Miss Harent[397] from Lyon, 44 years old, entered as a postulant.

18

Miss Mechet, a native of Paris, entered as a postulant.

At the same time, Sister Magdeleine Raison, a professed coadjutrix of Amiens, left for Poitiers.

21

The 21st of the same month, Mother Bigeu left for Bordeaux accompanied by Sister Maillard; the purpose of the journey is to deal with the merger of a religious house with our Society. This house, governed by Mother Vincent, follows the rule of Saint Ignatius as we do. The same letter that determined that journey, written by Father Barat, gives hope, according to a conversation he had with Bishop Dubourg of New Orleans, that our Society will be able to be established in his diocese for the instruction of girls, a work all the more interesting because every resource is lacking in these abandoned regions.

November 1

On the feast of All Saints Sister Chatain arrived, a domestic worker from Grenoble whose health required a change of air.

12

And on the 12th, Miss Sophie d'Aster as a postulant.

13

This day is remarkable because of the visit of Prince de Leon, duke of Rohan, who exhibits great interest in our Society and that of the Jesuits, and who has received from the Holy Father the pope signs of his predilection. He has a precious relic of Saint Stanislaus Kostka, and at the request of our mother general, he was willing to give it to her.

---

397 Cecile Harent, RSCJ, made her first vows on Ascension Day in 1818, and went to Chambéry to be assistant, then was superior at Autun, where she died April 7, 1826.

On the same day, the 13th, feast of Saint Stanislaus Kostka, patron of the novitiate, the general retreat began for the novices, postulants, and several professed. Father Roger gave the opening and will continue the exercises and direct it entirely.

21

The retreat was interrupted to give a little relaxation to the novices and to have the moving ceremony of profession of Sister Antoinette de Gramont, who had arrived from Amiens expressly to make her consecration at the motherhouse in Paris. Father d'Astros, vicar general and superior of the house, gave the discourse and did the ceremony. He was assisted by Father Perreau, our respected councilor and protector, and by Father Gaston de Sambucy,[398] confessor to the new spouse of Jesus Christ. After the Mass, our superior saw the whole novitiate for the 1st time and brought it to a tender devotion to Mary, the dearest gift that Jesus Christ has left to us, since he has nothing that *he does not share with us.* He exhorted us to make this thought the habitual subject of our meditation.

22

The retreat was resumed the next day to continue on the mysteries of Jesus Christ until the 1st Sunday of Advent.

At the same time that the novices were making it here, their mistress, Mother Bigeu, undertook hers in Bordeaux. The purpose of her mission was not fulfilled, because of the opposition of the vicar general [Father Boyer], superior of the house of Mother Vincent. She and her daughters are disappointed and hope that at another happier time, it will be possible to effect the union with us that they desire.

The bishop of Quimper wrote at the same time to Mother de Gramont to ask her for an establishment for his episcopal city.

December 3

The feast of Saint Francis Xavier was celebrated here according to the ceremonial and ended the whole retreat, whose fruits are noticeable. The same day, Miss Harent took the holy habit of religion; she received

---

398 Gaston de Sambucy, former seminarian at Saint-Sulpice, was responsible in this parish for the "Major Catechism for Young Women," followed by Eugenie de Gramont when she returned from exile. Arrested during the Revolution and liberated after the fall of Robespierre, he was named by Cardinal Fesch master of ceremonies in the imperial chapel. He was vicar general of the diocese of Paris until 1830.

the veil from the hands of Father Roger, who gave a discourse for the ceremony and, in the evening, the panegyric of the saint.

8

The feast of the Immaculate Conception was very solemn. Again, Father Roger preached, always addressing his words to the students of the boarding school, who, according to the rule, made their first consecration to the Blessed Virgin on this day, which should be imitated in all our houses.

9

The next day, Mother Antonia de Gramont returned to Amiens, where she is first mistress of class.

13

On the 13th, we remembered the day when our mother general began the house of Grenoble, the second one in the Society.

14

We fasted on the 14th, vigil of the feast of the Holy Heart of Mary.

15

This is the first year in which, following the ceremonial, we celebrated solemnly the feast of the Holy Heart of Mary, the Sunday in the octave of the Immaculate Conception of the Blessed Virgin. There was exposition of the Blessed Sacrament and a sermon in the evening by Father Roger.

18

Letters of Mother Bigeu from Poitiers and Tours announce that the bishop of Quimper continues his efforts for an establishment of our Society, that he wrote to her in a most urgent manner, and that she is on the road to go to Quimper.

25

Midnight Mass and the solemn Masses during the day were said by Father Varin, and the other days by Father Dollet, our chaplain by his zeal, in as far as we have one. There was no sermon that day, but it was as if Father Varin had done it in advance, because when he saw the community to bless us as he returned from travel, he spoke of the

Infant Jesus, inviting us to consider him as already our victim and to make ourselves victim with him.

27

On the feast of Saint John, he preached on these words: "*God has so loved the world that he gave his son,*"[399] and drew from them these two thoughts on the love of God for us and the obligation for us to return it.

January 1, 1817

On the first of the year, he again favored us with a visit and an informal conversation on the mystery of the day. He showed us Jesus Christ, victim of humility and suffering, insisting on these words that he wants us to say always: "*Ita pater,* yes, father,*"* and he cried: "Happy is the soul that grounds itself in this great *Yes!*" After giving in detail the occasions for sacrifice, to which the soul always responds *Yes, my God!* he ended by saying: "at the last hour, God will say to that soul: come, my daughter, and she will respond again: *Yes, my God!*"

On January 11, we saw Mother Bigeu again, back from her journey with Sister Maillard, after being successively in Poitiers, Niort, and Bordeaux. From Bordeaux to Niort, Poitiers, and Quimper, they left this last city full of the wishes of its bishop and earnestly solicited one of our foundations to be made there as soon as possible. Miss de Saint-Pern is offering us a beautiful location, which cost her more than 100,000 francs, and the furniture that is in the house. There is a church, beautiful bells, woods, orchards, and vegetable gardens enclosed in walls. She herself wants to consecrate herself to God and embrace our institute.

Our mother general is very desirous to fulfill the wishes of this zealous and good bishop by having religious come from different houses.

She came on the 7th to send away to Grenoble two of the novices, one because of health: Sister Josephine Meneyroux, who arrived August 4; the other, coadjutrix Sister Catherine Berne, who arrived with the other novices in July.

14

On the 14th, the house of Paris was honored by the visit of the bishop of Louisiana, who came to continue to discuss with our mother general the project of an establishment in his vast diocese. He had already spoken in Bordeaux with Mother Bigeu, and he wanted six religious for May. He awaits her response when he returns from Belgium, where

---

399 John 3:16.

he is going to ask for help for the work of the missions in his diocese. Our mother general, after taking counsel, seems to want to prolong the departure up to 18 months or 2 years.

February 1st

Entrance of Scholastique Compas, who had left a house of Benedictines where she had not been definitively committed, through the intervention of Father d'Astros, vicar general and our superior, who offered her to our mother general.

February 2

Since the feast of the Purification falls on this Sunday of Septuagesima, we had only the blessing of candles today; the rest of the Office was postponed to the next day.

5

The feast of the Holy Martyrs of Japan, February 5, was well solemnized for us by the ceremony of the first vows of Sisters Angelique Gillot and Octavie Berthold. Father Vaclet did the ceremony and gave a very moving discourse. He was assisted by Father Dollet.

8

Departure of our mother general for Amiens, where her presence has become necessary because of the state of health and the continual sufferings of Mother Grosier, superior of that house, for whom the doctor suggests a change of air.

15

Arrival from Grenoble of Mother Victoire Paranque and Sisters Olympie Rombau, choir religious in first vows, and Agathe Gerard, coadjutrix in first vows, all three bound for the foundation of Quimper.

22

Return of our mother general with Mother Grosier, Sisters Seraphine Avignon and Celinie, choir novices from Beauvais; Miss Adele Lefebre, postulant from Amiens, and Miss Zoe Dehilly for the boarding school.

23

On the 1st Sunday of Lent, we had a solid and moving explanation of the Gospel by Father Dollet, who had already done the same for several Sundays and makes us hope for a continuation on the Sundays of the year.

24

Departure of Sister Angelique Gillot, the same one who made her vows on the fifth; she is going to our house in Beauvais to work in the numerous poor school, with more than three hundred children.

March
4

Departure of the little colony that will found one of our houses in Quimper. It is led by Mother Josephine Bigeu; as first assistant [general], whom our mother is giving to this new house to establish it, intending another superior for it [Mother de Gramont d'Aster]. The mothers and sisters leaving with Mother Bigeu are: Mother Victoire Paranque; Sister Olympie Rombau in first vows; Sisters Eugenie Audé and Seraphine Avignon, choir novices; Therese Pelletier, professed coadjutrix and Sister Agathe Giroud, coadjutrix in first vows. Novena to Saint Francis Xavier.

6

Entrance of Miss Josephine Rosé who had been for several years with the Sisters of Charity and who has been received into the Society as a coadjutrix.

8

Arrival from Poitiers of Mother Prevost, whom our mother general had pass through to Amiens. She had as traveling companion Miss Therese Dusaussoy,[400] who is coming to try her vocation.

On the same day, first distribution of prizes in our house in Paris, the boarding school composed of 18 students. There was no one from outside; the exercises took place in the morning from 9:00 to 11:30 and in the afternoon from 2:00 to 4:00; the prizes in the evening at 6:00. Misses de Prefontaine and Genny de Labeau had the two ribbons of merit and the prize for good conduct, *ex aequo* [tied]. There was only one in all the classes because of the small number of children, but the prize for application was given in each class.

---

400 Therese Dusaussoy, RSCJ (1799-1823), was one of Mother Barat's nieces. She died at Chambéry after having made her profession, June 1, 1823.

12

Last day of the novena to Saint Francis Xavier, apostle of the Indies.

The same day, Miss Aline Lefebvre, who had entered February 22 and had made her postulancy in Amiens, took the white veil as a choir novice. Father Fontaine, a long-professed Jesuit, gave the discourse and did the ceremony.

13

Departure for Amiens of Mother Grosier in a better state of health, accompanied by Mother Prevost,[401] who will be assistant, and Miss Dusaussoy.

26

Arrival from Amiens of Mother de Gramont d'Aster, destined to be superior at Quimper. She has to stay in Paris to finish some business here. Her traveling companion, Mother Lemeré,[402] is destined for Poitiers, where she is to replace Mother Prevost in the role of mistress of health.

31

Her departure took place on March 31. She is taking with her Sister Elisabeth Kerulvay, choir novice, to help in the boarding school.

April
1

On April 1, the boarding school was composed of 22 students.

2

On the 2nd, Holy Thursday, our mother general served at table in the refectory with Mother de Gramont d'Aster. In the afternoon, she washed the feet of 12 novices; the ceremony took place in the novitiate, where

---

401 Marie Elisabeth Prevost, RSCJ (1784-1871), born May 26, 1784, at Montfort, followed her father, a colonial official, to Santo Domingo in 1789. Returning to France in 1794, she entered the novitiate in Amiens, May 31, 1808. On May 3, 1809, while yet a novice, she was sent by Mother Baudemont as superior of the house of the Sisters of Notre Dame, whose foundress, Mother Julie Billiart, had been expelled by Father Sambucy de Saint Estève. She remained there for four years, until the return of Mother Julie, and made her first vows on February 5, 1811, and her profession April 20, 1813. In 1814, she went to Cuignières, then to Poitiers. Returning to Amiens as assistant in 1817, she was named superior in 1819. Elected general councilor in 1820, she brought about the union of the Society of the Sacred Heart of the foundation of Annonay and that of the Providence of Charleville (1831). She was provincial in the Midi in 1839, assistant general and vicar of the North in 1851, and superior of the house at the Rue de Varenne in Paris from 1854 to 1869. She died January 29, 1871, at Chambéry.

402 Henriette (Marie) Lemeré, RSCJ, born in 1781, died May 5 (or 7), 1821.

they had decorated a little altar; our mother read the Gospel. The offices of Thursday, Friday, and Saturday of Holy Week were done according to the ceremonial. The religious and the students took turns for night adoration on Holy Thursday. We did not have a Passion.

6

The feast of Easter was very solemn. For the day's recreation, our mother had saved the reading of the travel journal of our sisters of Quimper, who had been received in that city with general excitement, especially by the bishop and his vicars general. They were also visited by the prefect.

8

Departure of Miss Josephine Rosé, who was not judged to be right for the Society.

18

Arrival from Poitiers of our sisters Magdeleine Raison and Louise Blet, coadjutrix sisters.

28

Departure of Sister Magdeleine Raison for Amiens.

May
13

Investiture of Sister Scholastique Compas with the habit. Father d'Astros, our honorable superior, did the ceremony and the discourse. The same day, he conducted the examinations of Sister Adele Lefebvre for vows and Miss Adelaide de Prefontaine[403] for entry into the novitiate.

13

The same day, Miss Cousin entered as choir postulant.

16

The sixteenth of May is remarkable and dear because of the third visit of Bishop Dubourg, bishop of Louisiana, who continues to want one of our establishments in his diocese, for which he is leaving very soon. Our mother general has promised him six religious for next spring.

---

403 Adelaide de Prefontaine, RSCJ, while still a novice, left for the foundation of Quimper in 1818 and remained there until her death on April 12, 1853.

The novitiate and the boarding school were presented to him and he blessed them. He addressed to the novices a few words on the beauty of their vocation.

27

Departure for Quimper of Mother de Gramont d'Aster, destined to be its superior. She is taking with her Sister Scholastique Hinard,[404] choir novice, to be one of the teachers, and Sister Louise Blet, coadjutrix novice. The news that our mother has received from this foundation of Quimper is more and more consoling because of the regularity and peace that reign there, and because of the paternal care of its noteworthy bishop.

June
5

Celebration of Corpus Christi, which we solemnized as before the Concordat, and there was High Mass, vespers, and solemn Benediction; exposition of the Blessed Sacrament took place during the whole octave with special permission of Father d'Astros, our superior.

8

Celebration of Corpus Christi in the parishes. The procession of Saint Medard went through our street, and the Blessed Sacrament was placed in our repository. After Benediction, each student approached and the pastor placed on her head the ostensorium that contained Our Lord.

13

The most solemn feast for us, that of the Sacred Heart of Jesus. Father Varin said the community Mass after giving the veil to Sister Adelaide de Prefontaine. In the discourse that he addressed to her, he drew from his text: "Do not weep over me, but rather over yourselves"[405] a moving instruction, as much about his own happiness as about the dangers that his companions could encounter. At the moment of Communion, he gave another discourse about the renovation of vows, in which he developed the meaning and extent of the obligation, from the words of his text: "Lord, in the simplicity of my heart that is full of joy, I have

---

404 Marie Scholastique Hinard, RSCJ, born in 1798, was confided to the Ursulines of Beauvais at the age of three, then was a boarder at Cuignières and Amiens, where she began her novitiate, which she finished in Paris. She then left for the foundation at Quimper to be a teacher. She died in the course of an epidemic on September 18, 1819.
405 Luke 23:28.

offered you everything."[406] Those who renewed their vows were: our mother general, the Mothers de Gramont, Girard, de Portes, Balastron, Duchesne, for the choir religious; Sister Berthé for the professed coadjutrix sisters; Sisters Berthold and Laloux for those of five years; Sister Chatain, the same as coadjutrix. The feast was preceded by a retreat of three days for those renewing their vows. Father Varin preached the first day, Father de Clorivière the second.

15

Beginning of the retreat for the boarding school by Father Druilhet, who from that time is also responsible as their confessor, since Father de Grivel, rector of the Jesuit Fathers, cannot continue to do it. This retreat prevented exposition of the Blessed Sacrament during the octave of the Sacred Heart, permitted by Father d'Astros, though with hesitation. It did not take place on Monday, Tuesday, Wednesday and Thursday, except at Mass and the evening Benediction.

June 1817
20

On Friday, octave of the Sacred Heart, exposition lasted all day, as well as the 21st, feast of Saint Aloysius Gonzaga, the day that the boarding school retreat ended. The students received Communion before the community. Father Druilhet spoke to them before Mass on the words of the Canticle: "My beloved has gone down into his garden, etc."[407] He spoke again before and after Holy Communion, and in the evening on the virtues of their holy patron.

July 1817
Six

Visit of Fathers Varin, Roger, Gloriot, Ronsin and Druilhet, who have received an order from their general to cease communications with us, on account of certain calumnies coming from Rome, in a letter in which it was supposed that they were failing to observe the Jesuit constitutions in this regard, even though they render the same services to other communities. They came for the last time to give us the help that has been our consolation and our wealth since our establishment. Father Roger gave a discourse and Father Druilhet said Mass again. Since yesterday, we have been reduced to the Mass of Father Tuite, an English

---

406 1 Chron 19:17.
407 Cant 4:16.

priest who cannot even come on Sunday, when we must look for other resources…but no more sermons from the fathers, nor explanation of the Gospel on Sundays.

In the evening, Mother Grosier arrived from Amiens. She is still suffering from her health. She is going to take the waters at La Roche near Châtellerault. She is accompanied by Sister Rosalie Cardon.[408]

7

Departure for Beauvais of Sister Catherine Laloux,[409] a sister in first vows, who will devote herself to teaching, according to obedience.

13

Departure of Mother Grosier and Sister Rosalie for the waters of La Roche-Posay.

15

Anniversary of the blessing of the formation chapel in the house of Paris.

21

Several days' visit to the house from Mother Louise Naudet, former lady in waiting to the archduchess [Marie-Anne, sister of the emperor of Austria], one of the first stones of the 1st Society of daughters devoted to the Sacred Heart, called the *Dilette*, which did not last. Since the archduchess has died, Mother Louise could not keep up an establishment in London and is going to Verona in Italy, where her sister, Mother Leopoldine, also a former lady in waiting to the archduchess, has made an establishment.

22

Celebration of the feast of Saint Magdeleine, patron of our mother general. The evening before, the distinguished students came to ask her to come to the meadow, where they offered her their wishes; the novices and elders did it only after supper. The altar was decorated as on the greatest feasts, but there was no exposition of the Blessed Sacrament. After the evening Benediction, given by Father Perreau, he distributed to the students the prizes for the trimester.

---

408 Rosalie Cardon, RSCJ coadjutrix (1786-1838), entered October 15, 1808, in Amiens, where she made her vows. She was infirmarian, and died October 21, 1838.
409 Catherine Laloux, RSCJ, made her profession at the age of 34 years, and died in Poitiers April 5, 1820.

29

Arrival from Quimper of Mother Bigeu, who left the establishment in that city in good shape and brought the foundress, Miss de Saint-Pern, who will be a postulant for the novitiate along with Miss Prudence Defois and Adelaide Josse, from Laval.

31

Celebration of the feast of Saint Ignatius, as solemnly as possible, even though we did not sing High Mass. That of the community was said by Father Perreau, who during it gave a moving discourse on Saint Ignatius. Mr. Eugene de Montmorency with two English lords attended and received Communion. Father de Retz said the second Mass.

August
15

Celebration of the feast of the Assumption of the Blessed Virgin; a student made her First Communion, which is the 1st in the Paris house. That happy child is Miss Elisa de Montarby, daughter of the governor of Martinique, where she must go in the autumn. Father Perreau gave the discourse for First Communion and celebrated the Holy Mass. In the evening, he again gave the discourse before renovation of vows and the consecration of the students and the entire house to the Blessed Virgin.

16

The next day, his zeal and charity were again shown as he was willing to do the ceremony and the discourse for the taking of the habit by Misses de Saint-Pern and Cousin,[410] both choir novices, and to receive the 1st vows of Sisters Adele Lefebvre as choir religious and Catherine Maillard as coadjutrix sister. The Blessed Sacrament was exposed all day, and in the evening, the missionary Father Enfantin gave a discourse on the Blessed Virgin, which we did not have the evening before and which was well received. He also brought in congratulations and instructions for the four new fiancées and brides of Jesus Christ.

20

Departure for Amiens of our mother general and Mother de Gramont,

---

410 Victoire Cousin, RSCJ, born October 20, 1810, entered the novitiate October 30, 1842, in Avignon, and made her profession October 26, 1853. She was infirmarian for a long time, and died October 19, 1859, in the house of Saint Joseph in Marseille.

with three students and two young ladies [Armande and Olympe] de Causans.⁴¹¹

28

Return of Mother Grosier from the waters, with Sister Rosalie Cardon.

September
8

The day of the feast of the Nativity of the Virgin Mary; we had the 1st Communion of the second of the Montarby girls, because of her departure soon for a land without resources for the spiritual life. Her sister renewed it, and the next day, they were also confirmed at the house of the Religious of the Congregation.⁴¹²

18

Return of our mother general from Amiens and Beauvais.

The same day, Father Perreau was willing to do the extraordinary confessions of Quadragesima. Since July 21, when he began to say Mass for us every day, he has not ceased to prove by his many sacrifices his abundant and sensitive charity toward us. He has left off important business, his lodging, and his time of rest to pour out upon us the supports of religion. He says Mass for us every day, does an explication of the Gospel on Sundays, devotes himself for all our ceremonies, hears confessions, and even promises to become the community confessor, replacing Father Bourgeois.

21

Beginning of the illness of Miss Caroline de Monsaulerin, judged

---

411 Armande de Causans (1785-1866), RSCJ, entered the novitiate of the Sacred Heart at Paris at the age of 36 years, received the habit January 20, 1822, made her first vows November 13, 1823, and her profession December 8, 1824. Superior at the house in Turin in 1826, then at the foundation of the Trinità dei Monti in Rome, she was there from 1828 to 1838 and from 1851 to 1864. She died at the Villa Lante, Rome. Olympe de Causans, RSCJ (1796-1867), was born in Germany. She entered the novitiate of the Sacred Heart, Paris, at the age of 21, received the religious habit on February 24, 1818, and made her final profession, October 15, 1823. Timid and reserved, the opposite of her sister Armande, she was class mistress in the elementary school and with the orphans in Paris, then at the foundation of Berry Mead (England), in December 1842, then in Amiens, Orleans, Nancy and Niort, where she died on April 12, 1867.

412 It is difficult to identify this Congregation, but it is probably the Congregation Notre Dame, founded in 1597 by Pierre Fourier and Alix Le Clerc, known by the name of Canonesses of Saint Augustin. This name of "Religious of the Congregation" was also attributed to members of the Congregation of the Most Holy Virgin, under the title of The Purification, founded in Marseille in the 17th century under the direction of the Jesuits.

to be the same as that of Miss Pauline de Choqueuse, which has lasted since August 27, with serious symptoms but without danger.

28

The illness of Miss de Monsaulerin has become a malignant fever.

October
4

A parotid gland succeeded in giving her illness a mortal character, and today she gave over her beautiful soul to God, fortified by all the sacraments. For several days, a continual delirium left no hope that she would be able to have confession. Father Druilhet, her confessor, wanted nevertheless to see her, and against all human hope, her reason reappeared and was turned toward divine things. Not only that, she was able to confess with all necessary presence of mind; and more, being prepared for her 1st Communion, she wanted to make it in her bed and received Our Lord with the most consoling dispositions, in the midst of the sorrow we felt at losing her. Her illness was so edifying that one could not see in her the shadow of an imperfection; docile, patient, grateful, fervent in lucid moments. There can only be the well-founded hope that she is happy for eternity, which can make up for her loss. She was only 11 years old!

4

The same day, arrival of Mother Giraud from Amiens, a choir religious in 1st vows.

8

Arrival of Mother Eugenie de Gramont from Amiens.

4

At the same time that God afflicted us with the first death in this house, he prepared us with great consolations: the return of spiritual help from our fathers [Jesuits]. The letter that forbade them to give it to us had taken more than a year to come from Russia, and the one that calmed our sorrow came in much less time, which seemed to us to be a singular trait of loving Providence in our regard. Father Druilhet brought the 1st announcement of this good news, and Father Varin, whom we had not seen since July 6, came to confirm it.

8
   Entrance of Miss Cecile Camille,[413] choir postulant.
   Beginning of the illnesses of Miss de Rosac and de Couronnel, boarding students, and of Sister Lefebvre, novice.

10
   Beginning of those of Miss de Rouvroy elder and boarder, who has a fever and severe pain in the side, and that of Sister Chabert, who has a fluxion from the chest.

12
   Beginning of the jaundiced fever of Sister Marie, coadjutrix novice.

13
   Arrival from Amiens of Sister Marthe Vaillant,[414] professed coadjutrix sister.

14
   Beginning of the illness of Miss Desmier, niece of Miss de Saint-Pern, and of Miss Pulcherie de la Myre, the 1st with fluxion from the chest and jaundiced fever, the 2nd also with jaundiced fever.

15
   Beginning of the illness of Sister Pauline Pain, choir novice, who, as assistant infirmarian, has caught the illness that brought Miss de Monsaulerin to the grave.

21
   Beginning of the jaundiced fever of Miss Anais Dupont, the dysentery of Miss Cecile Camille, and the more benign fever of Miss de Saint-Pern.

22
   Departure of Sister Aline Lefebvre, novice. The doctors have great

---

413 Cecile Camille, RSCJ (1789-1827), born at Les Tuileries in Paris, was educated by Lady Elisabeth, sister of Louis XVI. Director of the boarding school at rue de Varenne, Paris, and in charge of the Marian congregation, she then left for Bordeaux in 1823 to replace Mother Bigeu as superior. She died October 4, 1827.

414 Marthe Vaillant, RSCJ coadjutrix, born January 1, 1784, entered at Amiens in 1802, took the habit December 25, 1805, made her profession November 21, 1809, then went to the foundation at Ghent. She returned to Amiens in 1814, went to Paris in 1817, then to Besançon and in 1827 to La Ferrandière (Lyon), where she died November 26, 1860.

fear for her chest. Mother is returning her to her family, at least for a while.

23

Death of Miss Cecile de Couronnel, nearly under the eyes of her tender mother who had come to help her. Like Miss de Monsaulerin, she died under the eyes of her father, who has followed her entire illness, which made the spectacle of her last moments more painful for us because of the pitiful state of her unhappy parents. The illness of Miss de Couronnel was complicated by a fluxion from the chest and a bilious fever; that of Miss de Rosac took a malignant turn, and from the first days, her parents took her away. Her death, followed from close by, was as afflicting as edifying, as well as that of her two companions, Misses de Monsaulerin and de Couronnel. Here is the letter that our students wrote to the boarders in other houses on the occasion of these two deaths:

Dear Companions.

When we told you about the loss of Miss Caroline de Monsaulerin, which we had just experienced, we were far from thinking that the Lord would visit us again, and that in few days we would again have to shed our tears. Nevertheless it is really true. Two young companions have just been taken from us one after the other: Miss Cecile de Couronnel and Miss Marie de Rosac.

We admit to you: however submissive we may be to the will of God, this double loss has torn our souls. Both were very dear to us. Both combined the most attractive qualities: piety, sweetness, and amiability. It seemed that, formed under the very eyes of the Lord to a virtue equally tender and solid, they would someday live a distinguished life in the midst of a world to which their birth destined them. The Lord has decreed otherwise; may his holy name be blessed! He hastened to withdraw them in order to hasten their happiness, no doubt; but this favor he did to them will cost us many tears for a long time.

Nevertheless, religion tempers bitterness in a special way, for both of them, in their painful illness, received extraordinary graces from the Lord. Miss de Couronnel, 11 and a half years old, had not made her 1st Communion. She made it with sentiments of faith and piety that drew tears from every eye. The very day of her death, she received Extreme Unction and the holy scapular. She pressed it tenderly to her heart, and one of her last words was: "Ah! How sweet is the name of Mary!"

Miss Rosac, 13 and a half years old, herself asked for the last sacraments from the first days of her illness, and she received them with the most edifying fervor. Since then, she suffered enormously but never with a complaint. Her crucifix, which she held ceaselessly to her lips, helped her to bear it all. The names of Jesus and Mary were her last smile, and a little after saying them, she fell asleep in the Lord.

We are assured, dear companions, that these touching details will satisfy your devotion and strengthen even more the ties that unite us.

Misses Caroline, Cecile, and Marie were your companions as they were ours. We recommend them to your most fervent prayers, though we have the intimate conviction that these three angelic souls are now with the Lord, and they beg him ardently for their sorrowful companions, so that the memory of their virtues is at the same time a subject of consolation and of sorrow.

We are, etc.

October
24

Illness and death do not leave our house. On the 24th, our sister novice Pauline Pain received the last sacraments. She made her vows for six months, in the presence of our mother general and Mother Bigeu, her mistress of novices.

The same day, Miss Caroline Botaffel entered as a choir postulant.

26

Arrival from Grenoble of Sister Veronique Pellat, coadjutrix novice.

27

Arrival from Amiens of Sister Magdeleine Raison, professed coadjutrix sister, whom our Mother General had come to help with the sick, especially Miss de la Myre, whose typhoid fever forced her to be separated to avoid contact.

27

Beginning of the illness of Miss Luce Morange, and death of Sister Pauline Pain, novice.

30

Arrival from Poitiers of Mother Bernard, Sister Rosalie Bouchère, professed coadjutrix sister, and Augustine Balin, coadjutrix postulant and cook.

Beginning of the illness of Miss Benjamine de la Coste.

31

Death of Sister Marie Chabert, who received the last sacraments on the 18th of the same month and had made her vows in the presence of the community. Since then she had received Holy Viaticum and constantly gave edification in her illness and death. One can see some details, as well as those concerning Sister Pain, in the book of the lives of the sisters.

The same day, beginning of the illness of Mother Bigeu, mistress of the novitiate, who for a long time gave concern about her health, which did not prevent her from keeping vigil and waiting on the sick, which contributed not a little to her illness.

November
1

Burial of Sister Chabert before the community Mass, said by the bishop of London,[415] who says Mass every day while he is in Paris.

2

Departure of Mother Bernard for Poitiers.

8

Beginning of the illness of Sister Celinie Thouvelot, choir novice, less than 16 years old.

9

Beginning of that of Miss Clara de Tourmonde, which threatens a typhoid fever, and fear about the state of Miss Luce Morange, who has fallen from a simple fever into a typhoid fever.

14

Reception of the last sacraments for Sister Celinie Thouvelot, in danger of death from fluxion of the chest and typhoid fever.

---

415 William Poynter (1762-1827), born in London and ordained priest at Douai in 1786, was consecrated bishop and named apostolic vicar of the London region in 1812. During his theological studies, he lived many years in France and spoke French fluently. He was then engaged in the politics of church jurisdiction and episcopal control between the French and English churches.

21
Renovation of vows in the presence of the bishop of London, who gave a discourse suitable for the ceremony; it was short, devotional, and touching. In the evening, Father Varin gave the sermon.

Father Soyer, vicar general of Poitiers, confessor of the boarding school and superior of the house of the Sacred Heart in that city, named by the pope to the bishopric of Luçon, usually comes every Sunday to say the Mass at 9 o'clock. And Father de Beauregard, sometimes.

Extreme Unction was given to Miss Luce Morange, in very grave danger of death from a putrid fever.

The danger continues for Sister Celinie.

The illness of Mother Bigeu does not present the same danger. By special permission of Father d'Astros, our superior (now named bishop of Bayeux), she has been able to receive Communion often in her bed, either early in the morning or at midnight from the hands of Father Perreau, whose charity for us seems to grow day by day, since he is totally given over to our spiritual needs.

29
Entrance of Miss Olympe de Causans, choir postulant. She is a students from the house of Grenoble and belongs to a respectable family distinguished for the devotion that reigns there.

December
8
Celebration of the feast of the [Immaculate] Conception. The bishop of London said the morning Mass, and Father de Villèle, named to the bishopric of Verdun, preached in the evening on the Blessed Virgin and had the students make their act of consecration.

Mother Bigeu, convalescing from her jaundiced fever, was at Mass. The two others who are sick, Sister Celinie and Miss Luce Morange, both of whom had received the last sacraments, are better.

16
Celebration of the feast of the Sacred Heart of Mary. We fasted on the vigil, and the community Mass was said by the bishop of London, the 2nd as usual by Father Perreau, and the third, which was sung, by Father Soyer. In the evening, Father Varin preached in a moving manner.

During this month, we had a visit several times from Father Martial, vicar general of Louisiana and general agent for his bishop in France.

He came to Paris for the business of the mission and to deal with our mother general about the departure of the little colony that she has destined for this land.

21

Entrance of Sister Josephine Meneyroux, novice from Grenoble.

(At this date, Mother Duchesne's entries in the journal cease.)

CHAPTER II

1818-1821

THE FIRST FOUNDATIONS

INTRODUCTION

Arrival in New Orleans

From childhood, Philippine Duchesne dreamed of being a missionary in foreign lands to bring the Gospel to China or to *les sauvages* of the Americas. Two years after her entrance into the Society of the Sacred Heart in 1804, the call became more insistent. Now that dream was to be fulfilled in a reality that would be somewhat different from what she had imagined.

After such long hoping and planning, the departure from Paris was sooner than expected, on February 8, 1818 rather than after Easter as they had planned, because of the advantage of traveling with Father Martial and other priests who were departing earlier. But once in Bordeaux, there was another long wait until March 19 before they actually set sail. The voyage took more than two months and was sometimes rough. Once they had reached the Caribbean area on May 11, it was still weeks before they arrived in New Orleans and disembarked in the middle of the night on May 29, Feast of the Sacred Heart.

The city to which they arrived had been founded by the French in 1718 along the Mississippi River, about one hundred miles upstream from the Gulf of Mexico. It soon became a major port, trading to the south with Mexico and the Caribbean and to the north by river traffic with the rest of "Louisiana," the entire area drained by the Mississippi River and most of the Missouri, what would become the entire center of the United States. In 1722, a hurricane destroyed most of the buildings of the city, and it was rebuilt on the grid pattern that still exists today in the French Quarter. In 1788, a major fire again destroyed many buildings, so that when the Religious of the Sacred Heart arrived in 1818, much of the city was relatively new, including the Cathedral of Saint Louis.

In 1763, Louisiana and New Orleans along with it had been ceded to the Spanish, who governed it for forty years. Early in 1803, the territory was returned to the French and quickly sold by Napoleon, who needed funds, to the United States in April of the same year. The

American envoys who arrived in France to negotiate the purchase of New Orleans were astonished when they were offered the whole of Louisiana. The United States purchased the Louisiana Territory for fifteen million dollars, approximately three cents an acre, and thus doubled the size of the country. New Orleans quickly became one of the wealthiest cities of the United States, thriving from commerce both to the south and to the north. One of the items of commerce was the slave markets, and there were considerable numbers of slaves in the city, but also a population of free blacks from the time of Spanish occupation. The city was a target of the British in the War of 1812 between their military and the United States, but the British were never able to conquer it.

Once arrived in New Orleans, Philippine and her companions were overwhelmed with the generous hospitality of the Ursuline Sisters, who had been in the city for almost a century, since 1727, and who provided everything for them. Philippine had expected word from Bishop Dubourg when she arrived, but there was no direct communication. In New Orleans, Philippine caught her first glimpses of Native Americans and had her first encounter with slavery, which she found incredible to accept (letter 94, written the day after arrival). Within a few days, however, she was observant and involved with the blacks (letter 97 to the students at home in France). In little more than a week, she was thinking about how to serve all racial groups (letter 100 to Mother Barat).

Philippine was disillusioned by the state of the church in this thriving port city. Her idealism had led her to expect nothing but saints. She heard sermons of doubtful theology by one priest, which she said would never have been accepted in France. The Cathedral was under the sway of Capuchin Father Antonio de Sedella,[1] venerated as a saint by many and vilified by others, who was immensely loved by his parishioners and refused either to cede the cathedral or even to accept the authority of Bishop Dubourg and his vicar, Father Louis Sibourd. While in New Orleans, she also met John Mullanphy, a wealthy merchant from Saint Louis who would in later years be a major benefactor.

The Ursulines urged the nuns to stay in New Orleans rather than going north. Only their promise in Paris to go where the bishop wanted

---

1 Antoine de Sedella (1748-1829), OFM Cap., first arrived in Louisiana as agent of the Inquisition in 1779, returned to Spain in 1783, then returned and remained in possession of the cathedral of New Orleans from 1795 until his death. He was venerated as a saint by many of his parishioners, and was the cause of their opposition and prevention against the episcopal authority of Bishop Dubourg. Philippine's comments about him express this ambiguity.

them, as intended in Mother Barat's blessing on the venture, made Philippine determined to continue to Saint Louis. After six weeks in New Orleans to recover from the voyage, during which they wrote interesting observations back to France, the five religious began another long trip by steamboat up the Mississippi River to Saint Louis. Philippine used her well-developed powers of observation to record what she saw and was told along the way for the students and others in France who she knew would enjoy the details. Some of the information given her was unreliable, but nevertheless it contributed to colorful letters and reports that would fascinate her readers back in France.

North to Saint Louis

Steamboats had been plying the Mississippi only since 1811, and the journey was still a perilous one. The Saint Louis at which they arrived on August 22 had been founded by French fur traders Pierre Laclede and Auguste Chouteau in 1764 at a strategic location on the Mississippi River near its junction with the Missouri. It quickly became a major center of the fur trade to the north and west. In 1770, it went briefly to Spain as part of "Louisiana," was returned to France and sold immediately to the United States in the Louisiana Purchase in 1803. It then became famous as the starting point of the Lewis and Clark Expedition that began there in May 1804, commissioned by President Thomas Jefferson to explore the United States' new purchase and seek a waterway to the Pacific coast. The explorers spent the last night in Saint Charles, then set off to find the headwaters of the Missouri River. They did reach the Pacific coast on the Columbia River in November 1805, and returned to Saint Louis only in September 1806, nearly two and a half years later. They were welcomed as heroes. Meriwether Lewis died in 1809, but William Clark became governor of the Missouri Territory from 1813 to 1820, with residence in Saint Louis, where he died in 1838.

Once arrived in Saint Louis, the nuns were given hospitality for a short time with the Pratte family.[2] General Bernard Pratte and Pierre Chouteau were among the wealthiest residents of the city and major agents of the booming fur trade that came down the Missouri River. Philippine wrote that Mrs. Pratte was well known throughout the town. The Pratte house at the corner of Main and Market Streets was

---

2   General Bernard A. Pratte (1771-1836) made his fortune in trade and furs, and in 1794 married Emilie Sauveur Labbadie (1777-1841). He served in the War of 1812 between the United States and England as an officer from the Louisiana Territory. The Prattes had seven children. Their second son of the same name was fourth mayor of Saint Louis in 1844-1846. Two of their five girls, Emilie and Therese, were the first boarders in the school in Saint Charles.

a typical French colonial wood structure, two stories with a gallery and detached kitchen behind. The year before the nuns' arrival, General Pratte had remodeled the house and added another two-story brick building containing his dry goods and sundries store.[3] It is probable that Philippine met Governor William Clark while staying at the house of the prominent General Pratte in the summer of 1818, though she did not write about it. Later, in 1822, she would be godmother for the baptism of his stepdaughter (letter 190).

To Saint Charles

The understanding, and Mother Barat's wish, was that they would be established in Saint Louis. Unable to find a suitable house for them there, Bishop Dubourg sent them west to Saint Charles, a small village on the Missouri River about twenty-five miles away. The town had been founded for the fur trade by Louis Blanchette in 1769, under the name *Les Petites Côtes* (The Little Hills) because of its location nestled between the Missouri River and a rise of small hills behind. The town was under Spanish control 1762-1800 with the new name of San Carlos Borromeo. It was part of the Louisiana Purchase in 1803 and was the actual departure point of the Lewis and Clark Expedition up the Missouri River in May 1804. William Clark arrived in Saint Charles on May 14 with a large contingent of men. Several times in the next days, he dined at the Saint Charles home of the Duquettes, the house that would later be turned over to the religious. Meriwether Lewis, Clark's co-leader of the expedition, arrived late in the day on May 20. The next day, the two of them had dinner at the Duquette home before setting sail for their historic journey on the afternoon of May 21, 1804.

Fourteen years later, the religious arrived in Saint Charles, on September 7, 1818, and took up residence in the Duquette house. A week later, on September 14, 1818, they opened the free school, the first Sacred Heart School in the New World. On October 3, they opened the boarding school. Two of their three boarders were Emilie and Therese Pratte, daughters of their Saint Louis host, Bernard Pratte. The third was their cousin Pelagie Chouteau.

When Philippine and her companions arrived in Saint Louis, the population was nearly all French and Catholic, but the immigration of Protestant Americans from the East was well underway. Already

---

3   Callan, *Philippine Duchesne*, 256; cf. "Earliest Picture of St. Louis," in *Glimpses of the Past* (Missouri Historical Society, 1941) 8.7-9.

when they arrived in Saint Louis in August 1818, Philippine wrote to her sisters that Missouri was about to become a state. Just three years after their arrival, Missouri did become a state of the Union in a process called "The Missouri Compromise," which lasted from 1819 to 1821. Tensions were already building between slave and free states, tensions that would erupt years later in the American Civil War (1861-1865). Missouri was admitted to the Union in 1821 as a state where slavery was legal, to balance the admission of Maine as a free state at the same time. This meant that instead of living in a French colony as the territory had previously been, or even in newly American territory, Philippine and her companions were, almost immediately after their arrival, living in the United States, something they had not expected. No evidence exists that she or any of her first companions ever became American citizens. They probably remained citizens of France.

With the arrival of statehood in 1821, Saint Charles was the first state capital of Missouri from 1821 to 1826, but during those years, the religious were not there. A considerable population of French descendants remained in the new American territory, many with a long history in the fur trade and, therefore, with excellent relationships with the surrounding Indian tribes. As more American settlers moved rapidly westward into the vast new territory to the west and north, the older French population gradually became a minority but managed to negotiate political influence. By the 1830s, English was the prevalent language in the area, and the older French inhabitants found themselves surrounded increasingly by Protestant majorities.

The feeling of isolation for the religious in Saint Charles was acute. Letters were slow to arrive and sometimes lost. Months went by with little communication with the home in France that they had left behind. Philippine had not wanted to be superior of the missionary band, but she was the oldest and the obvious choice. She was inexperienced in this kind of leadership, having been only mistress general of the school at Grenoble and secretary general at the motherhouse. She had amazing powers of observation and was a good writer, but she did not know the best way to give account of the religious under her charge or to give them spiritual leadership. She could often be quite critical rather than understanding in these new situations of stress. She was critical as well of many of the Americans she met, whom she considered lazy lovers of independence and luxury despite their poverty.

Chapter 2

Changing Life on the Frontier

From early on, there was the need for the missionaries to change and adjust some of their ideas. They found themselves in a culture in which the norms of social status from the Old World would not hold, and all free persons considered themselves social equals, yet ironically there was also slavery, the greatest social inequality. The religious were unaccustomed to the practice of slavery, but it was everywhere around them and they had to accept it. From the earliest years on the frontier, Philippine raised the question of admission of black women to religious life and even of a new religious order for them. These ideas could not be realized, and black children could not be accepted into the boarding or day school, but they were given basic religious education whenever possible.

Already in 1819, Bishop Dubourg told them that having two classes of sisters, the choir religious and the coadjutrix sisters, even with different habits, would not work on the American frontier. Philippine tenaciously clung to the difference, however, knowing that that was the way it was done in France with its traditional social hierarchy, and that they would be able this way to attract vocations of women who were not able to teach. Even in the first year at Saint Charles, Catherine Lamarre was pushing the boundaries of the two ranks, wanting to teach (letter 124). By 1821, however, Philippine writes to Mother Barat that the bishop has ceased his objections (letter 163). The first postulant who persevered, Mary Layton, was a coadjutrix sister. The religious needed to adjust their ideas of cloister, which was simply impossible to maintain; all they could do was stay at home, the object of many curious visitors, with a few planks delineating the idea of a fence around the house.

The custom of having paying day students was beginning to develop in France. From the beginning, it was part of the education offered by the religious in America (letter 119). Many parents who could afford to pay wanted this education for their daughters but were not willing to consign them to the complete and nearly all year long seclusion of the boarding school. Parents of the boarding students also pressured for more access to their daughters, pressure that Philippine resisted. In her letters, she often laments the negative effect of contact with families and home visits on the boarding students. The ideal for character formation was a total convent environment.

From the beginning, they all realized how important it was to learn English in this land that was quickly changing from French colonial to American. Octavie Berthold was said already to be fluent in English. The others had studied it before departing and along the way. Eugenie learned English well enough, though Philippine wrote that the Americans found her accent hard to understand. For Philippine, not gifted for languages, it was a lifelong trial. Over the years, she learned to read and understand English, but never trusted herself to speak it fluently, though there were certainly many occasions on which she did have to speak it.

True to their counter-Reformation European background, the little group of nuns considered Protestant churches, which abounded in the frontier setting, as heretical, yet they accepted Protestant children in their schools, hoping of course to convert them. They felt a strong competition with Protestant missionaries who were often more successful. Even though the religious were imbued with a spirituality of love through their formation in devotion to the Sacred Heart, yet elements of the religious extremes of Jansenism remained in their reactions. Philippine's eagerness for sacramental confession when she hardly had any opportunity to sin seems strange to us. In reality, confession was a way to have personal spiritual direction, which was sorely needed by these women thrust into a strange land, in their own language. Yet the constant fear of not responding to grace was deeply felt, keeping Philippine and others like her in deep self-doubt.

In the Catholic Church of the nineteenth century, priests were considered the religious experts because of their education and ordination. Moreover, the prevailing ecclesiastical organization actually gave to some of these clerics the position and title of superior of houses of nuns. While strong female spiritual leaders such as Sophie Barat were able to exercise some spiritual guidance, yet the authoritative expectation fell on the priests with their seminary education, though they did not always welcome the obligations of the pastoral care of nuns. As a result, the necessity of having as spiritual advisor the confessor with whom the nuns also had to negotiate business affairs was very awkward.

Florissant

The religious wanted a house in Saint Louis right away, where there would be greater opportunity for potential students to reach them; but the housing market was such that no affordable house was available, hence the first foundation in Saint Charles, west of the Missouri River. Bishop Dubourg, courageous and bold, was not a realistic manager, and he made arbitrary decisions that affected their welfare. Only a year after settling them in Saint Charles, he found land for them at Saint Ferdinand in Florissant on the east side of the Missouri, closer to Saint Louis, and insisted that they move there.

Fleurissant, the original name, was anglicized to Florissant, a small village that had been settled in the late 1700s by the French, called Saint Ferdinand under interim Spanish occupation. There had been a Catholic church there from 1790. Because of Bishop Dubourg's insistence, the religious had no choice but to move in September 1819, before the beginning of classes, though the house would still not be completed for another three months. Meanwhile they lived and ran their school in a nearby farmhouse also owned by the bishop. The final move into the new house and chapel took place in cold and snow on the days just before Christmas. By 1820, the boarding school counted seventeen girls, who together wrote to Mother Barat in France to congratulate her for her feast day. The same year, a novitiate was opened in Florissant that began almost immediately to prosper: in 1821, there were six novices, three of them from among the seventeen students who wrote to Mother Barat the year before: the two Hamilton sisters[4] and Emilie St-Cyr.[5]

When the religious left Saint Charles in September 1819 after only one year, the residents were distressed. At first there was thought to leave there Eugenie, Catherine, and the postulant Mary Mullen to continue the day school (Letter 124), but that plan was not followed. By 1822, a doctor in Saint Charles with daughters in the school in

---

4   Mathilde (Xavier) Hamilton (1802-1827) and Eulalie (Regis) Hamilton (1805-1888) were born in Sainte Genevieve, Missouri, of a family of English and Irish origins settled in Maryland and Kentucky. The Hamilton sisters joined the boarding school in Florissant, Mathilde in autumn 1819 and Eulalie at Christmas of the same year. Mathilde (Xavier) had a tremendous struggle with her family with regard to her vocation, but entered after her younger sister, taking the habit June 16, 1821. She made first vows March 19, 1823, and final vows after only two years, on April 17, 1825, in order to accompany Eugenie Audé to the foundation at St. Michael. There she held positions of responsibility until her sudden death on April 1, 1827. Eulalie (Regis) entered the novitiate first, in 1821 at the age of sixteen. She was mistress general at the City House in 1835, and assistant and superior. She was then superior at Saint Charles in 1841, at Saint-Jacques in Canada in 1847, then at Eden Hall and Detroit. She returned to Saint Charles in November 1851 at the request of Philippine. Sent to Chicago in 1865, she remained there until her death.
5   Emilie Saint-Cyr, RSCJ (1806-1883), called Josephine, born in Saint Louis, was Mother Duchesne's student at Florissant, and entered the novitiate in 1821. She was the second postulant, after Mary Layton, who persevered. She took the habit on March 19, 1821, made her first vows July 16, 1822, and left the next day with Philippine for Grand Coteau, where she made her profession in 1831. She was assistant and superior in several houses, including Saint Charles, where she was sent by Elisabeth Galitzine and remained for the largest part of Philippine's retirement there. The two religious were united by reciprocal affection, but Philippine always thought that Emilie did not have the gifts necessary to govern a house.

Florissant offered to build them a house. By 1825, the Jesuits were building their church there and hoping the religious would return, which they finally did in 1828. Since then, the house at Saint Charles has been in continuous existence and remains today.

Through these years and beyond, there is frequent mention in Philippine's letters to Mother Barat of a possible foundation in New Orleans, where French Catholic influence was still strong. That was not to happen until 1867, well after Mother Duchesne's death. However, only three years after their arrival in Missouri, the year 1821 would bring them back to Louisiana, to a little town up the Mississippi River called Grand Coteau or Opelousas, where the widow Mrs. Smith was offering land and a house. This meant splitting the little band of five who had come together across the sea, though a flow of new American vocations had begun and other missionaries were promised from France. Bishop Dubourg was insistent that the founders of the new establishment go to Louisiana before the arrival of the reinforcements who were on the way from France, Lucile Mathevon and Anna Xavier Murphy. So on August 5, 1821, Mother Eugenie Audé and the novice Mary Layton boarded a steamboat for Louisiana to found the second Sacred Heart community and school in America. When the two new nuns from France did eventually arrive, they were split up: Xavier Murphy would go to Opelousas, where she would become superior when four years later Eugenie struck out for yet another new foundation at Saint Michael. Lucile Mathevon traveled north to Saint Louis. She would later be the one to refound Saint Charles in 1828 and, eventually, to be the leader of the pioneer band to the Indian mission at Sugar Creek in 1841. Because of the closing of all houses in France for a brief period in the early twentieth century, the house at Grand Coteau, begun in 1821, is the oldest house of the Society of the Sacred Heart in the world in continuous existence.

LETTERS

Letter 92   **L. 1 to Mother Vincent**

SS. C. J. et M.

[May 1818]
For Mother Vincent[6]

My very good Mother,

    We are approaching the end of our journey. I have been led to hope that we are going to meet a ship heading to France; I am profiting by it to express my gratitude for so much kindness and my regrets at our separation. I have often looked for you in the divine center that unites us in spite of the geographical distance; and I have often seen you there, far ahead of me who have so few of the virtues that give one entrance to it.

    Father Barat will let you read our journal; therefore, I will not tell you anything about our voyage. One of our most pleasant recreations has been to remember those we had together with you and to recall your kindness, the virtues that adorn your holy house and our desire to bring them into ours. We don't see it yet: we are still on the sea; and after the sea, another voyage is to be faced, almost as long as the first.

    Father Martial has written to Mrs. Fournier; we are waiting to write ourselves until we arrive in New Orleans, where I hope we will receive news of her dear brother, our holy bishop. Father Martial is also in charge of the journal; it is not for us to add anything to his. Our journal is for our houses.

    A thousand greetings from me and my sisters to your dear daughters; our regards to the respectable Father Boyer.

---

6 Original autograph, C-VII 2) c Duchesne to RSCJ and Children, Box 4. Copy: C-VII 2) c Duchesne-Varia, Box 9, *Cahier Y, Lettres de la Mère Duchesne*, pp. 50-53.

I am yours in the Sacred Heart.

[no signature]

If there were an occasion to offer our respects to the Archbishop of Bordeaux, we would be very happy to convey the expression of our gratitude. Please do the same to Mrs. Fournier and Mr. Louis Dubourg.

We have just entered the waters of the Mississippi, which flows into the sea, but ten leagues from the mouth; the water is fresh and is wonderfully different from seawater at the point where they join.[7]

[On the reverse:]
To Madame
Madame Vincent
Residing rue Lalande N° 46
Opposite the School of Medicine
Bordeaux

Letter 93   L. 8 to Mother Barat

SS. C. J. et M.

[A] Near Havana, on the island of Cuba; we are sailing along the channel between this island and the Great Bahama Bank, 180 leagues from New Orleans, May 16, 1818.[8]
(This letter is for you alone.)

Very Reverend Mother,

Last year at this very hour and on this day, we received the last visit of the bishop of Louisiana, and you gave your consent to a foundation in the New World. However content I was at the time, I never thought the anniversary would find us so near the end of the first stage of our journey; for what is 180 leagues in comparison with the 2,200 we have traveled in fair weather and foul since leaving Royan?

7 This letter was written, therefore, between May 25, the first day the *Rebecca* navigated the waters of the Mississippi in the Gulf, and May 29, the day of the arrival in New Orleans.
8 On the original, the bottom of pages 3 and 4 were cut off; the letter was reconstructed by J. de Charry from three manuscript sources: [A] Original autograph, C-VII 2) c Duchesne to Barat, Box 2; [B] and [C] Partial copies: C-III USA Foundation, Haute-Louisiane, *Lettres de la Haute-Louisiane* 1818-1823, I, pp. 5-7; J. de Charry: *Correspondence*, II 1, L. 92, pp. 56-66; Hogg: pp. 38-45. Cf. Ch. Paisant, pp. 108-113.

An officer, detained because of some irregularity in his passport, joined us at night in a small boat. He informed us that some disturbances had taken place in Paris and in Bordeaux. The idea that you and other beloved persons would be suffering from them was the greatest sorrow I could have; for if we had perished at sea, it would have been the destruction of but one branch of the tree, a branch useless until now, but if the trunk of the tree were attacked!

How impatiently we are awaiting one of your letters. We are living in the hope of finding one in New Orleans; for if the ship that was to have left after us made a quicker voyage, I do not doubt the possibility that it brought us letters. I gave strict instructions that all be forwarded to us, but certainly one of those I wrote to you from Bordeaux was lost. I told you that I would have time to receive an answer, and that time was exceeded before the departure.

We are nearly at the end of our voyage and are in fairly good health. The weather has allowed us to sail along the coast of Cuba, a route not ordinarily taken because of the currents. It shortens the voyage by 400 leagues. The ordinary route is between Martinique and Guadeloupe. We avoided that detour, but we were so becalmed south of the Tropic that there was question of passing between Santo Domingo and Puerto Rico, taking a northerly course and then coming south through the Bahama Channel, which separates Florida from the Great Bahama Bank near the United States.

We have been 52 days seeing nothing but sea and sky; only on May 11 did we sight land from a distance; this was Caicos, the first of the Lucayan Archipelago, which belongs to the English. We passed between it and Marignane. At one moment we passed over the Bahama Sand Bank, the following days in a spot where the water was deep enough to keep the ship afloat. Everyone rejoiced at seeing that Lucayan island, as the land is so much more appealing than the sea.

That sea is terrible; at certain moments, I thought of writing to you to beg you not to send anyone else before receiving more precise news of us and being assured of the worth of so much sacrifice. I would greatly regret missing the opportunity of Father Velai and the Ursulines in September, but all things considered, you will not be able to have news of us from Saint Louis or to estimate our needs before October at the earliest. So if you are thinking of sending us help, I shall count on nothing before next spring;[9] and I will be the first to beg you to send no one to this mission who is not mature, without conceit, and in

---

9 The first reinforcements arrived only in 1822.

whom you see a well-marked vocation from God rather than desires expressed only in words.

We had bad weather the first three weeks. Catherine was beside herself; I feared she was out of her mind with terror. She gave many signs of it and kept repeating that she had certainly said clearly to Father Sellier, to Mother Prevost[10] and even to you, that she did not feel that she had the courage to go so far away. I answered her that I was sure that you would not have chosen her if she had not really been willing and had even asked to go; at that she replied that she had *indeed asked to go to Martinique because she believed it was near but that she had always felt repugnance for Louisiana*. During the bad weather, she turned night into day and day into night. In the end I told her one day that if she wanted to get up, she should come to share my bed; she chose to stay put. At present, she is better, declaring that once on land everything will be marvelous and that she would not want to go back.

I know and quite understand that those who are going to the same place as we are describe only its beauty in order to discourage no one. That is Father M[artial]'s request. But I must tell you the whole truth, hiding nothing, whether it be the perils of the sea or my cowardice. A storm at sea is a truly terrifying spectacle. The noise from the breaking waves and roaring wind would drown any thunder or cannonade. It is absolutely deafening, and added to that is the rolling of the vessel itself. The sailors shout to encourage one another in their work; it is a lugubrious sound, but their silence is more dismal, and still worse is the sight of the captain pacing the deck in an anxious mood. The ship tossing violently in an angry sea gives the impression of the confusion of the last day. The sky seems to roll up rapidly behind the mountains of water, dragging the stars with it. The sea, nearly black in the storm, constantly gapes wide, disclosing bottomless depths; the waves sweep over the deck as the ship rolls and pitches. Twice the waves have forced open our little portholes and drenched our beds at night. The masts bend, the sails are furled or torn; the helm is abandoned in order not to strain the vessel. All this is no laughing matter unless one sees God in the storm.

[B] The odor that pervades the ship is another trial. The foul air, the tar, the pipes, the hold above all cause sickness that is relieved only by going on deck to get fresh air; but this is not always possible in bad weather or in the evening when the men are going to bed, in the

---

10 Marie-Elisabeth Prevost (1584-1871), RSCJ, was the superior of the house of the Sacred Heart in Amiens where Catherine Lamarre lived. Louis Sellier, SJ (1784-1854), was prefect of studies and spiritual father at the minor seminary, Saint-Acheul, near Amiens.

morning when they are getting up or in bright sunlight. Some days we have been the only ones, with one other lady, not to sleep on deck. Besides all this, we are condemned to stay in our little holes very late because people are getting dressed in the lounge.

[A] But if I have thought regretfully that some would not overcome their fear, I have realized with even more pain that a great number, above all you, Mother, Mother Bigeu and others, would not be able to survive the stifling atmosphere of the cabins, the hard, narrow berths, the incessant noise, the handling of the ship's rigging, which is often carried out at night. Talking is as loud as in the daytime. Eating and drinking go on in the lounge, where two of us sleep, and the cabin of the other three opens onto this lounge.

Seasickness is a wretched malady. Besides making one feel as if one had had four or five emetics in a row, it affects the head as well as the stomach. One is incapable of anything, even a short consecutive thought; short aspirations can hardly draw any affection from a cold heart. I could say only *Ita Pater*,[11] or "I have left everything for you, O my God." And in this state if one asks for water, it often arrives five or six hours later, the same for tea. When one can take only broth, it is cabbage broth laden with grease and often made with spoiled meat. It is a mistake to think that one must eat during this illness. For several days, I took only one or two cups of broth in twenty-four hours and that while lying down; and afterwards I felt quite well. Eugenie and Marguerite have suffered less; either they are more courageous or in better health. However, for two or three days, we were all in such a state that we could not help one another, and the steward had to render us humiliating services. Either he or the captain's servant came and opened our curtains to give us tea or broth.

As for Father M[artial], we did not see him at all; he was very unwell also. [C] For a fortnight, he suffered severe digestive trouble. I cured him by means of Glauber salts.[12] During our sickness, the ship rolled terribly; one fell at every step. Either the captain or another had to give us his arm to go to the latrine, and they waited for us at the door. If one used a glass, the rolling ship whisked it from one's hand spilling the contents on the ground or over us, and one risked breaking the precious utensil.

We have left Havana behind us, good Mother, and maybe we will see New Orleans before the end of the week. We long to visit our Beloved at leisure, and my heart beat fast on seeing the steeples of

---

11 "Yes, Father," Mt 11:26.
12 A remedy bearing the name of the pharmacist, Jean Rodophe Glauber (1604-1668), who discovered the curative properties of sodium sulfate.

Havana, whose churches are magnificent, they say! When shall we see these holy temples? However, God has allowed us to have Mass about three times a week, and Communion, too, except from Wednesday of Holy Week until Quasimodo [the first Sunday after Easter], when the bad weather and sickness deprived us of everything. God took from me the memory of all that could make me want the end of the voyage and all hope of success, and during the long nights of storm and insomnia, in the silence in which God seemed deaf to all our prayers, I often asked myself if I should have repented of having risked lives so precious to the Society, so many resources that would perhaps be more useful elsewhere, to have pursued our project of emigration too far; but this feeling was never able to penetrate my heart. The peace was bitter, but it was always peace.[13] The will of God has been shown by your consent, Reverend Mother. We have been helped by so many fervent prayers; my only anxiety was not being able to confess, because Father Martial, who was as sick as I was but less concerned about the outcome than I, when I asked him if he was going to let us die without absolution, answered: "At the end of the week." I remember how Fathers Perreau, Joseph [Varin], and Louis [Barat] were always ready to listen, in less grave circumstances.

In Bordeaux, the captain had been advised not to take priests and religious, which would lead to certain shipwreck. He answered: "I have found that they do not bring misfortune." At the end of three weeks of misfortunes, one day someone said to the captain at table: "If by tomorrow the weather does not change, we will have to draw lots to see who is bringing the bad luck. On other voyages, we used to strip and beat the cabin boys, and that brought good weather." We prayed very much and the next day, at the end of twenty-four hours, the captain told me: "We are saved! We are now on good seas, under the influence of the trade winds near the Tropic, which we have crossed and recrossed seven or eight times."

We were wearing only our winter habits in the tropics because we could not unpack our luggage, which was in the hold. For all voyages, we must remember that when leaving even in December, they may need their summer habits. Excellent sea air is needed to counteract so many disadvantages. Octavie left off her flannel underwear and felt her rheumatism only when we neared land. We had to watch ourselves in the midst of so many religions and different opinions! So much impious talking, banter and revolutionary songs, from "Ça ira!" and "Aux armes,

---

13 "Behold, my bitterness changed into wellbeing" (Isa 38:17).

citoyens!"[14] Nevertheless, their conduct was decent, and we were able to follow our spiritual exercises. But because of lack of space to have Mass just for us, Father Martial was miserly about it. He has a gift of getting along well with everyone; he is of very cheerful character.

God has taken away all pride during this voyage. I thank him for it. I have found it a remedy against the seven capital sins. Oh, how good it is to see only God, and he hides his gifts! I always await them, and after this, I hope for martyrdom, which will be the crowning glory. My soul expands at this thought, and I embrace this happy lot in advance!...

Nothing can be less sure than our foundation in Saint Louis. Bishop Flaget[15] of Bardstown, Kentucky, who is more familiar with this city than Bishop Dubourg, advises him rather to choose Sainte Genevieve, inhabited by the Irish, who are offering to build his cathedral for him. The steamboats do not go all the way to Saint Louis; we will have to go 50 leagues by land, and the cold is such in winter that the ground freezes to a depth of six inches, and all the little plants are destroyed. If you want details about the United States, you will find much that is true in the work entitled: *Journey through the two Louisianas* [1801-1803] by Mr. Perrin du Lac. Since then, Louisiana has become part of the United States and has made much progress.

Philippine Duchesne

Letter 94   L. 1 to Mother Bigeu

SS. C. J. et M.

From New Orleans, May 30, 1818[16]

My very good Mother,

---

14 Refrain from *La Marseillaise* written in April 1792 by the military officer C. J. Rouget de Lisle, sung by the Marseillais, to whom it owes its name, when they entered Paris in August 1792. In 1795, it was declared the national anthem by the Convention, then prohibited from 1815 to 1870, and officially restored as national anthem in 1879.

15 Benedict Flaget, SS (1763-1850), born in Auvergne, France, joined the Sulpicians in 1783, and was ordained a priest in 1787. He arrived in Baltimore in 1792. He became the first bishop of Bardstown, Kentucky, in 1808, and transferred the diocesan center to Louisville in 1839. He traveled much for his pastoral work and spent four years in Europe to recruit missionaries (1835-1839). Renowned for his holiness and pastoral effectiveness, he died in Kentucky in 1850.

16 Copies: C-VII 2) c Duchesne to RSCJ and Children, Box 4; C-III 1: USA Foundation Haute Louisiane, Box 1, *Lettres de la Haute Louisiane I 1818-1823*, pp. 161-168. Cf. Ch. Paisant, pp. 116-121.

Here we are since two o'clock in the morning in New Orleans. Yesterday we renewed our vows on board the vessel in union with you and all our friends, and the Heart of our good Master carried on a little rivalry with that of his Mother for answering our prayers after that holy ceremony. It was the feast of the Sacred Heart at 8 o'clock in the evening that I set foot on land, which I had not touched since Holy Thursday—and which I kissed reverently under cover of darkness—this land that has been the object of so many prayers whose vivacity surged up as we drew near to it. The Ursuline religious, whose kind welcome simply overwhelms us, having been warned of our arrival, sent us carriages from 7 leagues away to where the ship docked for lack of wind. We rode in procession and arrived at two o'clock in the morning on the last Saturday of the month of Mary. That is why I said that there was some rivalry with her son to favor us.

So as not to disturb the order of the convent, we went with our reverend leader [Father Martial] and his two companions, to the home of their friends who were waiting for us, one of whom is the vicar general of the bishop. I had the three thorns that I felt the evening before in the midst of the happiness that our modest celebration gave to my heart. 1) No direct news from the bishop for us. 2) No school or boarding school in the episcopal city, Saint Louis, where the cathedral was already ten feet high when he wrote. Where will we be? I do not know. Someone is seeing to it, but at 12 miles and the school at 30 miles away. 3) The vicar general highly praised the Lancaster Method,[17] blamed the brothers for refusing to use it, and predicted that they will not succeed because the Protestants have the advantage with it. What will be asked of us about this? How shall we decide? When will we have an answer? I had a moment of feeling crushed and would have redirected my thinking to Havana if the destination had not been fixed by obedience. Here is what made me think this.

We encountered a ship whose captain asked us to take a passenger from that city to New Orleans. He was French, Basque in origin, and 12 years in the islands. His piety attached him to Father Martial. He learned the reason for our voyage and came one morning to give me out of generosity a roll of money, 212 F in all, saying that he was very eager to contribute to our foundation, adding with a simplicity that reassured me: "If you do not succeed in Saint Louis, and if you should have projects in Havana, I will give you everything you could want." When

---

17 From the name of its originator, Joseph Lancaster (1778-1838), English Quaker, this educational method used older or better students as tutors to teach younger or weaker students.

he departed, he also left us his supply of paper and pens. Havana is a Spanish city, adorned with superb churches. There are already several convents, among them one of Spanish Ursulines, who had left New Orleans at a moment of crisis. The city has a population of 80,000. Its morals are corrupt because of a series of bad priests cast out of Spain. The island has many Negroes and Indians.

In the future one can hope for an interesting foundation, but that one, ours and so many others that can be set up at enormous distances, made me think of asking: 1) Our mother to change the statute of a single novitiate, but rather to follow the example of our fathers who have them at great distances. I know that is permitted for us, but it is preferable to see a match between what one reads in the Rule and what one does. 2) I had the same thought about the postulants for recreations. 3) About access for our benefactors that is more restricted than for others. 4) Pardon one more thought: that nothing is specified about accusations and penances. Can they be made before the assistant superior when the superior is absent? 5) But the biggest difficulty is cloister; I was not one hour with our holy sisters than they said to me: "You will see, at such great distances, one cannot do the same as in France." They spoke especially about cloister: their Negroes and Negresses, large and small, are in the cloister, what cloister! A child could jump over it: a few planks!... I have not seen a single stone all along the Mississippi. 6) The Negroes are slaves, they have about 32. Can this be? The civil law that makes them free is not observed except in a small part of the United States, especially in New York. I have already embraced these little Negresses of the sisters, one month old, one year, three years. That one would be sold for 2000 F and her father, for up to 12,000 F. We have not yet seen any Indians, even though there are many in the city who willingly make themselves known.

You see, dear Mother, how important these questions are. You can present them to our mother, with whom this letter is meant to be shared, but it was pleasing to me to put your name above, as witness of my remembrance and my gratitude for so much concern for us. Once the decision is taken after advice from Father Varin and Father Perreau, I beg you to send it to me by way of their friends in Georgetown, to whom I will give my address when I know it. I did not expect this trial. Is Bishop Dubourg afraid that we will be a burden? Does he fear a repetition of the atrocious calumnies against him and his daughters here, like those against Saint Francis de Sales? By dividing his foundations, does he want to divide his resources and spread the light of faith, having in a space of 500 leagues only twelve priests?

Yellow fever is not here, as it was feared. The doctor visited our ship 7 leagues from the city. Would you believe, dear Mother, that I was so ungrateful as to forget that, according to the vow to Saint Regis that our mother permitted me to make, at the moment of boarding the ship we should have had a novena of Masses said to Saint Regis? I am writing to Mrs. de Mauduit to ask her to have it done. If she pays for it, she will write to you; but if not, please send her the amount by way of Mr. Rollin or someone else. Pray much for us, good Mother, not only because of the dark veil that covers the future of our efforts, but also because of so many losses of spiritual goods. We counted 36 Communions, 48 Masses, 24 expositions of the Blessed Sacrament, 60 Benedictions, 24 sermons, and Fathers Joseph, Louis, Perreau, and our dear mothers.

I await impatiently the blessing of the Holy Father. He himself wrote to the superior of this house, when she was in Montpellier. She wrote to him, without the knowledge of her confessor or bishop, to decide whether to come here. The answer was prompt and favorable, and Bishop Fournier told her that it was a unique case for a pope to answer the letter of an individual person without consulting the bishop.

This very hospitable house is composed of several Creoles, one of whom is the daughter of one of the first inhabitants of this city, born about.... Two came from Pont Saint Esprit 32 years ago, and I have had the pleasure of repeating to them all that I remembered then about their voyage. Their third companion is dead. Eight came from Montpellier with the superior 8 years ago, by way of Philadelphia and Baltimore. In the latter city, they were discouraged, but a holy gentleman told them that a lay sister had predicted that the banks of the Mississippi would one day see many religious houses. That encouraged them. The others are those chosen by Bishop Dubourg. Our foundation will be the second at 500 leagues up the river, and when will it deserve the name? Father Martial is full of goodness. He has many connections with Mr. de La Grée of Grenoble, always something to please us.

My letter to our mother went with those of my sisters on a ship that passed us on the Mississippi. I told her of my disappointment in not having news from her, especially since they said that there are troubles in France. I told her about our voyage, as did Octavie. There was bad weather for three weeks, then good weather afterwards, but delay caused by periods of calm. It took only 15 days from Havana here, a distance of 180 leagues, but our ship is one of the lucky ones: another that left before us took 78 days to Havana, and another that had only a quarter of our route, 35 days.

How necessary it is for these enterprises to have persons who are strongly silent, mortified, and with judgment. The Americans are not courtly and do not like delicacies. They admire culture as much as the French do, but they do not like them, disdain their customs, their language, and deny their ability in certain sciences and arts. It is said that they are the most industrious people in the world and the most capable of civilizing North America. The Methodist sect, which has missionaries, is spreading fast and makes the Catholics realize the need for a similar movement for Catholic instruction instead of a resident pastor at too great distances (the thinking of an advocate of the Lancaster Method).

The Ursuline sisters are a haven for religion here. Besides the five of us, they now usually support six ecclesiastics, and they usually feed and lodge the two who reside here, who have nothing else. Here there are no revenues provided for ecclesiastics. If they combine together in a region, they come under the law and their apostolic efforts are censured. Cotton, linen, black material and bread are reasonably priced here, as well as crockery, but food and lodging are very expensive: one chicken, 5 F; two chicks, 5 F; a monthly rented room, 100 F; a visit to the doctor, 10 F; a daily hotel rate, 10 F; a day's wages for a worker, 10 or 15 F; porters earn up to 20 or 30 F a day.

Nevertheless, I count little on boarders; those here, who are very impressive looking, intelligent and would not look out of place in Paris, are nearly all from the islands and plantations, and are placed here only for First Communion, for 3 months, 6 months, a year, almost never two. How can we succeed in so little time to form them to virtue and religion, and then they are withdrawn? Here they give 900 F; that is 300 F in Paris, but these sisters are rich and God permits it for the good of religion. The priests have nothing except from them, and that good work alone costs them 15,000 F a year. A chaplain costs them 50 gourdes a month besides lodging and food, or 3000 a year, and that is not a Father Perreau or Father Rambaud, to be sure.

The gospel this Sunday, May 31, and today's epistle revived my heart a little, and I had the first Benediction since Passion Friday. God allowed me in a free moment to express to the superior a certain opposition against the priest who praised the Lancaster Method, etc. She told me that my approach made it easier to make hers to me. She opposes his title of vicar general and told me many things that show that he is not entirely devoted to the mission and has opinions at odds with those of the bishop. Opinion is generally so in favor of him that one must hope. God is good; nevertheless, he does not forbid foresight, and in the fear that the bishop's preparations for us will cost only 10,000 F, which we will owe him, I hope to avoid other expenses and have something left to eat. A garden and some cows will be enough for us. So I would like a sister gardener and with her a domestic of Father Martial's whom the bishop wanted to bring; but he left him because he has too familiar a manner, but he expressed his desire. He is a good man, in good health; he bakes bread, does the garden, makes furniture, and would be able to accompany our sisters en route. Father Vincent and Father Barat know him and could propose this good work to him, not very lucrative. He has enough to pay his voyage, and his deposit of 3 or 400 F.

The French Consul who came to see us before I had presented the letters of recommendation confirmed to me that one is better off with regard to religion and morals under the American captains, and he assures us that the royal ships never carry women, that there is a rule in that regard. This consul is a man of the world who is completely honest, religious, obliging. While he said that he has little power, he offered that we could address all our letters to him. He is *Mr. Guillemin, Consul General of France in New Orleans.*

Father Martial has shown us the first fruits of his apostolate in the New World by giving First Communion to 40 young people of color. The paper is running out. Get many blessings for us from our mother and our fathers. Many good wishes to our mothers and sisters. Those here are writing and the consul will take the letters.

Letter 95 L. 8 to Mrs. de Mauduit, at Crest (Drôme)

New Orleans, 2 June 1818[18]

My dearest Sisters and Brother,

I suspect that the friendship that unites us will have given you some anxiety about the outcome of my voyage, anxiety that may be increased by the length of our trip; but here I am on land, in a city where the language and customs could make me believe I am in France, and the house that welcomed us could be one of ours. In none would we have received greater signs of affection and numerous attentions; the ship stopped six leagues below the city because of lack of wind. The Ursulines, to whom our bishop had recommended us, sent for us in a

---

18 Copies: *Cahier, Lettres de la Mère Duchesne à sa famille*, pp. 92-95; *Lettres dactylographiées.* C-VII 2) c Duchesne to her family and lay people, Box 5.

carriage that must have cost them at least fifty *écus*; still they thought it very little.

Once we arrived at their house, we found not only touching examples of every virtue of hospitality but the most comprehensive care: medicines to guard against change of temperature, baths, cool drinks, carefully chosen food, all kinds of clothing; ours was taken and washed the same day by the Negro women. Mothers could not have done more for their children. They are even talking about giving us several things for the continuation of our travels; we still have four or five hundred leagues up the Mississippi in a steamboat, an admirable invention that can make the trip in twenty days, while only two years ago it took the people of this country six months. There are now forty of these boats going up and down the Mississippi; commerce is becoming greater by the day, and Upper Louisiana, where we are going, is making progress daily toward civilization.

Our bishop's church is almost finished, and our house is being readied as well as the school; the priest who accompanied us on the voyage will direct it. Upon arriving, he found several students in a hurry to follow him and the parents still happier to be able to raise their children in a Christian manner. How many educational establishments would be needed in this country! We see young people eighteen years old who have learned only how to eat and to run around, even among the wealthiest inhabitants; they have been taught so little about how to pray that they don't even know how to make the sign of the cross or genuflect or name the principal mysteries of the faith.

How much better are our fortunes than the colossal fortunes that cause the soul to revolve around only material things! Prices here are all in proportion to the amount of money; the Ursuline nuns, lodging us, are saving us more than fifty F a day that we would have to spend if we were paying for our stay here while waiting for the boat to Saint Louis.

When we see so much fertile land uncultivated, we are surprised that so many people who in France are arguing over a few square feet of land do not come to the banks of the Mississippi to harvest the fruits of their labors in a very short time.

I beg my brother not to neglect to withdraw the income that is completely due for 1817.

I told Melanie [Visitandine at Romans] that upon arrival I wrote to the superior of Georgetown to recommend myself to her prayers; I met one of their boarders here who, seeing my cross that reminded her of theirs, was very much touched. I had asked her for a few articles for the sacristy, but I withdrew my request because of the enormous cost of transporting them, which maybe we could not afford. She will be sure to tell my aunts and cousins and her mother superior how much I count on their prayers.

A businessman from Havana, French in origin, joined us near Cuba. He was so interested in our work that on his own initiative he very modestly gave us more than 200 F, wishing, he said, to cooperate in it.

I would like to have written to the two Amelies [de Mauduit and Jouve], to my godson [Henry Jouve], and to the oldest Lebrument girls [Caroline and Henriette], but I have so much to write as my departure may be very soon, that I beg them to read what is in my heart and, if they want details, to ask Constance [Jouve] for our journal.

I do not despair of seeing some of my nephews or nieces in this country one day, whether like us to save souls or to earn in a few years what they will need to live on for the rest of their life.

I am all yours in the heart of Our Lord,

Philippine

I beg Mrs. de Mauduit to have nine Masses said for me at La Louvesc; Mother Barat will repay her, unless she wishes to make me a gift of them, and then she can tell her so.

Letter 96 L. 7 to Mother Maillucheau

SS. C. J. et M.

New Orleans, June 3 [1818][19]

My very good Mother,

I wrote to you from Bordeaux and to Aloysia, too. I do not know the fate of my letters, but I carried with me the loving memory of a mother and a friend whom I cannot forget, more a friend at the moment of our separation, when you were so devoted in everything that could advance our mission. We are still 400 leagues away. Our house is being arranged, and the bishop's church is being built. While waiting, we are enjoying a good example of perfect charity with the Ursuline sisters, whose care for us is that of the tenderest of mothers, and far from finding us a burden, which in fact we are, they speak only of the pain of our leaving.

---

19 Original autograph, C-VII 2) c Duchesne to RSCJ and Children, Box 4. Copy: C-VII 2) c Duchesne-Varia, Box 9, *Cahier Y, Lettres de la Mère Duchesne*, pp. 53-57.

I will not give any details of our voyage, since I think that our mother will have shared the two letters that have already gone and the journal with them. If it has not reached you, we will resend a copy with what follows up to our arrival in New Orleans. I am also writing a letter to the students and sending with it a little basket for you, made by an Indian.

I beg you not to forget me to anyone. If the bishop speaks to you of me, offer him my very humble respects. I offer them also to Fathers Rivet and Rambaud, whose goodness is just as present to me as when I saw the effects more closely. I count very much on their prayers and on those of Father d'Hyères; we would have great need in this diocese of some workers like him, and of his children. In September, we count on Father Velai, but if that is not known, do not say anything.

I would like to say a word to each of my sisters individually; neither the time nor the distance permit it, but I do not forget anyone before God, and I name here especially Mothers Rivet and Second, my first companions, Mothers Lavauden, Adrienne [Michel], Morelin, Fournon, J. de Coriolis,[20] de Rambery, Rombau; my former daughters, Foussala, Boisson, Françoise, my companions at work; finally, everyone, including the students and the poor. Tell these last that I was present Sunday at the religious instruction of the Ursuline sisters; there were more than 300 of all colors and all faces, especially some good old black women, who would really have liked it if we stayed with their mothers in the faith. The same day, there was in their church a First Communion of 40 blacks, Creoles, Mulattos, etc. When will we see so many in our church?

This Ursuline convent, as old as the city, was built as a regular house at the expense of Louis XV. The first sisters nearly perished of misery, living more in the marshes than on land. Now they are rich and are nearly the only ones supporting religion in the city. We could not repay what they are doing for us.

Goodbye, dear Mother. Octavie and Eugenie offer you their respects.

---

20 Josephine de Coriolis, RSCJ (1799-1859), entered the novitiate December 21, 1817, made her first vows in Grenoble, December 21, 1819, and her profession in Paris, December 11, 1825. She was for a long time superior at the Trinità dei Monti, and permitted the young postulant Pauline Perdrau to paint the fresco of "Mater Admirabilis" in one of the cloisters in 1844, erected a chapel there, where a good number of conversions and healings happened, and propagated devotion to this miraculous image of the Virgin Mary throughout the world. She gave hospitality from 1845 to 1848 to Mother Makrena Mieczyslawska, Basilian abbess of Minsk, of whom Philippine speaks in her letter to Amelie Jouve on August 30, 1848. During the revolutionary troubles of 1849 in Rome, she acted wisely and courageously to welcome Mother de Limminghe and the community of the Villa Lante. Back in Paris in 1850, she was mistress general at the Hôtel Biron. Later she re-opened the house in Parma, where she died on March 11, 1859. She is the author of *l'Histoire de la Société du Sacré-Cœur*, A-II 2)-b) General History of the Society.

Letter 97   **Letter to the boarding schools
of Paris and Grenoble**

SS. C. J. M.

New Orleans, June 3, 1818[21]

My very dear Friends,

Your names carried upon my heart and in my heart are always present to me; I have added to this the pleasure of telling you so. I do not know when this letter will reach you, but however late it arrives, it will always tell you that I will never forget you, at the same time that I attest that it is sweet to leave all for God who has given himself entirely to us.

I have already seen these Indians for the love of whom we have come so far. There are many who come to sell the little baskets, some of which you will see, or blackberries that they collect in the woods. The skill with which they make their little trinkets and the craftiness with which they sell them prove that they are capable of reflection and thus to come one day to the knowledge of God, if one takes care to make of them human beings in order then to make them Christians. But in this city, which is more corrupted by luxury and grandeur than any city of France, people are accustomed to despise them like animals. They experience only rejection, and they are wilier than those we will find in Upper Louisiana. They are cruel, vindictive, and reject everything said to them about religion. Even when they understand French, they answer: *"Not me that, me Indian."* Those who come to the door of the Ursuline Sisters call them *the women of the Great Spirit*. Those I have seen are completely covered like the representations of Our Lord at the moment of the *Ecce Homo*, but the mantle that covers them is much more bizarre. One of them who came to put his head in at the door of the church on Sunday looked like a devil wanting to put his head in at the door of paradise. He then made off like a thief.

The same day, I was going to the halls where the Ursuline Sisters give instruction to more than 300 Creoles, mixed race, and black women; there are some who live like saints. One of them came to me all joyful, her two hands together, to know if I was staying here. She devoured

---

21 Copies: C-VII 2) c Duchesne to RSCJ and Children, Box 4; C-III 1: USA Foundation Haute Louisiane, Box 1, Part B, *Lettres de personnes variées*, 1818-1828, pp. 32-39; C-VII 2) c Duchesne to her family and lay people, Box 5, *Lettres à Mme de Rollin N° 9, Cahier*, pp. 13-21. Cf. Ch. Paisant, pp. 127-131.

us with her eyes and was very sad when we told her that we were going farther away. But alongside the few good ones, how many are ignorant and love only finery when they can get it from New York or Philadelphia, where there are no slaves. They go barefoot frequently on workdays, and on Sundays in dresses and hats of pink or blue taffeta, undoubtedly to offset the black of their face. Here several wear tulle dresses or at least of bright white fabric.

The slaves, who do not have what they need to appease their vanity, wait until their masters are absent, then go to the ball dressed in their clothing. The women who iron do the same on Sunday with the dresses that are left with them. Ah! Pray much for people so ignorant and sinful; the laborers are lacking to instruct them. When an Indian can explain himself and excuse himself, he says: "*Up to now, no one teaches us.*"

They group around a fire, which is as pleasant to them in summer as in winter; they even sleep around it. The blacks, too, never go to bed without warming themselves in every season. The condition of these slaves is not always unhappy: they have two or three hours a day for themselves, which they use to cultivate a little ground that is given to them, which they call *desert*, or they go to work elsewhere and earn as much in a little time as those who work all day in France. The pope has permitted them to work on Sunday also. They each have their little house; all of them together form a camp. They are all clothed. I have seen along the Mississippi plantations where there are up to 100. Their master with these alone is rich by more than a million, since every slave is worth more than 10,000 F. In Cuba, which is called here Great Cuba, there are plantations with more than 400 blacks. There are individual ones that produce 250,000 F in sugar per year. Does that make them happy? I would really rather instruct one Indian woman and eat like her, than to see myself in such great abundance with the responsibility for so many persons, for the salvation of whom they are so indifferent that they leave them without instruction, without religious practices.

I will try to include with my letter the plan of the ship in which we came. After you have seen it, please send it to the Misses de Vidaud and de Jonquières in Grenoble, to whom I promised to write. The Seine that you know in Paris, the Rhone so beautiful and rapid, the Loire so lovely in Tours, finally the Garonne, have nothing on the Mississippi. The width of a fifth branch at its entry is equal to those of the Loire when they are united [to the Gironde]. Its entry is frightful: from the Gulf of Mexico, one passes through what is called *white water* (which is really green) and there, one begins to be able to find the sea bottom at several leagues from the mouth of the river. Its waters are carried on those of the sea without mixing either to right or left, and the ship as it plies leaves behind a visible trace of the seawater that it has turned over.

The struggle between the sea and the river is visible at its mouth. To push it back, the sea has accumulated sand, which is held by the edge of the land and the rocks, whose tops are visible, to form a bank. The river has very little depth and leaves only enough water to carry a boat, which, in a space that is too narrow, is surrounded by reefs and enormous tree trunks that float and land on the ground. The captain is then in full activity; the best sailor is at the rudder; another, with a probe in hand, repeatedly throws it and calls out the number of fathoms that he finds; the coastal pilot is at the front of the boat with the long view to see the actual area between two objects he has observed, which must fix the course. The other sailors and the passengers keep a dismal silence and do not begin to speak until the captain says: "We are in the river."

There is no tide as in the Gironde. To go upstream, one has to be pushed by a favorable wind, which often dies. Therefore, it takes quite a long time to go 32 leagues. We were not so favored, or delayed. After the horrors of the entrance, we enjoyed the beauty that was offered: an undergrowth of trees of the loveliest green forms a long, pleasant curtain that is not interrupted by any devastation, since the river is so peaceful that the bank alone contains it with no dike, but along it are little cabins and large plantations where one can see orange trees, pomegranates, myrtle, pink and white laurel on open ground, fields of tobacco, corn, cotton, and sugar cane, among which herds of cows or other animals graze. The cows' milk must be sugared. When you buy it on the boat, the vendor includes a piece of sugar cane.

At half the distance to New Orleans, the woods are no longer only undergrowth, but they are good timber trees: the green oak, the sycamore, thorns, high poplars, and willows. Along the water are enormous palm trees whose leaves are very large, and when tied together by the stems, they make a large fan. These leaves make brooms, adorn the loveliest straw hats, and are used by the Indians to make their baskets. They paint them with different designs to make them in the manner that you will see. The Mexican Indians are natural artists and make very beautiful things of shells.

To finish what I want to tell you about the banks of the Mississippi: the part in the neighborhood of New Orleans is cleared of these trees, which good cultivation will not replace. The marshy areas are not right for good vegetation. Vines die and dry up; cherries and currants do not produce fruit; the best plums are like our worst; peaches rot, and vegetables are very expensive. Figs and oranges do well, but this winter, which was extremely cold for this region, caused many oranges to die, and in the best years, they do not compare to those of Cuba. They gave us some en route, much better than those of France, with pineapple and bananas. Cuba also exports tobacco and sugar cane, which cannot mature enough to have its full sweetness; we eat it raw here; the refined kind comes from France and is also expensive.

The sea is gray during storms, the color of slate in good weather, and beautiful blue with rays of violet in full sun. It is often hardly brighter than the moon when the setting sun seems to sink into the water. At other times, it looks like a blazing furnace. Its rising and setting are even more beautiful on land where the horizon is wider. At sea, one can see for only 3 leagues, and it looks like the distance from our house to Val-de-Grâce, because it all looks the same. I have not seen any whales or even sharks or dogfish, though several were caught on the hook, but we came upon several groups of dolphins, very big fish, and they caught 2 large porpoises or "sea pigs" and rainbow-colored sea bream, a cod, a huge turtle which, instead of feet like those on the ground, has 4 strong fins; flying fish; crocodiles in the Mississippi that look like gray lizards; many snakes, sea polyps, and shellfish by the millions; there were a thousand on a cedar trunk found in the sea, having come from the coasts of Virginia and Carolina. The mosquitos that we encountered at the entrance to the river make themselves more heard than seen; they much resemble their venomous cousins of France. The only native bird that sings is called the *mockingbird.* There are also *popes, cardinals*, and *bishops.* The pope is easier to feed than the cardinal; we have also seen pelicans and herons.

In the house of the Ursuline Sisters, who have the goodness to lodge us, there are nearly 60 boarders, 20 orphans, and some day students. They are all *white*, except those who come for Sunday religious instruction; on the contrary, we will have more girls of color. I commend our mission to you, and I have already recognized the effects of your prayers. To finish well is everything. The country where we are going to win souls sends much cargo to this city, which has received more than 500 ships this year, not counting the 300 that will take what remains of cotton, sugar, tobacco, and flour.

In two words, I conclude by telling you that I have you all in my heart, and I try to put mine in the Heart of Jesus.

Philippine

Special Features of the Country[22]

They told us about a Cuban plant that attaches like ivy to walls and inflames the hand as soon as one approaches it. There one finds a flea that burrows under the skin, lays its eggs there, and forms a little wound. It happens often here that when one goes for a walk, little red things as small as the point of a needle attach to one's legs, causing a terrible itch with inflammation. The way to get rid of them is to wash with soap. The ants are so abundant that one has to take great precautions against them. They carpet the walls sometimes and even come into beds where they bite. The mosquitos are like our cousins; divine Providence takes care of the suffering by sending them only in the evening or the morning when the heat is heavy. They attack the locals less, do not trouble one walking, and from December to May. This year, there were few.

New Orleans is [built] on silt. The land has only a certain depth; however little you dig, there is abundant water, but it is bad; they drink the river water that is not clear, but it is healthy. Few people mix it with wine because of the price. The Mississippi is so deep that whatever attempt is made to measure its depth at the city is as impossible as knowing that of the open sea. Wood here so resists water that wooden foundations made 80 years ago have been found nearly intact. They cover houses with wooden shingles, cut like slate and with the same slope. They eat quantities of blackberries brought by the Indians. They season them like strawberries. They eat little salad because oil is rare and expensive. They are dispensed from Saturday abstinence.

Cows cannot subsist here closed in.[23] They are let go during the day and they go into the woods. Their calves that are kept behind make them come back. They are milked only once a day, and their milk does not make much butter. That of Saint Louis is much better. The woods to the right and left along the Mississippi are 90 leagues deep in certain places. One would be afraid to get lost in the marshes that are interspersed in them. To the west of these woods are very rich areas. Snakes are so common in Martinique that in a sugar field one year there were so many that the blacks could not take a step to remove the weeds, which is necessary. The owner, seeing that he had to sacrifice the harvest, set it on fire. The snakes, feeling the heat, all went to the

---

22 Copy: C-III USA Foundation Haute Louisiane, Box 1, *Part B: Lettres de personnes variées 1818-1828*, pp. 41-45. The four sections (Special Features of the Country; Edifying Characteristics; Note on Upper Louisiana; and Notice on Louisiana and the Edifying Life of Miss Isabelle) are not dated and are not part of letter 97, but they were surely written upon arrival in America and sent to the students. We therefore place them after this letter.

23 Enclosed in a fenced pasture.

middle and piled up to the height of a house. I must say that the houses in the region are low because of the winds. They often cover them in brick and surround them with galleries.

There are no poisonous animals in Cuba. The vipers are not dangerous. The scorpions cause a light illness. Yellow fever is easily healed when caught in time.

Edifying Characteristics

1. We see children of color come every day for 2 or 3 consecutive hours in the church, and in the evening, not tired, they surround the altar steps and kiss them several times, bowing to make reparation.[24]
2. A good Mulatto woman has such faith, that when she does the ironing, she will not take money for ironing the church linen (she asks for convents for Mulattos).
3. Another is going to go 400 leagues at her own expense to offer her services to the bishop.
4. They have just buried Miss Marie, a great model of charity. She was a chambermaid to a rich inhabitant of Santo Domingo, who had 250,000 F in revenue, lost it all in one day in the revolt of the blacks, and arrived in New Orleans. Marie supported her mistress and 2 children by her work, repairing lace and stockings. God blessed her work. She was soon in a position to buy a black woman who gave her some children and earned income by their work. She found herself able to care for her mistress during a revolting illness and infection that lasted 18 months, during which time she ruined 6 mattresses. She went as far in her charity as to sleep near her while her infection prevented her own child from visiting her, and she wept much at her death. After her mistress, she closed the eyes of her son, who had nothing but debts to pay her for her services. Finally, to crown her merits, she took in, cared for, and closed the eyes of 2 missionaries who died of yellow fever and were saints. She herself suffered much, and before she died, she freed her black women.
5. The Catholic Acadians, expelled from Acadia when the English seized it, took refuge here and make up a good quarter of the city, keeping their good principles.

---

[24] This act of reparation was made after Benediction to repair for outrages committed against the Heart of Jesus.

6. One is very human here: there is dispute over a foundling who is being raised like one's own child. A woman whose house was burned was later given a collection of 50,000 F, but unfortunately, they would not have given so much for a church or a religious work.
7. Several good black women who could have earned 25 F a night and their food during the illness last year risked their life to watch for free at the Ursulines. During the whole of Lent, they give up tobacco.
8. One of them named Catherine and her daughter Lucette were among the group. Catherine spends her life in prayer, serving the sick and burying the dead. She was from Santo Domingo and was converted by the bishop. For having been slightly impatient, she deprives herself of her coffee, which is very necessary here. Having known God a little late, she says like Saint Augustine: "I have loved you late, O my God!" Having heard that God likes short prayers, she said: "I not capable of leaving my prayer, I must pray long, prayer in heaps, when sad, prayer consoles me, I not know how to suffer; well! I promise not to eat breakfast." She retired and spent 5 years keeping an old blind man, still has her work at home, and besides her family, four foundling children.

[By Mother Duchesne]

Note on Upper Louisiana[25]

Saint Louis, right bank of the Mississippi
Elevation: 39th degree latitude
Population: 136 families. A presbytery of 4 *arpents*.[26]

Fleurissant[27]
15 miles north-west of Saint Louis
36 families

Sainte Genevieve, right bank
60 miles south-west
44 families. A good presbytery and 144 *arpents* of land.

---

25 Copy: C-III 1: USA Foundation Haute Louisiane, Box 1, *Lettres de la Haute Louisiane I 1818-1823*, pp. 31-32. Cf. J. de Charry, II 1, pp. xxi-xxii; Hogg, pp. xv-xvi; Ch. Paisant, pp. 131-132.
26 Old measure of length, equivalent to 58 to 71 m., according to region. By extension, the square arpent carré (acre) became the surface measure that was equivalent to 35 to 51 ares, depending on the region.
27 French word for Florissant, which Philippine uses thereafter.

The Barrens
81 miles, south-west
80 families. Many Protestants who harass the Catholics.

The climate is extremely cold in winter. Mass cannot be said without difficulty and many precautions must be taken. Sometimes those present have to beat their feet against the floor so as not to freeze.

The soil is of unbelievable fertility but is not cultivated because of the low number of inhabitants. They are increasing visibly, and the immigration of families that arrive from Europe, especially Germany and England, is continuous, so that in a few years, this region will be flourishing.

Religion enjoys complete freedom. All follow their own as they wish. Catholic priests are respected here, perhaps more than in France, and even the heretics come willingly to hear them preach. There is much more to endure for the exercise of the ministry than in Europe. But the terrain is less ungrateful because grace has been less abused. The poor people are docile but lack instruction. They have never had any but bad priests, the rejects of Europe, who by their bad example destroy the good that their preaching could accomplish.

We cannot hope to work so soon and in an effective way for the conversion of the Indians. There is no way until there is a beneficial revolution in religion among the whites, who belong to several sects and among whom Catholics are such only in name.... The Indians know that with regard to religion, a great diversity of sentiment reigns; and they say to the missionaries who reach them that when the whites agree among themselves on the same faith, it will be their turn to adopt it also....

Otherwise, they approach the villages with great security and freedom and speak with pleasure to the missionaries. They come on horseback in this country, sell their game, and buy ammunition. They are half-naked, with silver pendants from ears and nose, their faces colored red or blue, etc.

Wars among them are frequent and they kill many, without fear or regret for those who survive. By tradition, they retain several informal traits of Christianity that fathers have communicated to their children, since the Jesuits came to sow the first seeds. However proud and intractable, they have a great liking for the priests, whom they call black robes in their language, and God is called by them the Master of Life. Many of them who still make the sign of the cross do it with the left hand because they say the left one is closest to the heart.

Notice about Louisiana and the Edifying Life of Miss Isabelle[28]

Louisiana was given to Spain at the end of the last century, about 1782. It had been discovered at the beginning of the same century. The Jesuits came there soon, and the country had not yet been settled when they called the Ursuline Sisters to instruct young girls and take charge of the first hospital built next to their house. But the establishment that began in suffering prospered through devotion to the Blessed Virgin. A sister brought her statue from France, one that she had found in a garret, cleaned with respect and promised to her good mother that she would have it honored in America. This little statue is still there. It is set with honor under glass above the superior's place in the choir. Louis XV had the convent built thirty years ago, and it cost him so much that he said: "These religious must be better housed than I." But he was mistaken. Everything that came from France on the royal ships for the religious arrived duty free; the governors protected them.

Under the Spanish, the king paid their chaplain and board for eight religious, and the laws permitted that a girl who converted, whose religion would have been in danger with her parents, no longer had to obey them.

Isabelle wanted to take advantage of it, and here is her abridged story. She was from Natchez and born of Protestant parents. They gave her a good education by worldly standards and she had artistic skills. At 17 years, they sent her to New Orleans to learn French; they had acquaintances there. But the young woman, passing by the Ursuline Convent, felt an overwhelming attraction to enter it, asked to do so, and after many difficulties, they gave their consent because she said she would learn French there in the same way as with private tutors.

From the first day, she was all eyes and ears to instruction about religion, but she understood nothing. Finally, God worked in her in a marvelous manner. After eight days, she said she could follow and when she listened, she shed many tears. The religion teacher took her aside and asked her the reason: "Ah!" she said, "my good Mother, I have lived like an animal, I did not know my Savior, Jesus Christ, nor his Holy Mother, so what good is everything else?" The love of Jesus Christ and that of Mary took complete possession of her heart. Without human respect, she asked the youngest boarders to help instruct her and stayed with them continuously. After two months, she asked for

---

28   Copy: C-III USA Foundation Haute-Louisiane, Box 1, *Lettres de la Haute-Louisiane I 1818-1823*, pp. 38-40. Cf. Ch. Paisant, pp. 132-134.

holy baptism. The mistress examined her about her instruction, found that she had not lost a word of anything she had been taught, and as to her dispositions, she was ready to die, to suffer everything rather than to break her baptismal promises. It was a solemn one, and she had for godparents the Spanish governor and his wife. It was clear that she had received the fullness of grace; she grew in perfection each day, and her prayer became sublime. It was a simple act of making herself nothing before the great majesty of God. She dissolved in tears and believed that it was an imperfection in her not to have many spiritual thoughts. A mother who loses a child has less sorrow than she brought to her first confession, when she was told that her faults were not serious. "Ah!" she answered, "if they are not because of the matter, they are because of ingratitude." The purity of her soul astonished her confessor, and she was prepared for her First Communion. When her parents learned of her change and her desire to become a religious, they came to take her. The sisters wanted to enforce the Spanish laws, but the bishop decided that she had to return to her family. He confirmed her before her departure and she made her First Communion. The father consented, but he did not want this to be inside the convent; it was in the external church. She did not have permission to re-enter except to gather her clothes. But finding the image of the Blessed Virgin, she prostrated before her, saying in sobs: "Holy Mother! What has been my pride and temerity, aspiring to be the spouse of your divine son, and was I worthy? Oh! Support me, dear Mother, in my struggles." She arose to try to pack her things, but finding other images of the Blessed Virgin, at each one, she renewed her protestations, her prayers and sobs. There was no one in the house who did not weep with her, so much did they love her and fear that she would be persecuted. Indeed she was, but that did not prevent her from persevering in her vocation for seven years. After that time, everything made her despair of being able to fulfill it, but both before that time and after, up to her death, which was not far away, she always persevered in faith, piety, and zealous actions, instructing the ignorant and baptizing all the children, Indians, blacks, and others who were in danger of death. Thus, she got a great number to heaven ahead of her.

The end.

Letter 98   **L. 1 to Father Varin**

SS. C. J. et M.

[June 4, 1818][29]

My very good Father,

Here we are, almost at the end of our journey, for four or five hundred leagues are very little when one has traveled thousands, and a trip on a gentle and beautiful river is a pleasure after one has seen the ocean and its storms. The Mississippi is not very formidable except at its mouth. It will soon be as heavily navigated as our rivers of France, so greatly is commerce progressing on its shores.

The doctor who attends the convent where we are staying has pictured New Orleans to us, perhaps too optimistically, as becoming very soon the equal of Bordeaux, and St. Louis becoming like New Orleans, and all Upper Louisiana transformed in a few years into another France, as far as climate, fertility, commerce, and civilization are concerned. The idea of so much progress in so little time has sent my thoughts flying after my heart. They have raced to the far northwest and across the South Sea to Korea or Japan to gain the martyr's palm. That is the way with ambition in this world—never satisfied. But I can assure you that mine would stop there, and after martyrdom I will want nothing.

Before attaining this happiness, which may still be far away, I allow myself to form other wishes concerning our mission; and the most important for it and for us will certainly be to see some of your sons out here. If only you would work to bring this about!

How much my soul was constrained—expecting to find here only saints and meeting almost immediately a priest (not the one who has caused the schism, but another) who holds opinions bordering on heresy, who has no love for the august name that it is such an honor for us to bear, and who makes trouble for a convent which, after God, is the main support of religion in this city. The Lancaster Method, very much in fashion in this country, pleases him a great deal. I do not know what will be proposed to us in this regard. I have spoken of it in two letters to our mother so that she can speak to you about it, as well as several other issues, the most important of which is the admission of persons of color among us and our children. This would bring vilification upon us, but how I would cherish such vilification! Arrogance and

---

29 Original autograph. C-VII 2) c Writings Duchesne to various Eccles. Box 8. (See French, p. 347.)

distinctions are as common here as anywhere; only the names change, and wealth is the idol instead of titles.

The closer I approach it, the more clearly I realize how very difficult our work is going to be and how meager are our means for getting started. But God is in the work; his will was manifest, and far from feeling an increase of that dryness of heart, which was such a trial for me in Bordeaux and on the ocean voyage, I feel my heart expand now with hope. I am the more blameworthy for not being more virtuous, since I have to recognize the fact that so many graces have been poured out on us. Help me by your prayers, and recommend me, I beg you, to the prayers of all your sons. I beg the same favor from Fathers Roger and Druilhet, to whom I offer respectful regards.

I am with respect, good Father, your unworthy daughter.

Philippine Duchesne

June 4, 1818

> [On the reverse:]
> To Mother
> Mother Girard[30]
> Rue des Postes, N° 40
> For Father Joseph
> *Paris*

Letter 99 **L. 1 to Mother de Gramont**

SS. C. J. et M.

First Friday of June [1818], New Orleans[31]

My very good Mother,

I wrote to you from Bordeaux. I do not know what happened to my letters, as I had no answer, and the time passed in that city was long enough to have brought us that consolation. I live in expectation of the consolation that the answer of our mother will bring. With what eyes and what heart we will devour it!

---

30 Mother Girard, secretary general of the Society of the Sacred Heart, distributed the mail.
31 Original autograph, C-VII 2) c Duchesne to RSCJ and Children, Box 4.

We are sustained in its absence and that of yours by the thought of the great merit that might be attached to our sacrifices and by the signs of Providence that reveal the goodness of God in our regard. We have been received by the Ursuline Sisters with great charity and good will. But one of these sisters, a relative of Father de Sambucy, of Mrs. Sabatier, and of Mother Philippine at Sainte-Marie, was astonished and even annoyed that these persons did not give any advance notice of our arrival. We said that they did not know about our departure, but she answered that you knew what was happening and had informed her nieces and cousins. Please make up for that omission. She is called Mother Saint Joseph, assistant superior, and seems like a saint who overwhelms us with attention, as does the superior.

They have indicated a wish that we would spend the summer with them in order to allow time for our house to be finished. They refrain from insisting only because of the usual illnesses of the month of August, to which nearly all foreigners fall victim. They say that I will be immune, since I had a strong fever resulting from mosquito bites that set me on fire; they also think I had scurvy. I was very embarrassed since I was with these sisters. They have pressed charity as far as to be pleased, saying that I am safe and that it is better to be ill with them, where nothing is lacking. Finally, they touched my hand and offered me tobacco to show that they were not afraid.

The mosquitoes are nothing compared to other years when, at sunset, they were on heads and into mouths by the millions. One can do nothing in the evening but fan them off or stay under one's mosquito net. The heat is also moderate this year, which is even more surprising because there has not been rain. At present, there is no fruit for refreshment. The boarders and the community have coffee *au lait* and butter every morning, even the Negresses in the kitchen. They also serve milk at dinner and *goûter*.

Mother Girard would laugh to see me every morning take not only a little coffee without sugar covertly, but a large cup of coffee *au lait* sugared like syrup, etc. Seeing that I did not want to eat breakfast, the superior had me ordered to do so by the doctor, who says it is absolutely necessary here, and it would be rather better not to eat supper. So this is what I do.

All my sisters are well except for mosquito bites. How our dear mother would suffer from this! There are no mosquitoes near Saint Louis. The milk is also very healthy and delicious there, the fruit more abundant, especially apples; but what is better, we will find more goodness, piety, and innocence. There they speak more English than French, so we continue to study it with a postulant who had been a boarder at the Visitation in Georgetown, where there are 38 religious. We do not have the glory of bringing devotion to the Sacred Heart to the United States; I saw a book printed in this city full of prayers to the Sacred Heart. There is also a beautiful picture painted in Rome.

I beg you earnestly to give me some details about Mother and the children. I am all yours *in Corde Jesu,*

Philippine

This city is corrupt and not very religious, but I hope that alms will draw down blessings: there is question of an orphan, a foundling, who is raised as one's own child.

[On the reverse:]
To Mother
Mother de Gramont
Rue des Postes N° 40
Paris

Letter 100   **L. 10 to Mother Barat**[32]

SS. C. J. et M.

New Orleans, June 7, 1818[33]

My very dear Mother,

The longer the time since God separated me from you, the more ardently I long for news of you and of those who are our fathers and mothers and sisters. As I am uncertain whether you have received the letters I wrote in the middle of May when we were near Cuba and also one from here to Mother Bigeu that I sent via Georgetown, I will go back a little to what I said in those two; it is customary to repeat when letters are sent by sea. The French Consul promised to send our mail by a vessel sailing to Le Havre in a few days. Letters for Bordeaux will wait for the *Rebecca*, which leaves at the end of the month.

---

32 In the present edition, letter 9 to Mother Barat is intentionally absent. It is an account of the Atlantic crossing, written by Eugenie Audé, not by Philippine Duchesne. Jeanne de Charry nevertheless included it in her collection (letter 93), while recognizing that it was not written by Philippine.
33 Original autograph, C-VII 2) c Duchesne to Barat, Box 2. Cf. J. de Charry, II 1, L. 94, pp. 77-85; Hogg, pp. 52-58; Ch. Paisant, pp. 137-142.

In my last letter, I noted the sad events at the beginning of the voyage. The beautiful weather that followed restored our health and finally came the joy of our arrival. Everything we saw fulfilled so many of our most earnest desires. Catherine, who had shown the most weakness, was therefore the happiest one to see the land; I beg you to ask Mother Prevost about this tearfulness that makes me fear harm to the tear ducts. Marguerite, calm, obedient and humble, savors the joy of her vocation; but I am afraid that her deafness, from which she suffered even in France, will limit her usefulness. Octavie has shown several signs of lack of experience, which have given rise to unfavorable comments actually expressed with contempt. During the voyage, her health was excellent, but as we neared land, she suffered palpitations and weakening of her sight. She said this was due to a blood condition that clouded her vision; she had the same problem in Grenoble. Eugenie is the only one who can do close work; both the sisters wear glasses. The fervor of this good religious has increased enormously. Overheating caused by the diet at sea brought on hemorrhoids and swollen ankles, but they have disappeared now. Only find out, if you please, whether something should be done about this.

I do not know whether we shall learn something about Saint Louis before I close this letter. The bishop does not write, which is hardly encouraging. I have met one wealthy man from that district who told us they are waiting with great impatience for both the college and the girls' boarding school, and that the college would be in Saint Louis and the boarding school three leagues away in a village called Florissant or Saint Ferdinand, in beautiful, healthy, and fertile country. Apparently, there is no house available, but it is said that in that country construction is quick though not very solid; there is no question of using stone; all is made in brick and wood. In this house, for instance, all the dividing walls between cells and other rooms and even the roof are made of wooden planks. I have never seen such beautiful houses.

We are wonderfully treated in this house; they even want us to stay longer and have no fear of illness. These religious have had various things bought for us; they wanted to pay for them, saying we could settle with them later. We are always sure to receive, as a present, a piece of cloth worth fifty F. The superior told me today that her house would always be our stopping place and that when more companions come to join us, they must choose a season that would allow them a longer rest here; she also wishes to look after all our business for Saint Louis.

I hope that in time we shall have many more establishments in this country, but it is essential to train both English and Spanish women.

In Saint Louis, language and customs are more English than French. Here English is as common as French; nearly all the pupils speak both languages, and many of the parents, only English. No one could be better turned out or more amicable than the Creoles. Those of the "habitations" [large rural estates] are often neglected, but for the Americans in towns, education is first class. I saw a little ten-year-old girl today whose schooling must end when she is twelve, but to keep her occupied up to her ability she is learning Latin; her twelve-year-old brother speaks and writes both languages, also Latin, and now he is studying Greek. He will come with us to Saint Louis. His mother, a true Mother of the Maccabees,[34] is perfectly capable of teaching him herself, but she prefers to send him 400 leagues away to be sure he will be taught by holy priests. Father Martial is in charge of him. He already has three pupils and his Masses at five F. He is sorry about the man of whom I spoke to Mother Bigeu, a carpenter, gardener, baker, whom I promised I would help come to this country. He will perhaps love us better than him, feeling that he has been deserted. He would have suited us very well; Mother Vincent knows him and so does Father Barat.

The same merchant [Mr. Mullanphy] who comes from Saint Louis is leaving for Philadelphia; from there he will take four of his daughters to France to place them in boarding schools for two years. They were all pupils here, and the eldest, who is over twenty, would like to become a religious. He does not want to leave her here with these nuns and says that she has to spend two years in France. I spoke to him about our house in Poitiers without settling anything. He seemed pleased with the discovery. Mother Grosier would do well not to refuse these girls if he takes them there. They are good girls, as rich as the father, who in his will has provided for an income of 10,000 F so that they will not have to ask anything of a guardian in case of his death. Someone has just spoken to me of two other sisters who are also going to France.

The Ursulines, who have recently made a foundation in Havana, are now going to Puerto Rico.[35] It is easy to make foundations with the Spanish. These nuns in Havana have received 125,000 F from the bishop, 30,000 in a collection in two days and 300,000 F as dowry of one of their members.

I believe that we will find everything necessary for clothing. Black cloth is common and not expensive, likewise cotton and other materials; these nuns have found good bargains in times of plenty. But the

---

34 The mother of the seven brothers suffered martyrdom (2 Macc chapter 7).
35 The Ursulines, who had been in New Orleans since 1727, made the foundation in Havana in 1803. Puerto Rico and Cuba were then Spanish colonies.

Americans' taking of Pensacola from the Spanish following a war with neighboring Indians has caused all prices to go up suddenly.[36]

Do not forget, dear Mother, the school rule, the plan of studies, the astronomy text, an atlas, breviaries, the formula for final vows, the Summary of the Constitutions, the verses on geography, the poem on Religion, *Esther*.

Answers required:

1. Regarding the admission of colored children to the boarding school or to the Society, there will have to be separation, as we have vowed to give instruction to the colored people, and the white people do not want to associate with them.

2. Enclosure can be secured only by wooden planks and hedges. If we possess land, how can we look after it?

3. I have asked if we do not state that postulants may come to ordinary recreations, how can we get to know them? And at great distances from novitiates, that benefactors be not excluded from coming in; that there be a method for accusations and conferences.

4. That we employ enslaved persons in service only with extreme caution; they are unreliable in important matters. However, God has his own everywhere.

5. If you send us a Sister to be the gardener, it is useless to entrust costly goods to her. The essential is 1) stockings—the sole can be changed—leather gloves to guard against mosquito bites; 2) a small mosquito net; 3) she must know how to make soft shoes; 4) she must have very light clothing for the part of the voyage in the Tropics and on the river with long sleeved chemises; 5) she will need bouillon cubes or bottles of consommé to make broth with hot water when she is sick; these can be bought in Bordeaux for three F; 6) a coffee pot to heat water with a lamp; peppermint drops; sweet wine. It is so necessary to have means of refreshment. I had laughed at all the provisions we were made to bring along, but nothing was superfluous. A syringe is also very necessary for those who need it.

I inquire often and nothing has arrived from France; the answer is always a cruel "No." How we long for news from you!

Every day we expect the boat from Saint Louis; but some of our belongings are still locked up in the ship. The sisters went yesterday to pick up our beds, etc. The nuns' wagon with five Negroes (who do the

---

36   During these years, the Americans had invaded the Spanish territory of the Floridas, where Pensacola was the westernmost city. In 1821, the United States purchased Florida from Spain.

work of one) went with them. When they appeared, there was general rejoicing. The sailors greeted them eagerly. The cook, in spite of his shrunken body after thirty years in the army, rushed to offer them a seat; in fact, all vied with one another to see who could best receive them. The captain's little boy ran to Sister Catherine with tears in his eyes; she had often looked after his cuts and bruises. And Carlin, his pretty little dog, more amiable than Tobit's,[37] jumped and welcomed them with dancing steps. The captain was not there, but he had said he had never had such pleasant passengers. Not wishing to exaggerate, I did not tell him I would never forget him, but that I would always remember the *Rebecca*. That seemed to please him.

Our hostesses are worried about our journey. If they had their way, we would travel at a low cost. I would not be surprised if they contribute to the cost. I am in real difficulty, as I cannot count on the 10,000 F sent through Philadelphia. If a building has been undertaken or purchased, this sum may have already been spent. I ought not to be astonished at the strokes of Providence. French money, which can be acquired with difficulty, is practically worthless here. If you ever make a foundation here, there must be a rich benefactor on the spot; otherwise, you will be ruined. The Ursulines told me that the voyage of the eight religious who came from France eight years ago cost 21,000 F. (It is true that they spent five months in Baltimore.) Only four of those eight remain. And those who came last year, before we did, cost 15,000, including their stay in Bordeaux. Sometimes it is possible to obtain leave to make one's own meals aboard ship, and that is cheaper; that is what Mr. de Marseuil did. Sometimes poor people get a free passage by working on the ship. These are not admitted to the saloon or the dining room.

At my astonishment that only Negroes are employed in menial tasks in this country, while so many people are dying of hunger in France, I was told that they are preferred in spite of their bad habits. White people are spoiled both as to work and to equality. Asserting, "We have the same skin as you," they all acquire the right to be "gentlemen." Here is a surprising example that affected me deeply. These religious, who want to do everything for us, arranged to have our clothes washed at their expense by their Negroes. I gave Catherine a small amount to do in the same room. After several difficulties, she came to tell me that she did not like working alongside the Negro women, that here white people did not do so. I answered that Negroes also have souls, redeemed by the same sacred Blood and received into the same church, and that if

---

37 Tob 11:9.

she was not willing to work with them, she had better take passage on a ship returning shortly, since we came here for the Negro. She was so unreasonable that she did not recover her good humor until evening.

I understand that we may be here for a long time. Father Martial is going into the countryside for a fortnight.

I am asking [Mr. Jouve] in Lyon to do a service for our kind religious whose goodness to us is overwhelming. They are expecting a priest and three nuns who will leave France in September. If you could provide them with a pretty embroidered flounce for an alb, I would be so grateful. They do not have any here.

Reverend Mother, the paper is at an end. Another ship leaves at the end of the month. It will repeat that I am your unworthy but obedient daughter.

Philippine

Letter 101   L. 1 to a professed religious in Paris

New Orleans, June 8, 1818[38]

My very dear Mother,

I was informed somewhat late about the departure of our ship. For a long time I have wanted to renew our connections, and here I am very embarrassed to have to be brief. But, good Mother, you who see things only through the merciful Heart of Jesus will let pass both the brevity and the delay in writing, which will make me forget to write what I do not forget to feel: the sweet, strong bonds that unite me to all my mothers and sisters.

I hope that the weighty affairs of my first mothers will not hinder their remembrance of me to all their children. Please do more and recommend me to our good fathers, to Father Perreau, to your dear sister, to Mother Desportes for the sacristy equipment that seems not to have suffered any damage, to Mother Balastron for the clothing that was completely saved from any mishap on such a long voyage, to Sisters Giraud, Lefevre, Harant, Eugenie, Aglae, Zoe, Berthé, Genevieve, Marthe, Madeleine, Veronique, Rosalie, etc. But I have run out of time; add the names. Yes, my heart gathers them all.

---

38   Copy: *Lettres intéressantes concernant la Société des Dames du Sacré-Cœur de Jésus, depuis 1816*, p. 68. A-II 2) g, Box 2.

I have seen some Indians, very touching with their unhappy attitude, with the body almost naked and 18 rows of pearls at their throat, their hair unruly; impossible to make oneself understood, but I have hope for the future.

Goodbye, good Mother, in Corde Jesu,

Philippine, your sister

Letter 102　　　L. 1 to Father Barat

SS. C. J. et M.

[June 21, 1818] Feast of Saint Aloysius Gonzaga[39]

My very dear Father,

I have already written to you, but I do not know the fate of my letter. It would be very good to have a response. I was still at sea when I wrote, on the Mississippi when the letter was sent, and now we have been with the Ursuline Sisters in New Orleans for three weeks, not knowing when we will set out again.[40]

At the beginning and during the greater part of our voyage, I experienced that aridity that had already caused me such suffering at Bordeaux. My soul rejoiced as we drew near to this land I have so desired, but it was in order to be able to carry the weight of a heavy trial: that of hearing on arrival a priest who had been highly praised to us speak about the affairs of this diocese, of instruction, etc., etc., in a manner that greatly astonished me, since I imagined I would find only saints. He almost completely gave himself away in a sermon I heard, after which someone had the courage to tell him: *"If you had preached that way in Italy, you would have been forbidden to preach before you got down from the pulpit."* In short, he saw that he had displeased especially the religious and he left, leaving them however in great deprivation, since Father Sibourd[41] had just left for Philadelphia, where he went to have a polyp removed from his nose, a very bad growth. He seems to be lost for the mission.

39　Original autograph, C-VII 2) c Writings Duchesne to various Eccles., Box 8. Copies, C-III USA Foundation, Haute-Louisiane, Box 1, *Lettres de la Haute-Louisiane, II, 1823-1830*, pp. 168-170; C-VII 2) c Writings, List-Varia, Box 9, *Cahier Y, Lettres de la Mère Duchesne*, pp. 78-93.
40　At her arrival in New Orleans she found no information about when and where Bishop Dubourg expected them.
41　Although the manuscript reads the name as Sibona or Sibono, it is probably Louis Sibourd, vicar general in New Orleans until 1826.

The excellent Father Moni has left his parish eight leagues from here, where he is greatly loved, in order to lend help to this city,[42] but his meager capacity in French hinders the good that he could do. He spoke to me about you and loves the Society [of Jesus] very much; he hoped that you would come. Oh! What a harvest you would find! And how rare are the harvesters! The parish here is pitiful; the partisans of Father Antoine [Antonio de Sedella] bought him a miter and brought it to him, saying that they wanted him for bishop. Fortunately, he answered that they do not make bishops that way. They show some signs of dependence, just enough to prevent a schism. He is very much loved, very charitable, very approachable, very penitent, with an exterior of sanctity that enhances his ministry.

Up north, they say, everything moves slowly but solidly toward good. The Protestants leave their sermons to go every Sunday to hear the holy pastor who preaches in English; they love him as much as the Catholics do.

Generally, people encourage us about our future. I see many difficulties, but I see them with great peace, even though I have never been with so little consolation. I have left everything spiritual and human without promise of any success. I see my powerlessness to direct souls. I fear to hinder the good, and nevertheless I cannot regret what I have done. It always seems to me that God wants this work. It appears that we will not be in Saint Louis. Many want us here, especially the charitable religious who are taking such care of us. They also want to retain Father Martial, and I would like him to be for them since their interests are very dear to me. He listens to that with one ear but would gladly help the religious. We do not know to whom we will belong. God is there; my sisters are well, especially since we reached cloister, so necessary for Octavie. Catherine talks too much. They will tell you more. We are all in a trying situation. How we want to be living our own rule!

I am sending you the packet for our mother, so would you please send it to her by occasion or by coach and distribute the letters, after you have examined the interesting work of the Indians and seen the accompanying note.

I am, with profound respect, your unworthy daughter.

Philippine

---

42   Louis Léopold Moni, OSB, was pastor at Destrehan, Louisiana, but functioned as vicar general in New Orleans in the absence of Father Sibourd.

[On the reverse:]
To Father
Father Barat
At the minor seminary
Bordeaux

Letter 103 **L. 11 to Mother Barat**

New Orleans, June 22, 1818[43]

Dear Reverend Mother,

Our captain is going back to France before the date previously announced. I am taking advantage of his good will to send you some handiwork done by the Indians. I think they will be as precious to you as they have been to me. An enclosed note gives a full explanation.

I wrote to you when we were near Cuba, to Mother Bigeu when we arrived here, sending it via Georgetown, and since then via the consul who has now entrusted the packet to the captain of a ship going to Le Havre. My letter contained several others for the fathers, mothers, and sisters and the children; here at last is my fourth letter. I have rambled in all of them; or rather, I have often contradicted myself in speaking of events and quoting differing opinions. Moreover, the heart suffers from its sacrifices whose price is often hidden by faith and hope; but love even in distress declares to God: "My God, *laetus obtuli omnia.*"[44]

I experienced this sentiment when the doctor announced to me with a sinister look that I had scurvy. The questions he asked showed his astonishment that the doctor who had come aboard on the river had not detected it; others say to me: why did I leave France? Octavie came to tell me aloud in the refectory, "Reverend Mother, do not worry, I beg you…" I was far from being troubled, but I thought seriously that God did not want anything more from me; that Eugenie could captain the ship, that she would do better. I was happier than Moses; I had at least entered the Promised Land. I assure you death had a great attraction for me, for I often feared I would spoil the work of our foundation. God only shows me more of his love! After a few days treatment my legs, which were very swollen, enflamed, and blotchy, became nearly

---

43 Original autograph. C-VII 2) c Duchesne to Barat, Box 2. J. deCharry, II 1, L. 95, pp. 86-92. Cf. Ch. Paisant, pp. 144-147.
44 "I have joyfully offered everything" (1 Chron 29:17).

normal. I trust the doctor was mistaken. At sea, I did not have any stains on my hands, which I always used to get, or trouble with my gums; it is only on land that I have had these lumps and blotches, for which I blame insect bites. My teeth and gums were never worth much in France, and he, the doctor, has judged me on them. Anyway, here I am, perfectly well; Catherine had something similar, and without naming her illness, I made her share my treatment. Octavie has had her pain and palpitations but not the clouding of vision. Eugenie sleeps and eats very little; Marguerite is not very regular. I cannot express my gratitude for the touching kindness shown by the Ursuline superior. It is unbelievable how we are the continual object of her attention and that of her daughters. Having looked after us in our troublesome illnesses, she now wants to contribute to the cost of our journey. She talks of 500 F as the widow's mite in the Gospel. I told her frankly about the 10,000 F sent from Philadelphia but did not hide from her my fear that it would all be spent by the time of our arrival. She shared my anxiety and wanted me to write to the bishop; she approved of my letter and asked me to say nothing to her daughters about the 10,000 F, so as not to diminish their interest. Here everything is discussed in Chapter. We shall never be deceived by these religious; so of your great kindness please send to Mr. Jouve the necessary information for the commission they have sent to Lyon. They like Octavie and Eugenie very much. They would like us to remain in this town and promise us great success. They would help us with admirable disinterestedness; nevertheless, they think, as we do, that it is more for the glory of God to go to Saint Louis of the Illinois. While they want to contribute to our work, everything in their own house is utterly simple: the church is just a room with bare walls as the choir is also, wooden benches in the parlors, great difficulty in lodging their pupils, etc.

The vocation of the superior held no attraction for her but was decided by the Pope himself. She came here eight years ago at the time when this state was becoming one of the United States. Sixteen Spaniards left this house to go to Havana, which was under Spanish rule. The Ursuline superior had seven companions; ten more came last year. They need more, especially well-formed religious of their own order, which will pay the cost of their passage. Here are real saints who have been giving classes for the last thirty years and have saved many souls.

The kind merchant from Havana came to see us. He would welcome us in Havana but promises nothing. The Ursulines who know Spanish say we should not go there. But my impression of that island is of an earthly paradise and that the Spanish contribute freely and generously to religious establishments. The island, although it is nearer to the equator, has a healthier and lower temperature than New Orleans; there are no poisonous insects; yellow fever is easily cured if taken in time, and women are far less likely to be attacked by it. The main difficulty is, of course, the language; we should have at least one who speaks Spanish perfectly.

English is proving to be very difficult. Octavie is the most advanced, and she cannot converse freely with the parents, most of whom are Americans in Saint Louis; nothing mediocre will pass with the Americans; they can go far; nothing European is above them. The Creoles, who form the greater number here, are more lazy, light-minded, and pleasure-loving; they marry at twelve to fifteen, as sixteen is too late. One of them after a month's music lessons is already fit to compose; they are like trees that grow quickly and perish equally promptly. Their looks are charming, nothing irregular in their figure or height.

I beg you not to forget our novena at La Louvesc, which I have asked my sister Mrs. de Mauduit, to have said. In leaving France, it was forgotten, and we owe it in conscience for our vow.[45]

Yesterday was the feast of Saint Aloysius Gonzaga, patron of the noviceship, who will be patron of the minor seminary. Father Martial preached; he is well liked here, and his health is good.

I have written to you to tell you that the Consul of France allows us to address our letters to him; there will be no cost and he will send them on. He will also take small packets. As for the large ones, which must be stored, the Ursulines will see to it at no cost to us, and they are willing to keep parcels that are waiting. School effects, like books, instruments etc. must be declared exactly and addressed to the house of education in Saint Louis. They will not be charged customs, which are high here: one year it gave the government 40 million. Commerce is becoming very important.

We do not yet know how much we owe; what is certain is that all our luggage is here in the convent and in good condition (except the wine, half was lost in storms). Through the influence of the consul, nothing was opened at the customs. They were content with the declaration; it is important that our packages in tarred wrappings are not spoiled before our second sailing; they say it is without any danger and that the captain, who knows we are coming, is a very wise man. These steamboats are strictly regulated; the women are entirely separate from the men, so there will be no Mass, no Communion, no Confessions the whole of that time. We do not know the exact date of departure;

---

45 The vow made to Saint Francis Regis to obtain her departure.

nothing direct has come from the bishop. Travelers from Saint Louis say they are waiting for us eagerly and that we should lack nothing, that we shall be completely successful. We would need an English woman if one offers herself, but it could be another Sister Benoît as regards health.[46] Catherine already resembles her too closely in that respect, and she talks too much.

The priest whom we have seen here is a Benedictine from Florence; he wanted to be a Jesuit and loves them. He looked on us as his sisters and daughters. We like him in spite of the difference in language; he was pleased to be understood by Octavie and Eugenie in Italian; he belongs to one of the noblest families in Florence. The man whose opinions horrified me on our arrival is suspended; he has done harm here,[47] they are trying to repair it.

To go back to the subject of Havana: the Ursulines have told me that the Spanish are not attracted by devotion to the Sacred Heart; that when they were in Spain the king paid for their chaplain and the board of eight religious. Under Louis XV, who had the convent built, every object arrived from France postage free. The Jesuits were the ones to get them their establishment, and the first one I got to know myself found them the postulants they needed. The details of the trials of this house and the intervention of Providence, which has sustained it, are very striking. To me that is a sign of the Blessed Virgin, similar to my feeling about my picture of Saint Francis Regis.

From my sisters' letters you can see how they are tried; happily, they are given something to do; Octavie is very good with the people of her own class; Eugenie almost irreproachable and so is Marguerite. All live in holy impatience for letters from our good fathers, mothers, sisters, and children. The long silence is not your fault, but the slow progress of ships, which are all delayed this year; while we offer the privation of news from your dear self and your advice and comments, it is still a consolation to tell you that my sisters pray a great deal for you.

I am at your feet.

Philippine

---

46 Claudine Maujot, RSCJ, called Benoît.
47 This is probably one of the assistants of Father Antoine (Antonio de Sedella), Spanish Capuchin supported by the "trustees." He opposed Bishop Dubourg and wanted to remain pastor of the cathedral.

[On the reverse]
To Mother
Mother Barat
Superior General of the Society of the Sacred Heart
Rue des Postes, N° 40
Paris

Note on the contents of the basket, the folder, etc.[48]

1. The large and small baskets are the work of the Indians.
2. The little vase is half a coconut, fruit from Havana. This fruit, covered by its double shell, a piece of which I enclose, is very heavy; nevertheless, the branches of the lovely tree that bears it, which are very narrow and very flexible, carry 4 or 5 each one. This kind of closed container in its second shell encloses a very white flesh that tastes like a nut; in the middle is a refreshing liquid that is drunk and with which one washes the face to improve the complexion.
3. Some nuts from this country, relatively rare but as good as those of France and carried on a tree that resembles our walnut.
4. A piece of the shell of the lace tree that splits open in the shape of a piece of lace that we include. From it they make fairly large and fairly beautiful ones for bags and shirts, which one can wash.
5. There are two leaves of the palm, a large plant about which we have already spoken.
6. The fine little herb is a parasitic plant like ivy that attaches itself to all the old trees. Those on the banks of the Mississippi are so covered with it that they look as if someone has hung long pieces of hair on them. This plant when mature is put in piles, decays; and when they take off the first part, leaves a hair very similar to that of horses, from which they make mattresses. Those for the winter here are made of cotton because wool is too expensive.
7. The long plant serves as a sponge to wash tables and dishes. It grows easily; the grain is in the creases and grows well.
8. The little fruit that looks like a bottle-shaped squash comes from it, so large that one can make buckets out of it by digging it out.

---

48 Copy: C-III USA Foundation Haute Louisiane, Box 1, *Part B: Lettres de personnes variées 1818-1828*, pp. 39-40.

Letter 104   L. 2 to Father Barat

SS. C. J. et M.

June 22, 1818, N-Orleans[49]

My very good Father,

Do not be offended by my large paper; it costs 25 sols a quire. I am addressing to you a packet of articles made by the Indians, not to satisfy your avarice but to mortify your inclination, allowing you only the sight of these charming objects, and asking you to send them on to Paris by coach, if there is no other occasion. My letter for our mother should reach her.

Please do not be so mortified as to not look at everything carefully and leave the letters addressed to you in the Indian packet.

I ask you to distribute the others and to have everything repackaged by John F., who is used to rendering service for us, and to put "for Paris" on the address. The explanation for our poor gifts is in the large sheet that covers the packet.

I am with respect, my good Father, your unworthy servant.

Philippine

Mrs. Fournier told me about the picture, but the *Gustavus* will not unload before the departure of the *Rebecca*, so I cannot give you any news about it.

[Added on the reverse of the letter:]

My very good Father,

I had already sealed my two letters when the captain of the *Gustavus* brought us your two and those with them. My first impulse was to go to thank our good Master and renew my offering. Mrs. Fournier is the best person to know of opportunities, since she is so interested in the mission. She spent 12.6 F for us, which I beg Father Debrosse to repay and charge to our mother. If anyone sends books, please ask Mrs. Fournier to direct the packing. Sister Nativity[50] would be well received here.

---

49   Original autograph, C-VII 2) c Writings Duchesne to various Eccles., Box 8. Copy, C-VII 2) c Writings, List-Varia, Box 9, *Cahier Y, Lettres de la Mère Duchesne*, pp. 93-96.
50   Jeanne le Royer (1731-1798), called Sister Nativity, was born in Beaulot, Brittany. Having entered the convent of the Poor Clares-Urbanist of Fougères, she had visions and made prophecies

We are very grateful for the Masses of our fathers and have often received Communion for them. Father Martial told me yesterday that he will stay here for a while. The reason is too long to explain but it is urgent. God blesses his sacrifices. He is well and attracts many people.

Please examine our poor gifts to our mother, send off all of it and distribute the letters that are not for Paris.

I am with profound respect,

Philippine

The letters for Bordeaux are in the Indian packet.

[On the reverse:]
To Father
Father Louis Barat
At the secondary school
The former poorhouse

Letter 105   L. 12 to Mother Barat

SS. C. J. et M.

June 24 [1818] New Orleans[51]

My dear Reverend Mother,

God who loves to console his own has allowed the *Rebecca* to delay her departure so that I would have time to receive your letters along with those from Mother Bigeu and your brother, which the *Gustavus* brought me. As the ship has not yet unloaded, we have not received our picture;[52] but Mrs. Fournier tells me that it was taken on board by the captain.

I will not repeat anything from my first letter to you. Yours was taken to the foot of the altar before we read it; indeed, we must thanks God for this great gift; we were all greatly heartened, as you can well understand.

When she handed over to us the treasure of your loving heart, the

---

that were edited under her dictation a little before her death. Cf. *Vie et Révélations de la Sœur Nativité*, Edition Beaucé, Paris, 1817.
51 Original autograph, C-VII 2) c Duchesne to Barat, Box 2. Cf. J. de Charry, II 1, L. 96, pp. 95-97; Hogg, pp. 64-66; Ch. Paisant, pp. 148-149.
52 The picture of the Sacred Heart that Mother Bigeu was to send.

superior of the Ursulines graciously asked us to send you her regards and said that she earnestly hopes to be able to meet you; she is really a great soul. She would like all who are coming this way to stay in her house. They could make themselves useful by demonstrating how to make flowers; they could bring a leaden hammer (they have molds) or teach them how to mend lace, to do needlepoint and different knitting and embroidery stitches.

There are some distinguished religious here, and they are humble enough to praise Eugenie and Octavie, who both please everyone. They are both well. It has proved better for Eugenie to go to Communion less often; I think the confessor at Quimper thought too highly of her. She showed grave arrogance on some occasions at the beginning, which I pointed out to her. She has now greatly improved and will be your consolation; she is irreproachable. My one fear for her is the impact of the high spirituality in which she has been encouraged; she appears to despise all unction (as if that which flooded Saint Xavier and Saint Teresa were imperfections) and to feel the cross but not to apprehend it. I can see her coming to believe that there is no perfection except being frustrated or bored.

Catherine will always make mistakes. She appeared to be sorry yesterday for a fault that I had written about to Mother Bigeu for her to communicate to you; my letter to you was too full and already sealed. I beg you to open the letter to Mother Bigeu if she is not in Paris; I had the same intention when I sent you the letter addressed to her when we arrived here. If I talk to her of business affairs that concern you directly, it is because I know you trust her completely, and your humility always makes you tend to consult others.

Forgive me for my letter from Bordeaux,[53] like so many other faults that you have put up with so patiently. It seemed natural to me to express all my fears regarding my office. I am always more and more convinced that I have no gift for guiding souls; but God does it by himself and my sisters are content; they will tell you so.

Father Martial will stay here longer than we do. Since I finished my letter, everyone says such encouraging things about our future in Saint Louis and here, if we make a foundation here. Mother Rivet would not be too old; women of fifty-two have come here; but one must be steadfast, especially at sea, and ready to face death.

Believe, my incomparable Mother, in the deep respect of your too guilty daughter who is at your feet very humbly.

Philippine

---

53 This letter has not been saved.

Letter 106   **L. 13 to Mother Barat**

New Orleans[54]
Begun July 9, 1818

SS. C. J. et M.

Very Reverend Mother,

This is the fifth time I have written to you since our arrival, and I calculate with pain that it will be a long time before we get an answer. The *Gustavus* brought me some of your letters that were rather old, also two from your brother and our picture of the Sacred Heart. Mrs. Fournier included in the same consignment a small packet for the bishop that she did not declare; therefore, we cannot withdraw the consignment from the customs office. The government in Washington has made such strict rules that the inclusion of a single object found in a package and not declared means confiscation of everything, to the profit of the officials. At this moment, they are holding back a piece of cloth because a box worth fifteen *sols* was not included on the form. One lady has had all her luggage held back because it contained a few dolls that were not declared. These laws are quite new but are followed to the letter; I beg you, therefore, to make this fact known every time something is sent. All articles of different kinds must be declared; for example, *a box marked (certain address) containing sewing needles, embroidery silk, gold lace of such and such value; a bale of cloth for vestments, such and such a price; supplies for different kinds of needlework, etc.*

No duty is paid on objects carried by the passenger, but information must always be given so that they are allowed to pass, for example, *used linen and habits for women.* Things for the school are not subject to duty; therefore, books for study and other school effects: material for needlework, maps, globes etc., cost nothing, but they must be marked: *For the House of Instruction of Saint Louis.* Nothing will be opened. However, nothing should be inserted that requires duty, since it would be confiscated if they happened to open the package. Some of the customs officers are lenient; others with the [penetrating] eyes of an Argos are adamant. I sent them Mrs. Fournier's letter so that they could see that we were unaware of the packet put in with our picture, which,

---

54   Original autograph, C-VII 2) c Duchesne to Barat, Box 2. Cf. J. de Charry, II 1, L. 98, pp. 100-109; Hogg, pp. 68-75; Ch. Paisant, pp. 152-158.

moreover, being of a devotional nature, did not tempt them much. We hope to get the picture by Sunday, the day we leave here; it was to be tomorrow. Our luggage is already on the steamboat for Saint Louis; we have not unpacked anything. Everything arrived in good condition; we are using only what we had in our small bags. Each week these religious have had our clothes washed. We have bought some light cotton dresses, black with one white thread running through the goods. (The doctor and the religious insisted on this measure.) The sisters have purple, almost black, cotton dresses. We wore our religious habit on the ship, and no one took offence; on the contrary, several said it was well chosen and could offend no one in the world. The Ursulines, even those who have come in the last thirty years, have travelled in secular dress; we shall have to do so to some extent on the steamboat. We shall also be unable to gather for Mass and confession and such.

Father Martial is being kept here for various important reasons. Our companion from Father Liotar's is coming with us; some distance on the way we shall pick up another priest; we have been warned not to approach him, as he is very scrupulous. Lately he was traveling in a ship that was sinking; he did not even notice it or the fright and general disorder because he was saying his Office; they were obliged to force him to get into a boiler, which kept him afloat. Another time a priest traveled seven leagues to go to confession to him but had to return unshriven because the priest was saying his Office and refused to be disturbed.

Father Martial would like to come to Saint Louis soon; he has sent all his luggage in advance and has put it entirely in our charge. He is beginning to find us not such a responsibility (I am almost angry at this). Our fathers in France cannot be forgotten. I asked him to write a word to you; I do not know whether he did it, but he was not pleased at my request, saying he had no complaints to make and that as for praise, it would be obvious this had been asked for. He reprimanded me for what I told you about Catherine; and when I told him we had to report everything, he replied: "Yes, in due time, when you are able to write the good with the bad; at these distances one should not give an unfavorable impression that cannot be undone." I tell you this so you will ignore what I say that is due to my rigid character.

He shows himself very fatherly towards us and has not abandoned us for confessions. I admit I skipped going to him three or four times,[55] for there is an Italian priest here, kindly as Father Perreau, pious, loving

---

55 She went to confession to a priest other than the habitual confessor.

the Society, whose soul is as noble as his birth; Eugenie says he comes from one of the most illustrious families in Florence. He has shown great interest in us, and I suspect that he gave part of the 1500 F that we are to be given on leaving for the unknown costs of our journey. The reverend superior of this house will present them saying modestly that she is responsible for only 500 F; but how many other things do we not owe to her generosity: medicine, crockery, a gross of plates, remedies, material, candles, laundry and food, which, if calculated at the same price asked of the pupils, would come to 1500 F in silver, and if the gifts for our establishment were counted, at least 3000 F. It would be even more had it included the cost of lodgings, doctors in the city, etc.

When I mention the doctor, do not be anxious; it is true he thought at one moment that I had scurvy, but he was mistaken. I am in better health than I have been for a year; that is to say, I am perfectly well. I brave the sun and the humidity, the spicy and salty food customary in this country, which they think you must take to give tone to the stomach, which becomes sluggish in this damp heat. Marguerite has a slight case of hemorrhoids; the doctor thinks it is better for her that they be stabilized, and he wants to bring them on. Eugenie has had them for the third time since leaving France and his advice, on the contrary, for her is to control them by cold baths. Octavie is well; her pains and palpitations are felt less often; she has a rash caused by the heat, and she is being treated for it; Catherine also, she is the one who will be the least accustomed to the climate, because between real or imaginary illness, there will always be something wrong; at present she is not showing fear, but in the future: wind, the failure of the steamboat, fire that can break out, contagion, all these build up and prevent sleep; work in the kitchen heats and harms the sight; active occupations cause the legs to swell. Mother Prevost would have rendered us a service by warning us of all these things; you would have given me [Marie] Berthé;[56] it is important to have someone for the more practical, menial tasks to avoid using the Negroes who do practically nothing.

But why should I be thinking of the future with apprehension, since at the present moment Providence is always for us and our mission? Not one of the vessels involved has had an accident for a hundred years, whereas accidents are so frequent. The *Paterson*, which left a little after we did, perished near the Windward Islands in the Antilles; happily, the passengers and part of the cargo were saved, but details are not

---

56 Marie Berthé assisted Philippine in setting up the motherhouse on the Rue des Postes in Paris in 1815-1816.

known. The *Rebecca*, in spite of bad weather, fire, an encounter with a fearsome corsair, suffered nothing while we were aboard; when she was going out of the river, she was pillaged by pirates; they took 40,000 F from a passenger. I do not know what happened to our many letters and the parcel containing handiwork of the Indians, which I sent to your good brother for you.

As I am unsure whether you have received my requests, I repeat them here: the timetable of the boarding school, Plan of Studies, book of astronomy, poem of religion, geography by Gathis, forms of greetings, our office books, geographical verse, atlas, red ribbons of merit, small globes and spheres. Ships often come here from Le Havre, and if Mrs. de Rollin gave you an address to send goods going out or to receive those coming in, this would be more advantageous than sending everything via Bordeaux. I do not know how we shall manage with the Plan of Studies of France; can we follow the same plan with students in classes with sixteen-year-old children who know neither how to read nor to pray to God and others, eight years old, who speak both languages perfectly? Here reading is a priority: for English readers to extend their range, for the French with a language mixed with Spanish, Creole or Negro; there are five languages in use at the school.

In spite of many difficulties, I am thinking seriously of an establishment in New Orleans. The Ursulines with singular disinterestedness are most eager for this and would not let us down. They stressed especially the lateness of the arrival of the steamboat, the bishop's silence, the impossibility of acquiring funds for the rest of our voyage, fearing that the 10,000 F already sent have been spent without our knowing for what purpose and by whom. Finally, the needs of the city and the drop in income of the greater number present difficulties. They added that there are many people in the city saying that we must stay. I opposed these wishes with the following: 1. Our mission is for Saint Louis. 2. The air. 3. Our vocation for the Indians, etc. 4. The small number to begin in a large city. They answered: 1. That it was almost impossible to begin in Saint Louis at the moment because nothing was ready. 2. The voyage was dangerous in the hot season. 3. That there were plenty of Indians, Negroes and mulattos here, 4. That several people were working in education with fewer means and managed their business very well; that we should not offer ourselves but wait until we are asked; that there was a fund ready for such an establishment; that there were not enough churches here; we would ensure that one more was built in a suburb where it is healthier; it would be at a distance from the Ursulines, but since we both keep enclosure, that was no problem. We could come to an understanding about our taking boarders; that when theirs diminished in number, there would be no problem; they would take more day pupils. 5. That it was absolutely necessary to have a house here that would be the center for all those we might have in America; that the noviceship would be better in this center, a city where there is an abundance of everything and where one meets people from the four corners of the world; that if the cold climate of Saint Louis did not agree with certain people, they could come here, and vice versa, as needs arose. 6. Lastly, they made it very clear that they welcomed us and all those who would come later, but it might happen that it would no longer be possible, etc. etc.

I felt the force of these arguments. I have always been in opposition to the will of God being indicated for Saint Louis. Father Martial thinks the same. He asks for no repayment for all he has paid out for our baggage or dues on the ship. At last the steamboat from Saint Louis has arrived; there was no letter either for Father Martial or for us, but the bishop again recommends us to these religious and says that he has promised a house with garden and orchard where we can function on our arrival, which is awaited with impatience.

I interrupt myself to tell you that we have the picture of the Sacred Heart in our hands. And so we are leaving.

All the thoughts that were for staying in New Orleans have disappeared as also those for Havana. We see the will of God in this.

However, I am so touched by the strength of the reasons that make an establishment of our Society desirable in this city, that I ask this of you for the following spring.[57] I shall say a word to the bishop and to the Consul of France, if I can see them before leaving this city; I will send you their reply and hope you will not put the small number of subjects as an objection. As nothing is going ahead in France, we must work elsewhere and fulfill so many promises for these countries. I am so happy to have come here that new sacrifices made in order to extend our apostolate will not be felt; whether it means facing the terrors of the sea anew or crossing the least frequented forests. I seem to be ready. I am only envious of Father Martial, who has more work than he can cope with, while we are living in idleness.

Women religious in this country should be a great body rarely seen, lest they scandalize the Americans who are very reserved and not very indulgent towards our sex. They even say that it would be very difficult to remain in New Orleans without grilles, but I do not agree. New Orleans

---

57 The foundation in New Orleans would be made only in 1867.

is corrupted by the influx of foreigners. They increase daily; we have seen more than twenty vessels in two days, but what good needs to be done! All these little mulattos, Negroes, Creoles, even white people follow Father Martial like sheep; there are three numerous catechism classes each day. And the girls would be the same if they were given the chance. That is why I come back to my request for an establishment here. Is Mother Rivet not willing to come? At her age, it is easier to get acclimated. Mother Thévenin has asked to come. The life here is fitting for her, and her gentleness, education, and facility for languages would be most useful. Great learning is not needed; more in Saint Louis perhaps, for the Americans are less frivolous than the Creoles.

You could consider Eugenie as a superior; I think you would have nothing to fear. She is mature, does everything with wisdom and in the presence of God. The difficulty is that she would be too young for the big city; and if Octavie were left in the North, as seems necessary for English, which she understands better, and for the studies, still more for her temperament and the character of the inhabitants, less corrupt than here where there is always a tendency to speak and interpret others' words in an evil way, I do not think she will ever acquire the experience necessary to be in charge or even to have much contact with people from outside. Her excellent character and her humility will help her to work under a younger person. We would have great need of a good domestic and one or two Sisters like Agatha [Gauthier].[58]

Forgive all the mistakes in my letter, good and respected Mother. I have been constantly interrupted by the preparations for our departure, and I have neither time nor paper to begin again (the supply of thin paper is exhausted, that is to say, what we had for the voyage; the rest is still packed away in our baggage. Here it costs two *sols* a sheet.)

These sisters are also very concerned to provide us with everything; one of them cleaned our mouths like a dentist; another brought us fifty pounds of coffee and sugar; the superior, a purse of 15,000 F. All this has not distracted me from you, and my greatest pleasure is to write to you; but all these gifts deserve some recognition and still greater gratitude to the charitable people who treat us so well.

In spite of all the distractions of a departure and the uncertainty of events and the punishments that I have reason to expect, I see my past; I realize how much pain I have cost you, and I am now at your knees to receive forgiveness.

Your unworthy daughter,
Philippine Duchesne

---

58 Her ardent desire for the missions of America was never realized.

Letter 107   L. 3 to Father Barat

SS. C. J. et M.

Saturday July 11, 1818[59]

My good Father,

Finally, the departure for Saint Louis has come; I am writing to you at night, no longer having the day to put all our effects on board. Tomorrow we will leave this city after Mass, and the holy house that received us. Father Martial, who has one foot in the parish and whom the trustees would like to make pastor of the city after the death of Father Antoine, cannot leave it, in order to take advantage of the good will and to bring it back to complete union.[60] There is yet a way to go and many call Bishop Dubourg *bishop of Illinois*.

Father Martial has three catechism lessons every day full of simple young people, straightforward and fervent, a group of whom already wants to be brothers in a college. So, if his former domestic servant did not come here because it requires too high a salary, the conditions being too onerous, I do not lose hope that we will be able to find someone else in this country. Father Moni is acquiring a Negro from Baltimore, educated in secondary school, who is perfect.

The *Gustavus* has brought us our painting and your precious letters. How paternal you are, and you sense the needs of your daughters when you promise them to take advantage of every occasion to write to them! You are the only one who gave us interesting details about our homeland, and I passed them on to our priests. The letter from Grenoble about your nieces and Father de Vidaud also interested me a great deal.

Two weeks ago I sent on the *Rebecca* to your address a packet for Paris and several letters for Father Debrosse, you, Madame Donthée, Madame and Mademoiselle Marange and for our houses. Perhaps it is all lost because we know that that ship was pillaged as it left the river.

I ask you to thank Father Debrosse for the Masses he has had said for us; we have all offered our Communions for you, but what kind of exchange is that? Keep up your charitable care; one runs the chance of

---

59 Original autograph, C-VII 2) c Writings Duchesne to various Eccles., Box 8. Copies, C-III USA Foundation, Haute-Louisiane, Box 1, *Lettres de la Haute-Louisiane, II, 1823-1830*, pp. 175-176; C-VII 2) c Writings, List-Varia, Box 9, Archives de Quadrille, Bordeaux, *Recueil de lettres de La Nouvelle-Orléans, de Saint-Louis et de Saint-Charles (Mères Duchesne et Audé)*, pp. 10-12.
60 This was an anticipation, because Father Antoine died only in 1829.

more than one danger in travel and setting up an establishment so far away. The bishop has not written to us at all,[61] but recommended us to the Ursuline Sisters and told them that he has rented a house with garden and orchard for us, and that they are waiting for us impatiently. I am impatient to get to work, and I am envious of Father Martial who is already so needed. He would like to be working on his college, but a much greater good holds him back, and he is preparing some candidates. How hopeful I am about thriving Louisiana; perhaps we will soon have several establishments here, and I will ask our mother for them. They would like to keep us here, and it would be an advantage to have a foothold here and a boarding school.

The religious especially pressed us, and since they cannot keep us in the city, they have filled us with good things. We have been lodged, nourished, healed, and laundered at their expense; and as we leave, besides many gifts in kind, they procured for us 500 F in beautiful piasters with an inexpressible charity. We needed that gift of Providence because a voyage like ours is completely ruinous. The end of the paper and the late hour oblige me to finish.

My sisters are well and offer you their respects.

Philippine

[On the reverse:]
To Father
Father Barat
At the minor seminary
Bordeaux

Letter 108   L. 1 to Mother de Charbonnel

New Orleans, 1818[62]

[Fragments of a letter]

(…) In these United States, as spread out as Europe, there are only 9 million inhabitants. The States gave permission to French refugees

---

61 Bishop Dubourg wrote to her on June 28, 1818, but the letter had not yet arrived. The promises made in France were far from confirmed: "a thousand difficulties could arise, and your foundation could be delayed. To physical privations could be added more painful ones, lack of spiritual help in some circumstances. Wait for everything." Copy, C-III USA Foundation Haute-Louisiane, Box 1, *Lettres de la Louisiane Part A*, pp. 3-4.

62 Copy: C-III 1: USA Foundation Haute Louisiane, Box 1, *Part B: Lettres de personnes variées 1818-1828*, pp. 55-56.

to build 4 cities; and those that were built a long time ago are gaining every day under the Americans, people who they say are the most industrious. They have so developed the banks of the Mississippi that tobacco, cotton, etc. that gave 18,000 units 4 or 5 years ago, produced 36,000 last year and 50,000 this year. When they have not made 50,000 F per year on sugar, they are not happy. The bread is better here than in Paris and proportionally not more expensive. Besides this, certain materials, of which I sent you samples, are not expensive, and with that in mind, the making of habits could be more expensive than the material. Father Martial was asked 50 F for an "*anglaise*"[63] whose material was worth 18 or 20 F. We made it ourselves and happily did it well....

Please send us a man and a Sister, good workers. (...) The black women are full of vice and lazy. A good worker from France would do 4 times as much work as they do, and it would be done better. A black man put up for sale, a thief, drunkard, night prowler, because he was a mason was sold for 10,500 F. The Ursuline Sisters emancipated several but they omitted a formality in the deed, and they profited by bringing a lawsuit demanding wages. The nuns will almost lose 50,000 F that they are asking for. This is what happens with them (...)

I am in the Sacred Heart,

Philippine

Here there are 8 black women in the kitchen. Two girls would do as much at home. I think 2 men would not be too many.

Letter 109   L. 14 to Mother Barat

SS. C. J. et M.

Saint Louis, August 22, 1818[64]

Very Reverend Mother,

We are close to 3,000 leagues away from you, yet I am always near you in my desire to conform to your intentions and to follow your ideas. But at this vast distance, one can only groan sometimes seeing how we are overtaken by events, which deny us the possibility of receiving light from you.

63 A coat.
64 Original autograph, C-VII 2) c Duchesne to Barat, Box 2. Cf. J. de Charry, II 1, L.101, pp. 134-139; Hogg, pp. 91-95; Ch. Paisant pp. 173-176.

Here we are at our third temporary halt since leaving Paris. Bordeaux and New Orleans left us with no regret except the delay in achieving our ultimate happiness; Saint Louis, where we hoped to stay, is our third encampment. We are in a very respectable house where we are getting to know our first boarders. We leave here in a week's time to go to Saint Charles, where our establishment will begin in a rented house. The bishop is to take us there and stay for a time to settle us in himself. Today he was kind enough to hear our confessions, and he said he regretted that he was unable to keep us in Saint Louis where there is not one room to rent. He made us see the great advantage of going to Saint Charles, which he thinks will be one of the most important cities in North America. It is on the Missouri; the banks are more populated every day, and one of the new states of the Federal Republic is to be named after it.[65] Not a day passes without four or five families with all their baggage passing through to settle in territories that are growing at an astonishing rate. And if a plan is carried out to build a canal connecting with New York through the Ohio and the Mississippi, our communications with France would be quicker than through New Orleans.

We departed on the steamboat *Franklin*, on July 12 and arrived only today, August 22, that is, the boat arrived. However, I left the boat on the evening of the 21st with Octavie, as we were only a mile away. The captain accompanied us to meet the bishop who welcomed us kindly and took us himself to the lodging that his fatherly kindness had arranged for us. He will give us as chaplain a priest who knows your brother, Father Barat, very well; it is thought that he was with the fathers. His name is Father [Benedict] Richard.[66] The bishop promises to come often to Saint Charles and says that it is a morning's journey.

Even though Sainte Genevieve is a little bit farther, I proposed that he place us there. When the steamboat arrived there, the parish priest, a native of this country but educated by the Sulpicians in Canada, came to see us, bringing a carriage to take us to his house for Mass and breakfast. The captain did not allow him enough time. He was very distressed and said he had asked the bishop to send us to his parish, that he loved Sisters, that he been brought up by them in Canada, that there were more than forty young women who would run to the steamboat to see us if only they had known we were there, etc., etc. This visit consoled us; we seemed to be listening to a father and an apostle; he fulfills the difficult duties of a parish of two hundred leagues all alone. He told us

---

65 The state was admitted to the Union in 1821.
66 Benedict Richard, OSB, arrived in Louisiana in 1817 and ministered in Saint Louis and Saint Charles before becoming chaplain to the Ursulines in New Orleans. He died in 1833 during a cholera epidemic.

that the Indians of this part of the country still remember the Jesuits and are happy to see priests, have their children baptized and have them bless the crosses they wear, but that nevertheless he does little among them and among the Negroes. What can be done with such a dearth of priests, while throughout the States Protestant ministers abound, even among Catholics, and are paid and supported, even among the Indians?

At New Madrid, a village on our route almost completely French, more than 150 persons have not had the ceremonies of baptism; they are in only civil marriages, have not made their First Communion and go to the Methodist church to hear moral teaching, so they say. At Kaskaskia, another small village with a large church, the pastor of another parish comes only every two weeks; he is old and cannot give instruction. The Catholics have no instruction at all, so they go to a Protestant school and learn to read only English. The district will become increasingly only English speaking and Protestant as to religion, if no help is forthcoming. More and more settlers are from cities on the East Coast, Swiss, Germans, etc.

The bishop says we must wait for a foundation in New Orleans, that the Ursulines are already distressed, that the town is in danger of losing the faith (if the good already done by Father Martial is not sustained). As for Sainte Genevieve, he says it is losing land every day because the Mississippi is eroding the riverbank, that it has no commerce and no hope of having any, whereas the Missouri is becoming an increasingly rich country. In fact, you will see in the diary, which will be sent from New Orleans, that from Natchez, 100 leagues north of New Orleans as far as the Ohio, rather close to Sainte Genevieve, on the left bank there are only woods, inhabited by Indians, and on the right bank more woods broken up by a few poor dwellings; neither river bank has stone with which to build nor anyone to cut back the woods. At the approach to the Ohio, one sees Kentucky on the left bank, and on the right, there are several villages. The scenery changes completely, no longer a uniform green curtain of trees, often impenetrable, but rocks, pleasant hills, more houses, flocks and crops. In Kaskaskia, surrounded by Indians, we saw Catholics who work and live in the village and go to the church we visited. The chief of the Illinois and the princesses came to the riverbank to see the steamboat, which had never before been seen on this tributary, which has the same name as the village. Our steamboat went up this river to deliver merchandise. The chief and the princesses were on horseback with their attendants. They were dressed in embroidered garments and, seen from a distance, did not seem at all ridiculous; in fact, they presented an imposing and interesting sight.

The diary will note other incidents. Our only wish is that you have no fears on our account. You knew that we should have much to put up with, but the example of our holy bishop, who could have had a brilliant career in Paris but instead chose poverty and hard work, is enough to encourage us. Before we left the ship and entered the land we were to inhabit, I reread the words of Deuteronomy, a text that had previously made a deep impression on me: "*Audi, Israel; tu transgredieris hodie Jordanem...Ne dicas in corde tuo...propter justitiam meam introduxit me Dominus in terram, hanc possidendam...Observa et cave, nequando obliviscaris Domini Dei tui et negligas mandata ejus atque judicia et ceremonias quas ego praecipio tibi hodie.*"[67]

Such is our resolution: may God bless it. I am more and more convinced that Sister Eugenie has the qualities required for employments involving relationships with people from outside; I have thought of asking you to name her assistant instead of Octavie; but latterly I have begun to fear harming the one by a secret elevation and the other by discouragement. However, Octavie has been both cheerful and amiable during our last voyage; and she is useful, as she has learned the most English, but she does not yet know enough for our needs. The bishop is sending us a convert from Protestantism from Philadelphia; she has a vocation and speaks English.

Please, I beg you to think of sending us [coadjutrix] Sisters. The Negroes and the whites are all equal here, as in New Orleans. Catherine clings to the idea of teaching, yet she knows nothing about it. I no longer have a place for her.

I throw myself at your feet together with my sisters to be blessed by our loving mother.

Philippine

I cannot think how we are going to manage with the studies together with English and so many difficulties. Please give my regards to our fathers, mothers and sisters.

We were hoping to find letters from you here; we have been very disappointed.

[On the reverse:]
To Mother
Mother Barat
Superior General of the Ladies of the Sacred Heart
Rue des Postes, N°40
Paris

---

67 "Listen, Israel..." Dt 4:1, 6:4; Jos 1:11; Dt 9:4, 8:11.

Letter 110   **L. 4 to Father Barat**

SS. C. J. et M.

Saint Louis, Missouri, August 29, 1818[68]

My very good Father,

God deprives us of news from France and the sacrifice is great. Since the letter brought by the *Gustavus*, we have seen nothing. I was hoping to find something in Saint Louis, since Father Debrosse promised to send us some letters by way of Georgetown. Fearing that his ignorance of our address held them back, I wrote to the father rector, but a mistake was made in our address; the error that has delayed the mail will be rectified. In any case, I am giving him my address.

I told you when I left New Orleans that Father Martial was remaining there to see if he is able to do anything for the good of religion. We have had as traveling companion Father Richard, who knows you and who will be pastor at Saint Charles, Missouri, where we are going to live in a little rented house. The bishop, who would like to have you here as well, has enough trouble to build his church, to replace the one in badly disintegrating wood where worship is now held. He has not been able to do anything for us, and he shows us by his example how we should be in this country. His episcopal palace resembles one of our least farmhouses; he gathers several sick priests, four or five, who with him have their sleeping quarters, refectory, and study, in a very little room. They are doing better now but are still poorly lodged.

The seminary is being built 60 miles from here, in an American congregation that resembles a picture of the early church. It took them only six weeks to build a church under the direction of a good Trappist who instructed them and who resembles Father Enfantin in his success. He has an open and simple manner. He wanted us at Saint Ferdinand or Florissant, his parish, but his very lovely town is not as yet sufficiently inhabited or established. The pastor at Sainte Genevieve, who is from there and trained in Canada, someone with admirable zeal, came to see us on the steamboat and showed the same desire to have us and the interest of the young girls of his area.

The situation of our distance from Saint Louis made me remark to the bishop that perhaps we would be better at Sainte Genevieve because of the excellent pastor, the proximity of the seminary, and the nature of the inhabitants. He had reasons against this; then he said: "Well, you will

---

68 Original autograph, C-VII 2) c Writings Duchesne to various Eccles., Box 8.

also go to Sainte Genevieve." Kaskaskia, where we disembarked and which has been for several months the capital of the State of Illinois, is also completely without resources. They send the children to American schools, where they learn not a word about religion nor learn to read French, so they know and understand only what the Protestants know; and among the Methodists there are many missionaries.

Now that I am on the spot, I see the impossibility of a large establishment. The most we can do would be as at Cuignières or Sainte-Pezenne;[69] by spreading out into those little towns as we grow, we would do a thousand times more good than in one large house. The novitiate could be at Sainte Genevieve while waiting for a better place, because, absent a stroke of Providence, nothing will bring us back to Saint Louis. The children want us, and they would leave their parents who spoil them to come with us, but they do not realize the price of a Christian education. While even the slaves contribute to outrageous luxury as they build halls for show and for balls, temples, etc., not one even among the triple-millionaires would give a sol for a house of education. English has become indispensable, and we bite it off with difficulty. It is an overwhelming obstacle to the plan for our houses. Here reading and all sorts of instruction are done in two languages, and reading will take up the greater part of the classes. Badly lodged, few in number, without cloister—how to keep it? I am going to write to our mother; my situation is very difficult.

The half-civilized Indians would offer a rich harvest, but we need priests to bring them. I have only seen some along the way, which increases my interest in them, but I cannot make myself understood. Nothing is begun, nothing can even be planned for our houses. The bishop shows us his position and that of the first Ursuline Sisters, and tells us to love our abjection now, that the fruits will come in the future. In his presence I was like a rock pounded by hammers. I proceed with closed eyes. Providence will open the way if he wishes. They say China has been converted. Is it true?

I beg Mrs. Fournier to read our journal, since she wants to, and then to send it to you to send it immediately to Paris when there is an occasion, because the paper is too heavy for the post, and all our sealed packets leave us with nothing. One has to make such journeys to learn how to conquer fastidiousness and to practice poverty.

The letters, the summary of the voyage, and the journal cannot go by post, but we need to have the books soon, several with gilding.

---

69 The house at Cuignières was a small foundation made in 1808 by the community of Amiens; the establishment was transferred to Beauvais in 1814. Sainte-Pezenne was a little annex of the house of the Sacred Heart at Niort.

In New Orleans and here at Saint Charles, they drink only water from the Mississippi and the Missouri Rivers, dirtier than or as dirty as that of the Seine.

My sisters are courageous and more fervent than I. They see the cross and embrace it. Please tell our mother your opinion about the plan of study, cloister, and the multiplication of houses. Only by dividing can we do anything. The distances are too great and zeal too little to go to the other side of the Missouri.

My respects to Fathers Debrosse and Wrints and to Mother Vincent and her daughters.

I am your daughter at your feet.

Philippine

August 31:

Just as we were leaving for Saint Charles, they wanted to keep us in Saint Louis or at Florissant, 3 or 4 miles away.

I am asking for books in English and French, whatever you select. They are rare here.

[On the reverse:]
To Father
Father Barat
At the minor seminary, secondary school
Bordeaux

Letter 111   L. 8 to Therese Maillucheau

SS. C. J. et M.

Saint Louis, Missouri, August 29, 1818[70]
Recommended to St. Anthony of Padua

My very good Mother,

I wrote to you from New Orleans, where I received the picture; and it is here with me, though I have not yet been able to see it. Before going by land and water again to Saint Charles on the Missouri, at 12 leagues from here, it is not a good idea to unwrap it or to unpack the trunks.

Keep the other gifts, because in Saint Charles we will be in a very little rented house and the roads are difficult, so it could happen that

---

70   Original autograph, C-VII 2) c Duchesne to RSCJ and Children, Box 4.

the transport charges could be more than the actual value and cannot be paid, for we are in dire poverty here. Besides, many necessary things are available here including clothing. Except for shoes that cost 15 F, clothing and linens are at the same price as in France. Silk, pearls, silk cords, spangles, rings, buckles, etc., in small quantities would reach us by way of New Orleans, addressed to the boarding school for girls in Saint Charles on the Missouri. That way we can avoid customs charges, a privilege for houses of education.

How God is testing me by depriving me of news about the dear house in Grenoble! He is also trying me by sending me so far away from the bishop, from the center of light. Here there is no other house like ours in France. It would cost millions to build them, and it definitely seems that we will sow in tears. But this is our happy lot if it procures for others the ability to reap in joy[71] and to see the children of our prayers surround them eagerly!

I have seen all kinds of Indians. They come to the banks of the Mississippi, are almost completely clothed and good, some of them half-civilized, and they speak French or English. Many keep the memory of *(word torn)*, give their blessing upon entering a house, have their children baptized, and bless themselves with the crosses that they wear. They say to the Methodists who want to instruct them: "*Who are you? You have a wife. The black robes do not. Go away.*"

I cannot write to Aloysia [Jouve], but she will not doubt my interest. I wish her to be able to go to China; they say it has been converted, and she is young enough to learn the language.

How much a zealous soul can do! The bishops of Boston and Kentucky are having marvelous results, even among the Indians. But what poverty! What journeys, what dangers! Here one speaks of a journey of 300 leagues the way you would of 30 in France.

Remember me to Fathers Rivet, Rambaud, and d'Hyères, and to all your daughters, my dear sisters. I do not forget the children.

I am with deep sentiment, in the Heart of Jesus, good Mother,

Philippine

[On the reverse:]
To Mother
Mother Therese Maillucheau
At Sainte-Marie d'En-Haut
Grenoble
Isère

---

71 Ps. 126:5.

Letter 112   **L. to Mrs. Fournier**

SS. C. J. et M.[72]

[Saint Louis, August 29, 1818]

Now that I am near our holy pastor, I must express my gratitude for all the care you have taken to secure this happiness for me. I have spoken to him very much of you, and it is easy to see how much the memory of you moves him. He said one day to the person with whom we are lodging, showing your picture: "Here is a person to whom I would very much like to introduce you." His health is good, although he suffers from nervous stress, from the unusual heat of this year in Saint Louis and from travel on horseback. He suffers even more on account of the health of his missionaries. Father Andreis is exhausted from overwork and austerity; he is weak and often at the moment of preaching he makes a sign that he cannot speak; then the bishop with his ordinary facility speaks in his place, whether in English or in French. In one of these situations, he made a paraphrase of the Our Father that was unsurpassed. Father Garti is dying of a chest condition. Fathers Niel[73] and Evremond have fever, but they are not in bed.

The bishop is not keeping us in Saint Louis, a city that has grown so much in two years that there is not a room to rent; and families coming here to live are obliged to go farther up the Missouri, which will see us on its banks, in Saint Charles, twelve leagues from here. It costs us to be far away from the bishop: he told us not to spare him these first days; and encouraged by his remarks, we did not wait a week for confession; then he told me *to take care not to abuse the priests' time*. He has an enormous amount of business, interminable correspondence, and continual visits. He welcomes everyone with the affability you know. Recourse to the sacraments, all but forgotten, is beginning to revive, and the veneration of the bishop is universal. His church will be ready for use this winter; the side aisles are not being built for the present. Father Andreis has the reputation of a saint here; it is considered a marvel that he can preach in English; he does so less agreeably than the bishop, but

---

72 Copy, C-VII 2) c Writings, List-Varia, Box 9, Archives of Quadrille, Bordeaux, *Recueil des lettres de la Nouvelle-Orléans de Saint-Louis et de Saint-Charles (Mères Duchesne et E. Audé)*, pp. 30-32.
73 Francis Niel, first rector of the school in Saint Louis, then pastor of the cathedral, had a stroke in 1824 and went to France to obtain his subsidies but did not return to America. In Paris he encouraged Mother Barat to establish a house quickly in Saint Louis. Cf. Letter of M. S. Barat to Philippine, June 16, 1826.

his forceful expression and unction attract to his sermons many people who ignore his accent.

In order to keep my promise, I am sending you the journal from New Orleans to Saint Louis. I beg you not to keep it or copy it but send it right away to Father Barat at the minor seminary or, if he is away, To *Madame Barat, rue des Postes N° 40, à Paris*, our superior, for whom my sisters have made a single copy. She is awaiting it eagerly.

Please give my respects to Father Boyer and to Mother Vincent to whom I have written several times. My sisters, who are all very well, send you and Mr. Louis Dubourg their regards, as do I with them.

The bishop is going to come to spend a few days with us in Saint Charles where he will install Father Richard as parish priest and our chaplain. I am with respect, Madame, your devoted servant.

Philippine Duchesne

Saint Louis, 29 August 1818

P. S. Since I finished this letter, I have learned that perhaps we are not going to Saint Charles and will be closer to the bishop.

Letter 113   L. 48 to Mrs. Jouve, in Lyons

Saint Louis, August 29, 1818[74]

My dearest Sisters,

I am writing today to Mrs. de Rollin by way of Washington. Since I can send only one letter by that route, I am taking advantage of the return of the steamboat that brought us here to give you some news. Our journey from New Orleans here lasted twenty days and was quite pleasant. We are leaving again the day after tomorrow for Saint Charles on the Missouri, where we will live for the present.

This country is going to be made a state, which will enter the Union of the United States; it is now just a territory. Saint Louis will be the major city; its population is growing daily; building is going on everywhere and lodging is not to be found; accommodations are more expensive than in Paris and so is food. Luxury is a strange thing; it reaches even among some half civilized Indians. Since the bishop's arrival, religion is

---

74 Copies: *Cahier, Lettres de la Mère Duchesne à sa famille*, pp. 95-97; *Lettres dactylographiés*. C-VII 2) c Duchesne to her family and lay people, Box 5.

being revived, and it is being established in Kentucky, by the apostolic zeal of Bishop Flaget, the bishop there; before he came, the people had no religion at all. He has had several churches built; I saw many made of wood.

It is a long time since I have had news from France that would tell me how you all are. My health is good, and our holy bishop's health survives in spite of his hard labors. If you would like some details of our voyage, my niece in Grenoble could copy some of our journal, which is going to arrive later by way of Paris.

Dear Sisters, believe that my prayers to heaven always include you and that your happiness is always my heart's wish. All yours in the Heart of our good Master.

Kisses to all your children,

Philippine Duchesne

Letter 114   L. 15 to Mother Barat

SS. C. J. et M.

Saint Louis, August 31, 1818[75]

Very Reverend Mother,

It is very hard to have no news from you and to be so out of touch when we have such need of your guidance. When we arrived here on the 24th, I hastened to write to you through Georgetown and since then to Mrs. de Rollin in care of the French Consul in Washington. In spite of these letters and the five preceding ones from Havana on, I have so many things to tell you that sentiment is giving way to business and the details of our travels, so my letters are terribly dry; still I ought to be brief in order to say more.

If you have received my last letter of July 11 from New Orleans and the one from here at the end of August, you will have seen that our journey on the Mississippi took forty days, happily for all of us, for almost all the passengers were sick, some seriously so, as a result of the heat; we had only some discomfort.

---

75 Original autograph, C-VII 2) c Duchesne to Barat, Box 2. Stamped: Paris, December 8, 1818. Cf. J. de Charry, II 1, L. 102, pp. 140-149; Hogg, pp. 95-104; Ch. Paisant, pp. 185-190.

The bishop's palace on the outside resembles a little barn in France, and the church is wooden with gaps between the logs; he is having one built at the expense of the people of Saint Louis, who are finding it burdensome. He was able to rent a house for us only in Saint Charles, a small town about twelve leagues away. The kind welcome we received from the parish priest in Sainte Genevieve when we passed through there and the urging of some young people of the city prompted me to ask you to send us there. The bishop was opposed for the many reasons that I told you about, but he let me hope for a second foundation there later; he does not favor one in New Orleans. I rejected Florissant, for we would have to build there. The countryside is beautiful but not sufficiently populated. Saint Louis seems out of the question. For two years, that city has been growing at such a rate that land that formerly cost 20 F is now worth 100; one person refused 120 F for his land. A property with a house that would have fewer advantages for us than Paris could not be had for 50,000. The bishop rented for 2000 F four poor little rooms to begin his school [in Saint Louis]; as they are not yet occupied, he offered them to us along with land on which to build. But a house no bigger than Cuignières would cost at least 36,000 F, and it would be necessary to rent in the meantime.

Mr. Pratte, the brother of the priest in Sainte Genevieve,[76] who is housing and feeding us while we are house hunting, has no desire to keep a carriage to go to Saint Charles; he wanted to buy a house here for 40,000 F and rent it to us; it is of the size that would cost 36,000 to build. I saw it; it is well located, quite new, but would need alterations that could be done only if we owned it. I proposed to him that we buy it, after asking the bishop's advice, for his house would not have enough ground for gardens.[77] The house to be bought would have sufficient land, and we would be able to arrange the terms.[78] I realize we would have to act with great caution. Of the money the bishop received it seems only 7000 F remain. I am relying on the kindness of the Ursulines to lend us money without interest; my hope remains with them and even with the kind merchant from Havana, to whom I shall write. And Mr. Pratte, who intends to send us his five daughters, one after the other, maybe will lend us something. I have called him our temporal father, and he well deserves the title. He has a well-stocked store with moderate

---

76 Henri Pratte, brother of General Bernard Pratte, was born in Sainte Geneviève about 1788, studied with the Sulpicians and was ordained a priest in 1815. Then he returned as pastor in his native town, where he was very much loved. He died of yellow fever in 1822.
77 The house he was proposing in Saint Louis.
78 Dates settled on for partial payments until the total had been paid.

prices, and he will give us as much credit as we need. His wife is the most esteemed person in the city; she has five daughters, excessively spoiled; they love us so much that they all want to leave their parents to come to the convent. When we go out, they are worried lest we are going away. Celeste especially, four or five times a day in season and out, begs her parents, who would like to wait to send her. These five attractive children have the happiest of dispositions and charming voices. They are related to so many people in the city that there is a swarm of cousins, all delightfully well mannered, who have come to see us and would like to follow us. One of them did not sleep for joy the day we arrived. I attribute this enthusiasm to their good angels.

It is the same for the little colored girls; they look at us open-mouthed, and when Mother Octavie seated one beside her in church, the others all said, "How happy you must be!" You can see that all this youth is very appealing, as well as the Indians we often see. With the bishop's presence here and your intention in sending us, we would rather wait and be inconvenienced here than go elsewhere and be worse off.

We must not imagine a very large establishment here; for many years we can be only another Cuignières, nothing more. The houses resemble huts in the vineyard or workers' cottages. That will be a reason to divide to do more good in a wider area. If the inhabitants of Sainte Genevieve and Kaskaskia would want to give us lodging, I think those would be the two places to choose: the first because a few leagues away a seminary is going to open in an American congregation modeled on the primitive church;[79] the second is the capital city of the State of Illinois, which entered the Union with this title.[80] There are French Catholics there with no other school than the American Protestant one. The church is large, and one could build alongside it. I cannot give up the idea of New Orleans and the great good we might be able to do there. (Do not read aloud.) It would not be impossible for Father Martial to be the bishop there one day, and our good friends in that city [the Ursulines], who in a few years will have a payment of 300,000 F would do something for us, even at the risk of having fewer children. They foresee that, but it does not make them less generous. I do not know if they are aware of how much their education displeases some because they have kept former kinds of punishment (all that is for you alone, I beg you).

79   It is probably a reference to "trustees," corporations that owned ecclesiastical properties, which often formed the basic structure for Catholic churches in the States.
80   Illinois became a state of the United States that year, 1818.

Here I am reaching out to many places without having a firm foothold, but desires cannot be curbed when there are so many needs. The Illinois, half civilized, are next to Kaskaskia; they have left the banks of the Illinois, pushed back by other nations. Several speak French, others English. The bishop says that language is as necessary as bread, but at fifty, one cannot learn it. Think about that. But coadjutrix Sisters can get along without it, and if you have not thought about sending us some, do not forget it, especially someone for the garden. A day's wages is 10 F. Whites do not wish to be servants; neither do free Negroes. Manual labor is costly because there are so many houses to build and fields to cultivate that workers can earn as much as they want. (Do not read aloud.) Slaves say that the misfortune of their situation affects everything. In the house where we are, two Negresses have families but are not married; the third is a known thief. When she was accused of taking 50 F, she said she thought it was only 15. Their children would like to come with us also and would be good, without their mothers.

Mr. Pratte just asked to see me; he is working to get us a house and a number of boarders to begin with. The parents themselves have set the fee for room and board, including laundry, at 225 *gourdes*, that is 1125 F for us. If I have not learned the results of his research before the steamboat leaves for New Orleans, I will write to you through one of the eastern cities, and it may be that that letter will reach you before this one does. The bishop is not at all opposed to the Lancastrian method. He is annoyed that the brothers have not taken it up and says that he would not forbid it here at present.

His kindness does not keep him from being quite firm; he knows me already and sets me straight. He likes Eugenie and Octavie very much and so do the parents. He reproached me for preferring Eugenie; I had not noticed that, but told him, as I have told you, that I find she has more poise. However, I am not pleased about two things, although she is not insisting: 1) without saying anything to me, she proposed to the bishop that she be placed alone in a household where only English is spoken so that she would have to speak it; 2) now in Saint Louis according to your wishes and regarding Saint Charles as the tomb of this little offshoot of the Society, she is making minute comments that everything should be as it is in France *(that is impossible)*; we have to make allowances; we are happy to be as close as possible. We will be obliged not to have beds exactly like yours, for we will have to fold them up during the day for lack of space etc., etc. Enclosure will be very different until we have enough money.

Here is how we will be able to arrive at that: the father of four or five young ladies, about whom I have already spoken to you, wants to send them to Poitiers upon the advice of the Ursulines who began their education. The eldest wants to be a religious; he is opposed, but he ended by saying to the bishop: "All right, when she has spent time in France, if she persists, I will give her a nice piece of property in Florissant and she can found a convent." This man, Mr. Mullanphy, is very rich; he has nine million in *piastres* and lands; he is lord of almost the whole village of Florissant. We could then have a large house, safe and convenient; and the father would be flattered, like the master of the whole country, to have a fine establishment. His daughter is very promising. Bishops in the eastern cities where she has been have confidence in her ability to engage in good works. The bishop, who is her director, without knowing what we said to the father in New Orleans, wrote to tell her to ask to go to Poitiers and to join our Society there. Alert Mother Grosier if needed. The father will not allow her to go farther. It is very important to attract her strongly to our work; otherwise there may be a rupture in the future since, they say, she has everything necessary to be in charge. Make sure of her yourself, and it would be very pleasing to me to have her, or anyone else of your choice, in authority over me.[81]

There is a Mrs. de Perdroville here with two attractive and talented daughters. She wants to open a boarding school. Mr. de Perdroville was in Napoleon's suite. Although Mr. Pratte is connected with him, he wants to entrust his two eldest daughters to us at once and be in on the ground floor. He is returning just now, having been with the bishop and several fathers of families; he himself has turned them towards Florissant,[82] saying that instead of 4000 F for this house in Saint Louis, it would take 8000 to equip one in Florissant to house twenty-five children (The bishop says we will have Protestants and that they will stay,)

Wherever we are, at least it does not seem doubtful that Saint Charles is the place and that we will soon have a number of children, but wealthy ones who insist on developing their talents. There is a piano teacher but no piano; that would be the most necessary thing for us, and the fees would pay us back quickly. Among other necessary items: six candelabra and a processional cross for the church; two seals, one for the school and one for us; a large cross and a smaller one in case of accidental loss; ribbons of merit, red for the fourth class, a medallion; samples of English penmanship, the only form taught here; supplies

---

81   This plan was never carried out, and it seems that Miss Mullanphy did not persevere in the Society.
82   Mr. Pratte is no longer thinking about a boarding school in Saint Louis, but in Florissant.

for flowers, cord and models for burses, silk, chenille, gold and silver thread, spangles and brilliants for embroidery, with prices for everything; embroidery patterns, needles of all kinds. By addressing packages to *Maison d'Institution in Saint Louis,* you can avoid customs duties. But the bill is absolutely necessary in order to avoid confiscation or delays.

As for textbooks for the classes, I don't know what to tell you or how we are going to manage. Everything must be in the two languages, and I believe, as does Father Barat, that books in English are more available and at better prices in Bordeaux than in Paris.

1. Grammars must be English-French instead of French-English, as English is more common.

2. Geography in English only, very detailed of the United States. If these are not available, for example, a large atlas, then we must go to Philadelphia for them at great cost.

3. Summaries of history; maybe a general summary in English for English speakers could be found; history of the United States in both languages.

4. Mythology workbooks and a short summary in English.

5. I would not like Father Loriquet's[83] arithmetic; it is too confusing; besides, we cannot be sure that they use the same system here. We will prepare workbooks for the money and measures. I believe I have asked you for astronomies, the poem of Religion, and the school rule for the boarding school. The plan of studies will be very much changed because of English.

All these are very urgent as there are no books here, and the few that are available are very expensive, 10 or 12 F each. I ask you with confidence for all these things, as I know that 4000 F remain with Mother Geoffroy, 400 of which I received from the Ursulines for the albs; they must be used to reimburse Mr. Jouve.

Octavie has gained in maturity in so many different circumstances. She was our interpreter on the steamboat, as everything was in English.

Eugenie is again showing some arrogance; under pretext of advice formerly received, she has dispensed herself from certain practices like acts before feasts etc., which the others are doing; she thinks herself excused from the ordinary prayer and from certain rules of conduct. Will you please see her letter to Mother Bigeu, and based on what she says there, advise her and me; she so loves faith that she seems to count it more important than the charity that opens hearts and increases fervor.

---

83 Nicolas Loriquet, SJ, composed the first plan of studies for the houses of the Sacred Heart in 1804. He was also the author of numerous scholastic manuals, the use of which was required at that time in all the houses of the Society of the Sacred Heart.

The two Sisters are well; our health is good. All told, my four sisters have good will, love of their vocation and zeal.

I beg you to forgive the length of my letter and be my spokesperson to my fathers, mothers and sisters. How eager we are to have news of you!

The journal that I had Eugenie keep is paid for;[84] it will come to you by way of your brother, our common father.

At your feet,

Philippine

[On the reverse}
To Mother
Mother Henriette Girard
To give to Mother Sophie
Rue des Postes, n° 40, care of Mr. Roussel
Paris

Letter 115   L. 2 to Mother Bigeu

SS. C. J. et M.

Saint Louis, September 2, 1818[85]

My very good Mother,

Here I am in this land so desired; I drink the waters of the Mississippi, but I see only those for the love of whom we have undergone two difficult and dangerous voyages. I thank God for having hidden from me the obstacles that we are finding. Moreover, I thank him for having taken them on and wanting them overcome. I should be more than ever excited about the pursuit. It is no longer an attraction to challenge me; it is the realization of the pressing need that excites me; it is the disposition of children who attach themselves to us with conviction and bring us apples during Mass, pressing themselves against us to show us their eagerness. It is the example of holy pastors in this land whom zeal impels, especially the bishop of Canada, a certain Bishop

---

84 The cost of shipping has been paid.
85 Copy: C-III 1: USA Foundation Haute Louisiane, Box 1, *Lettres de la Haute Louisiane I 1818-1823*, pp. 86-88. Cf. Ch. Paisant, pp. 191-192. The name of the recipient is not indicated, but given the content and style of the letter, it is probably Mother Bigeu.

Cheverus of Boston, Bishop Flaget sleeping in a "house" [English word in the French text] of Indians, so flimsy that the pigs come in through the holes, serving several parishes, giving away his last shirt, without the two *sous* to pay his passage across a river, changing the face of Kentucky where no religion was known 10 years ago, having already founded several religious houses, one of which is of sisters so austere that in winter they go in bare feet in the snow to cut wood in the forest and carry it on their shoulders. [It is the example] of the bishop who makes himself everything to everyone, suffering with magnanimity, working without ceasing, with no other *resources* than those drawn from France or from a few people; nothing from *this city*.

It is a wager, in one sense, but not for the foundations. They waited for us; they complained of the few resources for education, but now it has all cooled off. I am no less determined nor less hopeful. I make use of the human means at my disposal. The bishop has his trials, but he is wonderful in their midst. There is no point in going around mournful.

Several things have changed since my letter to our mother, so I beg you to have her read this one, too; and for the same reason, I address it to Father Barat. We are still in someone else's home, with every display of charity, with Mr. Pratte in Saint Louis. This will be our address until we are settled. It seems that it will be Florissant. The bishop is giving us an empty property, which is valuable here. We will have to build in wood. You know that he promised nothing, and I am very careful not to raise his concerns. I pity him with his sick priests, the impieties, etc. He has given us a Sacred Heart on the breast of the Savior, a little one painted in Rome, a Saint Aloysius Gonzaga, and a reliquary with 300 authentic relics. He says, "It is to console you." He says he can come to see us every 15 days, but I don't count on it, only once a month. It is impossible out of Saint Louis, where everything conspires to exclude us.

Besides all my requests for our mother, I beg you to add that of several English dictionaries; one French; a bundle of *papier à la cloche* [paper 30 x 40 cm.]; it is available here at 50 F a packet; the English grammars of Peylepton and one of Cobbes; some wooden shoes or galoshes from Bordeaux, necessary for winter. There are none here and shoes cost 15 F. In the mud, what expense! I also ask you to get for us those very little spheres, or globes, to give the idea—it is a toy—and some patterns for purses.

Letter 116 **L. 16 to Mother Barat**

SS. C. J. et M.

> Saint Charles on the Missouri, September 12, 1818[86]
> Commended to St. Anthony of Padua

Very Reverend Mother,

Having walked around several ideas successively about Saint Louis, Sainte Genevieve, Florissant and Saint Charles, we saw that this last carried the day, putting us as far away from you as possible in America because of all the detours and halts necessary to get here. The bishop, who is very far seeing, considers this place very important; it is the best founded establishment on the Missouri, three miles from its confluence with the Mississippi (which has a less strong current at that point). American settlers from the East pour into this area every day. They are restless people but are sustained by the hope that Saint Charles will become a great link for commerce between the United States and China, for in the Upper Missouri region there is a river that flows into the Pacific at a place where crossing the ocean into Asia takes only two weeks.[87]

Meanwhile everything here is very scarce and costly; one cannot find workers for 10 F a day; we are renting a house that is too small and too expensive.

The town wants to give the bishop for us a piece of land, 180 feet across by 300 feet deep; but two Presbyterians have refused their signature, and it is possible that will put a stop to the donation. The bishop will consult with them, and then we would build on the land nearer the center and nearer the church. The pastor will be our chaplain and will celebrate Mass twice on Sundays.[88] If we are not given Saint Charles, we also have the possibility of a large property in Florissant; as for Saint Louis, I do not see staying there. The bishop has enough trouble there. He was most attentive to us on the trip to Saint Charles, accompanying

---

86 Original autograph, C-VII 2) c Duchesne to Barat, Box 2. Postmark: Paris, June 1, 1819. Cf. J. de Charry, II 1, L. 103, pp. 152-156; Hogg, pp. 104-107; Ch. Paisant, pp. 195-197.

87 Through the purchase of Louisiana from France in 1803, the United States acquired all the territory drained by the Missouri. The town of Saint Charles, situated on the Missouri, was well located to participate in the project of creating a commercial route to the Pacific through the Columbia River.

88 Because of the way enclosure was understood in the Society, the Religious of the Sacred Heart could not go to the parish. Therefore, the pastor came to celebrate Mass in their chapel on Sundays.

our carriage on horseback, helping us in and out of the ferry on the river, escorting us to our house where we have had frequent visits. He leaves again today, and I do not know when we will see him again. He spoke to me about writing to you, but he has not yet had time to read our Constitutions; but he said to follow them and that we would have a good penance if we failed to do so without necessity.

There is no difficulty concerning the habit, but cloister is no stricter than at Cuignières or Sainte Pezenne. We have a very small chapel in a room. We hope to open the school for the poor the day after tomorrow. We are assured of only two or three boarders and no Indians; those from here are less well-disposed than the Canadians who are good Catholics; nevertheless, the harvest is being prepared. A company has been established in Saint Louis for trade with Indians along the banks of the Missouri; they are friendly with the whites and come down the river at times. We met a group of them who were going to make a treaty with the representatives of the States in Saint Louis. They followed us as far as the river, touched the sisters' hands and kept us in view until they reached the other side.

The bishop is now sending some priests who are coming from Rome to the missions of Missouri; the Holy Father is showing great interest in this country, which is no longer being called Upper Louisiana but the territory of Missouri and soon the *state*.[89] Those who ferried us across the river and brought all our baggage by cart to the house would not take a *sou*, saying that we represented our Lord Jesus Christ. Protestants, whose daughters the bishop does not want us to refuse, say that when someone is educated by us, she can never leave. The bishop encourages us by his example; he says we are the mustard seed, that great good works are being prepared. He is very happy with our sacristy and even happier with Eugenie and Octavie; seeing them laughing while they were getting our poor house ready, he said, "Look at these young people who could have shone elsewhere and who are so merry in their situation. Oh, it's splendid, splendid; as for us, we're just old sinners." Another time he added, "Their dispositions are all so good, and some are making great strides." He had been afraid that we would be wasting the priests' time, but in the end, he was the first to mention confession.

I wrote you from Saint Louis. It is really hard for me not to get any letters; it takes six months for them to reach here, three or four for mine to go to you. I asked for books in English; here the prospectus, the newspapers, all the accounts, all the addresses are in English. The

---

89 It would become a state in 1821.

bishop is sending us an American postulant; in the meantime, Octavie is doing English.[90]

All our effects were intact, except the corner of one package that was not wrapped with straw and so was damaged.

I am worried about your health and that of Mothers Bigeu, de Gramont [Eugenie], and de Charbonnel. One has to be as far away as we are to realize what strong bonds of esteem, of gratitude and of love unite us to the best of mothers; my regards to our good fathers.

We have real need of a gardener, because we have a huge garden, and the daily wage is 10 or 12 F.

I am at your feet.

Philippine

My sisters are well; I still have a sore finger; my handwriting testifies to this.

[On the reverse:]
To Mother
Mother Barat, rue des Postes
n° 40, care of Mr. Roussel
Paris
France

Letter 117   L. 17 to Mother Barat

SS. C. J. et M.

Saint Charles, Missouri, October 8, 1818[91]
Commended to Saint Anthony of Padua

My venerable Mother,

After longing and sighing for news of our dear Society, finally we received three packets at the same time, two addressed by Father Barat and one by Mother Girard[92]; doubtless they arrived at different times in New Orleans, but the same steamboat brought them to Saint Louis, where they waited even longer and came by opportunity with our first

---

90 Teaching the English classes.
91 Original autograph, C-VII 2) c Duchesne to Barat, Box 2. Postmark: Paris, January 17, 1819. Cf. J. de Charry, II 1, L. 104, pp. 157-164; Hogg, pp. 107-113; Ch. Paisant, pp. 199-203.
92 Henriette Girard was then secretary general in Paris.

three boarders,[93] who arrived last Saturday with all the dear news from France. The Blessed Virgin on this day dedicated to her added to the many favors we owe her that of the foundation of our first American boarding school and the arrival of the copy of the letters from Rome.[94] We are invoking her under the title of Our Lady of Prompt Succor, as we promised the kind Ursulines we would do. We shed happy tears on learning that the Sovereign Pontiff [Pius VII] has added his approbation and blessing to the many signs that our mission is the will of God! Tomorrow we will sing the Te Deum and have a Mass of Thanksgiving offered. Imagine our joy in hoping for two new foundations, at the progress of our boarding schools and schools for the poor, in learning about your trip to La Louvesc and the conversion of the English lady, about the vows of our sisters and the enlargement of the house in Paris,[95] the retreat and the news of all our dear ones, even of the deaths of our sisters, so precious in God's sight.

I shall answer all these letters by way of New Orleans, as will my sisters; this one will be less voluminous, as it will go through Washington; that is how I sent the last letters I wrote from Saint Louis and the first from Saint Charles. You will have seen how Providence has brought us to the remotest village [a city here] in the United States. It is situated on the Missouri, which is frequented only by those who trade with the Indians. They do not live very far away from here, but I have not seen any little Indian girls in the month since coming here, only a half-breed who is promised to us as a domestic or postulant, depending on her ability; there is not the same prejudice against this race as there is against Negroes and mulattos. The bishop has said positively that we may not admit them to either of the schools and had appointed one day a week for the religious instruction of people of color; otherwise, he said, we would not keep white children in the schools. He told us about an experience of his at the college in Baltimore,[96] which shows how difficult it is to overcome racial prejudice in this country. He consulted his archbishop [Archbishop Carroll] on the matter and was told that this attitude would have to be maintained as the last safeguard of manners in this country.

---

93 Emilie and Therese Pratte, and their cousin, Pelagie Chouteau.
94 The copy of the letters of Cardinals Litta and Fontana to Father Perreau, about the approbation of the departure of Philippine and her companions to America by Pius VII.
95 The Society of the Sacred Heart rented the house on rue de l'Arbalète, adjoining that of rue des Postes.
96 Bishop Dubourg had been superior of the college at Baltimore before being named apostolic vicar of Louisiana. His archbishop was Bishop Carroll, a former Jesuit.

I am sending you the bishop's approbation,[97] as far as he has been able to give it without having read the Constitutions. He is now at the Barrens or *Bois-Brulé,* near Sainte Genevieve, where he is founding his seminary, paid for by a congregation made up of Americans from Kentucky, who have been instructed by Bishop Flaget and the Trappists. They live like the primitive Church in Jerusalem or like the Guarini in Paraguay.[98]

In Saint Charles where we are, it is quite a different country, although there are some signs of improvement. A few years ago, however, one might have witnessed conduct comparable to a pagan bacchanalia: girls scantily clad, holding a bottle of whiskey in one hand and a man with the other, dancing every day of the year and never doing any work. Now there is more exterior decency, but these people are as ignorant of morality as the Indians are. In our free school, we now have twenty-two children, and in proportion to the population, this equals a school of a hundred in France. These children have never heard of Our Lord, of his birth or of his death or of hell, and they listen open-mouthed to our instructions. I have to say to them continually, "Yes, this is really true." All except two are learning the alphabet. Among the children who pay a little tuition, there is the same ignorance. When we complain to the bishop that we have no "savages," he replies, "Indeed you have, and your work among these children will be wider and more lasting because of the influence over the poor." We have to combat worldliness as well as ignorance. Some of the boarders have more dresses than underclothes or handkerchiefs; they have embroidered dresses of brightly colored silk with lace trimmings and fancy sleeves of net or lace.[99] The pupils of the free school dress on Sundays like our boarders in Paris. They scorn black shoes and must have pink or blue, yellow or green ones, and the rest to match, but they do not use handkerchiefs. We have had to require them to do so at school.

We are very inconveniently lodged here and shall have to go elsewhere at the end of a year, for we are paying nearly 2000 F for seven

---

97 The establishments of the Society of the Sacred Heart were then diocesan and remained so until the approbation of the Constitutions by Leo XII in 1826. The house in Saint Charles in 1818, therefore, depended on Bishop Dubourg.
98 From 1609 the Jesuits organized in Paraguay a project of evangelization and human development in favor of the Guarani Indians, the famous "reductions," in which they sought to imitate the ideal of the early church. They disappeared after the suppression of the Society of Jesus in Spain and all Spanish territories (1768). The Trappists, under the leadership of Dom Augustin de Lestrange, were established in the United States in 1801.
99 Philippine specifies what kind of lace with two French words: "*la levantine*" is a light silk material; "*la blonde*" is a bobbin lace.

small rooms badly in need of repair, a large garden, orchard, and woods, left uncultivated, and we have no one to work them. We need a French gardener. Our baker and carpenter are French. As we cannot find a larger house, we shall have to build.

In this neighborhood there are more Americans who speak English than there are French or Creoles, but as both languages are fairly well understood and the children are accustomed to hearing both, Mother Octavie can take care of the English part of the school for the time being, as all these children are very ignorant. The bishop is not quite convinced of this. He had her read aloud to him and Eugenie, too, and he thinks it will be six months before she will be able to manage. She must have been intimidated by him. Everyone likes her, and when we are all three together, all eyes are on her, especially when she speaks, even in English. This pleases the Americans who disdain anything that is not American, and as they are not given to flattery, I see no harm in her pleasing them for the good of the boarding school. It seems that a complete change came over her on the steamboat; now she has the bearing and all that is needed here to be a mistress general; she is that as well as secretary and mistress of class, if you approve; her regularity is perfect with what you have already given her. Sister Eugenie is also very good; she is mistress general of the free school, sub-treasurer and *vestiaire*. Marguerite is sub-infirmarian and cook; she is virtuous but so slow at everything that it cannot last; it could even tax her virtue because she is so embarrassed. Catherine would have done better *(lines crossed out are illegible)*; she is exact in her employments as sub-*vestiaire*, portress, refectorian of our little household.

Our effects arrived in good condition. The bishop was very pleased with the chapel furnishings. The Blessed Virgin is over the tabernacle and touched the ceiling of our tiny chapel, about the size of the sanctuary in Paris. But everything is very devotional in the little corner. There is a picture of the Sacred Heart with more than fifty figures; it comes from Rome; one of the Savior opening his heart also came from Rome, a Nativity and an Adoration of the Magi, both ravishing; a reliquary containing fragments of the True Cross, the thorn, the sponge, the crèche, the straw and relics of all Jesus' family, of all the apostles, popes, doctors of the Church, etc., relics of Saint Ignatius and Saint Regis, more than you have, and some very devotional pictures and lastly the one of Saint Regis that was found in the trash in the church at Grenoble, which I had promised him to have honored if he brought me to America; it was above the tabernacle on the day it was framed and the Mass in honor of the saint was said.

All the notebooks that came from Grenoble, thanks to Mother Adrienne,[100] have all the French poetry we need; we need the English and geography in French verse[101] we need seeds for trees and vegetables and samples of English handwriting.

We would have great need of an English religious or someone who is fluent in English and knows petit point tapestry, crochet, lace design, and the piano. I have already asked for one, and I am emboldened by the kindness with which you tell us to tell you everything.

Time and paper leave me only the possibility of assuring you of the obedience of your daughters, of sending our greetings to our fathers, mothers and sisters and of being at your feet.

Philippine

[On the reverse:]
To Mother
Mother Barat, rue des Postes
n° 40, care of Mr. Roussel
Paris
France

Letter 118 **L. 18 to Mother Barat**

October 8, 1818[102]

My very good Mother,

Just as I was finishing my letter, we received a visit from a Sulpician from Canada, a French national; for twenty-three years, he has been parish priest in Detroit, the principal city of the territory of Michigan, having about 1,500 souls, as many French as Americans, Catholics and Protestants. He has formed a group of five young women to whom he gave First Communion and whom he has been directing for twelve years. The oldest is now about thirty and has been elected superior by her sisters; the election took place in the presence of Bishop Flaget of Kentucky, who confirmed it.

---

100 Adrienne Michel, RSCJ, was mistress general and mistress of studies in Grenoble from 1815.
101 In her letter of November 9 to Mother Barat, Philippine also speaks of a geography and of verses "from the hand of Mother Balastron."
102 Original autograph, C-VII 2) c Duchesne to Barat, Box 2. Cf. J. de Charry, II 1, L. 105, pp. 164-167; Hogg, pp. 113-115; Ch. Paisant, pp. 203-204.

This good priest, Father [Gabriel] Richard[103] by name, a Jesuit at heart, and a zealous missionary in the fullest sense of the term, has had them read Rodriguez ten times, has given them a rule and they have made temporary vows. Bishop Flaget wanted them to have a noviceship under a superior who knows religious life before they make permanent commitments, and he wanted to send some of his own religious, Sisters of Charity with an adapted rule[104] or penitents like Trappistines. Funds were lacking for such a long trip, so nothing was done, and Father Richard and his daughters, who are Canadians, do not like the idea of joining with Americans; they would like to be formed by a French religious, and Father Richard has asked us for a superior.

I answered that it was not possible at the moment and, besides, that we would have to have your consent. I promised him to write to you. Detroit has the same climate as Canada; heating is needed in September; the area is poor; there will be few boarders at 450 F; even few day pupils who can pay, but the cost of living is low, and there are many neglected people.

The trip, at least a month long, is possible: 1) by going up the entire length of the Illinois River, going three leagues overland to join another river that flows into Lake Michigan, the length of which is crossed by boat, one arrives at Michilimackinac, and one would cross Lake Huron from the Illinois River to Detroit. There is a route by land, but it is known only to the Indians. It would take two weeks, camping out every night in the woods, no matter what the temperature. 2) The other way to make the trip is to take the Mississippi as far as the Ohio, then go up to Louisville and from there by land to Detroit. It is thought that there will be a bishop there soon,[105] maybe Father Nerinckx,[106] a Flemish priest, or perhaps a Russian. There is already a new bishop in Cincinnati in Ohio, who will probably be administrator in Michigan in place of Bishop Flaget; he will bring Dominicans from Rome.

[no ending, no signature]

---

103 Gabriel Richard, PSS (1767-1832), born in Saintes, France, was the apostle of Michigan. Pastor in Detroit, where he would die in 1832, he wanted to found a house of the Sacred Heart there; a foundation would not be made until 1851.
104 These were the Sisters of Charity of Nazareth, founded in 1812 by Mother Catherine Spalding (1793-1858).
105 Edward Fenwick, OP, born in Maryland in 1768, was the first bishop of Cincinnati, a diocese erected in 1821. He died in 1832 of cholera.
106 Charles Nerinckx, born in Belgium in 1761, was ordained a priest in the diocese of Malines in 1785. He was a missionary in Kentucky from 1804 to 1824, and in 1812, founded at Loretto, the congregation of "Friends of Mary at the Foot of the Cross," called the Sisters of Loretto. He died at Sainte Genevieve, Missouri, August 12, 1824.

Letter 119 **L. 19 to Mother Barat**

SS. C. J. et M.

Commended to Saint Anthony of Padua
November 9, 1818[107]

Very Reverend Mother,

In this remote corner of the world with the barriers of the Missouri and the Mississippi, I still do not know if you have received a single one of our letters, but I have had the indescribable consolation of receiving several from you, from Mother Bigeu, and from Father Barat before he had had any news from us. However, your good brother knew that the *Rebecca* had arrived in New Orleans. Our first letters sent immediately when we reached the mouth of the river should have gotten to you, unless, of course, the vessel did not reach Bordeaux before the other one, in spite of taking a shorter route. Perhaps God allowed this so that you could not read some sentences that might have alarmed you. As everything in this world is variable, the situation is now changed. My second letter was to Mother Bigeu, via Washington; the third from New Orleans through the kindness of the French Consul; the fourth when the *Rebecca* returned; the fifth via the consul when we left New Orleans; the sixth on our arrival in Saint Louis via Washington; the seventh via the steamboat returning to New Orleans; the eighth on our arrival in Saint Charles through Washington; the ninth also or through Philadelphia. Here is the tenth.

I cannot repeat all I have already said in so many different situations, said and unsaid. What interests you is our present situation; it is what we have desired, hidden under thorns, with difficulties, but sweetened by the unction of grace and confirmed by the all-bountiful Providence, which never leaves us and is perceived at every crisis. My greatest consolation came from the letters from the cardinals, from the Holy Father's blessing, the two projected foundations in France,[108] the establishment of the novitiate in Paris in spite of the increase in the boarding school, your trip to La Louvesc and to my dear Sainte-Marie.

---

107 Original autograph, C-VII 2) c Duchesne to Barat, Box 2. Stamped: Colonies – Bordeaux. Cf. J. de Charry, II 1, L. 106, pp. 167-174; Hogg, pp. 115-121; Ch. Paisant, pp. 211-215.
108 In 1819, the foundation of La Ferrandière took place at Villeurbanne, near Lyon, and the orphanage directed by Mother Lalanne in Bordeaux was joined to the Society of the Sacred Heart.

The fatherly kindness of your dear brother who follows us at such a great distance is a pledge of that of our Spouse.

We had a disappointment when we opened your packages: no paper thinner than this, no Nouet,[109] the same for the *Sufferings*,[110] only Lent and the retreat of Bourdaloue,[111] no catechism of Constance or of Charency, very little on religious life, but in compensation a notebook of samples of Greek themes, a geography, and the verses in Mother Balastron's handwriting and spelling, all of which we use.

Among all the things we need and for which I have already asked you, the most useful will be what will help us to live, as in this world the soul is subject to the body; therefore, a gardener or workman and a factotum are absolutely necessary, but of our religion; otherwise, they will be an expense for us, for all white people here consider themselves equals; they are on the same footing as their employers and no longer wish to be of service. All the French domestics who have come to this country have forgotten what it means to be grateful for benefits and have undertaken a life of independence or idleness. It is necessary to have slaves in order to have service; here there are very few Negroes, and they are no use to us. It is impossible to get day laborers, even at 10 F a day; our garden and orchard are uncultivated; one cannot even get through them. We look on potatoes and cabbages as the most sought after delicacies. There is no market; a pound of butter and eggs are like a fortune; and in spite of our wishes, we have had to profit from the permission to eat meat on Saturday all year. At this time of year, the hunting season, we can get venison and geese, but in spring and summer, there is nothing except salted meat and fish. There are many cows but practically no milk; ours hardly gives enough for the boarders and Mother Octavie who eats with them; if we buy it, only with difficulty can we find it for twelve sous a bottle, twenty-five in winter. And with all the salted food, we lack water; the well on the place is dry; we have to send to the Missouri for water at twelve sous for each trip for two small pailfuls.

---

109 Jacques Nouet, SJ (1605-1684), *L'homme d'oraison, ses méditations et entretiens pour tous les jours de l'année,* 1st edition, Paris, 1674. The French Library in the house at Saint Charles possesses *Les Méditations*, in ten volumes and *L'homme d'oraison*, in eight volumes.
110 *Bouquet de myrrhe, ou considération sur les plaies de Jésus-Christ*, translation of the work of Father Vincent Caraffa, general of the Society of Jesus, 1st edition, Paris, 1643.
111 *Sermons d'Avent et de Carême*. Louis Bourdaloue, SJ (1632-1704), a brilliant preacher, made "the interior life" one of the important themes of his *Sermons* and the object of several publications. He was also the author of *Pensées* and *Retraites spirituelles*. He combatted quietism, a kind of religious mysticism in French Catholicism that advocated living only for God, outside of society.

So many difficulties make me think about building elsewhere. But the inhabitants have gotten together and formed a committee with a president who has obtained all the signatures of the townspeople to go to cut wood in the common forest and raise the framework and roof of our house; we shall have only to plaster it and divide it inside. It will be only 36 feet long and 25 wide, but that is considered large here where there are only wooden cabins covered with mud that comes off freely and leaves gaps everywhere. Marguerite sleeps in the kitchen; I am in the day pupils' classroom, my other sisters, among the pupils who cannot be more than ten; they are still only three, but some others have applied. Besides, we have six day pupils who pay 15 F per month and 24 in the free school in a separate classroom; we must be careful not to call them poor; that would wound the parents and prevent them from coming.

We see by experience what faith tells us, that those who are lost, are lost through their own fault. These Indians, who show consideration for the priests, why don't they go to them for religious instruction, as they go in crowds to ask for whiskey in order to get drunk, in spite of the state of fury they know they will be in after drinking? We had the lovely idea of instructing the women who would be docile and innocent, but laziness and drunkenness affect the women as much as the men; they would need priests living among them to make men of them before succeeding in making them good Christians. The total success of the small number of priests is to re-convert a few and support those who are already Christians. We have so far had contact only with half-breeds, who are born of Indians and whites; there are many in Saint Charles.

I am persuaded, however, that God had his designs in bringing us here. Already pictures of the Sacred Heart adorn several churches, for I have revived my old talent for painting and making paper flowers, and we have made decorations for several tabernacles. In Saint Charles, no one knew how to answer *Amen* in church; now our day pupils sing Benediction and have already learned some of Father Barat's chants, especially to the Sacred Heart. They are eager to learn and they learn easily. Father Richard, the pastor and our chaplain, was delighted on All Saints' Day, which ended for them with a three-day retreat. He is a priest who has been at Belley and resembles Father d'Hyères[112] without his exaggerated mannerisms; he is not at all scrupulous, as was said.[113] He is just what we need, since there are none of our fathers [Jesuits] here.

---

112 He looks like Father d'Hyères, director of the seminary in Grenoble. He knew Father Barat in Belley.
113 See the tale of the shipwreck in her letter of July 9, 1818.

The neighboring priests have been very kind to us. The one in Florissant, a Trappist, [M.-J. Dunand],[114] who wants us, is urging the people of Saint Charles to build a house for us in order to keep us here. We cannot remain where we are, but it will cost a good deal to build and furnish a house. I am already hard pressed to provide for our household on what comes in from the fees of the three boarders, for the prices are exorbitant. We must live from day to day and even ration drinking water, but there is consolation in this deprivation and daily dependence on the visible help of Providence. I see my strength diminishing in both body and soul; that humbles me before God and warns me that death may be near.

I see with pleasure that Octavie and Eugenie are liked better than I am; I only help them. Octavie is in charge of the boarders; Eugenie helps her with the day pupils. God blesses their work. Octavie has grown in every way since we left New Orleans; she is exact, fervent and is learning to control the children. Eugenie holds more to her own ideas and would be happier if she saw that the Jesuit missionaries in their sodalities[115] had as much if not more merit than those who were working in well-run schools. The bishop is saddened when we speak of what we had in France. He says, "Did you expect to find it here? You have to forget it; you will never be as unhappy as I was!" Our habit, our order of day, our spiritual exercises are absolutely safeguarded. It is only the classes that are different; most of the children are illiterate; some read English, others French, and the day pupils require us to put the afternoon class early so that they can leave at four o'clock. Marguerite is learning the cooking and other exterior tasks. Catherine helps her but not very well, through either infirmity or the desire to do something else; I would like you to disabuse her of the notion. She has nothing of what is needed to teach here; the children cannot abide her.

We are making so many friends with our paintings and paper flowers that we would need carmine and rose coloring, needles, pins, thread, Mass cards—in Grenoble they cost practically nothing—as well as two cinctures,[116] a warmer, a pruning knife. We cook without a pot hook,

---

114 Marie-Joseph Dunand, OCSO, born in Lorraine in 1774, was a Trappist of the monastery of La Valsainte, in Switzerland, and contributed to the settlement of the women's monastery of La Riedra in the spring of 1804. He came to America in 1805 and to Missouri in 1808. He was pastor at Florissant from 1814 and so when the religious arrived in 1819; he oversaw the building of the convent there. He was replaced in 1820 by Father Delacroix and returned to France in 1822.
115 In the sodalities of the faithful under their guidance.
116 From the Latin *cingulus*, cincture, a cord or band of material that the priest celebrant puts around his waist over alb and under chasuble, a symbol of the cords with which Christ was

kitchen garden, warmer, spit, mortar, etc., etc., a bellows for the whole house. A grill costs 10 to 25 F, and an iron stove costs more than 200 F, and that is on the black market; we have no saw to cut wood or a man to do it for us.

If the vocations we hear about are true ones, we shall need a separate house for a novitiate. I had this idea: by the end of the year, the new convent here in Saint Charles will be built and ready for use, and the two younger nuns, who are successful and have gained the confidence of outsiders, could conduct this school, and I could open a novitiate in Florissant. The pastor in Sainte Genevieve, a distinguished priest, is training some good postulants, and there are some possibilities in the free school here. I would put Octavie ahead of Eugenie now. I fear that the latter has too much confidence in her own ideas. However, if she were superior, she would see that one cannot always do what one would like.

No more room, I kiss your hands and your feet.

No signature

[P.S. on the first page:]
Seeds for vegetables, fruits and above all for shrubs to enclose the property.

[On the reverse:]
To Father
Father Louis Barat
The Secondary School
Former workhouse
Bordeaux

Letter 120   **To the Religious and Students**

SS. C. J. et M.

(November 20, 1818) from Saint Charles, Missouri[117]
Recommended to St. Anthony of Padua

bound in the Garden of Olives.

117 Original autograph, C-VII 2) c Duchesne to RSCJ and Children, Box 4. Copies: C-III 1: USA Foundation Haute Louisiane, Box 1, *Lettres de la Louisiane Part A 1818-1822*, pp. 24-28; C-VII 2) c Writings, Duchesne-Varia, Box 9, Archives de Quadrille, Bordeaux, *Recueil de lettres de La Nouvelle-Orléans, de Saint-Louis et de Saint-Charles (Mères Duchesne et E. Audé)*, pp. 32-39. Cf. Ch. Paisant, pp. 215-218.

To my Mothers, Sisters, and Students of the Society of the Sacred Heart,

Our New Year wishes will reach you late, but the Heart of Jesus who unites time as well as distance will make them pleasing to you whenever, especially when we tell him that we wish to be completely his in union with you.

We do not yet know if you have received any of our letters. We have had the happiness of having several of yours, containing among other things the copy of that of Cardinals Litta and Fontana, which filled us with consolation, and of which I have already announced reception to our mother by way of Washington. Our Father Barat has given us dear proofs of his interest in us by writing to us regularly. I already have five of his letters; the last one is not very consoling with regard to our desire to see him in this land, given the trials to which one is submitted by the difference in customs, climate, and the lack of many things.

But Providence, which looks on this land with mercy, has inspired the superior at Georgetown to buy some land in Upper Missouri. It is very much sought after, and every day American families pass by here, especially from Kentucky; they are going to establish a settlement at Booneslick, where there are good salt mines. Not far from there is the town of Franklin, where the fathers will place their school; and from there, in small settlements, they will extend 200 leagues farther than here into lands where the faith has never been known. A society is needed for such a grand enterprise. This will be the third one of men who will water with their sweat the earth of this vast diocese. The Lazarists have begun their seminary at the Barrens, or Burnt Woods, the most fervent area in the region. The young ecclesiastics of Father Liotard are beginning their school in Saint Louis. We continue to believe that these lands will become important and that Missouri will form a new State this winter, of which Saint Louis will be the chief city, as New Orleans is of the state that alone keeps the name of *Louisiana*.

To the left of the Mississippi we find the State of Mississippi, with Natchez as capital; that of Tennessee, of Kentucky with capital at Bardstown; that of Illinois with capital at Kaskaskia, previously a considerable city with a stone church, a rare thing here, and a house of Jesuits. When they were destroyed, the local Indians, learning of the departure of the last [Jesuit], jumped into their canoes, pursued them, and brought them back forcefully, saying that they wanted their father and would protect him in their midst. There was no safety when traveling around them except in the black robe, and several seculars were obliged to wear it in order to travel safely near Kaskaskia. That city was nearly ruined by a flooding of the Mississippi; the waters stopped only when a holy priest who was there went in procession before the waters, planted a cross, and said: "*You will not go beyond it.*"

This love of the Indians for the black robes (the priests) is common in all these lands and even with the Sioux, a very barbarous nation. The priest who knows them best comes here often, and he told me that they would furnish him all his meat if he wanted to accept it; but he does not want to take anything from them to avoid the request for whiskey, a corn liquor that puts them in such a state that a drunken Indian, here in Saint Charles, held his child in one hand and his sword in the other to cut him in two. They took hold of him forcefully to save the child, who was baptized. These unhappy people will give anything for this liquor, and they go sometimes in groups to the priest, even at midnight, to ask him for it. But he is careful not to have a drop of it.

In this state of things, we have to be very careful not to have them get too familiar with us. Providence has its moments. Here is the conversion of one of them, very striking. He was very sick, and told himself: "I went to see the author of life (he had been very sick another time) and he told me: 'Go back, it is not time.' But now, I will go to the author of life." François, a Christian Iroquois who was there, said to him: "The author of life undoubtedly sent you back to have water poured on your head." The Sioux replied: "I do believe that this is why he told me: 'Go back.'" François answered: "Do you want me to go get the black robe who will pour the water for you?" The Sioux: "Go quickly because it is urgent." The priest did not delay in coming, was happy with the answers of the dying man, baptized him, and he died immediately. He buried him solemnly and baptized his son who was also very sick.

This happy event happened near us. The priest was Father Acquaroni, a Roman Lazarist, one of our zealous friends. Another, who is a Trappist, told us similar stories about the love of the Indians for him. He is always on the road, encounters them often, and does not experience anything bad from them. When he went to *Prairie du Chien*, which is called that because the Indians have only tents made of deerskin, movable and dragged by dogs, all the women come out of the tents, bringing him their children so he can touch them. Men and women run to his Mass, but he can do nothing with them because of their different languages.

A severe law among them is that a wife must take care of her husband when he is drunk, under pain of execution by the chief, or a considerable punishment. The husband also takes care of his wife when he allows her the pleasure of drunkenness. The wives are veritable slaves; if the household moves, the woman will have three children on her back, and the Indian walks freely with his weapon. If he kills a bear or a deer, he leaves it in place; and if it is too heavy, he cuts it up. He goes to the tent, tells his wife where she will find the beast, and she has no rest until it is all at the tent. Even if it is 10 o'clock in the evening, she has to go.

We do not have a real school for Indian girls, but for the half-breeds born of Indians and whites. One is in service with us and will perhaps someday be a religious. Her father, out of avarice, married or sold her at 12 years old. She never wanted to go with her husband, always held herself back, speaks very little, and is gentle, pious, and speaks of giving herself to God. I am sending an Indian bag and some shoes that will show you their industriousness.

They give names of animals to those who go to them. They call the pastor at Sainte Genevieve "the son of the white fish." They welcomed him one day and, seeing the bishop behind him, asked him who that was. The pastor answered that he is the father of the black robes. Immediately, the whole group came up to him and greeted him, even though they were drunk.

Much commerce is being developed on the Missouri with the Sioux and other nations. The merchants in Saint Louis, who go up the river in barges, suffer as much as the missionaries. Often they have nothing to eat, and this trip lasts eleven months.

The Canadian Catholics are supported by the English government, which is interested in keeping up the population in the country. They have beautiful churches; gold shimmers in all the vaults, and they have 5 religious communities and nearly 500 priests, while in this enormous diocese, there are perhaps 20 or 24.

A Canadian Iroquois had been at Florissant near Saint Louis and died in his own country at a time when one could not travel. His father hollowed out a log with his weapon, put him inside, and attached it to a tree. The following spring, someone told him that the child was crying: "Let's go to Florissant." His father carried him here, 600 leagues, and gave 200 F to the pastor for a Catholic funeral. In the church, near the Sioux, the altar was decorated with cut out figures of Venus and Bacchus. Now the Heart of Jesus shines on the door of the tabernacle.

[without conclusion or signature]

Letter 121   **L. 5 to Father Barat**

Saint Charles, Missouri, November 21, [1818][118]

My very good Father,

I put here a sheet for our dear mothers and sisters that I did not have time to continue because the bishop is leaving today and asks for our mail to put on the steamboat, which, however, may not leave for a long time, since it cannot go upstream since the closing of the Ohio River because of low water levels.

We await impatiently the crate that you said was coming and the letters that I hope will accompany it. Those you have already written fill us with gratitude. So as not to repeat, please read the sheet for my mothers and sisters.

The bishop has been here for 18 days to see to the business of our foundation. The inhabitants want to supply wood for us, but the land offered to us leaves some worries about the firmness of the donation. The town thinks it belongs to them; others say that it belongs to Congress, which could distribute it to others; they would not give it to a religious community! Nevertheless, I lean toward staying in Saint Charles so as not to eat up in travel and carriage what we have left. We would not be better at Fleurissant than we are here.[119]

We have profited well from the bishop's visit. He did the distribution of prizes, and he liked it so much that he will return after Easter to give them again and see progress, and at the end of the year, too. He heard all our confessions and will have us renew our vows. The freezing or overflow of the Missouri deprives us of seeing him all winter. Today when he spoke to all of us together, he said that he would take the greatest care to see that the rule was followed exactly without alteration, and that he regarded our arrival in his diocese as a great benefit from God, who would promise the greatest results.

I feel all the thorns of leadership and the situation in which we are. Nevertheless, I am at peace and disposed to lose the hope of a too glorious martyrdom by blood in exchange for obstacles, contradictions, and humiliations. I am sending you our prospectus, changed since the bishop brought it to us. One sentence pained me very much; you will see, the bishop declared that the Church forbids baptizing the child of

---

118 Copy, *Recueil de lettres de La Nouvelle-Orléans et de Saint-Louis, 1818-1819*, Archives de Quadrille, pp. 39-41. C VII 2 Philippine's writings (varia) box 9.
119 Fleurissant is the French for Florissant, which Philippine will later use.

an unbeliever without the permission of the parents, except in danger of death.

I must leave you, my dear Father. How good it would be to see you again! We sing and learn your songs; the bishop liked them very much. My respects to Fathers Debrosse, Wrints, Mother Vincent and her dear family. I am your daughter in the Sacred Heart.

Philippine Duchesne

Letter 122   L. 9 to Therese Maillucheau

SS. C. J. et M.

Saint Charles, December 16, 1818
Recommended to St. Anthony of Padua[120]

My very good Mother,

Just a few days ago, I sent to New Orleans letters from myself and my sisters for our common mother in Paris. They were confided to the Consul of France, through whom they should be delivered. Now, the brother of one of our students is going to Philadelphia, so I am taking advantage of his good will to write to you by this way, which will be shorter. Nevertheless, I am very happy: your letter, those of our mothers and students dated July 6, and those that left France at the same time as one from Father Barat, dated August 31, have reached us. That is less than three and a half months. You did not yet have any of my letters, but from Bordeaux, they told me of the arrival of those written in New Orleans, which makes me think that you should also have received the others at the right time.

All the news from France fills us with joy and lightens the pain of separation. Thank you for Aloysia's journal and especially for the details about the two new foundations. God is good in thus making this plant of the Society grow. You see that Louisiana is not your rival: we were good only for this half-civilized country. I do not know what to call the place where we are, inhabited by a mixture of Americans who have come from the East, Creoles of French and Canadian origin, Germans, Irish, Flemish, French, and finally half-breeds, born of white and Indian, who combine the moral failings of both groups. As for real Indians, we

---

120 Original autograph, C-VII 2) c Duchesne to RSCJ and Children, Box 4.

do not see them. Since the expansion of Americans from the East and their wars with the Indians, they have retreated farther away; and it takes Jesuits to bring them to us, like Marie of the Incarnation. We would attract them more surely with liquor than with our sermons. They will give anything to have it, but in conscience, we cannot offer it to them, given the frenzy it puts them in, which makes them quite dangerous.

God permits that certain glimmers of religion sometimes produce conversions, but it is rare. A low moral state is general; and the diversity of languages, the enormous distances, and the difficulties of travel make any connection impossible for the moment. God, who wanted us here, has permitted us to see some Indians, but he puts in their place people with the same needs with whom instruction can obtain greater benefits by offering us vocations. We already see many vocations developing, and from the Indians there would be none. Their laziness, their free life that knows no shame, and their difficulty in acquiring a certain level of instruction give only a very distant hope to have any among us.

Among the day students, we have several half-breeds and mulatto girls. The others are Creole or American. We have just received our first postulant, Miss Mary Mullen, who was raised in two religious communities in Baltimore and Kentucky. She understands only English, and I despair of speaking it and understanding it well; to read and understand what one reads, even to write it is not so bad, but the pronunciation is off-putting. Mother Octavie is doing all right, Eugenie less so.

Please pass this letter on to Mother Barat. *(Two lines have been crossed out.)*

Thank you for your offers. Nothing is to be refused in a country that is so deprived, especially when we are established in a community and boarding school and so cannot live like the poor. We have had the happiness of doing without bread and water. I expected the first deprivation but did not imagine that on the banks of the Missouri, seeing its abundant waters flowing by, we could lack it ourselves; but since we cannot go to take it, no one wants to carry it here. Marguerite returned today from two springs, carrying two buckets, one half full, ice in the other. The Missouri is nearly frozen over; it is so cold that water freezes next to the fire, as does the laundry placed in front of it to dry. Neither doors nor windows close, and no one in the area knows how to make a foot warmer. You would not get one for less than 25 or 30 F. We got a little stove for 250 F. Our wood is in pieces that are too big, and there is no one to cut it and no saw to help us do it. Laziness is the local vice; these are customs *(word torn in opening the letter)*; people work only for the need of the moment and they have too much *(word torn)* to look mercenary. Also, for food there is only corn, pork, and apples; no eggs, no butter, no oil, no fruits, no vegetables.

So, good Mother, what would be most helpful to us and for sure less expensive than here: fruit and vegetable seeds of all kinds, and seed to raise bushes to make an enclosure; the tools that Jean François had packed, a little iron stove with its pipe jointed to save space; a few English books on religious life, church history, etc. You can find these books in Bordeaux, and to avoid paying import tax, if you no longer have the tools, it would be better to have Jean François buy them and pack them up together at Bordeaux. A case of Mass wine would be even more precious for us, and olive oil. Also, there is no vegetable oil, and bear grease is revolting to people. But if you can get some for us, so that it will not spill *(torn line)*. I do not know how we will get through Lent: fish without oil or butter, and not a single egg until spring. We are content in this state of want. There is nothing that we brought from France or New Orleans that has not been very useful to us.

I really do not know what I am writing. It is late at night, and tomorrow will be too late. I cannot reply to so many lovely letters that I have received. Please make it up for me, especially with Mother Bigeu, who should have several of my letters. Nevertheless, I suspect that some are lost by way of Washington, because when I asked for the address of the superior of the Jesuit Fathers' school, they gave me another that was wrong. *Fiat.*

My sisters are well enough; I gave more details to our mother. I am without exception the worst; Octavie and Eugenie are very virtuous.

In Corde Jesu,

Philippine

[On the reverse:]
To Mother
Mother Therese Mailucheau
At Sainte-Marie d'En-Haut
Grenoble
France
Département de l'Isère

Letter 123   **L. 9 to Mrs. de Rollin**
Rue des Vieux Jésuites, Grenoble

SS. C. J. et M.

1819[121]

My good Cousin,

Having arrived at the end of our journey, I was surely expecting that your tender friendship would follow me; it is as precious to me as when I tasted all the sweetness that drew us together in our childhood, and I will never forget my first and most intimate friend.

We are all happy because we have found the cross we were looking for; but since the true crosses are those we do not choose, God has prepared for us some trials we were not expecting: we thought we would find ignorance and innocence combined, and we meet children whose fathers are lazy and drunken and mothers consumed with love of fancy clothes and dancing, indifferent as to whether their children know more than they themselves. But the children are irresistibly attracted to us; they are the ones who beg to come to school and who cry to be allowed to do so. We cannot teach them to sew; they have no materials: a skein of cotton for knitting costs 5 F, thimbles, thread, needles are expensive; and even if we had room enough to house them, we could not keep them occupied. Here, where everything is poor, each one makes her own chemise, dress, even her shoes, and one must speak of these things in the singular, so poverty-stricken are these people.

We are paying almost 2000 F rent for the only house that could be found available; this part of the country is newly settled and not yet built up. As the voyage was enormously costly, only 5000 F remain to build a small house that would cost 15,000, without a second floor; everything is so expensive, especially labor. The bishop is giving us land for a house and garden with a cabin for day students. We are well thought of in Saint Louis; we will be closer to the city when we leave this location.

Since you tell me to confide my troubles to you, here are the ones that are weighing on me without discouraging me, for opinion of us in Saint-Louis is becoming more favorable daily; we shall have enough pupils there to enable us to pay back our loans; see if you can obtain

---

121 *Copies of Letters of Philippine Duchesne to M*^{me} *de Rollin and a few others, No. 9; Cahier, Lettres à M*^{me} *de Rollin*, pp. 18-21; *Lettres dactylographiées.* C-VII 2) c Duchesne to her family and lay people, Box 5.

something for us; I will pay it back as soon as possible. I have given Mother Barat the address of a banker in Philadelphia who has an agent in Saint Charles; he has rendered us a thousand services. The quickest and safest way to send money would be through him.

The winter was mild for this climate; there is a bread shortage in this little town; we have had to do without it at times, and we suffer also from lack of water where we are; we have had to go to the Missouri to get it. But no white person wants to work as a servant here, and we are not rich enough to buy slaves; we care for the cow and the chickens ourselves; we dig in the garden and fetch water when there is a spring running near our house; otherwise we have to pay for it.

Do not think that all of this is difficult for us; what costs me is never to be able to reach the little Indian girls, the objects of all my desires; but it is necessary to take them at four or five years of age to save them from brutalizing vices at later ages: the fathers and mothers are all addicted to liquor; they will give anything for a bottle of kirsch. If the boarding school provides us with revenue, we will get the Indian parents to let us raise their little girls from an early age. The only way to instruct them is to take entire charge of them and to give them board and room.

Would you believe that among the Creoles of every nation there is proportionally more luxury and corruption than in Paris?

Thank you for all the details about your family and mine; give my good wishes to everyone, especially to my aunt, to your husband, Mr. and Mrs. Perier, to my brother and sister-in-law. Upon leaving Paris, I sent my brother my life certificate so that he could collect my entire income for 1817. I am coming now to send him a new one to withdraw the income for 1818. I don't know if it will be accepted; I will be informed a year from now; ask my brother if he has received these two documents and assure him of my tender affection. You know how devoted I am to you, my good cousin. Everything here reminds me of your generosity, our chapel above all, decorated entirely by you.

All yours in Our Lord Jesus Christ,

Philippine Duchesne

Letter 124   **L. 21 to Mother Barat**

SS. C. J. et M

Saint Charles (Missouri territory) January 25, 1819[122]
Recom. to St. Anthony of Padua

Very Reverend Mother,

My last letter was at the end of November or the beginning of December. I am afraid that I may have caused you some anxiety about our situation and the state of my soul, which, thanks be to God, is content amid trials; and in fact little generosity is needed, for the goodness of God and his Providence are evident everywhere. First of all, the bishop is very well disposed towards us, as you will see from the copy of two of his letters.

It seems Sister Catherine is very unbalanced; however astonishing her proposal to the bishop, it did not surprise me;[123] there is more disorder in her imagination than bad will in her heart; she wants to be an apostle and relies for guidance on the opinion of Father de la Marche[124] and for the truth of her inspiration on Father Sellier, finally on your promise to employ her in education. To calm this feverish desire, she has been given a mulatto slave girl to teach and she reads the catechism aloud when supervising the study time of one or several who, not knowing how to read, can study only if the teacher repeats the lessons; finally, she teaches singing to a young woman whom one of the neighboring parishes wants trained. All this does not make her happy; however, on New Year's Day, she made good resolutions and, as Marguerite was in retreat, she graciously replaced her at that moment. But, as it is impossible to know what effect her health will have on her mind, and I see her holding on stubbornly to what she is given for her use, I beg you to let me know as soon as possible, if you have not already done so, whether:
1. You would approve her setting up a foundation alone, while still a part of the Society; I fear that being apart would be harmful to her.

---

122 Original autograph, C-VII 2) c Duchesne to Barat, Box 2. Cf. J. de Charry, II 1, L. 108, pp. 185-193; Hogg, pp. 127-133; Ch. Paisant, pp. 224-228.
123 She suggested herself as a class mistress or director of a day school in Saint Louis.
124 Father de la Marche was the chaplain of the community at Cuignières. Before the French Revolution, he had been the chaplain of the Carmelites of Compiègne.

2. What claim she would have on what we have brought from France.
3. What relationship we ought to have with her.

God preserve me from ever being a witness to a separation like this, as her letter and Eugenie's will prove to you that she has thought about it; I have need of your guidance. Her relations with Marguerite have been hurtful to the latter; following conversations about which I was told, she did not stop complaining about her trying situation, and her refrain concerning the kitchen was, "You have to be there to know." Eugenie has been ready to replace her, and I have thought seriously about taking her place myself if the children's observation, a reputation for stinginess or poverty, and finally the necessity of helping Octavie had not stopped me. She has so little sense of appropriate timing; one incident will show you: she came to the table at noon one day with her veil lowered. I asked her why it was like that, and she told me that she had not had time to raise it since morning Mass (seven o'clock). Call that what you will. But it is certain that the milder weather, water delivered to us in a cart, bread no longer lacking and baked by a Parisian baker, an abundance of wood, easy to get, enough meat—all this makes our situation comfortable rather than painful, and it would be very ungrateful to complain. I even hope to have supplies enough for the Lenten fast; I have been able to get butter and eggs.

But it is good to learn by experience who is suitable for this life. These good Sisters will soon be unable to be of service; Marguerite, because of slowness and awkwardness, lacks foresight. Catherine, because of weak health; against every kind of work she opposes either rheumatism or problems with her kidneys or lungs or stomach or eyes. That is also why she says she is not suited to the work of coadjutrix sisters. However, I fear her behavior in front of the children and later the postulants; certain gestures and remarks betray her feelings: at table rejecting a dish she doesn't like, speaking of singing and saying, "That's all I have in the world." Mother Octavie suffers from palpitations and sometimes from her throat through too much speaking with the children, because with those who cannot study by themselves, the teacher has to talk all the time. However, she is very cheerful, and her soul has expanded to the point that, far from fearing Holy Communion, she longs for it and communicates more frequently and deserves it by her fidelity. The children love her, as do all who know her. The same is true of Sister Eugenie; all her clouds have dispersed.

From the bishop's letter, you see that he is insisting on Florissant, and he has forbidden the priest who was raising money to build here for us to come to see us so often. I foresee that all this will remain but a promise if the inhabitants are not encouraged, and no one will do that except this priest through his zeal and the knowledge he has of the people.

Here are my thoughts, which I want to submit to you in this regard: to build here, using what we can collect of materials promised, a small house to maintain the school for day pupils, some of whom would pay and provide for the three persons dedicated to the work; the others would be taught gratis. This part of the country will not furnish boarders for a long time. People are too poor and too lazy to overcome their poverty until there is a new generation. The present one is almost all half-breeds who appreciate nothing except their independence. This work would be entrusted for the time being to Mother Eugenie, Marguerite and an American postulant [Mary Mullen] for the English-speaking pupils. This person is not sufficiently well mannered to be with the boarders, who make fun of her. When we shall have trained a teacher for the paying day pupils, Eugenie can withdraw and Marguerite would remain at the head. Mother Geoffroy had destined her for Sainte-Pezenne, and our town is the equivalent. She who cannot do much active work can give religious instruction and lead them to God. The greatest need of your family in this country would be a superior or a mistress of novices who has excellent command of English; otherwise, it will be difficult to form people to religious life; they would receive only a foreign formation. Mother Octavie, who is the most advanced, often does not understand; and for students aspiring to religious life, she is too eager to be loved. The bishop says that people my age never learn English well. I try out a few sentences with our postulant; I write it, but I do not understand her when she speaks, and Mother Octavie does not always understand either.

I will go to Florissant, therefore, with Octavie, whom all the boarders love and who has more talents than Eugenie; for our children being from Saint-Louis, all the parents will want them closer. Besides, she knows both languages best, so she is best equipped to teach them, whether the French who are learning English or the Americans who are learning French. The same can be said of her regarding novices; I see it with our postulant, a rather mediocre candidate about whom we cannot make a decision until we know her better. Reading, writing, and speaking this language are less difficult than understanding spoken English.

Judging by what we see, we will have to be content with less than we would like. The habits of neglect, the laziness, ignorance, and sensuality make our holy state difficult to understand; someone who appears to be an angel to her confessor does not know how to do or suffer anything;

she sits by the fire drinking coffee or tea, leaves everything in disorder rather than taking action; that is the character we have to overcome. We would have more hope with the boarders of French background; one of them calls you *her mother* and your reverend brother *her father*; another thinks only of Saint Francis Xavier, and what is astonishing, another, even before knowing his life, in prayer always gets close to the picture of Saint Francis Regis, etc.

The wardrobe of the Americans can be judged by that of our first one: two ragged chemises, two little sheets, two poor handkerchiefs, one pair of stockings, and shoes. When one stocking was missing, instead of looking for it, she went to Mass with just one stocking on a very cold day. We have gotten a little more activity out of her, but she is not yet known in depth regarding her vocation.

As repulsive as the parents here are by their laziness, drunkenness, and love of dances—there is one every week given by people who lack everything—there is hope in the children; they seem inclined to love us. A Protestant girl who wants to convert wants no other godmother but us; two intelligent Negro slaves came by themselves to be instructed. You would have been touched by their manner, their admiration of the picture of Our Lady in the chapel; they did not even know the Our Father, or what religion they were born into, or whether they were baptized. They understood only English.

Do not be surprised, good and zealous Mother, if we wish to divide ourselves in two or even four to preserve the good begun here and to go to do even greater good near Saint Louis, the center of the state that is going to be created in Missouri (that of Illinois is separated from us by the river). There we will be closer to the source of help, to the wishes of our bishop, and nearer to Father Martial, who, it is said, is coming up the Mississippi with students from New Orleans whom he is bringing to the academy the bishop is opening in Saint Louis, of which Father Martial will be the head. We cannot wait for your answer before beginning the house here or in Florissant, but we can wait for a decision about our individual destinations on September 1, again taking advantage of navigation.

I hope Father Martial will bring us the package your good brother has said was coming; we are longing to have it, especially because of the letters. We have received a packet from Quimper, containing fourteen letters to Eugenie from the boarders; she has hardly read them all, and I am afraid we shall have an enormous bill in Saint Louis that we will not be able to pay.[125] Would you please see that letters that

---

125 The cost of postage was paid by the recipient.

can wait are put in the packages that come to us from time to time; it is not rare here for a letter to cost 15 F and to obtain sixty of them we had to sell some of our brand new extra clothes; we needed them for ourselves as well as for our postulants without trousseau. My last letter was sent through Philadelphia; this one will go by the same route; and if you wish to answer the same way, here is the safe address: *Messrs. J. and G. COLLIER, St Charles, Missouri territory. To the care of Messrs. FASSILL and LANGSTROTH. South-West corner of Market and Second Street. PHILADELPHIA.*

A ship going from France to Philadelphia takes a month at most and a second will bring us your answer.

[no ending or signature]

Letter 125   L. 22 to Mother Barat

SS. C. J. et M.

Saint Charles, Missouri Territory, February 15, 1819[126]
Rec. St. Anthony of Padua

Very Reverend Mother,

Just a few days ago, I received from New Orleans a letter from Father Martial, four months old. He is coming to Saint Louis. And there was one from the bishop written six months ago,[127] but it depicts so well what one can expect to find in this country that I thought it might interest you. The second, quite recent, concerns our transfer to Florissant.[128] The experience of a winter here, and that a very mild one, has made us realize that we would only vegetate in this place, without accomplishing the little good we might do elsewhere. But it is hard to abandon so many interesting children, several of whom will belong to the Heart of Jesus, and it seems to me necessary to leave Sister Eugenie here for the moment. Before long, Marguerite, who will be with her,

---

126   Original autograph, C-VII 2) c Duchesne to Barat, Box 2. Cf. J. de Charry, II 1, L. 109, pp. 193-202; Hogg, pp. 133-139; Ch. Paisant, pp. 228-233.
127   "When you are here you will see that in all of Upper Louisiana, I would not have been able to find a situation more suitable for a beginning. (...) One must prepare the ground before cultivating," June 28, 1818, C-VII 2) c Duchesne to various Eccles., Box 8.
128   "I approve completely your plan to divide your community and to leave at Saint Charles only the day school under the direction of Mother Eugenie, your good sister and Miss Mullen. Your boarding school will do much better in every way in Florissant." January 29, 1819, *Idem*.

will be able to take charge of this day school with some young persons to assist her. There are several spoken about, and in the meantime our present postulant [Mary Mullen], who is being trained, can teach English and interpret; she still has six months to get accustomed to French, and study of it is developing her mind.

Mother Eugenie is loved in her school. She has just made her retreat, and she was greeted with tears of joy that made her own flow; and since it was said that maybe we are leaving, several of the older girls are saying, "Soon I'll be packing my things, too," and the youngest are begging us to take them with us, saying that they are asking that of the Heart of Jesus. If we were not so short of funds, we could do much good by educating several of them at our own expense, but what can we do without lodging or provisions! We cannot remain in this house where one room like the parlor in Paris and six little ones cost almost 2000 F a year. The bishop was very mistaken in thinking we could house twenty-five boarders: not even ten, though we fold up the beds every morning.

The northern section of Missouri can never send us boarders who can pay; we can have here only a day school with very few children; we could not live on it. Pride tries to hide their misery, but we see these poor, hungry children coming barefooted, often in the coldest weather, with no other clothing than a very light dress with nothing under it. You see, good Mother, that forced as we are to give up the boarding school here, it is heartbreaking to leave no help at all for these children who could be nicely trained. In four months several have learned to read, write, the little catechism, a number of songs, the prayers for Benediction; they do all the singing now; before, the priest had no one who could even say *Amen*. I hope you will approve what the bishop desires so earnestly.

Yesterday, the 14th, was a very happy day. A young priest, Father Portier,[129] who came with us from New Orleans, asked for places for several boarders and told us of his mission to New Madrid, a small town, a center of earthquakes that have been felt as far as here. No priest has gone there for twenty years. Father Delacroix, another young Flemish priest, our extraordinary confessor, comes from Upper Missouri, country that has never seen a priest.[130] There are two missions there: one at

---

129 Michael Portier (1795-1859), born in Montbrison, France, ordained priest by Bishop Dubourg in 1818, accompanied Philippine and her sisters from New Orleans to Saint Louis, in July-August 1818. In 1829, he would become the first bishop of the diocese of Mobile, where he remained until his death.

130 Charles Delacroix (1792-1869), born in Belgium and ordained in France, arrived September

Côte Sans Dessein,[131] which he has dedicated to Saint Paul the Apostle and where there are twenty-two families; the other at Booneslick or Franklin, dedicated to Saint Francis de Sales. He gave a mission there; all the Catholics profited greatly, and some Protestants came to hear him. Several promised to allow him to teach catechism to their children. A catechist has been appointed. Father Delacroix confirmed for us what the bishop had told us, that the Fathers [Jesuits] from Georgetown are going to buy land there and work for the glory of God. The field of labor is immense, but the population sparse and poor; I would let my desires run in that direction if English were not the only language spoken.

I come back now to the 14th, when I received four letters: one from Mr. Petry, French Consul in Washington, who is offering me his services to send letters; I am taking advantage of it today. His letter is extremely polite but dated three months ago. From Grenoble, a newspaper five months old; a letter from Mother Bigeu, dated four months ago. We had much joy in reading them. It seems that these dear letters, while binding us to the whole Society, are uniting us more closely to one another, as they remind us of the grace God has given us in the Society of his Heart.

Mother Bigeu did not give me any details and spoke of earlier letters that I have not received, but I am hoping. I tell myself that there will be one from you in the packet; you would not leave us without that consolation. Father Perreau shows that he is still a father, and I am still his daughter, for I do not find anyone here to replace him and do not hope to. This solitude of the heart, which finds nothing on earth that answers its desires, forces one to throw oneself into the Heart of Jesus. Thank this good father for his letter,[132] dated almost six months ago, and for the joy he has obtained for us through this third blessing

---

14, 1817, at Annapolis with Bishop Dubourg and in Saint Louis in January 1818. He was named treasurer and resided at the farm, which he vacated for the sisters, whose house was not finished. Bishop Dubourg then named him pastor of Florissant. His journeys to the Indian missions damaged his health, and in June 1823 he went down to Saint Michael, Louisiana, where he built a church. In 1824, he proposed to the Religious of the Sacred Heart that they make a foundation there, which they did in 1825. He returned finally to Europe in 1839.

131 Côte Sans Dessein at that time was a growing commercial village situated on the north bank of the Missouri, across from the Osage River, about twelve miles from Jefferson City.

132 Father Perreau answered Philippine's questions concerning: a foundation in the country, temporal independence, the admission of persons of color to the boarding school and to the novitiate, religious vows, cloister, and division into two houses. On this last point, his advice was the opposite of Bishop Dubourg's: "I believe you must insist particularly on two things, even with regard to the bishop: 1) to have an ecclesiastic in your establishment every day, at least in the morning; 2) not to form two houses at present, as from your correspondence it seems there is a desire. (...) It is better at first not to try to do all the good that presents itself, for one risks thereby ending badly oneself and perhaps for others." Letter of August 29, 1818, *Notebook N° 92*, pp. 17-24.

of the Holy Father and the hope of the Brief for the Confraternity of the Sacred Heart, which will be precious for us.

The admission of persons of color is not practicable for the boarding school; the bishop has decided, relying on the bishop of Baltimore [Bishop Carroll] who told him that the disdain for them is a *prejudice*; but a *prejudice* that must be preserved as a safeguard of behavior. In this country, Indians are on a par with whites when they are not of mixed blood, but everyone agrees that the little girls must be taken in at four or five years of age before they have become incapable of learning; then we would have to lodge and feed them! And we do not have the wherewithal.

As to enclosure, there is not a single wall in the whole country for 500 leagues around; there are wooden fences that serve to keep the animals out but not people; our cloister consists of staying at home, but people come in when and as they wish and make entrances without asking us. We will have to be in our own house to establish regularity; in this house, it is impossible. Even though we are living in practically uncultivated territory, we do not have an inch of land; it is all held in common or owned by Congress, which has made no definite law. One can build with certainty only on land purchased from individual owners, and the price is high. Therefore, we have no need of the persons Father Perreau has in view. I do not know if there are already some in Florissant, for those who are going to cultivate the land the bishop has acquired there are Flemish.[133] He is going to give us a portion for a house and garden for the boarding school only.

If our sisters imagine us surrounded by Indians, they are quite mistaken. I have seen only a few old women who made their First Communion at the age of fifty or sixty when all passion is spent. But to compensate, I am learning new trades, along with Mothers Octavie and Eugenie: we dig in the garden, carry out the manure, water the cow, clean out her little stable, the only one around, as all the animals roam at large; and all this with as much joy as if we were teaching Indians, since God wishes it so, and our poverty, along with the false pride of the inhabitants prevents our finding servants. Catherine has rheumatism; Marguerite finds everything external so foreign that she is quite confused. She is doing well in the school, and that would be a good place for her if we could find a cook. I spoke about it in my last letter of January 25, which also contained two letters from the bishop. The letters of Sister Marie de l'Incarnation can give you an idea of our

---

133 Bishop Dubourg had appealed to a society of brothers who were farm workers.

country, since it was populated only forty years ago by Canadians; the first inhabitants all speak French therefore.

Priestly ministry has little success and costs a good deal of trouble. One priest, not being able to live in one of his parishes, where there is a dance three times a week, and where he was being left to die of hunger in a poor hut, moved to another parish this winter to the house of the principal inhabitant who has two beds: one for the father and mother, one for the priest; all the children sleep under skins on the floor. This priest, therefore, is in a room with no fire, no casements, rough boards closing up the windows, enduring crying children day and night, obliged to warm himself at the kitchen fire when it is so cold that even wine freezes, and he has problems with his eyes. Moreover, he has no consolation at all in his ministry, no one at his Mass on working days, and twelve or fifteen on Sundays, etc. Bishop Flaget, bishop of Kentucky, traveled hundreds of leagues for a meeting between the Americans and the Indians to get them to agree to accept "black robes" (priests). A Protestant minister, one of the delegates, contradicted him, so Bishop Flaget gained nothing but a severe illness in a cabin where there was no one to care for him.

The weather has been very beautiful since we arrived, but I am told that there are often furious winds and bad thunderstorms and light earthquakes. As the country does not yet have a constitution, it is easy to get away with things and to escape. Fires are set deliberately, and there are poisonings attributed to slaves, but they are not numerous. People sometimes set fire to the woods and prairies when the grass is tall and dry. One night, the Americans of Saint Charles stayed up watching so that the fire did not reach the town, for it was spreading like a whirlwind. In autumn, we see it on all sides and in the forest across from us on the other side of the Missouri.

The money is another inconvenience; gold and silver, which abound in New Orleans, are lacking here; we pay with paper money from private or individual state banks, and the bank notes decrease in value constantly, even while you hold them. One believes a debt has been paid, and the creditor comes back saying, "This bill is worthless." It would be necessary to have a new list of reliable banks every day.

The soil is very good here but left practically uncultivated through laziness. The half-breeds among the inhabitants share the Indians' hatred for work and love of drink; in some villages or in almost all, there are drunkards in every house. The girls are crazy about dancing, dance parties every week: one of them is queen, dressed at the expense of her king; she opens the dance and embraces all those taking part; the others, who often have neither bread nor lingerie, have at least gowns of decorated mousseline etc. This mania will be cured only in future generations. Saints would be needed to work in these hearts so poorly prepared. It is all the more painful for me not to be one; I see the two sisters [Catherine and Marguerite] losing instead of gaining, and I am the cause of it. As for Octavie and Eugenie, they are running in the way of perfection, and the little good done here is due to them. You will have two superiors in them, and if you cannot replace me by an English woman, Octavie will be able to fill in. We will soon have more Americans than French-speaking Creoles. What good will I be able to do without facility in English? I experience it with our postulant, and for her good and the good of others, I would with pleasure see myself in the lowest employments in the house. Besides, you know me: people are afraid of me, and a superior must be liked by everyone.

Father Perreau, who forgets nothing that might interest me, gives me news of our fathers. Will you please recommend me to the prayers of all, especially Father Varin. I believe that if you and they were here, you would think with the bishop and with us that what is needed is a Sainte-Pezenne[134] and that a boarding school could not thrive. If Eugenie were taken off suddenly, her children would abandon everything. Do listen to me, Reverend Mother.

I am at your feet your obedient daughter.

Philippine

I beg Mothers de Gramont, de Charbonnel, Giraud, Balastron, and all those with you, Sisters and children, to pray for us.

I beg you to please put in an envelope the enclosed letter from a Frenchman who has had no news for two years; please remove the band I put round the letter to lighten the envelope.

Letter 126   L. 2 to Mother Vincent

SS. C. J. et M.

Saint Charles, Missouri, March 2 [1819][135]

My very good Mother,

It has been a long time since I have had news of you, perhaps

---

134 A day school and an orphanage, and the transfer of the boarding school to Florissant.
135 Original autograph, C-VII 2) c Duchesne to RSCJ and Children, Box 4.

because the steamboat that brings me the letters that are so desired cannot stay in Saint Louis, and no one can assure me, so I am answering you in haste so as not to miss its departure; and because of our eagerness, I must sacrifice responding to your dear Aloysia and to Sister Dosithée. I sincerely congratulate the former for the happiness she has obtained, and all of you for such a good retreat given by your two fathers, which makes us jealous of you, since we are such dissipated travelers and now less apostles than farmers. We have great need for your sister workers to tighten our doors and windows, but even more to animate us by their fervor. We often speak of the Sacred Heart of Bordeaux,[136] of so much goodness, care, and charity exercised in our regard. If giving alms enriches, you must have great abundance.

I have learned with sorrow that your health is completely weakened and that you cough continually. We pray for your recovery, which is so necessary for your work.

We do not yet know how things will be for us. We have spent some very painful moments when we arrived, almost not knowing which way to turn. Everything is getting a little clearer, but we are beginning a very difficult year, needing to build with very little in funds in a country with few resources. Nevertheless, we are all happy, persuaded that God has wanted this work and that he will sustain it.

We will find everything for clothing here, but the furnishings for needlework, books, and objects for church and classes are not to be found. If you could send us some samples of English penmanship, it would be really essential for us.

But what would be even better are your prayers, which I ask you to grant us without ceasing. Please give our affectionate respects to Mrs. Fournier. Our holy bishop has many labors and successes to come, for the soil is unresponsive but everything is prepared for a good outcome. He willingly takes on difficulties so as to bring consolation to his successors. He is fairly well.

Father Boyer will be glad to receive our profound respects and you, my dear and very honorable Mother, our ardent wishes for you and your daughters in the Heart of Jesus.

Philippine Duchesne

---

136 Their community had taken this name, which could cause confusion, since they were not yet part of the Society of the Sacred Heart.

[On the reverse:]
To Mother
Mother Vincent
Superior of the Sisters of the Sacred Heart
Rue Lalande

Letter 127   **L. 23 to Mother Barat**

Saint-Charles, Missouri Territory, [March] 5, 1819[137]
Rec. to St. Anthony

Very Reverend Mother,

    I am not afraid of being reproached for my silence but rather for indiscretion. I figure I have written to you about twelve or fourteen times, and I think I can write regularly every month, either through New Orleans or one of the eastern cities by the opportunity of travels of persons known to us. Six or seven hundred leagues are nothing in this country; it is like fifty or sixty in France, although there are many more dangers. The steamboat *Franklin*, in which we came up here, on its next trip ran aground a fourth of the way up and was stuck on the sand for three months; when it was afloat again and continuing its route, it struck one of the tree trunks that are a hazard to navigation on the Mississippi, and it filled with water and sank. No one perished, but all the merchandise is at the bottom of the river in the shallows. Why did that accident not happen while we were aboard? A new act of Providence in our regard and a sign of God's will for our sojourn here! What's more, it was reported that it was carrying goods for us, but I have just learned that, for no apparent reason, they were consigned to the *Washington*, which fortunately made the trip from New Orleans to Saint Louis, in thirty days. We are waiting eagerly for the box that Father Barat promised us and your letters that were delayed, for the last from Mother Bigeu refers to others written previously, which will be the first since you have heard from us from New Orleans.

    Our benefactors in that city [the Ursulines], seemed to have forgotten us, to judge by their silence; one of their letters tells me the contrary. They have sent prepaid to us, in the same steamboat, four kettles, soap,

---

137 Original autograph, C-VII 2) c Duchesne to Barat, Box 2. Cf. J. de Charry, II 1, L. 110, pp. 217-223; Hogg, pp. 148-152; Ch. Paisant, pp. 237-240.

bluing, candles, a case of raisins, one of codfish from one of the boarders, a barrel of cassonade (raw sugar), and several other cases the contents of which I do not know; the letters were enclosed. The cassonade alone is a considerable gift: maple sugar sells at 25 *sols* for 14 French ounces and is not very palatable; the other went up to almost five F a pound in the cold season. We use a great deal because most often we can give the pupils only coffee at breakfast; there is nothing else.

Providence is wonderful for us: one day when we did not know how we could pay the baker, the laundress, the salt bill, etc., we began a novena to divine Providence and Our Lady of Prompt Succor; the next day, Father Richard, our parish priest and confessor, told us that he absolutely insisted on paying his board, as he had received something for his services. In spite of my resistance, he settled on 600 F for the year and gave me 350 immediately, which took us out of debt. We resolved to continue the Litany of Providence every day; and at once we received news of the charitable gifts of the Ursulines, from whom, however, we are asking for a loan of 1500 F, following the bishop's advice; he assures us that they will lend it (as if he were sure of their answer). Doubtless, he knows of their desire to help with our building. Moreover, the inhabitants of Saint Charles are becoming active about our house here; they have already brought to the spot huge logs forty feet long to build the house; it will overlook the Missouri, as Sainte-Marie does the Isère, and the view would be just as beautiful if the fields were cultivated.

My good Mother, the letter I wrote and sent through Mr. Petry, Consul of France in Washington, and a preceding one, inform you of our plan to divide between Florissant and Saint Charles and submit it to you; I enclosed in those last two letters four copies of letters from the bishop concerning and approving what I am proposing to you. Since then, he met us in Florissant. On Shrove Monday, I went with Mother Octavie; he arrived an hour after we did at the pastor's house. He showed us the place he is giving us and the plan of a house, a third of which will be built this year, 36 feet long and 32 wide. It is on a good piece of land between a small stream that never runs dry and a creek that dries up in summer. This house will be made of brick and will cost 15,000 F. Now we have no more in hand than 5800 at the most, with our rent and the journeys paid. Besides, we will have 300 or 400 to pay for finishing the house in Saint Charles that the inhabitants have promised only to build and put the roof on. It will be constructed of large logs laid one upon the other to form the walls and roofed with wood.

The bishop told me he has written to you to ask for money, but I told him not to hope for much from that quarter, knowing the expenses you have; that we would be able to ask the parents for the yearly fees in advance; that is my only human resource. But I do not doubt Providence or God's will for the propagation of our work in this country. The bishop added that opinion in Saint Louis is changing very much in favor of us, but no one is very rich there yet. He asked a great many questions about our whole household here and told me that Sister Catherine had quite misunderstood his answer to her, and he thinks she is mentally unbalanced. While saying that, he added, "If there were more of you, I would ask for two for a day school in Saint Louis."

Sister Eugenie has weathered her storm and goes forward in the way of perfection; she could do any work anyone would wish to give her. She seems to be in the prayer of quiet and finds particular acts troublesome, like so many acts of virtue a day. I beg you to tell me how to guide her in this. Mother Octavie is also very fervent and is gaining in self-assurance; her children like her very much, and she will be happy to follow them to Florissant, without envying the independence Sister Eugenie will have here. Marguerite is still out of her element regarding exterior life. Catherine is better, but her behavior depends on the state of her health, little suited to a life like ours, which is fatiguing. The priests have a worse time than we do; I know of one who had about two cartloads of snow come into his room in one night through openings in the spaces between the boards. Almost the same thing happened to the brothers who work the bishop's farm. Their little house will be left for us, and we will set up the day school there at the end of the garden.

All the letters from France give us a great deal of enjoyment. We have been able to follow you in all your travels, and the progress of the Society makes us very happy. Reading this dear news makes it seem as if we are in France. It will seem even closer when a canal from the state of New York connecting with the Ohio River will make it possible for us to have news of you in a month and a half. This canal will be finished in one or two years, they say.

Another response of Providence to our novena is that we have been able to buy a second cow, which in a month and a half will have given enough milk to pay for herself and will make it possible for us to fast the whole of Lent. Only the boarders will have meat four days a week, according to the custom in the United States. We were told these cows would become frenzied if we tethered them on our grounds, but they are behaving nicely and follow us around like two big dogs; they even try to come into the house after us.

Would you be kind enough to tell me whether, in our situation, it would be contrary to our spirit to accept gifts from the day pupils, such as eggs, meat, etc., and to accept payment from those who wish to give five F per month for their children in the free school. Several would not come without paying through a kind of pride. May we sell some produce from our garden to help support ourselves?

I beg you to commend me to the prayers of our fathers and to think about replacing me. I believe I must be dreaming when someone calls me the superior, and more and more I feel I am hindering the good we might do.

I am with profound devotedness, very Reverend Mother, your quite unworthy daughter.

Philippine Duchesne

I have just received your letters, which I thought were lost; I will try to become what you desire, my beloved Mother; how I would like to be a comfort to you.

[On the reverse:]
To Mother
Mother Barat
Superior General of the Religious of the Sacred Heart
Rue des Postes N° 40
Paris

Letter 128 **L. 6 to Father Barat**

SS. C. J. et M.

Saint Charles, Missouri Territory, March 15, 1819[138]
Recommended to St. Anthony of Padua

My very dear Father,

A few days ago, I wrote briefly to you, having left the letter to our mother open so you could read it and so avoid repetitions. Today it is the opposite: I write a letter to my father, which he will share with my mother.

---

138 Original autograph, C-VII 2) c Writings Duchesne to various Eccles., Box 8.

As we are in a time of trial, God has allowed that all I told you about our situation has changed; and for lodging, we have no other resources than the good will of the inhabitants of Saint Charles, who show eagerness to raise the skeleton of a house for us. It is said that they will slow down and instead of being raised in a month, it might not be ready until autumn. God knows, let us abandon it to his care.

As to Florissant, everything is delayed for three reasons: 1) the religious in New Orleans have lost a lawsuit and have had to borrow to sustain themselves; they cannot help us, nor can those in Havana; 2) you and our mother tell me of a shortage of subjects and money; 3) when I saw the contractor's plans for Florissant, I saw only extortion, excessive spending that would ruin us. Having learned this, I wrote to the bishop refusing the assistance of the contractor and telling him that all our resources were in what he was holding for us. I told him how we had managed at Grenoble without a contractor, several striking examples of their voracity and the ruin of so many religious houses through debt. His answer was that he had thought well about it and since he could not help us, it was necessary to stop the project at Florissant, but to write to him myself so that it came from me. I did not delay in doing so and that is where we are. The local residents are having a meeting again today about our work. It is incontrovertible that they show us more interest here. The boarding school will proceed slowly because of crossing the Missouri, but let us have patience.

Another reason, a fourth, is very serious: it is the little help we can expect from our two sisters. Catherine [Lamarre] has gone so far as to propose herself to the bishop for a foundation in Saint Louis, modeled on Sainte-Pezenne, where a lay sister was superior. Therefore, without her suspecting, I emphasized the fate of Mother Benoît who put this house on the level of that of the Society. The other [Marguerite Manteau], who is out of her element in dealing with outsiders, is completely off track and seems not to have overcome her haste for her retreat; when she cannot worry about her own work, she busies herself about whether we are doing ours. Oh, how good it is never to have been put forward!

Mothers Octavie and Audé are completely devoted. Deprivation, overwork, strange diet, nothing repels them and privations are their joy. One can always expect more from the upper classes. They give themselves willingly to everything. So I rather regret saying in my last letter that Mother Lucille is not fit for this country; there will be enough French girls to keep her busy. By a stroke of Providence, of which I do not yet see the outcome, the young person who always followed us to church in Saint Louis and brought us apples has since then lost her mother at Christmas, and her brother was drowned while trying to help pull out the [steamboat] *Franklin*. The bishop sent her to us to serve, and we received her without realizing that it was the same child who by instinct attached herself to us so strongly. She knows how to read, write, and speaks the two languages. In this sense she will be more useful to us than the first postulant [Miss Mullen] who was without a vocation and very indolent. This one is intelligent, and we will train her for work with the poor.

My good Father, I had written my letters before going to the bottom of the crate that you took the trouble to send us. Nothing is as precious to us as your own work; reading it is to find you again; it is to serve the Heart of Jesus Christ by practicing and savoring its teaching. I regretted finding ourselves there, even indirectly, for it is still very doubtful that we are worthy to serve the glory of God here. One goes on, one takes great steps forward and then a thousand little ones backward, which leave one at the starting point or less; unhappily, I experience this. I do not know who our benefactors are, except those of Quimper and Niort, for the trinkets, rosaries, etc. Mother Eugenie thanked Quimper; I ask you to do the same for us for Niort.

Father Debrosse was good enough to answer me and to tell me that we owe him nothing; please thank him. We must keep limits this year; the essential is to have our own home. You could not believe how difficult it is to have order and regularity where we are: nothing locks, and we can be accosted at any moment by strangers.

Among the letters that have gone out, I answered Mother Vincent, but I am never hesitant to convey to her our union with her in the Heart of Jesus. In spite of your fears, I hope her house is prospering and yours, too, even more useful. Julie [Bazire][139] and her companion told me about their entrance into the novitiate [at Sainte-Marie d'En-Haut]; just imagine whether I am happy to see successively such dear students give themselves to God. The greatest conversion would be that of Miss Pernety, whose letter was simply perfect. We have some here who call

---

139 Julie Bazire, RSCJ, born on August 15, 1806, in France, entered the novitiate August 12, 1825, and made her first vows in 1827. Arrived in Saint Louis in 1829, she made profession May 8, 1830. She was superior at La Fourche in 1831, then at Saint Michael and at Grand Coteau, in 1837. Back in France in 1843, she went to the foundation in Lemberg, then in Austrian territory, according to Philippine's letter to Mother Gonzague Boilvin, October 18, 1843. She returned to America from 1847 to 1850, and left the Society of the Sacred Heart on an uncertain date. On August 28, 1851, she wrote to Bishop Blanc of New Orleans, expressing to him her desire to return to Louisiana as a religious of the Sacred Heart (Archives of the University of Notre Dame, photocopy sent to the Archives of the Province of the United States-Canada). She died in France, February 22, 1883.

you their father; the stories from Europe amused them as much as those from America entertain the children in France.

As for the domestic servant about whom I told you, the bishop, who knows him well, does not think he should come. They have suggested a young couple from Grenoble for our service; this would be very useful, but the expense...! And the climate is a great trial for those without the vocation...! And the isolation from one's acquaintances exposes them to so many things! At Florissant we will have the help of the brothers who cultivate the bishop's land.

The situation of our holy bishop is a long trial. The health of several of his priests wavers: Father de Andreis is in danger, and he is the right hand of his pastor. Even Father Martial cannot replace him, since he does not understand English and cannot direct the seminary confided to the Lazarists. When one sees his difficulties at close hand, his limitations, etc., one would want to devote oneself to working with him without personal interest for the glory of the One who gives him such generosity. They say, however, that things are going better in New Orleans, and that everything is leading to a reunion.

The superior of the Ursuline Sisters told me with feeling about your letter and that of our mother; it had a good effect. She continues to regret that we are not in her city or near it, since every day she turns away students whom she would send us; but she does not dare insist, since the bishop showed his displeasure that they had dreamed of keeping us there without consulting him. She regrets that, at such great distance, she cannot share with us their abundance in a thousand little ways that we lack here. She cannot get her embroidery box out of customs without the invoice, which Mrs. Jouve must have put inside it.

I thought it useful, my good Father, to write to you at once so that if our mother becomes upset at seeing us in two places, you will reassure her. But this cannot be delayed long, given our obligations toward Saint Charles and the necessity of a large boarding school to feed the novitiate and the orphans, our only hope for service personnel, since we do not have slaves, and there are no whites who will do service work.

It will be a question here whether we can speak of lay sisters for the domestic work. In New Orleans, the difference is imperceptible; the only difference is Office. Two different habits will be noticed. Already Catherine wants ours, without daring to say it. It comes at her from all sides, poor dear! She has good moments that make me believe that her faults are more in her badly organized head than in her heart. It proves that for this country we need healthy bodies that can resist the attacks that temperament brings, and not too old. What a difference there is among these four [religious] with regard to courage, devotion, and the taste for poverty and humiliations!

I thought I had lost my health, but it is renewed and I do not suffer from anything. But I will have much to expiate because in this change, the degree of consolation outweighs the suffering. What a joy! To see the Holy Father praise our journey and see by this single event the will of God lifted from me that cruel suffering that perhaps under the pretext of following a call, I did my own will. The rules and the letter of Saint Ignatius teach that one does not obey when one tries to lead superiors to one's own desire. So my prayer is only an outpouring of gratitude for the knowledge that this will of God so much desired will be even better when the Sacred Heart and its daughters will spread the reign of Jesus Christ in these new lands.

I am with respect your daughter,

Philippine Duchesne

March 15, 1819

The good God is trying us: our first boarder, a ribbon of merit, is dangerously ill. She is the oldest daughter of the lady [Mrs. Pratte] who received us so well in Saint Louis. If she dies as I well fear, this will be according to human thinking a severe blow for us; but God can do all. I always think there are several letters lost, not having had an answer to certain questions about the health of my sisters. Mother Octavie and Catherine are often suffering.

[On the reverse:]
To Father
Father Barat
At the minor seminary
Bordeaux
France

Letter 129   L. to Miss Constance Jouve

SS. C. J. et M.

March 1819[140]

---

140   Original autograph, C-VII 2) c Duchesne to her family and lay people, Box 5.

My dearest Niece,

My answer is a little late, but I don't love you any the less. At such great distances, our relationships must often be kept up in the divine Heart of Jesus. How you must love him now that he is showing you his love in giving you the grace of making your First Communion. Always keep the fruits of this grace so as not to be ungrateful.

Give my regards to your dear parents. I have learned that your good Papa has done the favor I asked of him for the Ursulines of New Orleans, but they are afraid that they cannot get the box out of customs, as they do not have the required bill. If it has not already been sent, it would be necessary to send it to their address, *Dames Ursulines*; there can be no mistake.

I sent my certificate of annuity in a letter to my brother in Grenoble. I hope he has received it. If he withdraws from the last two years, 1817 et 1818, that will serve to pay Mr. Jouve for his service to the nuns or for so many other things that I do not cease to ask of him. These nuns have given me an advance payment that I have spent.

Tell my brothers and sisters that I am very well, that I never forget them and my interest in them does not lessen. I am going to be very busy about our lodging. Building is beginning and our financial resources are very weak.

Good-bye, my dear girl. I love you tenderly in the Sacred Heart of Jesus.

Philippine

I send my love to my nieces and your companions.
Give my best wishes especially to Amelie de Mauduit, Amelie Jouve and the four eldest Lebrument girls.

Letter 130 **L. 3 to Mother Bigeu**

SS. C. J. et M.

Saint Charles, April 25, 1819[141]
Recommended to Saint Anthony of Padua

---

141 Copy: C-III 1: USA Foundation Haute Louisiane, Box 1, *Lettres de la Haute Louisiane I 1818-1823*, pp. 131-135. Cf. Ch. Paisant, pp. 245-248.

My very good Mother,

I wrote to you and our mother general on March 8, the 12th to Father Barat, begging him to communicate my letter to our mother general, to whom I wrote again about April 12, sending a letter by post to Father Martial, who is still in New Orleans for at least a year, because it has worked out well for the union of spirits in the obedience due to their pastor.

I was in a hurry to send my letter, since I was in a state of anxiety about our foundation. In each of my letters, I have said something contradictory, and after having told father that we would all stay in Saint Charles, I told our mother that the bishop opposes this foundation and transported us all to Florissant to a house that is not yet built, which we are beginning at our expense; since we do not have enough, we will borrow. My observations about fear of debts and taking on exaggerated expenses did not convince the bishop. He finds that I lack confidence, and to remove all cause of distress, he will take care of arranging everything himself.

When I think about the fact that we must pay everything back through doubtful boarding school operations, which have disappointed us, and that we are left with four after the departure of one who was sick, I am afraid; but when I say that we cannot have much extra income from boarders, I am answered: "Nevertheless, you are living with just so much, and I fear that it is not always being kept in balance." I answered that we had advances, a wardrobe made, no sickness, and no purchased furniture. I hope that Providence will either decrease expenses or take from me my fear that many promise their daughters but will not send them. Here we are very rich in words and reduced in effect... Who would have told us that on the wild banks of the Missouri there would be a Paris of such luxury, softness, laziness, corruption, and ignorance that it does not seem worthwhile to learn and teach? The unjust judgments towards a woman who had a school in Saint Louis make me see what awaits us of opinion and gratitude; but all for God! Happy to work beneath the shadow of the naked cross!

When leaving more than 50 children of different classes at Saint Charles, I experienced the regret that Saint Francis Xavier had when he left the Socotorians[142] who stretched out their arms to him. This area, the first that welcomed us, will always be dear to us; and it makes me want companions from France to be able to destine them to continue the

---

142 The inhabitants of Socotra, a small archipelago in the Indian Ocean.

good work begun, already so evident that several families are distressed at our departure, and especially the pastor [Father Richard] who told me: "If you stay, everything I will have will be yours." But the bishop, who did not want us in Saint Louis, now would like a day school run by two of us, which would not allow a return to Saint Charles. Remember that he told you in my presence that we would have to have 30,000 F when we arrived here? I told him that my mother could not make more sacrifices for us, and that if we could not maintain ourselves here, she would certainly recall us. I would be upset and so would he, but I wanted to impress on him that we have to limit the expenses of our house so as to be able to balance receipts and expenses for a few years.

In two letters to our mother, I sent the address of a merchant in Philadelphia who has an agent in Saint Charles, a very obliging man. I do not know if the letter he sent by that city has arrived, but it is sure that this would be a very convenient route, because everything that goes to New Orleans is addressed directly by his brother to the bishop, and there have already been some mix-ups. Besides, since he enters into all the details, it would be good to know exactly what is coming from France. But not having tried the way through Philadelphia, though it should be sure, I cannot refrain from seeing that everything that comes to Saint Louis is brought from New Orleans; and every day there are more connections between these two cities. God will inspire the direction to take, always under the protection of Saint Anthony of Padua; everything that is recommended to him gets through. This gentleman will help us even at Saint Charles, but he will be more useful for letters. For packages, it is better through New Orleans.

The bishop made a retreat here and was full of interest in us and our work. He admires our Constitutions.

We have had two fire alarms, the first in a chimney, without damage; the second in the chapel on Holy Thursday. All the decorations of the altar and the chapel were burnt, and even the upper story up to the ceiling was burning. The sacred Host was found intact on the paten, which had fallen onto the altar, under the pall that was completely burnt. On cannot imagine a moment like that. God's Providence granted us that it had rained the night before. Water in a boat nearby gave us the means of throwing out whatever was on fire and attacking the flames that filled the chapel, so that with a little work, our chapel was ready for Easter Day; the vestments were far from the fire.

The rumor of our move will keep boarding students from coming here. According to all appearances, we will have to manage with four until autumn. So impress upon those who will come to expect poverty, not in theory, not in unrealized desires, but in reality. While we had our sick student [Miss Pratte], it was impossible to find meat from fowl to make soup; her mother sent it from 5 or 6 miles away. During this season, we have only salted pork. Laziness prevents cultivation and raising of fowl. But the poverty of accommodation is really something else: never to be alone here day or night, neither in health nor in sickness. This is what one must expect at Florissant as well as here. Our physician has seen 32 sick in one house, with nothing but salted meat and corn for food and remedies. We who want poverty are not quite there.

One day when I had grabbed a calf by the tail at the same time as Eugenie had it by the neck to separate it from its mother and make it go a little way, I thought afterwards that I was a superior more worthy of that office than of government. Ah! If only God would hear the wishes that I make for the good of our mission here! Help them along, I beg you, by asking for someone else in my place.

We have had winter in spring here. The cold killed one of our heifers, made the seedlings die in the garden, which will not yield much, and often covered our poor cow, who does not want to be fenced in, with ice, with which she came in the morning to offer us her milk and ask for her feed. Our two cows are worthy of mention: one of them kissed the bishop's hands, and often kisses ours. We have trouble keeping them from coming right into our rooms looking for something. They made Lent a little easier and now supply meat. [...]

Letter 131   **L. to Mister Jouve**

SS. C. J. et M.

St. Charles Missouri Territory, April 25 [1819][143]

My dear Brother,

I have just learned from the Ursulines nuns in New Orleans that they have received the box of things you sent them, with which they are very happy. I have asked our mothers in France to send you payment for the cost from some money that should have been sent to me. If that has not yet been paid, please remind Mother Therese [Maillucheau] in

---

143 Copies: *Cahier, Lettres de la Mère Duchesne à sa famille*, pp. 101-102; *Lettres dactylographiées*. C-VII 2) c Duchesne to her family and lay people, Box 5. This letter is addressed to her brother-in-law, Mr. Jean Joseph Jouve.

Grenoble, for I have received and spent here most of the sum in question, promising the Ursulines who made us the advance that I would have it reimbursed in France.

These nuns tell me by mail that they are sending me letters from France by opportunity, in particular, those that were addressed to me in the box. I think there is one from my sister, and I ask you to assure her of my satisfaction.

We already have a number of children; but as we do not have a suitable house in Saint Charles, we are leaving here in order to be closer to Saint Louis, in a place where the parents will have less difficulty in sending their children. Crossing the Missouri is often very difficult.

A sore finger keeps me from continuing. Believe in my undying attachment and assure my sister and your children of it.

In friendship,

Philippine

To Mister
Mr. Jouve
Rue Royale
Maison Monicaule
Lyon

Letter 132   L. 24 to Mother Barat

SS. C. J. et M.

Saint Charles, Missouri, July 29, 1819[144]

Very Reverend Mother,

Following your recommendation, I have begun to number my letters. Number 1 was to Father Barat.[145] We have never been such a long time without writing or receiving letters from France. The last was from Sophie Lacroix and told me only what other earlier ones had told me about your travels. What caused delay were the steamboats we are always waiting for, which shallow waters prevent from moving.

---

144   Original autograph, C-VII 2) c Duchesne to Barat, Box 2. Cf. J. de Charry, II 1, L. 114, pp. 233-240; Hogg, pp. 159-163; Ch. Paisant, pp. 248-252.

145   This letter to Father Barat may be the one of April 20, 1819, about which M.S. Barat wrote on September 27, 1819.

Besides, at our distance from Saint Louis, we miss many opportunities of sending mail. We complain among ourselves about this state of privation, not to express regrets, but to add fuel to the fire of our sacrifice and so renew it.

The captain who brought us over from France is said to have just arrived in Saint Louis; that is why we are writing now and hoping for letters from the nuns in New Orleans that will contain some from you; that is our dearest hope.

I received a second letter from Mr. Petry, Consul of France in Washington, which contained one from Mrs. de Rollin, one from Mrs. Jouve, and from Aloysia; from these letters, it seems that all those sent here through Rouen are lost. My sister spoke of theirs of the month of September. I am told that the pupils of Paris have written to us, but we have seen nothing from them or from Mother de Gramont, or from several to whom we wrote upon landing. The most recent from you is from January. Mother Giraud wrote to us about foundations in Lyon and Nîmes.

Since then, the good God has favored us with his cross. The greatest, without doubt, the heaviest, is the lack of success of our work. If a saint were in charge, it would all go better; that is what makes my burden heavier. Every day I see that I do not have what is necessary to fulfill my office. Sister Octavie is growing in fervor and regularity. Her health often gives her something to suffer. In the last six to eight months, she has seen the doctor three times and, even so, is still suffering from palpitations; pains from rheumatism and stomach troubles are worse at this time. According to the opinion of Mr. Laënnec in Paris, we cannot expect complete relief for her. She continues to take her class, but I find that, in spite of her talents, she does not hold the children well; they do not get anything out of it. A pupil said the other day: "We have as much fun as we wish in there."

That is not a minor disadvantage among children, several of whom easily criticize their mistresses and speak about them; one day they put Sister Catherine in the lowest grade for virtue, because, they said, "*She is not obedient*; she tells us that we argue, but she does it with M. D. [Mother Duchesne] more than we do." That shows their bad spirit. Children here consider themselves equal to their parents. When one tells them how docile French children are, they reply: "We are not French children." They drink in independence with their mother's milk. When they do obey, they always find that someone is making fun of them: "You're obeying like a slave," etc. Some are being prepared for

First Communion. Mother Octavie threatened one of them with being delayed: "*I've done with all that*," she said. We will just manage to have six or eight First Communions before we go to Florissant. They will take place on the feast of the Assumption.

Corruption surpasses lack of docility; wealthy people have unmarried Negro women with children in their houses; they see all that and do not leave their mothers' arms the whole of their childhood; they are embraced continually; their food is minced for them; in effect, they adopt indolent attitudes and manners. There is an excess of luxury and love of dancing; at each ball there is a queen costumed from head to toe by her boyfriend; they have shoes of silver cloth costing 40 F; they wear garlands, not on the head but around the neck, and make-up in three colors; their dresses are of tulle or lace, which reveal the whole figure.

It seemed to us that our children appreciated what we were saying to them about these excesses; but *one*, our ribbon of merit, whom we believed to be an *angel*, left because of illness, seeming to desire only Heaven; and one sojourn of two months in Saint Louis robbed her of all her docility, her piety, her sensitivity: "I pay enough to be well served," she said one day. It took the experience of such a change for Mother Octavie to be convinced that the children must be grounded in religious principles and that not every devotional practice is necessarily solid. That child was her dear spiritual daughter. Another had among her things a book beautifully bound, printed and illustrated; on opening it, I saw: *Sacrifice to Venus*, with an engraving that showed all the indignity of the sacrifice; this book was given to her by her mother and came out of the father's library, which contains many similar works. (The Blessed Virgin will save that one.) While in Saint Louis not a single spiritual book is for sale nor is there a place to order one. All the works of Rousseau and Voltaire are available and enough luxurious objects to supply all of Paris with knick-knacks, feathers, flowers, tulle, and not only for the rich, but even for those who come to our school barefoot, even in winter.

Mother Eugenie also has some disappointments in her day school. Her health has come back, but after Easter, she had the appearance of exhaustion that Mother Bigeu often has. She maintains her fervor and devotedness by continual mortification and the presence of God.

Sister Marguerite is getting nowhere. Her external work has utterly defeated her, so much so that it has been necessary to take her out of the kitchen where she was making continual mistakes in her confusion. We have placed there an American orphan, fifteen years old, who is managing better as to order, but badly as to economy; but we had to make a sacrifice for the good of a soul. What I feared the most was fire.

The chimney caught fire the third day she was in the employment; that made her a little more careful. That is the third fire alarm we have had this winter. I told you about the other two in my last letter. On Holy Thursday, above all, almost everything was burned in our chapel. The sacred host was found on the altar, out of the chalice; the tabernacle was only damaged.

I have already told you everything about Catherine in reporting the children's remarks. Her health causes her a great deal of suffering, especially her head, which made her refuse to go to the kitchen; she will be saved, but I am very much afraid she will always be imperfect. With two Sisters who cannot manage the kitchen and the laundry (for which we are paying a Negro woman) and with so few people, I doubt whether a great number of coadjutrix Sisters from France would be very useful for us; they would be spoiled before they arrived, unless they were very virtuous. The two young choir nuns never complain of anything; the other two are very difficult to please, especially Catherine.

That tells me that our progress in this country will be very slow; It will be impossible to maintain the two ranks; all must be equal; there will be differences in fact by reason of talents, education, and employments assigned; but to say to someone when accepting her, "It is for service," not even one of the Indians would accept that. Several Americans are inquiring about us; they would have to be sisters; but they are already asking whether we share the cooking in turn, a week at a time. It would take your presence and your prudence to sort out all this; but since I don't expect to see you here, I turn to a little picture of Our Lady of Good Counsel with a prayer for my situation.

The house in Florissant is coming along; we are told we will be able to move in the first of September. The bishop will have returned from the Barrens [*Bois-Brûlé*] then; his seminary has kept him there. Someone told me that Father Martial had joined him. I trust in Providence for the debts this house will incur and for the transportation. One day I had almost nothing left; the banks whose notes I had all failed at the same time. However, payment is made only with this money. God will be our resource.

I am still convinced that he wants us here, and it is my only consolation to see that all five of us feel the same, even the one whose vocation I doubted [Catherine Lamarre].

If for a few instants we are feeling the thorns that pierce us everywhere, we know that we are your daughters and that we have fathers, mothers, sisters, and children who pray for us, and our courage cannot fail.

There is little hope of working with the Indians. In the days of Marie de l'Incarnation, the Jesuits went everywhere and collected the children, appeased the parents, interpreted their varied languages, and committed them to writing in dictionaries and books they composed. These works surpassed what individual missionaries can do alone; when one is here one can see that easily. My desire to devote myself to these poor souls has not lessened, if God only opens the way.

I am with profound respect, Reverend and loving Mother, your unworthy daughter.

Philippine Duchesne

Letter 133   **L. 25 to Mother Barat**

SS. C. J. et M.

No. 4
Saint Charles, Missouri, August 28, 1819[146]
Rec. to St. Anthony of Padua

Very dear Reverend Mother,

It is a real suffering for us when we count the months and realize that we have had no word from France since January; and even then I had only five or six lines from you in a letter from Mother Girard, who told me about Mother de Charbonnel's departure for Lyon and the critical state of three of our sisters, Mothers de Saint-Pern,[147] Mourat of Amiens, and Victoire [Ollier, coadjutrix novice] in Beauvais; but we don't know if the good God has taken them.

I did not write myself between April and July, as there were no opportunities to send letters. In April, I sent letter #1 to Father Barat; on July 29, I wrote #2 to you, and in August, letter #3 to Mother Bigeu.

I gave myself the consolation of rereading your letters and others from France; I felt both consoled and encouraged; I don't say they bind me more closely to you, because the bond between us could hardly be

---

146 Original autograph, C-VII 2) c Duchesne to Barat, Box 2. Cf. J. de Charry, II 1, L. 115, p. 240-247; Hogg, pp. 164-168. Ch. Paisant, pp. 255-258.
147 Marie de Saint-Pern (1768-1819) was the donor of the house at Quimper. Henriette Mourat, RSCJ (1787-1819), made her first vows in Amiens and died in Poitiers shortly after her profession. Victoire Ollier, coadjutrix novice, died in Beauvais, February 4, 1819.

drawn tighter. That is why it gave me great joy when the bishop said one day, speaking of us "*Oh! C'est bien de la race,*" "Oh! That's a family trait."

Nevertheless, good Mother, I believe that there will always be some differences because of different nations and climates; summer here was as oppressive as last year in New Orleans. I do not think it possible to close all the windows at night in a dormitory for twenty children, as we have in Florissant. The children do not wish to put up with closed curtains: here the beds are placed in front of doors, windows, fireplaces, with no concern for drafts; here everyone sleeps with doors and windows open when it is very hot. It is the same in Martinique, where I am told there are no shutters on the windows.

We are going to give the prizes in spite of the difficulty of awarding them based on the whole year; you will understand how hard it is to maintain a class here. Pupils arrive for three months not knowing how to read; the mistresses exhaust themselves teaching them the catechism and other things with little success. Some read English instead of French; others both languages, still others French only; it is the same for grammar, geography, and arithmetic. One cannot ask them to buy books; several have neither pens nor paper nor sewing materials; scissors, thimble, needles, thread, all are lacking. "Mama has none," they say, "We cannot find any." We have five Protestant day pupils, sisters or cousins. There is only one diocesan catechism for all of them. Finally, we gave them a second one and a few prayer books from those given by the pupils at Grenoble. Textbooks, also given by Grenoble, are our treasure; all the classes use them, lending them to one another, but they are already well worn. Even if a few parents of good will would like to provide books, there are none to be had. We learned from an English teacher, whom the bishop hired for his academy in Saint Louis, that in the whole of the United States, he has not been able to obtain what he needs.

Mother Octavie took advantage of the presence of this teacher to have him judge which of her little Americans deserved the prize for English reading; she herself spoke with him and read to him, and he said without flattering that she read and pronounced well; that pleased me very much, for to whom could I entrust the teaching of English if she could not do it? Our American postulant [Miss Mullen] is already married; others have withdrawn, and I see no sure vocation except in a few pupils, still too young and all French speaking. This *English* makes Mother Octavie stand out; they speak only of her; national pride causes them to despise those who do not know it, and in fact, it is of prime necessity here. However, the bishop does not think Mother Octavie writes English well enough, and often she does not understand the native Americans when they speak too fast.

You see that God has not given us the gift of tongues. Maybe God wants women missionaries to thrive on abjection rather than on success; I think so when I see the bishop's clergy ready to preach in English at the end of a few months. I despair of speaking it; Mother Eugenie is quite behind; but she has enough to do to teach the French-speaking pupils; she is venerated by her class. For First Communion on the feast of the Assumption, she went with her children to the parish church; I believed that was in line with your intention; without that supervision there would have been no order or devotion. When she came back with her little troop of ten or twelve, people seeing her said, "*There she is, the good virgin.*"

As your answers are long in coming, and as it is in her class in the free school that the first vocations are in preparation, for her children have complete confidence in her, I have thought that if we have novices, she would be the best one to form them. Besides, there are persons born to command, people to whom God gives this gift; she has it. As I told you in the past about Mother Emilie Mial, I fear only one thing: it is that in that employment she would often find opposition and that she would also annoy others.

You know that great virtue always has its shadow. In Saint Louis, where ideas are carnal as in New Orleans, people had her renouncing the religious state and marrying a young priest who had been sent to Saint Louis and who, they said, went to Rome *to be laicized*. As for me, I was a widow who had left her children in New Orleans. This was the talk of the whole town.

It is First Communion that has made us think that many of the children are capable of great virtue; one of them, sent away and taken back by her old grandfather, threw herself at his feet and kissed them; another carried eight buckets of water, one after the other, in front of people she thought had made fun of her, for here big girls blush to carry a bucket of water; they make little boys and girls do that. It was the Holy Spirit who inspired them to do those two acts, according to our recommendation to make five acts every day; from time to time, they have to give an account. Some carry it too far.

It seemed to me that Mr. Jouve should in no way be troubled about paying for the others; he owes 450 F every year to Aloysia for her whole life; he could hold it back. I have used up the 4000 F that Niort owes us for all the commissions I have given you; I understand your position and expect nothing else; God will help us. This cost of the house in

Florissant will go well up to 30,000 F; we have about 5000; the rest we will get little by little from the fees. And there we have spent 2000 on a location unsuitable for pupils. I do not think we will go to Florissant before October. The bishop does not answer me; I know that he was deceived at the Barrens [Bois-Brûlé] about his seminary and had all kinds of crosses.

He wants two of us for a free school in Saint Louis.[148] We are promising Saint Charles to come back here to reopen the day school, and nevertheless, how can we ask you for personnel when you have nothing with which to pay for their journey? If God inspires you to do that, have the kindness, I beg you, to send us fairly young persons. Catherine is good only for dreaming up projects; now she wants to stay in Saint Charles to run the school, or so it seems. Marguerite made a strenuous effort at the beginning. Now she is altogether worn out, quite asleep; she does little.

Kissing your feet, I am with respect, Reverend Mother, your unworthy daughter.

Philippine Duchesne

My regards to my fathers and mothers, Father Perreau especially. Remembrances to everyone.

[On the reverse:]
To Mother
Mother Barat
Rue des Postes n° 40
Paris

Letter 134   **L. 10 to Messrs. Perier and Mrs. de Rollin Rue Neuve du Luxembourg, Paris**

SS. C. J. et M.

Saint Charles, Missouri Territory, August 29, 1819[149]

---

148 The foundation in Saint Louis would take place in 1827 and the return to Saint Charles in 1828. In 1819, the whole community moved to Florissant.

149 *Copies of letters of Philippine Duchesne to Mme de Rollin and a few others, No. 10; Cahier, Lettres à Mme de Rollin,* p. 21-24; *Lettres dactylographiées* C-VII 2) c Duchesne to her family and lay people, Box 5.

My very good Cousin,

It is a year today since I wrote to you from Saint Louis after our arrival.[150] I received your answer to that letter through Mr. Petry, the consul in Washington, who added a very obliging one of his own. I could not give you all the specific details, as I kept a journal of our whole trip that Mother Barat will certainly be happy to let you read if you ask her for it.

Since that time, our situation, although precarious, offers few variations; we have had very few boarders, as Saint Charles and the northern part of Missouri are to too poor to send any. And because that river separates us from Saint Louis and is subject to terrible floods, winds and ice, mothers consider this an insurmountable obstacle to sending their children to boarding school. A house is being built for us in Fleurissant, nearer to Saint Louis. We will pay for it little by little, and we will abandon Saint Charles next month, with regret at leaving a more populous place where the children, day pupils, are well disposed, and the location is much more advantageous than that of Fleurissant; it will be an important town one day, for commerce on the Missouri with the Indians or the new American establishments at Booneslick, Franklin, etc., in Upper Missouri is increasing by the day. To foster this, the government has just placed troops and mounted cannon on steamboats, which were never before seen on the Missouri.

In Saint Charles, about twenty houses have been built since we have been here. The inhabitants allotted us a piece of land; but to get title to it, we have to have a grant from the Congress, and I am asking Mr. Petry to request it. There is nothing more difficult in this unsettled country than to obtain land; everything belongs to the Congress; nothing is regulated. If one is not provided with permission, it could happen that a settler is ousted by others who have gotten ahead of them with the government.

Mr. Wallein will have seen that it is not easy to secure land in Saint Louis and that it is extremely expensive. I am told that he remained there a very short time and that, invited by some friends who had found other land, he was probably somewhere on the banks of the Ohio.

We have been without news from France since receiving your letter of December first and one from January from Paris, never such a long silence. It has made me fear political disturbances in my country that may have caused harm to my relatives and friends. I am praying to God for them, and his Providence is never lacking.

---

150   We do not have this letter.

You knew my heart so well, my good Friend, when you told me all that concerned so many persons who are so dear to me. My ambition for my brother is for better gifts than a fortune, although I am quite sure that as a good brother, he will help Mr. Lebrument with the estate of our aunt Gueymar. I was very moved by the death of Mr. Pascal, especially because it will have affected my aunt, your dear Mama,[151] now the only surviving member of her generation of our family. Camille's [Jordan] health worries me a great deal; tell him of my concern. You know also how much gratitude I owe Mr. de Rollin and Mr. Teisseire; so please remember me to them and to my sisters. Mr. Lebrument tells me in a letter that they wrote to me through Le Havre, but I haven't received their letters; the shortest and safest way is through Bordeaux to New Orleans; ships and steamboats are moving continually between Bordeaux and New Orleans and from there to Saint Louis, which is growing steadily. From now on address letters to us, general delivery there. Someone can pick them up and send them to Fleurissant, which is in the country where there is no post office. Someone told me about a steamboat that went from New York to New Orleans by sea with boilers and wheels in ten days; it left its masts in New Orleans and went up the Mississippi without masts like other steamboats; that's the first example of such a crossing, also of steamboats on the Missouri; we have seen the first four.

In leaving France, I sent my annuity certificate to my brother and since then another dated from Saint Charles; I could send a third by the next opportunity for New Orleans, because it needs the attestation of the consul. As for the income from Mr. Lebrument, it was agreed that it would be applied to the fees of one of his daughters at Sainte-Marie; as soon as Mother Barat has cancelled that arrangement, you may give it back to him.

I am fifty years old today, my dear Friend; that age makes me feel how unfit I am for the undertaking in which I am engaged, but it has cooled not at all the tender sentiments that bind me to you, to Augustin, to Camille, for so many years. You were my first friends in the world, and though I left that world, the feelings of friendship have survived even such a death. I thank you for your loving interest; your letter touched the deepest chords of my heart. My companions are much loved here and are doing good; they ask to be remembered to you. You heard about our accident on Holy Thursday, when we had used all your gifts to our chapel; your generosity has made it possible for us to have even

---

151 Alexandre-Charles Pascal (1751-1818) was the brother of Mrs. Claude Perier, née Marie-Charlotte Pascal (1749-1821), Josephine's mother. He was a King's councilor and knight of the Legion of Honor.

more from your hand on Easter; many things in this holy place remind me of Josephine and her loving and attentive solicitude.

The difficulty now is our lodging; the bishop is having a house built but at our expense. Where shall we find 30,000 F when we have no more than 5? I won't know the exact amount until we are in it; I dread it, yet I do not lose trust in Providence; as a way out, I grasped at the proposition in one of your letters, enclosed with one from Father Dumolard, to acquaint you with our situation. I asked you for a small loan to assist us; but if it is not possible, do not count any less on my gratitude and constant remembrance of you before God and my eternal friendship.

All yours in the Heart of Jesus,

Philippine

My respectful good wishes to my aunt and her family.

Letter 135   **L. 7 to Father Barat**

SS. C. J. et M.

Florissant, September 17, 1819
No. 5[152]

My very good Father,

You give us good proof that we are always your daughters, for your care for us does not diminish and, on the contrary, seems to increase in our favor. Your letters to Mothers Octavie and Eugenie did them the greatest good and strengthened them in the path of perfection, where they are very determined to walk. Far from being frightened by difficulties, they are never more content than when they have something to suffer.

During Lent we received a crate that came from you where were found the glasses of the lady who gave us so much out of her goodness. If she is still well disposed toward us, nothing would be more useful than some English books for the boarding school. Please express to her continually, I beg you, our gratitude for her generous offerings. That

---

152   Original autograph, C-VII 2) c Writings Duchesne to various Eccles., Box 8. Philippine numbered her letters because some had been lost.

crate contained the work of Sister Nativity, your own precious collection, and devotional objects.

A second crate was sent to us by the bishop, larger and filled with the same kinds of things. I do not know who enriches us the best. Our good mother speaks to us only of shortage in all the houses, which makes me regret having made so many requests in so many letters that must have weighed you down. I based my boldness on 4000 F that the house at Niort owes us; but now, 600 F were sent to Lyon for the religious in New Orleans, 1000 F are coming to me from that city for payment of the port tax for two big crates, no. 1 and no. 2 containing a piano, some chandeliers, some silks, and some material with which to make flowers. Those crates should arrive here soon; they are in care of Mr. Dubourg, the bishop's brother. But in announcing these two crates or boxes, he said nothing about two others that you mentioned in a note of April 18, attached to a letter from our mother, which no doubt contained the paper coming from Poitiers and the books about which our mother speaks. I hope that all these things have not been sent at her expense, but that she has drawn on the money that Niort owes us.

The scarcity of money is felt also in the United States. A large number of banks have stopped payment, and this means total loss for all who hold their notes, the common currency of the country. It is rare to find a few dollars or other coins among the paper money we receive. I know that the bishop, for want of money, wanted to stop the work on our house. Nevertheless, it is advancing and we will be in it in a month, even if they do not plaster until spring.

We had the pleasure of a visit from the bishop yesterday. He still wants three of us and treats us like daughters. We are in a house that belongs to him, from which we are discovering Florissant, surrounded by woods, orchards, and cultivated land where we take what we lack. The bishop was delighted to learn of the establishment of a little house of ours in Bordeaux[153] and made a great deal of the lady who has united herself to the Society there.[154]

153 Father Barat had written to Philippine on April 28, 1819: "You will have a little house at Bordeaux. That will at least be a foothold. The bishop has just written to Mother Sophie to begin a house in the diocese. The House of Providence, similar to that at Niort, has offered itself to the Society of the Sacred Heart. It is the establishment of Mrs. Lalanne who presents herself to be received. Your bishop should know this house." *Lettres du P. Barat à Mère Duchesne*, C-VII Duch. 2)- c) Box 8.
154 Catherine Suzanne Felicity Dudevant Lalanne (1756-1835), born April 10, 1756, in Bordeaux, married Mr. de Lalanne in 1776. In 1784, in Bordeaux, she founded the "Providence" orphanage. At the death of her husband in 1816, she consecrated herself to God. In 1818, in order to save her work, she asked to join the Society of the Sacred Heart. At that time the orphanage counted about fifty orphans and four or five teachers. On May 13, Mother Barat accepted, and

I was displeased that a little momentary embarrassing detail caused you and our fathers and mothers any concern about us. I assure you that such moments are truly a delight and that we must be careful not to take pride in them. Divine Providence does not keep us waiting very long, and in spite of the uneasiness of moving into our house with debts of perhaps 20,000 F—they do not yet say exactly how much—I do not doubt that we will recover it in a short time, since we were able to live at Saint Charles with so few children without incurring the least debt.

I will try to get my annuity certificate in order to send it with these letters. I would be grateful if you would send it to Sainte-Marie to have it sent to my brother to withdraw a little income from the estate.

It will probably be Father Martial who will carry these letters to New Orleans. He is returning there with regret, but the astonishing change that he has brought there by his industrious devotion and his zeal should make him attached to this place that was so long ungrateful and that now offers hopes, but not such that the bishop can yet go there. That would awake old jealousies and prejudices. The bishop is very tired from traveling. He will probably have Father Rosati as coadjutor, and Bishop Flaget has Father David. Father de Andreis' health is too poor to allow him to travel, and Father Martial has refused to learn English, which is necessary for a bishop. They talk about assigning one to Detroit, which would relieve Bishop Flaget, and another one to Cincinnati.

Among so many holy ministers, I do not find *(the rest of the sentence is cut out)*. I feel as if my soul were quite alone, but I have too little feeling to be distressed about it. I do not know what my state of soul is; I am unfaithful, and I do not worry; I am haughty and impatient, and I taste only the sweetness of Jesus. I rarely humble myself, yet the strongest conviction I experience is that of God's goodness to me. Father Richard did not handle me gently, and I am grateful for that, but I feel with him as with our pastor, that respect does not call forth that confidence that puts the heart at ease. Mine is as if hanging and cannot have an energetic movement except toward the heart of Jesus or Mary or Saint Francis Regis.

Please distribute our letters and assure Father Debrosse and others who are perhaps near you, of our profound veneration, as we ask for their prayers.

It is nighttime and I am nodding away.

The last thing is to thank you on the part of the bishop for the work of Sister Nativity, which he took before knowing that it was for him.

on July 13 Mothers Geoffroy and Messoria arrived in Bordeaux to carry out the union. On August 6, 1819, Mother de Lalanne pronounced her vows in the Society of the Sacred Heart.

One cannot hide anything from him; his eyes see all: the outside and inside, the spiritual and the temporal.

I am at your feet in the Sacred Heart, your unworthy daughter.

Ph. Duchesne

Letter 136   L. 10 to Mother Maillucheau

SS. C. J. et M.

Florissant, September 26, 1819
Recommended to St. Anthony of Padua[155]

My very good Mother,

I am no longer in Saint Charles from the beginning of this month, the end of the situation that we had no wish to renew, since it was too expensive. The pastor at Saint Charles offered his presbytery until the house at Florissant would be ready. But meanwhile, the bishop, when he visited, did not approve that moving plan and wanted us to move to Florissant, not to our own house, but to a little house of his. This is where we are now for another month yet, after which we hope to move into our new brick house.

It was during that visit of the bishop that I learned through Father Martial, our guide on the sea voyage, that a large crate has arrived in New Orleans containing a piano and a package of silk and material for flowers; these two things should be sent to us promptly. I did not have to guess from where these objects of such value came. I know that in what concerns our mission, no house has been more eager and more generous than the house of Grenoble, and that was confirmed for me by our mother, who told me that the piano is in part a gift from you, along with everything about the flowers and embroidery. We give you our sincere thanks, or rather, the Heart of Jesus, so generous and rich, will reward you.

I answered your different letters, all full of offers of service, and I am embarrassed to have made so many requests of you, several of which are not useful, like that of olive oil that could have many mishaps, go bad, and cost money that is right now completely absorbed in our building, which will still leave us a great debt.

---

155   Original autograph, C-VII 2) c Duchesne to RSCJ and Children, Box 4.

Yes, dear Mother, I withdraw all the requests that I have made to you for different kinds of furnishings. At present, our situation in this new area is getting better, and every day it is in better communication with Philadelphia and New Orleans. I see that we will have everything necessary for life and for the first needs of the boarding school. As for conveniences and material comforts, they are not what we are looking for, and I hope that God will never provide them for us. We are much happier offering him a few privations.

There are only two things necessary to go along with the piano and help the students with handwriting: 1. Some examples of English penmanship, which you have in several large, unused notebooks in the house in Grenoble, and which would be helpful here; 2. Sheet music for the piano.

I charged you with receiving the several journals of Aloysia's up to September 1818, and I said what interest they have for us. I would have liked a few words in your letters about Fathers Rambaud and Rivet, of whom I would like to hear news. Give them my respects, as well as to Father d'Hyères.

I do not think I can write this time to several of our sisters and students of your family; we are only camped out here and disturbed endlessly, because a single room is parlor, portry, classroom, dormitory, refectory, and student infirmary for nine of them. The other room, a hovel, is kitchen and community room. All the beds are put on the floor at night and taken up in the morning. In this vast house, I received a letter addressed to the *Palace of the Bishop.*

If only you, dear Mother, receive the expression of my sentiments for so many cherished objects, please communicate them. Aloysia knows what I am for her and how much I want her sisters to follow her example, especially my little Constance [Jouve], whom I still seem to see walking solemnly in the lower garden, dressed in the religious habit, and who has so often wanted this.

Sisters de Coriolis, de Rambery, Dusaussoy, and L. de Vidaud know of my ardent wishes for their perfection. I do no less for Sister Dumoulin whom I knew well at the home of Mr. and Mrs. Bernard. I beg her to remember me to them through the maid Manette. If I do not name all my sisters, it is for lack of time and paper. I even omit details about us and will send them only to the motherhouse in a sort of journal, and our mother will share them with you, with no doubt that the holy union that centers us in the Heart of Jesus will be the subject of a holy and charitable interest in what concerns us.

In the lovable Heart of Jesus, I am your longtime friend and daughter,
Philippine

I beg my nieces to give news of me to my sisters. I wrote them last July.

Our health is holding up and courage does not diminish. All my sisters offer you their regards.

> [On the reverse:]
> To Mother
> Mother Therese Mailluchcau
> At Sainte-Marie d'En-Haut
> Grenoble

Letter 137   **L. 26 to Mother Barat**

SS. C. J. et M.

> Florissant, September 27, 1819[156]
> No. 5
> Rec. to Saint Anthony of Padua

Very Reverend Mother,

It was hard for me to learn that you have been anxious about us, but it was very sweet to hear you say: "I would like to have a letter from you every month." I had not yet had that loving invitation when I went without writing from April to July; but besides the letter at the end of July, I wrote again on August 20, no. 3, and on August 28, no. 4, by way of the consul in Washington.

Father Martial, who came to see us in Saint Charles on his way from New Orleans, told us about the arrival in that city of the piano and the bundle of silk fabric, with the bill for the contents and more than 1000 F for the expense. We are awaiting the arrival momentarily of the two shipments, numbers 1 and 2. How eagerly we welcome everything that comes from France, our birthplace, from the center of the Society and from our mother who holds the place of Jesus Christ.

---

156 Original autograph, C-VII 2) c Duchesne to Barat, Box 2. Cf. J. de Charry, II 1, L. 116, pp. 248-253; Hogg, pp. 169-173; Ch. Paisant, pp. 272-275.

A long time ago, the nuns in New Orleans received the article that Mr. Jouve was commissioned to obtain for them, and they are very happy with it; they have told me of their gratitude and have paid the cost. These 600 F, added to the 1000 received in New Orleans, reduce to 2400 what remains at the house in Niort, and even less if Father Barat has fulfilled the request for books and metal fixtures that I gave him. I would like to delay a few of them, not that they would not all be useful, but because I see that several of them can be obtained here, and the essential for us at this moment is money. The bishop's funds are exhausted by his seminary at the Barrens and his college in Saint Louis, not to mention the cathedral; our house overwhelms him with trouble, and it will be urgent that we repay him. Except for this reason that depresses me every time I see him, I would ask you to keep the money at Niort, seeing how useful it would be to you and preferring to deprive myself rather than to know that you have burdens, which I share. Therefore, as the need for this money is urgent, I have sent to France the address of the agent in Philadelphia and of a merchant in Saint Charles who wishes us well. I know that this agent sent on my letter in the month of May.[157] I don't know if it has reached you yet; I gave you this address in another letter, and here it is for the third time: *Messrs. J. and G. Collier, Saint Charles, Missouri Territory. To the care of Messrs. Fassil and Langstroth, Southwest corner of Market and Second Streets, Philadelphia.*

I do not yet know the debt we have contracted because of our building. The bishop was having it stopped for the moment for want of money; the pastor in Florissant [Marie-Joseph Dunand] has taken on himself to move the work along, even to adding another floor, giving the bricklayers land in payment and spending his last *sou*. He is extraordinarily eager to have us in his parish, already calling us his daughters; and behold, the bishop is forbidding us to go to him for direction, either ourselves or the pupils. That is going to put me in a very difficult position, for the bishop does not want him to know that it is because of his order that we refuse to go to confession to the pastor. He has designated a young Flemish priest [Father Delacroix] who can hear confessions in four languages and who will live in Florissant, in a little house belonging to the bishop, nearer to us. We will have to feed him, as we do Father Richard, who is a real loss for us. As he understands religious life well and the spirit of our father,[158] he regrets losing us very much.

157 Letter 130, of April 25, 1819, addressed to Mother Bigeu.
158 Probably Father de Tournély, whom Father Dunand could have known, because the Fathers of the Sacred Heart were in contact with the Trappists of la Valsainte, in Switzerland.

In spite of the concerns we are causing him, the bishop still wants three of us and wishes to so overwhelm you with letters that you will be forced to agree to sending them; I have left him little hope, based on your letters. I don't know if he sees now that we would have been much better in Saint Louis: here we will be besieged by parents with their carriages. At this distance of four or five leagues, how can we set days and times for visits? It will be necessary to arrange business early, etc. The situation with the doctor is difficult; the one in Saint Charles was good, a more skilled surgeon than those I saw in Paris who could not even bleed Mother Octavie, who had that treatment by the one here; he was very attached to our house, even though he was a Protestant. The one here is a drunk. There are twenty-four in Saint Louis, most of whom will charge 50 F to come here; they have to earn enough to gain their livelihood in such a small city.

I was touched all the more by your gift of the piano, as it was paid for out of what you needed. O my good Mother! Believe me, we suffer only when we learn that you are suffering; your letter of April 18 worried me about your financial difficulties and the excessive work that is falling on you. We are invoking divine Providence, both for you and for us; I have still more devotion to Providence; it has shown itself favorable to us so often.

Mother de Marbeuf will please accept our humble thanks as well as Miss de Cassini and another young woman [Miss de Saint-Marc], whose name appears after hers, but I cannot read it. How many benefactors and benefactresses our little establishment has already! If you are giving us the gift of Julie [Bazire], English is the most necessary thing she should learn, but it is not enough to have lessons; one must speak, speak incessantly; neither Eugenie nor I can understand it yet, and Octavie, in spite of her fluency, her assurance, her continual study, often cannot understand certain Americans or make herself understood. I believe a miracle takes place for the priests; several of them, after a few months, were able to minister in that language; but the bishop places them for a time with Americans where only English is understood, and they are forced to apply themselves to it. Spanish is useless here at the moment. In these regions, there are many Irish, a few Flemings and Germans. French Creoles and native-born Americans are becoming the most numerous, moving continually from the East to the West.

I am enclosing a letter from Cuba [from Sister Sainte-Monique Ramos, superior of the house of the Ursulines in Cuba], in answer to a request for money that I had made to help us to exist, as they say; but the wealth of the Ursuline house had been exaggerated; it is nothing, as you see.

You tell me little for my soul, but that little would do a great deal of good if I were faithful. I ask only that grace of God, for consolations are lost. My heart seeks someone to lean on and finds God alone; in this bent to seek comfort, I was casting my eyes on Bishop Flaget of Bardstown in Kentucky; but though he was to come, now there is no sign of him. I thought of Father de Andreis, provincial of the Lazarists, but he is so often sick and has to be away that it is necessary to remain with God alone. My soul has not been able to open itself since I left France. The ones I named are two saints of universal reputation whose ministry God blesses.

My sisters were delighted with your letters and those from your good brother whose advice, along with yours, sustains all five of us; to my mind, he wrote in letters of gold to Sister Eugenie, who showed it to me, and in gold also to Mother Octavie, in another sense: against the thoughts of the one and against the tendencies of the other. They are well thought of by their bishop and by their mother. Marguerite is doing well.

The opportunity is leaving for Saint Louis.

I am at your feet, Reverend Mother, your unworthy daughter.

Philippine

[On the reverse:]
To our Reverend Mother Barat

Letter 138   L. 3 to Mother Vincent

SS. C. J. et M.

Florissant, September 27 [1819][159]

My very good Mother,

I have learned from the bishop and then from a letter from Father Barat of the loss that you have suffered in the person of Father Boyer, in whom you had a worthy minister of Jesus Christ, the father and special protector of your establishment and our benefactor. During the happy time of our stay with you, he welcomed us, encouraged us, and prayed

---

159   Original autograph, C-VII 2) c Duchesne to RSCJ and Children, Box 4. A note in another handwriting: "Essential No. 5."

for us. We felt bound to him by gratitude, and we will express it at the feet of Our Lord when we also pray for him; but I hope he is already in the place from where he can draw the most abundant graces upon you and upon us. *May they be graces that unite us in the same Society, as we are united to you by esteem, attachment, and gratitude.*

Father Barat notes to us that the moment of Providence has not come for that, *that your holy archbishop is opposed to the union. It is a new trial, but I hope that before our death, it will happen. What a happiness it would be if it procured for us the advantage of having here one of those souls formed by your care, so humble, so docile, so much according to the rule and, therefore, so united to the divine Heart of Jesus and so perfect for his work.*

We often speak of you, always with benefit for our souls. Our health is good, or rather, taking its course, for you know that Mother Octavie and Sister Catherine do not have much of it. How is yours, dear Mother? It was quite suffering when we were with you, and since then, that of your dear mistress of novices, of her assistant, and of so many others who all deserve our dearest remembrance.

We are no longer in Saint Charles. We have crossed back across the Missouri to be nearer to Saint Louis, at Florissant, a little village where the ground is fertile. We are still only in temporary lodging at the parish. Our house is not yet finished. Since it is in brick, we will be able to move in right away. We are waiting in a house with two rooms that belongs to the bishop. We have 9 boarders there, and we will surely have twenty when we move into the large house that will have 10 or twelve rooms, large and small. That is quite a bit for this region. And you see that we cannot have a large boarding school, such as the lack of Catholic churches should require, for the Protestant ones are not lacking. They are held in the smallest groups in houses, most often by ministers who set themselves up even with the Indians.

Pray for us, dear Mother, pray for so many souls that perish. You will do more in your fervent prayers than we will in our feeble efforts.

I am with profound respect, dear Mother, your humble servant.

Philippine Duchesne

Greetings and respects from all my sisters to all your dear and holy daughters.

Letter 139   **L. 26 to Mother Barat**

**Journal of the Little House of Florissant
of the Sacred Heart of Missouri**

[September 1819[160]]

This little colony has had nothing important happen since the event of fire in the chapel until the distribution of prizes, which followed the most important event of the First Communion of several children. On the feast of the Assumption, they had this happiness, and I spoke of it to our mother general in a letter that followed soon after [August 28, 1819] and went off to Washington.

We were waiting impatiently for the arrival of the bishop from the Barrens to determine the length of our temporary lodging until our house was finished in Florissant. He arrived in Saint Charles the last days of August, after having celebrated magnificently in Saint Louis in his church. He was accompanied by Father Martial and Father Delacroix. He came in the evening and wanted to depart the next day. He spoke about our affairs and decided that our lodging would be at his farm until our building is finished.

The boarders engaged him to distribute their prizes, and this took place the next day at nine o'clock in the morning. He began with the free day students, to whom questions were addressed before him about the catechism and Bible history. They left after the distribution, and the paying day students, combined with the boarders, recited different parts of verses and stories, copies of which I had from Father Reyre, a Jesuit.[161] The bishop found them perfect for instruction of young persons; several were recited by Miss Odile de Lassus, who received the prize of good conduct and the ribbon of merit. The bishop left before noon on horseback, testifying to his satisfaction at the little feast.

At daybreak, we began to pack our things, and on September 3, they were taken in carts to the Missouri, where they were placed on two boats that took them down river as far as Fleurissant, where they were unloaded on the opposite bank.[162] They were guarded there in

---

160 Original autograph, C-VII 2) c Duchesne to Barat, Box 2. Copies: C-III USA Foundation Haute Louisiane, Box 1, Part A, *Lettres de la Louisiane, 1818-1822,* pp. 46-49; A-II 2) g, Box2, *Lettres intéressantes de la Société,* pp. 192-195. Cf. J. de Charry, II 1, L. 117, pp. 255-261; Hogg, pp. 174-177; Ch. Paisant, pp. 267-270.

161 Joseph Reyre, SJ (1735-1812), was author of pedagogical works such as: *Mentor of Children, Maxims, Historical Events,* and *Fables in Verse,* first edition 1809, Paris, Audot.

162 Florissant is eighteen miles east of Saint Charles, on the opposite bank of the Missouri, and nine miles from Saint Louis.

the hot sun by Mother Eugenie who had gone by water with Sister Catherine and three boarders. The pastor of Florissant [Father Dunand] had carts brought from our building, and Father Delacroix, the ones from the bishop's farm. There were seventeen trips that day; that is not to say that we have great possessions, for a one-horse cart can carry only three people or baggage in proportion.

This first expedition was followed by a second, when Mother Octavie left with two of the older girls in an open carriage sent by the father of one of them. I intended to bring up the rear that afternoon with the cows, the calves, the chickens, and Sister Marguerite. But our cows revolted when they found themselves tied and obliged to walk in the sun, so we had to wait until early the next morning, when the rest of our belongings was packed into three carts, along with cabbages to appease the cows. These animals started off on a rampage, but soon they were mastered by their ropes and by fatigue, and they decided to follow with their calves. I perched on top of a cart, dividing my attention between the care of my reliquaries and that of the chickens. After driving about ten miles, we crossed the Missouri in a small boat just opposite Florissant. When we landed, Marguerite lined up the chickens with motherly tenderness and gave them food and water. I did the same for the cows with my cabbages. Then Father Delacroix appeared on horseback to show us the way. As we had let the cows loose, he had to gallop after them every time they tried to run into the woods.

By evening I reached the little farmhouse where I learned with sorrow that Father Delacroix, who was living there as the bishop's manager, had left it and established himself in a hut as open as a birdcage. It was there that he had fever for several days, and we could not get even a chair to pass through the little hole that served as both door and window. When the bishop learned of his state of health, he ordered a wooden house to be built to give him a bedroom and a chapel. With a few workmen, this house was built and completed in a week. Father Delacroix now has a roof over his head; the Blessed Sacrament has been left in the chapel, and we are settled in the way we most desired, *for the one who has Jesus has everything*. The farm tenants caught the fever and were not able to care for themselves, so Sister Marguerite cooked for them. Mother Eugenie had six cows to milk, morning and evening, two belonging to us and four to the farm. That lasted but a short while, only to give way to another trial. Mother Octavie and two of the boarders also got the fever. As there was only one room for the pupils and one for us, we thought everyone would catch it, but Providence was there, and today, September 28, everyone is well.

The bishop came the day before yesterday; he gave us Father Delacroix for our chaplain; he has been alternately the bishop's secretary and treasurer; he calls him his angel. He is a young Flemish priest, one of those in the seminary in Ghent whom Napoleon sent into his army; therefore, he is a good horseman, and on difficult missions he easily crosses formidable rivers by swimming his horse across. He is the first priest anyone in the Upper Missouri has ever seen. He will live in Florissant in a small house belonging to the bishop, on the same property as ours. This will also serve as *pied-à-terre* for the bishop when he visits his properties.

The bishop was coming from Saint Charles when he saw us. He spoke of the regret our departure caused and tears still being shed. Mother Eugenie is the chief cause. The children loved her very much; they said good-bye to her on the riverbank like [the elders of Ephesus] to St. Paul.[163] I thought I would thwart these poor children by having Mother Eugenie depart first, but they were on to it and ran to the boats; we could not send them back; it was the same with several mothers who would willingly have left us their children, in spite of the pride of the region that made them refuse to serve us, but it was impossible.

I had all the unpleasantness of closing the house; it was necessary to tell our landlady [Mme Duquette] that we could not pay the rent at once; she was polite but cold, and I am going to try to use the income from one child to close out this debt.

We would be very wrong to complain, as divine Providence has been so good to us. A small bag of rice of 20 or 25 pounds has lasted us all year, and we eat it often. We have bought no coffee and very little brown sugar; the apples from Saint Charles that ripened last year in October were ready this year at the beginning of August and have been a considerable saving of vegetables and of bread, without doing any harm. We are swimming in abundance, and we have sold enough for two months' worth of bread. Here we have the same abundance of fruits and vegetables; we have salted down a little bullock, and we get bread and flour from Florissant on credit for six months. The wood left over from making the bricks will provide fuel for the early winter months. Thirty chickens, several of which will give eggs all winter, were waiting for us upon our arrival.

Finally, the frequent visits of the bishop and of his missionaries, the assurance of the presence of Father Delacroix and of the pastor [Father

---

163 Acts 20:17-38 describes how the Christians of Ephesus accompanied Paul as far as the ship that was taking him to Jerusalem, weeping because they would never see him again.

Dunand], who is using every cent he has to pay our workmen; all this makes us realize that we would be very ungrateful and very wrong to mistrust divine Providence in either spiritual or temporal needs.

I am opposed to storing provisions; last year a supply of fish spoiled. The children would not eat it; we buried it, but early one morning the dogs dug it up and scattered big pieces of rotten fish all around the house and in the fireplace. Passersby seeing it said we were going to have sickness because we were feeding the pupils rotten food.

Letter 140   L. 28 to Mother Barat

SS. C. J. et M.

[Florissant, October 10, 1819][164]

Very Reverend Mother,

I am profiting from Father Martial's return to New Orleans to give you news of us and to tell you of our departure from Saint Charles to go to Florissant. The bishop has welcomed us there in a house belonging to him, until our house is livable; that will not be until the month of December. That month, already so memorable and so dear, since it brought me back almost miraculously to the blessed solitude where you adopted me and where I saw you with such joy for the first time [December 13, 1804], where we celebrated the feast of Saint Francis Xavier, the object of your love and of mine, that month is going to become meaningful for me again as we open the first house of the Society in the New World. The bishop will add to our happiness by having a retreat given to us soon after; it will enliven us anew for the work that is going to increase, since at that time several children will be added to our number, whom the small size of the house does not allow us to take now.

The bishop has had the kindness to visit us a few times and see the pupils who are preparing to come and the needs of Saint Charles, whose poor children are still grieving Mother Eugenie's absence. He desires that you send an increase of at least three persons; they would not be too many for one house, and I would very much like two for

---

164 Original autograph, C-VII 2) c Duchesne to Barat, Box 2. Cf. J. de Charry, II 1, L. 119, pp. 265-268; Hogg, pp. 180-182; Ch. Paisant, pp. 275-276.

Saint Charles, if you do not continue refusing your consent to a small establishment for day pupils only or orphans, as in Bordeaux.[165] You understand how consoling and necessary the arrival of our sisters would be. I long for your dear Julie [Bazire], but English is the only language she needs to speak here, along with French.

Our benefactresses in New Orleans have promised us to welcome all our sisters, and they will keep their word.

We will receive Communion on the 15th for our dear Mother Therese [Maillucheau] and for your niece [Therese Dusaussoy].

Please accept the constant prayers and good wishes we offer you, which we renew today in union with all your families for the New Year. In rivaling them in tenderness and respect for you, may we not be behind them in merit before God!

With respect, I am in the Sacred Heart, very Reverend Mother, your poor, unworthy daughter.

                                    Philippine Duchesne

Florissant, October 10, 1819

My sisters are in the same state as when I wrote my last letter.

[On the reverse:]
To Mother
Mother Barat
Superior General of the Ladies of the Sacred Heart
Rue des Postes n° 40
Paris

Letter 141   **L. 28 to Mother Barat**

SS. C. J. et M.

No. 6
Recommended to Saint Anthony of Padua
November [15], 1819[166]

---

165 The orphanage of Mother de Lalanne united with the Society of the Sacred Heart on July 13, 1819.
166 Original autograph, C-VII 2) c Duchesne to Barat, Box 2. Postmark: Colonies via Bordeaux, 20* 1820. Arrived March 20, 1820. Cf. J. de Charry, II 1, L. 120, pp. 268-275; Hogg, pp. 182-187; Ch. Paisant, pp. 282-285.

Dear Reverend Mother,

I wrote to you on September 28 and also to several of our mothers and sisters. These letters will be much delayed because I gave them to Father Martial on his departure from Saint Louis, but the steamboat that carried him failed several times between here and Sainte Genevieve; and although it is afloat now, it will not continue its route until spring, since the river does not have enough water. As a result, we shall have to wait a long time for the piano and two other packets about whose arrival in New Orleans we have learned, unless they have been put on the *Henriette*, a lighter steamboat that can easily run its course. These letters of September 28 should have been no. 5, but I think I forgot to number them.[167] The last news we had from France is from the month of April, both yours and your good brother's and Mother Bigeu's. We are now very impatient to read the letters that are in the packets that are announced, or other more recent ones; our only pleasure is to have news of you.

We had hoped to be in the house that is being built by the beginning of November, but we will be lucky to be there by January 1. While waiting, we are living at the bishop's farm; he has made the legal transfer of the donation of land where the house is. This donation cannot be made to the community because the law would not recognize it, but must be made to one [religious], who will then make her will in favor of another, and so reciprocally. I do not know if the land where we were at Saint Charles remains ours, since we have left the area, because it was given on the condition of an establishment that has not happened. No one has regretted our departure as much as the good and beneficent Father Richard, pastor of the place and our confessor; he seems to despair of having a Catholic school before he reaches old age. He has always been ill since then. One of his visits shattered me.

Dear Mother, a holy and judicious priest from New Orleans has offered several persons of color with useful skills to the Lazarist Fathers to be a kind of third order attached to them, and through the bishop, has made a similar proposition with regard to girls of color who want religious life. It seems to me that the role of commissioner sisters would suit them perfectly, and with that title, they could render services just as important as those of the coadjutrix sisters. It would be difficult to have them among the whites, since all are equal here. Our two good Sisters are aging very much, and I have been forced to put Sister Marguerite

---

167 In fact, her letter of September 28 is marked as no. 5.

back in the kitchen for a while to give our American orphan time to prepare for her First Communion. Marguerite takes on too much and is as anxious in mind as in the past. She surely is not very gifted, but who is? As for the other Sister [Catherine Lamarre], her head is working constantly; when she cannot complain about things, she says: "You thought *that* of me." She has threatened impulsively to complain to the bishop if he were accessible to her. He knew this and said: "Let her come; she is bad spirited." I can deal with this only with patience, and I do not have much hope for a cure, but everything happens menacingly. The bad example is the most worrying; we live so close to one another that moods are catching, the bad more than the good.

The remainder of my little emigrant family tends toward perfection with all their strength. They are the ones who contribute most to the work and will see it prosper. I do not deserve it and I still have all the faults that made you groan. I fear very much to hinder the grace of God: we have neither postulants nor space to lodge them. We are perhaps the only ones in the Society who kept the feast of Saint Stanislaus [Kostka] without them. But a recruitment of persons over 60 years old who are still in France is offered us. You see that hope is far away, but this is how it is: the bishop knows of two ladies in Montpellier who are older but with many talents and virtues. They have made vows in religion, and even to consecrate themselves to the mission in Louisiana. They are kept at home by a mother who is 80 years old. They await her death in order to accomplish their vow. At first, they thought of the Ursulines, but now, of us. I wrote to the bishop that they would have to write to you and spend some time in one of our houses, if you so judge, while awaiting their departure. He assures me that they have a childlike spirit and uncommon virtue. Their name is the Misses Roi.

If we have some girls of color and some orphans, this would be enough for domestic service. As for a man, one of the Flemish domestics the bishop brought here has offered to be attached to our house, and he fits in in every way: he will live with Father Delacroix, a Flemish priest to whom the bishop has entrusted us.

The bishop complains of not having received your answer to his letter, and he wants to write to you again to ask you for more sisters. He has in mind several establishments, notably at Sainte Genevieve. But Saint Charles offers a thousand more resources and is growing, while Sainte Genevieve, lost in the country and with bad soil, declines daily. [Surely] the bishop's plan is to confide *(words torn)* of all kinds of girls in his diocese to our Society. This presupposes a multitude of small divisions. We could, if you think so, form something like a third order of Daughters of the Heart of Mary[168] who would be for the small schools. If you think this is good, please send their rules. For the rest, the bishop has to send a priest to France to see you about the expansion of our work. If something does not go well, I beg of you not to speak of it to Mrs. Fournier, the bishop's sister, who is easily upset by what concerns him. He reproached me once about what I was writing to France.

We have just borrowed 10,000 F from the rich Mr. Mullanphy to finish the house. His three daughters, who I told you were in Poitiers, are instead in Lyon.

I hope you will not mind if our chaplain sends some cloth from Flanders to you in Paris, so that you can send it for him to Bordeaux, to have it sent here: it is Father Delacroix, and he has great need of it!

Our consolation in these woods is that our boarders are doing better than in Saint Charles. Several give signs of a vocation, but we must be prudent because of their wealth and their family. The order of day is like that in Grenoble, and the uniform is magenta edged with black velvet. We had to explain that we do not want feathers or flowers or tulle and lace as trimming.

One thing that is very annoying here is that the Americans, especially the Protestants, consider it scandalous to have the slightest game or outing on Sundays. I spoke to the bishop about it, and he thinks we have to give in to the local opinion. He had the same thing at the college in Baltimore.

The bishop has such a strong desire that we have more choir religious, that if the little money that remains at Niort has not been used or sent, it would be better to keep it for travel. As for a trousseau, we can find everything here for our habit at a moderate price. We have only crepe for a veil. Mother Eugenie lost her cross, but happily found it again. Marguerite's ring is broken. If someone comes, I would like them to bring a pair of sabots to provide a model; we are always in water, chasing after the cattle that do not have a stable. The kitchen is separate because of the danger of fire. The prairie and forest fires have been ravaging this year; we have seen them at close range.

This is enough about material things, dear Mother, but my heart is with you and the two Societies in the Heart of Jesus. When I think that I belong to them, my soul expands and opens to tears of gratitude, and

---

168 Philippine is thinking of this congregation modeled on the Daughters of the Heart of Mary, an institute founded in 1790 by Father de Clorivière, SJ (1735-1820), and Miss Adélaïde de Cicé (1749-1818), with help from Father Varin.

I see nothing but happiness in privations. Could God grant me other favors? There is only martyrdom left for him to give me. But on my part, what sorrow! How badly I have responded!

I am at your feet *in Corde Jesu*.

Philippine

You know what my heart says to our fathers, mothers, sisters and children. Your letters and those of your brother make us impatient here when we do not have your answers.

[On the reverse:]
To Mother
Mother Barat
Rue des Postes, n° 40, care of Mr. Roussel
Paris

Letter 142   **L. 29 to Mother Barat**

SS. C. J. et M.

No. 7
[Florissant] December 1, 1819[169]
Rec. to St. Ant. of Padua

Reverend and honored Founder,

I wrote to you at the departure of Father Martial, and my companions did, too; I know that he has been very much delayed in route, and I expect that our letters, which should have been under no. 5, which was forgotten, have also experienced long delays; they were dated September 28. I have tried to repeat what I said in a letter I wrote to you on November 15, no. 6, which would have taken a month to get to New Orleans. I seem to have exhausted all the subjects that would interest you, but I feel that with you, they are inexhaustible and that, beyond the necessary business, the heart will always want to have more.

I have filled out my annuity certificate for the end of this year, but the absence of the governor and assistant governor of Saint Louis, whose *visa* is necessary, keeps it here.

---

169   Original autograph, C-VII 2) c Duchesne to Barat, Box 2. Postmark: Paris, April 18, 1820. Cf. J. de Charry, II 1, L. 121, pp. 276-286; Hogg, pp. 188-195; Ch. Paisant, pp. 286-290.

I have had more trouble getting possession of all the goods sent from France in April and stuck in customs in New Orleans since then. They have just written to say that I must send an attestation made in the presence of a judge, to testify that we were informed of their arrival in order to collect them. This formality is not usually necessary, and I thought perhaps that they wanted to spare us the regulations in the public interest. I have not been able to find the judge, and in any case, the ice and low water will hinder us from receiving anything before spring. It is sad, especially because of the letters that your kind brother enclosed.

On November 21, we had the consolation of uniting ourselves with you; our grandfather came to spend the whole feast with us and talked to us together and individually.[170] But I did not notice any pleasantness; I found him discontented with everything,[171] which I had not seen before in general, because for me personally, since my arrival, I have had the idea that his first glance was not favorable. I had the same impression of those who have followed him, just what I needed in a place where so many desires have taken me and where I would have deliciously enjoyed the benevolence of my father. "God alone" and "*Ita Pater*" have a new meaning in the situation in which I sense that divine Providence will not abandon me. It seems to me that I am invested with it and can touch it with my heart and my hands.

Grandfather says he has written to you to make several requests, excluding the coadjutrix Sisters, whom he does not want, saying that the system does not work for the country. Everything I have told him about the *Plan of the Church* and *of the Society* is of no value, and he has quoted your grandfather as knowing when to bend to all the customs. So he wants *one habit, a single rank*, and that *health alone* be the criterion for menial employments, to which even the head [the superior] must apply herself. He consents, however, that Sisters Catherine and Marguerite remain as they are.

The conversation with Audé also heated up, so that we felt ourselves *(torn word)* very little in control of the building, that we were hardly consulted about our *(torn word)* residence; I told him that with us, once the grandfather [bishop] had given permission for an establishment, he left to us the choice of place. Up to now, he has crushed us with a weight of authority. He stopped and left us, unhappy. I did not

---

170 Philippine uses this pseudonym for Bishop Dubourg or another bishop when she treats delicate subjects.
171 This displeasure was probably caused by the refusal of the religious to make certain changes to their Constitutions and by their desire to found a second house at Sainte Genevieve rather than at Saint Charles.

know how to heal the wound, since I am liable to resist again, unless you tell me to let it all go, but would you? With a creative spirit, one who has plans can go far. Besides, if one takes a near-sighted view of the temporal, our expenses would be too far-reaching; *we must* be in charge of them as soon as we are in our own house.

Money is very scarce here; even the richest property owners do not have it now. The stagnation of commerce in Europe extends its influence here, and several failed banks have incalculable difficulties in making payments. I went with 500 F in notes to pay our rent, but they did not want to take them. I saw there our first Raphael[172] [Father Richard]. He advised me to remain firm. We have borrowed 20,000 F, but we do not know if it will be enough for the house, let alone our unknown debts with the foreman of the work.

The land on which we are to live has been given to me legally by my grandfather; it comprises orchard and garden to be planted—the land is all in one piece—and I have made my will in favor of my two friends [Audé and Berthold].[173] I forgot at the time that I had taken away the right to receive and give; I have told you about it, as had Father Perreau. I was informed again of the necessity of doing this in this country and the example of our friends [Jesuits] at Georgetown. What do you and Father Perreau think of this? Either for that or for the rest, I have not had a moment of peace since the 21st.

To return to the institute, I see a middle ground: to accept girls of color as coadjutrix; but besides the fact that they do not come except from a distance, their vocation would have to be discerned for a long time. How many poor girls unable to be in the first rank would be marvelous in the second, if their ideas were changed after a while by spending time in their future residence and receiving instruction? To bring them closer, I imagined giving them the same form of dress, bonnet with flat pleats, without cross or choir cloak, for up to seven years. When they are sufficiently formed, they could perhaps be accepted in whichever rank. I say "perhaps," because is it not true that authority figures can accept the spirit of a country uncritically in order to gain hearts, and so not challenge a pride that is sustained by general opinion.

In my last letter, I praised the Misses Roi of Montpellier, women 60 years old who have made a vow to come here, and whom I have asked to write to you; they are of the greatest merit.

---

172 A guide like the angel Raphael for the young Tobit (Tob 5:12).
173 "Bishop Dubourg had Mothers Duchesne, Berthold, and Audé make their wills on the subject of his donation of land at Saint Ferdinand, which we give to each other by bequest in case of death." *JSA*, November 28, 1819.

I repeat the request that nothing of what I have written reach the sister of grandfather [Mrs. Fournier]. At this distance, the meaning of words can change. I have already received a reproach that makes me aware that this precaution is necessary.

We have a good Prussian for our work, so much the better because he knows neither Prussian nor Flemish nor English nor French, so he can only say what is necessary. Flemish is the language he speaks best.

Our health is good. Divine Providence has made the weather so mild that neither we nor the children suffer from the drawbacks of our lodging *(torn word)*, or from colds, even though half of us have only the roof as a ceiling. I do not have *(torn word)* the night. They are always telling us that we will move into the house this month. Several of our students want to enter the Confraternity of the Sacred [Heart]. It is a new joy to be inscribed in Paris. Please make it known.

December 10

My letter, begun on the 1st, was interrupted by lack of opportunity and need to see more clearly the subject of my letter, and by a retreat that is not yet finished. The absence of our Ananias[174] has advanced it. It was to have taken place after our move, but grandfather did not want the local pastor [Father Dunand]; he sent us the leader of the sons of the patron of our schools [Father de Andreis]. He is a saint, a well of knowledge; his talks are solid and profound, in the spirit of our friends [Jesuits], whom he loves very much.

As regards my vow, he cited the example of the Augustinians who, though strictly religious, receive and bear witness to secure their possessions here. On my situation with grandfather, he said it is delicate and that he was in the same position; that in Rome there is a Congregation of cardinals for the *Regulars*[175] in order to judge these kinds of questions, for those in danger of losing their spirit and their original form if they yield to the desires of their pastors. It is enough for you to know that I need an answer; the surest and fastest way would be via Mr. Petry, Consul General of France in Washington, to whom I am sending this.

Sister Marguerite is more and more muddled about external things, and the little American does not have much head, so I am always in difficulty with regard to the kitchen. Some colored women from New

---

[174] This is a reference to Father Delacroix, on mission in Gasconade. Ananias is a guide for Saint Paul (Acts 9:10-19).

[175] The Congregation for Bishops and Regulars, instituted in 1600 by Clement VIII, after several transformations became The Congregation for Institutes of Consecrated Life and Societies of Apostolic Life. Cf. John Paul II, Constitution *Pastor Bonus*, June 28, 1988.

Orleans have been suggested, but the bishop has written that they must wait until he has written to you.

I see painfully that *equality* is the obstacle to many vocations, even with a single rank, because merit, etc., will always make a difference and self-love will always find reason to complain: some who know nothing would like to be teachers. And if the class teachers also did the housework, where would they find the time? And personal neatness? And if they do not do it, there would be a distinction. All things considered, perhaps it is better to stay as we are and put up with fewer vocations. We will expand less here and do it later in a region where the spirit of subordination has less hold over self-love. When the *superior* takes her turn in the kitchen, several will also want to take a turn at being *superior*.

Nevertheless, I have no other desire than your will.

A thousand greetings to Fathers Joseph [Varin] and Perreau, who surely will want to advise you in your response, as well as *our dear mothers* [assistants general].

I am, with profound respect to my dear benefactor, your humble servant *in Corde Jesu*.

Philippine Duchesne

December 16, 1819

P.S. I have just received your letter. I have not yet given Catherine hers. She was bled yesterday and is peaceful at the moment. Mothers Lucile [Mathevon] and Dutour[176] are not appropriate for coming here: it needs more external style and talents, and especially knowledge of English.

[On the reverse:]
To Mother
Mother Barat
Rue des Postes n° 40 care of
Mr. Roussel
in Paris

---

176 They were nevertheless sent to America: Lucile Mathevon in 1821; Helene Dutour in 1827.

Letter 143   L. to P. Provenchère

[Report of three financial transactions][177]

No. 6

Mother Philippine Duchesne to P. Provenchère

1819		
Nov. 23	Record of the sale by Bishop. L. G. Dubourg. Paid to Mr. Gamble	$150
Dec, 15	Mortgage and debt to Mr. J. Mullanphy	$ 5
1820		
Jan. 27	Record of the above mortgage, paid to Mr. Gamble	$225
		$875
Sum received on the above account by Bishop L. G. Dubourg St. Louis, February 4, 1820 P. Provenchère		

Letter 144   L. 8 to Father Barat

SS. C. J. et M.

Recommended to St. Anthony of Padua
Beginning, 1820[178]

My good Father,

I wrote (letter) no. 7 to your sister [and] our mother on September 16. My letter mailed should have gone by Philadelphia. It is a long time since I wrote to you yourself; I have made it up by speaking of you often and remembering your advice. We often say that we will never see you again, but you often said to us: "'God alone' means giving up consolation." It is very true that in our relations with you, there has

---

177 *Philippine Duchesne à P. Provenchère*, 1819-1820. Original autograph. Report of financial transactions and receipt, signed by P. Provenchère. Series XII, C. Callan, Box 7, packet 2, Letters to lay people. Archives of the Province of the United States-Canada.

178 Original autograph, C-VII 2) c Writings Duchesne to various Eccles., Box 8.

been something more solid than consolation, but God has caused this separation, this privation; it is enough to be resigned to it. At the same time, he has put into the people of God who surround us a zeal, an interest that we do not merit. Everyone assures us that we will not lack for support, and I have every reason to believe that Bishop Dubourg, not wanting the direction of the pastor of Florissant for us, has attached to our house a priest very appropriate for our work. Besides food, he says to give him 1000 F, a difficult amount to find in our situation, because for a house that will cost 30,000 F, only 7500 remains from what we brought from France. Good Father Richard, who is dying of regret that we are away from his parish, instead of asking for anything, gave us all he could and would have continued, but he cannot be here, since he has not learned English in spite of much study.

English is just as important at Saint Charles and everywhere in this diocese, in spite of being a difficult language. I do not speak or understand it. Mother Eugenie stammers it and Mother Octavie, in spite of her facility for language, speaks it badly and will never be able to teach it, says the bishop, because of the extreme difficulty of pronunciation and the extreme sensitivity of hearing of those who speak English. Nevertheless, all the parents require its study, and we have no one with us to do it. Mother Octavie is aided by an American boarder, whom I beg you to ask God to join us, please. Her strength of character and other dispositions would make of her an outstanding subject and just what we need for teaching English.

Novices are yet to come, and the way of their entering is now the most difficult thing for us. I spoke to our mother in my last letter. The bishop himself has asked that we have only one rank and a single habit; as a result, there would be no [coadjutrix] Sisters. We gave our opinion in our letter and ended by saying that we will do whatever our mother decides for us, but I am afraid this adjustment will not be enough for self-love. If one cannot complain of difference in rank and habit, one will do it about occupations that only talent and merit can give. The more I think about this, the more I see the great difficulty of doing it all, for how will we change the opinion of a whole nation that is sustained by the tendencies of human nature? Nevertheless, we will leave Sisters Marguerite and Catherine as they are. The latter has received a letter from our mother that hurt her but did not change her inclination that will always be a torment to her. She says that her letter was misunderstood and that undoubtedly someone wrote against her. I believe that she wants to remain faithful. God is helping her, and the bishop does not listen to her anymore about that; he has neither the will nor the money to help her in the matter of a foundation. His funds are exhausted, and he made us borrow 10,000 F for our building, which will not be enough to finish it, but at least we are under cover. We will go step by step to finish it.

We moved into our house on December 24 in great cold that has continued and makes this winter worse than any they have had for a long time, for twenty years. Our health is holding up, but the expected children have not come, and that is another problem, to know how we will cover our expenses. I am waiting every day for the 3000 F from Niort. That will have to come to me directly. The bishop has given us by legal deed the land on which our convent stands, including garden, orchard, and courtyard. We have a very good man attached to the house, who costs us almost nothing for this country, only 620 F plus food, etc. All the banks of the States have failed, which puts the whole country in a crisis such as has not been seen before. The only paper money that is valid is that of the Bank of Missouri.

We have not received the piano and other boxes and crates. Nothing is getting up the Mississippi, which is entirely frozen. Certain provisions are lacking in Saint Louis. Sugar is priceless.

The opening of the new cathedral was on Sunday after the feast of the Kings, although it is far from finished. Nevertheless, it is astonishing that the bishop has been able to do so much in two years. He counts 40 priests in his diocese. They say that Canada has no more than two hundred, with six communities of women well established.

We all persevere in the hope that we will be, too, some day. But now the shadows are too deep to see it. We have experienced that happiness can be had with much suffering. We are happy with our destination; we have nothing to regret, and we are disposed to live in peace in the midst of poor success. Poverty does not cost us when it means only privation for us. It is the debts that tear at the heart, but an abject poverty, dependent, repugnant, is that of Our Lord, and we embrace it as coming from the Heart of Jesus; and what I express to you is the single sentiment of your daughters in Louisiana, who all call themselves your humble daughters in Corde Jesu.

The second day [of January 1820]

Ph. Duchesne

Tell our good mother not to have any anxiety about us. The holy Father Richard says that we will succeed. I believe that man of God more than I believe the worldly people who say the opposite. We are happy; our 16 children are good.

A thousand wishes of respect to Father Debrosse and Mother Vincent. What a sacrifice for us that all those letters are in customs in New Orleans! My respects to my fathers and mothers when you give them news of us. The bishop is going down to Lower Louisiana for several months.

The students who wrote to you are awaiting an answer. One of them, Miss Emilie, who is 16 or 17, had only bad books and believed that all religions were the same. When she came to us, she was so changed by her sudden devotion to the Blessed Virgin that, though promised in marriage for several years, she told her intended not to count on her; he was not angry because she did not choose someone else but wanted to be a religious. Her mother said she would die of sorrow. She answered: "You will be blessed because 'happy are those who suffer.'" She is now in Saint Louis in the midst of a struggle so that they will not accuse Bishop Dubourg of having pushed her into the path she is taking. She does not see him and stands on her own. Father de Andreis is her confessor and does not oppose her. He gave us a retreat and never stops saying how happy he was in our solitude. This worship of God in the untouched wilderness delighted him. You cannot imagine, he says, the interest he takes in us.

They say that my dear Sister Julie [Bazire] wants to come here. How I would like it! It would be most useful for her to improve her music and art rather than English. Father de Andreis cannot master the pronunciation though he studied it in Rome.

I am at your feet, your very unworthy daughter.

Philippine

[On the reverse:]
To Father
Father Barat, priest
At the minor seminary
Bordeaux
France

Letter 145   L. 1 to Father Debrosse

SS. C. J. et M.

Recommended to the Holy Angels, February 29, 1820[179]

---

179 Original autograph, C-VII 2) c Writings Duchesne to various Eccles., Box 8.

My very dear Father,

I owe you many thanks: first of all, for answering my first letter and finally for having been willing to take care of all kinds of expenses for us. The good God, who gives you this charity toward us, will keep track of it. It is just as necessary for us now as we undertake a house whose building is costing four times what we have. This fourfold will be paid back little by little by boarding fees, with interest. But there is still plenty to do to fence us in and establish a garden and orchard. The daily costs[180] always bring us up dry, and we would stop all spending if it were possible not to be enclosed; but our security and comfort require it, as does regularity of life, and we cannot do without it. Since there are no shutters, anyone could enter our house at night by removing the sliding window frames. That would not be so strange in this country where people sleep with open doors.

For the moment, I do not ask for anything to be sent from France because of the impossibility of paying the import fees. Mr. de Vidaud speaks of a shipment of wine; as useful as that would be, I beg you to stop it if he is sending it by Bordeaux, since we can find enough wine here for the Mass; or even better, if he does not ask for a statement of expenses, keep the same amount in cash for us. That would help for the voyage of one or two of our sisters, whom our Father Louis [Barat] thinks will not be able to come any other way than being picked up and transported like Habakkuk.[181]

My brother offered me money to return to France, and I am going to write to him that I would prefer that he use his money to get me a companion by paying for her voyage. If this resource fails, I have hope in Mr. Inglesi,[182] son of an ambassador in Rome, who has devoted himself to the Louisiana missions. He will be ordained at Easter and will set out immediately to help them in every way by going to Europe. He wants to see our mother; he is especially interested in us and says that he will

---

180 Wages paid to the workers.
181 Dan 14:33-39: the prophet Habakkuk is seized by the hair by an angel who carries him from Judea to Babylon to feed Daniel in the lions' den.
182 Added by an archivist: "Mr. Inglesi joined the Hogan schism." Angelo Inglesi presented himself as a Roman count who wanted to be a missionary. He made a strong impression in Saint Louis in 1819, was ordained quickly by Bishop Dubourg in March 1820, and undertook numerous journeys, recruiting missionaries and collecting funds. He met Mother Barat in Paris. In Rome in 1821, he contributed to the creation of the Society for the Propagation of the Faith, but a serious moral affair in which he was implicated obliged him to leave precipitously. Back in America, he joined the schism of William Hogan in Philadelphia. A. Inglesi died of yellow fever on June 13, 1825, in Santo Domingo. "The Inglesi Affair" was one of the reasons for the departure of Bishop Dubourg in 1826.

take care of the financial difficulty about sending subjects to join us. He has just said that we should prepare to sing his first Mass on Easter Monday. He will preach for us and take our correspondence to France. The Spirit of God will tell Mother [Barat] what we need: as for talents, the study of English for a French person counts for almost nothing. It is the ear more than the eyes that must become accustomed to this language. Father Barat tells me to have printed the "*Pensez-y bien,*" but it is already in print. We can get it from the cities of the East as well as *L'Imitation, Le Combat spirituel, L'Introduction à la Vie dévote, L'Âme élevée à Dieu* and excellent and devotional catechisms, and all in good quality English. It is the classic books that are missing. A student has translated several notebooks into English, which will soon be the only language of the country. Meanwhile, the French Creoles enjoy your precious collections, but they are a small number. The failure of many banks puts everyone in a squeeze, and this is one of the most damaging factors for our establishment.

I am with respect, Reverend Father, in the Sacred Hearts of Jesus and Mary, in union with the Holy Angels, your humble servant.

Philippine Duchesne

Saint Ferdinand or Florissant, March 1, 1820

Would you like to know how much the piano cost them to get it to Florissant, to say nothing of having it come up the Mississippi by steamboat? 4 *sols* per pound. The bishop had trees brought from Paris to bring to Saint Louis. I wrote quickly from New Orleans that they should plant them there, and not be obliged to put the trees in the boat and pay the weight of 4 *sols* per pound.

Father Inglesi will not be able to return to America before next spring. You will have time to choose your subjects. Where are you on your projected establishment in Bordeaux? And where is the house? They call you Providence: that is a joke on those who talk like that. It would be wonderful for Florissant, but ridiculous for Bordeaux.[183]

[On the reverse:]
To Father
Mother Barat
Father Debrosse
Superior of the minor seminary
Bordeaux

---

183 Father Robert Debrosse was then rector of the Jesuit College in Bordeaux.

Letter 146 **L. 1 to the young religious of the house of Grenoble**[184]

SS. C. J. et M

To my dear Sisters Aloysia, Louise de Rambert,[185] Josephine de Coriolis, Louise de Vidaud, and Julie Dusaussoy
March 1 [1820][186]

[1st sheet]

I have just received, very dear Sisters, by a steamboat long halted in the ice of the Mississippi, a little packet of letters, some dated February 1819, the others April and May of the same year, which gives me double letters from Sisters Aloysia and Louise de Vidaud. Since the steamboat is stopping only briefly, and I want to take advantage of its return, I find it impossible to multiply letters. And what prevents me on the same paper from thanking my dear Aloysia for her interesting journals, to congratulate Sisters Louise de Vidaud and Julie Dusaussoy for their generous resolution and their happiness that is also mine, since I find myself fortunate to have new bonds with them!

Finally, I owe to all of you together the fulfillment of a promise. Do you remember that sometimes when we talked together while reading the *Edifying Letters,* and I let escape my wishes to go to uncivilized lands, you made me promise that if I ever went, I would send you accounts? It is time to do them, but I cannot make them very interesting: this country, which seems just recently to have emerged from barbarism, offers neither singular deeds for us, nor the curiosities that would be offered by a country that is distant but civilized.

The State of Lower Louisiana, with New Orleans as its principal city, has only that considerable city; much land, though good, goes uncultivated, but establishments are going up on all sides: there are French, Spanish, and Americans. This last name is given to citizens of the United States, whether born here as civilized or descendants of the English. The air around New Orleans is unhealthy; higher up, it becomes better. Upper Louisiana, with Saint Louis as a center, is still only a "Territory,"

---

184 This letter is addressed to the young religious of Sainte-Marie d'En-Haut whom Philippine had had as students. Euphrosine (Aloysia) Jouve had the charge of sub-mistress of novices.
185 Louise de Rambert entered the novitiate in Grenoble and made her first vows on the feast of the Sacred Heart, in June 1819.
186 Original autograph, C-VII 2) c Duchesne to RSCJ and Children, Box 4. Copies, C-III 1: USA Foundation Haute Louisiane, Box 1, *Part A, Lettres de la Louisiane, 1818-1822,* pp. 53-61; *Part B, Lettres de personnes variées, 1818-1828,* pp. 123-133; A-II 2) g, Box 2, *Lettres intéressantes de la Société depuis 1816 N° 1,* pp. 216-222. Cf. Ch. Paisant, pp. 295-301.

that is, a dependency of the States without participation in government. The country is healthy for the most part, except in the areas where there is stagnant water; nevertheless, especially this year, there are contagious diseases. The long trips on water in the heat and deprivation cause many illnesses among the travelers, who spread them when they arrive.

The passion for travel is very great and does much damage to young people. Those who go to Philadelphia for business bring back all sorts of luxury objects, such that the poor here often have more than our most well-off students in France. The inhabitant in the countryside, after having eaten his salted meat and cornbread, washed his laundry, and cooked, puts on his hat with flowers and ribbons, his colored shoes, his parasol, his embroidered shirt, etc., to go out. Those who go up the Missouri and Mississippi 5 or 600 leagues for the trade in furs, etc., with the Indians, bring back their loose morals, passion for profit, and ferocity. Yesterday a man here came into the house of a neighbor who was binding brooms; the neighbor asked him: "Am I not doing a good job?" The other answered: "You would not know how to kill a man."

For those who go up the Missouri, hunting provides food, but in the remote establishments in the direction of the sources of the Mississippi, hunger so takes hold of travelers that they eat each other; and I have been told that we have in our town those who eat human flesh, not Indians, but from civilized nations, perhaps even *French*. This is how it happens: the leader of the expedition hires the men at a certain amount for the trip; some go ahead while others go out at certain times in search of the objects of their business. Snow or other accidents prevent them from rejoining the group at the determined point. Then, if the snow prevents them from collecting wild moss to eat, they get together to cast lots on who will be food for the others. They sit in a circle, the lot is cast, and a gun is ready to fire on the one on whom it settles. The others make him their food. When there are only two, the stronger kills the weaker. This is what they face for a little money. And what do they do to save souls?...

I have learned that in this land there is earth that has all the properties of soap and can be used in the same ways. The Indians wash with it and soften their furs, which they trade for gunpowder, jewelry, blankets, and liquor. Drunkenness is a widespread vice for the Indians and the civilized. Dance is another danger that leads to the most violent passions.

All here make their own soap with water that has remained in ashes and filtered back for several days. They boil this with all sorts of old grasses, skins, spoiled oil, and bones. They boil it for several days. The result is a rough soap, but fairly good. They make their own candles, and they burn them in the church, where they drip less than the yellow wax candles that are easily found but are not purified.

The woods between Saint Charles and Florissant are full of trees from which they extract *sugar* that is sold like the other. It is mainly the *maple* that produces it. There is also quite a bit of *honey,* and wild nuts of which the *nut* cannot be used because the shell is too hard, clusters of wild *grapes* from which they make a passable wine, but it is often impossible to reach them because the clusters grow at inaccessible heights around the big trees. It is the same with the fruit of the persimmon that is better than our medlar tree and is also eaten when soft. It is the same with the *assemine* (paw paw), fruit in the shape of a cucumber with the flesh of a fig. You have seen the fruit called pecan, which is the local nut and has taste, but they do not make oil from it. Here there is only bear oil, which is a grease that does not flow very well and is often rare. We will spend our Lent without fish or oil or vinegar, and that with ease. Vinegar is made here with rainwater in which one places a certain amount of whiskey, a liquor made with corn and sugar. They leave it out in the sun.

The type of *horse* is very pretty. There are more of them than people, and no one goes anywhere without being on a horse. On Sunday, the door of the church looks like a horse fair; the women go only seated with their children in their arms. The *cows* wander everywhere without being fenced in; their calves are kept in to make them come back evening and morning, but what trouble it is to get rid of the calf when you want to lead the cow! Not only does it resist human force, but it moves in a direction violently and drags the person holding it. The oxen and horses return to their stable where they are attracted by salted corn, etc., but often they are lost; then, one must search the woods to find them. The *oxen,* accustomed to the freedom, are sometimes difficult to harness for work; then, to save time and trouble, they leave them harnessed together for whole months at a time, night and day. In my opinion, the goat is the prettiest animal in the country. Its head is one of the prettiest, and it is so tender that as soon as you approach, it comes forward to kiss you. It has all the gentleness of the lamb and adapts easily.

As for plants and grains, the most common is *corn,* from which one makes bread like this: they lay out the flour in hot water to a certain thickness and then put it into an earthen oven that has been greased, and they put fire above and below. We eat it often, and the Americans prefer it to *wheat,* which grows well here, as do green beans, pumpkins, French *melons, watermelons,* and other garden *vegetables. Potatoes* are very much used: there are *white, red, yellow, blue or violet,* and finally *sweet* ones that have a taste just like chestnuts, which are not like the ones here, but this kind does not keep well. The *lentil* is unknown. *Rice* comes from Lower Louisiana *and* is expensive. Besides the fruits already named, the woods furnish many blackberries that are eaten with sugar, like strawberries that also grow here, as well as a little fruit that has a form and taste a little like the *citron* and goes by that name. You find everywhere an herb called *belladonna* that grows like spinach and has that taste. Corn is eaten in its early stages and cooked in water or, in later stages, washed to remove the sheath and cooked in wine, and many other ways. It is given as a tisane frequently; it is the flour soaking in water. It is called *gruau* and is taken as a purgative. It supplements the herb bouillon. In a plaster with mustard on top, it has the appearance of our mustard plasters and even of a vesicatory. Mercury is much used here in remedies.

I wrote to you that we left Saint Charles the first days of September. We spent up to the 24th of December in the house owned by the bishop in the midst of our beautiful woods. There we had the visit of Father Inglesi, son of a Roman ambassador; he was still a child in the pope's party at the crowning of Bonaparte. Since the invasion of Rome, he has traveled much and finally, in Canada, decided to devote himself to the missions. He will be ordained at Easter, will come to us to say Mass, preach, and then he will leave for Europe to advance the business of mission and perhaps as well our business with our mother about sending more sisters.

Another visit no less interesting was that of Father de Andreis, provincial of the Lazarists. The bishop told us to sing for him the beautiful hymn to the Name of Mary, by Father Barat. Mother Octavie and the students obeyed, but the good saint missed giving us the spectacle of Saint John of the Cross in ecstasy at the singing of the Carmelites. He blushed, paled, trembled, planted himself in his chair, let himself fall down, and wept. Then he gave us a retreat. He has so much enjoyed the solitude of these woods that he never stopped saying that he had spent in these days his most beautiful days in America, and that he would never forget it. The songs of Sion, sung in this strange land, enchanted him. He had already sailed the length of the Ohio to proclaim the names of *Jesus* and *Mary* where they have never been heard.

[2nd sheet]

At the moment, we have our wealthiest student at odds with her family over becoming a religious. She had never read anything but bad books before coming, but the Blessed Virgin, by whom her heart is taken, obtained for her the gift of faith that she did not have, contempt of the world, detachment, a religious vocation, and above all such a love for the Blessed Virgin that when someone else speaks of her, she is seized with irritation as if one infringed upon the rights of an only daughter; she has that kind of jealous love for her. Several of her companions profess the same attraction, but we must not count very much on perseverance; rather, more on the persecution that could come from it.

We left the bishop's property in great cold. The pastor [Father Dunand] of Saint Ferdinand (or Florissant) had written to me that the *holy land* will be open to us the week before Christmas. I went there myself with a young American orphan who serves as our interpreter, since all the workers speak English. When I arrived in the town, I heard the bells ring for Mass and went first to the church. The words of the priest told me that it was the feast of Saint Thomas the Apostle, and my soul was elated by the joy of setting foot in our establishment on such a day. He and Saints Francis Xavier and Regis were in turn the ones who particularly attracted me to beg Jesus and Mary that it would be to the glory of their Hearts.

On the 23, Mother Octavie, Sister Catherine and six of the older boarders came on foot to find me; they were wrapped in wool blankets, their stockings on the outside of their shoes so as not to slip on the ice. A wagon with our effects followed them. I took advantage of its return to our house to go wrap up the last packages and pack the things for the chapel. On the evening of the same day, the rest of the boarding students left by wagon, escorted by Father Delacroix on horseback.

The next day, 24th, Mother Eugenie, Marguerite and I heard the last Mass in our little Bethlehem. No other chapel has represented it better: the good God was without windows for several days, with such large holes in the ceiling above that large apples fell through and decayed behind the tabernacle. It was often sown with beans and corn that fell through the cracks! As for the floor, there was no difficulty getting rid of what was swept up because each plank had a hole big enough to let it fall through. Nevertheless, it was where the bishop, Father de Andreis, preacher of the sacred college, and we all were often filled with consolation.

We had extreme difficulty packing up this chapel, so much did the cold hinder our movement. Finally it was done, as well as almost everything that remained. Marguerite was supposed to come with a little cart; I left on foot with Mother Eugenie to lead our last cow in a friendly manner, because we had not been able to tie her, and she did not have a calf to attract her. I filled my apron with corn to make her follow me, but she preferred her freedom and ran in the snow and brush of the woods that we were crossing through. We were often stuck in the snow following her, catching our veils and habits on branches. The weather was getting worse, so we let her go back to the old house, while we headed for Florissant following only the tracks of the pigs to guide us in the snow. We were so oddly dressed that we frightened a whole flock of these animals that were almost wild. I had my money and papers in my pockets and bag, but suddenly the cord broke, and everything fell and was buried in the snow, along with my watch. Mother Eugenie came to help me, but the wind had blown snow into my gloves, and they were frozen on my hands. I did not have the strength in my fingers to carry anything; we had to put everything in a dirty handkerchief, and I had to carry my bag and my pockets under my arm. When we arrived at Florissant, they were already concerned about us; the wagon we had counted on following had gone on well ahead of us because we had lost the right road.

The place destined for the chapel was emptied of the wood it contained. Curtains made up the back wall; the freezing made it impossible to do otherwise. The altar was prepared during the evening and *veillée* was spent adorning it and going to confession. At midnight, Father Delacroix said Mass. The whole house was present except the two youngest boarders; the workers came too and received Communion, since all were devout.

The next day, 26th, the bishop arrived and preached the parish Mass to exhort the parishioners to contribute for the day school. Two gatherings of this kind took place, after Mass and before Vespers. He had dinner with the pastor and did not come to us until evening, accompanied by Father Inglesi and Father Delacroix, our confessor and our pastor. The students were all in purple uniforms bordered with black velvet. With us they asked for his blessing, then standing in a semi-circle in the parlor, they sang him some verses of gratitude written by Mother Octavie, followed by a couplet for Father Marie-Joseph Dunand, Trappist, pastor of the place, who had managed all the work on our house with money that he did not have, bought seven horses for the carts that he did not succeed in having made, lodged the drivers and cooked for them himself, cleaned the place, burned the brushwood, etc. It is still he who will build the building for the day students, since the inhabitants withdrew or made unacceptable proposals.

Before he was a Trappist, this good father was in the army of the Revolution, deserted, and entered La Trappe. He took part in all the travel in Russia of Father Augustin [de Lestrange], was his procurator general, and had built the house for the religious in Switzerland, then the one for men in Kentucky that was burned. When illness decimated their second establishment near Kaskaskia in Illinois, he remained alone in the country on mission. He made a number of conversions, was among the most solitary in the diocese, and had to defend himself from prairie fires in his travels, from tigers and rattle snakes, and he saw lightning next to him. His greatest cross is not to have eliminated vices. His zeal made him quite a few enemies, and he says that he had not had any consolation until we came here. Nevertheless, we always give him trouble; when money is lacking to pay a worker, he advances it. That is enough so that we should pray for him.

To return to the bishop's visit, on the feast of Saint John [December 27], he gave First Communion to two of our children, blessed the house, and left. Passing by the classroom, he saw the remains of breakfast on a bench, since our only table was for him, and yet the legs were about to fall off.

We saw our worthy bishop again on March 1. He really wants to leave us tranquil about the advances he has made and says that we will repay him without becoming too worried about it. He told us that Father Martial began his secondary school in Baton Rouge, a pretty little town in the State of Mississippi, 37 leagues from New Orleans on the other side of the river. Natchez is the principal place; it is a Sodom, but he accomplished the same good there as he had in New Orleans, stirring up the few Catholics to ask for the visit of their bishop. The bishop went at their invitation and, on the return, will visit his 4th secondary school, created last year on a piece of land of 400 acres given by a widow who is also having a house built. It is a gift of 200,000 F, entirely new.

The four secondary schools born this year are: 1. The one at the Barrens, which is a seminary at the same time, conducted by Father Rosati, Italian Lazarist; 2. The one in Saint Louis, conducted by Father Niel of the house of Father Liotard in Paris; 3. Father Martial's at Baton Rouge; 4. The one in *Opelousas* (if I have remembered the name correctly), conducted by Father Brassac.[187]

My dear Sisters, this is what comes to me about this country. Excuse the disorder of the account; it was often interrupted. And ask God that we might have the happiness to make him loved and to love him ourselves with an effective and generous love.

---

187 Hercule Brassac arrived in 1817 to work with Bishop Dubourg, the first priest of the new church at Grand Coteau (1819-1822). He played a key role in the acquisition of the property of Mrs. Charles Smith for the Sacred Heart foundation at Grand Coteau. He was a priest in Baton Rouge in 1834 and at Donaldsonville in 1835. He returned to France in 1837 and worked as vicar general of the European bishops in America from 1839 to 1861.

I am in the Sacred Heart, your sister,

Ph. Duchesne

Letter 147   **L. 30 to Mother Barat**

SS. C. J. et M.

No. 10
March 3, 1820[188] Recommended to St. Ant. of Padua
For Reverend Mother Barat

My dear Mother,

I wrote to you on January 25 and since then to your dear brother. The two words are for three objects. The first, for you, announces that we know the price of our house. It is 30,000 F, of which 10 is paid from what we have or from boarding income; 10 is borrowed for two years at 10 per cent; and 10 is advanced by the bishop, for which he doesn't even want a document [attesting to the loan], not wanting, in the case of death, that we should be concerned about it. He told me with great kindness: "You will repay it when you can." Moreover, he is allowing us this year to cultivate land that belongs to him, next to ours.

He also wants to relieve us of the support of a chaplain by placing Father Delacroix elsewhere, and does not see a problem with putting us under the care of Father Marie-Joseph [Dunand], who showed great virtue when he saw that our confidence was going elsewhere, who has great care for us, and whose talent is necessary for us to finish our buildings. Nothing is plastered yet, there are no shutters, no staircase to the attic, and no clock tower—which leaves an opening in the roof that soaks us. All finished, the house will cost 35,000 F. We are sorry about Father Delacroix; he is an angel of peace.

The bishop was here yesterday and showed much interest in us. He read us your letter in which you complain that we are not in Saint Louis. He still thinks that place is not right for the principal house in this country, saying that then the parents would not have placed their children as boarders, but as day students, or would have visited them. They would go out continually for dances, etc. For the novitiate, life there is very expensive. But he wants us to have a house there for

---

188   Original autograph, C-VII 2) c Duchesne to Barat, Box 2. Cf. J. de Charry, II 1, L. 123, pp. 297-299; Hogg, pp. 202-203; Ch. Paisant, pp. 302-303. The letter of January 25 to which Philippine alludes is lost.

day students, for the people and the little children who are too young to be boarders. You are aware that this project and our only existing house demand the help of at least two sisters, capable (as he says) of preserving the spirit and being superiors someday. I am calculating with pleasure that the three years have begun. It would be important for us to have Americans for the English that is becoming widespread, and those who will come should be young enough to learn it. I nearly despair about it for myself.

The bishop gave his opinion yesterday for the first time that Mothers Octavie and Eugenie read well.

May all your sacrifices and the use of the money from Niort be to support us. As for the crates and packages, they will have to wait until we can pay the port fees. The first ones have not arrived.

My regards to our fathers; I ask their prayers and those of all our mothers and sisters. I am at your feet, Reverend and good Mother.

Philippine Duchesne

We have sixteen students. The bank failures have prevented several from coming.

[On the reverse:]
To Father
or to Mother Barat
In Bordeaux or in Paris

Letter 148   **L. 9 to Father Barat**

SS. C. J. et M.

[March 20, 1820]
Rec. to St Anthony of Padua[189]

My very good Father,

Father Inglesi,[190] who is very willing to take our commissions for France, is one of the great gifts that God has made to this mission. Born in Rome of a distinguished family and acquainted with almost all of

---

189 Original autograph, C-VII 2) c Writings Duchesne to various Eccles., Box 8. Copy, C-III USA Foundation, Haute-Louisiane, Box 1, *Lettres de la Haute-Louisiane, II, 1823-1830*, pp. 184-186.
190 In a note, in another handwriting: "This priest was later involved in schism. Do not speak of him."

Europe, he has devoted himself to humble ministries in this country and is traveling in the interests of this church in Louisiana. He was ordained yesterday, feast of Saint Joseph, and is coming in the evening to say his first Mass sung by our sisters and the students. Two priests came to assist, and we will have five priests in the chapel at one time, something never before seen in Florissant. Father Inglesi takes a particular interest in us. On the way back from Rome, he will go to Paris and see our mother in our interest. He is going to be coadjutor to Bishop Dubourg and will reside in New Orleans.

We received day before yesterday the cases sent from France in April and September. Here is the whole list of what we have received at several different times:

1. one case of toys and books, in which were the glasses of Madame X;
2. one larger case, partly filled with your precious collection;
3. a small case containing material for making flowers;
4. the large case with the piano;
5. the one with candlesticks and seeds;
6. the one with books from Amiens, toys, cloth, irons;
7. the one with papers;
8. the one with globes.

These last two were left with the bishop by mistake.

He recommends that nothing useless be sent to us because of the high freight charges. Actually, the charge for these six cases will be, they say, from New Orleans here, 80 *gourdes* or 400 F, which we do not have. Fortunately, a friend of ours who was on the steamboat will take care of that for the bishop. He expects much more from us.

Counting on divine Providence, which never abandons us, we had nothing but joy in seeing so many things that remind us of the charity of our fathers, mothers, and sisters of France, who leave us no time to want or to lack.

Father Inglesi, seeing his departure advanced by the delay of that of the bishop and the opportunity of a steamboat, does not leave us time to answer all our letters. I am especially unhappy not to be able to answer Mother Emilie [Giraud], my first and very dear daughter, but she will not count any less on my remembrance.

The last steamboat carried a packet of our letters, but they do not answer every one that has arrived for us:

1. Mother Vincent in a roll of samples of handwriting and songs;
2. In one packet, sent by mail to Saint Charles, that Father Richard sent on to me and that you said in your letter had been sent to Father Asselin;

3. In a case with the Plan of Studies. We replied to the packets sealed in oilcloth by doing the same with our response [for waterproofing].

Father Martial gave me a receipt for the 1000 F that you paid for me, but there is no news about the other 1000 F that you told me about in your last letter. The customs charges for the six cases went up to 500, but even if they had been higher, they would have been satisfactory to us since they came from you and our mothers and contained real wealth for our situation that has nothing painful about it, even for weak human nature, except for the debts.

[*Several lines have been cut out.*]

Add to your kindnesses by giving me some special advice. I cause harm to souls rather than helping them, and without even considering the delicious peace I wish for, I would like to be replaced.

I am displeased not to have the time to write to Mothers Vincent and Agatha to thank them. I beg you to do it for me by offering them my affectionate remembrance in the Heart of Jesus. Our children who wrote to you are burning to have an answer to their letter.

I am, my good Father, with profound respect, your humble servant.

Philippine Duchesne

Saint Ferdinand, March 20, 1820

In the last letter of March 3, there was something for Fathers Debrosse, Wrints, and Mother Lalanne, our good and generous sister.

[On the reverse:]
To Father
Father Louis Barat, priest
At the minor seminary
Bordeaux
France

Letter 149   **L. 31 to Mother Barat**

SS. C. J. et M.

Florissant, March 20, 1820[191]

Dear Reverend Mother,

I wrote to you only 17 days ago, no. 10, but the opportunity through Father Inglesi, future coadjutor of the bishop, who is traveling on church business, was too good to let it get away. After his journey to Rome, Father Inglesi will return via the North and wants to see you, to request of you religious for this mission, provided that his desires, those of the bishop, and ours are fulfilled and the meeting of the [General] Council produces a priority in favor of our mission.

We have received six crates or packages: 1) a piano in good condition; 2) candle sticks in good condition, and a crate of books from Amiens and others that make up the third; 4) the little box of flower decorations; 5) a package of paper; 6) a crate of globes, one of which is broken. It was a great joy to unpack all of this, nothing of which is useless, and several things are indispensable. Nevertheless, I think it prudent, in view of the state of our debts, included here, and the enormous shipping fees on the Mississippi, to stop any other shipments. They told me about a podium that cost 30 F in fees; our crates will go as far as 400 F; the charges went up to 500 F. The one thousand F went in freight charges; the rest was dispersed, and we owe the fee to the parent of a student, who is willing to wait for it.

The bishop has shown us great kindness. Since the land destined to be our garden is not ready, we will plant it this year on his land that includes some large apple trees that we will enjoy.

The day school is being built by subscription and the active zeal of the pastor. It will be ready to open in a month. A postulant, an American widow whom we are delaying, could be employed for those of her nation.

Tell me about your dear health. I have only time to be at your feet to be blessed in the name of the Sacred Heart. I attach here the summary of expenses and a floorplan of the house drawn in haste and showing the land too small. It is enough for the garden, orchard, and courtyard.

---

191 Copy, C-III 1: USA Foundation Haute Louisiane, Box 1, *Lettres de la Haute Louisiane II 1823-1830*, pp. 183-184. Cf. Ch. Paisant, pp. 308-309. On March 20, 1820, Philippine also wrote to Father Barat.

Please, good Mother, convey for me all the thanks that we owe for so many benefits. We love to see their source in your heart, after that of Jesus.

Philippine

Letter 150   **L. 49 to Mrs. Jouve at Lyon**

March 27, 1820[192]

My dear Brothers and Sisters,

In a mailing that came to us but very delayed, I found two letters from you, accompanying a superb present that will make our humble chapel look like the churches of France when we produce our beautiful vestment. This is the second one I have received from you, and it will be very dear to me because it is an indicator that you have not forgotten a sister who herself is often concerned before God with your happiness, to solicit it by her feeble prayers.

All the information you give me about the family and especially about your children interests me very much. Euphrosine already keeps me up to date, and I know through her that Amelie's health is not as good as I had thought. God has his ways in making her suffer; he will remove the taste of the world from her.

I will not speak of my situation so as not to repeat too much. Since September 14, we are in the house that is our first in the United States. We owe much for the building. Half of this debt will be taken care of by our reverend bishop, who has procured an advance for when and how we can pay, but over 10,000 other F are due to an individual of this place, with interest.

My dear Sister, you ask me what would give me pleasure. I have few desires and confide myself mostly to Providence. Nevertheless, our state of debt requires that we get along with only what is indispensable; I could not make up our beautiful vestment without gold braid. But pick one of the simpler ones. I cannot find any in the whole of the United States. A little sewing thread and green silk would also be really necessary for us, with a short *Abridged Ancient and Roman History*,

---

192 Copies: *Cahier, Lettres de la Mère Duchesne à sa famille*, pp. 101-102; *Lettres dactylographiées*. C-VII 2) c Duchesne to her family and lay people, Box 5.

because I want to present our house like those of France. We will have a boarding school and a day school.

Remember me to my brothers and sisters. What you tell me about Mrs. Lebrument consoles me greatly.

I am your very loving sister *in Corde Jesu*,

Philippine Duchesne

Letter 151   L. 9 to Mrs. de Mauduit

March 27, 1820[193]

My dear Sister,

I have just received one of your letters, completely appropriate to encourage a heart so sensitive to tenderness. Mine suffers for you to see you so isolated. I have learned through several letters of the marriage and pregnancy of your dear Amelie, the departure of Augustine and your profound solitude. May you find peace of heart, that consolation of the soul that brings happiness, often in the midst of suffering. I ask Saint Francis Regis, our common friend, to give you by his prayers all the consolation that my heart wants for you. I am delighted that you offer me *(torn word)* with him and I ask you to have a Mass said for me at his tomb.

Remember me to my aunts at Romans and to Melanie. I count very much on their prayers to become holy. Give my regards to Mr. de Mauduit and to your two lovely daughters, especially Amelie, who is nearer to you and whom I love so much. Suggest to her for me that she frequent the sacraments every month and practice devotion to the Heart of Jesus and to his Holy Mother.

I have a pressing engagement, little time, and several letters to write. I leave you, sure of your understanding and friendship. All yours *in Corde Jesu*,

Philippine

---

193 Copies: *Cahier, Lettres de la Mère Duchesne à sa famille*, pp. 101-102; *Lettres dactylographiées.* C-VII 2) c Duchesne to her family and lay people, Box 5.

Letter 152   **L. to the novices
of our house in Paris**

SS. C. J. M.

Florissant, March 28, 1820[194]

My very dear Sisters,

How many wonderful things we have received from our houses in France at the arrival of the *Etna*, which brought us 6 boxes or bundles making up two shipments from Bordeaux at different times. We do not know what sentiments to feel: gratitude, the interest that inspires unity, the choice of details, everything combined to have us spend the happiest day. We read your letters at several recreations; as for me, I received nearly forty at that time, but one was two years old, others 18 months. The most recent were those of November 1819, not in the bundles but confided to a missionary who stayed in New Orleans and sent them by post. The others were mixed in with all kinds of different objects, after having gone through customs. If ever you send them like this, they must be bound together in a packet, for I fear that some were lost, especially those from Fathers Joseph and Perreau that I think our mother said were coming, and the privation of which is a great sacrifice for me.

You, my good Sisters, who live under their gentle influence, take advantage of this happy time. Perhaps one day, nourished on strange milk, you will regret that of your spiritual infancy, and you will be in danger of starving your soul, if from now on, your constitution in the spiritual life is not well established.[195] Tell these holy fathers sometimes that their distant daughters have great need of their counsel and their prayers.

We congratulate you for being finally united in one house, the cradle of the Society, since it is there that you are being born for it, and for being under the care of such a good nurse [Mother Deshayes]. Remember me to her, and do not think that she is lacking in gifts because I left her guidance very imperfect. The fault is mine alone, and I expect of your charity prayer to continue her mission in me.

Most of you, dear Sisters, have expressed to me the desire to come to our country, and *declare it to me*, as if I could help you accomplish it;

---

194   Copy, A-II 2) g Box 2, *Lettres intéressantes de la Société depuis 1816, N° 1*, pp. 223-224.
195   1 Pet 2:2; 1 Cor 3:2; Heb 5:12.

but it is the business of our mother general and her council. It takes all her wisdom and the spirit of God who inspires such a decision. When I see people who were all eager to come to this country and now are at the point of returning to their homeland, I think such a project has to be carefully nourished. It takes detachment, mortification, humility, and a desire to suffer that can sustain you in moments of trial. As for me, who am astonished at the goodness of God in my regard, who has given to me according to my desires and not according to my virtues, I can do nothing except make known to our mother the needs of our mission.

I thank Miss de Clausel[196] for the news that God has chosen her for his spouse. How this dear novitiate gives hope as it does to the Society.

Pray, Sisters, work at your perfection, and if you are Berchmans,[197] we will be astonished at you, since we do not have the least of his virtues in such a sublime vocation.

Philippine

We have had in one week two first Masses of two priests ordained on the feast of Saint Joseph. These Masses were sung with deacon and subdeacon. The Heart of Jesus was pleased to have his gentleness felt in our chapel, where these holy priests said that they experienced something they had never felt before, that they were caught up outside themselves, that our house was a true paradise, and that these innocent manners (speaking to our children) enchanted them, so that they would be very happy to come often.

Letter 153   L. 32 to Mother Barat

[May 8, 1820][198]

Dear Reverend Mother,

---

196 Henriette de Clausel, RSCJ (1800-1852), born December 28, 1800, received the habit in the novitiate of Paris on August 28, 1820, and made her profession December 7, 1831. One of her first tasks was to be involved in the education of the princess of Brazil, Isabel, daughter of Peter II and heir to the throne. After several years in Paris, she went to Niort, where she died on February 2, 1852.

197 Saint John Berchmans was born in 1599 in Brabant, Belgium. He entered the Company of Jesus in 1616 and made first vows in 1618. He was an excellent theology student and finished his studies in Rome, where he died in 1621 at the age of twenty-two. In 1866, the cure of Mary Wilson at Grand Coteau, Louisiana, was the miracle accepted for his canonization in 1888.

198 Original autograph, C-VII 2) c Duchesne to Barat, Box 2. Cf. J. de Charry, II 1, L. 127, pp. 305-308; Hogg, pp. 207-209; Ch. Paisant, pp. 311-312.

Besides the inestimable services that we have received from the Reverend Father Marie-Joseph Dunand, a religious of La Trappe, we owe him 1000 F for having undertaken and advanced the work of our building, and for having contributed his labors and funds advanced to us to buy different useful objects for us, under an agreement to pay it back to Father de Lestrange in France or to himself, since he was getting ready to return.

I beg you therefore to acquit this debt to our worthy benefactor from the money owed to us by Niort. Added to all these kind acts is his fear to inconvenience us by naming a firm date for payment, but his desire and mine is that this be done as soon as Mother Geoffroy can manage it; it is a sacred duty for us.

I am writing to Father Barat for the same reason, for you have paid out 1000 F twice on our account, and I might fear that you would not be able to furnish this payment that concerns us more than any other.

I am with profound respect, Reverend Mother, your very humble daughter and unworthy servant.

Philippine Duchesne

Saint Ferdinand, May 8, 1820

P.S. I was counting on including this letter in the one of Father Dunand, but he has sent it back to me with his own for me to send. So I add these words to reiterate my loving and respectful sentiments and to ask you again for two good religious, one to be superior of all, the other a coadjutrix to direct the kitchen, now given over to the children, with serious consequences for their conscience and for our interests.

If God inspires you and makes it easy to send more people, it would fulfill all our wishes and would be exceedingly useful. If you see Father Inglesi or Father Dunand, I am sure you will be pleased to learn about us from eyewitnesses.

I venture to announce to you Father Inglesi as the future coadjutor of the bishop, which he is not now.

Please offer my respects to Fathers Perreau, Varin, Roger and all my mothers and sisters.

I am at your feet, your unworthy daughter.

Philippine

My sisters are well, that is to say, as they were in France, which is quite something. Mother Eugenie, though, has a fever from time to time that worries me, since she does not take care of herself. God also seems to be testing her by keeping her in a state of fear. She avoids Communion, which she wanted one or two years ago.

[On the reverse:]
To Mother
Mother Barat
Superior General of the Religious of the Sacred Heart
Rue des Postes n° 40 care of...
Paris

Letter 154   **L. 10 to Father Barat**

SS. C. J. et M.

[May 8, 1820]
Rec. to St Anthony of Padua[199]

My very dear Father,

I wrote to you and to our reverend mother in March by way of Father Inglesi, a Roman by birth and a priest of Louisiana who is traveling for the interests of the mission and for ours, which he has much at heart. He expects to see our mother and wanted to have a letter for her. I wrote of him to her and to you as the future coadjutor of Bishop Dubourg, but since then he has contradicted me and seemed astonished that anyone could have thought that because of his youth.

Perhaps you will see another priest from this country sometime this year [Marie-Joseph Dunand], religious of La Trappe. He is the chief reason for my letter, because we owe him 1000 F, which he agrees to get back in France, which is very helpful to us, since we are always short of money here, and we know that dear, good Mother Geoffroy still has something for Louisiana. I beg you to warn her as well as our mother to keep 1000 F to pay our debt to this good father, who wishes the 1000 F sent to his father, Dom Augustin de Lestrange, or to him when he arrives next winter. If by any chance you would have 1000 F available for us, I beg you to save it for the payment of this sacred debt, unless there is enough left in our fund to pay it. I dare not expect

---

199   Original autograph, C-VII 2) c Writings Duchesne to various Eccles., Box 8. Copy, C-III USA Foundation, Haute-Louisiane, Box 1, *Lettres de la Haute-Louisiane, II, 1823-1830*, pp. 189-190.

that, for then it would happen that this good father would not be paid because everything that comes through Bishop Dubourg will go toward paying our debt to him, and he always hopes for the 15,000 F that he has asked. I have not harbored such a delusion.

The father to whom we owe these 1000 F is the same one who directed the building of our house. It was watered by his sweat, the witness of his care for us, and we would not be living in it still if he had not procured the advance of money that would have been lacking without him. How every active effort arouses opposition! After having labored fifteen years in this mission and having been alone for a long time, he is giving way before accusations and complaints against him, and he is being replaced in this parish. The apparent pretext was his desire to return to his monastery. We went through a difficult time. We owed this father a great deal, and nevertheless another kind of direction is more suitable for us. From every side they wanted us to take sides, and we could neither go against gratitude nor against the good of our house. We left it for authority to act and commended the whole thing to God. It would have been very despicable for us to say a word that would have contributed to the alienation of him who sacrificed everything for us in his parish.

We have 20 boarders now, good for the most part. We are trying to fence in our property without success, for in this country fences are made like ladders. (A little sketch is inserted here.) We are not rich enough to have a board fence like that of the sisters in New Orleans. As for stone, there is none.

Repeat to our mother the request for subjects. Three American postulants have left, having neither vocation nor talent. Vocations are rare here. For our welfare, we need a good superior and a good cook. Neither the health nor the talents of our sisters are up to the latter job, so it is entrusted to children who are not totally to be trusted. Reasons of conscience have necessitated a change in relationships there between two sisters. The surveillance of these three orphans is more difficult than that of the twenty-one boarders. I think the bishop is beginning to understand that we cannot get along without [coadjutrix] sisters. He said recently to Mother Eugenie that her hands were too darkened and that when she did that kind of dirty work, she should wear gloves.

I think his good judgment will above all make him approve a change of superior, and there is no one who would suffer from it. I will never attract confidence either within or outside with others, but my two companions do, and they make good use of it. Sister Catherine received from our mother the real medicine she needed and she has been well since then. The one from Niort [Marguerite] is less well, not very active, hurried, restless, etc. I am the useless one, happy to be able to share the hard work. I would like to be devoted only to that, and I would be happy. It is deadly after such lively desires to see success hindered and languish and finally to realize that I am the obstacle. Happy too would I be if, having no support from anyone on earth near me, I were deprived even of those consolations that are too sweet for a life that is a dying in Jesus Christ. That is what I desire, though I am not preparing for it by my fervor.

I beg you to repeat to all our mothers our great gratitude for the gifts of each one. They would enjoy the joy we experienced when opening the cases containing so many proofs of their tender solicitude for us. My respects to Reverend Father Debrosse, to Mother Vincent, to Mrs. Fournier—but do not tell her anything that would be unpleasant for her to hear.

I am with profound respect, my good Father, your humble servant and daughter.

Philippine Duchesne

May 8, 1820

[On the reverse:]
To Father Barat
At the minor seminary
Bordeaux

Letter 155 **L. 1 to Mothers Bigeu, Lalanne, and Messoria**

SS. C. J. et M.

Rec. to St. Ant. of Padua[200]
May 8, 1820

My dear Mother,

The last news we had from France came from your house in a little

---

200 Original autograph, C-VII 2) c Duchesne to RSCJ and Children, Box 4. Letter addressed to Mothers Bigeu, Lalanne and Messoria, kept in the series to Mother de Lalanne because of the address bearing her name. Copy: C-III 1: USA Foundation Haute Louisiane, Box 1, *Lettres de la Haute Louisiane II 1823-1830*, pp. 191-192.

packet that contained a pair of stockings and the interesting account of your establishment written by Mother Messoria.

How precious it is to us to be united with a house where God is so well served and where he manifests his loving Providence. He also lets us experience his continual benefits. Pray to him for us, not in fear that it will be lacking, but with just dread that we will not respond to his favors.

Please recommend all my sisters to the fervent prayers of your daughters. They have the happiness to be more missionary than we, who do nothing for God except resign ourselves to do little.

I am with respect, dear Mother, your humble servant,

Philippine Duchesne

Saint Ferdinand, May 8, 1820

P.S.:

Dear Mother,

I missed the immediate opportunity I thought I had, so I am adding a few words for Mothers de Lalanne and Messoria in Bordeaux, for you must have found me very brief, telling you nothing about our situation.

When we realize that we have been less than two years in this country, we cannot but marvel at the ways of divine Providence; for after some delays and unimportant privations, God has put us in our own house, kept us in good health, established in such a way that we can hope to pay the debts contracted for our building, and provided with spiritual resources, even abundantly. Isn't this wonderful?

Even more wonderful is the work of the bishop: in less than two years, he has seen his cathedral built, his seminary built and in operation, and three or four secondary schools located throughout his immense diocese, all the parts of which are at least visited by priests. From places where the low population does not warrant a resident priest, we have some well-disposed boarders.

So agree with us that God is good!

[On the second leaf:]

To Mother Messoria

My good Mother,

I owe you my thanks for your interesting account. You are fortunate to work at such a beautiful activity as that of caring for, forming, and instructing so many young children. You are far away from our first mothers, but with the *Ita Pater* of Father Joseph [Varin], there was consent to everything and they are happy, no matter what happens.

The situation does not leave me time to answer Mother Geoffroy. Please give her my regrets and my devotion.

I am with a heart that is all yours, your servant.

Philippine Duchesne
Your sister *in Corde Jesu*

Saint Ferdinand, May 8.

Please post the two letters for Dom Augustin of La Trappe and Father Dunand. The others, except the one to our mother general, can wait for an opportunity.

[On the reverse:]
To Mother
Mother de Lalanne
Superior of the house of La Providence
Rue Mercière N° 9
Bordeaux
France

Letter 156   L. 11 to Mrs. de Rollin, in Grenoble

SS. C. J. et M.

August 27, 1820[201]

My dear Cousin,

It has been a long time since I wrote to you, but I knew you intended to go sometime to Rue des Postes, where you could always get the most recent news of me, and that way content your good heart that is so faithful to your old friend. They sometimes say that old hearts

---

201 *Copies of letters of Philippine Duchesne to Mme de Rollin and a few others, N° 11; Cahier, Lettres à Mme de Rollin,* pp. 24-29; *Lettres dactylographiées* C-VII 2) c Duchesne to her family and lay people, Box 5.

become hardened or lessen the sharpness of feeling; but I can say the opposite from experience: the names of Josephine, Marine, Augustin, and Camille always bring me a sentiment of pure and tender friendship and gratitude.

Now that the people these names recall to me are no longer the almost immediate instruments of divine Providence for me, it makes use of other resources to show me divine favor. We left Saint Charles, Missouri, last September. Among many amusing aspects of our move, we were very aware of the tears of the children we left behind without seeing any other means of education for them. The house at Florissant or Saint Ferdinand was not ready, so then we lived temporarily in another house until Christmas Eve, when we moved into our own house, that is, a house built for us and for part of which we are in debt, having borrowed in order to make it habitable. I do not doubt that divine Providence, which has led us here amid so many dangers and difficulties, will accomplish its work by imperceptible means that seem to undermine its activities, but leave it no less admirable to the eyes of those who follow it along its ways of goodness.

We have twenty boarders, who are remarkable by being from established families that are influential in the area, where we are seen as much better than we deserve. The Protestants as well as the Catholics look on our establishment favorably. The failure of almost all the banks and the stagnation of commerce have prevented many boarders. Money is very rare. The health of Mothers Octavie and Eugenie does not permit vigorous activities, and we have quite enough to do. Mother Eugenie is threatened by tuberculosis; this is the greatest cross that I have to bear here. The loss of such a religious would be a great blow to our work. Since the building for the day students is not finished, we still do not admit any.

I have to thank you for all the information you have sent me about our families; the remembrance of Mr. de Rollin is pleasing to me, as is that of your good parents. Please remember me to them and give news of me to my sisters. Mrs. Jouve asked what would give me pleasure, and I answered that I received material for a chasuble, but here there is no ribbon to adorn it. I would also like some cards for the canon of the Mass, bound together, with two or three cinctures and a little semi-fine gold fringe. None of these things can be found here, but for our clothing, we lack nothing that can be bought with money, since commerce supplies everything and at very moderate prices.

Missouri has become one of the federal States of the Republic this year. Saint Louis is the principal city for ten years, and the father of our first boarders will have great influence. He is very attached to us. The laws of the state are being discussed. The point most discussed and debated is the admission of slavery. It seems that those who have slaves will keep them permanently, and their children who belong to them, but they will not be able to carry on slave trade with Africans. We do not want them and cannot buy them, and so I do not know how we will get the service work done, especially since we do not go out. No one hires out as a domestic; everyone wants to be of the same status. Up to now, we have had young orphans up to the age of 21 given to us by a judge.

Believe in my unshakable attachment.

All yours *in Corde Jesu,*

Philippine

Letter 157   L. 33 to Mother Barat

SS. C. J. et M.

August 29, 1820[202]
Rec. to St. Ant. of Padua

Dear Reverend Mother,

The last news we have had from France was from you, for me and Mother Eugenie, dated February 29, 1820, no. 4 or 5. This letter was received with our usual transport of joy, but it also left me a little sad, since you had nothing settled about sending us help. Divine Providence had buoyed us up with this hope and with the expectation of soon having among us a very good American vocation. Unfortunately, she has upset all our plans just when I saw Mothers Octavie and Eugenie declining visibly and, as a result, the entire work along with them.

We cannot count on vocations here; the frivolity of some, the insolence of others, the resistance of parents to our way of life, the obstacle of language and the colored people, all seem to restrict us to a small number. I would willingly withdraw into our narrow sphere if I did not think it would create an obstacle to our growth. My two little mothers would be better fitted, or anyone else whom you would send. But in

---

202   Original autograph, C-VII 2) c Duchesne to Barat, Box 2. Cf. J. de Charry, II 1, L. 130, pp. 315-321; Hogg, pp. 214-218; Ch. Paisant, pp. 317-320.

spite of my preference for Mother Lucile [Mathevon], I doubt that she would please the bishop, who values externals and talents, since more of them are needed here than elsewhere; a pleasing appearance is usually found here; and as for knowledge, the less one has, the more one thinks to find it infused and universal in the persons who teach. If Sister Josephine Meneyroux has calmed down, she could easily replace Mother Eugenie in case of her illness or that of others.[203]

In my last two letters, I told you about the change in her health caused by the little care she has given to it and by several acts of imprudence. The largest one happened recently. She was convinced that the cause of her irritation was having too much blood. She was bled very severely, but that was not enough; an hour or two afterwards, she went out into a cornfield, took off the bandage and let the blood flow freely, which made her fall several times. When she had recovered a little, she dragged herself to the house and fell on the doorstep, white as a sheet, in front of me who did not know about this little madness; she had hidden it from me for several days. I assure you that the opinion of the doctors, combined with her lack of docility with regard to her body, makes me very anxious. I had already told you that she was in a very suffering state of soul. I cannot sort out if it is all a trial, but it is sure that she has shown several spiritual faults, which is troubling to me in light of what she would be capable of becoming for the Society through her devotion and her ability. God blesses her work with the children visibly; she holds them better than Octavie.

I am only at peace when I think that God wants our work and he will bring it about; but the difficulties are great. Mother Octavie has had *(word crossed out and illegible)* from which she has recovered. Her health is the same as it was in Paris; Sister Catherine, as she was in Amiens, and Sister Marguerite falls often. She must have complete tranquility, and how can we achieve this when we are so few and I am now the only strong one?

Moreover, the beginnings of Paris and of Grenoble are nothing compared to this: there is never any rest. At least in Paris and Grenoble, we were poor and modest, while here, we must be poor and magnificent. This month I found myself with 6 and 1/2 *sous* in the purse, besides

---

203 Rosalie Meneyroux, called Josephine, an aspirant in Paris in 1820, returned to her father for health reasons. In Bordeaux she met Father Barat, who encouraged her intent to go to America. She embarked without the agreement of Mother Barat, and even without telling her. She arrived in New Orleans December 24, 1821, stayed with the Ursulines until February 1, 1822, then went to Grand Coteau, where she was much appreciated, but she returned to France in May 1822.

the debts. Every day, besides our own table, we provide another for the priests, three or four of them.

The bishop himself spent ten days with us. He has never shown us so much goodness. He worries much about the health of Mothers Octavie and Eugenie and would like the latter to take some excursions on horseback, but since happily her cough has stopped, I made her understand that her nerves contributed more to it than her lungs. He still wants a day school in Saint Louis, in spite of the fact that he is waiting for some religious from the East for the little hospital that he is establishing. He also wants a school in Lower Louisiana, where, 60 leagues from New Orleans, a lady has already founded Father Brassac's college and is building a convent that she will endow.[204] After speaking about her project, the bishop said that if you were less intransigent, he would address himself to you, but the location does not fit us at all. It is in the countryside where there would be no boarders and few day students.

I still regret that we do not have a foothold in New Orleans. Nevertheless, the Ursulines are going to leave it. Their property has been cut by a street, which puts them in a thoroughfare. Besides that, there are the illnesses each year, the proximity of the hospital, etc. All this has made them move two miles out of town to a superb acquisition where they will build a convent. Father Martial, who has been living in the house where they are, is quite against this project, which has the consent of the bishop since he knows that it is the wish of *all* these religious, that they will give him use of their church and support the priest who will serve them. They will sell the rest of their property at a good price. That is where I would have liked to have a foothold in order to communicate with you. See if you are in time to propose this to them and to subscribe to this work. As for us, we were refused a loan because they have themselves borrowed for this enormous acquisition. They have always been full of attention toward us. We have just received a second barrel of brown sugar and a case of china. All of it is of the greatest usefulness for us. They have promised us some rice.

---

204 This is the foundation of Grand Coteau, 6 miles southwest of Opelousas, about 150 miles from New Orleans. The Smith family came from Maryland, in 1803, and had an immense property where they cultivated fields and raised cattle. After the sudden death of her husband in 1819, Mrs. Smith wanted to accomplish the projects of her beloved husband: to finish construction of the church for Father Brassac and found two educational establishments, one for boys and the other for girls. The foundation of the girls' school would be realized the following year by the Society of the Sacred Heart. That for boys was begun by the Jesuits in 1838 and closed in 1922. Berchmans Academy, opened by the Society of the Sacred Heart in 2006, has continued that mission. Upon their arrival in Grand Coteau, the religious learned that Mrs. Smith, now a widow, intended to live with them. Employing her remarkable charm, Eugenie Aude succeeded in convincing her that this was impossible.

I have been told that the bishop, in his affection for us, wants to enlarge our property and establish a small farm. I am not impressed by this donation because it will bring about more frequent visits than ever, along the lines of the bishop's ideas, with cost for us. This causes a great deal of expense, time, and especially irregularity. I am happy because these poor priests find a little rest and healthy air in Florissant, where they can be received only by us; this makes me fulfill that part of my vocation when I said: "I will only do the priests' cooking and I will be content."

The important part of your letter was about the day students. It has already been agreed with the bishop that we will not bring any more into the house, and since here there are no poor and no social distinctions, the paying students and those who do not pay will form a single class of day students. If our health is restored and we get help, we could open it at the beginning of winter.

The scarcity of money prevents many boarders. I have no desire for great success; I see everything with greater tranquility than before, even what is the result of my failings and my inability to do what I have to do. It is a means for nourishing abjection and nothingness. Dear Mother, do not consider my happiness but the good of the house, which is the work of God; one cannot doubt it.

My respects to Fathers Varin and Perreau (they are very silent). I forget neither fathers nor mothers nor sisters; everything is seen and felt in the Heart of Jesus.

I am at your feet,

Philippine Duchesne

[On the reverse:]
To Mother
Mother Barat
Superior General of the Religious of the Sacred Heart
Hôtel de Biron
Rue de Varenne
Paris

Letter 158 **L. 1 to Mother Deshayes
mistress of novices in Paris**

SS. C. J. et M.

August 29, 1820
Rec. to St. Anthony of Padua[205]

My very dear Mother and my dear Sisters,

I would often like to be in your midst to profit from your holy recreations. I am sure that I would gain much. I would like to do nothing but listen, but you would say to me: "It is up to you who have crossed the seas to tell us stories." I am very rusty at that, and even though I would try, I would often have to be silent.

While we wait to see each other again, which will be in heaven, I hope, I have collected a few things to obtain your prayers in return.

What most pleases me is the delegation of the Osage, an Indian nation, to Bishop Dubourg. The chief came to Saint Louis to ask him to go to their country. He will go there next month with some merchants from Missouri who have promised to help in every way to see that his identity is respected among this people, somewhat as all the Portuguese merchants did for Saint Francis Xavier. The Anabaptists are trying to push ahead. Their leader has had a dozen of his henchmen sent to that country. I hope they will have no success. The bishop gave this chief a crucifix, which he received with respect and afterwards went into a store in Saint Louis. The owner wanted to know if he realized what the crucifix was, so he offered in exchange a beautiful saddle, some liquor and finally much money. The Indian refused it all saying that *he would never undo what the one who speaks of the author of life gave him*. Father de Andreis, superior of the Lazarists, who is a saint, said in a prophetic tone: "*It is as sure that I will go to the Osage as it is sure that I will go to bed this evening.*" I will let you know about the success of this voyage of the bishop, who would like very much to see the Jesuits from Georgetown established in Franklin or Booneslick in upper Missouri.

---

205 Original autograph and copy: C-VII 2) c Duchesne to RSCJ and Children, Box 4. Other copies: A-II 2) g Box 2, *Lettres intéressantes de la Société depuis 1816* N° 1, pp. 228-232; C-III 1: USA Foundation Haute Louisiane Box 1, Part A: *Lettres de la Louisiane 1818-1822*, pp. 63-69; Partial copy: Part B: *Lettres de personnes variées, 1818-1828*, pp. 134-137. Cf. Ch. Paisant, pp. 320-325.

We had for supper yesterday the two heads of the Lazarist seminary in *Bois brûlé* or *the Barrens*. They are at the same time pastors of the first church of the parish. Every Sunday there are more than 60 Communions and about twenty on Saturday, and often more men than women. There are not even 8 people in this parish who do not receive Communion every month. One doesn't see dances or cabarets that you find elsewhere. If someone finds a coat, a tunic, etc., it is hung on a tree near the church so that the owner who is looking for it will find it the most easily. Often the thing hangs there for a month and no one else touches it.

I had news from the bishop himself about the foundation of the Sisters of Charity, from M. X. near Baltimore. He directed a widow in New York who had three daughters and no fortune. She spoke to him of the frequent inspirations she had after Communion about an establishment for Christian education, and she followed the bishop to Baltimore in the hope of succeeding. One day she came to tell him: "You refuse this establishment for lack of means, but after Communion it was said to me that M. X. would give 30,000 F for an educational establishment. The bishop did not want to accept it until a long enough time had passed without the gentleman's changing his mind. They began the buildings of the convent that now contains 50 religious or novices and 60 boarders. They have taken the rules of the Sisters of Charity with a habit something like ours. A gentleman who recently saw them told me that there are some capable women there. The founder always lives with one or two of her daughters. She puts aside every year a sum big enough to help now with the building. They have established foundations in Philadelphia, New York, and Kentucky, where they are again making changes. The house in New York is very unstable, as is the existence of the bishop, since there is a division between the Irish Catholics and the others.[206]

In these dioceses and that of Boston, there are very few priests. Bishop Dubourg is the richest in personnel. He will soon have ten Lazarist priests and several brothers who work their land. A society of brother workers in Milan recruited them. There are more than forty priests in this diocese, and in Canada more than 200, and five or six

---

[206] Elizabeth Ann Bayley Seton, SC (1774-1821), from an important Episcopalian family in New York, married at the age of 19. She gave birth to five children before the death of her husband in 1803. In 1805, she converted to Catholicism and under the influence of Louis William Dubourg, then a priest of Baltimore and president of Saint Mary's College, she founded the Sisters of Charity, the first American women's congregation, which established schools and hospitals. A few years later, their sisters founded the first hospital in Saint Louis. Canonized in 1975, Elizabeth Ann Bayley Seton was the first saint born in America.

well-established convents and a good seminary. The English government protects our holy religion there; the governor and the group go to the processions.

A Methodist minister of good faith wanted to go to convert the Catholics of Canada and thought that the best way to begin would be to win the seminary. He began his mission and was himself converted to our holy religion, about which he was completely ignorant. There are more than 90 sects in the United States. There are some who do not marry, others in which one spins in the meetings until he falls into a crisis, and then the minister comes to listen to the inspired speech that he speaks.

Someone formed one of the most dangerous: a priest unhappy with the archbishop of Baltimore wrote to another Flemish priest who was unhappy with the court at Rome, to go to have himself consecrated bishop by the one in Utrecht (Jansenist), then to come to the United States where a party was gathered of whom he would be the leader, under the title: *Bishop of the Catholic and Independent Church*. The Flemish priest was horrified at the plot and revealed the correspondence, which the archbishop of Baltimore made public.

Father Anduze,[207] who will be a Priest of the Mission [Lazarists] at Christmas, spoke to me much about Father Barat and said he was 18 months at his school in Bordeaux. He has great talents and serves in the college in Saint Louis.

At Baltimore there is a holy gentleman who, to break the hold of the world where he appeared very comfortable, pulled out his own teeth to disfigure himself.

In Kentucky, there have been so many demonstrations against Catholics that they asked the priests to show their feet to see if they have horns like the one they put on devils in pictures. They confused them with that.

In Kentucky, there are three or four convents of Sisters of Charity and of Trappists. In one of those houses, they were reduced to such poverty that they had nothing to eat. One day when the sisters went barefoot in the forest to cut wood, as was their custom, a beautiful deer presented itself to them and let itself be taken. They killed it and it furnished meat for a long time.

---

207 Aristide Anduze, CM, former student of Father Barat at Bordeaux, arrived in America in 1818. Ordained priest in 1821, he was a professor in the college in Saint Louis. He then exercised his ministry in Louisiana and returned to France in 1844.

Bishop Flaget of Kentucky has lost three of his missionaries who have returned to Europe. One of them is the founder of a group of penitential sisters and is considered a saint.

A rich widow of Lower Louisiana founded a college there at 60 leagues from New Orleans and is now building a convent that will probably be occupied by the Sisters of Charity. It will be in an area where there are few children.

We have four from Prairie du Chien, a month's travel from here; it is the American location where most of the Indian chiefs come. When they come to deal with the governor of the States, they carpet the entire assembly room with the skins of otter, beaver, etc. The most able delivers a discourse that always begins in the same way: "*That the author of life created everything and made the earth for human beings who should all have a part in it.*" The conclusion asks for liquor, gunpowder, and bread. The iron works are always of great finesse, the "English irons" as they call them in France; the cast iron stoves are very ornamental and very expensive.

The pottery is painted with great variety and style. The Indians often use it for a course in sacred history, or to portray a winter evening, the traits of freemasonry, or the exploits of Bonaparte. We have his portrait on a handkerchief, on another the whole calendar, on another all the signs of the zodiac, all with explanations printed on the material.

On the feast of Saint Magdalene, we celebrated the feast of our mother. The students played the last act of the Louisiana play, which was repeated after the distribution of prizes at the request of the bishop.

The visit he made at Florissant and his next departure for the Osage made us have the prizes early. The students will return on September 1. Since several students also had to leave, our numbers would have been too reduced for a later distribution.

On the feast of Saint Magdalene, Mother Octavie added to the play the following verses, which she had me recite:

[Translator's note: The following verses are in rhymed couplets in French. The first stanza is translated in verse to convey the impression.]

> If from our eyes flows forth a tear
> At remembrance of a mother most dear,
> Never believe that on our part
> Wild regret could tear our heart.
> No, our hearts with the same flame burn
> And the same zeal, to which they turn.

Of that divine work, however unworthy instruments,
We are the children of the dear Society.
Are you still remembered, O Reverend Mother?

Under the wings of our guardian angel Regis,
From the day when we left our beloved shores,
Without casting upon them our painful regrets.
Our hearts were already on the distant shore,
That would replace the banks of the Seine.
The right hand of the Lord deflected the dangers.
The Star of the Sea guided the ferrymen,
And the ship as it glided along the water
Seemed to follow the hand of the divine guide.

Regis took care of his little flock,
And we finally arrived at our desired land.
What was our joy! Your heart, O Mother,
Thanked our God for a successful voyage.

"So it is here, Lord," you say with love,
"That you would prepare for me a happy dwelling.
It is upon this dry land that you have cast me
Since my tender childhood, night and day, by your earnest wishes.
You heard, my God, the desire of my heart,
And in this single wish, I have found my happiness.
How often in a pious reverie
Have I not thought I could gain the palm of martyrdom.
No, it is not a dream, it is real,
The divine spirit always tells the truth.
For the glorious martyrdom that I believe awaits me,
I find another more hidden, but that cannot be brushed away.
In these wild forests I find only beauty,
For I see *the wood of the Cross* everywhere.
O precious Cross, my life companion!
At your feet I am ever nourished by my tears!"

This is your wish. Ah! It is ours, too,
Since the head with the members is tenderly united.

Draw near, children, come on this beautiful day,
Another Madeleine deserves your love,
In the heart of our God. In this unique center,
America is France and France is America.

Couplet:
Although I always remember
The beloved things of our France,
I would with pleasure suffer
Their absence,
If I can glorify my God in this place.

Letter 159   L. 1 to Mother Desmarquest, superior of the house in Beauvais

Florissant, September 26, 1820[208]

A letter from our reverend mother tells me of the shipment of a piano, to the purchase of which you willingly contributed. We all want to thank you and tell you that this instrument, seemingly a frivolous item, will contribute indirectly to the glory of God by attracting to religious instruction, by the lure of a gracious art, many people who would disdain our services if they were only spiritual.

One must come to this country to see in the children all the unhappy effects of the three concupiscences in the rough. We expect to find innocence, and we see only defects with no covering to disguise them. But at the same time, that they have no idea of what education is, God permits that they begin to feel the cost; and we do not despair of being able to graft the cultivated olive branch onto the wild one.[209] The children here generally have good memory and intelligence, and here as elsewhere, grace chooses whom it will favor. Those we have left at Saint Charles for the most part long to be with us; but for all of them, that time is delayed by various complications of age and other obstacles that God permits for our mutual testing.

I hope that Mother Deshayes will willingly receive here my respect and gratitude. I recommend our efforts to her prayers and those of

---

208 Copy: A-II 2) g Box 2, *Lettres intéressantes concernant la Société des Dames du Sacré-Cœur de Jésus depuis 1816 N° 1*, p. 195; C-III 1: *USA Foundation Haute Louisiane*, Box 3, *Lettres de la Louisiane II,* pp.203-205.
209   Rom 11:17, 24.

Mother de la Marche and of all my sisters whom I know and those I do not know, but whom the Sacred Heart of Jesus encloses with me in the same love for the Society.

I am in him yours devotedly,

Philippine

Letter 160   L. 34 to Mother Barat

SS. C. J. et M.

No. 16
[October 30, 1820][210]
Rec. to Saint Anthony of Padua

Dear Reverend Mother,

I have never had such need of your letters and never have had to wait so long. At last, we have received the packet of letters entrusted to Mr. de Menou; we are consoled by yours, those of dear Father Varin, those of my sisters, and the hope that they will come. My preceding letters must have disquieted you about the health of Mothers Octavie and Eugenie; they will have made you feel the need for reinforcements, and this one will prove the same. After those two generous sick ones were delivered from all their bleedings and blistering, I myself fell ill; and with convalescence, it lasted two months. I received Holy Viaticum and was never so close to seeing God. After so many times of burning desire to be with him, at the moment when I could hope for it, I felt the emptiness of my accomplishments, the strictness of God's judgment, and the hardness of my heart.

My illness was erysipelas, which affected my whole body and was accompanied by fever, which, when it was gone, turned into a gastric infection. Since my head was so painful, the bishop, who was good enough to come with his physician, made me have another three blisterings and two mustard poultices. After that, I was no longer delirious, nor did I take any more *mercury*, which is much used in American medicine, and of which I have felt the bad effects: mouth trouble, continual salivation, weakness in my legs and my *head*, to such an extent that

---

210 Original autograph, C-VII 2) c Duchesne to Barat, Box 2. Postmark: Paris, March 18, 1821. Copies: J. de Charry, II 1, L. 131, pp. 322-336; Hogg, pp. 218-228; Ch. Paisant, pp. 325-332.

for a long time I was operating on the idea that I was two people: if one dies, I said, the other will still remain. And I searched for that other one. Before finishing with me, I must make you admire Providence. A young American physician treated me with all the tenderness of a son for his mother, finding in me a resemblance to her. He came up to four times in one morning and wanted nothing for his visits.

I had hardly recovered my strength when Mother Octavie fell with her beautiful black velvet shoes from France that are very *slippery* underneath. She has broken a bone in her leg and is therefore confined to bed for thirty or forty days. She is only at the seventh day and yesterday was delirious with fever. She is better today but is already tired of being in bed.

Before I finish the recital of illness, please tell us what Mr. Laënnec[211] thinks about *mercury*. Here it is regarded as the best cure for fever, and necessary against *yellow fever,* but it is used for nearly all illnesses. I have been so ill with it that I told the bishop that the remedy was worse than the illness and that I would come to an understanding with our doctors in the future that they would never use it for us. He thought that was a good idea.

The bishop, the whole diocese, and we in particular have had a great loss in the person of Father de Andreis, provincial of the Lazarists, first vicar general, of great sanctity and talents for ministry, with prodigious learning. A putrid fever carried him off just as I was beginning to get better. All Saint Louis, even the Protestants and the Jews, followed his coffin and regretted his loss. Several miracles have already been attributed to him. We have inherited his *Imitation* [*of Jesus Christ*] and other precious relics that he always carried with him. Father Richard, our first confessor, replaces him with regard to holiness and as vicar general; but he has not been able to learn English and does not have as much learning. I am happy that the Missouri no longer separates him from us;[212] he will be useful for retreats and he loves us very much.

Father Rosati is now head of the Lazarists. He has sent us a postulant [Mary Layton] from the Barrens and proposes to send another. She is certainly the best we have had so far, but she can be only a coadjutrix sister. The bishop has agreed. The other one has more education. But how difficult it is to make people understand religious life when their language is different and they have no idea of it, whose customs with regard to food and clothing are completely different. These postulants

---

211 The famous Doctor R. Laënnec (1781-1826) who had cared for Octavie in Paris.
212 Father Richard was until then pastor in Saint Charles; now in Saint Louis, the Missouri River no longer separated him from Florissant.

arrive with nothing for support or trousseau: one sheet, two pairs of stockings, two chemises, one handkerchief, with eight or ten dresses as light as gauze; this is usual here. Little by little, we diminish our trousseaux to help them. That does nothing for us if they leave, but we still have the merit of charity. We must be Providence for them as God is for us.

We are living, but always down to our last *sou*. Money is becoming scarcer every day. Children are withdrawn or they do not pay…you know the burden of debts. You will have received one letter, or two, asking the house at Niort to acquit us of our debt to the Abbot of La Trappe, 1000 F that one of his religious advanced to us here, to enable us to buy a mare and cart, etc., which are very necessary for us. There has been such a drought that our well and the two streams that surround us and have flooded us are now dry. We send our cart for water for drinking and for the kitchen, and it is only at a league from here that we could find water for the students to wash, and it is very costly. If I had the last 1000 F from Niort, I could pay my debt to the merchant who received us; we have always borrowed from the fees of his daughters, but he has paid so far in advance that we must necessarily settle this account once and for all. Then, with no building, we will resume with his daughters' fees.

Our children are very good, to the number of about 20. Some parents are also very good, others not very prompt with their payments.

As my brother wished to give me the sum of 6 or 700 pounds, I have asked him to pay them also to Father Abbot by way of Mr. Rusand, but this is quite apart from the other 1000 F. The certificates of annuity that I was sending him have been returned to me from New Orleans as not legitimated. Since then I have not been able to get others, since our justice of the peace was very ill, then I was ill, and now he is dead without being replaced. Everything is so impeded in such a small place, especially since we do not go out.

I have shared with the two mothers your disappointment that we will not be in Saint Louis; but all three of us are of the opinion that Florissant will be better: it is less hot in summer, there are fewer illnesses, there are no mosquitoes, and there are not as many visits, especially since we have declared firmly that the parents must have houses to eat in, and that we would rather close the boarding school than become an inn with continual distractions. Everything has been settled for our tranquility. We offer nothing except to the bishop and other priests who come to eat with us and stay at the parish. In Saint Louis, they will know everything that happens with us, and we will be the talk of the town.

For a hurt finger, they withdraw the children, and it becomes harder for them to adjust. Even *holy* visits can be a problem. Nevertheless, the bishop seems to want a day school of our Society in Saint Louis; but I redirect his attention toward New Orleans, reminding him of the poverty of the countryside, the lack of even day students, and the impossibility of being able to sustain a novitiate that an establishment in a city could help. Father Martial already has in Lower Louisiana 40 well-selected children and here in the college, 18 who give him plenty of worry.

The bishop, who is going to visit his whole diocese and even attempt to be received in New Orleans,[213] agrees with all my ideas for New Orleans, but you realize that it will cost you religious. If you have seen Father Inglesi, he will have spoken to you about our needs. We cannot count on having many houses here for quite a few years; if we were to have land, we would have to build, and it is impossible to have the land cultivated. The cost would take away all the profit from the harvest. The shortest day's work costs 5 F and wheat costs 50 or 60 *sols* per bushel; corn at 25 or 30 *sols*, potatoes at 50 *sols*. A bushel is twice a quart[214] in Grenoble. We cannot sustain our Society in this country without the income from the boarding school, and there will always be few here because of the small population, lack of money, and the many religions: there are more than 40 in the United States. If we were in a position to have day students, we would have to think about teachers.

As for Indian girls, God's time has not yet come. The Jesuits will have to do it first. The bishop is asking for them, but he does not have them. We are going to dismiss the daughter of an Indian whom we have. She has no intelligence except for evil, and she is lazy and stupid. In a year and a half, she does not know the alphabet or her prayers or the catechism. In church, she knows only how to tear paper or step on our trains[215] when we pass. She behaves like an animal; we cannot do anything with her.

Another establishment close by, for which I thought the bishop would get religious, is at Opelousas. A rich lady [Mrs. Smith] has built a church there and a little college, and she is keeping funds for a convent for girls. She will pay for the trip and would join them. In the case that she did not fit, the bishop would take the responsibility to tell her.

213 After the expulsion of two schismatic priests from New Orleans, Fathers Martial, Moni, and Portier were preparing for the arrival of Bishop Dubourg, who lived there in 1823, when the divisions were overcome.
214 The word "*quartaut*" that Philippine uses is Burgundian patois that designates a small barrel of 57 liters, a quarter of a cask of wine.
215 Trains on choir mantles. They were eliminated in 1836.

Lately he has been very relaxed with us. He says that no one loves us as much as he does. He has asked me whether I have spoken to you about this lady. He says that he would rather have us there than any others, and that though it is truly in the country, it has a rich harvest of sugar. These three establishments: the one here, New Orleans, and Opelousas would be spread through the whole length of Louisiana. May God give us the means to work for his glory. Sister Lucile [Mathevon] could be superior of one house, Sister Eugenie of another. As for me, you will put me where you wish. I have no other desire than to do the will of God, and my illness has put me deeper into indifference. The bishop has ordered me to look after myself, and I do so simply. This is my first letter today. I have four meals and stay in bed until seven o'clock, etc.

Mother Eugenie has served me with a zeal, a care, an attention that cannot be described, and, forgetting herself, she has completely recovered her health. But as soon as I was better, she no longer looked after the house *herself.* Mother Octavie has a *laisser faire* attitude; the pallor, the sadness, the moods have begun again. Sometimes I have read a letter she has written to you, and I was not happy with it; sometimes she knows that I am unhappy, etc. She has a distinguished manner, but she is made to govern alone. Too young for New Orleans, she would do perfectly in Opelousas. She would leave me with a large empty hole, especially for the work with the students, but I should put everything before your eyes. There was a storm the first day that I wanted to go to Mass. Mother Octavie was afraid of it; the sisters hardly liked it, and she suffered on account of their bad manners. To all our miseries is joined the aging of Sister Marguerite who is weakening, especially since she had a fever for some days. Sister Catherine keeps up better. She is also better since your letter and the change in the bishop's attitude toward her. What joy you have given to your poor daughters, Reverend Mother, by the hope of seeing three new sisters. Please send them to us quickly.

The school building is finished by means of 1000 F that we borrowed and that we will eventually reimburse. The residents have not kept their promises. We could open the school with one extra [religious], because the distance from the houses does not allow us to have the children for more than a few hours each day. They never have needlework or thread, thimble, needle, etc. so that once the prayers and lessons have been said and the catechism done, it is best to send them home, otherwise they become restless and talkative.

We have a special need for the Irish religious [Anna Murphy, called Xavier]. But if she knows only Irish, that is not English. We have many

Irish in this country whom the Americans, who speak English, cannot understand. You can get some idea of their sensitive ear and the difficulty of pronunciation. We have only Mother Octavie for this instruction, and she is far from what should be. Mother Eugenie is beginning to understand and speak; she is the one who forms the postulant [Mary Layton]. She is truly good at this, and she knows how to keep up respect. In spite of the goodness of Mother Octavie, most of the students give their confidence to Mother Eugenie, and God blesses her efforts. I think God permits all the work of her imagination, which often makes her serious and disagreeable, in order to test her and to give her the experience of different states of soul. Her little class benefits from her care.

I had trouble beginning this letter, and here I am at the eighth page with no fatigue, only with the desire to keep going. However, what my strength would allow, time takes away from me. Our brick house has holes, so before the great cold, it has been necessary to *plaster*, as they say here, but in France we say *rough cast,* for walls that are incomplete, since we cannot finish everything. Mother Octavie, who is in bed, has left me part of her class with mine, and spending time in bed shortens my day. So I must conclude and even deprive myself of answering several letters. My sisters and your children who are so good will excuse a convalescent. Mother Deshayes has a letter from me that will cross with hers.

I am convinced that our house will not be finished without having cost 50,000 F.

Taking advantage of your goodness in asking us to tell you our needs, I go to the most pressing: what is necessary for the formation of our young people. We have already received: *Employments,* the *Imitation,* "*Think Well about It,*" the *Spiritual Combat,* the *Devout Life,* a good *Catechism, The Soul Raised to God,* and the *Historical Catechism,*[216] but not a good *Bible History* or an abridgement of the Old and New Testaments. They cannot be found here. There is a single copy of Rodriguez on *Christian Perfection* at the seminary, but they will not part with it. So there are two books that we need badly. We have all we need of books of French devotion, even several duplicates, but none for the children. Nor do we have an Ancient History or Roman History or American History. The old Bible Histories given by the students [of France] and the old historical catechisms are all worn out. Our children

---

216 *The Holy Daily Employments of a Good Religious,* 1688; the *Imitation of Jesus Christ* by Thomas A. Kempis (15th c.); the "Think Well about It": *Little Essay on Final Ends,* Besançon, 1726; *The Spiritual Combat* by Lorenzo Scupoli, 1549; *Introduction to the Devout Life* by Saint Francis de Sales, 1604; the *Treatise on Christian Perfection* by P. Alfonso Rodriguez, SJ, 1609.

have to borrow everything; otherwise they would have *nothing* for study, often not even pens or paper.

You will be pleased to know that Father Delacroix, a Flemish priest now our confessor, suits us perfectly. He is devout, zealous, interested in our work, and has the candor of a child. Finally, he is a man of peace. He speaks English and French, which is very useful for the Americans to whom he gives instruction every week. Since he is pastor of the parish, we have only to give him his food, and we no longer have to give him what would have been expected in money. He says his Mass twice a week in the parish, and we have him the other five days. This will be every day when the parish church is rebuilt on land that belongs to the bishop adjoining our house. Our chapel will become, as at Grenoble, a side chapel looking into the sanctuary, and we will benefit from all the services. This will be especially helpful when there is a scarcity of priests.

I would have regretted dying before raising an oratory to the Sacred Heart in this county. I was thinking about doing a chapel in his honor in the church, opposite our side chapel. I talked to the bishop about it, and he decided that the church of Florissant would be dedicated to the Sacred Heart, that Saint Ferdinand would be second patron of the church, that the chapel of the Blessed Virgin would be opposite our chapel, and that the one of Saint Francis Regis, which I also asked for, would be in a corner of our chapel. In the opposite corner, we will find a fitting place for all our beautiful relics: there are already four of the Holy Cross and two of the Holy Thorns, etc. We will be very devout there, and it will be our fault if we are not fervent.

The death of our dear Sisters Laloux and de Sylguy[217] caused us great affliction and will make more difficult the help that we are asking, but you will make an effort for your poor Louisiana that extends its arms but cannot reach fathers, mothers, or sisters. When I was sick, they were already saying in Saint Louis: "What is going to happen to this establishment?" If Mother Octavie were not here, we would have to abandon the Americans.

Receive, dear Mother, the expression of my deep respect and my eternal devotedness. Your unworthy daughter,

Philippine Duchesne

October 30, 1820

---

217 Catherine (Marie Josephine) Laloux, RSCJ, died age 36, two years after profession on April 5, 1820, in Beauvais. Victoire de Sylguy, RSCJ, entered in Paris and died at the age of 23 on April 2, 1820, at Quimper.

[On the reverse:]
To Mother
Mother Barat
Rue des Postes N° 40
Paris

Letter 161   **L. 11 to Mother Maillucheau**

SS. C. J. et M.

Recommended to St. Anthony of Padua
November 30, 1820[218]

My very dear Mother,

I wrote a long letter to our mother in the month of October, and later at the bishop's departure for New Orleans. I cannot satisfy my heart's desire to have an intimate conversation with you, first because of weakness from an illness and also because of the multiplication of work, since so many things were delayed because of my illness and Mother Octavie's fractured leg that left her thirty days in bed. Besides, I know that they send you from Paris all the details that can interest you. I will just assure you, to keep you from worrying, that the health of all of us is now normal except for Mother Eugenie who, although she is better than in the spring, is not yet really well; but she has always been like this, and it is difficult to take care of her.

We are going to try to begin a day school. We have been promised that they will build the house at village expense, but it has only been begun and we will owe 1500 F. But this is an expense done with pleasure; we have found a way to borrow this amount.

We renewed our vows on the 21st and had the consolation to all be at the ceremony. Mother Octavie was out of bed just for the solemnity. The next day, feast of Saint Cecilia, our students, who are naturally gifted for singing, sang the Holy Mass, and very well. We also left the altar decorated from the vigil and took advantage of the solemnity to give more adornment to the first taking of the habit in Upper Louisiana since the beginning of the world, and to see there a chosen one of the Sacred Heart besides. This happy person is Mary Layton. She is from

---

218   Original autograph, C-VII 2) c Duchesne to RSCJ and Children, Box 4.

the parish, which can be seen here as the early church. She is 21 years old and is received as a coadjutrix.

We are lacking the consolations that come with an abundance of resources. The bishop, who usually comes to see us rather often, is gone all winter to visit his diocese. Father de Andreis, superior of the Lazarists, has died a death as saintly as he lived; and Father Richard, our first confessor whom we saw come closer to us when he went to Saint Louis, is destined as confessor to the Ursulines. If we return to New Orleans, we would have the great happiness of finding him again, and he is another saint, just right for us. Our pastor is now on mission in the Upper Mississippi; he went alone. During his absence, we have to make another relationship, one that is preparing us a postulant.

Please tell my brother that my documents are leaving for Washington (that is where they should be retrieved), and please give news of me to my sisters. According to the last letter from Sister Josephine [de Coriolis], it *seemed* that Aloysia was more ill. We must imitate her in her resignation, but it costs me much, and I would like to see her here. I will never make myself understood; I am too old. Mother Octavie is the most advanced in English, and Mother Eugenie is far enough along to serve as director of our postulant and to give [religious] instruction to the Americans who do not understand French, while I take charge of the French. That is still the greater number, but it is diminishing while the other grows.

Ask God to send us vocations here, because if we wait for them from France, the dangers and cost of the voyage and the difficulties of adjustment will always leave us with a very small number.

I commend myself with great affection to all my mothers and sisters. Those here join with me. My respects to Fathers Rambaud, Dumolard, Rivet, and d'Hyères, even more to the bishop if you see him. I ask for prayers, for we have great need of them. I ask my nieces to send my regards to the Religious of the Visitation at Romans. A very affectionate greeting to Aloysia and dear Louise [de Vidaud].

I am all yours *in Corde Jesu*,

Philippine

[On the reverse:]
To Mother
Mother Therese Maillucheau
Superior of Sainte-Marie d'En-Haut
Grenoble

Letter 162 L. 3 to the students of Sainte-Marie d'En-Haut[219]

[1820]

Notes on some of the nations of North America, mainly on the Algonquins

These peoples call themselves *Children of Heaven* and call us *Children of the Earth*. Here is the fable that tells of their origin.

The one whom they recognize as God made those of us from beyond the sea children of the earth and their fathers, children of heaven. Here is how they fell to earth: "A young man and a young woman wanted to get married. As they were at some distance from their parents, they did not consult them. They walked along on the sky, which is made of glass that is less thick in some places. It happened that they came to a weak spot; the sky cracked and they both fell to earth. Not seeing any possible means of getting back up to heaven, they married and from them came all these Indian peoples. But one of their prophets announced that when some bearded men came into their country, they would become their servants."

These bearded men were the Europeans. The Indians had no beards themselves; they continually pull out their hair; the men keep only a little tuft because in warfare it is the practice to bring back the scalp of one's victim. Having only a little tuft, they suffer less when they are scalped, for the flesh must adhere to the hair. The women keep their hair arranged in such a way as to form a part on the head, which they paint red as well as their cheeks, their eyebrows and eyelids. For clothing they wear only a skirt above the knee and a man's shirt buckled. As it is considered very immodest to have bare legs, they wear red leggings; they like bracelets, earrings and nose rings. The men wear only a belt and voluminous trousers in the woods, but as it is not suitable to come into the village wearing the trousers, they put them over their arms, as men here might do with a hat. Their clothing consists of tattoos on their bodies of birds and animals, and when they go to church or some sort of ceremony, their blankets envelop them completely. Ordinarily they have only a baptismal name and give themselves surnames of animals; if someone is a fast runner, he is called the hare; if another is a good hunter, he is the wolf and so on.

The Algonquin language is soft and pleasant; but it is missing some words, for example, they cannot say: *there are three persons in God*, but they express the mystery of the Trinity by saying: They are three in one.

219 C-VII 2-c) Duchesne Writings History of Society, Box 1.

The life of the Indians is quite similar to that of animals. The French have built several villages for them, but they never repair the houses; if the stairs or the roof fall down or the floor has holes, they make no repairs. They do not even maintain the property. Even in the house of the king himself, the children's waste is left, like the dogs', in all the corners of the house; they stay there for only three months; the other nine months they hunt in the woods. They do that from August to May.

There are 400,000 Catholics in the country, counting both Indians and Europeans, 30,000 Protestants, mostly English. When they tell the Indians that there are only three sacraments, they answer: "Look at these English; they don't know their religion; the French have told us that there are seven! The bishop, the head of the Church, has assured us of this fact. If the English come to tell us the contrary, we will mistreat them."

But the English, far from opposing the priests, take pride in treating them well and favor them in everything. They esteem the priests more than their own ministers; the Sulpicians have a seminary in Montreal; and on the other side of their church, there is a community of nuns. There are six different orders in Canada:[220] the Ursulines of Mother Marie of the Incarnation, Carmelites, Hospitallers of St. Augustine,[221] Sisters of Charity, Religious of Notre Dame of Peter Fourier[222] and of Notre Dame of Mme de Lestonnac[223] or Jesuitesses. But the Indians are not inclined to religious life and do not remain virgins. In one community, they accepted a young girl who made her vows; after she had made them and had developed, the blood began to boil in her veins, making a quiet life unbearable; she could not be managed, especially in springtime. They had to confine her on an island in the river where she ran about like a

---

220 In France, the Council of Trent and the Counter-Reformation were at the origin of a great missionary movement. In 1625, the Jesuits were established in Canada; they founded or invited religious congregations of women to educate young girls and to care for the sick.
221 In 1639, the Augustinian Hospitallers of Mercy from Dieppe (France) founded the Hôtel-Dieu of Québec, the first hospital in America. Catherine Simon de Longpré (1632-1668), in religion Marie-Catherine de Saint-Augustin, joined them in 1647. She is considered a co-founder of the Church in Canada.
222 In 1597, Alix Le Clerc (1576-1622) founded with Saint Peter Fourier (1565-1640) the Congrégation Notre-Dame (Canonesses of Saint Augustine) in Lorraine, France, for the education of girls. Peter Fourier, trained at the Jesuit university of Pont-à-Mousson, drafted the plan of studies based on the teaching method of the Jesuits. Father Nicolas Loriquet, SJ, was inspired by it in composing the plan of the Society of the Sacred Heart in 1804. Cf. M.-F. Carreel, *Sophie Barat, Un Projet éducatif pour aujourd'hui*, Paris, Ed. Don Bosco, 2003, pp. 80 ff.
223 Jeanne de Lestonnac (1556-1640), born in Bordeaux of a Catholic father and a Calvinist mother, a niece of the philosopher Montaigne, married Gaston de Montferrant, Baron de Landiras. Having been widowed, she brought up her five children and, in 1607, founded the Company of Mary-Notre-Dame for the education of girls; her educational project was inspired by the *Ratio studiorum* of the Jesuits. She was canonized in 1949.

rabbit and killed all the rats and mice that she found. The religious habit exhausted her; one day before prayer, she got the idea to cut it off just above the knee and came into the church that way. The superior was not able to make her understand that this was not good, and from that time on, they have not accepted any Indians. It seems that their nature demands that they run about in the woods as their ancestors have been doing for 2,000 years.

When it is very cold, they build large open cabins out of tree branches; they have an opening in the roof to allow the smoke from the fire in the middle of the cabin to escape; the ground is covered with pine and fir branches on which they all sleep, but as they feel cold on one side and the heat from the fire on the other, they turn like roasts on spit, and they are so accustomed to it that they turn over even in their sleep. As for what they eat, they do nothing; when they have nothing left, they go hunting and kill a bear, but they don't bring it back. The women with their children go to get the animal in a sled, cut it up and cook it. The food of the smallest children is their mother's milk; after that, they are given tree bark to suck, then they eat meat. They are not acquainted with bread; in great need they make a little baked dough and eat it like a nut to sustain life.

That is the Indians' life from birth: they come into the world hardly causing their mother any pain; she does not go to bed at all. And here is a little story: a missionary was going down the river in a little boat with an Indian and his wife; he was reciting his breviary. Suddenly the Indian said to the father, "Let's stop here for a moment." They got out of the boat, and the priest continued saying his breviary. After half an hour all three got back in the boat. A few minutes later the priest heard a baby cry, he said, "But I didn't see any baby." The Indian informed him that at the moment they had left the boat the wife gave birth. She had wrapped it like a little kitten in a corner of her blanket and continued the journey. Once arrived at the village, she took all the baggage out of the boat, helped to bring it ashore and went to the church saying to the priest, "Here is my baby; baptize it."

These poor women love their children very much; and when they have them baptized, the priest cannot give them any greater pleasure than to say that they are pretty, even better if he kisses them. But as they are dirtier than a dog that has wallowed in the mire, it is really disgusting. One missionary was kissing only the child's eye; its mother noticed this repugnance and spit on the child's face to wash it.

Children run about in the woods with their parents as soon as they can; they are carried if they cannot walk; but after three months sojourn in the village all leave in a very light birch bark boat. Everyone gets in: father, mother, children, the dog, the cat and a little bit of flour. If someone in the band dies during the nine months, the body is put on the top of tree so that it will not be eaten by animals; coming back they enclose the body in wood, load it onto the boat; they sit down and eat on top of it, then take it to the church and tell the priest: "Here is So-and-so who has died." The priest buries it. If it is too badly decayed upon return, it is buried, and the next year they come back to collect the bones.

When a girl is fourteen or fifteen years old, her mother without her knowledge, says to the father, "Our daughter is of an age to marry. To whom shall we give her? So-and-so has a son, let's give her to him." The boy's father consents; the two young people are taken to the church and they marry, often never having seen each other. Once it was announced at high Mass that Mathias was to marry Catherine; but unfortunately, there was another Mathias in the village; people told him: "You are going to get married tomorrow." "I know nothing about it." "But you were named." Just in case, this Mathias went to the church and found himself on his knees in front of the priest; two Mathias and only one Catherine. The priest was embarrassed; he investigated and told one of the Mathias to withdraw. He went home as tranquilly as he had come.

These Algonquins learn to read or to write in eight or ten days; but they never read fluently, only by syllables; they do not have enough ambition to perfect their skill. The women have superb voices and learn the most difficult of our melodies in several parts, one after the other in quick succession; they have to sing a great deal because all the prayers and the catechism are sung. When they are singing, they leave a small opening for the mouth in the blanket in which they are wrapped.

The Algonquins, like the Illinois, are very gentle. The Iroquois are wicked and through wars are reduced to a few hundred. The greatest defect of these peoples is a passion for drink, especially rum; when they are drunk, they are out of control.

The king also goes around naked or with a blanket and lives as simply as the others. Here is a description of a wedding banquet for a prince. Beef, mutton, pork, flour are all put in huge cauldrons. When everything is cooked, the cauldrons are carried into an immense hall; all the guests crowd around the cauldrons, the king, the princes and a missionary at one end of the room. A speech on temperance is delivered; the priest is asked to bless the food so that it does not make anyone sick; then everyone takes his portion: dogs, children, women, men. The meal lasts from nine in the morning until one o'clock. The poor children can hardly move; and one missionary, as he was leaving, was astonished to see them lying on the floor and their mothers rubbing their stomachs to aid digestion.

One day the missionary went to the king's house and saw the queen making crêpes *(massepains)*. As he wanted to be courteous, he said to the king, "The queen makes crêpes very well." The king, pleased with the compliment, answered, "I will have you eat some." Later there were three missionaries at table with an Englishman; there was a knock at the door, and as no one opened, the king announced himself. Then he was received courteously; he opened his blanket, took three crêpes from under his dirty, naked arm, and threw them on the table saying, "Here you are, eat." The missionary would rather have vomited than have eaten them, but in order not to displease the king, he pulled out from the middle of the stack the crêpe that had not touched the skin; he cut it in four pieces and each one ate a portion. The king drank a glass of wine and withdrew with his entourage, which he had left at the door.

As three Englishmen wanted to see the queen, the missionary offered to introduce them to her. She answered, "It doesn't please me, but let them come." She was seated on her bed wrapped in her blanket; the Englishmen told the missionary to ask her some questions; she answered, "They are very curious." Then she had them leave suddenly because she had noticed that one of them was looking rather indecently at her lady in waiting, for in this nation the women are very modest. The people are also quite indifferent to life; the sick are placed at the door, and when they see that they are going to heaven, those who have faith rejoice and say to the priest, "I am going to be put outdoors; I will soon go the author of life. I am very happy." They are placed in a cabin made of branches with a hole beside the mat on which they lie; they are pulled over onto the hole when necessary. Then the hole is covered with bark. To hear the dying person's confession, the missionary must lie down beside him, sometimes on top of the hole. When he brings the Blessed Sacrament into these poor cabins, he is preceded by a sister who puts some decent clothing on the patient. The priest carries his sick call set in a box like a small desk with everything needed. The Indians do not want to go to the hospital and get out of bed quickly and lie down on the ground. They do not mourn the dead. One father said to another, "Your boy is going to die; tell him to say hello to mine; he is in paradise because he was very good."

When they go to confession, the priest has to arm himself with patience in order to listen to all they have done in the past nine months of absence. "I left on such and such a day; the sun was at this angle; I put my boat in the water and with my wife, my children, my dog, and my provisions." The wife says "My husband has drunk rum; he is quite tipsy, etc." But at the same time that much time is lost in listening to their story, it is consoling to see how innocent they are. Sometimes in this confession of nine months, the priest cannot find even one venial sin. He says to the wife, "Were you impatient when your husband was drunk?" "How would I have done that? I would have displeased the author of life whom I had just received and whom I was guarding with my hand on my heart." "Were you angry when you hadn't enough to eat?" "The author of life remained without eating for forty days; the longest I was without food was six days; I have not suffered as much as he." It is often the same story. These poor women with nothing to eat sing their hymns all day long and make their children sing in order to forget the hunger that is gnawing at them.

This is how they pray in the church during the three months sojourn in the village: They converse with all the saints whose pictures they see in the church. There are many beautiful pictures to instruct them by looking at them. To the Infant Jesus: "How beautiful you are and how kind to have left heaven to come be with us." To Jesus suffering: "It must have cost you greatly when they preferred Barabbas to you; you said nothing, and I, the other day, was angry about an insult." "Ah! These wicked scoundrels, how they have treated you! Would that some Algonquins had been there, they would have defended you." To the Blessed Virgin: "You are very happy to have been the mother of the author of life; I would have liked that also. What have you done to deserve that? Nothing, but the author of life chose you because he wished to."

On the feast of the Assumption, a beautiful silver statue of the Blessed Virgin is carried in a celebrated procession. One of the princes who was to carry it wanted to appear handsome. He bought a trimmed jacket from an Englishman, and a beautiful pair of silk stockings; he was all decked out to carry the Blessed Virgin. The only thing lacking was a pair of trousers over his shirt.

When they return from the hunt, they bring skins that they sell at a high price for sugar, etc. They keep their money beside them in a bag of bark. The country people who know they have some arrive with a leg of lamb and a dish of strawberries. The Indian takes it and tosses the farmer a *piastre* worth $5; the farmer takes advantage of the naiveté of the Indian and says, "That is not enough." The Indian is not happy! But he throws another *piastre* and before long has emptied his purse. When there is nothing left, he goes elsewhere to ask for food.

There are missionaries 1,200 leagues beyond Montreal; there are some in the Rocky Mountains more than 400 leagues away in a terrible place. There is proof that soon the faith will have been preached everywhere, even among people at the farthest distance in the North: one of their chiefs was found wearing an ornament around his neck; it was the paten from a chalice taken from a missionary who had been killed.

Bishop Flaget, a Sulpician, the bishop of Kentucky, had his cathedral dedicated [in 1819] and the local authorities, dependent on the United States took part in the ceremony.

The bishop of Georgetown has Sulpicians and Visitandines in his diocese.

We have learned recently of the martyrdom of the last French bishop in China;[224] it is an irreparable loss.

[On the envelope, numbered No. 29]
To the young ladies of the boarding school
of Sainte-Marie

Letter 163   **L. 35 to Mother Barat**

SS. C. J. et M.

No. 20
Saint Ferdinand, February 18, 1821[225]
Rec. to St. Anthony of Padua

Dear Reverend Mother,

I have been deprived of news from you for a long time; the ice on the Mississippi has kept back the steamboats on the river during the winter. At last, a boat has arrived because of the thaw and has brought me several packets of letters, several of which are 19 months old, others from April, May, and most recently August. More than a month ago, I had one in September from Father Barat, our dear protector.[226] He has

---

224 Jean François-Régis Clet, CM (1748-1820), martyr, born in Grenoble, was imprisoned, tortured, and executed on February 18, 1820, at Ou-Tchang-Fou, China. He was canonized October 1, 2000.
225 Original autograph, C-VII 2) c Duchesne to Barat, Box 2. Cf. J. de Charry, II 1, L. 133, pp. 339-349; Hogg, pp. 229-236; Ch. Paisant, pp. 340-343.
226 Father Barat announced the sending of this sum on May 15, 1820, hoping that it would arrive before winter. Philippine received it only on March 1, 1821: "Letters from France and receipt of 5,710 F that we paid to Mr. Mullanphy, toward our debt [of 10,000 F]" (JSA).

sent me the triplicate of the bill of exchange of 571 *gourdes* (or 5710 F), which I promptly paid to the one to whom we owe 10,000 F and who, they say, has his eyes on our house, since he relied on the mortgage and the extreme difficulties for persons like us to obtain any money. I would rather reject this thought as dishonorable to him and to the bounty of God, whose Providence has been shown to us over and over again.

Our father [Bishop Dubourg] no longer gives us difficulty about the two ranks of religious: the first one to be received [Mary Layton] is a coadjutrix. Of three postulants, there will still be one more if she perseveres.

Tomorrow the first stone will be laid of the bishop's church adjoining ours, and it will serve the parish. It will be dedicated to the Sacred Heart, and on the façade will be this inscription: *et erit Cor meum tibi* [my Heart will be with you]. It will also be consecrated to Saint Ferdinand, patron of the parish, and to Saint Regis, our patron. We are not able to contribute to this building because we have debts. It will be paid for by subscription and will belong to the bishop, who will leave it in our care. Our pastor is full of confidence for its success.[227]

The day school is finished at our expense and paid for. When everything was ready, no one came, giving the bad roads and the cold as the reason. It will be all right in the spring. By then I hope we will have two novices who can do an American class. Mother Octavie does the one in the boarding school, but it is so impossible for a French woman to pronounce English well that she has to have help from an older English-speaking boarder, and sometimes the Americans do not understand her because of bad pronunciation. Nevertheless, she is the phoenix of our group; it is she of whom people speak, it is she whom they want, it is she who pleases everyone and whom it would be good to have as leader, if her great goodness did not make it almost impossible for her to be firm. Besides, this country is full of suspicions. She has such a lovely face and her speech is so pleasant that I fear that she is too attractive to some persons: a young physician, especially one not married, and a young confessor, both of interesting appearance. It makes me want Sister Lucile very much, in case I am not there. This good Mother Octavie often suffers from heart trouble; you know she is not well.[228] If she were not here, our establishment would be dealt a mortal blow. Nevertheless, she makes herself more and more worthy of

---

227 "Though it is a parish, the church will belong to the bishop [and not to the trustees], since it is built on his property." JSA, February 19, 1821.
228 In Paris, Octavie Berthold had consulted Dr. R. Laënnec, inventor of the stethoscope and medical diagnostic by auscultation.

her Beloved; her gentleness, her submission, and her exactitude never fail. (One incident that concerns her.) One day a Protestant came to offer her some almanacs. She met him, conducted the business, and spoke to him with such charm that he went right away to a shop and said, "I have seen the most beautiful religious that the Creator has placed on earth; her religion must be good, because she is so happy! But she has left the world in the flower of her life."

Mother Eugenie has had a year very painful for herself and for those around her. A retreat, in which God spoke to her heart, has dispelled the clouds of shadows that oppressed her and left her unendurable to herself. I am more and more convinced that this trial was given by God himself to make her increasingly understanding for leading others. She has a special talent that inspires confidence with no softness. She benefits from this experience, and if the retreat has filled her heart with unction and peace, the life of Saint Teresa, of which she has made a summary in English, has enlightened her on certain points where I had feared a bit of illusion. The remembrance of the Society is for her the taste of honey in the mouth, and she is fundamentally humble, loving to be reprimanded and attracted to everything that is lowly and poor.

The sisters are better as regards peace. Sister Marguerite falls often and becomes outwardly confused, but she is happy to be in America. To Sister Catherine, too, you have applied the right remedy. She makes herself very useful, especially for washing and ironing. The boarders love her when she takes surveillances.

I am always the worst one and the biggest obstacle to the good. I do not merit, nor do I obtain, the confidence of those who arrive [the postulants], who give it quite naturally to my two companions. How I long to be of inferior status! I am disposed to obey anyone, whoever it might be. I would only be sorry to have the care of temporal matters, still a heavy load. Our mothers adjust to it quite naturally, and I cannot speak English. Mother Octavie has no difficulty in speaking to physicians, workers, and merchants. Mother Eugenie has enough English to work with the children and to guide our novice, who perseveres in all humility, complaining only that she is not corrected enough. You can have no idea of what she puts up with in milking the cows in mud, snow, and ice, often soaked with rain; she becomes so cold she cannot move. One day we had to cut the milk with a knife and hammer, as if it were sugar. Nevertheless, this winter has been less severe than last year.

Father Barat's letter informs me that you are at the Hôtel Biron for the assembly.[229] I am waiting impatiently for the details of this interesting meeting and the results of the decisions that should regulate our conduct. As for the Irish woman [Anna Murphy], I was delighted with her letter, and as regards English, she will be very useful. But I think we must give her a true picture of our position here: inconvenience everywhere, above all for lodging, not even knowing where to put our work, our writing, no table to oneself, food often unattractive with not much variety, rigorous cold and overwhelming heat, and no spring. God alone and the desire for his glory: there is nothing else.

After a novena made for this intention, three vocations have been decided from the boarding school: young people from 16 to 18 years old, two Americans [Mary Ann Summers and Eulalie Hamilton] and one French [Emilie Saint-Cyr]. The last one has permission; she needs only that of the bishop,[230] who is in New Orleans. The second one does not yet have it. The third is an orphan, and her guardian makes no difficulty.[231] She is sixteen years old, looks after the kitchen with astonishing ease and attends to everything. She would be very fit for studies if it were not to her soul's advantage to remain for a while in lowliness. She has such a good memory that she will be able to learn quickly what is necessary if you allow her to be a choir religious. She could not be a teacher here because of the family from which she comes, but she could do so without difficulty in another house. She speaks both languages well and writes and reads them with an intelligence to which nothing needs to be added.

If the clothing ceremony takes place on the feast of Saint Joseph, as I hope it will, they will take advantage of the steamboat to write to you, as I will also, as well as to my very dear Mothers Bigeu, de Gramont, Grosier, and to your dear Julie [Bazire], who so loves Louisiana, and to Father Barat. Tell him that he has a letter from me, no. 19, via New York in January. The shipment of books, about which he was concerned,

---

229 The General Council ran from August 15 to October 13, 1820. Officially convoked to revise the Plan of Studies, it also dealt with other urgent questions: requests for foundations and the purchase of the Hôtel Biron.
230 Given the particular situation of the American mission, the permission of the local bishop was required for admission of a postulant.
231 Mary Ann Summers, RSCJ (1804-1826), was born December 28, 1804, in Baltimore, Maryland, of an Irish family. After having moved to Saint Louis, her parents died, leaving four orphans. Mary Ann, the oldest, was sent by Bishop Dubourg to the boarding school at Saint Charles to help with domestic work. Mr. Hubert Guyon, her guardian, allowed her to take the habit at the age of sixteen on March 19, 1821. Admitted as a coadjutrix sister, she became a choir religious at her first vows, made at Saint Ferdinand in 1823, before being sent to Grand Coteau, where she died suddenly and prematurely on May 20, 1826.

has arrived in very good condition with his precious hymns. Could he also compose one in English for the poor Americans, who have just as many privations as we do?

I have received the answer from Father Joseph [Varin], without hope of ever seeing him again. The sentence from his letter: "…will leave to guide these kind girls…" misled us for a moment. I believed we would have him. Father Perreau has forgotten me altogether; I beg you to let him know my distress and to ask him for a word for me.

So now all the money from Niort is in America. I fear that the father abbot [Dom Augustin de Lestrange] will pursue us. His religious [Father Dunand], who is very kind to us, only laughed at what I had given to our principal creditor [Mr. Mullanphy], that is, to credit the sum to his name in France. I do not know how we will pay him. Since I do not know the lady [Mrs. de la Granville] who gave the 200 F, would you kindly thank her for us.

And you, Reverend Mother, what can we say in recognition of all your care for us? To love the Heart of Jesus deeply and to be in him your humble daughters.

I am at your feet, your most unworthy

Philippine

What I told you about the confessor [Father Delacroix] is only with regard to bad people, because he is an angel of peace and simplicity. Besides those already named, greetings to Mothers [Gabrielle Charlotte] de Gramont, Deshayes, Josephine [Bigeu], Eugenie [de Gramont], and the whole novitiate.

[On the reverse:]
To Mother
Mother Barat
Superior General of the Religious
of the Society of the Sacred Heart of Jesus
PARIS

Letter 164   **L. 12 to Mrs. de Rollin**

SS. C. J. M.

Saint Ferdinand, Missouri Territory, February 18, 1821[232]
Rec. to St. Ant. of Padua

My dear Cousin,

It has been a long time since I have received news of you, but I knew that you were thinking of me, and Mother [Barat] told me in a message she sent me, that you have given 500 F. I really recognized in that your heart and your zeal for good works. No matter how little in importance our work is and that we are unworthy servants, nevertheless God who sees the intention will reward the purity of your vision and will give you the promised hundredfold. He does not forbid adding a new sentiment of gratitude for so much attention and generosity on your part. When I go over in detail the holdings of our little sacristy, I say to my sisters with pleasure: "This came from Mrs. de Rollin," and I am not easily finished. Everything you have given us is even more precious because I can no longer ask for things from France for fear of not being able to pay the import tax. If one day, as I hope and await, we separate into two houses, one of which will be in New Orleans, the customs fees will be cut by more than half.

We are the grain poured out on the earth. At the moment, we can hardly sort things out, but we are full of confidence, all of us inspired to perseverance in the hope that it will bear fruit someday. It is not important to taste it in this life, as long as God is served.

God permitted that, when we arrived in Saint Louis, money was plentiful, land and houses at excessive prices. It seemed better to build where we are. This was not my opinion, but it was necessary to follow that of others and to borrow in order to finish it. Now that the failure of all the banks has made the bills disappear, almost the only kind of money used here, we could have land and houses for nothing in Saint Louis. Instead, we have to pay back what was borrowed at a time when money is worth ten times more. These are unexpected events against which human prudence can do nothing. But Providence is there, and

---

232 *Copies of letters of Philippine Duchesne to Mme de Rollin and a few others, No. 12; Cahier, Lettres à Mme de Rollin*, pp. 32-37; *Lettres dactylographiées.* C-VII 2) c Duchesne to her family and lay people, Box 5.

we count on it so much that we remain firmly at our post. We are so persuaded that God placed us here himself that no one regrets it.

The children who are not of mixed blood with Indians or Negroes are generally docile and easy to guide and just as intelligent as those in France. As for those of mixed blood, there is little to do with them, so strong is the negative tendency; and if we receive them in the boarding school, the whites will withdraw, but we do not have the difficulty of refusing them. They do not come.

I fear, dear Cousin, that you have had much difficulty since we left you; I have been told that Aunt Perier was very ill, and I have heard nothing better. Her age makes me fear the worst.[233] I know this suffering, and I can imagine others for you, for they abound in this painful life; happy are those who, like you, often cast their view upon eternity, where their virtues give them the assurance of rediscovering forever their friends who are as virtuous as they are. It is dear to me to carry in my breast this sweet hope that I will see again my dear Josephine in the place where there are no tears or sorrows.

Give my greetings to Mr. de Rollin, to Mr. Teisseire and to my cousins. Tell Mrs. Lebrument that I have received her letter, which was nearly a year old. To avoid these delays, I now send them by way of New York, which is the shortest for letters, and I stamp them as far as the port.

Could you please find out if my brother has remitted to Mr. Rusand the total sum that he offered me, and that I asked him to turn over in France to the agent of a priest who advanced it to me here. Thank him again, and also for the trouble he is taking about my certificates, if he has received them.

I would have liked you to see in Paris a priest of this diocese who belongs to one of the great families of Rome; he was in the papal group at the crowning of Bonaparte, and he is generously devoted to this difficult mission. He is traveling for its interests and his own business. He does not want to return without bringing or procuring passage for one of our religious, and I think he will push for our establishment in New Orleans, since he was at the blessing of our house, where he chose to say his first Mass. If you had listened to him, it would have been as if you were seeing us.

Goodbye, dear Cousin, I am taking the liberty to attach here a letter for our mother, since I do not know her address.

I am all yours in the divine Heart of Jesus,

Philippine Duchesne

---

233 Marie-Charlotte Perier, Philippine's aunt and Josephine's mother, died July 31, 1821.

Letter 165 **L. 11 to Father Barat**

SS. C. J. et M.

No. 21
Recommended to St Anthony of Padua, March 7, 1821[234]

My dear Father,

With what pleasure have we learned from your last letters that you were still in Bordeaux, and so you can still be the father of our little colony. No one else except our mother has been of more support, sympathy, and goodness. I am so embarrassed by all the trouble taken for us and by all the expenses we cause that it would make me capable of regretting my efforts to come here, if I were not ever persuaded that it is the will of God that we be here. I quiet my anxieties by thinking that the Sacred Heart for whom you want to work by helping us in every way is the great rewarder.

I do not know if we should lament or rejoice over the departure of our fathers from Russia. If some of them from Siberia want to find the same climate and the same work for part of the year, they can come to our area. It takes souls of that quality to persevere out here; and if they go to the Indians, they can still hope that martyrdom will be their lot, even perhaps more surely among the lawless men who trade with them. There is polygamy, fraud, etc.

In several of your letters, you mention Mr. Le Torneur.[235] He lives in Florissant, but we never see him. He has never given me a sign of life, even after the letter I sent him that was enclosed in yours. He believed that his wife was dead and told someone that he was sending for his children. Later he said that he was going to join her. He is trying to sell his property, even at a loss, but it will be very difficult given the extreme scarcity of money. Everything is worthless. One hears only talk of auctions[236] for payment of debts and the execution of justice in all its rigor, of unfortunate poor people who see a life's work come to

---

234 Original autograph, C-VII 2) c Writings Duchesne to various Eccles., Box 8. Postmark: St. Louis Mo., Mar. 10. Copy, C-III USA Foundation, Haute-Louisiane, Box 1, *Lettres de la Haute-Louisiane I 1818-1823*, pp. 207-210.
235 He was captain of the *Rebecca*, the ship that brought the first religious to America. In her account of the voyage, Philippine emphasizes his goodness and solicitude toward them. It is not clear why he was later in Florissant.
236 Philippine wrote here in her letter in French "aucans," attempting to use the English word "auctions."

nothing because of a small debt. A pair of oxen cost $3, that is 15 F for us; 18,000 *arpents* of land paid for with $100, that is 500 F.

In such a situation, one is never at ease with debts. We still have one for 15,000 F, of which 10,000 is a mortgage on our house, about which the creditor boasts. Providence will not allow him to foreclose on it; it has been on our side too often for that. But he has dealt with us as with his other debtors. Since he can find no buyer for our house, he could probably get just the amount of our debt at auction, though it cost nearly 40,000 F. This situation is very different from that of Grenoble where we never had a single *sou* of debt piling up. But it is right that having sinned all the more, I should do more penance and that the happiness of establishing a house of the Sacred Heart here should be purchased at the price of a few worries.

I had a moment of hope that the $571 that came through New York was an entirely new gift from Providence. When I saw that it was almost all that I had counted on to pay the Trappist father and Mr. Petit Clair,[237] I was very dismayed, because I had already turned over the note to our principal creditor who holds the mortgage. I did not know how to explain matters to the others. Fortunately, the good Trappist religious who loves us sincerely, told me: "I prefer that you owe me rather than the other man. I will never foreclose on you." He also got the note of Mr. Petit Clair changed into one without interest and without the stipulation that it be payable in France. So I beg you, *if it is not already done*, to give nothing to the family of Mr. Petit Clair. I would prefer, if you have something for us, that you keep it for the Trappist father who will return in the spring and through whom you will have news of us in great detail. He had the house built and says Mass for us every day since the bishop named another pastor.

You ask for news of Miss Emilie Chouteau. She has gone home for the third time, without difficulty, wanting, she says, to get out of the state of incertitude and obtain the consent of her family. She will not get that for a long time; and from here to there, it is much to be feared that she will give in to so many offers of marriage directed to her and so many allurements of affection and pleasure. Miss Emilie Pratte already gave in more easily. She is about to be married, but in a very Christian way. Her parents are delighted, and she is worthy of praise. Miss de Lassus, who also left, has refused three offers of marriage, but she will give in one day, as will a really superior American who could have been the Aloysia of America, except for her precipitous departure and return

---

237   A baker from Florissant who had returned to France. Cf. Letter to M.-S. Barat, August 15, 1821.

to a family that is devout but the only Catholics in the area, without a priest, with no religious support. Father Richard predicted that she will return; I hope so. Meanwhile, her sister, very likeable but less capable, asks admission but does not yet have parental consent. We will have two receive the habit on the 19th.

I wrote that to our mother last month by way of New York. She told me, and you too, about the agony of my dear Aloysia; but when one is here, having crossed the ocean, one no longer has friends to see again except in heaven. It is there that I will see all of them, even though I become more and more earth-bound. I was in a *(torn word)* naturally as a servant. It requires something quite different to guide souls, but God does it himself: my two young mothers are more and more perfect and so relish their poverty and abjection that they would suffer greatly to find themselves well-off. This should be the disposition of those who expect to join us: to anticipate suffering, and *God alone* as support.

I must always come back to that wretched issue of money, and I forgot to tell you that I have now received: 1) 1000 F from Niort; 2) 1000 other F; and in third place, your note for 571 *gourdes*, which completes the 4000 F from Niort, plus a gift from different people whom our mother names. I also received in very good condition the case of books that came from the thrift of Mother de Gramont from Quimper. If you also have the 400 *livres* that you told me about, keep them for our debts.

As for books, we already have some duplicates, and I have indicated to our mother some that we need, if Grenoble wants to make us a gift of chronologies, history books, beautiful geography books and books that contain the Office of the Blessed Virgin. It is all most needed for the children. But in the end, this difficult year will be a year of privation for all. By the first steamboat, I will give you details about our library so that you can know what we have.

I am with lively gratitude in the Sacred Heart, your humble daughter and unworthy servant.

Philippine

My respects to Father Debrosse and Mothers Vincent and de Lalanne. Our mothers and sisters are well enough with regard to health and I, more vigorous than ever, with few teeth.

My four sisters ask your blessing.

[On the reverse:]
To Father
Father Barat
At the minor seminary
Bordeaux
In France
By way of New York

Letter 166 **L. 1 to Father Rosati**

SS. C. J. et M.[238]

[March 21, 1821]

Dear Father,

I have a precious opportunity to remind you of myself and to recommend myself to your prayers, along with all my sisters and our children. One of them, Miss Hamilton, greatly desires to consecrate herself to God in our house. She fears that she will be called for before she receives an answer to the three letters in which she asked her mother's consent to become a religious. We know that letters are often lost between here and Fredonia;[239] perhaps that is the reason for the silence on the part of *(illeg.)* Mrs. Hamilton. We hope that through your mediation, this *(illeg.)* will reach her, and we shall receive an answer.

Your zeal for the salvation and perfection of souls has encouraged us to write this letter, which has the glory of God for its object. We are also eager to express our deep regard for you and to tell you of the many prayers we say for your holy house.

I am with profound respect, Father, your very humble and devoted servant,

Philippine Duchesne, sup.
r.S.C.

March 21, 1821

238 Original autograph, C-VII 2) c Writings Duchesne to Rosati, Box 6. Reverse: "March 21, 1821, Mother Duchesne, Florissant."
239 There are several towns in the Midwest named after Fredonia in New York State. One such was being established in Indiana at just the same time as these events, but it is not clear that it is the one to which Philippine is referring.

[On the reverse:]
Reverend M. Rosati
Priest in the Seminary
The Barrens

Letter 167   L. to Sister Louise de Vidaud and her novitiate companions

SS. C. J. et M.

Recommended to St. Ant. of Padua
April 10, 1821[240]

My very dear Sister Louise and your happy companions,

 I remember when I was still in Grenoble and carried away in desire to the lands about which we were reading in *Edifying Letters*, I said to the lovely children who made up my class that if God ever gave me the grace actually to go there for the instruction of the poor and ignorant, I would not fail to write to them about what I know would be curious or of interest.

 I have already fulfilled part of my promise by the different journals that have gone out from here and by the letters to the novices of Paris and Grenoble, where the greater number of those are to whom I made my promises. Now that divine Providence has separated nearly all of them for the glory of his divine Heart, I take a secret pleasure in finding at the source of the Society my dear and beloved Louise who, in her dreams while she was in the third class in Grenoble, competed with me *to be the first to go to martyrdom and already to experience the happiness of following the Lamb wherever he goes*. Her holy father was happy to see in her these holy thoughts that presaged her vocation. I have the firm hope that she has persevered and that now the triple bond of the vows has united her to our divine Savior.

 I would encounter here our children of France and would see in our boarding school the skill of some and the devotion of others, if they had time to be strengthened in their principles and to be instructed in

---

240 Original autograph, CVII-2) Duchesne: *Letters to RSCJ and children*, Box 4. Copies, A-II 2) g, Box 2, *Lettres intéressantes de la Société*, pp. 243-249. C-III USA Foundation Haute Louisiane, Box 1, *Lettres de la Louisiane, 1818-1822, Part A*, pp. 77-83; *Lettres de personnes variées, 1818-1828, Part B*, pp. 141-149; *Lettres de la Haute-Louisiane, II, 1818-1823*, pp. 210-217 b. Cf. Ch. Paisant, pp. 348-352.

depth. But whether it is lack of money that makes the price of boarding school too high, or the custom to marry girls too young, or the natural shallowness of the children, all this provides entry for the enemy of all good. One does not dare to convert a young person, instructed in so many apostasies as she may be. One girl, persuaded by the instructions of a holy priest, was baptized, received Communion, and was confirmed. When she returned to her family, won over by her parents and friends, solicited by [Protestant] ministers, alone to fight against error, she let herself be won over; she apostatized and went to one of those sects that abound in these regions where often a Catholic finds herself without priest or resources. Marriage is often another danger; nevertheless, it is also sometimes the only moment that establishes a convert for good. Here there is no retreat house for innocence exposed, where faith finds a way to avoid seduction. When someone converts, we must be sure of the parents, or snatch the victim away to Jesus Christ when they want to corrupt her; and the country has no resources for that: no great buildings, no money to endow an establishment, and no work to provide an honest subsistence labor.

We have among our students a young Protestant, charming, docile, devoted, who loves very much to go to church and tries to imitate her companions by making the sign of the cross, etc. Well, if she became a Catholic when her parents did not want it, we are pretty sure that she would return to her first religion. The only good thing to do is to instruct her well. Then, at the time for marriage, at an age when she can make her own decisions, she could follow the religion of which she has had a taste, or even make her choice at the moment of death. But how apostasy makes us tremble! We have had under our eyes young people who even seemed fervent. One of them as a penance wrote the whole catechism by moonlight. She ended up abandoning it all and getting married before a judge without confession, as did one of our day students from Saint Charles whom we had judged the most devoted of all. It makes me tremble. Two other day students were sent into a region entirely Protestant to force them to abandon our holy religion, that of their mother who made them promise on her deathbed to remain faithful.

Besides this multitude of religions that count up to 40, there is the imminent danger of adornment and of balls. Everywhere, they dance with fury. In the fervor of the dance, they marry, taking the dancers as witnesses. That is all their religion. There were balls in Saint Louis in which one of the rules was that girls could not be taken there by their fathers or brothers.

There is a town in which is gathered everyone of a religion in which one cannot marry. On Sunday, the men and women go to church in separate groups of men and women. When everyone is there, the preaching begins; then they also begin convulsive movements: everything in the church spins, the women make an umbrella with their skirts and when they fall from turning too fast, as well as the men, the minister listens to the words spoken in this swoon, and they collect them as oracles of the Holy Spirit.

It's a completely other thing in a certain camp in the country, near some cities of the East. These really bring on mania, and even the spectators experience unexplained upset. I know it from eyewitnesses.

A fanatic in another religion imagined that he should not work and that God would take care of his family's needs. While waiting, the wife and children were dying of hunger. Finally, he had the inspiration to tell his wife, to calm her fears, to put some stones in a furnace and they would become bread. His hope was mistaken, but he was not persuaded otherwise.

Another imagined that God would raise him to heaven; but to help with his assumption, he attached large wings to his back and went up like that to the roof of his house, telling his wife to say: "Go up, go up!" but it was all futile. He stayed on earth.

Another incident of fanaticism is much more tragic. To care for his six children, a widower took a Methodist girl who seemed very virtuous. She ate little, kept silence, and always had the Bible in hand. Finally, her imagination got away with her so much that she came to think that the six children would be in danger of being lost when she was no longer with them; and to avoid this misfortune, she killed all six of them and killed herself after them.

Duels are also rather frequent, and very near here, they were preparing for a public one. Each antagonist was looking for his friends to support his side. When the pastor, a pious Lazarist, heard about it, he went to the field of battle to try to reconcile the two enemies. He found one too hardened to listen; he went to the other, who knew him, loved him, and was moved when he saw him. The pastor took advantage of this to win him away and was on the point of succeeding when the other, like a demon, insisted on fighting. So the desperate pastor threw himself on his knees to beg him to think of his soul, which he was exposing to being lost in such an obvious way. It was all futile, and seized with sorrow, he fell back exhausted. This was the moment of grace: the enemies agreed to separate. But the father of the less wicked one was unhappy and told the priest that he should give his attention to saying Mass and not to other people's business. It is always like this in this land: the fathers are worse than the children.

The same Lazarist runs a school, and funded by Providence, he keeps several young people with him and nourishes and forms them with care. One of them, very devout, wanted to enter the ecclesiastical state. His mother arrived furious, took him and told him: "I would prefer to see you dead at my feet than to see you as a priest." The same priest, when preaching at a wedding on the unity of the marriage bond and its indissolubility, had an unhappy old man say out loud: "Well, I have had thirty wives."

Blood mingled with that of the Indians and blacks forms a race that is difficult to lead to virtue. We had to send away a child of this kind, unable to do anything with her. She was indolent, lazy, violent, and a glutton. In church, she did nothing but tear up paper that she stuffed into cracks or our books. Finally, she said one day to her companions that I had the devil for a husband and that I caressed him often.

Everything that you have read in the *Edifying Letters* about the cruelty of our Indians is still true today in Upper Mississippi and Upper Missouri. At the time of the war they waged against the United States, there were some who burned white men, their prisoners, on a little fire and forced their wives or their brothers to eat their bloody, roasted flesh with which they fed themselves. Even today, without being savages, men have been seen cutting the breast of a woman, roasting and eat it.

Let us leave these horrors to speak about our hopes. Our children are easy to lead and very conducive to devotion. One of them, who is only 10 or 11 years old, when hearing a hymn to Saint Aloysius Gonzaga, said: "O Mother, what I love best is that it says that *he chose the thorn to attach himself to the Cross.*" On another one in honor of the name of Jesus: "O how I love these words: *He is sweet as honey.*" She often passes up a time of recreation, turned toward the picture of Saint Aloysius Gonzaga, singing hymns.

Among the children, there is admiration for the saints and their affection is always well motivated. Two of them are carried away with love for Saint Francis Xavier, and when a companion comes along, they snatch her away to make her love their saint by telling her about the saint's virtues.

One day, the littlest class was left alone by mistake, so they arranged themselves in silence and studied their best without saying a word. Mother Eugenie arrived and asked what they were doing, since it was still the time of recreation. "Oh! Mother," they answered, "Did we do badly by devoting ourselves to study?" Several times in my class, someone looked in the book while supposedly reciting from memory, but before the end, she fell to her knees and accused herself aloud and of her own accord.

Yesterday the oldest girl spoke unkindly of her companions and was rebuked. In the evening, they saw this big girl kneel in the middle of the refectory before her companions to ask pardon, of her own volition. There are some who have asked for recreation all day, but it was in order to make a retreat and spend the day in the chapel.

Several of the students who have left have carried their vocation into the world, but I do not think that they will be able to overcome the extreme resistance of their parents, nor fight continually against the seduction of pleasure, flattery, of stupid pleasantries, and of frequent propositions of marriage. We also have several in the boarding school who long for our holy state, but if they do not keep quiet about it, they are quickly withdrawn.

On the feast of Saint Joseph, we had the clothing as a novice of a boarder fifteen years old and an orphan in our service, sixteen years old. The boarders were charmed, and one of them said on the way out that seeing the two novices embrace was like seeing justice and peace embrace. The next day, 5 or 6 of the youngest students wrote to their parents to ask permission to receive our holy habit. We stopped these letters, but they were comical to read, especially of one who exhorted her father to enter the Society of Jesus. That poor child and her sister worry us very much. They will come to get them in a month to go to Prairie du Chien, 400 leagues from any priest. One man did go there alone. Once they wanted to throw him in the river; then they suggested that he crown his work in the region by *permitting a ball*. This is the home of these poor children, without a mother, in a house where they receive the troops and the chiefs of the neighboring Indians, with no one to supervise them but the daughter of an Indian woman and a neglectful father. I suggested reducing the cost of the boarding school if it was too much; he was offended. One of his daughters is a pleasure seeker; pray much for both of them.

Other than the ceremony of taking the habit, we have had two other devotional ceremonies.

The first on February 19: with our pastor, I laid the first stone of the church that will adjoin our house, dedicated to the Sacred Heart under the patronage of Saint Regis. It will be built by subscription. The second was on March 25, feast of the Annunciation, when 5 children made their First Communion.

We have proposed to open the school at the beginning of winter; the cold, the bad roads, and parental neglect have so far prevented the opening of classes in the day school. They only began on April 2.

This is my answer to the two letters from my dear Sister Louise de Vidaud. Her sacrifice fills me with consolation. I will already have enough, if I learn that Mrs. de Chabannes, her sister, is keeping up her devotion.

I am in the Sacred Heart your devoted servant.

Philippine

My respects to your good mistress, my former mother.

Letter 168   L. 5 to Euphrosine and Amelie Jouve

SS. C. J. et M.

April 11 [1821][241]

My dear Aloysia and dearly beloved Amelie,

Father Barat has written to me to tell me that one of you is confined to bed and the other is a postulant, that one must exercise patience and the other still fight against the resistance of their parents, but courage, both one and the other! What can someone fear in illness who has left everything for God? And what could Amelie find in the world that would equal her divine spouse who invites her to give herself to him? I can have no sweeter satisfaction than to learn that my good Amelie and my dear Caroline [Lebrument], whom I have always counted on for the future, want to leave everything for the Heart of Jesus. He will repay them fully for their sacrifices; they will find the hundredfold in this life for themselves, and God habitually blesses the families that give him the first fruits, of which he is jealous.

It is very sweet to think of that house that is so dear, that was my place of origin three times over, to see that God who is so good attracts

---

241 Original autograph and copy: C-VII 2) c Duchesne to RSCJ and Children, Box 4. An archivist dated the letter to 1821. If this is correct, Philippine does not know that Euphrosine (Aloysia) died January 21, 1821.

to it little by little my dear nieces and students. You are a planting that when transplanted will spread its shadow far. We have three novices, three postulants, 20 boarders, and 10 day students. After classes, we find time to work in the garden, gather wood, and help one another with the laundry, since we have to do that of the students.

Since I burned some of my notebooks in Paris and have almost nothing in English for class, we have had to rewrite much in French, having only incomplete or useless things in the old notebooks, and to draw some of it for English. As for me, I have summarized the whole Bible, from a very good Catholic Bible that someone loaned us, since I could not find any summary in English that was not altered. Mother Eugenie has summarized in English the life of Saint Teresa, and Saint Francis Xavier is about to fall to me [she will have to take charge of the translation of his life]. We do not know what to give our novice, who knows only English, to read. With time and work, we will have what is essential. The Jesuit Fathers at Georgetown and the Sulpicians in Baltimore have already produced by subscription several books of devotion in English, and we buy them.

All yours in the Heart of Jesus

Philippine

I am writing by the same occasion to my sisters.

[On the reverse:]
To Mother
Mother Maillucheau
Superior of the house of Sainte-Marie d'En Haut
Grenoble

Letter 169   L. 12 to Therese Maillucheau

SS. C. J. et M.

April 11, 1821
Recommended to St Anthony of Padua[242]

My very dear Mother,

---

242 Original autograph and copy: C-VII 2) c Duchesne to RSCJ and Children, Box 4.

It has been a long time since I received any of your letters directly, but Father Barat makes up for this. Knowing when there is an opportunity to send letters, he never fails to write to us. He told me about your trip to Paris, the purchase of the Hôtel Biron, the heartbreaking condition of my dear Aloysia [Jouve], and the vocation and entrance of her sister [Amelie]. All of that was interesting and stirred up so many different sentiments in my soul that all come together in the holy will of God.

We always have a very limited field of action, but the few people we serve would have no one without us, and would never know well their religion and the loving Heart of Jesus. We are firm in perseverance. Not one of us regrets having come here, and each of us desires to die here. Far from resenting our state of need, we love it and would be unhappy in a condition of wellbeing. We laugh about our lowly occupations as others do about their feasts, and we will never become ill out of sadness. Please tell this to the honorable Father Rambaud, my good father, who tells me that Bishop [Claude Simon] of Grenoble and Father Bouchard have had the kindness to remember us. Please tell them of my gratitude, and tell the bishop that his name is often on my lips.

God consoles us with three young novices who are well disposed, by the hope that they will soon be joined by two Americans [Mathilde and Eulalie Hamilton], who alone will be enough to sustain our work when God calls us to himself. The bishop had sent several priests to their home so that, hearing only English, they will become accustomed to speak it. The older one learned French with us in very little time and is able to translate into her language for us many works of devotion and class work, which are completely lacking for this people. A French woman will never become capable of writing English really correctly.

Through the letters of Mothers and Sisters Furnon, Chauvin, and Bonabaud, I see the immense good that is being done in your classes, which should fill you with consolation. Since time is flying and I have already missed two steamboats, I cannot tell them individually how much we are all conscious of their remembrance of us. Their letters arrived only yesterday.

Mother Octavie is the phoenix of the group. She pleases everyone, and people are so surprised to see a person vowed [to Jesus Christ] who is content and happy, which she knows so well how to express that a number of Protestants have already said that it is a proof that our religion is the best one. She is loved in the boarding school. She and Mother Eugenie greet in the Heart of Jesus all their sisters and their dear place of origin and offer you their loving respects.

I am in the Sacred Heart your humble servant.

Philippine

I have heard of the death of F. d'Hyères.

Letter 170 **L. 36 to Mother Barat**

SS. C. J. et M.

Florissant, April 12, 1821[243]

Dear Reverend Mother,

I learned today through a letter from good Father Barat, that you are definitely at the Hôtel Biron and that our fathers have replaced you at no. 40 [rue des Postes].[244] I am so happy that this house that has been his will always be dedicated to his divine Heart. I am also most consoled that your real father [Varin] again directs your little flock, which one day must be a good influence in the world. I do not hear anything more about Father Perreau, all of which proves that he seeks only to be hidden. I am very annoyed that he has forgotten me; several letters have had no answer. However, I still like to call myself his daughter! In three years, I have received one letter from him and one from Father Joseph. But tell them that this silence, however it distresses me, reminds me of what I keep in the Heart of Jesus, where one converses without saying anything, and that it is there that I will make my remembrances and my gratitude heard.

The letters from your good brother are the most recent of all, one in September and the last on October 31; nevertheless, it took six months to arrive. He tells us nothing about the results of the assembly, except for your change of house, nor anything about the departure of several sisters.[245] This is distressing. If you agree with the projected establishment in New Orleans that the bishop and Father Inglesi want; he will protect it; that will be essential.

---

243 Copies, C-III 1: USA Foundation Haute Louisiane, Box 1, *Lettres de la Haute Louisiane I 1818-1823*, pp. 222-224; C-VII 2) c Duchesne to Barat, Box 3. Cf. J. de Charry, II 1, L. 135, pp. 354-358; Hogg, pp. 239-242; Ch. Paisant, pp. 358-360.

244 From 1814, the Jesuits occupied the Hôtel de Juigné, also on rue des Postes. In 1818, Father Varin was named superior of the Jesuits in Paris.

245 The departure of Lucile Mathevon and Anna Murphy for Louisiana.

You know that Mother Octavie was examined by Dr. Laënnec and has heart trouble, the symptoms of which are increasing and could take her away at any time; but she may live for a long time. This illness strikes like lightning, and its progress cannot be tracked. She is much loved in this country, inside and out, and she likes it, too.

In this country of tolerance, it does not matter to which religion one belongs. Some have changed theirs as many as twenty times.

Mother Eugenie is becoming more and more fit for government. She has fine judgment, prudence in not acting hastily, much zeal and firmness; she is agreeable in appearance and expression. She knows enough English to guide the Americans and give them religious instruction, but the American class is reserved to Mother Octavie, who does it very well, even though she makes many mistakes, both in speaking and in writing, as our physician tells her frankly. Marguerite is always good but weak. Catherine has the linen room for the children, is surveillante, and washes and irons. Marguerite helps her with the last mentioned and in the pantry and with the day students, who are few in number.

The letters through New York arrive more quickly by post than the one I received by another route, which brought me the first 570 *gourdes* that were applied to pay a part of our debts. I answered you through New York in a letter to Mrs. de Rollin. According to your advice, I thanked her and you even more, asking you to thank Mrs. de la Grandville on our behalf.

We have received the *Lives of Our Deceased Sisters* as far as Mother de Sylguy. I am waiting for that of Aloysia, and I have learned with consolation that her sister Amelie is a postulant and that Caroline [Lebrument, her cousin], who has already experienced your kindness in the boarding school, will perhaps also experience it in the novitiate.

If Mr. Mullanphy himself brings you my letter, please welcome him, but very simply, as he will decidedly be himself. You would not be able to tell that he is the most powerful man in the country, who could buy all of Saint Louis, and one of the most able financiers. He is going to get his daughters in France and see his son in Paris. He has loaned us 10,000 F at 10% to finish our house, and your contribution of 3000 has lessened our debt.

Yesterday I had some good news: the best of our students, an American [Eulalie Hamilton], has obtained her mother's consent to take the veil. She will later be a good teacher. Her older sister [Mathilde] is considering it and has outstanding talents for us. Father Rosati, superior of the Lazarists, is directing her with vigor.

I am with respect, dear Reverend Mother, your unworthy daughter.
Philippine

Letter 171   **L. 50 to Mrs. Jouve, in Lyon**

April 1821
Saint Ferdinand, State of Missouri, by way of Saint Louis[246]

My dear Sisters,

A gentlemen from our country who is going to France to bring back several of his girls who have been educated there gives me a good opportunity to write to you, and thus maintain the tender bond of friendship that unites us and that the distance only seals into my heart; for if we must become spiritual to last through an entire eternity, it is no less true of nature and religion. And if I am distanced from you in this life, I have the firm hope that we will only be closer in heaven, and that our reunion will even be more delightful. What I say for you, I repeat for my brothers-in-law and those of your children whom I have known, several of whom were in my care. It will be the most consoling news for me if I learn that Amelie, Mrs. Bergasse, Amelie Jouve, and the four oldest Lebruments [Caroline, Henriette, Eugenie and Marine] have completely embraced the cause of virtue and are worthy and faithful daughters of the Church, in the purity of faith, as in observance of the commandments.[247]

I wrote to my brother, by the post on the first of this month, to ask him to send to the Abbot of La Trappe by way of Mr. Rusand an amount that he promised me and that I owe to said abbot, having received it from one of his religious. I have yet to learn that the debt has been paid.

The Ursuline religious of New Orleans were not cleared of debt immediately with Mr. Jouve, since they understood that I would work it out with him. I wrote to them that I had nothing on his account and that they should please pay him, which should be done through the mediation of Mrs. Fournier of Bordeaux, sister of our bishop, who is at this moment in Lower Louisiana. The enemies of religion had closed him out up to the present time, but the time of God's mercy on this country having arrived, he attempted his visit and was received everywhere with extraordinary enthusiasm. He wrote to us from a parish where there will be more than 700 Confirmations.

---

246 Copy certified to be same as original, Paris, November 18, 1895. The vicar general: R. Bureau v.g. Seal of the Archdiocese of Paris. Other copies: *Cahier, Lettres de la Mère Duchesne à sa famille*, pp. 104-107; *Lettres dactylographiées*. C-VII 2) c Duchesne to her family and lay people, Box 5.

247 Mrs. Bergasse was her niece, Amélie de Mauduit, who married Henri Bergasse in 1818.

The Ursuline religious are continuing their generous interest in us. They just about keep us in sugar, dried fish, rice, and cooking ware, not counting many other things that they sent us, postage paid. They would see us with pleasure in New Orleans, and I do hope that we will have a foundation there in a few years. The bishop wants it, too. The only difficulty is money. When we were there, people threw *piastres* from wagons when we went by, and now the richest go wanting.

I hope that my sister Melanie, a religious at Romans, will not cease to help me with her prayers as did our distinguished aunt[248] of whose holy death I have learned, as well as the responsibility laid on my aunt Euphrosine [Claire Julie Duchesne]. I beseech her to recommend me to her holy community, in whose good works I certainly desire to participate.

I have seen with difficulty that several French artists who hoped to make a fortune in these lands have had to return with less money than when they came. The family of Mr. de Perdroville, previously attached to Bonaparte, has not been able to survive and has gone back. I have learned this since they stayed in Lower Louisiana, where the lady, who had a good education and played the piano well, gave instruction to young ladies, making it possible for her children to live.

Goodbye, my dear Sisters, pray for me and have your children pray. I am in the Heart of Jesus your faithful friend.

Philippine Duchesne

Letter 172   L. 2 to Father Rosati

SS. C. J. et M.[249]

[Saint Ferdinand, May 20, 1821]

Dear Father,

I am most grateful to you and Father Potini,[250] because in deciding the vocation of Miss Hamilton and in making it easier for her to leave her family, you have not only acted for the glory of God and the good of

---

248   Marie Louise Duchesne (Sister Françoise Melanie) died in 1820 at the Visitation in Romans.
249   Original autograph, C-VII 2) c Writings Duchesne to Rosati, Box 6. On reverse: "May 20, 1821, Mother Duchesne, Florissant."
250   Anthony Potini, C.M., of Velletri, Italy, was born in 1799. He came to America in 1818 and was at the Barrens in 1820.

her soul, but also for that of our house, which had only weak and worn out supports and which God has been pleased to renew by drawing many young persons to the service of his divine Heart. Of these, no one is more suitable to us than the two young persons from your parish. These two sisters, although very different in character, are nevertheless well suited to the work of our institute.

Miss Mary Layton, a sister of ours for some time, is distinguished by her humility and gentleness. She took the holy habit on November 22 and Sister Eulalie Hamilton on the first Friday of this month. Her sister must still wait a few weeks.

It would be very pleasant to have a house near you and under your care, but the time for it has not come. It is necessary for our young plants to fortify themselves in the shadow of our holy retreat in humble duties. Such is the inviolable rule of our Society.

Father Ferrari,[251] whom we have had the happiness of having in the absence of Father Delacroix, gave a retreat to our children. Soon we will not be able to count all the good that your holy Society [the Congregation of the Mission] has already procured for us. Ours, still quite weak, recommends itself to you and asks the continuation of your interest.

I am with profound respect, Father, your very unworthy and devoted servant,

Philippine Duchesne

Saint Ferdinand, May 20, 1821

[On the reverse:]
To Father
Father Rosati
Superior of the Seminary
At the Barrens

---

251 Andrew Ferrari, C.M., born in 1792 in Port Maurice, near Genoa, came to America in 1816 with Fathers de Andreis, Rosati and Acquaroni, recruited by Bishop Dubourg. After ministering in Vincennes, A. Ferrari arrived in St. Louis in 1820. He accompanied Eugenie Audé to Louisiana in 1821; he died of yellow fever in New Orleans on November 2, 1822. Esteemed everywhere for his generosity and *joie de vivre*, he was the second Vincentian to die in the New World, after Father de Andreis. Cf. John E. Rybolt, C.M., "A Life of Andrew Ferrari, C.M." Vincentian Heritage Journal 7.1 (1986) 27-66.

Letter 173   L. 37 to Mother Barat and
letter of Mathilde and Eulalie Hamilton

Florissant, May [6] 1821[252]

Very dear Reverend Mother,

I have just received a letter from your good brother telling me that the General Council has ended; he also said he had sent 360 F; they are undoubtedly in New Orleans.

He said nothing about sisters for us, *fiat*.

Letter from a postulant of Louisiana to Mother Barat

Reverend Mother,

With inexpressible joy I come to tell you of the happy destiny of my sister and myself, since God, not judging the merits of either of us, has drawn us out of the vain pleasures of a corrupt world, to place us in the holy sanctuary that his Sacred Heart has prepared for us. O Reverend Mother, how can we show our gratitude for the generosity of these zealous mothers who have sacrificed all that was most dear to them in the world and have come to search out the lost sheep in the solitary deserts of Louisiana? We have no other compensation to offer them than to try to lessen their laborious work by trying our best to make ourselves worthy of our heavenly spouse who has chosen us. We beg you to honor us by giving us your salutary advice in such an important matter.

My sister has taken the white veil before me [on May 4], even though she is younger. For, after a year in the boarding school, I gave in to the wishes of my parents and returned to the family, so my entry into the novitiate was delayed. Nevertheless, our respected Mother Duchesne has promised to shorten the time as much as possible, for I long for nothing more ardently than the happy day when I will see myself clothed in the habit of Our Lord. We are waiting with great impatience for the arrival of three religious from France, who will be the subject of true pleasure to our little community.

---

252 Copies, C-III 1: USA Foundation Haute Louisiane, Box 1, *Lettres de la Haute Louisiane I 1818-1823*, pp. 225-227; C-VII 2) c Duchesne to Barat, Box 3. Cf. J. de Charry, II 1, L. 136, pp. 359-362; Hogg, pp. 242-244; Ch. Paisant, pp. 360-362.

We commend ourselves to your most fervent prayers, Reverend Mother, and to those of the community. Pray that we may become worthy members of the Society, particularly I, who am the most unworthy of all.

We have the honor to be, in the Sacred Hearts of Jesus and Mary, your submissive and obedient servants.

Mathilde Hamilton
Eulalie Regis Hamilton

[On the same sheet:]

Dear Reverend Mother,

This letter was written by the two subjects whom I regard as the foundation of the Society in the American nation. The younger one took the veil on the first Friday of May. You have no other novice with such a distinguished appearance and such a likeable character; she has taken the name of Regis. The older one, who entered only four days ago, will take that of Xavier, whose character she has. She brings together everything that could make a good superior. She is a strong soul. She has both languages and is well educated.

A letter received today from a priest in New Orleans tells me that three religious are on the way.[253] With that news, joy broke out on all faces, but I suppose it was the thought of having delayed letters from you. The one that told me of the death of Mr. Dusaussoy[254] was one of the late arrivals, which is why I had told neither you nor the rest of that dear family how sorry we were.

Nothing direct has come to tell me of your move to the Hôtel Biron and the result of the Council.

I am told that there are about 313 pounds for us in New Orleans. Money is always scarce here; nevertheless, we still have twenty boarders, but they are not punctual in payment.

I am with profound respect, dear and precious Mother, your very humble and submissive daughter.

Philippine Duchesne

---

253 There were to be only two, and they would embark only in November 1821.
254 This was Étienne Prudent Dusaussoy, married to Marie Louise Barat, older sister of Madeleine Sophie Barat.

Letter 174   L. 4 to Mother Bigeu[255]

SS. C. J. et M.[256]

[June 23, 1821]

My dear Reverend Mother,

Many things have happened since I last wrote to you or received your letter. I see your kindness in going through the list of houses and stopping at each one at what could interest this little branch of the Society thrown into Louisiana, where all are thanking God for being brought, and who often turn toward the trunk that has produced it and from which it ever seeks to draw the nourishment that sustains it. This little branch interests you because it is almost completely composed of your former daughters; good mothers are attached to those who have cost them the most concern. I know thereof all that I owe to my mothers, and how could I ever forget!

To write to you, I am taking advantage of the return to France of a baker from Bordeaux. He is the very one who loaned us 1000 F; I asked that it be repaid to his family at Niort before they sailed. Now there is nothing to give him. We are reimbursing the bishop who will take care of our debt to him and settle it. This man loaned to us without interest and in a most agreeable manner. He deserves our gratitude and every mark of esteem.

I am writing at the same time by way of New York to our Mother Barat to give her the details of the agreement that the bishop asked of us, to leave in Lower Louisiana the sisters who are arriving. There a widow offers a house, lands, Negroes, and money for a religious establishment dedicated to education. Rather than costing, it will help us pay our debts. The reception of five novices and the expectation of just as many postulants will make easier a division that will extend the reign of the Sacred Heart. It would seem that Sister Eugenie is the best to govern this establishment, since she can speak English and French, has an agreeable manner and an attachment to her vocation. To that, nothing is to be added.

---

255 At this period, Mother Bigeu was in Bordeaux to open a boarding school in the house of Mrs. de Lalanne. She was accompanied by Mother Néline Bruyer de Warvillers, RSCJ (1792-1841), originally from Santo Domingo, alumna of Amiens, novice in Paris in 1819, sent as mistress general of the new foundation in Bordeaux, where she died.

256 Original autograph, C-VII 2) c Duchesne to RSCJ and Children, Box 4.

Mother Octavie has a great fear of hot climates and does better in the cold. Besides, since Paris all the way here, I have had some fears for her when traveling. Some *verses* I enclose in this packet will show the reason. She is nevertheless a model of regularity, of sweetness and goodness, but she attracts affective friendships too much.

Our last taking of the habit, which the bishop did himself, was of a student who had left and returned, who has a character like that of Aloysia [Jouve] and who has taken the name of *Xavier* [Hamilton]; her sister, who is called *Regis*, is an angel of gentleness and innocence, with a very distinguished manner. Both of them understand the two languages and are the hope of this house. One needs this consolation for the loss of Aloysia.

Dear Mother, how worried I am about your health, but I have seen it badly undermined twice. At the same time that I complain about your suffering, I count on the return of your strength that is so useful to the glory of God.

I am with respect your unworthy child *in Corde Jesu*.

Philippine

June 23, 1821

[On the reverse:]
To Mother
Mother Bigeu
Assistant General
of the Society of the Sacred Heart

Letter 175   L. 13 to Therese Maillucheau

SS. C. J. et M.

Rec. to St. Anthony of Padua
Saint Ferdinand, State of Missouri[257]
June 23, 1821

My very dear Mother,

I received the summary of the life and virtues of our dear Aloysia. I was deeply moved as I read it and not without many tears, as I saw

---

257   Original autograph, C-VII 2) c Duchesne to RSCJ and Children, Box 4.

this course so well fulfilled in very little time, while mine, already rather long, shows no real virtues that could count for that eternity to which I am drawing so near. How true the saying is: *"We carry ourselves with us everywhere."* One is as imperfect overseas as one is in one's own country. *Martha* devotes herself actively with good intentions, but it is *Mary*, the soul that is humble, solitary, and recollected that merits the approval of Jesus.[258] But it is very difficult to change one's character, and if God still leaves me on earth, it seems to me that I could still set foot in South America, either in Lima under the protection of Saint Rose, my patron, or at Cartagena under that of Father Claver.[259] We will perhaps come closer with an establishment 400 leagues farther south, where the bishop has the project of putting our sisters who are promised to us. Five novices and several postulants and the appreciation for religious life that is developing in this country suggest that we will be able to increase.

But let us return to Aloysia. While she was on her deathbed, one of our students, who seemed to have forgotten her vocation in order to find happiness with a truly holy mother and grandmother, was awakened from her somnolence by the suffering that follows tepidity and infidelity to grace. A few months were enough to show her the emptiness of the world. She left it generously to walk in the steps of Saint Xavier, whose name she has taken. The bishop gave her the veil on the feast of Saint Regis. Her sister took the habit on the first Friday of May.[260] Her humility and meekness make the example of Saint Regis dear to her, and she carries his name.

The parish church that is being built will be dedicated to the Sacred Heart under the invocation of Saint Regis and Saint Ferdinand, patron of the town. You see that I always rely on the protection of Saint Regis, and I want to give him the testimony of my devotion on every occasion. On the day of his feast, the bishop said the Mass, two other priests said Low Masses, and a fourth, the High Mass that the students sang with music, accompanied by two priest musicians. We are hoping for a beautiful picture that represents our patron on his deathbed. It is very beautiful and will be a new gift from the bishop.

I tell Saint Regis that he ought to consider his own reputation and

---

258   Luke 10:38-42.
259   Peter Claver, SJ, was born June 26, 1580, in Catalonia, Spain. He entered the Jesuit novitiate in 1600, and did his philosophy studies in Palma de Majorca, where Alphonsus Rodriguez also was. Sent in 1610 to Cartagena in the Indies, New Grenada (Colombia today), he devoted himself for forty years to enslaved Africans arriving in the holds of ships, confined in inhuman conditions. He was canonized in 1888, and declared a "defender of human rights" in 1985. He is the patron saint of Colombia.
260   The two sisters Hamilton, Mathilde (called Xavier) and Eulalie (called Regis).

not leave me so wicked, while Saint Aloysius Gonzaga made Aloysia so good through his intercession. God gave her to you for a moment in order to console you for having made nothing of me, and after God and her patron, she owes everything to you. It is you who brought down the arrogance of her character and turned her pride toward the noble ambition of being a saint. May Mother de Lacroix and Sister de Coriolis make up to you the emptiness that Aloysia leaves. They have everything needed for this.

I was hoping to have from you yourself the details of this precious death. I still think that they were entrusted to our travelers, but if they stay in the South, I will wait a long time for them.

Everything you have sent us has been useful, but I am asking for nothing more so as not to be a nuisance. Besides, the customs duties are enormous. Nevertheless, since certain things are not to be found in all of America, if it does not inconvenience you, you can send them prepaid as far as Bordeaux and we can do the rest. This would be: a pair of galoshes and one of clogs as *models* so that we can use them as exemplars; some sacristy objects like galloon, fringes, cinctures,[261] books of Roman chant for Mass; books that your students wanted to give us for the day school because we have to furnish everything, as none of the students has a penny; a pair of cruets, a Roman missal, altar cards; four little candle holders; the *Conferences of Saint Francis de Sales*; two manuscript books of *Collections of the Instructions of Saint Jane de Chantal*; several books of Fathers Surin, Guilloré, and Lallemand; *The Large Life of Saint Regis; the Exercises of Saint Ignatius*; a notebook of English penmanship (you have some that are not used); and some disciplines.

I learned with consolation of the vocation of Amelie Jouve and of Caroline [Lebrument]; I have already told them of my happiness and I pray for their perseverance. They should also pray for me in that house so favored by my patron. Please tell my sister in Romans that I answered her some months ago. I commend myself to your holy community that has sent me an affiliation.

My respects to the bishop of Grenoble, to Fathers Bouchaud, Rivet, Dumolard, and my good Father Rambaud whom I will never forget. I have received one of his precious letters here.

May all my sisters find here the expression of my tender devotion in the Heart of Jesus in whom I am all yours,

Philippine

---

261 Cord that the priest wears over his alb, around his waist.

I have learned of the death of Father d'Hyères.

> [On the reverse:]
> To Mother
> Mother Therese Maillucheau
> At Sainte-Marie d'En-Haut
> Grenoble
> *Dépt. de l'Isère*

Letter 176   L. 38 to Mother Barat

SS. C. J. et M.

No. 24
Rec. To St. Anthony of Padua
[June 24, 1821][262]

Dear Reverend Mother,

I have received your letters enclosing the life of Aloysia,[263] and those from her cousins. I was expecting this loss, and it has made me examine my own life all the more. Hers was so short, so full, that it forces me to look at the uselessness of my own and my abuse of so many graces that leave me very imperfect and unmortified. The more I think of them, the more they astonish me and make me tremble. Above all, I single out the grace of belonging to the dear Society. I procured Aloysia for it; may her merits cover my faults and obtain for me from God reparation of the past!

After these letters, I received a little packet of an earlier date, containing the book of our good father, the account of the visit of two august princesses[264] to the Hôtel Biron, and that of Quimper on the abjuration of a Protestant [Appoline Douduit].

These different packets tell me the choice made for the three sisters for us, led by Mother Lucile. This news has filled us with joy, and the

---

262 Original autograph, C-VII 2) c Duchesne to Barat, Box 2. The date is missing, but the following letter (August 15, 1821) indicates it. Postal stamp: St. Louis Mo. June 30, 1821. By way of Le Havre. Cf. J. de Charry, II 1, L. 138, pp. 366-371; Ch. Paisant, pp. 365-368.
263 *Life of Euphrosine Aloysia Jouve, professed religious of the Society of the Sacred Heart*, by Therese Maillucheau.
264 Two stepdaughters of the Count of Artois, the future Charles X: Marie Therese de Bourbon, daughter of Louis XVI and Marie Antoinette, and Marie Caroline de Bourbon-Sicile.

bishop, just arrived from New Orleans after the feast of the Ascension, says he has letters more recent than what we have, that is, from the middle of February. He has spoken to us of four sisters on the way, of a postulant in New Orleans and of Father Dusaussoy.[265] The great praise of him by Father Anduze has made him determine to keep him in New Orleans for the needs of that city. He also has something in view for our sisters that I will explain to you.

Mrs. Smith, a rich widow, lives sixty leagues from New Orleans in an area called Grand Coteau, where she founded a parish and had a church built. She wants to give an educational establishment for that part of Louisiana, and she has made a donation to the bishop of 4,000 *arpents* of land, partly woods, partly ground sown in corn and cotton. They are building a house larger than ours for it. She offers to pay the expenses of several religious for a year, to give them a family of Negroes for service, to furnish the house and to pay all the expenses of a journey from Paris. The bishop sees the advantage of this foundation that would repeat in Lower Louisiana the good we try to do here, without exposure to the cold of winter and the sicknesses of New Orleans, which force the parents either to keep their children at home or to take them back each year during the summer. Since that part of Louisiana is rich, it will supply more students than here.

The bishop suggested that I should go to see Mrs. Smith, but considering: 1) the expense of a long voyage; 2) that Mothers Octavie and Eugenie cannot go without an intermediary [superior]; 3) that Mother Eugenie, because of her appearance, her virtue, her sensitive manner, and the facility with which she can make herself understood in English, would be able to obtain the greatest good, I have proposed to the bishop to put her in charge of the establishment, ready to have her return if you wish; or those who come from France, but the bishop did not want to leave them in New Orleans should they arrive. He directed before his departure that they should be sent to the country to the home of one of his nieces, who would send them off according to what I will decide in their regard at Florissant.

Our unanimous opinion is for a second establishment: 1) because Lower Louisiana is essential for the existence of Upper Louisiana; 2)

---

265 Louis Dusaussoy (1794-1873) was the oldest son of Étienne Dusaussoy and Marie Louise Barat, sister of Madeleine Sophie. He was the first novice not a priest admitted on September 20, 1814, into the Company of Jesus, which he left in 1822, after being ordained. In 1825, he left for America, but returned to France in 1829. His instability took him to Italy, Belgium, England, and Chile. He was chaplain of the house of the Sacred Heart in New York in 1856, but left the next year for Kientzheim, France, where he stayed for more than ten years. He died at Lille.

because of the mild climate, good for certain temperaments; 3) because the cost of the trip being covered puts us immediately in a state to pay off our most difficult debt, of which we see no way to free ourselves without outside help, since it is 15,000 F; 4) because, since we have received five good novices, we will remain in sufficient number and can receive three postulants who want to come, which would be impossible if our sisters had arrived [in Florissant], since several sleep in the attic, not possible in winter. Even without more people, we have to make up our beds every night in the classroom, refectory, etc.

Two establishments, far from involving us in further debt, would partly solve our problem. We can double the number of religious, students, and the poor, extend the devotion to the Sacred Heart and multiply its altars. These are very definite reasons. It is not a matter of indifference to make religious travel, only to return immediately to another destination, which seems to be your intention. So I wrote to my sisters to follow the way laid out by the bishop, promising them Mother Eugenie who, I hope, will free Mother Lucile, necessary here because of her age, if I go missing. If you write to these good sisters, it would be good, since I do not know their address, to send the letters to the bishop at Sainte Colombe, New Orleans, who knows it better than I.

When Mrs. Smith left the bishop, she threw herself at his feet asking him what more she could do for religion. He suggested that she provide enough revenue for the maintenance of four priests, hoping, after the promises of Father de Grivel, to have twelve Jesuits, put four with Mrs. Smith, four in Upper Missouri, and four elsewhere, as much for the missions as for a college. He asked for our very dear Father Barat as leader of the mission and addressed it to the pope. If this is nothing but a beautiful dream, it is at least sweet to feed on it. Mother Eugenie weeps with joy when she thinks about it, and will go with courage to her destination when we have news of the arrival of our sisters. God has made her for governance. The postulant announced is Miss Girard, sister of one of your daughters, who speaks English and French and is a great musician.[266] This climate discourages her entirely, as it does another.

I am extremely sorry for the worry that I have given you by so many requests for money, but every request was directed towards Niort, and I did not know it was on the way to us.

I have recently paid the baker and have paid something on the account to Father of La Trappe,[267] not knowing yet whether my brother paid it according to his offer.

---

266 The sister of Mother H. Girard did not remain in the Society.
267 Father M.-J. Dunand left Florissant November 4, 1821, to return to France.

How much we await with impatience so many packets that our sisters are bringing. We hope for many letters. We are writing now by an opportunity.

I am at your feet, dear and Reverend Mother, your unworthy daughter and servant. My regards to our fathers, our mothers, and to all your dear daughters of the Sacred Heart.

Philippine

[On the reverse:]
To Mother
Mother Barat
House of the Sacred Heart, Hôtel de Biron
Rue de Grenelle, Faubourg St Germain
Paris
France
By way of New York

Letter 177   **L. 3 to Father Rosati**

SS. C. J. et M.[268]

[Saint Ferdinand, June 27, 1821]

Dear Father,

I received your letter, and it is a joy to know that divine Providence arranges communications with you and gives us for sisters persons formed by you, a fact that I look upon as a promise for the future for our Society. The father prior corresponded with me for some time about the acceptance of Miss Manning, about whom I have received the highest recommendations from both the father prior himself and Father Delacroix.

Judge Moore has also written in behalf of his daughter, but his letter arrived only a month after he wrote it. The father prior could not answer him before his departure for Saint Charles, where (Mr. Moore) received a verbal answer today from the father prior who passed through Saint Charles on his way to Portage. He goes at the invitation of Father Acquaroni.[269]

---

268 Original autograph, C-VII 2) c Writings Duchesne to Rosati, Box 6. On reverse: "June 27, 1821, Mother Duchesne, Florissant."

269 John Baptist Acquaroni, C.M., born in Port Maurice near Genoa, arrived with Fathers de

Since the consent of the father has been given in advance, the two young ladies can leave together, if that is convenient for them. They bring only their trousseau, their bed, that is to say the mattress, either woolen or feather, and blankets, shoes and the black cloth for their habit, in the event that they receive it. I know that they cannot bring money.

But what is most important, and something that I am sure they have already learned from you, is the spirit of renunciation, because it is more essential here than in Europe. Two difficult points with us are the change of house that may come and entire indifference to employments, as I assume these young ladies are not prepared for the work of education. This fact places them in a kind of inferiority that is very difficult to bear in this country. I beg you to prepare them for this and to add to your zealous care for this house by giving me your opinion of the capabilities of these young ladies and of their readiness to acquire what they lack. Also, I would like to have your opinion on the attitude of their parents in allowing them to come. We do not want to hurt anyone, or to admit as teachers persons who would destroy the confidence of fastidious parents.

We are indebted to the Society of the Mission for many reasons. Father Ferrari gave us a retreat that reminded us of those of Father de Andreis, whose memory will never be lost among us.

The two Misses Hamilton have received the holy habit. The younger received hers from Father Ferrari on the first Friday of May, the day after the arrival of her sister, who was clothed on the feast of Saint Regis, our patron, by Bishop Dubourg himself. Both are very happy, and we expect much from them. Sister Mary Layton is also very virtuous.

I am, with respect, Father, your very humble and obedient servant,
Philippine Duchesne

Saint Ferdinand, June 27, 1821

[On the reverse:]
To Father
Father Rosati Superior
of the Mission and of the Seminary
At the Barrens

Andreis, Rosati, Joseph Carretti and Andrew Ferrari in Baltimore in 1816. He ministered in the St. Louis region from 1818 to 1822, then in New Orleans where he fell ill and returned to Italy in 1824.

Letter 178   **L. 13 to Mrs. de Rollin**

SS. C. J. et M.

June 29, 1821[270]
Rec. to St. Anthony

My very good Friend,

At the arrival of one of our sisters from France, I received a remembrance from you that is very precious: I am told that it contains some of Aloysia's hair, but with several blond hairs that are hers, there are also some very black, that I hope are yours. We cannot have devotion to the living, and I really hope that you will still be among them when I will leave this earth, but if God disposes otherwise, may he destine me to be an old oak that lives among the storms that destroy younger and healthier plants. It would be very sweet to me to venerate in the same devotion the remains of two relatives and friends who by a different path are united at the central point of all happiness and all pure affection in the Heart of Jesus.

Aloysia will be sanctified in obscurity and by suffering, and my first friend, by traversing on a grand stage of virtue the difficulties that have not beaten her down. The one was built up in solitude, the other will have forced the world to honor religion, she who in such an amiable manner, wins her victories. This is what makes me so appreciate the memory, but I hope that as witness of your virtues, God will not destine me to outlive you to venerate them.[271]

My remembrances to Mrs. Teisseire, Perier, Bergasse, to their husbands, but above all to Mr. de Rollin, my benefactor.

All yours in the Heart of Jesus,

Philippine

---

[270] *Copies of letters of Philippine Duchesne to Mme de Rollin and a few others, No. 13; Cahier, Lettres à Mme de Rollin* pp. 36-37. C-VII 2) c *Duchesne to her family and lay people*, Box 5.
[271] Josephine died September 23, 1850, two years before Philippine.

Letter 179   **L. 39 to Mother Barat**

SS. C. J. et M.

No. 25
Recommended to St. Ant. of Padua, August 15, 1821,
feast of the Assumption[272]

Dear Reverend Mother,

Through various letters, we believed that our dear sisters were due to leave in March to come to us. However, a letter from Bordeaux, written to the bishop on May 1, makes no mention of any embarkation concerning the mission, which has caused us much pain. And the bishop himself does not know what to think. He wanted our sisters all the more because he was dreaming of a second establishment in Opelousas, as I told you in detail in my letters of June 24, no. 24.

I am afraid that this new house and the consent I gave to it have displeased you, but I repeat the strong reasons that made me decide:

1) The small size of our house that will not permit reception of any more boarders or novices.

2) The reimbursement of the travel of our sisters by the founder that will help us with our debts that have risen to 13,000 F.

3) The advantages of this foundation that will not be found again in a hundred years in a country like this one. The founder, a rich widow, a converted Protestant [Mrs. Smith], who will give a house, land, a family of Negroes and maintenance of the religious working there for a year, besides the furniture.

4) The bishop, who is expecting some of our fathers [Jesuits], proposes to send some of them to this region.

5) Mother Eugenie has felt herself singularly attracted to this work, and I think she is more fitted for it than I am because she can understand English and express herself in that language. She is right for government, both in the community and without, and can deal with everything and see to all the needs of a house. On the other hand, her health is visibly declining and she needs a warmer climate for her chest. It is true that here there is overwhelming heat, but it changes rapidly to rigorous cold, against which we have had difficulty in getting her to take precautions.

---

272 Original autograph, C-VII 2) c Duchesne to Barat, Box 2. Postal stamp: St. Louis Mo., Aug. 17; Paris, 31 October 1821, through New York and Le Havre. Cf. J. de Charry, II 1, L. 139, pp.376-382; Hogg, pp. 253-258; Ch. Paisant, pp. 377-380.

We thought we would lose her last year; her spirit was more affected than her body. Her recovery was of short duration; a considerable eye problem that was difficult to remove, with alternating cough and fever made me fear a decline in her health. God seems to have manifested his will in making her very well disposed to take on the governance of a house, even though her humility will suffer from it.

At first it was said that she would not leave before news of the arrival of our sisters; but the uncertainty now has made her wonder if for that reason we should abandon the advantageous offer of Mrs. Smith, and if it would not be better that she go there now so as to arrange everything, and when our sisters arrive, they can live a regular life right away. At first I was astonished at these ideas and gave the impression that I was not listening, but they made an impression on me. The bishop liked them very much; and on the eve of the feast of Saint Ignatius, it was decided that Mother Eugenie would leave here with our first novice, Sister Mary Layton, on the following Sunday [August 5] by the steamboat [the *Rapide*], that is supposed to carry to New Orleans the devout and serious Lazarist [Father Ferrari] who has given us a retreat, and several students from the bishop's school, confided to a very good black woman sent by their family, and who has promised to give a little care to Eugenie.

I have given her 500 F for the journey and what is necessary for the chapel and vestments, thinking that she will be provided for by those who are coming from France. As regards books, she has taken all our duplicates, the Constitutions, and the notebooks and books for class, one of each kind. She will have them copied, as we do here by our novices and students. The bishop has added some books, decorations, candlesticks, and four superb pictures.

No one has lost more than I have at this departure. Mother Eugenie was my right hand, and through her, I was sure to be informed about everything. Her character worked better with mine than with that of Mother Octavie, whom she found weak, so there was not a close bond between the two, nor with the sisters. She was often abrupt with them, which provoked biting words that often caused her chagrin, either because she reproached herself for having contributed to it, or because she saw that she was an occasion for someone else's fault. Nevertheless, I can assure you that the pure desire to follow our holy laws and our lovable devotion to the Sacred Heart *has transformed and sustained her courage*. The bishop was very taken by her; he would have given her his whole house if he could. He wrote to the pastor of the place and to the founder the most flattering letter about our Society and about her in particular, with the wish that no one interfere in any way in the government and administration of the house, saying that he wants it and that it is better that way.

Since the bishop has taken charge of our debt toward Mr. Petit-Clair, the baker, who has returned to France, we have nothing to pay back to him in France. So now we have only two creditors: the bishop and Mr. Mullanphy, *whom you must have seen in Paris, where his son is in boarding school.*

Mother Octavie's health varies. She generally has a pleasing appearance. Sister Marguerite is losing strength. She is mainly charged with the day school, where there are 24 French girls. The good effected here is still in its early stages. Sister Catherine does surveillances and ironing. Her attitude varies considerably, but her health contributes to it and affects her mind. Mother Eugenie did not want her, and she would not have worked out there. We still have 22 boarders. I do not know if the failure of the Bank of Missouri, about which I learned today, the only one whose bills are acceptable here, may affect the boarding school.

The four remaining novices are good ones, especially the Americans, and among them, Sister Regis [Eulalie Hamilton], a real angel of candor, gentleness, and devotion. She is the most fit to replace Mother Eugenie for the work and the pantry, but like her, she eats too little and does not take care of herself. The novices are learning from Rodriguez, the Catechism of Constance, and Bible History. Since there is no orthodox abridged version,[273] I made a summary of the English text of a large Catholic Bible. A copy of the summary is studied and memorized. I have translated and extracted from the English a History of America and Roman History and made an abridged Ancient History. All these were useful for class summaries, since education is so brief; there is no [French] Grammar by Lhomond[274] left, so I also made a summary that all study from their own copy. It has also been necessary to redo the Arithmetic and Geography notebooks for this country in English. I hope that you will not blame us for this necessary work because of the lack of books; very few children can buy them. No one has any money.

The bishop and Father Inglesi still hope to have Father Barat, and we are immersed in that hope, because I think he will be placed in Saint Louis.

When I arrived here, I thought I had no more ambition, but I feel eaten up by Peru. But these desires are quieter than those in France that

---

273 There were only Protestant books on the Bible available. The young religious and the students did not have access to the whole Bible, but to extracts and summaries.
274 Charles François Lhomond (1724-1794), French priest, grammarian, and Latinist.

so disturbed you. Mother Octavie has just written via New Orleans. We commend ourselves to our fathers and our mothers, and we are your daughters, most attached to you in the Heart of Jesus.

Philippine

[On the reverse:]
To Mother
Mother Barat, Superior General
of the houses of the Sacred Heart
Rue de Grenelle, Faubourg Saint-Germain
Paris
France
By way of New York

Letter 180   **L. 40 to Mother Barat**

SS. C. J. et M.

No. 26
Rec. to St. Anthony of Padua
September 24, 1821[275]

Dear Reverend Mother,

This letter will be handed on to you by Reverend Father Joseph Dunand, religious of La Trappe. After having worked with great zeal in the vineyard of the Lord in this county that is still so uncivilized, with much fatigue and danger, he established two houses of his order, one in Kentucky, the other in Illinois, where fire, illnesses, and other calamities have destroyed everything. Now he will take up again with joy the monastic life of his order, which he has nevertheless practiced as much as possible as a missionary. The good father is one of our principal benefactors, having made infinite efforts to have our house built and having rendered us whatever service he possibly could.

The bishop's church next to our house is making progress. It will serve as the parish, and we will be less vulnerable to missing Mass because of the dearth of priests.

---

275   Original autograph, C-VII 2) c Duchesne to Barat, Box 2. Cf. J. de Charry, II 1, L. 142, pp. 389-391; Hogg, pp. 262-264; Ch. Paisant, pp. 403-404.

Some news from France lets us hope to see here our good father, your worthy brother, which brings us great joy. Mother Eugenie, of whom we have as yet no news, also lives in the hope of sharing our happiness in having some of our good fathers in her region.

I am with profound respect your very unworthy daughter, my unique Mother.

Philippine Duchesne

Letter 181   L. 41 to Mother Barat

SS. C. J. et M.

No. 27
Saint Ferdinand, State of Missouri, near Saint Louis
October 7, 1821[276]
Rec. to St. Anthony of Padua

Reverend and very dear Mother,

I wrote to you a few days ago, and also to some of our sisters, by the return to Europe of one of Dom Augustin's [de Lestrange] religious who has been of great service to us and who loaned us money that you and my brother have been kind enough to reimburse according to the intentions of Father Abbot. Since my brother tells me in one of his letters that he has paid 600 F instead of the 750 that I owed, I made up the balance before the departure of this good father, and it was agreed that, even if my brother had given more than 600 F, there would be nothing else to be paid. I would like to have helped in any way to facilitate his departure, 1) because of the desire and need he had to return to his "ark"; 2) because he was a cause of division here, having had disagreements with the bishop and several others, which made a bad impression. As for us, we had nothing but praise for him. Please tell him of our gratitude; but if, as it is said, he will return in two years, it would be good to inform Father Abbot that it would not go well for religion in this diocese and that the bishop would not give him faculties. All of this in secret; it would be too bitter for him if he knew that I told you, for it is important that he not be in doubt. He was not

---

[276] Original autograph, C-VII 2) c Duchesne to Barat, Box 2. Cf. J. de Charry, II 1, L. 144, pp. 394-405; Hogg, pp. 265-272; Ch. Paisant, pp. 403-404.

too sure whether he would go to England first, so that letters from us that he has might arrive late, which would explain their sequence of events. They contain nothing urgent. I held back to write via New York, ordinarily the fastest way, especially in winter when the steamboats cannot come here.

The most important thing is to help Mother Eugenie in Opelousas, not with money, but with religious. Several of my letters told you of her departure, the reasons that decided it, and the advantages offered by an establishment in Lower Louisiana to sustain that of the Upper. When she left, we believed that our sisters were already in New Orleans, that the bishop said there were as many as four, and that they could divide up between her and us. Your letter of the month of March tells me of a delay until September,[277] which will be a great setback for Eugenie. If at least the delay came from the desire to wait for Father Barat, whom we hope for, I would be consoled, but the delay is long!

Our house is coming along with the four remaining novices, the oldest one [Mary Layton] being the companion of Mother Eugenie, who directed her formation. She is American and is beginning to speak French. That language is more used in Opelousas.

The boarding school can only diminish here, since the Bank of Missouri failed after those of the other states, and money is so rare that the greatest landowners have none. Business is carried on by exchange. People want the creation of new *bank notes* with the value of the 36th part of the uncultivated land that Congress has given to this state. Until they appear, we will receive little from anyone, and as the creditors can refuse them, without a stroke of Providence we cannot pay our debts on time, which is the month of December 1821. The ways of Providence upon which I count are: first, the arrival of our sisters, who can go to Opelousas and will receive reimbursement for their voyage that Mrs. Smith has agreed to do. The second is the intention of the one whom we owe [Mr. Mullanphy] to provide a fund for some orphans, and the bishop should get him to give it to us here instead of doing it in Saint Louis. The third would be, if he is willing, to make of our debt a dowry for a little relative of his who wants to be a religious, but that is very doubtful. This child is Irish, has been with us for a year, understands French and never stops asking to enter.[278] The bishop is of the opinion to accept her. She is strong and we have had her doing a little of everything.

277 In fact, they did not leave until November 1821.
278 Mary Frances Mullanphy, a relative of Mr. Mullanphy, was born in Ireland in 1804, entered at Florissant in 1821, and made her first vows in 1825 at Grand Coteau. She then went to Saint Michael, where she left the Society of the Sacred Heart in 1831.

The four novices here are doing well. *Sister Xavier* [Mathilde Hamilton], the best one for teaching classes and for governance, is nevertheless not right for the leadership in what I told you. She has singular lapses of memory; she reads the martyrology every day and never knows the count[279] nor the saint of the day. Nevertheless, she learns by heart easily and translates well in both languages, which is useful for putting our French notebooks into English, which Mother Octavie with her language facility cannot do, so difficult is English for foreigners.

Sister Regis [Eulalie Hamilton] is better for external things and is replacing Mother Eugenie in the pantry. She teaches a class and teaches handwriting to the day students. She does not have her sister's perception, but she does everything quietly and exactly. Grace finds no obstacle in her and flows gently in her soul like pure water in a land that is well prepared. Her appearance is serious and very appealing by that combination of regularity, candor, and innocence. She speaks French but cannot translate it exactly.

Sister Mary Ann [Summers] does the kitchen and in that difficult job maintains great gentleness. She is very intelligent but without gifts for study, contrary to what I had first thought.

Sister Josephine [Emilie Saint-Cyr], who is only fifteen, has few abilities but much devotion. Even though she is a choir religious, she milks the cows, bakes bread, and has a day class.

We had counted on replacing Sister Mary [Layton], companion of Mother Eugenie, with two postulants from her area [the Barrens], but one of them has already left, saying herself that she had no vocation, and the other has broken her arm. Seeing the necessity of forming our future sisters ourselves, we are going to accept a sister of Sister Mary Ann, an orphan, whom she will train for the kitchen.

We continue to accept postulants, even with the expectation that the boarding school will diminish, because since we already have several fees paid in merchandise or commodities, we can live. The lack of money has made everything very cheap: corn meal at 25 *sous* per bushel, meat at 2 ½ or 3 *sous*, and soap at 8 *sous*.

You knew that the bishop had wanted to divide his diocese. He has returned to this project. Neither he nor his priests could live without the help of Lower Louisiana, and it is also Lower Louisiana that lends us a hand to help the Upper. The bishop is thinking seriously of placing us in New Orleans. When Father Inglesi, his coadjutor, returns, there will be two places, each with its own advantages. The one that would

---

279 The number that designates the day of the month.

most please me is the one where there is a house, because building brings financial ruin. Miss Girard will probably have left New Orleans by that time. Her confessor writes to the bishop that she has decided to go to find Mother Eugenie. I had a letter from this good mother at her debarkation, and the pastor of the place told the bishop of her arrival at the destination. She has written to you, and you know more than I about what regards her.

The superior of the seminary at the Barrens [Father Rosati] wants one of us for his parish. The house would be built at the cost of the inhabitants, who have all that is necessary. He will give the religious all the wheat they need and would supply the chaplain and the physician. The sisters there would be paid only in kind, since there is no money. But the establishment that would be the most direct toward the goal of our mission would be Portage des Sioux, the parish farthest north up to the lakes, except for Canada, which has no boundary to the west all the way to Asia.[280]

There is an apostolic man there, pastor of three parishes, schoolmaster, choir master, farmer, father of the poor and living like them. His village is the place where all the Indian canoes stop on their way down the Mississippi, and where all the merchants' boats also stop on their way through these immense lands in the search for furs. In their different posts, away for entire years from their wives, they momentarily choose among the Indian women and, not knowing what to do with the children who are born of these illicit alliances, they abandon them to their mothers, and these children born of baptized fathers are raised like savages with their mothers. Nevertheless, since many of these travelers are rich, there is no doubt that if they knew where to place their children, they would give them an education. Now this is a project of this good pastor. He is going to build a house, create a farm there, which he will leave to the establishment of his house for orphans or half-breeds; and he thinks, with reason, that since provisions cost nothing here, they will live by salting meat, etc. The Indians of these regions often kill deer

---

280 On the proposal of Bishop Dubourg in 1818, the Lazarists established their seminary at the Barrens, about 80 miles south of Saint Louis. Portage des Sioux is about 10 miles north of Saint Charles, on the south bank of the Mississippi. It was created by the French as an outpost against Spanish and American colonists. Situated on the narrow band of land between the Missouri and the Mississippi just before their confluence, it was thus named because it was the place where the Indians landed to cross from one river to the other, carrying their canoes, thus saving about 25 miles of sailing. It was acquired by the United States in the Louisiana Purchase of 1803 and was the location in 1815 of an important treaty between the United States and several local Indian tribes, by which the Indians, ceding all their lands north of the confluence, were required to leave and locate farther west.

just for the skins and, without thinking of the future, they abandon the meat or sell it for practically nothing.

This kind of establishment is the most useful to set up and the easiest to run. It is also the most similar to those of Marie de l'Incarnation and the nearest to our aims in coming here. I would have no other desire but to consecrate my life to this work if God wills it. If Providence does what I have written above to pay our debts, we could help this establishment beginning this year. Sister Marguerite would be just right for it. Her strength is diminishing, and one can have her do only quiet occupations. This would be to her liking and not above her capacity. You have never told me anything about the project of these little scattered establishments. This was the Jesuits' method in this country: extend education by dividing up. The bishop would like only our Society in his diocese, and he is too poor to have large houses: a little one here, another there, will survive with a little land or income, and for habits, they could receive enough from the boarding school. When one has lodging and something to eat, little is needed for clothing. I think it necessary to represent this to you for the good of religion and the salvation of many souls.

In his last two visits, the bishop has never shown us so much interest, and he says that he does not want our debt to him to cause us any deprivation or anxiety. He does not want gratitude and only made me note what remained after paying several sums on account. He is going again to Lower Louisiana and to Florida, which is also his.

He thinks it would be wise for the novices to make vows for five years after the first year of novitiate, and he permits them to be examined by any priests we wish.

Several of our students are persevering in their vocation, but Miss Chouteau especially has great obstacles.

Girls are free here at 18, so why could we not give the habit at 11 or 12 years? We would soon have some of that age and could make something of them. They are as developed in body and soul as they are in France at 14 years.

I have received the vow formula written by Mother Ducis[281] without any encouragement in your letter to use it. That weighs negatively for me and it frightened me. I feel that with my character and the awkward circumstances in which I could find myself, I would need a support such as your brother to sustain me. So I am waiting for this, in case

---

281 Henriette Ducis was named secretary general at the General Council of 1820. We know nothing of this vow formula.

that would be your advice; otherwise, my novitiate is yet to be made for that commitment.

Your whole family in Florissant is united to their mother to offer their most ardent [New Year] wishes for your prosperity, that of the whole Society, and of our fathers, particularly Fathers Varin and Perreau.

I am at your feet, your most unworthy daughter, but very devoted in the Sacred Heart of Jesus.

Philippine Duchesne

Pondering my duty to make my daughters profit in every way, I have sometimes thought that I was to blame for not urging them more to the holy practices of penance, but when I see these 15- or 16-year-olds labor, milk cows, survey the dormitory and take the kitchen, with at most one recreation because of the day school, I am afraid I will destroy them by overburdening them. It seems to me that self-maceration will be for the time when work is more divided and when they have a stronger constitution.

When I spoke of Portage des Sioux, I forgot to tell you that one can go there from here and return in the same day, but there is the Missouri to cross.

Have everyone pray for a student whose father, a Methodist Protestant, came to take her to have her baptized in his religion. I said that these excursions are contrary to our rules, that if she went out, she would not return, and that we do not force her to embrace our religion. In this country, there are many conversions followed by apostasies, and the child does not give assurance that she would have the courage to hold up in our religion against the will of her parents. Nevertheless, she would like it and she really loves the Blessed Virgin.

An Indian chief negotiating with Congress has asked for a *black robe* [a priest] of the religion of the French to instruct them.

[On the reverse:]
To Mother
Mother Barat, Superior of
the House of the Sacred Heart, Hôtel Biron
Faubourg Saint-Germain
PARIS, in France
By way of New York
Colonies through Le Havre

Letter 182   **L. 4 to Father Rosati**

SS. C. J. et M.[282]

[October 18, 1821]

Dear Father,

What joy I felt in learning that you are well enough to travel; it is joined to the sorrow of not seeing you for ten months. I hope that you will not forget our request for a retreat next year. The one Father De Andreis gave us makes us long for an equally happy one.

A letter from one of our sisters who has gone to Opelousas tells me that Father Ferrari has recovered from his fever and that he is very kind to her. This help is very necessary for her in the trials she has experienced in a very short time. Two of our companions have been ill, and I would be worried about it if I did not know that all the most solid foundations are begun in suffering and privation. You have proved the truth of this by yours, which is the hope of the diocese and the object of our continual prayers for its prosperity.

I am writing to the bishop, but I pray you also to tell him face to face of our ardent prayer for his welfare.

If Father Richard is still with him, I ask you to offer him our respect also and to tell him frankly that I have spoken enthusiastically of his projects to our mother [Barat], but I do not think she is able to consent to them because of the difficulty of communications. Besides, the number of her daughters is quite sufficient to teach the children in such a small town, and children in many other places have no one.

I am with respect, Reverend Father, your very humble and obedient servant,

Philippine Duchesne

October 28, 1821

Mother Octavie sends you her regards.

---

[282] Original autograph, C-VII 2) c Writings Duchesne to Rosati, Box 6. On reverse: "Oct. 28, 1821, Mother Duchesne, Florissant."

[On the reverse:]
To Father
Father Rosati
Superior of the seminary at the Barrens
Saint Louis

Letter 183   L. 42 to Mother Barat

SS. C. J. et M.

Saint Ferdinand, December 17, 1821[283]

Dear Reverend Mother,

I have just received your letter of last June 4. It reminded me that at this very moment my sisters in France and above all those in Paris are about to wish you a very happy New Year. Even from afar, I am delighted to unite myself with them, and all my daughters express the same wish as I do, for you first of all, dear Mother, and especially for all they have had as mothers, and for all our dear fathers whom we had hoped to see here soon. But your brother has taken away even that hope because of the need to sustain the foundations in Germany and Sicily. There is no one of us in France who is more attached to him than this little colony. We think we would have no more privation if we had the spiritual guidance of the reverend father. Sister Xavier says she would die of joy if she saw Father Varin. All the children call your brother their father; they speak of him as if they had known him a long time, so much do we like to tell them about him.

The bishop is in Lower Louisiana and should see Mother Eugenie, which is necessary to work out the arrangements with Mrs. Smith, founder of the house at Opelousas. I will not repeat the reasons that determined making this foundation. They are repeated in several of my letters; or the details that concern it; you have received them directly from Mother Eugenie. Father Ferrari, a Lazarist, who was her traveling companion, tells me that he left her in good condition, and he tells me about the advantageous air, the climate, and the house where she lives. By now she should have three postulants and ten boarders.

---

[283]   Copy, A-II 2) g Box 2, *Lettres intéressantes de la Société depuis 1816 N° 1*, pp. 318-321. Cf. J. de Charry, II 2, L. 149, pp. 33-39; Hogg, pp. 21-27; Ch. Paisant, pp. 410-413.

Since she has no expenses, she has already commissioned a missionary in New Orleans to bank 1500 F towards payment for our debts. They say our creditor in France is dead.[284] He should have brought you [certain] of our letters. I would much rather have to deal with him alone than with his successors, who are very exacting. We still owe him more than 7000 F at ten percent, and I had hoped that having promised 1500 F to the bishop per year for the upkeep of two orphans, he would deduct this sum from our debts and so we would be free of the debt without our noticing it. This hope is not lost, since his death is not confirmed, and his children are sincere. Tell your good brother this, since he is interested in our affairs.

As for the 6500 F that we still owe to the bishop, it is interest free; he does not want us to be disturbed by it at all. He has given us a new gift of land, all that our man can cultivate. The man is Flemish and resembles Brother Fonsala[285] in devotion, industriousness, and even in the face. He is married. We have built him a little house next to the school, to be safeguarded in case of trouble, and we give him 1000 F per year with his firewood and food or care in illness at no cost. Our Irishman of last year had pretty much the same situation. He regretted leaving us, but the Flemish man is better for us. We have reduced the cost of boarding because money is so rare; it is now 700 F.

So you see, dear Mother, that our situation is nothing to complain about. In spite of the extreme lack of money, our boarders are still up to twenty, and thus they provide maintenance for the novitiate, from which we will never have any income. But it is essential that it grow. We gave the habit on the feast of Saint Stanislaus [Kostka] to an Irish girl [Mary Mullanphy], our sixth novice, and I hope for as many next year.

Mother Octavie improves every day in all respects. Her fervor is that of the best novices, and she is getting experience in external relationships, with the children, and about temporal affairs. I was very much hoping for the arrival of Mother Lucile, but there are always delays. I am very annoyed about the proposal to come by way of Martinique. A stay on that island can be very detrimental to her health; besides, it requires a second crossing of the Gulf of Mexico, where shipwrecks are more frequent than on the high sea. One saves very little money and risks losing people. The shortest and surest ways are through New York, Baltimore, and New Orleans. The last one is preferable because the

---

284 Mr. Mullanphy was not dead; in February he was in New York, where he posted a letter to Mother Duchesne.
285 Perhaps the brother of Sister Marie Fonsala, who entered at Grenoble in 1807.

lodging will cost nothing. I count little on the promises of the minister, and the delays are harmful to our establishments.

I am very consoled by all the details about Aloysia, about her brother's retreat, her sister [Amelie] and my niece Caroline [Lebrument].[286] Please tell them that I am very concerned about them before God.

Mother Bigeu's condition is a real sorrow for us all.[287] Please tell her how deeply we are concerned about her.

In my last letter, I spoke to you about a possible foundation in Detroit, Michigan, a two-month journey from here. The bishop was not pleased that I have given even a vague answer. He has a kind of jealous love for us and told me not to forget Saint Charles, which we loved so much and where he is going to place a very good priest, have the church rebuilt on its land; and he would like us to have a simple school nearby. This place is the capital of the State of Missouri for five years, and perhaps permanently.[288] The center of government draws many people, and there are no educational resources.

Our church was blessed on November 21 with much pomp. Our chapel is the choir, as at Sainte-Marie. The priest says the Mass at the hour of our choice on ordinary days. On Sunday, he says two: one for us at eight o'clock and the High Mass at eleven. He preaches in French before the Mass and in English afterwards. The male and female singers in the church are one choir, and we are the other, both at Mass and at Vespers. This brick church is very pretty. It is the first devoted to the Sacred Heart, perhaps in the whole New World. Opposite our choir is a chapel of the Blessed Virgin, which has a beautiful picture, and in our choir is the altar that I vowed to Saint Francis Regis, where Mass was being said when the cold froze the wine in the chalice. I assure you that these three objects of our tender devotion, the Sacred Heart, Mary, and Francis Regis, brought together under our eyes, fill the soul with consolation. We have more day students than at Saint Charles. Sister Catherine is learning to sing.

I think all the money promised by your brother has arrived. The bishop told me about 300 F reduction in our debt. The superior [of the Ursulines] in New Orleans told me of about the same sum, so I assumed they were the same, not knowing that Mr. Gary had something for us.

---

286 Henri Jouve entered the novitiate of the Jesuits; Amelie and Caroline at the Sacred Heart.
287 From the time of the General Council in 1820, Josephine Bigeu was ill. Nevertheless, in December 1821, she went to Bordeaux for the transfer of the orphanage of Mrs. de Lalanne and the opening of a boarding school at Sablonat.
288 The capital became Jefferson City in 1826.

That is why I did not mention it. Father Barat would like an answer in this regard. Moreover, he has used a sum of money in pounds coming to us from Mother de Gramont.

If our sisters have not left, which may be just as well after so many delays, could they bring a Roman Gradual,[289] braid for a stole and a vestment, and some thin paper with the Catechism of Charency. We gave ours to Mother Eugenie, but we do not have one in French. In English there are excellent ones.

Since we are without class books, we make up for them with notebooks. I was thinking about proposing the foundation of a Visitation convent in Detroit and to send them books, as at Georgetown.

I am in the Sacred Heart, with all respect and submission, your unworthy daughter.

Philippine Duchesne

---

289 At this period, liturgical norms were established for each diocese, but the Religious of the Sacred Heart had chosen those of Rome. Likewise, the office of the choir religious was that of the Roman Breviary.

CHAPTER III

1822-1828

IN FULL ACTIVITY

INTRODUCTION

Second and Third Foundations and First Journey to Louisiana

Upon departure from France in 1818, Philippine had been named superior and, because of the distances, given certain powers over new foundations that superiors would not normally have had. Only three years after their arrival from France, settled first in Saint Charles where they did not expect to be, then moved after only one year to Florissant at the insistence of Bishop Dubourg, they were, again at the bishop's insistence, split into two groups in order to found a new community far away in lower rural Louisiana, where Mrs. Smith offered her house and property at Opelousas (Grand Coteau). Meanwhile, the next contingent, two fresh missionaries, arrived from France: Lucile Mathevon and Irish-born Anna Xavier Murphy, but they had not yet set out when Eugenie and the novice Mary Layton boarded a steamboat south in August 1821 for Grand Coteau. Philippine wanted to delay the new foundation until the arrival of the two from France, but Bishop Dubourg wanted otherwise. Mothers Mathevon and Murphy set out from France in September 1821, and arrived in New Orleans on February 2, 1822 (Letter 189). Xavier Murphy went directly to Opelousas, while Lucile Mathevon joined Philippine and the others in Missouri. Now they were seven from their old world, but there were already vocations from the new world. The first was Mary Mullen, who had already entered and left during the first year in Saint Charles, but now at Florissant there were Mary Layton in 1820, and Emilie Saint-Cyr and the Hamilton sisters in 1821, soon to be followed by others.

The new foundation in Louisiana got off to a rough start when they learned, among other things, that their patroness, the widow Mrs. Smith, intended to keep a living space for herself in the convent, until Bishop Dubourg convinced her otherwise. The foundation, deftly led by the gracious Mother Eugenie Audé, began to flourish quickly and soon there were vocations there as well. The very next year, 1822, Philippine decided to make the long journey down the Mississippi to visit the new house in Louisiana. She set out taking with her two new vocations destined to remain: Emilie Saint-Cyr, who had just made her first vows at Florissant, and the novice Mary Mullanphy.[1] With them was Therese Pratte, a Florissant student and daughter of the Pratte family in whose house the original group had stayed when they first arrived in Saint Louis. She longed to see again her beloved Mother Eugenie and then return to Saint Louis with Mother Duchesne.

Steamboat travel was still new and very dangerous. The danger of fire or explosion on board was always present; large amounts of wood were burned for a boiler to produce the steam to move the paddlewheels. External dangers were always present in the possibility of running aground or snagging on floating debris. When the religious had first gone up the Mississippi River from New Orleans to Saint Louis in 1818, the journey took six weeks. This time, four years later, the steamboat journey downstream, going with the current instead of against it, took only seventeen days, but then came the torturous boat travel from disembarkation at Plaquemine, Louisiana, through the bayous to Grand Coteau. Philippine tells the harrowing story in Letter 196.

The visit itself went without incident. They arrived on August 7. One of the boarding students in the school at Grand Coteau was Mary Ann Hardey, who read the address of welcome in French for the distinguished visitor. Later, as Mother Aloysia Hardey, she would lead foundations in the eastern United States, Canada, and Cuba, and become the first American assistant general at the motherhouse in Paris in 1872.[2]

The return to Saint Louis was catastrophic: Philippine and Therese Pratte, the student traveling with her, left on September 3 to go by way of New Orleans to board the steamboat *Hecla* there for the journey north up the Mississippi River. They were assured that there was no yellow fever in New Orleans at the moment. By the time they arrived, there

---

1   A distant relative of John Mullanphy, not to be confused with his daughter of the same name who was later a student at Florissant, cf. Letter 250. She left the Society in 1831 (Letter 384).
2   Mary Ann (Aloysia) Hardey, RSCJ (1809-1886), was born on December 8, 1809, in Piscataway, Maryland. Her family moved to Louisiana when she was a child. She began her studies at Grand Coteau at the beginning of 1822. When Philippine came to visit in 1822, she gave the welcome address for the students. She entered the novitiate at Grand Coteau, September 29, 1825, and took the habit the next month, October 22, before going with Eugenie Audé the next day to the foundation of Saint Michael, where she made her first vows on March 15, 1827. She became mistress general two months later, after the death of Xavier Hamilton. She made her profession on July 19, 1833, at the age of 23, in order to be superior at Saint Michael. She was later superior vicar (1844-1872), responsible for the foundations of New York and Cuba, then assistant general to Reverend Mother Josephine Goetz (1872-1886). She died in Paris and was buried at Conflans. When all the French houses were closed in 1905, her body was returned to Kenwood, New York, which she had founded in 1852.

was a serious outbreak of the fearsome disease. Philippine contracted the dreaded illness before boarding the steamboat north. On the second day, three people on the boat died of it, including the captain and first mate! Philippine and Therese had to disembark at Natchez, where there was fear of admitting those who were ill into the town; the cause of yellow fever was not yet known, and they feared contagion. Philippine and Therese were finally given hospitality by a local family. Only after nearly three months from their departure from Grand Coteau in early September were they able to return home to Saint Louis on the steamboat *Cincinnati*.

Philippine returned to her life at Florissant with the small community, a growing number of novices, and a farm that in 1823 included seven cows and sixty chickens. Throughout these years, there are frequent references to a foundation in New Orleans, but decisions were made against it in July 1823 and again in February 1824. Instead, another foundation was made by Eugenie Audé at a location closer to the city, along the banks of the Mississippi at Saint Michael, Louisiana, in 1825. When Eugenie moved to Saint Michael, Grand Coteau was left in the capable hands of Mother Xavier Murphy. The two houses grew and prospered. Eugenie was highly successful wherever she went, and began to assume relative independence with regard to the authority of Philippine, who habitually compared herself unfavorably to others. There was thought on the part of Mothers Audé and Barat of Philippine moving south to one of the Louisiana houses because they were doing so well, but she was firmly against it: Florissant was poor and she liked it that way. The school at Florissant never prospered like those in Louisiana, but it did not do as poorly as the impression that Philippine sometimes gives.

Life at Florissant: Jesuits and an Indian School

An added attraction of Florissant was the establishment of the Jesuits nearby. In 1823, Bishop Dubourg had succeeded in attracting them to his diocese. With U.S. government backing for the establishment of Indian missions and the personal approval of President Monroe for the project, he hoped to set up in Missouri a school for Native Americans and a seminary for the training of future missionaries. For this purpose the bishop offered the Jesuits a valuable tract of land that he owned. The Jesuit contingent arrived from Maryland in May 1823: two priests, three lay brothers, seven young Belgian novices, and three young slave couples, all under the leadership of Father Charles Felix

Van Quickenborne.[3] Among the novices who had come to Maryland in 1821 to be trained for the American mission were Peter J. Verhaegen,[4] who would later in 1841 be the priest who insisted that Philippine be included in the missionary band to Sugar Creek and the pastor who buried Philippine in Saint Charles when she died in 1852; and Pierre Jean De Smet, who was to become the famous missionary to the West.

Philippine and the rest of her community at Florissant were elated by this sudden appearance of the Jesuit spiritual support to which they had been accustomed in France, even if the notoriously harsh Van Quickenborne and Philippine regularly clashed. She was unfailingly loyal to him and insisted that his spiritual training was for her good. His use of sacramental authority was sometimes abusive. It was he who one year, because of a disagreement between them, probably in June 1825, refused absolution to Philippine in confession so that she could not renew her vows on the coming Feast of the Sacred Heart. She could not be present at the Mass and not renew her vows publically, so she did the only thing she could think of to avoid the scandal of the superior not renewing her vows: she pretended to be sick and stayed in bed all day. At another time, Anna Shannon[5] remembered seeing Philippine approach the altar for Communion and be turned away by Father Van Quickenborne with no explanation.[6]

In addition to boarding school and free school, at Florissant they had tried to have a small school for Indian girls, begun in 1825, at the same time that the Jesuits began their school for Indian boys. This at last was

---

3 Charles Felix Van Quickenborne, SJ, born in Belgium in 1788, ordained priest in Ghent, entered the novitiate of the Society of Jesus, made his first vows in 1817 and left for America, Georgetown, to be master of novices there. He arrived in Missouri in 1823, with Father Timmermans and five Flemish novices, one of whom was Pierre De Smet, future apostle of Kansas and the Rocky Mountains. With a reputation for spiritual rigor, he sometimes gave evidence of it by his intransigent authority regarding Philippine. He died in 1837.

4 Peter Verhaegen, SJ, born in Belgium in 1800, arrived in America in 1821, and in Missouri in 1823 with the first group of Jesuits. He was ordained a priest in 1826, was first president of Saint Louis University in 1832, and superior of the Jesuit mission in Missouri. In 1841, it was he who insisted that Philippine be included in the mission to the Potawatomi, and he who escorted her back to Saint Charles a year later. In 1851, he was pastor of the parish church of Saint Charles Borromeo in Saint Charles; it was therefore he who presided at the funeral of Philippine in 1852. He returned to Saint Louis University as a professor in 1858, but had to withdraw from teaching because of bad health. He returned to Saint Charles, where he died in 1868.

5 Anna Josephine (Stanislaus) Shannon, RSCJ (1810-1896), was born in 1810 in County Wexford, Ireland, and came with her family to Missouri in 1820. She was raised in Florissant before entering the novitiate in 1826. She made her first vows April 16, 1827, before she was 17, and her profession March 7, 1836. She lived many years with Philippine, and her memoirs constitute one of the most important witnesses of her life. Two of Anna's sisters, Judith and Margaret, became RSCJ and a third, a Sister of Charity. Anna was vice-vicar in Louisiana (1863-1873) and superior at Saint Michael during the first years of the Civil War. She died at Maryville, Saint Louis, in 1896.

6 Testimonies of Aloysia Jouve and Anna Shannon; cf. Callan, 421, 452.

some fulfillment of Philippine's purpose in setting out for America. Not surprisingly, the attempts lasted only a few years: the Indian children, taken far from their family, did not want to be there, found it impossible to sit still for long periods in the European manner, and frequently ran away. At Saint Louis, there were boarding students, day students, and the orphanage. In every case, the instruction and care of each group was intended to remain separate from the others. With so many groups and such close quarters, it is difficult to imagine how that was done.

During these years, Philippine acted several times as godmother for children baptized in the parish. The names of Philippine and Octavie Berthold appear in the baptismal records of Saint Ferdinand in 1822, 1824, and 1825. Philippine's godchild of April 5, 1822, Marie Rose Radford, was the stepdaughter of General William Clark; her mother, Harriet Kennerly Radford, had married General Clark after the death of his first wife. In 1825, Octavie Berthold was also godmother to two Indian boys of the Iowa nation, ages about ten and thirteen, baptized Peter and Stanislas, and the two nuns were godmothers of two girls aged two and four, whom Philippine described as the "foundation stones" of the Florissant orphanage (Letter 190 to Sophie, April 16, 1822).

Fourth Foundation: The City House in Saint Louis

By 1825, Philippine seems preoccupied about death and how to provide for those around her if she died, perhaps because the state of medical practice was primitive and there was so much death around her. Instead of dying, she was to leave her dear Florissant in 1827 to begin a fourth foundation, this time finally in Saint Louis itself. Unable to find a suitable property any other way, she resorted to writing directly to John Mullanphy, whom she had originally met for the first time in New Orleans in 1818. He was a successful Irish immigrant, one of the wealthiest men in the city and a patron of social works for the needy. She asked him directly for the donation of a property, and he offered a spacious property with a house on the south side of the city. The population of the city was booming during these years, and would increase threefold in the next decade.

One of the conditions for Mullanphy's gift of the land and house to the Society of the Sacred Heart was that the school also provide for up to twenty orphan or indigent girls between the ages of four and eight, to be selected by himself or his daughters, who would remain until the age of eighteen. According to the agreement, he or later his heirs would provide ten dollars for each girl upon entrance, and five dollars each year following, an amount that even in those days did not suffice.[7] John Mullanphy continued to be mindful of the poor of the city, however: the next year, he also established the first hospital in Saint Louis, staffed by the Sisters of Charity. The new school at the City House opened on September 17, 1827.[8]

Philippine and John Mullanphy probably did not interact much before 1827, although they had originally met in New Orleans almost ten years earlier. Mullanphy's beloved country home was in Florissant, not far from Saint Ferdinand, where Philippine had lived from 1819 to 1827. In 1817, two years before the arrival of the religious in Florissant, he had given his country home to his newly married daughter Jane and her husband, Charles Chambers, who took up residence there in 1820. Though there is no surviving evidence of their interaction that early, in later years, Jane Mullanphy Chambers would also be a benefactor of the Saint Louis convent, and after her father's death in 1833, supervisor of admissions to the orphanage.[9]

Bishop Dubourg was increasingly besieged by problems and opposition, whether in New Orleans or Saint Louis. He was a great initiator and a poor administrator. It may be significant that the foundation in Saint Louis only happened after his departure, for he had opposed the presence of the religious in the city from the beginning, with the argument that the boarding school, always the financial foundation, would not flourish there, but rather needed to be located a distance away.

Finally, Dubourg had had enough of frontier life. He visited Saint Louis one last time in 1826 and left for France, where he resigned his episcopal appointment. He had said nothing about this before he left,

---

[7] At the time of his death in 1833, however, Mullanphy apportioned in his will one hundred dollars annually to the local bishop for the use of the orphanage, and for each "graduate" of the orphanage who married, "whose conduct has been proper and meritorious…the sum of one hundred Dollars at least, and more, if the situation of the fund will admit according to the respective merits of those entitled to a donation out of this fund." Published will of John Mullanphy, RSCJ archives.

[8] Girls admitted to the orphanage were not always strictly without parents, but the parents were unable to support them. The work of the orphanage at the City House continued beyond the death of John Mullanphy in 1833, administered by his daughter, Jane Mullanphy Chambers. Her handwritten notes admitting needy little girls to the orphanage are preserved in the RSCJ archives in Saint Louis. The orphanage would continue beyond the move of the school in 1893 to another site farther west, until 1947. The school at the new location of the City House continued for both girls and boys until its final closure in 1968.

[9] Julia Jane Mullanphy Chambers (1799-1891), daughter of their benefactor John Mullanphy, was born in Kentucky and married Charles Chambers (1784-1862) in 1817 in New York. The couple settled in Saint Louis at the initiative of her father, who gave them land and a house to the west of Saint Louis, a property called today "Taille de Noyer" in Florissant Valley. There they raised 17 children. Their daughter, Ann Biddle Chambers Thatcher (1828-1913), gave testimony in 1900 for the cause of Philippine.

so the news came as a great surprise to everyone.[10] No one was more surprised than Joseph Rosati, an Italian Lazarist (Vincentian) priest, earlier recruited and highly trusted by Dubourg, already appointed in 1823 coadjutor bishop of Dubourg's entire diocese from Missouri to Louisiana. He was immediately appointed apostolic administrator of the whole diocese. Before his consecration as bishop, however, the diocese was divided, and he became the first bishop of Saint Louis in March 1827, while remaining apostolic administrator of the new diocese of New Orleans until 1829, when Leo Raymond De Neckere[11] was named its bishop. Rosati remained bishop of Saint Louis as long as Philippine held the office of superior. Their relationship was a close one, and she had recourse to him frequently. One hundred forty-eight of her letters to him are extant.

Return to Saint Charles, Further Expansion

In all the intervening years since the abandonment of the first house in Saint Charles in 1819, there had been frequent negotiations with residents who wanted the religious to return (cf. for example, Letter 190 in 1822) and with the Jesuits who were building a stone church there on the same property. In the middle of the decade, Philippine often mentions her favorable response to the idea in letters to Sophie. By this time, the pastor there was the formidable Van Quickenborne. In 1828, the community at Saint Charles was reopened by Lucile Mathevon and Mary Ann O'Connor,[12] and the school opened on October 10, in the same log house that they had occupied ten years before. It would remain their school and residence until a newer building was built in 1835. The old log house was finally torn down in 1858.

Meanwhile in Louisiana, yet a third house was founded in 1828 at La Fourche, west of New Orleans, by Helene Dutour, who had arrived from France the year before. A small group of Daughters of the Holy Cross (Loretto Sisters) who were English-speaking had a school there that

---

10 Dubourg later became bishop of Montauban in France, and was named bishop of Besançon, but died soon after, in 1833.
11 Leo Raymond De Neckere, a Belgian, left for America, where he was ordained a priest by the Vincentians in 1822. In 1823, he was vice-rector and professor at the seminary at the Barrens. In 1829, he was consecrated bishop of New Orleans and died caring for victims of the yellow fever epidemic in 1833.
12 Mary Ann O'Connor, RSCJ (1785-1864), born in Ireland, came to America, entered the Society of the Sacred Heart in Florissant and made her first vows on April 17, 1825. The same year, she was given charge of the class of Indian girls; she made her profession in 1829. In 1841, she was one of the founders of the Sugar Creek mission to the Potawatomi and devoted herself there until her death.

was languishing in a French-speaking region. After prolonged negotiations with Bishop Rosati, Philippine, and Mother Barat, the school was turned over to French speakers of the Society of the Sacred Heart and the community of the Loretto Sisters was disbursed, with the option of entering the Society, which several of them did. The foundation at La Fourche never went smoothly, largely because Mother Dutour insisted on the same academic standards as in the other two Louisiana houses, but the population and the proximity to Grand Coteau could not support it. The house was eventually closed in 1832 with heavy debt that had to be paid off by the other Louisiana houses and the contributions of friends.

The Society was experiencing amazing growth in its new American home: ten years after the first arrival, there were now six houses of the Sacred Heart in America, three in the South and three in Missouri, with twenty-seven religious, only eleven of whom had come from Europe, and twenty-five American novices. In spite of this notable expansion, Philippine continued to perceive herself as a hindrance to the success of the work and begged continually to be removed from the office of superior. That was not to happen for another twelve years.

LETTERS

Letter 184   **L. 5 to Father Rosati**

SS. C. J. et M.[13]

[January 6, 1822]

Dear Father,

I was deeply moved by the greetings from you that have reached me. We have not forgotten to pray for your house; and at the beginning of the New Year, I have increased my prayers for you and your seminary, the hope of religion in this diocese.

I foresee with regret that we shall not see you until vacation, a fact that makes me sorry that your house is so far from ours. I am ever more convinced that I am unsuited to my charge and that to bear it I would often need your advice, as it is impossible to say everything in letters. In regard to the two doves you had the pleasure to see receive our holy habit, the elder is in a state of temptation that goes beyond my experience and makes me fear for her vocation. Nevertheless, she has remained firm as she has not been tempted to respond to her brother's invitation. There is no one here on whose decision I can fully rely, and I realize more and more how much I have lost in the death of Father de Andreis.

Fathers Ferrari and Borgna[14] have honored me with a letter; both are most solicitous for our dear sisters in Lower Louisiana. I am concerned

---

13 Original autograph, C-VII-2) c Writings Duchesne to Rosati, Box 6. On the reverse: "January 6, 1822, Mother Duchesne, Florissant."
14 Philip Borgna, Piedmontese Lazarist, arrived in Missouri in 1819 and was ordained priest by Bishop Dubourg in Saint Louis, March 19, 1820. Sent to New Orleans, he devoted himself there with Father Ferrari during the yellow fever epidemic in 1822. After Bishop Dubourg's departure in 1826, he was named Bishop Rosati's vicar general in Saint Louis. Later he left the Lazarists and exercised his ministry in the diocese of Philadelphia until 1846, when he went back to Italy.

for them because they are so far from anyone who is enlightened on religious obligations. This knowledge cannot be drawn entirely from books; experience and practice are even more necessary. Mother Eugenie feels this need; I commend her to your prayers. Although her sacrifice was generous, nevertheless I fear that she will become disheartened.

The young lady from Fort Vincennes has not arrived. This does not disappoint me. The example of Miss Moore and her friend proves to us more clearly than ever that the surest vocations are those formed among our pupils, whether they be day scholars or boarders. I beg you in no way to encourage her to come if she is still undecided.

I am with profound respect in the Sacred Hearts of Jesus and Mary, Reverend Father,

Your submissive and unworthy servant,

Philippine Duchesne

January 6, 1822

My sisters send you their regards.

[On the reverse:]
To Father
Father Rosati
Superior of the seminary
Barrens
Saint Louis

Letter 185 **L. 12 to Father Barat**

SS. C. J. et M.

Rec. to St. Anthony, February 18, 1822[15]

My very good Father,

Already congratulating myself on the happiness of seeing you in America and that the time was near, I already thought that my letters would no longer reach you in France and that they should be discontinued. Yours, in which you speak of the needs of the states that have

---

15 Original autograph, C-VII 2) c Writings Duchesne to various Eccles., Box 8. Postmark: Bordeaux, July 10, 1822.

accepted our good fathers, and even of the scarcity of vocations to form a foundation at Aix, have taken away my hopes and discouraged several others who, tired of the painful work with little fruit, counted on joining you and thus hoped for more success.

As for us, we see well that this privation will reduce us to eating dry bread for the rest of our lives. I do not go around looking for consolations, of which I merit too few; but I feel my inability for the work to which I am bound, especially to give edification and aid in the progress of my flock. It would have been reassuring to act only by your inspiration and to see these poor souls being pulled out of their languor! But I must say *fiat* on that subject. It is quite a different thing from material privations; you have too much compassion about those. I fear that it drove you to communicate with our dear mother about it. Also, when I send her the account of our expenses, I prove to her that this year we have reduced our debt; and by doing that each year, we will come clear. We have reduced the cost of boarding because of the scarcity of money, and [nevertheless] our boarding school is not reduced; it is now yielding a few vocations that with time will carry on education and even religion. I do not doubt that the multiplication of our foundations is the surest means to spread religion in this ungrateful country.

What should a priest do in this land where he finds neither lodging nor clothing nor food? A mediocre virtue does not stand up to such a trial, and the defection of several priests only proves it. Most of them would like very much to be attached to our houses; in fact, without worry about temporal needs, they could more easily give their attention to the spiritual. Several times we have had the happiness of giving linens to these poor workers for Jesus Christ, and just about all the material from Amiens is gone as well as some of our handkerchiefs.

I do not desire to be more comfortable except to spread good works. We have been offered several children free whom we have had to refuse. Nevertheless, I promised to accept two Presbyterian orphans of 5 and 6 years, who will be given to us until they are 18, the age of legal emancipation, with the written promise to let them become Catholics and even religious, if they want. Another patron also said that he wanted to give us his daughter (it is the custom here to give one's children by a legal act before a judge), and he sees that it would be best for her to become a Catholic. Several Protestant boarders also have permission from their parents to be baptized.

But pray much for a charming child with a sweet, heavenly face, who is asking the same favor but is doubtful of getting it. To obtain it more quickly, she asks all at once to be like us. The answer must come from 400 leagues away. She was like a rock when her parents left, and wanted to appear before them with a crucifix hanging from her neck. Her mother asked her: "Do they make you wear that?" "No, Mama, it is I who want it." That evening we could hear her saying her rosary or conversing with her crucifix; she is never tired of praying. An old grandmother, who adores her, showered her with presents before leaving the area, weeping and making those weep who saw her; afterwards, she brought in a large Negro who had an expression of tenderness on his face and his hand over his heart, saying his farewell with tears in his eyes. The child stayed the same and even showed joy when the door closed, and she could say: "I am staying." She wanted to make her declaration, but fear that she would be taken away to another area without religious resources made us advise her to delay until after their departure. If the parents refuse, would you see any obstacle to baptizing secretly? Here they say it is against the laws of the church, that the permission of parents is required because of the danger of apostasy. This is what the bishop wants.

The church dedicated to the Sacred Heart contiguous to our house is nearly finished. They have been saying Mass there since November 20. Every Sunday, the priest says two Masses: one in the morning for us and one at eleven with sermon in French, and the *credo* in English after Mass. It is always a high Mass, sung in full chant. We make up one choir and some outside people another. Other than that, there are French hymns before the Mass and English hymns at the elevation and Communion. Our singers sing these hymns in parts with two American gentlemen who stand near our choir, behind a curtain. It is very solemn. It lasts only one hour. In summer, it finishes at noon. Mother Octavie is distinguished for the music, Sister Catherine for the chant; and she teaches the novices and day students, who number nearly forty. The parish is going well; nearly all the men have been to confession.

There is a novice who could use your attention; I had hoped for this but I had to renounce it. Is her state simple temptation? Is it opposition to every dependence and mortification? This discernment is difficult; pray much that she will emerge victorious from the battle concerning her vocation, just like the other likeable child for her vocation.

February 18, 1822

I have not received the box from Mr. Jouve in Lyon that you told me I should have, but I have the letters it contained. To whom was it addressed, I ask? I have great need of its contents.

Bishop Dubourg saw Mother Eugenie at Opelousas. That took away some of my worries in her regard. The delay of our sisters has been very upsetting for that foundation. I explained the reasons to our mother but have not yet received a response. Please offer her my respects and submission; I await the thaw of the ice and a steamboat to write with ease, but I could not restrain the desire to offer you my respects and my wishes in the Heart of Jesus, in whom I am your little servant.

Philippine

My respects to Reverend Father Debrosse and to our sisters.

[On the reverse:]
To Father
Father Louis Barat
Rue de Sèvres N° 35
Paris

Letter 186   **L. 43 to Mother Barat**

SS. C. J. et M

Rec. to St. Anthony of Padua
February 28, 1822[16]
No. 29

Very Reverend Mother,

I answered the letter in which you told me about the journey of our sisters at the beginning of this year, on one of the King's ships, a favor that I value very little, as I told you, because of the serious disadvantage of passing through Martinique, an unhealthy island, and of threading one's way through a labyrinth of islands where there are frequent shipwrecks. However, I am awaiting the arrival of our sisters with lively impatience, as I am very troubled by Eugenie's solitude.[17] I

---

16 Original autograph, C-VII 2) c Duchesne to Barat, Box 2. On the reverse, Father Barat wrote: "I read this letter, at the invitation of Mother Philippine in another letter that I received in the same packet." Cf. J. de Charry, II, 2, L. 152, pp. 52-59; Hogg, pp. 32-38. Ch. Paisant, pp. 424-426.

17 Eugenie Audé and Mary Layton, who had arrived at the end of August in Mrs. Smith's house, would remain alone until the end of December.

count very little on Mother Girard.[18] Happily, the bishop was there and his presence was necessary to settle many matters, particularly the terms of Mrs. Smith's donation. All is settled now on that point, and the bishop writes that the lady and our good Eugenie are in perfect accord;[19] she has already had the happiness of making Jesus Christ known to one person who did not know him and of having her baptized, a happiness we are expecting also, but we are suffering delays awaiting the consent of her parents!

I have just made a new copy of our Constitutions and in examining them carefully, I have not seen one word about the election or the nomination of the ecclesiastical superior general,[20] which could become an issue at the moment of making vows.

If you approve, we would have second year novices make their first vows without waiting for the end of the second year in order to give them more authority in the classes and greater standing with outsiders, before whom I shall soon appear very little; half of the boarders are Americans now, and I am sure that even Mother Octavie herself is not always understood. I believe all these vocations are good. Several young people are applying, but they are all working class who will be useful only for the day school, when we become more numerous. These arrive [without trousseau and without any dowry] and this house, so indebted already, would not be able to take on this charge. Wealthy postulants do not get anything from their parents.

Nevertheless, in spite of the diversity of beliefs and opinions, God helps our powerlessness and changes the opinion of the best informed and most influential Protestants in the country in favor of this house. One is sending us in one day three of his nieces; another brought his daughter, saying he wanted her to be a *good Catholic*. Still another said he had never contributed to any cause with as much pleasure as he felt for the church in Florissant, that this establishment was the best that he knew. Another had wanted to take away one of our orphans and said afterwards that he had been thoughtless and brought us another and proposed bringing a third.

---

18 Mother Girard and Constance Frouard arrived in December, but they would not stay.
19 Mrs. Smith wanted to reserve two rooms in the convent for herself, but Bishop Dubourg convinced her to have a small house built for herself not far away and to give the property of Grand Coteau (the house and half of the land) to the Society of the Sacred Heart, on condition that an educational establishment be maintained there. The other half of the land was given to the bishop for a seminary.
20 Until then the role of the ecclesiastical superior general was assumed by the Grand Almoner of the Court of France, a structure that posed problems in other countries. In 1826, with the approbation of the Constitutions by the Holy See, the office was replaced by that of a cardinal protector, residing in Rome.

No one among the Americans interests me as much as Miss Sara Benton. She is waiting for consent to her baptism and her admission among us; it is very doubtful that she will receive it as she is quite young.[21]

Our Father Barat has told me that one of those who were to come to us is dying of lassitude and that Mother Bardot[22] will not come. I am not sorry, on account of her peculiar illnesses, about which Sister Catherine has told me. This country requires very level heads because of the trying climate. There are several notable examples.

I think, my good Mother, that because of the great distances and the unnecessary costs, I am dispensed from writing to the superiors of each house, as the Constitutions provide;[23] either I would repeat myself or write mere nothings. You are the universal center of all the business as well as of all our affection, and I think that communicating with my mothers and sisters through you will make any witness I give more acceptable.

The order of day for Sundays and that of the novitiate is upset on account of the Mass at 11 o'clock and Vespers at 3; the novitiate because the novices all have an employment, and it is difficult to have them meet at the specified hours.

The general regulation of the order of day that was sent to us is not the one that was being followed in Paris or in Grenoble; it contains besides some things that were abolished at the first Council [of 1815]; however, I am leaving it as is, hoping to receive the decisions of the second Council [of 1820], according to which we can correct it.

We still have five novices, twenty-six boarders at 140 *piastres* per year or 700 F, but everyone says that in two months there will be no more money, so we shall raise it on paper, with which one cannot pay one's debts; from now on several are paying only in kind and several have reductions.

The day school is free, except for a few eggs or chickens; that gives the consolation of saying that one has paid.

---

21 Bishop Dubourg opposed having "*young B.*" baptized without the consent of her parents, for "that would be against all the rules of the church." By receiving baptism at the hands of a Protestant minister, he told Philippine, on October 11, 1821, "she will not receive any the less the grace and the character of the child of God and of his Church if her heart is well disposed. That is what you may explain to her." *Letters of Bishop Dubourg, bishop of Louisiana, concerning the establishment of the Religious of the Sacred Heart in his diocese*, C-VII 2) c Duchesne to various Eccles., Box 8.

22 Adele Bardot, RSCJ (1781-1828), childhood friend of Sophie Barat, professed in Amiens in 1805.

23 Article 325 of the Constitutions of 1815: "It is with the same object that local superiors are encouraged to frequent communication with one another."

We have a man in our service of the type of Brother Fonsala; he has his wife and a little house that we had built for him; we have only to pay him.

I hope that Mother Bigeu has recovered. I would write to her if I did not fear missing this steamboat. I beg you to give her my regards as well as our fathers, Mother [Eugenie] de Gramont and all our mothers.

I am in the Heart of Jesus, with profound reverence, very worthy Mother, your very unworthy daughter.

Philippine Duchesne

Our sisters send you all their most tender regards.

[On the reverse:]
To Mother
Mother Barat
Superior General of the Ladies of the Sacred Heart
Rue de Varenne
Faubourg Saint-Germain
Paris

Letter 187   **L. 44 to Mother Barat**

SS. C. J. et M.

Rec. to St. Anthony of Padua
March 6, 1822[24]
No. 30

Very Reverend Mother,

I just wrote you on February 18 by the first steamboat that has departed this winter. It was useless to send letters through any of the eastern cities where navigation only begins to be possible in April. I am taking this route, for my letter will arrive in New York at the very moment when the port begins to operate. My letter will reach you sooner that way. But I believe yours will still arrive here faster if they come through

---

24 Original autograph, C-VII 2) c Duchesne to Barat, Box 2. Postmarks: St Louis, Mo., March 8; Paris, May 13, 1822. Cf. J. de Charry, II, 2, L. 153, pp. 60-65; Hogg, pp. 39-44. Ch. Paisant, pp. 432-435.

New Orleans; opportunities are frequent, and one avoids the postage. Besides, I have not noticed that any have gone astray.

Mr. Mullanphy must have arrived in New York before the freeze, for I received your letter by mail, stamped from that city, where he surely must have posted it since he could not set out himself. It is said, however, that since the arrival of the bishop, the routes that were impracticable for women before are much better now. I am very disappointed that you did not entrust our sisters to him.[25] It is to be feared that their journey will be as expensive and dangerous and much more unpleasant on a French ship than on an American one, as the American ones are quieter; the Mullanphy ladies are excellent people.

We are slow in letting you know how your letters touched our hearts. I do not know whether it is possible that they could increase our gratitude, especially mine, for I owe everything to you; but I know that now we are free from a heavy burden, and it is very good to be consoled by our mother.

One of my last letters must have already quieted your anxiety as it told you of our hope of aid from Mother Eugenie[26] and that the bishop has said not to worry about paying him. However, pressured by the lack of money, he wrote to tell me to put 1000 F on his treasurer's account, and the latter himself asked for 1500 immediately; that is exactly the sum Mother Eugenie had already left in New Orleans for us, which was known. Therefore, I am expecting other requests. They are justified, for he has great difficulty in supporting the seminary [the Barrens] and the priests in Upper Louisiana. Journeys are expensive. On December 26, he was in Opelousas; January 27, in New Orleans and now he is in Florida,[27] where his authority is still not recognized. He has a great deal of land, but I set little value on that wealth for those who cannot work it themselves or who do not have numbers of slaves who are then driven to work by whips. For us, in my experience, crops cost more than the harvests yield; they are destroyed constantly by wandering flocks. I make an exception for orchards and gardens etc. and the land overlooking ours; thus the intention of Mrs. de la Grandville[28] will be able to be fulfilled and to rid us of a trying neighbor who is threatening to kill our cows when we chase his pigs out of our property.

---

25 Mother Barat preferred to wait for a royal vessel so as to have the free voyage promised by the minister, but she had to choose a private ship in order to have safe accompaniment.
26 Mrs. Smith was to reimburse the travel expenses of the missionaries.
27 Having been a Spanish colony until 1819, Florida was incorporated into the United States, but it became a state only in 1845.
28 Her gifts were made to acquire land.

I find that more than 6400 F have been received since our arrival here:

March 1820	1. 1000 F received through Father Martial, who paid the freight charges and the duty	1000 F
April 1820	2. 1000 F received from the bishop as deduction from our debt	1000 F
Dec. 1820	3. 3000 F through a letter of exchange (reduced to 2855 by the exchange)	3000 F
June 1821	4. 1000 F sent for us to the Abbot of La Trappe	1000 F
Unknown date	5. to the Abbot of La Trappe	313 F
Another	6. to the Abbot of La Trappe	360 F
		6673 F

Besides all this, there are the two gifts from Mother de Gramont from Quimper, one of which was used for books, but it is difficult at this distance to tell you anything more precise about these small sums. I am told: "You have received a sum in New Orleans; it will remain until there is an opportunity." Or: "The bishop has kept back some money to repay himself or for *some* commissions for us;" or details are given only some months later. I do not know how to put all this together, but I believe that everything sent from France has arrived.

We are going to increase our devotion to Saint Anthony of Padua. I promised him in August that if, by the first of January, we were free of debt, we would accept a boarder without paying; and then your letter of September came to free us of our most thorny burden. What remains will not trouble us as much as I feared; therefore, I want to fulfill this promise, but I want to know if it is sufficient to take a child who is already in the house and whom we would have kept in any case for religious reasons. We are expecting four boarders who will complete the number of thirty, the most we can take, as our choir is separated from the church by a balustrade and cannot hold more people; neither can the dormitory, the classroom nor the refectory.

So, good Mother, you see our establishment in Opelousas strengthened, and do not be surprised that during the novena to Saint Francis Xavier, whose great heart embraced the whole world, that I ask you again to think of other colonies. That was the purpose of my last letter, in which I forgot to tell you that we cannot be numerous here in the same place; as we cannot teach accomplishments here, either in school or outside, we would not be able to have enough to occupy the novices, most of whom have no aptitude at all for study; but there is no dearth of applicants for the free schools. I have received with sorrow the response of Sara Benton's father, who refuses to let her become a Catholic. I am afraid they are coming to get her, and she herself believes that she will not be able to hold out alone. She does not yet know the sad news. How angry I am that she cannot be baptized without the consent of superiors! Please tell me what the fathers think about this *question*. She wants to become a religious and is already instructed.

Please tell your brother that here we have very good catechisms in English and that Father Anduze has written to the college in Georgetown for *Rodriguez* in English[29] and other good books; but the small box of braid, thread, and silk that Mrs. Jouve sent me has been lost. I would like to know to whom Mrs. Fournier, the bishop's sister, sent it and how she classified it. I have two white vestments that I cannot finish; and white is worn on all the feasts here, even the Sacred Heart. One of the two was given by Mrs. Jouve.

I am very happy about the new foundation in Le Mans and the graces given at Aloysia's tomb in that dear house.[30] The letter from the new Aloysia gave me much pleasure.

You see at your feet, Reverend Mother, your whole poor family. You do not speak of our novices. The most perfect, Sister Regis, is begging to make her vows at the end of the year in the month of May. I beg you to answer her request. We are well enough.

I am in the Sacred Heart, with deep veneration, Reverend Mother, your very unworthy daughter.

Philippine

Regards to our fathers, mothers and sisters.

---

29 The *Treatise on Christian Perfection* of Alphonsus Rodriguez, SJ (1526-1616), was then the basic text for the formation of novices. Father Anduze, Lazarist, a professor at the college in Saint Louis and a friend of the religious in Florissant, obtained a copy of it from the Jesuits at Georgetown.
30 After the death of Euphrosine (Aloysia) Jouve, miracles attributed to her intercession multiplied at her tomb at Sainte-Marie d'En-Haut. Her sister Amelie took her religious name, a practice that the General Council of 1826 would abolish.

[On the reverse:]
To Mother
Mother Barat Superior General
of the Religious of the Sacred Heart, rue de Varenne
Faubourg Saint-Germain
Paris, France
By way of New York

Letter 188   **L. 6 to Father Rosati**

SS. C. J. et M.[31]

[March 8, 1822]

Dear Father,

I received your answer to my two letters. Thank you for your promise for the vacation. I know the value of it, as do all my sisters.

You were good to answer me in the midst of all your occupations, especially with your bad arm. Father Cellini[32] gave us the good news of your recovery. We have a new acquaintance in your Society of the Mission: Father Dahmen[33] greatly interests us, and we beg you not to detain him in the absence of Father Delacroix, who will leave two days after Easter.

The suffering condition of the person about whom I spoke to you continues. She went to confession to Father Cellini; I look for greater peace for her after this helpful visit, which does not keep me from regretting the loss of one of yours [Father de Andreis]. She is tempted to

---

31 Original autograph, C-VII 2) c Writings Duchesne to Rosati, Box 6. On the reverse: "March 8, 1822, Mother Duchesne, Florissant."
32 Francis Cellini (1781-1849), a physician at Holy Spirit Hospital in Rome, arrived in Saint Louis in 1819; he entered the Vincentian novitiate at the Barrens. He practiced medicine in Louisiana for several years and was chaplain at the house in Grand Coteau from September to November 1822. But, as a result of conflict with Bishop Dubourg about Mrs. Smith's donation for the establishment of a school, he was replaced by Leo De Neckere. In 1825, he went to Rome, left the Congregation of the Mission but came back to Missouri in 1826 after Bishop Dubourg's departure. He died in Saint Louis in 1849.
33 Francis Xavier Dahmen, CM, born in Germany in 1789, was ordained priest in 1819. He performed several kinds of pastoral work at Vincennes, Indiana; Florissant, Sainte Geneviève, and Saint Louis. He returned to Europe in 1852 and died in Paris in 1866. Louise Callan notes: "Father Dahmen was one of the priests of the Saint Louis area in whom Mother Duchesne had the greatest confidence" (Callan, p. 772, n. 10).

think ill of our divine Savior and his ministers. I beg you to do for her with your prayers what distance prevents you from doing in an interview.

I am with respect in the Sacred Heart, Reverend Father, your very devoted servant,

Philippine Duchesne, sup.

March 8, [1822]

Letter 189   L. 13 to Father Barat

SS. C. J. et M.

Rec. to St Anthony of Padua[34]
April 1, 1822

My very good Father,

You have already learned from a previous letter and from one I wrote to my mother that I believe I have received all the money announced by your letters. The one of September 9 told me nothing about the departure of our sisters, and lo, they arrived safely on the wings of Providence, which is always good to us. It is also to be noticed that they arrived on February 2, feast of the Blessed Virgin. Bishop Dubourg was the first to give me the news. He had Mother Xavier [Murphy] depart for Opelousas, and he will himself bring Mother Lucile [Mathevon] back to us; she also wrote to me, but her letter, which gave details of her voyage, told me nothing about our fathers and our mothers in France. I concluded that she is not accustomed to writing much, and so she did not know what to choose that would interest us the most in a letter. Undoubtedly, she is bringing some for me, but she said not a word about that. That annoyed me as well as the detour to Opelousas for the decrees of councils, the summary of the Constitutions, etc., which we were awaiting so impatiently; they are all in Mother Xavier's trunk.

Mother Josephine Meyneroux also arrived in New Orleans on Christmas Eve. That news astonished me a great deal, as it did Mother Eugenie, with whom she already is. We do not know the reason for her voyage nor who sent her, and there is so much wandering from

---

34 Original autograph, C-VII 2) c Writings Duchesne to various Eccles., Box 8. Postmark: Bordeaux, August, 1822.

the subject in her letters that I see pretty clearly that she came against the will of our mother who, anyway, had already written to me that she was trying to dissuade her from coming. She is asking to make her final vows at once and says that you are the one who sent her and that you should have written to me about it. If this is so, the letter is lost, for I have not had a word from France about her coming.

Thank you for the hymn about Aloysia.[35] All that I learn about her adds to my confusion: I am far from being able to make the same vow as she did.[36] God has taken my admonitrix, Mother Eugenie, but has provided me another in the novice to whom you wrote, who, to my great confusion, fulfills this duty better than if she had been charged with it. They think she loves me and she does not even esteem me. The trials she is experiencing about this and the temptations against faith and loving virtue deprive her of any of the sweetness of the Lord's yoke. God will perform a great miracle if he can make the tempest in her heart to cease. Her character will make her judge her judges for a long time, but she does not communicate about her contradictions; one hardly notices them. So I hope that she will persevere. She has the kind of nature that is made to command, so obedience is costly. She is necessary to us for English, and she gives classes in both languages as if she had been doing it for ten years.[37]

I have thanked you several times for your precious collection. I received it at the right time. It is read with eagerness by all your children.

We must rejoice in the good of others, but you will not hinder me from being unhappy that we have no Jesuits. They are really necessary. One's soul is very much alone here.

---

35 *La reconnaissance à Aloysia Jouve. Complainte de Jésus (et autres chants religieux en vers).* Grenoble: Baratier, Imprimeur de l'Évêché, Grand'rue, 1821. Bibliothèques municipales de Grenoble, V. 1733.
36 "Mother Aloysia seemed so pure, so innocent in the eyes of those who directed her that she was allowed to make the beautiful vow that Saint Teresa made only with trepidation, that is, to do what she believed to be the most perfect. This commitment was even more sublime in that this mother was in a position very heavy for human nature, exposed to the testing brought on by great suffering. (...) She said sometimes to her superior: 'The vow that I have made is very powerful; by bringing me closer to Our Lord, it makes virtue easier for me. I would never have thought that it was so easy and so sweet to accomplish.'" Archives USC Province, Manuscript of Philippine Duchesne, *Vie de Mère Euphrosine Aloysia Jouve, religieuse du Sacré-Cœur,* Vol. 2, pp. 61-63. According to the *Dictionnaire de spiritualité,* "the vow to do the most perfect commits one to do what one judges to be better, more pleasing to God in the concrete present situation." Vol. XII, part 1, pp. 230-233 (Paris: Beauchesne, 1984).
37 The novices in Florissant then were Mary Ann Layton, Emilie Saint-Cyr, Xavier and Regis Hamilton. Xavier Hamilton died at Saint Michael in 1827 at the age of 24; Philippine mentions in her notice the hard combats that she endured in the novitiate and emphasized her gift for teaching.

Please give the news to our mother general to whom I have written to tender her my gratitude for the 6000 F paid to our creditor. A few days ago, he was at the junction of the Ohio, so we expect him any day. The ceremonies of Holy Week, a retreat for First Communion, and the preparation for baptism of several Protestant students; all of this absorbs our time.

Miss Sara Benton, child of my heart, feeds on tears. She wants to be a Catholic and a religious, but her parents are opposed. To temper her suffering, we have received her as a "Child of Mary." Pray much for her; she brings together every good quality. Yesterday I saw Miss Emilie; she says nothing. I saw that her heart was troubled, but she lacks strength.

Other than those in the boarding school, we have eight poor children, of whom five are completely our responsibility. I promised to receive a ninth. This way we might produce many Catholics if we can augment the number. Pray for our success.

I am in the divine Hearts, my good Father, your unworthy daughter.

Philippine

My loving remembrances to my mothers and sisters in the Sacred Heart.

[On the reverse:]
To Father
Father Barat
Rue de Sèvres N° 35
Paris

Letter 190   **L. 45 to Mother Barat**

Florissant, April 16, 1822[38]

Very Reverend Mother,

Yesterday, April 15, we had the happiness of seeing our beloved and much awaited Mother Lucile; she was welcomed as we had been in New Orleans and in Saint Louis. Mr. Pratte brought her here with his eldest daughter [Emilie], our first boarder.

---

38 Copy, C-III 1: USA Foundation Upper Louisiana, Box 1, *Lettres de la Haute Louisiane II 1823-1830*, pp. 207-208. Cf. J. de Charry, II, 2, L. 164 bis, pp. 121-126; Hogg, pp. 80-83. Ch. Paisant, pp. 467-469.

A few days ago, we had a visit from our physician, a Protestant, from Saint Charles. He proposed starting a campaign to build us a house, offering himself to contribute more than anyone else, saying that he had several nieces, Protestants like himself, whom he wishes to send us and who would become Catholics; that they could not come to Florissant because of their mother's feeling for them. He wanted to obtain our consent immediately, which I postponed giving, but I didn't say a definite *no*, anticipating so many possible conversions. All upper class, educated people appreciate the Catholic religion above all others; and even if the parents do not embrace it, they will all arrive before long at allowing their children to do so.

We would have liked to have several of our pupils baptized on Holy Saturday;[39] but so that the parents can assist at the ceremony, we waited until Easter Monday.[40] We decorated the baptismal font, and the pupils were in festive dress. I had as goddaughter the stepdaughter of Mr. Clark, governor general, the highest ranking person in Saint Louis. Mother Octavie was godmother to Miss Marthe Marie Madeleine, the daughter of a doctor. We have also been godmothers to two orphans, of whom we took charge on condition that they become Catholics. They are the foundation stones of our little orphanage at the day school where they are already. Besides these four children, there are five others, four little girls in the day school and a little boy who did not even have a pair of socks for the ceremony. We dressed and decked out these poor children so as to impress on their minds the blessings of the day. This consoling ceremony will be repeated often, I hope.

My dear Sara Benton and her companion, Caroline Hamilton, wept the whole day at not having the same happiness. The former will die of sorrow and longing if she does not obtain it.[41] It is very difficult not to be able to go ahead. Five other Protestant boarders hope only for the same advantage; they say that the subject they like best is *instruction* [religion]. They had never heard of the judgment; they remain amazed when we speak about it, and they say that they do not understand how one can believe it and still offend God. These last days there were also three men baptized in our Church of the Sacred Heart. God is already

---

39   Baptismal ceremonies were held during the Easter Vigil, at that time celebrated on the morning of Holy Saturday. First Communion, to which Philippine refers, took place on Holy Thursday.
40   Easter Monday, April 8, 1822. The custom then was to baptize Protestants conditionally. According to the Code of Canon Law of 1917, the godfather or godmother at a baptism was not to be "either a professed or a novice of a religious congregation," without the permission of the ecclesiastical superior. That was probably the case here.
41   She would be baptized and make her First Communion the night of May 23rd but would soon be taken away by her family.

granting great graces there. There were twelve First Communions on Holy Thursday and there will be more on the feast of the Assumption.

Our confessor [Father Delacroix] leaves tomorrow for the Osage,[42] who do not want Presbyterian ministers because of their short coats and their wives. A Lazarist [François-Xavier Dahmen] will replace him here. That society is very friendly towards us.

Our orphanage opened during the novena for the feast of Saint Joseph. The day school suffices for their lodging for the moment. Hand-me-downs from the boarders clothe them and food is not a problem. We have full pails of milk, meat at 2½ *sous* and we make corn bread for them. Mr. Mullanphy has given a sum of money for an establishment of this kind, and we hope to be able to use it to enlarge the building, which is made of wood.

Sometimes I weep for joy at seeing more than a hundred people who, in one way or another, are learning here to love Jesus through us. I do not know how to praise God for it.

Mother Eugenie will have more success; she is back on her feet. She is happy to have borne alone all the difficulties of the beginnings. God visibly blesses everything she does; it is really marvelous. I miss her so much here.

I am ... etc.

Philippine

Letter 191   L. 14 to Mother Mailluchaeu

SS. C. J. et M.

Rec. to St Ant. of Padua
April 16, 1822[43]

My much respected Mother,

I prefer to write a little to you rather than not at all. Sister Lucile [Mathevon] arrived yesterday. I have only the night to write my dear

---

42 This tribe took the name of the Osage River. The Indians numbered about 5800, divided into three bands: Great Osage, Little Osage, and Arkansas. Their principal village, of 4200 inhabitants, was located in Vernon County, Missouri, at the junction of the Marmiton and Little Osage Rivers, 80 miles south of Kansas City. They were evangelized by Father Marquette in 1674. Father Delacroix went on mission there periodically; he returned on May 23 and would leave again on August 9 and come back, quite ill, on September 17, 1822.
43 Original autograph, C-VII 2) c Duchesne to RSCJ and Children, Box 4.

letters and answer the most urgent; the steamboat will leave immediately, so I must finish before daybreak.

This nocturnal silence lends itself to sentiments of the heart. Mine is always amazed when I think of Mother Therese, of our two conversations, of the rock, of Morgane, of the Holy Father, etc. Those walls, the sight of which filled me with gratitude, have become much more dear to me now that they contain the mortal remains, not of a niece, a dear student, but of a spouse of the Sacred Heart to whom he united himself by suffering and whose humble fidelity he glorifies.[44] Thank you for having prepared the details of her precious life and having made sure that they reached me. See that I am prayed for at that tomb, which we had visited together one day without foreseeing that it would become a sanctuary. Send me some of her relics and those of Father d'Hyères.

Please offer my respects to the bishop, to Father Bouchard, to Fathers Rivet and Rambaud. All my good former sisters are present to me, but I cannot name them all. Please also, Mothers de La Croix, Balastron, and Second to receive especially my tender remembrances, and to offer them to their dear sisters and mine. I commend to you our children who are still without religion, who all desire baptism. Five received it the Sunday after Easter. The parents of the others are opposed to it, but many graces are prepared for us; it seems that many hearts want only to be open to grace. Pray that it will be given them.

I am all yours in the Heart of Jesus and Mary,

Philippine

[On the reverse:]
To Mother
Mother Therese Maillucheau
Superior of the Religious of the Sacred Heart
at Sainte-Marie
Grenoble
Isère

---

44 Euphrosine Jouve, called Aloysia, died on January 21, 1821.

Letter 192   **L. 46 to Mother Barat**

SS. C. J. et M.

Saint Ferdinand, June 24, 1822[45]
No. 32

Very Reverend Mother,

I am profiting by this beautiful season to send this letter by way of New York, in the hope that it will reach you more promptly; but don't you use the same route, for the letters Father Barat sent through the father rector of Washington took more than eight months to arrive, because on this side navigation is interrupted at the first frost; instead send them through New Orleans. It is a long time since I wrote to you; I put it off until the bishop's return.[46] But that is too long a wait and when he does arrive, if I have several interesting things to tell you, I will have the consolation of writing to you again.

He is surely going to propose an establishment for Saint Charles, as I have already told you, or for New Orleans. The inhabitants of Saint Charles want us there, even the Protestants; we would have a numerous day school there, but as money has almost disappeared, there would be very few boarders here and none at all there.[47] We will have trouble keeping our twenty children until the vacation (month of August), and we don't expect more than the two or three daughters of businessmen of Missouri and of a few surveyors or other employees of Congress; only these can pay. But in proportion to the dearth of money, the price of foodstuffs is lessened, so we can live, as well as our novices and the six orphans in our care. It would be the same in Saint Charles if we have a house built there, and we would have the unique advantage we expected in coming here, which is to extend the teaching and look after a priest, for no one in Upper Louisiana could be expected to live on the income derived from the parish.

If you approve of this plan, I would like you to decide who, whether Mother Lucile or Mother Octavie, should be at the head. Mother Lucile understands better how to run a house, but she doesn't know English,

---

45 Copy, A-II 2) g Box 2, *Lettres intéressantes de la Société depuis 1816 N° 1*, pp. 331-333. Cf. J. de Charry, II, 2, L. 157, pp. 76-80; Hogg, pp. 50-54. Ch. Paisant, pp. 473-475.
46 He was then in Lower Louisiana and Florida and would return to Saint Louis only in July.
47 Very few boarders in Florissant and none in Saint Charles.

and there would be difficulties if she had to have too much contact with the parents of our American novices. (…)

Mother Lucile has won the hearts of all in the house and in the day school. Everyone admires her devotedness and her other virtues, especially Mother Octavie (…).

As for Sister Catherine, her zeal cannot be confined to a village; she still has Saint Louis or New Orleans in mind (…).

The novice I told you about is better; the others are getting along very well. We have a new one, coadjutrix, born in Sainte Genevieve, named Judith Labruyère;[48] she took the habit with the name of Sister Ignatius, on the feast of the Sacred Heart.

We have had two months of blessings; the attractive child I told you about [Sara Benton], who wanted to be a Catholic and one of us, has withstood violent opposition and refusal still. In spite of that several priests advised baptizing her and having her make her First Communion; that took place on May 23 at midnight. She is an example to the boarders and is really under the influence of grace; every day we expect them to take her away; she is most steadfast. There have been two other baptisms of Protestants, and several earnestly desire it. Miss Emilie Chouteau,[49] about whom Father Inglesi spoke to you, is again thinking of a vocation but no hope of her parents' consent, no more than for others. Saint Louis is like Malacca in the time of Saint Xavier; that tells you everything.

You are fearful, Reverend Mother, at the thought of a new foundation; but believe me, it is the only way we can subsist, because there we will be able to take more postulants, as we will have the means to house and feed them. You see that in one year Mother Eugenie is going to find herself as far ahead as we are after four years. It will be the same in Saint Charles; the whole thing is to have the spirit of sacrifice.

If some priests make a foundation among the Osage, two sisters would also be wanted for catechetical instruction; but *there*, entire death

---

48 Judith (Ignatius) Labruyère, RSCJ (1801-1831), coadjutrix, was born January 1, 1801, in Sainte Geneviève, Missouri, arrived December 31, 1821, at Saint Ferdinand, entered the novitiate June 14, 1822, and made her first vows June 25, 1824. Sent to the foundation of Saint Michael, Louisiana, in 1825, she made her profession in 1830 at the time of the visit of Philippine. She died the following year. C-VII 2) c Duchesne-Writings about the history of the Society, Box 1, *Vies des religieuses du Sacré-Cœur en Amérique*. See Chap. 4, Notice 1.

49 Emilie Chouteau (1802-1843), one of the first pupils of the Sacred Heart at Florissant, was the daughter of Auguste Chouteau, co-founder of the city of Saint Louis, and of Marie Therese Cerré. Her parents refused their consent to her plan to enter religious life. In 1825, she married Major Thomas Floyd Smith of the American army.

to self. We would have to go against all prudence; however, I would be quite happy to devote myself there, if you judge it appropriate in time.

Mother Lucile told me that your sight is getting very weak; I was struck with fear lest that limit my correspondence with you; you must often have difficulty reading my writing, but we do not have the wherewithal to write well.

While our confessor was with the Osage, who welcomed him and promised him some land, we had at Saint Ferdinand a Lazarist [Father Dahmen] who, although he fought with Bonaparte for five years, has all the appearance, the virtue and even the voice of Father Rambaud, the younger one. It seems he is destined for Saint Charles.

The bishop has sent us two beautiful pictures, one for Mother Octavie, representing the vision of Saint Francis at the Portiuncula, the other for me, of Saint Regis dying supported by an angel, and seeing Jesus and Mary waiting for him; it is extremely touching. We have placed it on his altar in our choir in place of the one of Saint Michael.

We would need a banner of the Blessed Virgin; we carried our statue, already quite spoiled, in the procession of the Blessed Sacrament, which took place in our garden; everything went off well, even on the part of the Protestants who came. Next year we would like to have some banners that are not so shabby; they were just pictures on paper on a background of fabric. On the feast of the Sacred Heart we had another procession and had several Masses, one with deacon and sub-deacon.

In order not to make this letter too long, I end by throwing myself at your feet to be blessed by my mother whose unworthy daughter in the Sacred Heart I am.

Philippine

My regards to our Fathers Joseph [Varin], Perreau and Louis, your good brother. I am told that we shall have no letters from him during his long retreat.

Letter 193   **L. 10 to Mrs. de Mauduit,**
at Grâne near Loriol (Drôme)

Saint Ferdinand, June 29, 1822[50]

I learned, my good Friend, that you had been ill, and since then no one has said anything to me about you. So I am coming to find out for myself everything that concerns you; it seems to me that a special bond unites me to you; no doubt it is our common love for Saint Regis; I beg you to make a novena for me in the church at Grâne where he began to make me feel his protection.

We now have two foundations in America, 400 leagues from each other; and several others are being prepared, the success of which I ask you to recommend to Saint Regis. It is only by multiplying them that we will be able to fulfill our purpose: the country is too poor and the population too sparse to build great establishments here. It is good to work in obscurity, and that suits our littleness.

I beg you to remember me to your daughters, especially to Amelie; tell me if her piety is lasting; how many children has she? How is your husband? How are you getting on in your solitude? How I desire for you the abundance of consolation that is found in the Heart of Jesus and that makes up for the bitterest natural privations!

I think so often of my good sister and I do not cease to wish her all the happiness she deserves and that her sensitive soul prepared for others, as far as it was in her power. I am in the Heart of Jesus,

Your friend Philippine

Letter 194   **L. to Mother d'Olivier**
(at La Ferrandière, Lyon)[51]

50 Copy: *Cahier, Lettres de la Mère Duchesne à sa famille*, pp. 107-108; *Lettres dactylographiées*. C-VII 2) c Duchesne to her family and lay people, Box 5.
51 Marie d'Olivier was born in Nîmes in 1778, entered the novitiate in Amiens in July 1804, and made her vows in 1806. She rose quickly to a position of leadership by developing a concept of education for women that included not only boarding schools for the ruling classes, but also for the emerging middle class, as well as free schools for the poor, centers of formation for teachers, and programs on continuing formation. She suggested that the Society of the Sacred Heart should be engaged not only in all these projects, but should also publish a journal that would help young women in their lives after leaving school. Madeleine Sophie Barat was favorable to her ideas, which were far ahead of her time, but she lacked the necessary resources to carry them out well. In a letter to Madeleine Sophie on April 7, 1841, Marie compared herself to Philippine Duchesne as a pioneer in an unknown land. She was then superior of the house at Beauvais, but her disagreement with the decisions of the General Council of 1839 and her refusal to remove herself from one of the poor schools that Mother

July, 1822[52]

I have wanted to write to you for a long time, since I have learned from several persons with how much joy and zeal you give yourself to our mission. Among several things that have come to me from France, either in a box confided to Mr. Mullanphy or by Mother Lucile [Mathevon], I am not able to know clearly what came from you. I would have had real pleasure in knowing specifically, since I much appreciate the modesty with which you offer your gifts. It is important that you not tire, for if God gives us the grace to multiply our labors and our establishments, which go only to places that lack everything, we do need the help of charity everywhere.

There is almost no more money in this country; bills are without value, and even when there is some, one cannot find objects for divine worship in the United States. We have considerable trouble in decorating our three altars: two in the church, that of the Sacred Heart and that of the Blessed Virgin, and one in the choir of our chapel, that of Saint Francis Regis, which we have set up through the obligation of a vow made to obtain our passage to America. When I put on the main altar of the Sacred Heart the cross and candelabra given by Mother de Marbeuf, there was nothing worthwhile left for the others. Nevertheless, for the great feasts we have the Blessed Sacrament exposed in our choir, since the numbers of people of different religions who often come to the services in the church do not permit exposition there, in order to avoid acts of irreverence. The bishop does not permit it. This is what makes me want a second set of candelabra in gilded wood for the altar of the Blessed Sacrament, with iron vases painted white, or at least a packet of gold paper to cover our ugly wooden vases and our boxes of ashes in which to insert our paper flowers.

The large piece of lace that you undoubtedly sent in the little box was of the greatest service for the feast of Corpus Christi. It went twice

---

Barat wanted to close (1840-1841) led her to leave the Society of the Sacred Heart in 1842 or 1843 and to return to her family. She nevertheless continued to consider herself a Religious of the Sacred Heart until her death in 1868. She wrote short spiritual meditations and other writings, some of which were reprinted several times in the nineteenth century: *Lettres aux jeunes dames du monde, Correspondance de Marie, Correspondance de Sophie, Dialogues des vivants au XIXe siècle, Les Trois Paulines, Le Nouveau Robinson, Nouvelles et Légendes pour l'éducation des jeunes personnes, l'Imagination ou Charlotte de Drelincourt,* published by Librairie de l'Œuvre des agrégations, 19, rue de Sèvres, Paris. Cf. Phil Kilroy, *The Society of the Sacred Heart in Nineteenth-Century France, 1800-1865,* 2012, Cork, Ireland, Cork University Press, pp. 87-132.

52 Copies: C-VII 2) c Duchesne to RSCJ and Children, Box 4; C-III 1: USA Foundation Haute Louisiane, Box 1, *Part A: Lettres de la Louisiane 1818-1822,* pp. 110-113; *Part B: Lettres de la Haute-Louisiane II 1823-1830,* pp. 298-302.

around the canopy under which the Blessed Sacrament was carried in the procession. It was made of white cotton that had become discolored from age and streaked from gutter drippings and fly specks. Four bouquets of roses placed at the four corners replaced the goose or cock feathers that had been put there, which made it look rather elegant. It was carried by an American and a Frenchman. We were the closest to the Blessed Sacrament. Four of the oldest novices carried the triumphal arch, on which we put our Blessed Virgin, adorned with all the other lace and ribbons from the little box. Two ribbons of merit [students] held the first ribbons and led the singing with our sisters. The day students carried the banner of Saint Aloysius Gonzaga and the boarders that of the Sacred Heart. The women, who went before us, carried that of the Blessed Virgin; the men and young people, who were at the front, carried the cross and the banner of Saint Ferdinand and Saint Regis, made of two paper images that represented each of these saints, attached to pieces of taffeta.

The procession made the round of our field sowed with very green oats, in which a path was cut to follow, which made a most beautiful green carpet. The repository was in the highest part of the field. This procession was made with respect, even on the part of the Protestants, who were there in great numbers. This kind of devotion is much appreciated here, and I am remiss in not having made a banner of the Blessed Virgin that is less ugly, and one of our patron Saint Regis and one of Saint Sophie. If any of your companions knows how to paint, her talents could not be employed in a better way. I have dabbled in it previously, but I only covered some Italian immodesties. I gave Saint Agatha a neck covering, the Infant Jesus a gown, and a shadow on the body of an angel. From one of a female religious that someone gave me that had a rather male face I have even made a Saint Ignatius in chasuble, but the lack of colored paints and of skill keeps me from trying to do a face.

The Osage have promised to receive the priests who will go to them. They are an Indian nation that set the tone for several others. A priest should soon begin the foundation. He could not stay long the first time because it was hunting season when he arrived. He was accompanied by French traders and several half breeds to serve as interpreters and to help him eat, because with these people, it is a lack of civility to refuse anything, and he had to face thirty dinners offered to him on the same day. To extricate himself, he would take a little and then have it passed on to the half breeds, who eat like oxen, as do the Indians, who do not plan ahead, and so often go for days with nothing to eat.

On the day when he said Mass, he baptized many children. The French were put on one side and the Indian chiefs on the other. During the instruction, the Presbyterian ministers, who had come there with presents for the conversion of the infidels, also listened. It would be very interesting to gather impressions. They have not been given much credibility because they have wives. Besides, the Indians in this area prefer the French and what comes from them over the Americans (that is what they call those from the United States). It is reported of an Indian that he said to one of them: "They told us that the grandfather (the king) of Spain gave these lands to the grandfather (the king) of France, and then the trees of the forest fell, and there was a great fire and dancing. But then, they told us that the grandfather of France had given these lands to you, the Americans, and then the trees no longer fell, and there were no more fire and dancing, but only ashes (great lament)."

During our priest's Mass, they gave 2 pigs and a goat to 6 Indians to prepare in order to eat. They found the ceremony too long and among them ate everything. It shows the patience of these nations that the chiefs were not angry; they just said: "They must have been pretty hungry." Forty came at a full gallop in front of the priest to have the honor of kissing his hand first, and they returned to the same village to have the other honor of being the first to announce his arrival. In the council that they held to decide whether they would admit the priest, they answered him: "We are very happy to have you; we are upset at not having seen you earlier. Come and you will truly know what this means: you will obtain what you ask." Traders set themselves up in the middle of the nation; a church was built there; two priests are too far to be *(word missing)*. They say that the black ladies will be able to teach their daughters, and I do not doubt that some of us will go there one day.

I commend urgently to your prayers several of our students from Protestant families. Four have already received Catholic baptism, but two received it in secret, and the most solid one made her First Communion at midnight. Several others want to be Catholics. We also have several students in the world who long for admission [to the novitiate]. Our Society consists of 5 professed, 6 novices, one postulant, 25 boarders, and 50 day students. Among the day students are 10 children, 5 of whom are orphans entirely in our care. The 5 others live at a distance, so they always stay at the school. Three sleep there, and we bring them food. We also have three other kinds of good works. The singing in church is also almost completely our responsibility, and we have the consolation of using all the voice we have for God. Ask him for our hearts to be like that of Jesus.

I am, in him, all yours,

Philippine Duchesne

Our respects to the sisters in Lyon and Grenoble, especially the aspirants [those in first vows].

Letter 195   L. 47 to Mother Barat

SS. C. J. et M.

Florissant, July 19, 1822[53]

Very Reverend Mother,

The bishop arrived a few days ago; he informed me of the departure of Mother Josephine Meneyroux for France, that of a coadjutrix sister from New Orleans, the ceremony of [final] vows of Mother Xavier Murphy, the difficulty she is having getting accustomed, and finally, the urgent need of helping out Mother Eugenie. All that, joined to profound silence on her part, which is most unusual and makes me suspect some disloyalties among the commissioners, has made me decide to accompany the two young sisters I am sending her. One is a choir nun, [Emilie Saint-Cyr, called Josephine] who made her first vows today, in view of the long trip and her courage in convincing her parents to accept not seeing her anymore. The second, a coadjutrix novice [Mary Mullanphy], is going to do the cooking, which Mother Eugenie is still doing. Mother Lucile, who is up to everything, has made this journey possible, which the bishop decided on quickly so as to profit from the departure of four priests on the same steamboat. When it returns, it can bring me back before the frosts set in.

The bishop, who gave the prizes at Opelousas, says that the children there are making astounding progress. In Saint Louis it is said that the boarding school here has lost ground since Mother Eugenie's departure. It is not true.

---

53 Copy, C-III 1: USA Foundation Upper Louisiana, Box 1, *Lettres de la Haute Louisiane II 1823-1830*, pp. 209-210. Cf. J. de Charry, II, 2, L. 158, pp. 83-84; Hogg, pp. 54-56. Ch. Paisant, pp. 483-484.

Today we had First Communion and Confirmation in addition to the ceremony of first vows of Sister Josephine Saint-Cyr, which caused many tears. The bishop gave a beautiful homily. He is of a mind to have the other novices who have completed their first year make their vows. They are eager to do so, and I repeat the request so as to give them greater influence in the boarding school where they are continually working. All our Protestants want to become Catholics. The attractive Sara Benton[54] has been snatched away by her grandmother in a great fury; it is pitiable to see her; she will surely be persecuted and is in great danger of losing the grace of her baptism and First Communion. Miss Emilie Chouteau, who is eighteen now, asked me secretly to let her know when I will pass through Saint Louis; she may have a plan to follow me.

I am writing the night before my departure. The bishop will take us at dawn in the carriage that brought him.

I am, in the Sacred Heart of Jesus, Reverend Mother, your obedient daughter.

Philippine Duchesne

Letter 196   L. 48 to Mother Barat

SS. C. J. et M.

[Plaquemine], September 8, 1822[55]
Rec. to St. Anthony of Padua
No. 40

Very Reverend Mother,

I wrote to you by way of New York before leaving Saint Ferdinand to inform you that I was leaving for Opelousas and during my trip down the river I sent to the mother in Bordeaux [Mother de Lalanne] a

---

54 She was the niece of Senator Thomas Hart Benton of Missouri. In 1830, she married Captain Brant.
55 Original autograph, C-VII 2) c Duchesne to Barat, Box 2. A copy specifies that the letter had been written at Plaquemine, where Philippine Duchesne spent five days in the inn after her visit to Grand Coteau: C-III 1: USA Foundation Upper Louisiana, Box 1, *Lettres de la Haute Louisiane I 1818-1823*, pp. 303-308. Cf. J. de Charry, II, 2, L. 160, pp. 89-96; Hogg, pp. 59-65; Ch. Paisant, pp. 504-509.

packet of letters that had been forgotten in Saint Louis; I repeated the same news to her.

I had wanted to make this trip from the first moment I learned that Mother Eugenie was ill; I had lost track of her after I learned of the arrival of our sisters from France and of the boarding school under the direction of an excellent priest [Father Jeanjean].[56] But upon the bishop's return, I realized again that the visit was necessary as this house needed help. It was without a priest, as some of the parish priest's enemies had driven him away for good. The bishop withdrew the convent chaplain in such a high-handed manner, saying he would lose his faculties if he stayed beyond the day fixed for his departure.[57] Mother Josephine [Meneyroux] had left; Mother Xavier [Murphy] had not yet settled in; Mother Girard even less so. It was necessary, therefore, to bring help.

Two young novices with good will can help with outsiders and one of them can be a class mistress.[58] The house will be able to manage if the boarders do not exceed thirty; that will never happen, I think. It is impossible to imagine what this country is like without seeing it; there is a population of twenty thousand souls in four small towns, which are the only ones that will provide boarders, as the journey beyond the center is too difficult between the marshy woods and numerous bayous; two of these make a waterway into a kind of basin; but one is navigable only in the spring; the other is the one on which I traveled.

We left Saint Louis on July 20 by steamboat. A former boarder [Therese Pratte], who had confided in Mother Eugenie, got her parents to pay for a visit to her: thus we were four traveling together, with three priests who gave us no help en route. On Sunday, 21st, we were counting on having Mass at Sainte Genevieve, but the captain wanted to load a cargo of lead at Herculaneum, so we stayed there until evening. God took pity on us by allowing us to meet two little girls, who followed us step by step along the river bank with their dog: their father came soon after to ask us if we were Roman Catholics. We replied that we were and talked to him of his responsibility to have his children baptized;

---

56 Auguste Jeanjean, born in France in 1795, was recruited as a diocesan seminarian by Bishop Dubourg and arrived in America in 1817. He was ordained priest in 1818 by Bishop Flaget of Bardstown, Kentucky, to open a college at Vincennes, Indiana. When that did not happen, he was recalled to Saint Louis and sent to New Orleans. He was very much appreciated as chaplain to Sacred Heart houses in Louisiana. In 1835, he refused nomination as bishop of Louisiana but was vicar general of the diocese, where he died in 1841.

57 Father Hercule Brassac said good-bye to the religious of Grand Coteau on June 18, 1822, and arrived in Florissant with Bishop Dubourg on July 15, 1822.

58 Emilie Saint-Cyr, called Josephine, made her first vows on July 19, the eve of the departure. The coadjutrix novice, Mary Mullanphy, did not stay in the Society of the Sacred Heart.

the older one was already baptized, but he wanted the same for the little one who was too young to receive instruction. We called one of the priests and the baptism took place to the great joy of the parents. The alumna was godmother, and the priest promised to visit the place in the course of his mission rounds; there are very few Catholics there.

The 22nd [feast of Saint Mary Magdalene], we stopped at Sainte Genevieve; we had Mass there and the joy of offering our Communion in union with those of all our sisters for our common and very dear mother.

From then on until the 28th we could offer to God only the great discomfort of the intense heat of this season, the proximity of the boilers and the other arrangements on the steamboat. We were all covered with prickly heat and with mosquito bites. In the evening we had recreation on the deck and spent the time singing hymns led by Father Desmoulins, who has a beautiful voice that distinguished him even at Saint-Sulpice. He left us at Baton Rouge, on the left bank of the Mississippi, where he has been appointed parish priest. On Sunday, 28th, we hoped to arrive in Natchez in time for Mass, but it was already the elevation, and as the priest does not keep the reserve in the tabernacle when he is away, we were deprived of Holy Communion.

We had dinner with the pastor, Father Maenhaut, a young Flemish priest whose health is greatly undermined, more, I think, from heart-suffering than from physical toil; he has very few Catholics. The wooden church stands humbly amid beautiful Protestant churches: there are five different sects in the place. Such a crowd was entering a Presbyterian church that we followed along but were informed of our mistake and went with sad hearts to witness the solitude surrounding the Catholic church. Father Maenhaut told us that he sincerely regretted having allowed Mother Eugenie to leave Natchez; he says there is no doubt that a foundation would have been better located in that fairly prosperous town on the great river, where there is continual traffic, than in a hole like Opelousas where we can never reach more than a very restricted circle; but we were badly informed and God allowed it in order to recompense Mrs. Smith's faith and for the salvation of the children in those parts who are so idolized by their parents, who would never have had the courage to send them to school at a distance. There will be few day pupils and there cannot be a novitiate because of the difficulty of access in every season and of obtaining provisions: it is necessary to do so in spring by means of rafts, which cannot reach there at any other time, and the charges of transport are so high; to send one small *armoire* from New Orleans there cost 120 F; each chair, 5 F, etc.

The 29th we left the river to wait in Plaquemine in an inn for a chance to board the bayou steamboat. As it was undergoing repairs, we had to stay for seven days at twenty F a day, besides sixty F to go three leagues to the steamboat. Then we had to pay another thirty-five F apiece to travel for twenty-four hours on that boat. We had hoped to reach the landing in it, but the receding waters had left the place so miry that oxen could not be driven into it, so the boatmen decided to transfer us and our baggage to a small boat that cost us fifty F to travel four leagues on another little bayou that they said would take us to dry land.

As the captain considered this a good plan, I thought we had to do what the people who knew the country advised, so we got into the canoe. The rowers were soon tired, and from the second little bayou we passed into a third. You can form some idea of the place we were in if you recall what was said of the waters surrounding Tartarus: the water was black and evil-smelling. As far as the eye could see, it flowed through the most dismal forests that stand in water all but one or two months of the year. The treetops have only a little dark foliage high up, and this is almost hidden by the long gray beards that hang from every branch of the old trees. (This beard, a parasitic plant, when dried and beaten, becomes a kind of fiber with which the country folk stuff mattresses.) The farther we advanced, the denser the forest became; but there was no dry land in sight, not even a sign of it. The day wore on. We had only a little bread to feed the eight people in the boat. I said to the guide: "I think you have lost your way and that it would be prudent to return to a place where there is dry land, no matter where." He said that was impossible, and his embarrassed manner convinced me that we were lost in the swamp. At the same moment we heard shouting. He said, "Listen, they are calling from the bank to tell us they are waiting for us." I answered, "But notice, the shouts are coming from a very different direction."

At that same moment we saw coming rapidly from behind us a canoe filled with Indians, Negroes and whites, naked to the waist, the most frightful-looking men, yelling and whistling as they are represented when rushing to an assured victory. Our boatmen grew pale and not one of them would have been able to put up any resistance. My three young companions were terrified, though they never dreamed of dangers as great as those I was picturing to myself. I told them to pray earnestly to God and place themselves under the protection of the Blessed Virgin. I promised her promptly a novena of Masses and already the canoe had reached us.

These Indians stared at us as if petrified, then passed by after having stopped close beside us. They eyed our water bottles, which they could have thought were filled with the wine they are so crazy about. They had nothing to eat, yet they left us without asking for anything. I thought they had passed us by just to go ahead and wait for us at a place where they could attack us more easily, so I gave myself up to prayer, recommending my soul to God in preparation for death, but to my companions I suggested only prayer and patience. Seeing that the boatmen were exhausted with rowing, I feared my complaints might annoy them. At last just when I was more and more positive we were lost in the swamp, dry land appeared suddenly, and we saw a cart driven by four oxen waiting for us. It was like a resurrection; I really was not ready to die.

I will never forget these names: Flambeau, Rousseau, Gaillard, and Tout-Blanc, which were repeated every minute in the woods, for the driver had to urge them on continually over the muddy ground. They took us for the night to an inn where, a few days later, all the travelers were robbed. We were fine and left at two o'clock in the morning for the house of the Sacred Heart where we arrived at nine o'clock in the morning [August 7].

Father Rossi, pastor of another parish in Opelousas, was just leaving. He continued to say Mass for us twice a week while I was there. The priest, whom the bishop had named as chaplain for Mother Eugenie [Father Cellini], had not yet arrived.

I have been without news of France and of Saint Louis. Letters ordinarily take six weeks to reach here. I asked Mother Octavie to hold any that arrived for me, as I thought they would not reach me at Opelousas. Mother Eugenie struck me by her dejected air; so did her first companion [Mary Layton] who was ill while I was there. Mother Eugenie seemed better, but her eyes are often bad. Mother Xavier has a little fever that is the result of nerves, I think. Mother Girard could be knocked over by a gust of wind. The only people there who are healthy are my two novices and Sister Carmelite;[59] she is in her own country and is a great help. As I found that she has all the necessary qualities, I got Mother Eugenie to make her a choir nun. I was delighted with the progress of

---

59 Carmelite Landry, RSCJ (1792-1852), previously an Ursuline coadjutrix sister, entered at Grand Coteau as a choir religious. Born in La Fourche, Louisiana, in 1792, she was the first native-born woman from Louisiana to enter the Society of the Sacred Heart, on April 30, 1822. On the following August 30, she received the religious habit from the hands of Philippine, who had just arrived in the South. She made her profession September 10, 1825, at Grand Coteau, where she remained for the rest of her life as assistant, admonitrix, and mistress general of the orphans.

the pupils. The bishop and the parents are equally surprised. They are seventeen in number and soon will be twenty.

I left on September 2 in a wagon drawn by two horses. The one belonging to Mother Eugenie resembled those of the Apocalypse and did not want to move. In the end the two of them collapsed in the mud. The boarder and I tried in vain to pull them out; finally the Negro took the place of the horse and pulled out the wagon after making us empty it. We went back to using oxen for the marshy places and then the steamboat on the bayou. Lastly, the fourth change, by carriage we went back to the inn at Plaquemine. We have been waiting in vain for five days for a steamboat to pass by. If one comes up the river, we will go straight to Saint Louis. If it is going down, we will go to New Orleans and wait there for another vessel. The river is very low, so they are saying that it will be difficult to get as far as Saint Louis.

End, September 8, 1822

Loving regards to my fathers, mothers and good sisters.

[No ending, no signature, no postal stamp]

Letter 197   L. 2 to Mother de Lalanne[60]

To the superior of the Religious of the Sacred Heart at Bordeaux

SS. C. J. M.

New Orleans, September 11, 1822
Rec. to St. Ant. de Pad.

My very dear Mother,

Since I am closer to you and have often had great difficulties in getting my letters out of Saint Louis, I hasten to converse for a moment with you and I ask you to send on the letters enclosed. The one to Chambéry is a thank you for the contents of two crates that were

---

60 Original autograph and copy: C-VII 2) c Duchesne to RSCJ and Children, Box 4. Other copies: C-III 1 : USA Foundation Haute Louisiane, Box 1, *Lettres de la Haute Louisiane II 1823-1830*, pp. 308-309 ; A-II 2) g Box 2, *Lettres intéressantes de la Société depuis 1816 N° 1*, p. 344. On the same date, Philippine wrote to Mother Bigeu.

entrusted to a young missionary, and that spent three months at customs because of a missing invoice.

I also received a letter from our Mother Barat that announces the sending of the life of Mother Aloysia. I have not received it, but I hope it will have gone directly to Saint Louis or to Saint Ferdinand, where I had said not to send me anything, since I expect to return sooner. I went down the Mississippi to take two novices to Mother Eugenie and to see her. I was very consoled to see a house very much according to the Sacred Heart and Saint Regis, formed in so little time, where the children profit a great deal; they must be more than twenty.

I return today by steamboat that goes back up the river. It is a long and costly trip, but it is necessary, and divine Providence leaves out nothing that is necessary; you experience this every day. All the details about your house interested us very much. We still do not know if your boarding school is increasing. We work in a small field but we love it, knowing that God does not ask for great works, but for a heart that holds nothing back.

I am with profound respect in the Sacred Hearts, my good Mother, your devoted servant,

Philippine Duchesne

Letter 198   L. 1 to Mother Debrosse

SS. C. J. et M.

New Orleans, September 11, 1822
Rec. to St. Antony[61]

My very dear Mother,

I received your letter in New Orleans on the 9th of this month. I was obliged to come down here on the way back to Saint Louis from Opelousas, where I had taken two novices to Mother Eugenie to keep her from killing herself with work. There was no other way to go back

---

61 Copies: C-VII 2) c Duchesne to RSCJ and Children, Box 4; C-III 1: USA Foundation Haute Louisiane, Box 1, *Part A: Lettres de la Louisiane 1818-1822*, pp. 120-121; *Lettres de la Haute Louisiane I 1818-1823*, pp. 322-324. On a note at the top of the copy: "This letter is addressed to Mother Debrosse. She received it on February 9, 1823." Cf. J. de Charry, II 2, L. 161, pp. 99-101; Hogg, pp. 66-69.

up the river than to come here to find a boat that would go all the way to Saint Louis.

Our new house in Opelousas is charming. It is as large as the one in Florissant. The chapel is beautiful and devotional, and the sacristy is well equipped with sacred vessels through the generosity of several priests. The boarding school has 17 children and five or six others are expected in a few days. God has quite visibly blessed this house, which is well established at the end of a year and without debts. But even more evident is the astonishing progress of the children in piety and studies. One in particular had never heard of God; she swore and smoked like a man, wanting to associate only with the Negroes. She is now well instructed in religion, has been baptized, confirmed, made her First Communion with the most tender piety, and now makes her meditation every day. She did not know how to read or write. Now she reads English, French, and writes fluently, etc. The parents are all well pleased, and this school has roused a desire for a similar one here. Several priests are urging it, and two who are in the best position to help us told me yesterday about a large estate located out in one of the suburbs that a rich man is willing to give for educational purposes, a house he will loan to us for free use for two or three years. Finally, he will procure the money without interest, or at a very low rate, to build the building.

I am leaving here in a few hours and have already sealed my letter to our mother, having neither space nor time to add to it. Please give her this letter, which will show her more than ever the goodness of God in our regard. Please remember your sisters of Louisiana to dear Mother Grosier and all the community. We love to talk together about our sisters in France, for the ocean that separates us seems really to put no distance between us. Our hearts seem to cross it rapidly to unite themselves to you and share in your merits. We do very little here, but we hope we are preparing for a future that will bear more fruit.

My sisters at Saint Ferdinand will have more recent news from France than I have, for while I am running around the world, I cannot hope to receive letters that will not find me even if they are sent to me. I return with one of our boarding students, who received permission to come see *her Mother Eugenie* and who would gladly have stayed with her if she had the permission of her parents. There is another who says she will sell all her possessions to go find her, but she has a father and a mother and is an only daughter.

I am in the Sacred Hearts, good Mother, all yours.

Philippine

Letter 199   **L. 51 to Mrs. Jouve, in Lyon**

September 17, 1822[62]

My dear Sister,

I received your letter and one from my brother-in-law that must have been taken out at customs from the box you were so kind as to send me, which I have not yet received. I am very grateful for these gifts you send me that are so useful for us and that will reach me, I hope, by the earliest opportunity; your letter came by mail.

I already knew the consoling details about dear Aloysia, her sister and my dear godson. I will call you a happy mother, since your heart's suffering in separation from your children cannot equal the sweet consolation of giving saints to religion, protectors of the whole family before God.

I am writing to my good mother in Paris to indicate the use of the income, as I cannot dispose of it myself; but you must always keep the 150 F owed to you by the nuns in New Orleans, which I have received from them.

I would like to write to you at greater length, but eye trouble is a problem, and ice is impeding all steamboat travel at this season. I am inserting this little sheet in a letter that will go by way of New York,

Many warm greetings to my sisters whose news you and Mrs. de Rollin have given me to my great joy.

We have begun a second establishment in Lower Louisiana where a lady has given the house and land; it is 3 or 400 leagues from here; that is like 90 leagues in France, as long journeys are common here.

I am all yours; best regards to my brother-in-law,

Philippine Duchesne

---

62 Copies: *Cahier, Lettres de la Mère Duchesne à sa famille*, pp. 103-104; *Lettres dactylographiées.* C-VII 2) Duchesne, Letters to her family and other lay people, Box 5.

Letter 200   **L. 14 to Mrs. de Rollin**

SS. C. J. et M.

September 20, 1822[63]

My very dear Cousin,

I am sending the note you asked me for in order to support the petition that is so important to me. If Mr. de Rollin and Camille Jordan[64] are willing to support it, and if the fact that it would benefit me recommends it to them, speak to them of my great desire for its success, in which I must take some part; if the little we have is spent on the voyage, we will have a great deal of difficulty in working to assist the unfortunate and even support ourselves. I know that the reference to the unfortunate has a powerful effect on them.

Finally, I have nothing more to add for you because your views are much broader than mine, and you lack nothing to succeed in your good works. If this one is not to succeed, it is because God does not want it.

I am all yours,

Philippine

Note:

Mrs. de Rollin is being asked to be willing to recommend the petition of Father Martial, vicar general of the diocese of Louisiana, to the secretary of the Navy. He is asking for the same favor that had been granted to the bishop and the first priests, for the four clerics and six religious who remained from those destined for good works in Louisiana.

This favor was to be transported free with their baggage in one of the King's ships from Royan on the Garonne to one of the U.S. ports.

---

63 *Copies of letters of Philippine Duchesne to Mrs. de Rollin and a few others, No. 14; Cahier, Lettres à Mme de Rollin*, pp. 37-38. C-VII 2) c Duchesne to her family and lay people, Box 5.
64 Camille Jordan died May 19, 1821, in Paris. At the date of this letter, Philippine still did not know of his death.

Letter 201   L. 49 to Mother Barat

SS. C. J. et M.

> October 30, 1822, aboard the steamboat *Cincinnati*[65]
> Rec. to St. Anthony of Padua
> No. 34

Very Reverend Mother,

It will surely seem astonishing to you that, having written to you at the beginning of September from New Orleans, as I was about to leave that city, I have not yet arrived in Saint Louis; but God is punishing me for my faults by letting me wander the world without spiritual help for such a long time.

I had been assured that there was no question of yellow fever in New Orleans this year; so I went confidently to ask hospitality with the Ursulines, but the boarder who was travelling with me was unwell, and I developed a fever myself on the eve of departing. I realized that the nuns were quite frightened lest we contract the dreaded disease, which, they say, attacks only people who are not used to the climate. The doctor, the father superior, *et al.* thought it wise for us to leave at once in order to avoid the disease. I wanted to do so myself, though I knew I was in no condition to undertake a trip of 400 leagues in this wilderness, 300 leagues from Saint Louis. How I wished we had a house of the Sacred Heart there. The place they offer us is quite safe from the contagion of yellow fever, which is prevalent only in the central part of the city. But God seems only to hint at that foundation that I desire so much as a link with you and with Opelousas.

They ordered a carriage for us and I went in a kind of horror to the steamboat. There my fever went up again, and on the second day of the trip, within twenty-four hours there were three people dead on the boat: the captain, his first mate and a passenger. A young man sent from France from the hospital in Lyon was traveling with us. The same day he felt so ill that he left the boat at a village where they tell me he died. Fortunately there was a priest in the place. Serious cases of fever continued on the steamboat, and I was suffering in every way, seeing people die like animals with no help, human or divine, without even

---

65 Copies, C-VII 2) c Duchesne to Barat, Box 3; C-VII 2) c Duchesne to her family and lay people, Box 5, *Cahier: Lettres de la Mère Duchesne à sa famille*, pp. 108-112. Cf. J. de Charry, II, 2, L. 163, pp. 105-112; Hogg, pp. 69-75; Ch. Paisant, pp. 526-529.

the loving compassion that alleviates suffering, and hearing people singing cheerful songs beside the dead bodies. I thought it prudent to get off the boat in Natchez, 100 leagues from New Orleans. That is the last town or village before Saint Louis. But once we arrived there, we learned that we could not enter the town because we were coming from New Orleans, and the fear was that we might bring the yellow fever.

We got off the boat and remained on the sandy shore opposite the town while a passenger tried to find us lodging. We were refused at several houses, but finally a man took us in. He had lost his wife just three weeks before, and he gave us her bed, which still retained the odor of the medicines and other signs of illness. The bedding had not been washed. I was at the crisis of my fever, but I held myself as straight as I could in order to hide the fact. I succeeded to some extent for four days, for they spoke only English, and I remained in bed as much as I could, treating myself. And God blessed my efforts, for since then the high fever has gradually abated and for a week I have been quite well.

I wrote to the parish priest in Natchez [Father Maenhaut] in order that I might see him and find shelter where there were some women. He was ill himself, but on the fifth day he came to see us and had us received in a very fine home on the same side of the river where we had everything that could rest and relieve the body. The lady, a Mrs. Davis, was a Catholic of Spanish origin, who speaks English, Spanish and French perfectly. There was nothing she did not offer us even to carriage and horseback rides. The pastor had promised me to come to hear my confession, but I waited another week, for he did not have money for the river crossing. I tried to go into the town for Mass on Sunday. The doctors, along with several other people, met at our request and their answer was negative. It contributed not a little to the return of my fever. Never have I felt such a great need of the Mass and the sacraments. Death seen up close was the cause.

My fever was a good excuse not to appear at dinner when several officials from Natchez were present. They had been told that there was a nun in the house, a superior what's more, and they wanted to see what kind of animal that was. They kept on asking my traveling companion if I would not at least appear after dinner and how I was dressed. One in particular, who spoke French, said it would give him much pleasure to talk with me. All this was repeated to me that evening by the lady of the house; I told her how delighted I was to have had an excuse to stay in my room.

Two days later the pastor came with great charity to hear my confession, but that is the only spiritual help I have had since leaving New

Orleans: neither Mass nor Communion nor any other confession, ten or twelve days of fast, the most severe I have ever had in my life, even during the Revolution. However, amid these hard privations, I always see the arm of Providence extended over us. We have just come upon the steamboat *Hecla*,[66] which we left at Natchez; she could no longer navigate; her boilers had burst. The steam had killed two men and burned several others badly, and thirteen men died of fever on board. One could not imagine a sadder situation than that of the three men left to guard the boat in a place where they could procure nothing. There is no doubt that we also would have been among the number of those who died.

This steamboat [the *Cincinnati*] also had a death. I talked several times to the man during his illness. I hope the good God was lenient with him; he had no religion and therefore was not baptized.

I learned in Natchez that there had been much sickness in Saint Louis, that the bishop had been ill and had lost one of his best priests [Father Pratte], the very one for whom I told you Sister Catherine might have been able to run a school. I have heard nothing from Saint Ferdinand. The length of my trip and the accidents I have experienced have made it impossible for letters to reach me. All this makes me very eager to get home.

I had written to Mother Octavie that I would probably have to go back to Opelousas for the winter, but no steamboats went down river while we were in Natchez, and as this one was going upstream, I thought the will of God was indicated by that circumstance. I am only sorry that I held out that hope to Mother Eugenie who will be severely pained ... I don't know how one of her letters reached me in Natchez; it informed me that she and three or four of her sisters had the fever. That troubles me, all the more as I am going far away from her. But the fevers in that part of Louisiana are not dangerous and I am trusting in divine Providence.

Mother Eugenie is so attracted to New Orleans; she talked to me about it continually. I was obliged to warn her to make neither advances nor promises, for she is the one to whom they are writing on the subject. There are several priests who would obtain funds without interest, etc. I cannot keep from seeing that this foundation is possible and that it would be very advantageous in supporting the ones in the North.

Our confessor is for the Osage. I don't know what to think of such a mission, at such a great distance, with so few priests and without

---

66 The name of a volcano in southern Iceland.

government support. The Jesuits always had that support! During my trip I have been reading about the voyage of the Count de La Pérouse who, while writing as a philosopher, shows the good that is being accomplished in California.[67] There are two Catholic foundations, one established by the Jesuits with 12 to 15 parishes having 600 to 800 Catholic Indians each. These parishes are all named for saints to whom Jesuits have devotion. The others run by the Franciscans also have their patron saints and are to take the place of the Jesuits; they told La Pérouse that the King of Spain was giving each of them 1000 F a year and that besides that there were orders maintaining their authority over their parishes and preventing Catholic children from being returned to their idolatrous parents.... Each parish is like a community: common prayer in the church morning and evening, work together, a common kitchen. The more I was consoled in seeing all these details, the more I realize the impossibility of our doing anything approaching that, unless Congress were to choose the Catholic religion because of its ceremonies, which in fact has already been proposed in order to try to civilize the Indians living in the States.

[continuation:]

SS. C. J. M.

St. Anthony

Very Reverend Mother,

I expected to finish this letter only at Saint Ferdinand but our slow progress makes me want to close it now, so that if by good luck I can find an opportunity of mailing it before my arrival there, it will be ready.

I am making my retreat on the steamboat. Everyone on board speaks English and those who understand French do not speak it at all, so I took advantage of being alone with God, for I foresaw that it would be difficult to get my retreat in after I reach Florissant. I have no books except a Bible I found on the steamboat and my little Office book. For the meditations I try to recall those of Saint Ignatius and Bourdaloue. The woman who shares the cabin with me comes there only to go to bed.

---

67 Jean-François de Galaup (1741-1788), Count de la Pérouse. Charged by Louis XVI with a voyage of discovery, he left Brest with two frigates on August 1, 1785, sailed along the northwest coast of America before crossing the Pacific, to skirt Siberia and the Philippines and reach Australia. His onboard journals were published.

In New Orleans I received the letter in which you speak to me about Father Inglesi, and that it is necessary to wait until the age of twenty-one for final vows, even though one is of age at eighteen here.

I beg you to remember me to our fathers, to all our mothers and sisters, especially to Mother de Gramont and to my nieces.[68]

At your feet, I am your quite unworthy daughter.

Philippine Duchesne

I learned en route that Mother Eugenie and several of her daughters had the fever. Mother Xavier [Murphy] is expending her charity on them.

Letter 202   **L. 50 to Mother Barat**

SS. C. J. et M.

[Florissant], December 1, 1822[69]

Very Reverend Mother,

I do not wish to appear to forget the best of fathers; so tell him, I beg you, that I am not writing to him for two reasons: first, because I have been told he is making his tertianship and cannot engage in any correspondence; the second, because he is so near you, this good brother Barat, that I do not doubt that you keep him informed about our little mission.

We have not received news of the arrival of Father Inglesi. It is always a help to know from you how to behave if we see him again.

My last letter to you, written aboard the *Cincinnati*, was already sealed when the steamboat struck a sand bar in midstream about 100 leagues from Saint Louis near New Madrid. I wanted to finish the trip by the overland route, and that was quite possible; but in this land age must bow to youth. The boarder who was traveling with me did not want to go that way. People sided with her and built up imaginary fears in her mind; they tried to deceive me, and as I would not in conscience leave her to travel alone or make the difficult trip myself without a

---

68 Amelie Jouve and Caroline Lebrument were at the novitiate in Paris.
69 Copy, C-III 1: USA Foundation Upper Louisiana, Box 1, *Lettres de la Haute Louisiane I 1818-1823*, pp. 329-333. Cf. J. de Charry, II, 2, L. 164, pp. 113-119; Hogg, pp. 75-79; Ch. Paisant, pp. 536-539.

companion, I remained there doing nothing until divine Providence inspired a French lady in New Madrid [Mrs. McKay][70] to invite us to her home. We went there in a canoe and stayed five days until the water in the river rose and lifted the steamboat off the sand bar. Then we returned to the boat by canoe with two young ladies who were going to Saint Louis to make their First Communion. The first, twenty years old, knew very well how to curl her hair and dance and sing, but she could not make the Sign of the Cross or say the Our Father or the Hail Mary; nor did she know the meaning of Mass and Communion. The other, age fourteen, is going to our boarding school; she thought herself well instructed, but did not know what First Communion meant. Neither one of them had ever been to confession. I tried to teach them their catechism, and after much hard work on my part, one of them answered that Our Lord, on the night before he died, changed bread and wine into *stone.*

On this trip I have seen so much ignorance in the many little villages that have sprung up in the last four years on the bank of the Mississippi that I am more than ever convinced of the need of teachers who could be placed gradually in the larger towns where there would be a priest, like New Madrid where there are sixty or eighty Catholic families whose children, with one exception, are learning only Methodist catechism because religious instruction is given only by the Methodists. Mother Eugenie said she sent me a letter in which you forbade these small foundations; I have not received it. It is not that we could make such foundations at present, but we could train teachers. Answers from France come so slowly; I beg you to approve of our training some children of the day school who will be able afterwards to become sisters of another congregation, as they would not be suitable for ours, since they are from working class families. I cannot tell you what the bishop thinks of this idea, as he is away just now. He has been in Baltimore for two months. I did not know it, as I had received no news from my sisters here or from him since my departure because the stops of the trip were unknown. It ended fortunately the eve of the feast of Saint Andrew, during the novena to Saint Xavier.

I found everyone in good health, but nearly all had been ill, some dangerously so, including some children and three priests in the sacristy at the same time; and then the one who came back from the Osage was near death. All have recovered, and the mission to the Osage is only

---

70   McKay: *JSA* November 30, 1822; but Callan (769-770 n. 57) gives the name McCoy, member of a prominent New Madrid family.

in preparation. There has never been so much sickness in Florissant. That is true for the whole United States. There has never been so much yellow fever in Louisville; it has carried off many. Don't be surprised therefore, Reverend Mother, if I insist again on a foundation in New Orleans; besides the fact that it is said that yellow fever does not strike there, it seems to me that one could brave its risk to save souls, given that the theatrical director goes to France to recruit actors, only to lose souls. The theater kills any tendency to piety in this country. Father Martial attributes the hard-heartedness of young people to the theater.

I have forgotten to ask you not to accept people for the Sacred Heart, as you say, in view of our needs. What you did for the Misses Mullanphy brought no favors for us from their father. As to my relatives, I do not ask for anything that can trouble you.

I was told in Lower Louisiana that a far too laudatory account about this mission has come from Europe. It is thought that, as Father Inglesi was not able to have it printed in Rome, he did so in Turin. It made people here who see things up close either laugh or groan; we are mentioned, and in marginal notes inserted here the good we do is stated: *Please God that it is true.* The best thing would be to burn these exaggerated accounts. The bishop wanted to withdraw them, but it happened that they were too widespread.

I have had news today from Mother Eugenie who tells me that health has been restored among her sisters and that finally they have a priest. It is Father Cellini, a Roman nobleman, with whom I traveled going downriver; he is kind, very devout and very strong; he is a good physician and has the pope's permission to practice his skill. He is elderly and understands business matters. He speaks Italian, French and English.

I repeat that there is a priest who is so eager to see a house of the Sacred Heart in New Orleans that he will put aside for that purpose the sum of 3500 F, which he will lend us without interest, *whenever we want it.* Land has been given and a house loaned. Mother Lucile will do much good at Opelousas and then we can send Mother Eugenie who is better fitted to deal with the outside; she has knowledge of the world and ease in speaking English, all very necessary in New Orleans. I can send her Sister Xavier Hamilton from here to be an English teacher, as we cannot take the two heads from the house at the same time. Another priest has told me that money without interest would be found, and good Father Richard says he will collect some for us so that he can die at the Sacred Heart.

In spite of my repugnance for Negroes as servants, we will perhaps be obliged to take them. A single man has to be looked after and fed; a married man thinks of nothing but his children and of earning for their support. The one we have expected a raise in wages even though he has money from France, 1100 F, a small house, a garden, and cows that he tends on our time; and besides when his wife is not well we always have to lend him one of the orphans to do the housework. Mother Eugenie came across one who drank; some are too delicate to do hard work, and others are not acclimated. It's a problem. The young man who came from Lyon and was at Issy with Father Babad has died; he caught yellow fever on the steamboat we were on.

Mother Octavie steered the ship well. It was reported to me that the bishop would lodge at the rectory and would take his meals in one of the sacristy rooms so that we would have no distractions in the house.

During my trip, I lost one hundred twenty Masses, one a day, eighty Communions, about twenty confessions and almost all the benedictions for four months. It seems to me that all these sacrifices are not without value and will produce several future foundations, especially in Natchez and New Madrid, which is growing in spite of the earthquake of 1811, which destroyed forests and opened crevices that still give off sulfurous fumes.

Kneeling at your feet, Reverend Mother, I offer my prayers for you to the Heart of Jesus. May he bless the year that is beginning, preserve you and sustain you in carrying your burden, and grant that I will not increase it by my faults.

I am in him, my worthy Mother, your unworthy daughter.

Philippine

Letter 203   **L. 7 to Father Rosati**

SS. C. J. et M.[71]

[December 1, 1822]

Dear Father,

After a long and painful journey, I was looking forward to the joy of visiting the seminary if I were to return overland from New Madrid near where our steamboat ran aground. I could not follow this plan,

---

71 Original autograph, C-VII 2) c Writings Duchesne to Rosati, Box 6. Reverse: "December 1, 1822, Mother Duchesne, Florissant."

which I had very much at heart, for seeing at first hand the unfortunate condition of soul and body of those ill in the boats who are left aboard when they are very ill, and the lamentable ignorance of children who are going to be taught everywhere by heretical teachers, I thought about forming among our day pupils or others a novitiate of sisters who could eventually be sent to villages where there would be a priest and, at least here and there, a place of refuge for the dying and a Catholic school.

I cannot propose this plan to the bishop, who is away. I am presenting it to you with the desire of beginning as soon as possible, thinking that you hold his place and that he can only be pleased if you have approved of it.

It seems to me that in order to make this work permanent it should be undertaken under the patronage and the rule of Saint Vincent de Paul for the Sisters of Charity, who do so much good in France and whose rule permits groups in each parish in addition to large hospitals. I believe these exist in every parish in Paris. If you were to accept them under your jurisdiction, taking the steps you deem necessary, I feel sure the work would succeed.

I foresee two objections on your part, maybe three. The first: the bishop's absence. I answer that it is urgent; souls are being lost, and we can write to him. The second: Why would our Society not divide up in the parishes?[72] I answer that the bishop would like us to, but our mother general would be opposed to it, as our rule does not lend itself to the lack of cloister and for other reasons. The third objection: Why do I want a novitiate of sisters close to us who follow a different rule? I answer that these sisters, having no one to be a superior, need to be formed to religious life by those who know it until there can be found among them someone who can govern. As most of them would be drawn from our schools, they are too young to be left to themselves but they could be trained in our school as teachers.

I beg you, Father, to commend this work to God; I have already done so every day during my journey. I feel more and more moved to assist such a foundation, if not with money, as we are still in debt, at least by sharing essentials and by procuring a place for them.

I am in the Sacred Heart, Reverend Father, your devoted and very humble servant.

Philippine Duchesne

---

72 Philippine envisages teacher training, like that being practiced in Piedmont at the *Soccorso* in Turin.

Recommended to St. Anthony
I have learned the good news for us of Father Cellini's arrival in Opelousas and of Father Borgna's recovery. He was well when I saw him with Father Ferrari in New Orleans.

[On the reverse:]
Reverend
Rosati Superior of the seminary
The Barrens

Letter 204   **L. 51 to Mother Barat**

SS. C. J. et M.

[Florissant], January 4, 1823[73]
Recommended to St. Anthony of Padua
No. 35

Very Reverend Mother,

    This time of the year renews in my heart the keenest sentiments of gratitude to God and to you, reminding me of that famous retreat during which you admitted me into the dear Society. Too deeply attached as I was to the holy mountain [of Sainte-Marie d'En-Haut], I did not dream that one day I should find myself so far from you who captivated me with such loving bonds. God, who wished that I should be here, gave me the grace to break the chains I loved so dearly and I have reason to marvel at the power of his grace that makes me so happy and content in the separation from all I love the most and without the least success that could make me forget my sacrifices.

    After that long voyage, during which I thought several times that I would die outside a house of the Sacred Heart, and about which I wrote in my letters #33 from New Orleans and #34 upon arriving here a month ago, it was a sweet joy to be with my sisters again and able to live according to our holy rules, but the joy is mingled with sadness at learning that our former pupils are giving themselves up to worldly pleasures and forgetting God. It is true that dangers are great in Saint

---

73 Original autograph, C-VII 2) c Duchesne to Barat, Box 2. Postmarks: Paris, May 15, 1823. Through Le Havre. Cf. J. de Charry, II 2, L. 165, pp. 153-158; Hogg, pp. 100-104; Ch. Paisant, pp. 549-552.

Louis, but it is a new source of sorrow since we fear the same thing for those who remain.

I consider Saint Louis like Malacca at the time of Saint Xavier: after a moment of zeal and effervescence there has followed a time of indifference to religion and of excess in the pursuit of pleasure. Our children are taken to balls and theatricals, to [Protestant] sermons, have bad books in their hands and live in idleness, etc. Several vocations have already succumbed in the face of so many dangers, and I foresee that here, as in the times of Jesus Christ, the poor will be chosen by preference to work for him. Since my arrival, I have admitted two postulants, one of whom had only two chemises, one pair of stockings, two dresses, etc., the rest to match, no bedding, no comb, not even a pair of scissors. I hope they will be willing to learn, for the needs are great.

In New Madrid I saw twenty-year-old girls who did not know how to make the Sign of the Cross and were ignorant of the basic elements of religion. The boarding school was reduced to eighteen pupils who were in a strange mood of insubordination. They were calling their mistresses Devil, etc.; they were saying, "*I don't want* to work, study, keep silence." And these were everyday faults. Although people think they are doing us a favor by bringing their children to us, I have threatened and even sent away one of the most insolent. The lack of an ordinary confessor and the stay of two or three other priests at the same time, one of whom was gravely ill for fifty days, fevers that have attacked all our sisters, all that has disturbed regularity very much (…).[74] Dissipation, argument, these are the plagues I have found in the community. However, when I arrived, I was told that everything was going *very well*. Reverend Mother, pray that I do not increase these wrongs by my faults and that you have here as many good daughters as in France. That's a desire that pleases you, I'm sure, and it is my most ardent wish.

I could not correct some abuses without reproaching a little the one [Octavie Berthold] who through kindness was not able to maintain order; but if that is lacking, everything is lost here, where insubordination is a virtue. Even the orphans complain about the food and the work, saying that they are treated like slaves. We had to tell them they could leave if they did not like it. [In New Orleans] Father Martial carries on his work with a firm hand; and in Kentucky [in Bardstown] Bishop David, coadjutor of Bishop Flaget, has a flourishing school, even though he is strict; and near us [in Saint Louis] where they tried to be easy and indulgent with the pupils, the school is going downhill.

---

74 Several lines are crossed out thus rendering them illegible.

The state of religion is bad in Saint Louis. The church's debts are not paid; those who hold the mortgage want to sell the lands of the rectory and consequently the bishop's garden, house, etc. He is in Baltimore at the moment[75] and the priest who holds the power of attorney does not dare come forward to buy the church and take charge of the debts. It is a bitter blow for the bishop and for his priests, who, besides, are being treated with the greatest ingratitude and given no salary. I am told that he must come here; I don't know if that is to sound me out. Our church also has a debt of 3000 F. The pastor has nothing left and we are clothing him.

I beg you to answer me about a foundation in New Orleans and about forming sisters for the rural schools. Mother Eugenie tells me that you never want us to make foundations of three or four persons, but many towns would not be able to feed more. I have not seen that in any of your letters.

The statement I am including here does not agree exactly with the account of expenses in my ledger, either because I am not accounting for the loss of money from France, or because I am counting what I received from Mother Eugenie for my return: what I considered as expense for the house. *Food* is not in proportion to the rest, as it is very much supplemented by our garden that furnished 100 bushels of potatoes and many other things and by the milk from our eight good cows and the eggs from sixty chickens. The repairs include plastering of several rooms, wainscoting and a long enclosure made of planks instead of walls. We owe nothing to the bishop, but 250 F to a gentleman who had paid for us. That is our state of affairs after five years, while Mother Eugenie gave us more than 2000 F her first year. You can see from that the necessity of a house in New Orleans to support the work. Here far from receiving anything from anyone, our first duty is to help the priests and maybe even the bishop.

Mother Lucile is excellent, only she would go too quickly in incurring expense. Mother Octavie is always amiable and pleasing to everyone. The two sisters, although they have grown stout, still do useful work. The five novices have good will and are being formed. I insist very much on study and have assigned it to Mother Lucile, for if she is ever superior, she will need it.

In the journeys, of course, I included the one of our sisters coming from France.

---

75 In October 1822, Bishop Dubourg went to meet with his confreres in the East and to discuss certain matters with the federal government. He would return in the spring of 1823.

I have not received the life of Aloysia; so I have not copied it. It is always necessary to recommend letters to Saint Anthony of Padua; it never fails. I have no news from Father Inglesi, or of the arrival of Sister Josephine [Meneyroux] in Europe, nor directly from the La Trappe father [Father Dunand].

My last letter went by a steamboat that was held up by ice; this one will go by mail from New Orleans. I am addressing it to good Father Richard[76] who had yellow fever and has recovered, along with one of the vicars. Another succumbed to it; he is a great loss.

Would you be so kind, very Reverend and dear Mother, to forgive me for all the past and pray that I may be better in the future. I am with deep respect, in the Sacred Hearts, your unworthy and devoted daughter.

My sisters ask for your blessing. I ask that of our fathers and some remembrances from my mothers and sisters.

Philippine Duchesne

[On the reverse:]
To Mother
Mother Barat
Superior General of the houses of the Sacred Heart
Rue de Varenne
Paris

Letter 205   **L. 52 to Mother Barat**

SS. C. J. et M.

[Florissant] January 16, 1823[77]

Very Reverend Mother,

Yesterday I received two of your letters; it is a universal joy when we receive them; we believe we are closer to our mother and her dear family, and it is a very sweet illusion. Your first letter of the month of July went to Opelousas before reaching me: I don't know if it was enclosed

---

76 Father Richard, former chaplain at Saint Charles, was performing the same service at the Ursuline convent in New Orleans.
77 Copies, A-II 2) g Box 2, *Lettres intéressantes de la Société depuis 1816 N° 1*, pp. 363-365; C-III 1: USA Foundation Upper Louisiana, Box 1, *Lettres de la Haute Louisiane I 1818-1823*, pp. 337-340. Cf. J. de Charry, II 2, L. 166, pp. 159-164; Hogg, pp. 104-108; Ch. Paisant, pp. 552-555.

in a package that people always prefer to send to Mother Eugenie than to me, as she has so won the esteem and affection of all who wish the Society well in New Orleans.

That is what already happened to the box Mr. Jouve sent me, which I was very anxious to receive, as it contained the braid for a pretty vestment, for which he had already sent me the cloth; none of that is to be found in our country. I wrote so often for it that at last I got my braid, but everything else stayed there. I beg you, my very dear Mother, in sending us things not to mix what is for our two houses; it costs almost as much to go to Opelousas as here because of the difficulties of transportation; the costs of returning things and of the freight are enormous. Besides, Mother Eugenie's house is quite as well set up as ours, if not better, and she hasn't the same obligations or debts; she receives many gifts, just lately a beautiful clock. The inconvenience of not being in the same place causes so many mistakes in our letters. Some have been found in table drawers at the Ursulines' house after a long time; another time letters addressed to Bordeaux were sent in a ship going to Havre; it would have been better to wait. I take the precaution of warning the superior in Bordeaux to send only by opportunity those I indicate and that contain nothing urgent. In that case the kind of paper does not matter; we do not have here the kind of thin paper you have in France.

I am tired of being indiscreet and asking, and it is necessary to cut back in our country in order to exist. I really do not know where we will get the 6000 F that we owe; we are neither in Peru nor in Mexico nor in the islands; but [in] the neighborhood of Canada, which far from giving back to France, has cost her a great deal and is the most difficult for the mission. There are only souls to win and very few of them. It is the desire of supporting ourselves and of having more children that makes me speak of New Orleans so often. I am hoping that my letter from Opelousas and from New Orleans will change your decision, since we are not asking anything from you and it is necessary to make a change in Opelousas, because the two heads [Eugenie Audé and Xavier Murphy] do not fit in the same bonnet.[78] We are saying nothing at the moment, as we need to have your consent.

Our *seer* [Bishop Dubourg] is away, in Baltimore, I think, to straighten out a misunderstanding with his colleagues or else to ask our fathers for assistance for the Indians.[79] I do not believe anything will succeed without them. We are still caring for the priest who made the last trip

---

78 Xavier Murphy wrote to Mother Barat, expressing her lack of confidence in Eugenie Audé.
79 Bishop Dubourg and Archbishop Maréchal of Baltimore were in opposition over the question of the transfer of some Jesuits from Maryland to Missouri.

and returned in a pitiable condition. What is necessary for these poor people are several persons who will work together and live among them. Journeys are too long, too costly and too dangerous to be undertaken often, and where would we get the money? Oh! How hard it is to see a minister of the Gospel suffer in such a magnificent cause and be unable to help him!

Your second letter (September 1822)[80] came by way of New York and, I do not know how, was entrusted to the archbishop of Baltimore, who is a long way from here, and then to our bishop who was away at the time. From the newspaper I learned that there were four letters for me in the post office in Saint Louis, and I was advised to go to get them. How quickly I sent someone for them, expecting news from you and what joy not to be mistaken! We had a reprimand from the *Seer*. My letter had been unsealed, therefore, as well as a large package for him, which was sent to Baltimore; at Louisville it was unwrapped and sent back to Saint Louis. They do this kind of thing chiefly looking for money. People think he has plenty.

I am really chagrined and humiliated to think that you lost that note for 1000 F. It is the result of the simplicity of our sisters who, a quarter of an hour after their arrival, scrupulously handed over everything they had to the interested person [Bishop Dubourg]. He wrote to me the same day, summing up Josephine's wealth, pointing out the *beauty* of our position and saying that as a result he was going to use the 1000 F from Bordeaux. The same thing happened with the 1500 F that Mother Eugenie sent me, in spite of my cleverness in hiding it. We owed him that, however, so it was justice to pay him, especially since Mr. Mullanphy has been paid. Now we owe only 2500 F without interest to an individual and the 6000 F from France. Mother Eugenie will be able to pay for the candle holders after a little while, and she would do well to leave them in New Orleans. Miss Elisa is being raised by her sisters very near us, maybe too near; for from the two gardens one can hear everything that is said; this is very disagreeable, especially when the pupils call one another names like "Devil."

I sympathize greatly with you at the death of your dear and respectable mother. I very much regret that I did not know in Joigny the one who brought our good mother into the world. We will pray very especially for her and for the young sister novice.

---

80 In that letter of September 30, 1822, Mother Barat refused the foundation in New Orleans.

Mother Lucile has relieved my anxiety a little about the 6000 F, for she said that a similar amount from my income has been lent to the house in Lyon, which is sufficiently flourishing to pay it back if you wish.

In my last letter I sent you the statement of expenses, and I told you that I had found our children very unsatisfactory. I attribute it to the departure of the older girls, to poor supervision and to illness. Three priests to take care of at the same time (one for 50 days), and all the active persons in the house, sick one after the other; that causes extreme distraction.

I have been told that a subscription may be raised for the debts or that he will take over the responsibility by buying the church.[81] It is a fact that staying in Saint Louis is difficult. Pray for this poor diocese where the demon is making numerous efforts, but please keep all this for yourself, for here people like to speak only of the beauty. The story of the traveler [Father Inglesi] is well known here.[82] What a cross for the person who sent him!

I beg you not to reproach our dear Octavie in any way; she is too amiable and too susceptible to friendship. It is in her nature; she will never reform completely on that point, and she would be so upset by disapproval on your part that her health would suffer a great deal; she is very useful. Another word about Catherine: she has made many complaints about the one she is so fond of. Mother Eugenie absolutely wants none of it, and she is right. Do not believe, dear Mother, that she sent Josephine Meneyroux away; she was so saddened by her departure that she wrote me desolate, and when she spoke about her sorrow with the confessor, he wept at seeing the depth of affliction God was sending her. But to remove the scandal that was spread about in the area, she pretended to agree and the other, in her muddled way, was appreciated by many. I repeat that Mother Eugenie is remarkably wise.

I am in the Sacred Heart, at your feet, your unworthy daughter.

Philippine

---

81 Bishop Dubourg would buy the church in Florissant, which belonged to the religious of the Sacred Heart, in compensation for their debts.
82 Angelo Inglesi, ordained by Bishop Dubourg in 1819, was implicated in scandals in Rome and in Philadelphia.

Letter 206   **L. 8 to Father Rosati**

SS. C. J. et M.

February 17, 1823[83]

Reverend Father,

I received your two letters: the first in answer to one of mine, and the second asking for prayers. I had them begun immediately and await a successful outcome from the goodness of God, maybe not according to your wish, but for the greater good of the mission to which you have consecrated yourself.

I believe that what distressed you so much was the news that you are to be a bishop, as we have just heard. Although it is one of the laws of charity to mourn with those who mourn, it is impossible to obey in this instance. For a long time eyes have turned to you when Bishop Dubourg spoke of choosing a coadjutor, and I saw on my trip how general this wish was. Our own interest adds to our contentment. We have experienced such kindness, such pure zeal on the part of the members of your Society that it is very dear to us, and all that tends to strengthen it in this country contributes to our happiness.

I think it is very advantageous for the sisters from Kentucky to go to the Barrens. I still see much good to be done, especially for the sick, by the project that I submitted to you. It will be accomplished but only in the future, because I do not think an older person in this country could be formed to religious life, since the young are ready for it only after many trials. Already two whom we had selected for this purpose have withdrawn for easier work. Moreover there are very few from France who can get used to things here. I would say that particularly about hospital workers, who in France are paid and cared for, like the sick, at the expense of the cities and the government. Here they must often go without necessities in order to give to the poor, and they are repaid only by ingratitude. One must have had long experience in the privation of the country and have been at the school of crosses to be a hospital worker in this country. I have written to the bishop three times about this project. Now he is suggesting a widow who may, in the designs of God, be destined for it.

---

83   Original autograph, C-VII 2) c Writings Duchesne to Rosati, Box 6. Post mark: St. Louis, Feb. 22. On the reverse: "February 17, 1823, Mother Duchesne, Florissant."

I am told that Father Cellini has not got used to Opelousas; if that is true you are aware of it. If the choice of his successor is up to you, we would like it to fall on Father Dahmen in the event that he is no longer content at Sainte Genevieve. The bishop seemed to want to assign him to Opelousas and has already told my sisters how much they would profit by such a choice.

I am with deep veneration, Reverend Father, your most devoted servant.

Philippine Duchesne

February 17, 1823

Father Delacroix is recovering from his trip to the Osage.
The Sisters Hamilton send you their regards. They are very saddened at their mother's marriage.

[On the reverse:]
Right Reverend
Rosati Superior of the
Barrens Seminary
Settlement

Letter 207   **L. 3 to Mother de Lalanne**

SS. C. J. et M.

[February 20, 1823]
Recommended to St. Anthony of Padua[84]

My very dear Mother,

I am taking advantage of the departure for France of a gentleman[85] who is connected with the bishop's house, to commend myself to your prayers. If he stops in Bordeaux, he will tell you that he has been long absent and that many say that perhaps he will not return to Saint Louis.

---

84 Original autograph and copy: C-VII 2) c Duchesne to RSCJ and Children, Box 4. Other copies: A-II 2) g Box 2, *Lettres intéressantes de la Société depuis 1816 N° 1*, Box 2; C-III 1: USA Foundation Haute Louisiane, Box 1, *Lettres de la Haute Louisiane II 1823-1830*, pp. 18-20.
85 In her letter of March 20, 1823 to Mother Barat, Philippine alludes to "a gentleman from Saint Louis" to whom she had entrusted letters a month earlier.

But I expect from God's goodness that it will not be that way. What persuades me to the contrary is that he wrote to me and spoke of his stay in Baltimore as ending well. When I returned from Lower Louisiana, he had already left during my absence. The good God has visited that house with many illnesses; undoubtedly the cold ended them upon my return. But this month, Mothers Octavie and Lucile have had a little fever. They have recovered; we have only a few light colds.

I hope to write to Mother Bigeu when I write to Bordeaux. I learned with great joy that her health has returned; I bless God a thousand times for it and I would have wanted to be her nurse in her sufferings as I was in Paris and Grenoble.

None of the letters in a packet confided to Mr. Smith are urgent except the one to our mother general. If he reaches Bordeaux and is forced to stay there for whatever reason, I beg you to take the packet apart and send by post the one to Mother Barat and to the cities closest to Bordeaux. All the rest can wait for an occasion.

I hope Father Barat is in Paris. I hear next to nothing about our fathers in Bordeaux. I would be very ungrateful if I forgot good Father Debrosse. I beg you to give him my respects and to ask him for a Mass. I have great need of it. God puts us under the press. The work of God is very much hindered: on one side, impiety and the deliriousness of pleasure, and on the other, discouragement. The difficulties almost overcome the good that is begun. Do not say anything about this to Mrs. Fournier—it would worry her too much—but the bishop has enemies in Saint Louis as in New Orleans. We feel the effects of the hindrances that he attracts, but the evil is much less when attached to poor women like us, than to the leaders of religion in the area. Alas! The world speaks and everyone runs to it. God calls, attracting through the voice of his marvels, of his pastors, of his punishments, and he cannot obtain entry into hearts, so that at the end, there is lethargy and indifference.

Our children are extremely difficult when with us, and when they leave, they give in to every impression. How outraged the Heart of Jesus is!

Please tell our mothers and sisters of our lively and tender attachment to them in the Sacred Heart.

I am in him, honorable Mother, your most devoted servant.

Philippine Duchesne

February 20, 1823

My respects to Mrs. Fournier and Mother Vincent at the Sacred Heart.

[On the reverse:][86]
To Mother
Mother Superior
of the Religious of the Sacred Heart[87]
Rue Mercière
Bordeaux

Letter 208   **L. 9 to Father Rosati**

SS. C. J. et M.[88]

[March 18, 1823]

Dear Father,

I was delighted to hear from Father Borgna that you have decided to make your permanent residence in this vicinity in spite of the dignity of your reputation which calls you elsewhere. I am entirely confident that Saint Francis Regis will bless this diocese by keeping you here; this is our greatest wish.

The bishop tells me in a letter just received that he has had to leave at the beginning of this month to join you, and he seemed to be very eager to do so.

He would approve of the formation of some persons for the work on which I consulted you. But he insisted that they must join the sisters from Kentucky[89] or, even better, the sisters of Saint Charles whom Father Inglesi has promised him. If he can obtain these sisters, the success of the work would be more certain; I would spoil it if I had a part in it. Besides, we diminish instead of growing in financial help, and the

---

86 Note added on the address: "If Mr. Smith does not stop at Bordeaux, I ask him to put this letter with those to Paris."

87 To bring about this foundation, Mother Bigeu was at Bordeaux from December 1, 1821, to June 25, 1823, but the destined recipient is Mother de Lalanne: the address is the same of that of May 8, 1820.

88 Original autograph, C-VII 2) c Writings Duchesne to Rosati, Box 6. On the reverse: "March 18, 1823, Mother Duchesne, Florissant."

89 These are the Sisters of Loretto at the Foot of the Cross, founded in 1812 in Kentucky by Father Nerinckx. A group of twelve of them came to Missouri in 1823.

disappointment we experienced at the departure of two young postulants makes me hesitate to multiply these attempts.

A letter from Opelousas informs me that Father Cellini is trying to move the church near the convent. He wants this very much as he thinks he can then care for both the parish and the community. I do not know if they are well informed as to his real intentions. You would know more about him.

I am with deep veneration, Reverend Father, your very devoted servant.

Philippine Duchesne

March 18, 1823

[On the reverse:]
Right Reverend Rosati
Barrens

Letter 209   **L. 5 to Mother Bigeu**

SS. C. J. et M.

March 20 [1823]
Rec. to St. Ant. of Padua[90]
(No. 7)

My very dear Mother,

I have just received your letter of October 23 with one from Father Barat with the letters that I received from France. It seems that you are no longer in Bordeaux; I did not even dare to address there my last packets of letters. They rarely get through at present. The ships that leave New Orleans go more often to Le Havre, where it would be convenient to have a mailing address.

I was very happy to learn that your health is recovered.[91] Do not be thinking at present, I beg you, of the good things of which death deprives you, but of the good that you can still do for the honor of the

---

90 Original autograph, C-VII 2) c Duchesne to RSCJ and Children, Box 4. Copy: A-II 2) g Box 2, *Lettres intéressantes de la Société depuis 1816 N° 1*, pp. 380-381. Cf. Ch. Paisant, pp. 562-563.
91 Mother Bigeu, who was ill, was recalled to Paris. To replace her at Bordeaux, Mother Barat sent Cecile Camille, RSCJ, born at the Tuileries and educated by Madame Elisabeth, sister of

Sacred Heart, who awaits you later on loaded with even more merits. May I have the same hope and not fear too much with reason that I am preparing the fuel for the purifying fire of the next life *(three lines crossed out)*. It was humiliating to me to read the details about Aloysia, to find myself so far behind her whom I saw born according to nature and according to grace. Eugenie [Audé] leads me in some ways toward the same reflections. She is one of those victim souls united to the Sacred Heart who draw down graces around them. Her house is better established than ours, she is widely loved and esteemed, and she merits it by her devotedness and prudence.

I was with her for three weeks to rejoice in her work. The separation was painful and followed by a return voyage full of misadventures. It took three months to return, with different accidents prolonging a voyage that should have taken no more than twenty days, during which I thought several times that I would never again see a house of the Sacred Heart. Nevertheless, here I am, having received a novice and yesterday, March 19, the first vows of three older ones [Xavier and Regis Hamilton and Mary Ann Summers]. You were not forgotten by any of them.

The bishop was not in Saint Louis upon my return. He had left for Washington and will return around Easter. During this time he has had some great difficulties to swallow: the departure of two priests, the death of two of the best, and the ingratitude of a city that he has filled with benefits. A faction has arisen against him because of the debts on the newly built church. They wanted to sell the rectory and even a house that he had built on the same property. The tempest has died down, but the conditions remain and especially the spirit of worldliness and impiety that surpasses the zeal for religion that was shown for a moment. We come in for a share of the criticism and worldly opposition. I am not discouraged; we do not work for the world.

I beg you to have your daughters, our dear sisters, pray for us. I am with them in the Sacred Heart, your devoted daughter,

Philippine Duchesne

March 20, 1823

[On the reverse:]
To Mother
Bigeu Assistant General
of the Society of the Sacred Heart

Louis XVI. In 1823, she was a teacher and responsible for the Marian congregation in the boarding school at Rue de Varenne. She died in Bordeaux.

Letter 210   **L. 53 to Mother Barat**

SS. C. J. et M.

March 20, 1823[92]
Rec. to St. Anthony of Padua
No. 39

Very Reverend Mother,

Just a month ago I wrote no. 38 to you.[93] Now an opportunity to write again has turned up, too good to miss. The priest who will take this letter to you [Philip Borgna] is one of our most fervent Lazarist missionaries. His superior is sending him to Rome on business for the mission to which he is utterly devoted. For two years he braved the danger of death during epidemics in New Orleans; he counts on returning there in a year's time; if we are going to make a foundation there, it would be a good opportunity to have two religious travel with him. He carries out all our commissions in that city and gets all Mother Eugenie's supplies.

In this letter I shall make no doleful complaints, because on the Sunday within the octave of Saint Francis Xavier I had the consolation of witnessing the clothing of our Sister Elizabeth Hubert, a pupil of the day school, sixteen years old, a good worker and firm in her vocation.[94] An even greater joy was reserved for the feast of Saint Joseph. Our Sisters Xavier and Regis Hamilton and Mary Ann Summers all made their first vows. They are the elite of our novices, the first two especially. Sister Regis did not think she could get through the day without dying, so great was her joy. She repeated this so often that I began to be afraid it would happen. That would have been a terrible loss for us; there is no obstacle to grace in that soul, and she does all the good she can. Her capacity for study is mediocre, but she is not yet eighteen years old, although she is quite tall, so she may improve intellectually. Her sister has great facility in everything, except for the order of a house, which may well be her sister's lot. She has to work harder for perfection; but she has great courage and devotedness. All three have the advantage

---

92 Copies, A-II 2) g Box 2, *Lettres intéressantes de la Société depuis 1816 N° 1*, pp. 378-380; C-III 1: USA Foundation Upper Louisiana, Box 1, *Lettres de la Haute Louisiane I 1818-1823*, pp. 344-346. Cf. J. de Charry, II 2, L. 167, pp. 166-169; Hogg, pp. 109-111; Ch. Paisant, pp. 560-562.
93 This letter has been lost.
94 Although Philippine considered her firm in her vocation, she did not stay long, for she does not appear in any other document.

of speaking and writing the two languages; as they are Americans, they learned French with us.

We would have waited for the bishop for this touching ceremony, but the novices were already in retreat, when he wrote that he would be here soon; in Saint Louis they are expecting him any day. Father Anduze, who had accompanied him, has undoubtedly gone back to France; he did not like this country very much. Once it happened that when he was going some distance to see an invalid, he was obliged to stop at a small house to ask for something to eat. He was served some bacon and milk, and while he was eating, a rattlesnake fell from the ceiling onto the table. He complained to his hostess about such neighbors; she answered that she often had two or three hanging from her breast to drink her milk, and that then she took care not to move so as to avoid being bitten. What a life! Do we do anything as difficult as that for God?

I had difficulty in clothing our novices in new habits for their vow day. An old cassock left by the Trappist served as chapel cloak for one of them. Sister Mary Ann's fichu and veil were made from one of the boarders' dresses, and Sister Xavier has everything new except an old pelerine, so she wore the livery of her Spouse who chose to be poor. All this has been an advantage because here they have to lead a hard life with many privations. I admit that I fear for those who are used to a life of ease and convenience.... One of us milks the cows, not in a stable but often in mud ankle-deep, in rain or in snow. Another spends herself in the kitchen and another in the bakery. Constantly they have to cross the swampy yard that cannot be drained properly; our habits and our rooms smell as a result; wooden shoes and galoshes are unknown here.

A gentleman from Saint Louis was the bearer of my last letter; I hope it arrived.

Mother Octavie has just suffered a great deal from sores in her mouth, different small abscesses. She is better; my other sisters are well. We are awaiting impatiently the *Life of Aloysia*.

I am in the Sacred Hearts, Reverend Mother, your submissive daughter and servant.

Philippine Duchesne

Loving remembrances to my fathers, mothers and sisters.

Letter 211   **L. 52 to Mrs. Jouve, in Lyon**

March 21, 1823[95]

My dearest Sister,

I am eagerly awaiting news from you, and I have a way of getting news promptly through Father Borgna, a Lazarist missionary priest from this part of the world, who is going to Rome on business for his mission. He is a very deserving man who does everything he can for us. He will be in Lyon for two weeks and perhaps will be able to see you.

Every year I have sent my annuity certificates to my brother, without ever withdrawing any income from the State. This time I am also sending those same certificates to my cousin Augustin Perier, hoping that he would pursue the business zealously; and I asked him if any funds were withdrawn to buy me a clock like the one at Grâne, which cost only 100 F. Perhaps it is even less at present; here these things are very expensive.

The route from Bordeaux is much less quick now than the one from Le Havre; ships from there leave continually for New Orleans. I beg you to tell my cousin or my brother if they plan to send me the clock. It can be addressed to the Ursuline nuns to have it kept for me.

I hope that in a few years we will have a house there; the land has already been donated, but the difficulty is in the building.

If you go to Fourvière, don't fail to pray for our common mother. I will never forget you, or your husband or your children. All yours in the Sacred Heart,

Philippine Duchesne

Give my good wishes to all those in the family who remember me, especially Mrs. de Rollin. I am not writing to La Ferrandière, having done so recently; but if Father Borgna wanted to go to see our nuns, please have someone go with him or give him a letter as from me, identifying him as a benefactor.

---

95 Copies: *Cahier, Lettres de la Mère Duchesne à sa famille*, pp. 113-114; *Lettres dactylographiées*. C-VII 2) c Duchesne to her family and lay people, Box 5.

Letter 212   **L. 54 to Mother Barat**

SS. C. J. et M.

May 20, 1823[96]
Rec. to St. Anthony of Padua
No. 40

Very Reverend and beloved Mother,

It is a long time since I have heard from you and that is a great privation. None of your last letters have told me that you have received the ones in which I told you about my trip to Lower Louisiana, in the course of which I reminded you about the project of a foundation in New Orleans. Your responses to earlier proposals indicate well enough that it is not your intention.

The bishop, who had been one of the first to speak about such a foundation, now seems to have no interest in it. No doubt he thinks we are not strong enough without your assistance, which you are refusing, and he is right. He is now giving all his attention to a significant gift the Ursulines have just given him; they are going to build a convent one or two miles from the city, and they are leaving him and his successors their church and convent in the city; it is one of the finest buildings in New Orleans, built a long time ago at the expense of the King of France, which meant nothing was spared, so much so that in reviewing the accounts Louis XV remarked, "*These ladies are lodged better than I am.*" It is a beautiful and happy experience for these nuns, who have supported Catholic worship in their city, to be able to make sure that their bishop has housing, since the American government did not grant him even a penny.[97]

The bishop himself gave us this news when he came back from Baltimore. He hardly stopped in Saint Louis; he came on the feast of the Ascension to give Confirmation in our church and First Communion to fourteen pupils, day pupils and boarders. He left again the next day and that was his only visit, during which he made fewer inquiries than usual about the state of our house. People are saying he is no longer our bishop and that he is signing himself only bishop of New Orleans,

---

96 Original autograph, C-VII 2) c Duchesne to Barat, Box 2. Postmark: Paris, September 2, 1823. Copy: C-III 1: USA Foundation Upper Louisiana, Box 1, pp. 212-216. Cf. J. de Charry, II 2, L. 168, pp. 170-177; Hogg, pp. 111-117. Ch. Paisant, pp. 587-591.

97 A *sol* or *sou* is change equivalent to 5 *centimes*.

whereas before he wrote bishop of Louisiana. Some say the new bishop is a Sulpician; others that it is Father Rosati, a Lazarist from Rome. I think that one or the other will be just the coadjutor of Bishop Dubourg.[98] His hasty departure precipitated that of several priests; one is going to become a religious in Rome; others are going to be pastors in Lower Louisiana. Our own [Father Delacroix] is thinking about going down there, saying that the Jesuits will be enough for us.

If you do not yet know what took place at Georgetown between the bishop and the Jesuits, you will be very surprised at my last sentence. He did not explain any of the details of this good and invaluable acquisition for a country like this one where the motto, *the greater glory of God,* must be their sole riches and support. One priest told me that the superiors wanted to close the novitiate (because there were foreigners in it), and that seven ardent, zealous and devoted young Flemings raised such a cry and protested that they had been called to America, and they would only leave the house when they were assigned to another house of the Society. Hearing that, the superior decided to send them to the State of Missouri with their master of novices and his assistant, and a few brothers and slaves to serve them. They are coming, it is said, relying solely on Providence but all the happier for that.

By the agreement the bishop made with them, he is giving them his dwelling in Florissant, which he bought for 10,000 F, the horses and cattle on the place and, as the house is too small for the twelve or fifteen people who are coming, several will lodge in the rectory. Unhappily the roof and the ceiling are not yet finished, and we have not a *sou* to help them with the work; the pastor is going on with the work very slowly because he too relies solely on Providence for funds. The only furniture will be what we will try to share, not willing to take second place to the good fathers regarding trust in Providence. The bishop is assigning them the whole of Missouri to care for, including Saint Charles and two other towns. That is a great deal of work for two priests; the novices are not yet ordained. I suspect that, when they are more numerous, he will take some of them for a school in New Orleans in the Ursulines' former convent, when they vacate it. As they are building in the place Father Martial was occupying, it is said that he closed his boarding school.[99]

Mrs. Smith also wants to give the rest of her fortune for a second foundation of the Lazarists. It would be quite close to Mother Eugenie.

---

98 After long negotiations, Father Rosati, provincial of the Lazarists, superior of the seminary at the Barrens, vicar general of Bishop Dubourg, was named coadjutor bishop on June 25, 1823.
99 His school, established on the property of the Ursulines, would be transferred in 1824 to the school of Saint Joseph in Bardstown, Kentucky, Bishop Flaget's diocese.

I am no longer going to ask you for the small communities. When the bishop passed through Kentucky, he obtained the services of twelve of the sisters of a congregation established in the diocese by Father [Charles] Nerinckx, a Flemish priest. These sisters, called *Lovers of Jesus at the Foot of the Cross, Daughters of the Cross* for short, are very austere, so covered up in their habits that only their chins show; they go barefoot and do all kinds of heavy work: digging, sowing, reaping, cutting wood and looking after horses, etc. There are already several houses, and in a few years they have attained a hundred sisters. They give religious instruction to the poor, train them to work and do a great deal of good. They are already hoping for a mission to the Osage for girls, and I see that they will get ahead of us regarding many good works that we can only wish for, as their customs are adapted to poverty and to the needs of the country. Every half-hour a bell rings among them, reminding them to say these words: "*O suffering Jesus! O sorrowful Virgin!*" At other times, they sing the same hymns together without leaving aside their different employments, one sawing wood, another in the kitchen etc. The main house of these sisters in our diocese will be at the Barrens, near the seminary. It is being finished at this moment. From there they will go out in the surrounding country.

The house in Opelousas is prospering. Mother Eugenie is already thinking about a new building. I am very opposed to it, given the instability of foundations in this country; things change like the wind; one must go slowly and surely so as not to be submerged. It takes only one malicious tongue to lose all the boarders in one day. The Nuns of the Visitation had forty boarders and now have no more than fifteen without hope of an increase; the lack of money is being felt in the eastern cities also. We have only eighteen, several of whom we take gratis; some others pay very little. Besides those, we have six orphans and seven novices or postulants who do not even bring their own clothing. I would like to send away the pupils who do not pay, but several would lose their faith. We prefer to be deprived of everything. The foundation in New Orleans would have sustained this one. God does not want it, *fiat, fiat* for the scarcity; *fiat* for the illnesses!

I thought Mother Octavie was becoming consumptive; she is recovering from several abscesses in her mouth, one of which the doctor lanced. She suffers with great peace. Her fidelity made me think she was nearing her final reward. Her loss would have been less harmful to the house at the time of our recession, from which I do not think we will recover; I even expect to lose several children soon; money is too scarce.

Mother Lucile has had the fever at different times. She would not be at all able to replace Mother Eugenie, the only one fit to be superior in New Orleans. She can make herself understood in English, and she has a rare talent for government. If this house were to take place, I would suggest leaving Mother Xavier [Murphy] superior in Opelousas; she is much loved by the children and the parents who insist on English.

(...) with the children and (...)[100] she said one day to her little class, who do not like the truth; she absolutely could not take one of the higher classes; the children would pass judgment on her, and here, more than elsewhere, that has repercussions.

I believe I am stuck here for my whole life. Based on opinions he has heard, the bishop has told me that Mother Octavie could not be superior and I see it. The children love her, but she does not hold them at all.

The day school languishes. One cannot imagine children less rewarding to teach; they are careless and inept. God be praised in everything! All the privations, all the humiliations will not be too high a price to pay for the happiness of witnessing the success of our fathers and their heroic virtues. This happiness is such that I hardly dare think of it and fear lest we have built castles in Spain.

Apart from the sick whom I have mentioned, the others are getting along. We have a thirty-year-old postulant [Mary Ann O'Connor] who seems very promising and who can be formed for the studies, but she also has the fever from time to time.

Father de Clorivière, nephew of our Father de Clorivière and confessor at Georgetown Visitation, wrote to me when the bishop returned and sent me the circular of the nuns. I am going to answer them when an opportunity comes up.

The last letters from France were from Mother Prevost, entrusted [to a traveler], to whom we are going to respond. Yours were dated September. You spoke about a tabernacle and the *Life of Aloysia*; we have received nothing. The 600 F from Mrs. de la Grandville have been used, as you know, to pay Mr. Mullanphy. There was no possibility of buying with an equivalent sum: 1) funds are always low; 2) Mr. Mullanphy's land surrounds us on three sides, and on the other, the land belongs to a minor whose land cannot be sold; 3) to cultivate the land here if one has to pay costs more than its produce. A day's labor is still 3.50 F and a bushel of wheat, French measure, is 25 *sols*; corn is 18 *sols*, etc.

I must tell you that I am always the same, that I impede the work of God, and that I harm souls more than I help them. And nevertheless,

---

100   Illegible passages; they concern Octavie.

I do not reflect enough on death and the judgment that follows. My recourse is to your prayers to the Heart of Jesus, in whom I am your unworthy daughter.

Philippine D.

Remembrances to our fathers, mothers and sisters.

[On the reverse:]
To Mother
Mother Barat, Superior
of the houses of the Sacred Heart, rue de Varenne
Hôtel de Biron
Paris France

Letter 213   L. 1 to Father Delacroix

SS. C. J. et M.

June 16 [1823][101]

Reverend Father,

I am taking advantage of Mr. Isidore's departure to try to express to you by letter what grief at your leaving prevented us from saying when you left. The silence of each one of us must have said more to you than words could have done, since that silence was the result of our great sorrow over the fact that we would no longer be able to see and hear one who had been such a friend and had done us so much good.

I am encouraged, however, at the thought that you will come back to this part of the country. So if Divine Providence keeps us here, we shall have the consolation of seeing you again, for you have been one of the chief instruments of God's goodness to us.

My sisters, the boarding students, and the orphans above all, to whom you have given so many kind proofs of your generosity, all are eager to offer you their respects and their gratitude. I beg you to offer a Mass for me so that God will help me to bear the trials of the office of superior and forgive me my faults.

---

101   Original autograph, C-VII 2) c Writings Duchesne to various Eccles., Box 8. On the reverse: "from Mother Duchesne, 1823, June 16; her expressions of thanks. No.1."

Will you please inquire if there are letters for me from Opelousas. Mother Eugenie must be in need of help, but I do not want to send anyone except at her request; and if she is making one now, I would lose the opportunity to have one or two Sisters travel in such pleasant and safe circumstances.

If a reduction of the boarding fee would cause Mr. McKay to leave Caroline Lavallée longer at school, we would charge only $25 per quarter[102] in order to keep such a good student.

My respects to Fathers Niel, Anduze, Deys and Michaud,[103] to whom I entrust our letters if they do not follow now.

We were given hope that Father Anduze would come to preach on [the feast of] Saint Regis; perhaps we shall not even have high Mass.

I am with respect in the Sacred Heart, Reverend Father, your humble servant.

Philippine Duchesne

We will not fail to pray for your trip.

[On the reverse:]
Reverend Delacroix
Saint Louis

Letter 214   **L. 2 to Father Delacroix**

SS. C. J. et M.

[June] 18 [1823][104]

Reverend Father,

I received the little packet containing a few books and some unimportant letters. But following your advice and in the fear that our sisters at Opelousas will kill themselves with work, I decided to let Sisters

---

102 The fourth part of the academic year.
103 Leo Deys, Belgian seminarian, left for America in 1816 with Fathers Rosati and de Andreis. After exercising his ministry in Saint Louis, he returned to France in 1824. Eugene Michaud, born in France in 1798, went to New Orleans as a diocesan priest.
104 Original autograph, C-VII 2) c Writings Duchesne to various Eccles., Box 8. On the reverse: "from Mother Duchesne, 1823; June 18, to take two or three sisters. No. 2."

Marguerite and Marianne[105] go [south with you], being unable to find a better time or opportunity for their travel. Under your care they will feel less keenly the sacrifice of our separation. Sister Marianne, who is older than 18 and has made her first vows, is quite free to go and does so quite willingly. Still, if there is time, it would be good for her to see Mr. Hubert and Mrs. Pratte.[106] The first was her tutor and Mrs. Pratte was very good to her. But if they should raise any objections to her going, that would cause us great inconvenience. Please do what you think best.

As for the expense of the trip, I am giving them $50, which will suffice, I hope, for the travel; and if anything unforeseen happens, Mother Eugenie will pay the rest. I would prefer that the captain of the steamboat wait for the payment until New Orleans or even when he returns here. I beg you to arrange this and to guide them in everything.

It is better to lodge at Plaquemine with Mr. Desobri than in the inn where we were, which is too noisy. If the baggage cannot go in the carriage to the bayou steamboat, it would be better to hire a cart that would take the Sisters and their baggage.

Please give the letters for New Madrid to Father Dahmen; there is frequent communication between the Barrens and New Madrid.

I am sorry that time did not permit these priests to come see us. I was expecting them this morning. They certainly understood that we could not possibly give them lodging overnight, as we no longer have extra mattresses. But our prayers will always follow you and all those who have expended so much care and kindness on us.

My sisters send their respects. Please accept mine and the expression of my veneration and gratitude in the Heart of Jesus.

I am, Reverend Father, your devoted servant.

Philippine Duchesne

[June] 18 [1823]

I am asking Father Jeanjean, who handles the business affairs for Mother Eugenie, to pay for the two places.

[On the reverse:]
To Father Delacroix
At Saint Louis

---

105 Marguerite Manteau, one of the original group, and Mary Ann Summers, who had just made her first vows.
106 Emilie Labbadie Pratte from Saint Louis, wife of General Bernard Pratte. She had given hospitality in her home to Philippine and companions for three weeks when they arrived in Saint Louis in August 1818.

Letter 215   **L. 55 to Mother Barat**

SS. C. J. et M.

July 18, 1823[107]
Rec. To St. Anthony of Padua
No. 42

Very Reverend Mother,

My last letter of June 10[108] must have consoled you greatly, since I told you of the long desired arrival of our fathers; however, you must not think the situation is the same as in France. There is not the same concern; and four times already this month, I have been told that it is possible that we may be left (...), that the highest authority may wish it so (...).[109] It is possible to adapt ourselves to the hours of the day and to the days, and I am expecting that divine Providence will not leave us without bread. That would be so much more bitter as no one would pity us, thinking that we preferred the rev. fathers to everyone else and that three[110] who could have continued to care for us have gone down to Lower Louisiana. Sheer misery is felt there as with us here; before I was fully assured, seeing the small number of our sisters in Opelousas, their boarding school stronger than ours, Mother Xavier's [Murphy] weak health and the hot weather and seasonal fevers, I thought it necessary to send them help; so as I was not able to leave here, I sent them Sister Marguerite [Manteau], the eldest, and Sister Mary Ann Summers, an aspirant. They left with three priests on the best steamboat on the Mississippi, which, through the pilot's error, ran aground about 400 miles from here; they continued on another steamboat that was passing by, but I have no news yet of their arrival.

These good Sisters have left a hole, made larger by the dismissal of Sister Marguerite Tison, a coadjutrix of ten months who was giving

---

107 Copy, A-II 2) g Box 2, *Lettres intéressantes de la Société depuis 1816 N° 1*, pp. 383-384; USA Foundation Upper Louisiana, Box 1, *Lettres de la Haute Louisiane II 1823-1830*, pp. 209-210. Cf. J. de Charry, II 2, L. 170, pp. 185-188; Hogg, pp. 122-126. Ch. Paisant, pp. 592-594.
108 This letter (N° 41) is lost.
109 Words erased. Father Van Quickenborne asks his superior in Maryland for authorization to take charge of the spiritual direction of the Religious of the Sacred Heart. Father Francis Neale permits it "ad interim," while awaiting the agreement of the father general, whose answer would not come until autumn.
110 Among whom was the parish priest of Florissant, Father Delacroix, who said good-bye to the community on June 8.

continual doubts about her vocation.[111] She has been replaced by a French postulant, twenty-one years old, apt for study and apparently with a good disposition; her name is Therese Detchemendy.[112] In spite of our poverty, I have had to call in a physician from Saint Louis to treat Mother Octavie, who had an ugly ulcer near her mouth; it is now much smaller; she has been cauterized and is eating. The others have pretty good health. All are consoled by the direction of their father. He is rector [Van Quickenborne] and master of novices at the same time; he is a Father Balthazar Alvarez, a real Rodriguez.[113]

He told me that his brothers at Georgetown were very poor; their land produces tobacco, the price of which has gone down a great deal, and does not suffice for all their needs. They were seventy and are now divided into eight or nine small communities; they are refusing subjects. We have three good sermons every Sunday: one in English at the first Mass, in English and French at the second.

I have had no answer to the letters I have written to you for a year; the quickest and most important could be stamped as far as the sea and addressed here: to Saint Ferdinand, State of Missouri, by way of New York. A letter addressed to the father superior of Georgetown took more than a year to arrive. Besides, I am afraid of being a burden [to the Jesuits who would have to pay the postage]. It is said that they are rich, but I know that their riches, like ours and those of the bishop, are real burdens.

Lower Louisiana has been afflicted with several scourges that have brought extreme want. Mother Eugenie will feel this, and we must no longer think about a foundation in New Orleans. You were inspired when you rejected this project.

We have had the happiness of being severely criticized and, to succeed even more in impeding our good works, people are saying that we are leaving; there are many who would like that. Soon it will

---

111   Marguerite Aloysia Tison, born in 1800, entered the novitiate of Florissant, where Bishop Dubourg gave her the habit on August 15, 1822, in Mother Duchesne's absence. She left the Society in 1823, entered again, left in 1824 with Judith Labruyère for Grand Coteau, then Saint Michael, without having made her vows (her name does not appear in the register of Florissant). In 1825, she was one of those who went to found the house of Saint Michael, but left the Society of the Sacred Heart definitively in 1826.
112   Therese Detchemendy, RSCJ, born in Sainte Genevieve in 1802, was the daughter of Pascal Detchemendy, a French politician, one of the wealthiest people of the region. She entered the novitiate at Florissant, took the habit on September 14, 1823, and made her first vows June 21, 1825. She taught first in Saint Louis, then in 1829 at La Fourche and afterwards at Saint Michael, where she died of cholera on May 31, 1833.
113   Balthazar Alvarez (1533-1580), SJ, Spanish mystic, was the spiritual director of Saint Teresa of Avila.

be necessary to confine ourselves to work with the poor and our own perfection, happy to tread a thorny path and to be aided by these living models, imitators of those whom we propose to imitate. What joy I have had in making clothes like the ones I observed on our saintly protectors. Here they are wearing the correct habit. My respects to these fathers of France whom we never forget and to my mothers and sisters. I am at your feet, your unworthy daughter,

Philippine Duchesne

The father rector is going to distribute the prizes to the day pupils on the feast of Saint Vincent [de Paul, their patron]. They will sing the Mass themselves. Sometimes, but rarely, they are thirty. Sister Catherine [Lamarre] is replacing Sister Marguerite [Manteau]; that is what she has so much desired; she does not insist on silence, and Mother Lucile also is too afraid of scolding; order is not well maintained. We have only thirteen boarders. Our sisters ask your blessing. I promised a Mass at La Louvesc for Mother Octavie. Would you please have it said for me, Reverend Mother.

Letter 216   L. 3 to Father Delacroix

SS. C. J. et M.[114]

July 18, 1823

Reverend Father,

I received your three letters: the first from Saint Louis, the second from the steamboat *Dolphin,* and the third from New Madrid, which only reached me yesterday. I sympathize sincerely with the unpleasantness of your trip, and I am embarrassed that my sisters added to your burden. We are very concerned about you all, and we pray ardently for the success of all the good works that will follow these hard beginnings.

I sent the $20 to Mrs. Pratte. Mr. Hamtramck, who came a few days ago, cannot pay the $35 until next spring. I am delighted that Mr. McKay will leave Caroline with us; she is one of our best students. We have only 15 boarders, and they will diminish. Mr. Wood has no money. His house near Saint Charles and all his orchards were swept away by the

---

114 Original autograph, C-VII 2) c Writings Duchesne to various Eccles., Box 8. On the reverse: "from Mother Duchesne, July 18, 1823. No. 2 bis."

Missouri. Captain Hamilton is going 800 miles from here and will take Caroline.[115] Mr. Rolette is thinking of withdrawing his two children. The Shakford child will probably leave the first of August, etc.

There is much talk about the bishop's departure and yours. Now rumor has it that we are leaving, and also Mr. Mullanphy. The frenzy for pleasure keeps growing, and father superior has preached against the dances; but even as they left Mass, they ran to them with more license.

Mrs. Chevalier and Mrs. Christi have died at Saint Charles, which has caused Father Timmermans to make several trips.[116] These priests have suffered a great deal by the delay of the arrival of their belongings. Finally, they are here. They are all lodged in the house. One of them comes in the morning for Mass and returns at once, except on Sunday. We have sent Sister Tison home to her family; she did not have a vocation. Mr. Lepère[117] is our agent. He has saved us $40.

We always have before our eyes reminders of your kindness to us, which inspire us to gratitude; but this sentiment is so natural to us that we have no need to be reminded, and it will always be our happiness to remember.

I am in the Divine Hearts of Jesus and Mary, dear Father, your devoted servant.

Philippine Duchesne

July 18, 1823

Mother Octavie is just getting over a sore on her cheek that has caused her much suffering. Dr. Gober treated her. My other sisters are well, and all wish to be remembered in your prayers at the Holy Sacrifice.

[On the reverse:]
Reverend
Delacroix

---

115 Cf. the letter of February 18, 1824, to Father Delacroix. Caroline Hamilton lived near Prairie du Chien, Wisconsin.

116 Peter Joseph Timmermans, SJ, born in Belgium in 1788, was ordained priest in 1820 at Georgetown. He arrived in Missouri in 1823 and died the following year.

117 Martin Lepère is frequently mentioned in the correspondence as an employee at Florissant. He was responsible for repairs, mail, and upkeep of priests. Philippine had such confidence in him that she asked him to come with her to Saint Louis in 1827, in spite of the objections of Father Van Quickenborne. He spoke French and English and so could supervise construction of the new house. A few years later, he was sacristan of the parish; Philippine repaired vestments for him. On September 19, 1831, *JSA* mentions that he left employment at the convent with his family to begin a business, without specifying what it was. The letters that Philippine addressed to him in 1843 and 1844 suggest that it was a textile business. They also reveal that Philippine continued to produce altar linens during her last years at Saint Charles.

Letter 217   **L. 10 to Father Rosati**

SS. C. J. et M.

[August 7, 1823][118]

Dear Reverend Father,

Your letter of June 26 arrived only on August 7. I am so sorry there is so little time before the date on which the American gentleman wanted to place his daughter here. You can scarcely receive my letter before the vacation at the end of this month. It will be only a few days long, and classes will reopen on September 1.

The price of our boarding school has been reduced to $140. Since money is scarce, we often have to reduce it further for many children for various reasons. This may be the case for the young lady in question, especially if she pays in advance for six months instead of three. We can also furnish the bed for $2 a year to avoid the expense of moving one; but the bed does not include bed linen. The trousseau consists of two pairs of sheets, three coverlets, one of which should be white, six napkins, six chemises, six handkerchiefs, six pairs of stockings, one black dress, one white and three or four everyday dresses, two pairs of shoes, one white veil, six short capes or white neckerchiefs, a knife, fork, cup, toothbrush, combs etc., paper, pens.

The superior of the Jesuits was deeply touched by your remembrance of him. He asks me to express his gratitude and also his regret that he cannot visit your holy house.

My sisters commend themselves to your prayer, especially Mother Octavie who is suffering, and the Sisters Hamilton, who are ever more firm in the happy choice they have made.

I am with the greatest veneration in the Sacred Heart, Reverend Father, your devoted and very humble servant.

Philippine Duchesne

Saint Ferdinand, August 7, 1823

---

118 Original autograph, C-VII 2) c Writings Duchesne to Rosati, Box 6. Reverse: "August 27, 1823, Mother Duchesne, Florissant." Philippine dated the letter August 7, Father Rosati, on the 27.

Letter 218 **L. 56 to Mother Barat**

SS. C. J. et M.

[Florissant], September 25, 1823[119]
No. 44
Recommended to St. Anthony of Padua

Very Reverend Mother,

I am writing to you again by way of New York, as it is the fastest at this time when navigation on the Mississippi will be stopped or greatly delayed. Besides, I see that our commissions in New Orleans are no longer carried out well since the good Lazarist, Father Borgna, is not there anymore but has gone to Rome. You must have seen him in Paris, for he took several of our letters.

I don't know what is delaying yours or whether you have forgotten us. We have never been so long without news from you. The last ones from you were dated more than a year ago, and it is six months since I received them. The most recent news was from kind Father Barat. He must have experienced great consolation at learning that through his brothers he is on mission in this ungrateful country. They are the only ones who will be able to effect conversion. For that it is necessary to love suffering, have constant zeal and put up with the miseries of others to the highest degree. We see all that in these earthly guardian angels whom God has sent to care for us.

The more we see of the father rector, the more we appreciate his direction and recognize in him the spirit of his father [Saint Ignatius]. I have found a father master; I no longer do just what I want. Still he is not content; he would like a more interior life and more details in giving an account of one's soul, and you know that I do not have much to say. He gave a three-day retreat to the whole house on the occasion of a clothing and a First Communion, which took place on the 14th, feast of the Holy Name of Mary and the Holy Cross. One could wish only that it had been longer; he has a gift of persuading and of touching hearts. Seeing your daughters in such good hands, I have no anxiety about

---

119 Original autograph, C-VII 2) c Duchesne to Barat, Box 2. Postmark: St Louis, Oct. 3; Paris, 1 December 1823, through Le Havre. Copy, C-III 1: USA Foundation Upper Louisiana, Box 1, *Lettres de la Haute Louisiane II 1823-1830*, pp. 217-221. Cf. J. de Charry, II 2, L. 175, pp. 202-209; Hogg, pp. 133-140. Ch. Paisant, pp. 594-598.

their interior lives. This father knows many of ours in Paris. His name is Van Quickenborne. He knows Mother de Peñaranda.

He and his brothers are all Flemish. They would be capable of converting a kingdom and until now have done very little as this country is so spoiled. They are building a house for the bishop. I have done all I could to get them to choose a site near the church, but there was no way to persuade them. They do not want to be close to us. I was deeply sorry about that because I foresaw that, in spite of their courage, we would be without Mass often in the winter. They have their own chapel, and ours is terribly deserted. The townspeople come very little, and we have only eleven children, only two of whom are sure to stay the whole year, since their fees are paid in advance. As for the others, they may leave from one day to the next. So you see, we are entirely in the hands of Providence, and it is sweet to rest there.

We have never lacked necessities, and we have even more money than formerly when we had more children; that reassures me for the future. We have even been able to assist our fathers, who are poorer than we are. They *are suffering,* and I would like to see some of the superabundance in France be directed to their aid. Help will still be too late. A wealthy man has refused to lend to them; they tilled the land with great difficulty, and a frost in September took away all hope of any harvest. Once more, it is necessary to adore Providence and abandon oneself. Friends and protectors are not found here; everyone thinks of self. No one deprives himself of luxuries, of pleasures to give to good works. There is not enough faith for that. Our greatest sorrow is not to see ourselves mocked and calumniated by our old children in their social gatherings, but to see them rushing headlong to their peril through pleasure and frivolity. The one who was with us the longest and who left only three months ago has just died a holy death before being given up to worldliness [Pelagie Chouteau]. One of her best companions had preceded her in the same frame of mind. These are our only consolations: that these dear children's days are shortened, lest evil and worldly seduction come to corrupt them.

Mother Eugenie's house will suffer this year from the want that pervades Lower Louisiana. She has not finished paying the travel expenses of the sisters I sent to her. She wanted to improve things too quickly, and many will be of no use to her. Wise economy is absolutely necessary here, more than in another country, because nothing is stable under heaven where we live; fortunes and establishments are overturned in a moment. Several people owe us money and pay us with calumny.

The diminishing number of pupils is not my greatest worry for Opelousas; it is rather Mother Xavier's health. She has been advised to go to Mrs. Smith's to recover, and maybe she is there already.

The bishop, who sees everything as rosy and always presents it that way, is the reason the fathers are a little disconcerted. They were expecting more than they found. And to me, when I talked to him about the reduction in the number of pupils, he said he was offering me an establishment that would help us very much: it is thirty leagues above New Orleans, on the river, so that communications would be very easy. The townspeople would build the house. But for that he is asking for six *choir religious* from France, well-known for their wisdom and quality, no Sisters [coadjutrix]. I answered that I did not think you would accept this foundation and not to count on more religious or money and that Mother Octavie's illness would take away all hope of our separating here.

However, there is little hope of doing anything in Saint Louis, where we are almost held in horror, as is the bishop, and in view of Mother Xavier's [Murphy] extraordinary state of health, which I suspect is caused by habitual nervous tension, and seeing that she is not able to get along with Mother Eugenie, maybe even less now, I have had the thought that she might be one of those people who need both mental and physical activity for their well-being, like Mother Bigeu; she might be suitable for the direction of the foundation the bishop is proposing. He admires her very much, for her virtue as well as her English. She, for her part, has great confidence in him and would be living near him; for it seems he is going to settle at that distance from New Orleans, on the other side of the river, maybe to live in a healthier district and at the same time to watch over the most populous part of his diocese. I do not want him in Saint Louis; he would lack everything and have only pittances. As for us the fathers make up for everything. This establishment of La Fourche—that is the name of the place—would replace the one planned for New Orleans, where we would have no success for a long time: commerce there is in stagnation, and different scourges are overwhelming a place where God is too much ignored. We certainly could give a few religious to assist Mother Xavier. Her bishop in Ireland judged her suitable to be a superior, and Mother Eugenie believes her to be ready to direct a house. She is the only one to whom I have communicated my thought. There would be time to speak with the bishop after your answer, which I beg you to hasten.

I am afraid of remedies that require going out into the world. I would not give my consent. It has been proposed to Mother Octavie.

I saw her getting weaker, but happily the father helped me instead of ordering what was suggested. He is to give us a retreat in November, which, I hope, will strengthen the religious spirit in this poor house. Mother Octavie is still in the same state. I had hope for a cure at one moment, but now I have lost it. She is profiting by this state of suffering and says with great fervor: "I would not change my sufferings for all the crowns in the world."

I fear for Mother Lucile lest she have ills of the same nature, and one would find in her much less peace in suffering. She is not at all capable of keeping regularity and order in a house. And I do not believe you have in America a daughter who has more firmness, a better mind, more attractive manners and talents for government than Mother Eugenie. Join to that the greatest possible devotedness and a courage above that of her sex. Our Mother Xavier here [Mathilde Hamilton] is still being tempted but not about her vocation. Her sister, Mother Regis, is perfect, except in studies. Sister Ignatius [Judith Labruyère] is another Sister Chatain. Sister Catherine is happy with her day school class. We have, in addition to those already named, three good novices. I have spoken to you about the Irishwoman [Mary Ann O'Connor]. The last [Therese Detchemendy] is Creole from Sainte Genevieve; she is gifted for studies, tall, strong, and firm in her vocation, which is rare in these climates.

If, through bad health or the absence of Mother Xavier [Murphy], Mother Eugenie found herself alone, it seems to me that it would be good if Sister Marguerite [Manteau] were to be made a choir religious to take her place at certain times or in case of illness; she is already needed for the office. All the rest are very young.

We had wanted to plant cotton; it did not succeed and our little bit of corn froze. We have no more than three orphans who give a great deal of trouble. Finally, the cross does not leave us; may it be our consolation until death.

I am with profound veneration in the Sacred Heart, your very devoted servant and daughter, Reverend Mother.

Philippine Duchesne

Our Father Perreau forgets us entirely, but I forget neither him nor dear Father Varin nor all those who contribute so much to the Glory of the Sacred Heart.
I felt great joy upon learning through Mother de Charbonnel the reunion of Mother de Peñaranda. I regret not knowing her. All my sisters offer you their deep respect.

If you send a cross for Sister Marguerite [Manteau], would you please add three for the first who have made their vows?[120] If you are willing to grant them a dispensation from some of the five years, their vocation is solid. I learned that Eugenie Lebrument was at the Visitation. I would have preferred to have her here, but God's will be done in everything and always.

[On the reverse:]
To Mother
Mother Barat Superior General
of the houses of the Sacred Heart,
rue de Varenne, Faubourg Saint-Germain
Paris France
By way of New York

Letter 219   **L. 11 to Father Rosati**

SS. C. J. et M.[121]

[October 5, 1823]

Dear Father,

At the end of August, I received your letter of June 26 in which you asked me for a place in our boarding school for a young lady from your area who wanted to be here for the reopening of classes. I answered immediately that the vacation ended the first of September, that the board was $140, that she would be given a reduction if there was a sufficient reason, that on Sundays the pupils wear black, that she would therefore need a black dress and a white one for great feasts; otherwise ordinary clothes are worn; enough underwear for changing is necessary. Because of the distance, we can supply the bed for $3 per year, but not the blankets.

Maybe this repetition is unnecessary, but it is better to repeat than to fail to respond to the honor you have paid me, in case my first [letter] did not reach you.

---

120 Emilie Saint-Cyr, July 19, 1822; Mathilde and Eulalie Hamilton, March 19, 1823.
121 Original autograph, C-VII 2) c Writings Duchesne to Rosati, Box 6. On the reverse: "Oct. 5, 1823, Mother Duchesne, Florissant."

Our Sisters Hamilton are doing very well and have made their first vows with great happiness. They offer you their deep respect and ask you to see that the enclosed letters reach their destination.

The Jesuit superior was very touched by what you told me to say to him on your behalf; he is in the same situation you were in during the first year of your foundation, and he has no resources with which to build. A picture like that is necessary so as not to find too much consolation in poverty, for we cannot help them as we would like. Our boarding school is reduced by more than half because of the scarcity of money. It is necessary that God make us purchase by trial the happiness of being a witness and of enjoying an establishment that must contribute so much to the glory of God.

I will receive news of Father Borgna with the greatest pleasure; it seems that there is no life for us in New Orleans since he is no longer there, for we so often felt the effect of his thoughtful charity. The bishop writes that Father Acquaroni is to return to Portage. We will be very happy to see him as well as all the members of the society of which you are the head and to whom we owe so much gratitude.

I am with respect, Reverend Father, your very humble and devoted servant.

Philippine Duchesne, sup.

October 5, 1823

[On the reverse:]
Reverend
Rosati Superior of the Seminary
Barrens

Letter 220   **L. 4 to Father Delacroix**

[Postscript to a letter of Octavie Berthold, November 6, 1823]

Allow me once more, Father, to testify to you my respect and gratitude, my esteem and my wishes for your happiness.

Mr. Hamtramck has not yet taken any trees. He has talked about taking the chair from the church; I think it belonged to you and that you had given it. Mr. Chauvin does not think he supplied you with as many boards as you thought, and up to the amount that you gave me.

Please answer these two questions, and believe me to be with respect, all yours in the Heart of Jesus.

Philippine

[On the reverse:]
Recommended to the care of Father Jeanjean
Vicar of the Cathedral, *New Orleans*

Letter 221   Letter 1 to Father De Neckere

SS. C. J. et M.

Saint Ferdinand, November 12, 1823[122]

Father,

I do not know the laws of this country well enough to know if Sister [Eulalie] Hamilton, the younger, who is only eighteen years old, can sell her property and if her sister, whose land is merged with hers, can sell without her sister [Mathilde]. Bishop Rosati can judge these problems much better than I.

Regarding our customs, a sister does not renounce her possessions until final vows, and our Sisters Hamilton, from whom we have received nothing, cannot do so until their [perpetual] profession in favor of the Society to which they bind themselves. Thus if they can sell their property, they should themselves receive the proceeds of the sale without going through other hands. I think there is still more good in maintaining a work than in beginning a new one, so that all the sacrifices they will make will be in order to give preference to Father Nerinckx and not to expect the best price for the land.

The desire is in my heart and theirs to contribute as much as possible to the interesting work of Father Nerinckx; and if Providence had not tried us by giving us many failures, we would surely not have been the last to contribute to the work of the seminary and its preparation. But God wants us to practice the vow of poverty in the most rigorous way, by being ever unable to follow the impulse and the obligation to exercise charity. But those of our house have the first right to our care and by putting this affair in the hands of Bishop Rosati, I do not doubt

---

122   Original autograph, C-VII 2) c Writings Duchesne to various Eccles., Box 8.

in any way that he will understand the reason for asking a reasonable price for the land. Our sisters Hamilton are not irrevocably committed until final vows, so it is better not to abandon all precaution.

We pray for Bishop Rosati earnestly with all the interest and veneration he deserves. Saint Francis Regis was deaf to the pleas we addressed to him for Mother Octavie, my first companion, whom you saw at Saint Ferdinand. She has a cancer of the face that has resisted all treatments. Her suffering is already great, and such a sight is not the least of my crosses. I beg you to remember her and me at the Holy Sacrifice of the Mass and to obtain the same favor from Bishop Rosati.

I am with respect in the Sacred Heart of Jesus, Father, your very humble and very devoted servant.

Philippine Duchesne
Superior of the house of the Sacred Heart

[On the reverse:]
To Father
Father De Neckere
Priest of the Mission
Barrens

Letter 222   **L. To a Religious**   **House of D. ✱✱✱**

SS. C. J. et M.

Saint Ferdinand
November 27, 1823[123]
St. Anthony

My very dear and respected Mother,

I am fulfilling a very pleasant duty in spending a few moments with you to offer you my wishes for the New Year along with those of my sisters; those for last year are already fulfilled through the success you have in your work for the glory of God. Maybe you envied the great work we are doing, while we have only to blush at seeing ourselves incapable

---

123   Original autograph, C-VII 2) c Duchesne to Barat, Box 2. Cf. J. de Charry, II 2, L. 177, pp. 217-219; Hogg, pp. 143-145. Ch. Paisant, pp. 602-603. De Charry includes this letter in the collection to Mother Barat, but the general level of information and formal style suggest that it is to someone else.

of doing anything equal to the multitude of your good works. But we are, however, content with our lot; we embrace the cross we share, and we are happy because it is given to us by the heart of our spouse.

Mother Octavie, our dear assistant, has been attacked by cancer of the mouth, which has already eaten away her upper lip and often makes her suffer a great deal. There is no hope of a cure; four doctors have treated her without success, and God seems to refuse the miracle we have been asking for, since the suffering increases at each novena made for her. God has given her the strength to endure this state of humiliation and suffering; she often says with great fervor, "I would not exchange my state for all the crowns in the world." If she carries her cross so well, why would we not be encouraged to carry it with her? That of poverty is added, as we have only eight boarders who pay, and we are not sure of them. Even so, we must pay up to 40 F for each doctor's visit, but how can we neglect any means to restore the health of a capable person? Now we have stopped these visits, as they are useless, and we content ourselves with the village doctor who is less expensive.

With very little money, we are entirely responsible for the expenses of the church, the debts of which are not paid; no one is zealous enough for such a beautiful task, or their misery has frozen their generosity. It would trouble us very little if it did not deprive us of contributing to the most important work for religion, that of the novitiate of our fathers, a seed bed of saints and apostles. The father rector is a man of great merit. We compare him to Father Balthazar Alvarez. It would be great joy in speaking to you of this family to give you details of successes and consolations; but their lot is the cross, and we are happy to march under the same standard. I am going to give you a glimpse of it, not to sadden you, but to let you see their courage in living in such poverty that hinders their zeal and in winter allows no comfort. They sleep in the fierce cold under a leaking roof, no floor and no glass in the windows, which they block up with planks. Add to that the work on the building, as yet unfinished, and in the fields, and you will see death to nature. How much money spent on parties and adornments would be better used for their works! See if you cannot get something for them.

I am your unworthy servant in the Sacred Heart.

Philippine

Letter 223   **L. 57 to Mother Barat**

SS. C. J. et M.

November 27, 1823[124]

Very Reverend Mother,

I was waiting to write to our mothers and sisters, to avoid the costs of the post, until the departure for France of a priest from Saint Louis, Father Deys, who feels called to go to Europe in search of contemplative religious life. Unfortunately, in spite of his promise, I learned that he is leaving today without telling us beforehand. I am hastening to write in the hope that maybe bad weather will have delayed the steamboat.

I am feeling more than ever what happiness it would be to be near the center of authority, fearing as I do to be caught up in an undertaking from which we would not be able to withdraw. Two or three times I have already spoken to you about a proposed foundation, thirty leagues from New Orleans, on the river where the parish would give the land and have a house built. But several religious from France and money for the journey and furniture would be required. I have written to the bishop that I did not believe that you would consent and that from here we would not be able to contribute anything to this work.

Some letters and the religious unrest in this parish, formerly Father Valesano's,[125] made me think that no one was still thinking about it. However, I have just learned that the bishop has proposed to Mother Eugenie to send her power of attorney to conclude the agreement, saying that he authorizes it and that he will write to you. The frail condition of our two houses and the instability of the country where nothing is firm make me apprehensive about taking on a work that would be highly publicized and the failure of which would be all the more regrettable. Everything is so superficial here.

It is said that we ought to have a piano teacher in order to raise our reputation. I don't know even then whether people would be satisfied with our education. Our fathers have learned with joy about the success of the fathers in France and in Sardinia. They are still having trials; they are such that I beg you to encourage again our houses in France to

---

124 Copies, A-II 2) g Box 2, *Lettres intéressantes de la Société depuis 1816 N° 1*, pp. 388-389; C-III 1: USA Foundation Upper Louisiana, Box 1, *Lettres de la Haute Louisiane II 1823-1830*, pp. 1-4. Second letter dated November 27, 1823. Cf. J. de Charry, II 2, L. 178, pp. 220-222; Hogg, pp. 145-147. Ch. Paisant, pp. 604-605.
125 Italian missionary with whom Josephine Meneyroux returned to France, November 21, 1821.

send them money, directly to them. The needs are so great here that I would be afraid of confusing their interests with those of others.

Mother Octavie is no better; the rest of the house is in good health. We have only ten pupils, and they are not to be counted on. The fathers have not been able to build before winter; today they are at the mercy of the weather, and all are acting as masons or carpenters to create a room that will be both study and dormitory.

The retreat for us could not take place. The father rector is also sick.

Very Reverend Mother, please look upon your weak little flock of Saint Ferdinand and be good enough to bless it at this moment when it offers you the warmest good wishes. It is all yours *in Corde Jesu*.

I am at your feet, your unworthy daughter.

Philippine

P.S. I beg you to excuse my haste and the liberty I am taking in asking you to send each mother a copy of the enclosed letter, as I do not have time to write to everyone; besides I would only repeat myself if I wrote several letters. The priest who is kindly taking my letter is a friend of the house; he is very devout, a great musician and has given piano lessons to Mother Octavie during the vacation; she repeats the lessons with Sister Xavier [Hamilton] who teaches the children. That throws a little dust in the eyes, for we cannot make them skillful pianists. How I long for a letter from you; I have had no answers to mine of fifteen months ago; your last was dated fourteen months ago. What a great sacrifice it is! My respects to the fathers and mothers, especially Fathers Varin and Barat.

Letter 224   L. 11 to Mrs. de Mauduit

Saint Ferdinand, Missouri, near Saint Louis
December 28, 1823[126]

My dearest Sister,

I received your letter that gives a complete picture of your soul; it is so kind, expansive, and zealous for the good. You will not doubt the interest I have in everyone important to you! You have consolations

---

[126] Copies: *Cahier, Lettres de la Mère Duchesne à sa famille*, pp. 117-120; *Lettres dactylographiées*. C-VII 2) c Duchesne to her family and lay people, Box 5.

and you have sorrows; that is our lot in this life, where it seems that consolation, always passing, is given to us only to encourage us in bearing the cross that would depress us if God did not strengthen us with his favors.

Remember me to your husband, your children, dear Amelie [Bergasse] especially, whom I love in spite of her silence in my regard; remember me also to my sisters. It is difficult to correspond with all those one loves at such a great distance; our contacts must take place in the Heart of Jesus. I lay before him the needs of all my relatives, and you are not forgotten, especially in the wishes I send you for the coming New Year.

Your kind heart may be happy to know about our location in the New World; you will find it on the right bank of the Mississippi, between the junction of the Missouri and the Arkansas Rivers. They are each more than 500 leagues long. We are higher up than the Ohio, which joins with the Mississippi from the left. If your map is detailed and shows New Madrid and Sainte Genevieve, we are farther north than these two towns, which are only villages, especially New Madrid, which suffered a great deal from an earthquake of which it was the epicenter. I stopped there last year on my way up the river from Opelousas, where I took two of our sisters to our new foundation, which is already more numerous than ours, as the country is less poor. The steamboats are so advanced that it takes only two weeks to do the 400 leagues from New Orleans here, and I spent three months on this return journey. That does not give one a liking for travel; it is only the desire to work for God that can cause a religious to put up with the inconveniences of such a long trip.

My health is one of the strongest and would suffice for more work, but we have to be content with what God gives. I would not wish to choose rest through fear of trouble, but it would be desirable to have it before death, for natural satisfaction is so often mixed in even the holiest enterprises and makes us lose the merit of them.

If Father Saint-Ferréol is still alive, remember me to him and have my former acquaintances pray for me, especially those who go to La Louvesc.

The village where we are is five leagues from Saint Louis, the chief city of the new state of Missouri and the same distance from Saint Charles, our first place of residence, which is the seat of government; Sainte Genevieve, where we ought to have gone, is thirty leagues away and New Madrid, 100. Our house is made of brick and adjoins the parish, newly built in brick also. The bishop provided the land and made us a gift of our property, which includes a large field, a little wood along a creek and a garden with a yard for the animals; we have about 100 chickens, seven cows and one horse. It costs us nothing to feed them in the summer; we open the gate, and in the evening they all come back promptly to the same gate without any cowherds. I forgot to mention the five sheep and some beautiful geese. All these are fed in good weather in the common woods and meadows, and in winter these animals have no other shelter than a straw covering mounted on scaffolding. If there were an opportunity, I would like to have a few silk worms, but we would never be able to spin it here, and I haven't seen any mulberry trees at all, so don't trouble yourself about it.

Goodbye, dear Sister, all yours in the Hearts [of Jesus and Mary],

Philippine

Letter 225   L. 5 to Father Delacroix

SS. C. J. et M.

December 30, 1823
St. Anthony[127]

Father,

I recall that in former years at this season we had the happiness of offering you our good wishes for the New Year. Distance does not change our gratitude towards you, and it would be very pleasant to express it to you. All my sisters join me in offering their good wishes. Each one would do so individually if it were not inappropriate, but they will never forget to speak of you especially to the Heart of Jesus, to whom you are so devoted and whom you have taught us to love as you do.

We are eager to learn your destination and that you are happy. The bishop's crosses increase on all sides, and I fear he will succumb to them. Father Inglesi has joined the schismatic group in Philadelphia.[128] Everything is going badly in Saint Louis and not very well here. The churchgoers prefer to give up their pew or even the church rather than

---

127 Original autograph, C-VII 2) c Writings Duchesne to various Eccles., Box 8. On the reverse: "from Mother Duchesne, 1823, December 30. No. 3."
128 William Hogan, pastor of the church of Saint Mary in Philadelphia, set himself against his bishop, Henry Conwell, expelled him from the cathedral, and exhorted his followers to disobey the bishop. The conflict is known as the Hogan Schism.

to pay pew rent. Several are ill at the Jesuit house, and it is astonishing that there are not more who are sick because of the cold, because they have not finished building. They have only the old houses.

I am with profound respect, Father, your devoted and humble servant.

Philippine Duchesne

[On the reverse:]
To Father
Father Delacroix, priest
Parish of Saint Michael
Acadia

Letter 226 L. 12 to Bishop Rosati

SS. C. J. et M.

[January 2, 1824][129]

Dear Bishop,

We have good reason to praise God for his goodness to this diocese and to us in particular, since he has chosen you as his representative in this part of the country. Such a happy arrangement of divine Providence makes us thank him a thousand times for having listened to our prayers, above all to our request to Saint Regis for workers filled with his spirit. This good saint, our protector, could not have answered more satisfactorily the novena made last year at your request; it is true that it is not your wish, but it is for the glory of God. I am grateful to Father Delacroix for telling me you had received your bulls and that Bishop Dubourg will come to consecrate you as soon as the weather improves.

I am with profound veneration, Bishop, your very humble and devoted servant.

Philippine Duchesne

January 2, 1824

---

129 Original autograph, C-VII 2) c Writings Duchesne to Rosati, Box 6. Reverse: "January 2, 1824, Mother Duchesne, Florissant."

Letter 227   **L. 2 to Mother de Gramont**

SS. C. J. et M.

> Saint Ferdinand, near Saint Louis, State of Missouri, January 2, 1824[130]
> St. Ant.

My very good Mother,

I wrote to our common mother at the end of November,[131] no. 40, and hardly spent any time all during the year without giving her details about us, but I have received no letter from her in return. The last one I received from her was dated September 1822,[132] and I received it after a whole year, and shortly after, one from Mother de Charbonnel, a little more recently.[133] At Opelousas they also complain about the total silence. I do not know to what to attribute it, but it is very difficult for me. I think that I should have asked that they write to me by New York, but maybe they forgot to stamp the letter to the port in France, or misaddressed the letters. Several have reached me addressed by way of Illinois or Louisiana. But these are two states different from ours. We can no longer count on it being the way it was at the time of the Spanish or the French. Our address is the one above, at the date of my letter.

In such a long privation, I do not know where several of my mothers are. I suspect that our reverend mother is in Turin,[134] according to the report of a missionary. So it is you, dear Mother, who I suppose to be the most stable and sufficiently charitable to get me a prompt answer. Until I am sure of the speed and accuracy of New York, please again use the route through New Orleans, sending the letter via Le Havre, from where more ships leave for this city.

---

130   Copies: C-VII 2) c Duchesne to RSCJ and Children; Box 4; A-II 2) g Box 2, *Lettres intéressantes de la Société depuis 1816 N° 1*, pp. 392-394; C-III 1: USA Foundation Haute Louisiane, Box, *Lettres de la Haute Louisiane II 1823-1830*, p. 221-223, C-III USA Foundation, Haute-Louisiane, Box. Cf. J. de Charry, II 2, L. 181, pp. 229-233; Hogg, pp. 151-155.
131   Letter of the 27 of November 1823, confided to Father Leo Deys.
132   Letter of the 27 of September 1822. Mother Barat wrote eight letters during the year 1823: those of June 22, August 7, August 25, August 30, September 10, November 22, and December 5 and 22. None of them had come by January 4, 1824, but they would all eventually arrive. The sojourn of Mother Barat at Sainte-Marie d'En-Haut and the serious illness that she had in that house explain her silence between September 1822 and June 1823.
133   It was copied by Philippine in Collection 92, 1, pp. 83-84. It is dated Paris, November 1822.
134   In fact, Mother Barat did not go to Turin at that time, but only in May 1832.

I am not writing about our expenses to Mother de Charbonnel, since I think she is perhaps at Besançon.[135] Please explain to the one who will receive it in the absence of our mother that the entry "church" refers especially to the contribution for the priest; all the liturgical expenses are ours. The people supply nothing and would rather abandon the church, and the fathers have no means of supporting it.

How consoled I will be when I learn the state of health of the persons in the two Societies [Society of Jesus and Society of the Sacred Heart], especially of you whose health is so fragile, of our reverend mother, and of Mother Bigeu, who has been languishing for so long. It would be sweet for me to see you share our happiness in having here those who would go ahead of us to advance the work of God, and whose leader [Van Quickenborne] condemns me to silence when it comes to speaking about his family, not wanting to endure other praise, either in person or at a distance, being content that God approves his sufferings and his modest labors. The approbation of his superior in Rome has arrived to strengthen him, as we were ourselves, when we received the blessing of the Sovereign Pontiff,[136] whom God called to himself, among the misfortunes that we were tempted to believe were the just punishment of our temerity and self-will.

Bishop Dubourg now has a coadjutor, who has just received his documents from Rome. It is Father Rosati, a Roman priest, superior of the seminary here and of all the Lazarist missionaries. He is a man of great merit, devoted to our dear Society and to whom we owe our origins. He exercises the functions of bishop in Missouri; and Bishop Dubourg, who has not yet consecrated him[137] and who will undoubtedly reside in Louisiana, keeps for himself that part of his great diocese that he had intended to divide. But experience has shown him the impossibility. Several bishops could not be maintained, nor their seminaries. The present residence of Bishop Dubourg is 30 leagues from New Orleans, where I do not think he will be able to stay. The establishment that he wants to make is near him, on the other side of the river, but it does not seem that there is any certainty about obtaining the land.[138]

---

135 Mother de Charbonnel was general treasurer. At the end of 1823, she was at Besançon, and returned to Paris in July 1824.
136 Pius VII died August 20, 1823. He had sent his blessing to Philippine and her companions by means of two letters (April 3 and 12, 1818) of Cardinals Litta and Fontana, addressed to Father Perreau.
137 He consecrated him in Donaldsonville, Louisiana, in the Church of the Ascension, March 25, 1824.
138 In the spring of 1823, Bishop Dubourg came to Missouri, made a pastoral visit around the south of his diocese, and stayed at Saint Michael and at Donaldsonville. In December, he

My very dear Mother, please commend me to the prayers of our fathers, especially Father Perreau, and Fathers Joseph and Louis. Mother Octavie is better, and all the others are well.

I am in the Sacred Heart, my dear Mother, your submissive and humble servant,

Philippine

Letter 228 L. 6 to Mother Bigeu[139]

SS. C. J. et M.

from Saint Ferdinand near Saint Louis, State of Missouri
For the superior of the house of *
January 2, 1824
St. Ant.[140]

My very dear Mother,

It has been such a long time that we have been deprived of news from France that we do not know what has happened in each house, who are the present superiors and what is interesting about them, and the glory of God and the advancement of this little Society that distance makes even more dear.

Would that I could have, like Saint Xavier, the names of everyone in these houses, to carry them on my heart and offer them to the Heart that unites us all; but I am wrong to want it. The wishes of the soul are enough for him. He sees every need, he knows every wish, and his goodness will fulfill them.

We have learned of the death of our Holy Father the pope and the election of his successor through the public newspapers. I do not doubt that there will be miracles at his tomb, about which the details will interest us, like the marvels that were done by the German prince [Alexandre de Hohenlohe].[141] I thank the house at Grenoble for sending

---

returned to New Orleans.
139 The style and content of this letter indicates that the recipient is Mother Bigeu. On the same date, Philippine wrote to Mother E. de Gramont.
140 Original autograph, C-VII 2) c Duchesne to RSCJ and Children, Box 4. Copies: A-II 2) g Box 2, *Lettres intéressantes de la Société depuis 1816 N° 1,* pp. 390-392; C-III 1: USA Foundation Haute Louisiane, Box 1, *Lettres de la Haute Louisiane II 1823-1830,* pp. 223-226.
141 Alexandre de Hohenlohe-Waldenbourg-Schillingsfürst (1794-1849) was the son of Prince Charles Albert II of Hohenlohe-Waldenbourg-Schillingsfürst and of Princess Judith Reviczky

us the brochure that contained those of 1821 and 1822, as well as two attestations of miracles at the tomb of Mother Aloysia. We still do not have her life, so often announced and never received.

Mother Lucile [Mathevon] often tells us about its contents and raises our desire to have it. This good mother is well suited for this country because she has not looked for anything except God. Mother Octavie has been giving us plenty of worry about her health for a year and a half. At this moment, there is a perceptible improvement, but I do not dare to be too confident. She is appreciated everywhere, both within and without, and she merits it by her excellent qualities. As one often loves in a new and particular way, we are preparing for her a foundation in Saint Louis in hope of her cure. She will be at the head, and there will be three persons. I will stay at Saint Ferdinand; pupils will pay 75 *sous* per month for this day school. They are collecting subscriptions, and all this will be done without us, without our knowing other than by public notice.

This project cannot take long, nor another one in Lower Louisiana.

The health of Sister Catherine [Lamarre] has greatly worsened. She suffers from great stomach troubles. The time when she suffered most was exactly the time of a retreat for the six professed, the kind that you sometimes have the happiness of having from our fathers. It was also a father who gave it according to the method of Saint Ignatius. These eight days were truly a time of spiritual abundance. The devil was jealous, so he made nine big pigs that we had bought arrive the second day of retreat. We had to take on this disgusting work for two days, and I was the first victim. I took this as punishment for my lack of recollection. The following days were peaceful, and this happy retreat ended on the feast of the Immaculate Conception. We had five exercises per day and one instruction. Everything was very solid and even touching.

You have surely taken notice of the happy event that has placed us under the guidance of our fathers. We had much apprehension of being refused, but Saint Francis Regis affected the provincial who said that because of our deprivation and the proximity of the church that they serve, we could have their ministrations, provided that their house did not suffer because of it. It is half a league from here. The result is that sometimes we lack Mass when one of the priests is on mission. We did not have it for midnight at Christmas, which had not yet been lacking, but at 8 and 11 o'clock with three sermons and exposition [of

> von Revisnye, born a Hungarian baroness. He was a seminarian in Vienna, ordained priest in 1815, and bishop in 1844. In 1819, he cured the paralysis of Princess Mathilde of Schwarzenberg. He was author of a good number of works on Christian asceticism.

the Blessed Sacrament] in our choir. The bishop permits it in the church only rarely because of the people of so many other religions who come in. The last Mass was sung with deacon and subdeacon and four other ecclesiastics in surplice.

The first of the year, the father rector was willing to distribute the prizes to our eleven children and listen to a little play that they composed about the pleasures of carnival, following his sermons against balls. We recommend to your prayers this weak flock and their companions who have left, whose facile and inconstant character cannot withstand the dangers of the world that abound here in luxury of adornment and table, balls, comedies, idleness, and bad books.

Among our day students, two Indian girls have given us the most consolation. One was faultless and wanted to follow our first calling, which she could not yet obtain. The second in six months learned very well to read, to write, a great number of hymns; and since she speaks her own language, Spanish, French, and English, she has the means to be very useful, even to the white people of her country, many of whom do not know how to read. She has a great desire to teach and especially to baptize all the sick children, and she has learned well how she should do it.

Expecting our children to decrease even more, we are trying to do everything we can ourselves. We make our soap, our tallow candles, our altar candles, our hosts, our butter, our wool, cotton, and linen thread. We planted cotton this year, but it did not succeed, since the seed is not fit for this climate. We hope to succeed better this year, to buy a knitting machine and make cotton and wool cloth. We know how to dye in black, gray, and yellow from the local trees and plants without costing anything. We will try to grow indigo for blue dye, which is very easy. We can practically live off the salted pork and milk from our farm. But that is enough talk about animal life. I beg you to ask of the Sacred Heart of Jesus that he will assure us one day life eternal where we hope to see you again. We are in him all yours, and especially I,

Philippine Duchesne

Letter 229   L. 6 to Father Delacroix

SS. C. J. et M.

January 16, 1824
Rec. to St. Anthony[142]

Reverend Father,

A few days ago I received your letter of November 26. Thinking you were still at Grand Coteau, I wrote to you there, not being able to wait so long to express to you our gratitude and at the same time offer you our wishes for the new year. God has already heard them, since he placed you near the bishop as you wanted, and that is a consolation for you.

I shared your letter with Father Van Quickenborne so that he could enjoy the interesting things it contained. But at the same time, he received one from the bishop that contained a part of the same details. He was very touched at your remembrance.

Please present my remembrances to Fathers Brassac and Anduze. Knowing their interest in us, I think they will learn with pleasure that Mother Octavie is much better, and I hope that with care we may be able to keep her. The rest of the house are well. The day school is ever the same. On Sunday there are nearly 50 young people, but the boarding school has only eleven, two of whom give nothing at all, and the others are not reliable. Mr. McKay from New Madrid has sent nothing.

We continue to support the church, because the fathers would not be able to, and the people have no interest. They do not pay for the pews either in a day's work or in double provisions, which has made this year very difficult for the missionaries. They have not been able to finish building and are spending the winter in old houses.

Mr. Mullanphy does not want to give anything, he told me, because he is annoyed with the bishop and with you. I am very happy that Mother Eugenie was able to send you something. I have not given you everything that was returned to you by Mr. Hyacinthe. I have learned with pleasure that Peter followed you; his excellent qualities console us for not being able to serve you in any way, for he can do it so much better than we can.

---

142 Original autograph, C-VII 2) c Writings Duchesne to various Eccles., Box 8. Postmark: St Louis Mo., Jan. 21. On the reverse: "Mother Duchesne, *1824*, January 16. N°4."

I wrote to the bishop at the beginning of the year, to whom I beg you to offer our profound respect. You have more news of France than we do. I do not know by what misfortune we do not get more letters from our country. That is a great trial to me. We have seen in a letter from the bishop, published in a newspaper, that he is very well informed about the conduct of Father Inglesi. It is public knowledge in Saint Louis, even in Canada, they say.

I am with profound respect in the Sacred Heart, Reverend Father, your totally devoted,

Philippine Duchesne

All my sisters offer you their regards. Father superior has answered you. Mr. Hyacinthe is taking back 12 planks that were mixed in with yours, which he was unable to take because they had all been given to Mr. Mullanphy. If we get something from the trees, would you want to give him the sum for the planks? He is very suffering and cannot work. The cross is found everywhere; we are fortunate to have been instructed on how to recognize its price.

Our greetings to Peter.

Never forget a family that was the object of your care and that is still full of your goodness.

[On the reverse:]
To Father
Charles Delacroix
Pastor of Saint Michael, Acadian Coast
On the river opposite St. James
Louisiana

Letter 230   L. 1 to Mr. James Clemens[143]

[January 19, 1824]
Florissant

Sir,

No doubt our commissioner did not understand the contents of the note I sent him; he brought me things that we cannot use at all, but he told me that you are willing to exchange them.

---

143   Photocopy of the original, C-VII 2) c Duchesne to her family and lay people, Box 5. Clemens Family Collection, Missouri History Museum Archives, St. Louis, Missouri. James Clemens (1791-1878) was a successful merchant in Saint Louis.

The crêpe is too narrow, it must be wide enough to make veils out of it. I ask you to exchange it at the same price.

The taffeta is too reddish and too limp. We want it to be like the model as to stiffness and white satin in color, at the same price.

I beg you to excuse the mistake; our distance and the impossibility of making the choice ourselves make it pardonable.

I am, Sir, respectfully, your humble servant.

Philippine Duchesne

January 19, 1824

>[On the reverse:]
>To Mister
>Clemens
>Saint Louis

Letter 231   **L. 15 to Mrs. de Rollin**

SS. C. J. et M.

Saint-Ferdinand, State of Missouri, February 16, 1824[144]

My dearest Cousin and Friend,

I received your letter of last summer, and I have shared all your sorrows; my tears have mingled with yours, and they have been joined by all those who, like me, have benefited from your generosity. I have spoken to my companions about your goodness for a long time; it is a pleasure for me to tell them about my first friend, all she has done for me—and this is very apparent at our religious celebrations—about her life-companion who made her days so happy and who, by sharing her loving interest, was the first to open for me the road to happiness.[145]

My feelings of gratitude could never weaken, remembering the happy couple a thousand times blessed by God. Judge then, my beloved Friend, whether my sisters, hearing of the blow that has struck you, could not share your sorrow and offer the most urgent prayers: but I am the one, among all, who feel your sorrow; and the last mark of your

---

144 *Copies of letters of Philippine Duchesne to Mrs. de Rollin and a few others*, No. 16; *Cahier, Lettres à Mme de Rollin*, pp. 41-44. C-VII 2) c Duchesne to her family and lay people, Box 5.
145 Jacques-Fortunat Savoye de Rollin died on July 31, 1823 in Paris. General Foy (1775-1825) pronounced his eulogy during the funeral ceremony.

spouse's kindness for me was such as to touch the tenderest chord in my heart. In return, I will offer for him the Masses, Communions, and the few good works we do, and I hope God has already heard the many prayers you have had said for his eternal happiness. Our mother general wrote to me about you and about the donation you have sent her for us, and she is as grateful as I am.

The two among my sisters who know you, Mothers Lucile [Mathevon] and Octavie [Berthold], send you their respect and deep affection. The latter has suffered much this year: an abscess in her mouth lanced by a surgeon has opened on her cheek and is causing us to suspect cancer. After causing much pain, the wound has healed, but a continual series of illnesses makes me fear a return. She is a precious person for her devotion, her teaching, and her attractive character.

No doubt, dear Friend, you have received the letter I wrote you following my aunt's death.[146] I cannot think of all the sorrows God has sent you since we separated without being deeply touched. There would be no understanding these mysteries of sorrow if religion did not come like warnings to show us that our happiness is not to be found here below and that we must look forward to it in a happier city that will reunite virtuous spouses, friends who are one in desiring good, those who have carried the cross following the example and in the footsteps of Jesus Christ, who wished to be the first to open that city to us by way of sufferings.

God has prepared some suffering for me here, too; after beginnings promising success, the lack of money has caused the withdrawal of a number of our students: only ten remain. This situation, joined to the persecution our bishop is suffering in his corrupt city, has caused him to move 400 leagues from us; but the worst suffering is seeing our former pupils, even those who seemed the most fervent and solidly virtuous, relapse into their former neglect of religion through natural levity and the attraction of pleasure and bad example. I still hope that their faith is not dead and that age, reverses and other trials from the hand of God will reignite it one day. That is my only hope for them; but we also have the opportunity of offering to those whom God calls a shelter in which to practice virtue far from the world's contagion. That will be our most enduring work here, and it is already drawing down a thousand blessings through those who have cast their lot with us, who now number twelve both here and in Opelousas. Other foundations have been proposed to

---

146 Marie Charlotte Perier, née Pascal, died July 31, 1821. The letter Philippine refers to no longer exists.

us, but prudence does not allow us to undertake them just now, lacking personnel and money, which it is not possible to send us.

I learned through Mrs. Teisseire and Mother Barat that Marine had entered at the Sacred Heart to recover her health. I hope she will do so, that she will consecrate herself to God and that your sister will not regret giving back to God what she received from him. That lovable child would be very worthy of him who asks the first fruits and rejects a sacrifice grudgingly given.

You understand how consoling it was for me to learn that the first of my nieces to give herself to God closed her earthly career in so holy a manner. I have shed tears at this death, but more for myself than for her, seeing that in so short a time, she made use of the talent given her, while mine has produced nothing so far. However, the moment of giving an account is approaching; I have already had several indications of it. If I had any regret in giving up this life, it would be in leaving our work still so incomplete and in the hands of religious, some of whom are too young and the others too unwell, but God knows what he is doing.

I believe, however, that I will still have the pleasure of receiving several letters from you. I will always answer with that haste and tender affection that I have promised you in the Heart of Jesus. All yours, always,

Philippine Duchesne

Do not forget me with Augustin [Perier], his wife and the whole family.

Letter 232   L. 7 to Father Delacroix

SS. C. J. et M.

Saint Ferdinand, February 18, 1824
Recommended to St. Anthony of Padua[147]

Reverend and very dear Father,

I am tempted to accuse you of calumny when you say you are forgotten at Florissant. Your memory, always held in veneration, will be forever dear, not only to us who have known how to appreciate you, but also to all its inhabitants. Mr. Mullanphy, though annoyed with us,

---

147 Original autograph, C-VII 2) c Writings Duchesne to various Eccles., Box 8. Postmark: St Louis Mo., Feb. 25. On the reverse: "from Mother Duchesne, 1824, February 18. No. 5."

misses you, and there is no one here who does not speak of you with respect and gratitude.

Mr. Hyacinthe de Hêtre senior, who is very suffering, wants to know how he could have 12 beautiful planks mixed in with yours that were carried to Mr. Mullanphy. Mr. Hamtramck, now absent, gave us nothing for you, nor did he say anything about trees, and even asked for the arm chair from the church that you received in payment. I intend to refuse him unless there is an order from you to turn it over to him. The Flemish gentleman who cut your trees came to see them and said that you had offered him all that you did not give to us. I will not turn those over either without an order. Mr. Chauvin, the farmer, thinks he made a mistake to your disadvantage in your account with regard to the planks and would like a summary of the transaction.

Please give this letter to the bishop. I am telling him about our mother general's intentions with regard to our foundations. She wants no more in the countryside and will approve one in New Orleans only if that is possible, but it will not be before God inspires some generous souls to give us not only land but a house. The scarcity of money is so great everywhere that it would be to act against prudence to contract debts that one is not sure of being able to pay off. Our mother told me several times to act with economy and not to count on her for money. She even withheld from me 1800 F sent by my family, to partially pay our debt to Mr. Mullanphy.

I mention these details so that you will not put too much confidence in the hopes of Father Borgna, contradicted by several direct letters. It is hard for me to refuse a foundation right under your eyes, guided by your attentions, and which you would certainly direct; but I cannot go against the orders of our mother, and we cannot at this time dream of anything except holding on to provisions here, and we have nothing for travel or the cost of furniture.

If we had been established in Saint Louis at the beginning, we could keep at least the day students, but here there are only the poor who cost but give nothing, nor do the novices; but our cows help us very much to survive, as does the garden. The expenses of the church are still ours. There has been no more than $20 income for the pews. Mr. Mullanphy does not want to pay for his. Mr. Cyr *(the rest erased by moisture)*. The Jesuit Fathers have their own problems, but they know how to suffer. Nothing comes to them from Maryland.

The wound on Mother Octavie's jaw is completely closed, but she has a constant sore throat, which impedes her in teaching her classes. There has been a great deal of serious sore throat in the area and many have died of it. Mother Octavie's seems to be the result of the infection caused by the wound. She also often has fever, but she suffers with much patience. Mother Lucile and Sister Catherine carry on with their day class. Sisters Xavier and Regis are ever fervent as is Sister Ignace. The two new ones are also good.

The wife of Big Louis is dead, and also the mother of Mr. and Mrs. Roussel.

Father rector received your little letter and answered right away. His letter and several of mine went to Grand Coteau, hence the long delay. Father *Témérairement,* as Mrs. Roy calls Father Timmermans, has gone only once to La Côte Sans Dessein. Mrs. Roy told me, when she came to get one of her daughters, that all the inhabitants together could not pay the expense of a trip, and that they make no money *(the rest is illegible).* This father goes alternately every Sunday to Saint Charles or to Portage or to Dardenne, and does not return until Monday, so that we miss Mass that day. Father rector, too tired from his Sunday when he preaches three times, often comes in the evening from the residence and goes back again.

I am with profound respect, good Father, your very humble servant.
Philippine Duchesne

All my sisters and the children offer you their respectful remembrance; please offer mine to Father Brassac and Father Anduze.
Do you know about the holy death of Miss Pelagie Chouteau? Caroline Hamilton is at Saint Anthony Falls [Minnesota], farther than Prairie du Chien.[148] She seems still to be a good girl.

[On the reverse:]
To Father
Father Delacroix
Pastor of Saint Michael
Bringers Post Office
Louisiana

---

148 Saint Anthony Falls is 200 miles from Prairie du Chien, Wisconsin, situated between Saint Louis and Minneapolis-Saint Paul.

Letter 233   **L. 58 to Mother Barat**

SS. C. J. et M.

> Saint-Ferdinand, State of Missouri, February 19, 1824
> Rec. to St. Anthony of Padua[149]
> No. 48

Very Reverend Mother,

In my disappointment at having no news from you, I wrote No. 47, on January 2 to Mother de Gramont, asking that she would be willing to send me some, as she was more likely to be in Paris.

Finally, two weeks ago divine Providence arranged the arrival of letters from France, all at the same time, some dated March, others June and even September. There were four in your hand and two written for you in Grenoble by Mother Second[150] and in Paris by Mother Prevost [June 18, 1823]. I was so happy that day! God had taken care not to let me know of the tragedy threatening the Society through your illness, and I have learned it now only to thank God thousands of times with all my sisters for preserving our mother for us. All my sisters are united in praying that such a terrible blow does not strike us as long as we live; that rather he will give you the strength to carry the burden he has imposed on you; no one else would bear the weight of it with such devotion to the general good.

As you suggested, I have already written to Mrs. de Rollin to thank her and express my condolence in her sorrow.[151] That money and the income from the State would have been very acceptable to us, but if it is necessary in order to pay back what has been borrowed for us, it could not have been put to a more just use. I am only sorry that you consulted me as if I had any desire or possessed anything in my own name. It is yours to decide, and it is up to me to conform to your wishes, which I respect in advance and to which I submit.

I ask you to sell the personal effects [toiletries or sewing supplies] you spoke to me about. I would like it if Mrs. de Rollin, after fulfilling

---

149   Original autograph, C-VII 2) c Duchesne to Barat, Box 2. Cf. J. de Charry, II 2, L. 183, pp. 236-241; Hogg, pp. 157-162.
150   Adelaide Second, RSCJ (1782-1857), entered at Sainte-Marie d'En-Haut July 1, 1804, and made her novitiate and vows at the same time as Philippine.
151   Josephine Savoye de Rollin had just lost her husband, and she was sending Philippine a large amount of money.

all her duties in the world as a daughter and a wife, would consecrate herself to the lovable Heart of Jesus. Her wound is too fresh for such a proposal just now, but I would not be surprised if she wished to do so one day, and she would be useful in the Society.

Her little niece Marie's letter consoled me very much. I hope that God, who has done such marvelous things for us these last days, will not close so soon the kind hand that brings them about. We are so inundated with favors that we would be very ungrateful to speak of our crosses.

Have you any doubt now that God wants us here? Since Pope Pius VII blessed us and said to his Italian missionaries: "Make devotion to the Sacred Heart of Jesus appreciated in America." Since then we have received an unhoped for benefit in having so nearby a seed bed of Jesuits as fervent as Berchmans,[152] formed like ourselves by a Father Rodriguez or Alvarez; he is one of the two. Now he stays away from us less; his interest is quite steady. His reserve did not come from defective zeal but from fear of acting against his Rule.[153] In his direction he has much in common with your holy brother, from whom I have had two little letters and one from Father Perreau. Truly I would be very ungrateful to complain of my sufferings, seeing myself blessed and sustained by so many friends of God.

The same packet contained the associations [or confraternities] from Rome, obtained by Father Inglesi, which Mrs. Fournier sent us.

You know the sad end of this unworthy servant. It is public in Saint Louis, as it was noted in the newspapers in Philadelphia and Saint Louis, where letters from the bishop of Quebec and our bishop concerning him were inserted.[154] It is said that he joined Hogan's schism; he has happily gone back to England. We will see him no more; he fled from a resident of Saint Louis who met him in Philadelphia. It has been much talked of everywhere, especially among the enemies of religion, and another priest has been accused of apostasy. I still hope it is false, but I believe it is useful to inform you because of religious coming to this country. They need a good head and solid virtue. The change of climate and the different outlook on life all cause strange upheavals.

---

152 John Berchmans, SJ (1599-1621), born at Diest (Belgium), entered the novitiate at Malines, and died in Rome as a scholastic at the age of twenty-two. He was beatified in 1865 and canonized in 1888.
153 The rule used to forbid Jesuits to take charge of the spiritual direction of convents, except in mission countries. Father Van Quickenborne received this permission from his provincial.
154 When he arrived in Philadelphia, the trustees of Saint Mary's church wanted to name Father Inglesi pastor instead of William Hogan, who had revolted against his bishop and had been excommunicated, but Bishop Dubourg refused.

Yesterday I received another letter from our former chaplain [Charles Delacroix], who is taking a good deal of trouble to have us in his parish. I am answering him and also the bishop, who approves of his endeavor, that you want foundations only in cities. I do see how much better it would have been in principle to found in Saint Louis; the parish priest was getting a school ready for us, but the bishop had not been forewarned that you had permitted nothing; therefore, I refused. We have been obliged to send away two novices. The others can only profit from their excellent direction [from Father Van Quickenborne]. Nowhere in this diocese will they find its equal. That makes me favor this village for a novitiate, far from the world and from visits, etc.

You have been kind enough to ask us what would be useful to us: we need some veils like yours. The ones here are too transparent. Money can be sent by opportunity to one of the vicars of the cathedral in New Orleans. They all wish us well. It is useless to give a name as they change very often. The title vicar cannot be misunderstood. I would also like some braid and fringe for a cope and a very small ciborium for our chapel so that we can have the Blessed Sacrament there. Here we can get black cotton cloth very cheaply, and we will weave next year, as we are growing cotton.

The arrival of sisters from Kentucky banished any idea of small foundations.[155] They will fulfill the need, supervised by Bishop Rosati, coadjutor to Bishop Dubourg, of the Congregation of Saint Lazarus [Vincentians]. He is a very good choice and wishes us well.

It seems that the bishop is not coming back up here; he has asked for his vestments and library. It is in the parish where he will live that Father Delacroix wanted to prepare a new foundation for us.

Sister Catherine has received your letter. The father has allowed her to receive Communion every week.

I spoil everything. When you release me from office, you will do the greatest good. I acknowledge in advance that I deserve it, not as a favor but as a penalty, but I always want to be submissive to you, being your very obedient servant and daughter, Reverend Mother.

Philippine

Loving remembrances to our fathers, mothers and sisters. Mother Octavie is better.

---

155 The "Friends of Mary at the Foot of the Cross," called Sisters of Loretto, arrived at the Barrens on June 14, 1823, to found there a convent called "Bethlehem."

I am very glad to have your consent to a foundation in New Orleans, not that we can make it yet, but in order to take advantage of the first opportunity.

[On the reverse:]
To Mother
Mother Barat Superior General
of the houses of the Sacred Heart
Rue de Varenne
France
PARIS

Letter 234   **L. 7 to Mother Bigeu**

SS. C. J. et M.

Saint Ferdinand, March 18, 1824
Rec. to St. Ant. of Padua[156]

My very good Mother,

From the last letters I received from France, I learn that the all-powerful God, in spite of the weakness of your health, has once more opened a vast field for your zeal.[157] You are very fortunate to work under the protection of so good and holy a court, where the virtues of Princess Clotilde of France[158] still yield their perfume. You also have the good fortune to be near a numerous Jesuit establishment that will not leave you without the abundant and solid bread of the divine word.

The same help is given out to us here as our only earthly consolation. Otherwise we have every sort of cross that the good God nevertheless proportions to our littleness: *little success* with the novices, boarders, and day students. The pestilential winds of liberty and pleasure need only to blow for two days over these light and independent heads to

---

156 Original autograph, C-VII 2) c Duchesne to RSCJ and Children, Box 4.
157 On August 21, 1823, Josephine Bigeu arrived in Turin, capital of Piedmont, for the foundation requested by the king and queen of Sardinia-Piedmont, Victor Emmanuel I (1759-1824) and Marie Therese of Austria-Este (1773-1832).
158 Princess Marie Adelaide Clotilde of France (1759-1802), called Madame Clotilde, sister of kings Louis XVI, Louis XVIII and Charles X, at the age of 16 married the prince of Piedmont, future king Charles-Emmanuel IV of Sardinia-Piedmont (1796-1802). She was declared venerable in 1808.

carry away the seed of a vocation or of the most sacred projects of piety in the world.

Poverty: it is easy when it takes away only what is superfluous or causes certain privations, but when it halts the holiest projects, when it binds the arms in a way, when it delays the advancement of the reign of God, that is when it weighs down. But God also lightens the weight by the thought that he is jealous for his glory and that if he takes away the means to procure it, it is because his time has not yet come. How sweet it would have been if we could have helped the establishment of our fathers!

I hope, Reverend Mother, that when Father Borgna returns, you will send me the details about your interesting foundation, of those who are part of it, and of the help that God gives it.

I have recalled that the house at Grenoble had suffered from what should have made it prosperous for heaven. You have been there since that sad event. Tell me if too much attention has been given to Aloysia, and whether we can continue to pray privately to her.

Add to this account something about your health. It is very important to us because you have been our mother and because you are one of the principal supports of our Society.

Your Eugenie is putting into practice what she learned from you. She governs her house very well and is surrounded with general esteem. I do not know if I will see her again. My last voyage brought so many inconveniences that I have little taste for travel, and our permissions hardly allow going such large distances.

I have also received your helpful instructions, and I am far from being able to give the consoling testimony that I make good use of them. I hope that the merit of so many good works done in the Society, in which I share, will cover over before God so many faults that, without this help, would make me deserving of a terrible death. But the union of all our hearts in those of Jesus and Mary gives me full confidence.

Mother Octavie, after having given us the greatest concerns, has recovered. Mother Lucile and my other companions are well.

In your contacts with the house at Chambéry, I hope that you will recommend me to their prayers there, as well as to those of your dear daughters, happy to work often in such a good field.

I am with respect *in Corde Jesu*, my very dear Mother, your former and poor daughter,

Philippine Duchesne

All my sisters offer you their tender respects and greet in the Sacred Heart their good sisters of your community. We are six, with 9 boarders, 3 poor children as orphans, 30 free day pupils. We are grateful for the direction [spiritual direction of the Jesuits].

[On the reverse:]
To Mother
Mother Bigeu
Superior of the house of the Sacred Heart of Jesus
Turin
Piedmont

Letter 235   L. 8 to Father Delacroix

SS. C. J. et M.

Saint Ferdinand, April 22, 1824
Rec. to St. Anthony of Padua[159]

Reverend Father,

I received your letter of February 21 a few days ago, telling me of the consolations that your zeal has brought you in the parish of Saint Michael. It would be very pleasant to share in this more closely and to be able to receive again your care, which will always inspire gratitude; but from the two letters that I wrote you in the meantime, you have seen that our mother general is opposed to foundations in the country and will give her consent only for one in New Orleans, if it could be made without help.

I hope that these letters will not hinder you from making any effort towards an establishment. I would truly regret that; since I have never given you any consolation, it would be too hard for us if you were constrained on our account.

Foundations, especially of women, will never prosper in a small place; if one succeeded right away, it would be only a passing flame soon extinguished. This is true in France as it is here and everywhere. The Ursuline Sisters, in spite of sickness, wars, persecutions, and change of

---

159 Original autograph, C-VII 2) c Writings Duchesne to various Eccles., Box 8. Postmark: St Louis Mo., Apr. 28. On the reverse: "from Mother Duchesne, 1824, April 22. No. 7."

governments, are always sustained. In a small town, they would already have been destroyed. I am still wondering how we will support the two foundations already established, because I expect that of Opelousas will also decline, although it is well supplied with house and vocations.

The reverend fathers are conscious of your remembrance. Did you know that Mr. Mullanphy holds a large mortgage with the bishop on the residence that he gave them, and he speaks of putting it up for sale if the bishop does not pay it. I assure you that it takes plenty of devotedness to work in this region. When Father Niel appealed for money in Saint Louis, one of the assembly said: "Do we need these priests? We should set them adrift in the wake of a steamboat."

On the very day of Easter one of the girls gave the same scandal as Miss Roussel.

Miss Therese Pratte has married this Lent; her older sister will marry in two months, and Celeste is engaged. The Misses Emile and Bosseron will also marry.

The Misses Maria and Adeline Boilvin,[160] Robb and Campbell[161] made their First Communion the day after Easter. There were 18 children, as many boys as girls.

The Jesuits did all the solemn offices of Holy Week, and there was a retreat for everyone during the last three days.

Mr. Hamtramck has not appeared and perhaps will not return. Mr. Shakford, having paid the taxes due, has the right to take over his property; perhaps it is already done. Mr. Chauvin has not responded about the planks. I think nevertheless that he will give them to Mr. de Hêtre. I am none the less grateful for the surplus that you gave us, as well as the trees. Mr. Hamtramck will not take them. Mr. Lepère says that you promised him a tenth, and Mr. Audiament believes that you gave them to him. He has been very ill, and his wife, too. It seems that his situation was very grave at the time that they moved.

I was deeply touched by a remembrance from the bishop that father rector was charged with giving me. I would really like to assure him of the consolations he deserves on all sides, and I sympathize deeply with

---

160   Julie Adeline (Gonzague) Boilvin, RSCJ (1813-1848), born in Saint Louis, entered at Florissant in 1828 and was one of Philippine's most beloved novices. She made her first vows in 1831 in Saint Louis and her profession in 1838 at Florissant. She was superior in New York, McSherrystown and Philadelphia, Pennsylvania. She died at Saint-Vincent, Canada, where she had gone for a rest because of her health. Several letters of Philippine addressed to her are extant.

161   Catherine Campbell, RSCJ, born in Ireland in 1797, entered the novitiate in Saint Louis in 1837 and made her first vows in 1839. She died in 1841.

his crosses. I would consider myself very unfortunate and very guilty if I contributed to increasing them.

Our sisters and students, reduced to just nine now, offer you their respect and commend themselves to the prayers of their former father. The parish never forgets you, and your memory there is blessed.

I am with respect, Reverend Father, your very devoted servant.

Philippine Duchesne

My respects to Fathers Brassac and Anduze
Our greetings to Peter. The Lepère and de Hêtre families are well.

[On the reverse:]
To Father
Father Delacroix
Pastor at Saint Michael
Bringiers Post Office
Louisiana

Letter 236   **L. 59 to Mother Barat**

Saint Ferdinand, May 2, 1824[162]
No. 50

Reverend Mother,

Your feast is very near; we unite ourselves in advance to your daughters who will have the happiness of offering you their wishes close at hand. The Divine Heart of Jesus will make up for us who cannot express our devotedness, our filial love, and our wishes for the happiness of the best of mothers.

The last news from France told us about your illness last year, from which you seem hardly to have recovered.

We cannot rid ourselves of the fear that maybe you have been overcome by another illness. May the Heart of Jesus listen to our ardent desire for the preservation of health that is consecrated solely to his glory.

I am enclosing here a request from the father superior of the Jesuits to take 700 F from his family; he has the greatest need of it for sacred

---

162 Copies, A-II 2) g Box 2, *Lettres intéressantes de la Société depuis 1816 No. 1*, pp. 400-402; C-III 1: USA Foundation Upper Louisiana, Box 1, *Lettres de la Haute Louisiane II 1823-1830*, pp. 24-28. Cf. J. de Charry, II 2, L. 185, pp. 247-250; Hogg, pp. 165-168.

vessels that are lacking. He does not wish to buy any before the money is received so as to avoid debt. I thought I could assure him that you would be willing to have the bill made out in your name so that his commission would be carried out in a shorter time. He needs two small chalices and a silver ciborium ten inches tall and a silver-plated monstrance like ours; it seems to me that Mr. de Rollin, who bought it, did not pay more than 50 or 60 F, and vestments in the five colors, neat and full. It seems to me that you bought one for Quimper for 40 F, which was lovely; maybe in Lyon there would be a better bargain by settling the price with Mr. Jouve. I have calculated:

three silver vessels	350 F
monstrance	60 F
five vestments @ 50 F	250 F
	660 F

After the cost of packing, maybe there would be enough remaining for a monstrance and some candle-holders, if their friends in France, touched by their want, would give some of these articles; that would leave funds for the candle-holders. They have only two copper ones for the table; we have given a little picture and some red cloth to decorate their small chapel. I do not need to stir up your zeal for this commission, which is so important for the fitting celebration of the liturgy and to benefit the missions that lack chalices.

We had very solemn services for Holy Week: procession on Palm Sunday—we were not there; the father rector would not have permitted it—Passion sung in several voices; Office and Lamentations sung, procession in the church; Holy Thursday and Good Friday night adoration, veneration of the cross, etc. Besides that, on the last three days, three sermons in French and in English for a retreat to prepare for Easter and First Communion. We had twelve children, boarders or day pupils.

We still have only nineteen boarders. All are well.

Mrs. Smith, the founder in Opelousas, has given the Lazarists a donation for the same parish for an educational establishment for young boys. Their superior [Bishop Rosati], now the coadjutor to Bishop Dubourg since March 25, passed the donation to the Jesuits. I don't know if they will accept it since they are so few. I want them to be established there because of our house in Opelousas, but if it were to be at our expense, that is, by our losing the very same advantage, I do not know how I would bear that new cross. I hope the Heart of Jesus will not wish that on us. I would fear our ruin because of the lack of help and the mistrust of the secular priests. It would be difficult to get used to a new form of direction; after the little bit of reluctance caused by fear of breaking the Rule, we are seeing the steadiest zeal and attention to the advancement of souls that recall our good fathers in France.

The house is in the same condition that I told you about, with no hope of growth. It is an opportunity to work at one's own perfection. I do so very little myself, however, and I am rather an obstacle than a means of advancement for the others. I hope that you will provide for this deficiency and that, as this trial of my being superior has not succeeded, you will remedy the situation in your wisdom and charity. I am very happy to have any kind of work that you would give me as a subordinate.

Two years ago, you told us about sending a tabernacle, but we have not received it; maybe Mother Eugenie kept it. Mother Octavie is pretty well.

I am at your feet, Reverend Mother, with respect in the Heart of Jesus, your poor daughter.

Philippine

P.S. A respectful remembrance to our fathers, mothers and sisters.

Letter 237   L. 16 to Mrs. de Rollin

SS. C. J. et M.

[1824] [163]

My very dear Cousin,

Since the heart-breaking event you told me all about in your touching letter, you must have received at least one of my letters expressing the share I am taking in your understandable sorrow and my gratitude for the generous remembrance of your dear husband. Thoughts of him and of you have often a place in my heart, and I never pray for my dear Josephine without adding prayers for the happiness of him who made her so happy.

I see you now engaged in your good works; and as charity, whose flame is more ardent than that of ambition, never says "enough," I come

---

163 *Copies of letters of Philippine Duchesne to Mrs. de Rollin and a few others, No. 18; Cahier, Lettres à Mme de Rollin*, pp. 46-48. C-VII 2) c Duchesne to her family and lay people, Box 5.

to feed yours with a proposal that you will consider in your wisdom. The scarcity of money and our distance from the city have rendered our first undertakings among whites fruitless; besides they have many schools. We want to return to the objective that first drew our desires towards America: the civilization of the Indians.

A wealthy organization with a large membership sends Protestant ministers as far as the Orient and the farthest parts of the States; but as Catholics are the poorest and least numerous here, the result is that error has ample means and the true faith is without resources. The bishop, however, has obtained a grant for the support of four Catholics who will dedicate themselves to the civilization of the Indians. This promise made by the Secretary of War has not been carried out, and so far the government, which has lent some encouragement to establishments in favor of Indian men, has never done anything for those for women.

We would like to have little Indian girls, but it is really to tempt Providence to begin without a little fund to at least buy clothing for these children. See whether among your friends you can secure a small annual income to aid in this work; you would receive an exact account of its use, and perhaps very soon you would be able to have the joy of knowing that, in tending the needs of the body, you have been the means of bringing life to the souls of these poor children who are now plunged in the darkness of idolatry. Our present governor, although Protestant, is quite willing to prepare the way for a new State composed of several Indian nations for whom laws would be drawn up, and he wants to employ Catholic priests. Speak of this work to Mrs. Teisseire, to whom I send tender love, as well as to you.

I am all yours *in Corde Jesu*,

Philippine

Letter 238   L. to Mother Victoire Paranque

SS. C. J. et M.

Saint Ferdinand, May 2, 1824
Rec. to St. Ant. P.[164]

My very dear Mother,

---

164   Original autograph, C-VII 2) c Duchesne to RSCJ and Children, Box 4.

Despite all the changes that have happened to the house of Grenoble and the withdrawal of most of the mothers and sisters I knew, I am no less attached to that happy refuge reserved for the Sacred Heart, which contains his distinguished spouses and where I myself had the happiness to become one of them, after so many graces that I have received from the goodness of God.

One of them that I cannot forget is my unexpected return to that blessed house through the protection of Saint Francis Regis. Here, as in Grenoble, he is our faithful protector. I still believe that I owe him Mother Octavie's return to health, for which I promised him a Mass at his tomb and another for another intention.

Would you please, dear Mother, have the goodness to have these two Masses said at La Louvesc. Father Rivet or Father de la Grée, to whom I send my regards, will show you how. If not, then please ask my sister, Mother Xavier Duchesne,[165] Religious of the Visitation at Romans, asking her to pray for me.

I hope you will answer me, dear Mother. The surest and fastest way will be to address your letter, and affix the postage, to the Mother Superior of the Civil and Military Hospital at Havre de Grâce, Department of the Lower Seine, for Mother Duchesne, to Saint Ferdinand of the Missouri in America (in an envelope). I hope you will give me more details about Mother Aloysia, and whether they continue to call upon her with success,[166] and about my many sisters, the children, and the day students.

I remember my nieces and recommend to them the acquisition of wisdom and devotion to Mary to obtain it. I have received the little packet in which Amelie Jouve collected objects of her interest for the Indians. I answered her, as I did Amelie Lebrument. I do not know if they have received my letters. I also wrote to Ms. Anna de Chaléon.

Please send me if possible the *Conversations of Saint Francis de Sales*, the *Life of Sister Alacoque* by Bishop Languet,[167] the work of Father

---

165 Augustine Melanie (Xavier) Duchesne (1786-1828), younger sister of Philippine, a Visitandine at Romans.
166 Numerous miracles, conversions and healings were attributed to intercessions made to Euphrosine (Aloysia) Jouve, before her tomb. The tradition says that Mother Barat was so concerned about it that she told Euphrosine under obedience to stop the miracles.
167 Jean Joseph Languet de Gergy (1677-1753), anti-Jansenist theologian, was bishop of Soissons, elected a member of the *Académie française* in 1721, and named archbishop of Sens in 1730. The author of office books, catechisms and pastoral letters, he was violently attacked by the Jansenists opposed to devotion to the Sacred Heart because of his work, *Life of the Venerable Marguerite Marie Alacoque*.

Galliffet on the Sacred Heart,[168] and the works of Father Nepveu and Father Lallemand.[169]

All these, I think, are in double or triplicate in your library. A Roman missal would also be essential.

My greetings to the bishop, Father Bouchard, and Fathers Rivet and Dumolard.

All yours in the Sacred Hearts of Jesus and Mary.

Philippine

My sisters remember you and all your sisters, as I do; we are ten and have only 9 boarders and 30 free day students or something like that.

> [On the reverse:]
> To Mother
> Mother Superior
> of the house of the Sacred Heart
> Sainte-Marie d'En-Haut
> Grenoble
> France – Department of the Isère

Letter 239   **L. 60 to Mother Barat**

Rec. to St. Anthony of Padua
Saint Ferdinand, Missouri, June 10, 1824[170]
No. 51

Very Reverend Mother,

Since my last letter, no. 50, May 2, 1824, which enclosed a promissory note on Ghent from the father rector to buy sacred vessels in Paris, I have had the joy of receiving two letters from you in the same envelope with one from Mother de Gramont and one from Mother de Coriolis. We always await news impatiently, so these were received with eagerness. I beg to express my gratitude in particular to Mother de Gramont.

---

168   Joseph de Galliffet, SJ (1663-1749), was a zealous promoter of devotion to the Sacred Heart.
169   Louis Lallemand, SJ (1588-1635), was the author of the first important synthesis of Ignatian spirituality. François Nepveu, SJ, *Pensées ou Réflexions chrétiennes pour tous les jours de l'année*. Alex Leprieur, Paris, 1759.
170   Original autograph, C-VII 2) c Duchesne to Barat, Box 2. Postmark: St. Louis Mo. June 16. Copy, C-III 1: USA Foundation Upper Louisiana, Box 1, *Lettres de la Haute Louisiane II 1823-1830*, pp. 9-17. Cf. J. de Charry, II, 2, L. 187, pp. 254-261; Hogg, II, 2, L. 187, pp.170-177.

In our abject little establishment we experience from month to month shattering changes that always form the content of our correspondence, leaving expressions of respect, attachment and devotedness to the Heart of Jesus, our Divine Master.

I am unnecessarily preoccupied by as many worries for the fathers' establishment as for ours, even more so. I am wrong in so doing, for I have no more effect than the fly on the coach-wheel had to speed up the coach. They have trials, but they are never discouraged. The fine old spirit of zeal, courage, poverty, etc. lives again fully in them. The bishop, who is aware of the treasure he possesses in them, can do nothing more for them; he sees that the government has contributed nothing toward the work with the Indians, of which they will have five tomorrow, and is making different proposals. The first: land in Opelousas near Mother Eugenie, but what good is land in that country with no men and no money! It is the same as in this State where congressional lands, at seven *livres,* ten *sols* an *arpent,* find no buyers. I would like very much to have them in the neighborhood for the sake of my sisters; but as Mrs. Smith imposes several conditions on this new donation, it will be a long time before it can be accepted. The second thing the bishop is offering them is land in Saint Louis for a school, but they would have to build, and a loan could not be arranged. I hope that later this project will come about to facilitate extending their work and removing one of the chief obstacles to going into the city now, the change in direction.[171]

Alas! The poor father rector, the only priest of the Society in this State at the moment, has more to do than he can manage. His companion, Father Joseph Timmermans, from Antwerp, died suddenly a week ago, as a result of exhaustion suffered in missionary work at Eastertide; he had to travel through country either in flood or in drought, sleep in miserable huts made worse by standing water and filth, and only the bare floor for a bed. He is the first Jesuit to die in this State; the earlier ones confined their activity to the country of the Illinois. He is buried in our church near the altar. His brothers sang the Office solemnly.

The father rector, whose health is very weak, is left with four parishes and other, more distant missions separated by wide rivers, our house and his own, and the direction of the studies in the evening; his buildings will not be completed until September because of lack of money. His people are sick one after the other, brothers, Negroes, Indians. The first two Indians are dangerously ill with whooping cough, which has

---

171 The change of bishop. The bishop's college would be closed in July 1827, and that of the Jesuits officially opened in November 1829.

caused the death of more than a hundred children in Saint Louis, and causes severe suffering. I admit that when I see how calm he is amidst so many matters that demand his attention, I cannot help thinking that his soul is stabilized in those high regions of peace that are reached by complete renunciation and union with God. On Sundays he says two Masses, preaches three times in the morning, oversees the catechetical instruction and hears confessions between the services. To live in the neighborhood of saints has such an attraction that I prefer our poor country place to a brilliant establishment in a city.

When the government gives aid in civilizing the Indians, we must be in a position to follow the plan mandated by the Secretary of War regarding boys and girls. The fathers cannot take girls; we hope to take some, relying on Providence; food will cost little; we have room for lodging; we will beg clothes. The chief congressional agent in charge of dealing with the nations in this part of the country approves the plan and will see whether the Secretary in Washington, to whom he will appeal, will also give us a grant to increase the number of our pupils. It would be unprecedented for girls, and he has little hope; but we must neglect nothing for such an important work, the object of so many prayers, which brought us here and is in itself more significant and gives greater hope of success than any other. The father rector speaks with such satisfaction of the first little ones who are docile and innocent; one of them has already been baptized, as one day it was feared he was dying.

Last week a Catholic Iroquois[172] family came here; they had been in Missouri and were returning. They were carrying in sacks made of hide the bodies of two of their relatives who had died on the journey; they were buried here solemnly. I was godmother to an attractive little one named Marie and had as co-sponsor her Indian brother age twelve; he was comical in answering the priest, who delighted in the situation. He spoke French. The mother seemed to have some education.

It seems that our country is getting ready for the renewed apostolic work of many missionaries. The Sac nation has declared, "Until now we have not been willing to listen, but now we will and we wish to live like the Whites." I beg you to tell my nephew Henri [Jouve] that the harvest is ready, that it would be the time for him to come to reap where his holy patron, Saint Regis, so longed to clear the ground. We pray very much to him for the conversion of the Indians and add a

---

172 The Iroquois lived on the shores of the Saint Lawrence River and of Lakes Erie, Ontario and Huron.

forty days' prayer to obtain workers speedily; but they must be dead to everything, for there is nothing to satisfy nature. Faith alone and the love of Jesus crucified maintain one here.

The Visitation nuns in Georgetown, whose number had increased to fifty-six, are in great financial distress and may be obliged to separate. Formerly they had forty boarders; now they have none, and they have gone into much debt for their church. All the institutions in America are suffering these same sudden reversals. One must be prudent, therefore, and go step by step. I am expecting to see Mother Eugenie's house decline. How can it be avoided when the college of the fathers in Georgetown, with excellent professors, cannot support itself, with resulting debts that are giving them much anxiety.

Besides insecurity, these failures are caused partly because Catholics everywhere are the poorest. In Georgetown and Baltimore bankruptcy is almost general. Therefore, in these missions the treasure of poverty will never be lacking, while for societies established by Protestants in New York, Boston, etc., there is money in the amount of 1,250,000 F per year to send their missionaries even to the East, and they maintain schools for Indians in those areas where there are as many as eighty pupils. How sad it is not to be able to go ahead in doing good, when the work of the opposite camp is bursting with success! Without help from France, the missionaries will do little good here. If my flesh could become money, I would gladly give it to support the missions.

Bishop [Dubourg] now has Bishop Rosati as his coadjutor; he was consecrated on March 25. He paid us a short visit upon returning to this part of the diocese, which will fall to him in three years' time, according to the provisions of the papal documents. He showed much interest in us as well as in the Jesuits whom he urged to open a college in Saint Louis. He also urged us to go to Donaldsonville, a small town thirty or forty leagues above New Orleans. Bishop Dubourg, in a letter, strongly urged me to agree. As at that moment a friend was seeing about something more solid in New Orleans, I answered that you did not want any more foundations in small places. I could not be won over by the reasons he put forward in hope of success. These are passing flashes that soon come to nothing. It seems to me, therefore, that unless we are not wanted in New Orleans or nearby, it would be better, since we must be small, to work entirely for our Indians and settle where there will be apostolic men who will serve as models, keep a suitable distance and not make us waste time.

The father rector kept well away from us at the beginning; but happily, reading about the Missions of America introduced him to some reverend fathers, superior for both spiritual and temporal affairs of communities whose foundations they had prepared and cared for.

With what joy I saw those beautiful crosses you sent us. The two Hamilton sisters deserve to wear them, but their time is not yet up. I beg you only to allow that, if the older one changes house, her sacrifice may be rewarded by being admitted to profession, as you allowed for Mothers Octavie and Eugenie.[173] Sister Hamilton has completed a year and a half since first vows. I made a mistake in asking you for a change for Sister Marguerite; it would have been out of place; Mother Eugenie was against it and happily foresaw your wish.

I thank our good Father Barat for his four beautiful hymns for us. I have sent them to Opelousas, and we are enjoying them here. If only we could listen to that dear father here and enjoy his presence, as we did in Paris!

We have blessed God that Father Debrosse[174] escaped such a great danger, that Father Varin was founding a new house in Dole, and that the novitiate was flourishing. How good God is! Who would have said twenty-four years ago that we would see this dear resurrection[175] and that we would enjoy its precious fruits. The Heart of Jesus is very rich; how can one fear being poor with him?

If there were a third foundation, I still think that Mother Eugenie is the best person to direct it. In one of your letters you named Mother Lucile to replace her and I would stay here, nearer to the Indians, with Mother Octavie who could not govern a house on her own. Since the wound on her face healed, she has been having sore throats all the time and suffers from them often.

I beg you to offer my respects to good Father Perreau, to all our fathers and to our mothers.

I am at your feet, in union with the divine Hearts, your little and old daughter,

Philippine

P.S. We ask you to count us all among your most devoted daughters who, with their happy sisters, wish you a very happy feast.
We have nine boarders, two of whom do not pay; they would be lost if they left. I do not believe that we shall recover the 1700 F of fees in

---

173   Octavie Berthold had been admitted to profession on February 2, 1818, one year after her first vows, in view of her departure for America; the same was true for Eugenie Audé, after eight months, on February 8, in the morning, the day of the departure from Paris.
174   Robert Debrosse, SJ, was the uncle of Rosalie Debrosse, RSCJ.
175   The re-establishment of the Society of Jesus in the universal Church, not imagined in 1800.

arrears by parents deeply in debt. Mother Eugenie has sent me 1250 F this year in provisions or in money, which have served to pay our domestic servant, to buy Mass wine and many other indispensable things. We have six milk cows now; they are half our livelihood and cost very little.

> [On the reverse:]
> To Mother
> Mother Superior of the Civil and Military Hospital
> to hold for Mother Sophie Barat
> Hôtel Biron in Paris,
> *At Havre de Grace*
> France, Department of Lower Seine
> By way of New York

Letter 240   **L. 13 to Bishop Rosati**

SS. C. J. et M.

[June 24, 1824][176]

Dear Bishop,

Since the happy moment when we first saw you among us, with the new dignity that gives us to you in a special way, it seems our happiness has grown and that God has given us this latest proof of his providential care for us, and we thank him for it unceasingly.[177]

Doubtless you already know of the great and sudden loss the mission has suffered in the person of Father Timmermans, SJ, soon after his return from the coast. It looks as if the devil places the greatest obstacles in the way of the missionaries of Missouri: Father Delacroix returned ill the first time and dying the second; the good father whom we are mourning was exhausted the first time, and the second time he died.

Father Van Quickenborne is crushed by his poor health; and if he did not hope for two new priests, he would not be able to carry on. He

---

176 Original autograph, C-VII 2) c Writings Duchesne to Rosati, Box 6. Postmark: Jun. 29, St. Louis, Mo. Reverse: "June 24, 1824, Mother Duchesne, Florissant; received July 7; answered the 9."
177 Bishop Rosati was consecrated coadjutor in Donaldsonville, Louisiana, March 25, 1824. The preceding letters indicate that his nomination had been known for some time. After Bishop Dubourg's return to France, Bishop Rosati became bishop of Louisiana, March 20, 1827.

still serves the church and hears our confessions. At the Ember Days we went to confession to Father Timmermans. With your permission we could suspend this article of our Rule until the arrival of new priests who can direct us properly because they have the same rule. It would be hard to change for such a short time, and our distance is an added difficulty, coupled with the fact that the priests of St. Louis are not accustomed to serving religious communities.

Father Timmermans' death often deprives us of Mass and Communion because the father rector has to divide his time. We try to compensate for this by exposition of the Blessed Sacrament, which is frequent in our houses. There is the difficulty of replacing the Blessed Sacrament at night when it has been exposed in the morning. If in place of exposition, you would allow the tabernacle to remain open in our private chapel where we make our adoration and permit us to close it in the evening, we would have an equal benefit without giving the father the trouble of coming over, often impossible. Bishop Dubourg would not allow exposition in the church, doubtless because so few go there. But we beg you to let us have it there on the feasts we have in common with the Jesuits, because the proper solemnity can be had only in the church; our interior chapel is not suitable for exposition. Adorers will not be lacking on those days.

In anticipation of the happy time we look forward to in October, please accept the profound respect and veneration with which I am, Bishop, your Excellency's submissive and unworthy daughter,

Philippine Duchesne, sup.

June 24, 1824

[On the reverse:]
To His Excellency
Bishop Rosati
Barrens
Near Sainte Geneviève

Letter 241   **L. 61 to Mother Barat**

Saint Ferdinand, July 25, 1824[178]
Rec. to St. Anthony of Padua
No. 52

Very Reverend Mother,

We have just celebrated the feast of Saint Mary Magdalene, recalling such dear memories. We tried to rejoice in spirit with all our sisters who are gathered around you, trusting our love and good wishes to the Sacred Heart of Jesus. Mass, Holy Communion, and a little extra recreation were all circumstances permitted by way of celebration, but we do not want any community in the Society to outdo us in heartfelt affection and devotion to our loved mother.

I am afraid that news about different institutions in the States may make you uneasy about us, but I beg you not to worry; we wanted the cross, not honor, poverty and not ease, the will of God and not success. So even if God's work is hampered, we can always gather the precious advantage of being in a situation that can unite us closely to Jesus Christ, our divine Spouse. All the black veils have this disposition. Mothers Octavie and Lucile, Sisters Xavier, Regis, Catherine, and Sister Ignace, coadjutrix, who made her first vows on the feast of the Sacred Heart [June 25, 1824]. As for the novices, two are firm in their vocation; the third, a young Spaniard, wavers a good deal. If she leaves, it will be the third in a year; of all my trials, that is the most painful, for I am to blame for this lack of perseverance, which can be attributed to lack of care and good example on my part.

I am eagerly awaiting the happy moment that will set the seal of papal approbation on our Constitutions. I wanted to have Sister Xavier Hamilton translate them into English, but the thought that some changes or additions might have been made caused me to wait. We would like a copy of the vow formula for both first and final vows, and please tell me who should sign them besides the new Bride of Christ;[179] that is not indicated anywhere.

---

178 Original autograph, C-VII 2) c Duchesne to Barat, Box 2. Copies, A-II 2) g Box 2, *Lettres intéressantes de la Société depuis 1816 No. 1*, pp. 402-405; C-III 1: USA Foundation Upper Louisiana, Box 1, *Lettres de la Haute Louisiane II 1823-1830*, pp. 29-34. Cf. J. de Charry, II 2, L. 188, p. 265-270; Hogg, II 2, L. 188, pp. 177-184.

179 At this time vows were received by the bishop (or his delegate) who signed the vow document along with the new religious, the priest witnesses, the superior and her assistant.

I would like to know also the exact number of Masses we are to have offered each month; it seems to me that it is one a week for our deceased sisters, one for the Society and one for the dead; that makes six. It may happen at times that we cannot afford to have them said, as the stipend is fifty *sous*.

Father Borgna has not arrived. I hope you will entrust Miss Mathevon's money for the fathers to him; that is the best opportunity. But if you do not have enough, bankers in Paris would willingly issue a bill of exchange on New Orleans or Philadelphia or New York. It would be well placed; all our merchants do business there; there would be only the loss for the difference in exchange, either for transferring money or for the difference in currency: the *écu*, 6 F in ordinary use, gains 5 *sols* on our *gourde* or dollar, and the *napoléon* loses 5 *sols*. The two together are worth 2 *gourdes* or dollars. I believe there is less loss on a large sum.

There is so little silver of the country here that one sees only Spanish *piastres* or *écus* of France. Everything is accepted.

If you could send us a few books when there is an opportunity, here are the ones we do not have: Father de Galliffet [*The excellence of the devotion to the adorable Heart of Our Lord Jesus Christ*]; the *Large Life of Sister Alacoque; Christian Reflections [for every day of the year]* of Father P. Nepveu; Father Surin;[180] the [*Spiritual Maxims for the direction of souls*] of P. Guilloré; *Mental Prayer of* Father Grasset and his *Considerations on the Practice of Prayer and Meditation*; and *Mme Louise de France* [Carmelite at Saint-Denis].[181] Mother Xavier Murphy has asked in Ireland for [*the Treatise on Christian Perfection*] of Rodriguez in English. I don't know if it will come to us.

Since one of the Jesuit priests died we are often deprived of Mass, although father rector goes far beyond his strength in his efforts for us. If, with his weak health, he succumbs, then we will feel the weight of the cross; he no longer speaks of others coming to help him. It would be all the more desirable as the mission to the Indians begins to get underway. The governor in charge of commissions to several nations would like to unite them to have enough to form a new state and make use of the services of the Jesuits for this great undertaking. Although he is a Protestant, he maintains that only Catholics can civilize the

---

180 Jean Joseph Surin, SJ (1600-1665), *Spiritual Catechism of Christian Perfection*, Paris, 1659, 2 vol.; *Fundamentals of the Spiritual Life*, Paris, 1667; *Spiritual Dialogues in which perfection is explained for all kinds of persons*, Nantes, 1704-1709, 3 vol.
181 This list was one for the use of mistresses of novices in the Society of the Sacred Heart of Jesus.

Indians.[182] The fathers have five of them who give them a great deal of trouble.[183] They do not want to wear clothes; they want to sleep nude; they want to do nothing; they are very sensual. One day when they felt they had not been given enough meat, they went up to the scholastics, demonstrating that the skin on their stomachs was not stretched tight.

The Indian chief, father of two, fairly well clothed, passed through and said to us by means of an interpreter: "Mothers, I am leaving my children; pray for them every day to the God you worship and have pity on them."

I don't know when we shall be able to take the Indian girls; we all want to do so.[184] But this year has been disastrous; the Missouri rose considerably and swept away many homesteads and domestic animals and ruined the crops. There are hardly any wheat or vegetables. Soon we shall have only three or four pupils.

The main thing for the moment is to support our little community. The Visitation in Georgetown is obliged to divide the community on account of debts. Twenty are remaining; twelve or fourteen have asked shelter in Quebec and in New Orleans, and it is said that the Ursuline house in New Orleans that was doing so much good has gotten into financial difficulties because of a large building operation. These nuns had paid for the journey of several nuns from Canada whose return trip they have had to pay at great expense. I should be very sorry to begin a foundation in that city just now; it might look as if we were taking advantage of their misfortune.

I learned also that the father general does not want the school in Washington to continue; it takes only day pupils who pay nothing; therefore it would have to close unless the parents take measures to assure the livelihood of the teachers who have nothing; but here one can seldom count on promises. The Jesuits have not received for their Indians what the Secretary of War had promised. The father rector told me today that the work with the Indians is beginning to go well and that he is expecting others. He is inviting his brothers who are eager for their conversion to indicate their desires to the father general. Tell that to your dear brother, whom we want so much, and to my nephew who has the same vocation; he is of an age to learn English.

---

182   The term translated here as "civilize" is "*réduire*" "reduce;" it comes from the expression "the Reductions of Paraguay."
183   The Jesuits' boarding school for Indian boys opened May 11, 1824.
184   The boarding school for Indian girls would begin in Florissant, April 6, 1825, under the direction of Sister Mary Ann O'Connor.

The father rector thinks that the best way to send money is through the Bank of the United States, which is in debt to France, and he believes there would be little or no charge.

There is great fear here for the consequences of the flooding of the rivers in Lower Louisiana. If the harvest is lost, Mother Eugenie will soon be in the same state as ourselves. *Fiat.*

There are so many reverses of fortune here, such instability in enterprises, so little support, that one would almost need the visible finger of Providence to make any change of place. Here we no longer fear death from hunger; that's something. If God takes from us the means of making ourselves useful, we must accept his will. Sometimes I think that God is spoiling our first plans, our first work, in order to build up, little by little, the advantageous work of instructing the Indians. That must be merited by humiliation and other suffering. Don't worry about us; none of us is discouraged. I am the most dissatisfied because I have reason to think that I am turning aside blessings on our work.

It is up to you, Reverend Mother, to remedy that. I have no need to rouse my submissiveness in order to say I am your wholly devoted and obedient daughter *in Corde Jesu.*

Philippine Duchesne

I ask my kind mother to put this small sheet in an envelope for Mrs. de Rollin. Our sisters are all at your feet.

[On the reverse:][185]
To Mother
Mother Barat Superior General
of the houses of the Sacred Heart, rue de Varenne
Faubourg St Germain
Paris

Letter 242   **L. 14 to Bishop Rosati**

SS. C. J. et M.

[July 31, 1824][186]

---

185 Mother Barat added: For Fathers Varin and Barat, No. 4.
186 Original autograph, C-VII 2) c Writings Duchesne to Rosati, Box 6. On the reverse: "July 31, 1824, Mother Duchesne, Florissant."

Dear Bishop,

I received your letter in answer to mine. Father Van Quickenborne also received the one you wrote to him but twenty-four days later. Do not think, I beg you, that disappointments discourage us; we accept both success and failure as the will of God. We shall always be happy as long as we have your approval and protection. If God, seeing our desire to work for his glory, contents himself with our good will, we can do no more.

Father Nerinckx has never mentioned the property of the Hamilton sisters to me, and I did not think I should be the first to broach the subject, since I could give only the same answer we have already given.

In her last letter, Mother Eugenie did not seem to expect to see Father De Neckere in Opelousas, and I thought he was there. We are praying earnestly for the recovery of one who is so useful to the diocese, as well as that of Father Portini; but we pray constantly for the worthy pastor whom God in his mercy has given us.

I am with the most respectful veneration, Bishop, your Excellency's submissive and obedient daughter,

Philippine Duchesne

July 31, 1824

Letter 243   **L. 17 to Mrs. de Rollin**

SS. C. J. et M.

[1824][187]

My very dear Cousin,

How grateful I am for your kind remembrance and for the news you give me of your dear daughters [of the House of Providence] whom I cannot forget. Assure them all of my love and ask them to pray for their companions in Missouri that they may acquire a taste for school work, for they are better at dancing than at sewing and reading, and

---

187 *Copies of letters of Philippine Duchesne to Mrs. de Rollin and a few others, No. 20; Cahier, Lettres à Mme de Rollin*, pp.49-50. C-VII 2) c Duchesne to her family and lay people, Box 5.

we have great difficulty in checking their desire for pleasures that lead them into vanity and vice. However, several console us very much, and we show them good example by working on the land, even carrying manure, and in order to rid them of shame, doing in our poverty what the richest country inhabitants do in France.

Above all, pray for me, who am damaging the work, far from helping it.

All yours,

Philippine

Remember me to Mr. and Mrs. Teisseire.

To Mrs. Teisseire in Grenoble

Not knowing whether Mrs. de Rollin is in Grenoble, I take the liberty of addressing a letter for her to you.

Read it in her absence.

Letter 244   L. 15 to Bishop Rosati

SS. C. J. et M.

[August 20, 1824] [188]

Dear Bishop,

To the joy of seeing someone from your house who can give us news of you and the hope of a visit is joined the great sorrow that the mission has felt in the loss of Father Nerinckx.[189] I know of your grief especially and that above all increases ours. The Jesuit Fathers have offered to have a solemn service.

Although I hasten to pray for this venerable missionary whom I believe to be in heaven, I feel even more compelled to ask for the preservation of the ministers who remain and the success of their labors. Our wishes are directed principally to you, Bishop, as the one responsible for religion in this part of the world, whom God uses in a special way to guide and bless us.

---

188   Original autograph, C-VII 2) c Writings Duchesne to Rosati, Box 6. Reverse: "August 20, 1824, Mother Duchesne, Florissant; received the 25."
189   Father Nerinckx died at Sainte Genevieve on August 12, 1824.

We are impatient for your visit. There are some children to be confirmed, and we fear that they may leave us without this grace. The number of our children will soon be reduced to four or five. I am less concerned about this problem, which necessarily stops or delays other projects, than about obstacles to the founding of a school in St. Louis. The father general [of the Jesuits] does not wish to accept payment from day scholars, and it is impossible to find enough boarders to support the teachers. Father Niel, who does not know the customs of religious life, is proposing arrangements that the Jesuits cannot agree to. I make this observation because of my eagerness to see the youth of Saint Louis renewed, and by the desire I would have that settling this matter is sufficient reason to have you come to us.

Bishop Dubourg has not written to me since your return, but our superior general still wants us to have houses only in the larger cities. I am expecting that the house in Opelousas will undergo the same trial as this one, a common experience of religious houses. Mother Eugenie is very impatient for Father De Neckere's arrival.

I am with profound veneration, Bishop, your Excellency's devoted and unworthy daughter.

Philippine Duchesne, sup.

August 20, 1824

[On the reverse:]
To His Excellency
Bishop Rosati
Barrens

Letter 245   L. 62 to Mother Barat

SS. C. J. et M.

Saint Ferdinand, September 1, 1824[190]
Rec. To St Anthony
No. 53

Dear Reverend Mother,

---

190 Original autograph, C-VII 2) c Duchesne to Barat, Box 2. Postmark: St. Louis Mo. Sep. 8. Copy, C-III 1: USA Foundation Haute Louisiane, Box, *Lettres de la Haute Louisiane II 1823-1830*, pp. 226- 231. Cf. J. de Charry, II 2, L. 189, pp. 274-283; Hogg, pp. 184-189.

Ever since you made me hope for the approbation of our holy Rules, I have been waiting with lively impatience for the happy news to reach us. Following your recommendation, we are praying for its success without our sisters knowing why. It seems to me that there is nothing more I can hope for on this earth than that lone consolation. I am longing to leave it, not that I do not have plenty of fears for my last hour, but because I see that I am not suitable to advance the work of the Society in this country. This thought is confirmed in that the father rector has often told me to ask you for someone fit to govern. I have told him that I have begged you to do this, but that you have not promised us anyone, since you were too pressed for new foundations, but that, if my sisters made this request, you would take more notice since the necessity would be better proved. He did not appreciate this answer, so I am left with the discomfort of knowing that I am not fulfilling my duties, that souls suffer from it, and that nevertheless I do not see the end that will put me in my place. I beg you earnestly to weigh before God the needs of this part of your family, all the more dear because it is abject and suffering.

Yesterday I had a letter from Mother Eugenie, who is still hoping to have a house in New Orleans soon. She is well aware that she alone could govern it, and she thinks that Mother Anna [Xavier Murphy] with a good treasurer could suffice for the place where she is. I am expecting her house to decline like ours, and then it will be easier to manage. I fear that this would not go well with Mother Lucile [Mathevon] who, by her age and rank in religious life, would be senior to Mother Anna, but is quite inferior to her with regard to the conduct of the children, and she lacks firmness. She does not hold the day students well and does not understand a word of English, something really necessary for the leader because one is often obliged to make use of those of lesser rank for that language. If these two houses down river were settled, Mother Lucile could be at the head. I am well aware that I annoy her, but she must make these sacrifices and I will try to diminish them for her.

Please do not accede to a request of Mother Eugenie who would like me to move down river if there is a new foundation. I carry with me a strong apprehension that I ruin things wherever I am, because of a saying I once heard a long time ago: "You are destined to please me less by success than by failure." Whether that was illusion or the effect of a too-excited imagination, I have always held this conviction in my soul, and I fear to take on anything lest it fail. If I could only follow in obedience and do the works of others, I would not have the same anxieties.

The present state of our house could not be more suitable to confirm me in my opinion. Since the bishop has been obliged to retire, we are in total oblivion or, if one remembers us, it is with disdain and pity, the result of indifference. The children who leave all follow the easy path. Practically nothing is made of the day school with Mother Lucile, who was always willing to praise them and now finds them very difficult. The worries of the fathers are ours. They will succeed, I hope, but the setbacks, privations, and ingratitude they experience weigh heavily on my heart, which would be so happy if I could contribute generously to such an important work. I am even astonished to have been able, by some secret of Providence, to loan or give them something; for we have the responsibility of three orphans, all the expenses of the church, etc., and we only have seven boarders, of whom two pay nothing. They are going to diminish more, although the boarding fee is no more than 100 *gourdes*, almost half what it was at the beginning.

There is no money in the country. Anything that circulates is from France or Spain, and pleasure comes before anything else, so there is nothing left for a solid education. But there might be some local people who want to place their children with us, so we would always keep our big house for a boarding school, and we would create in the day school another boarding school more suitable to the poverty of the area; its fee in the value of 150 or 180 French F would be paid not in money, which you cannot find, but in maize, potatoes, lard, beef and butter. This will be the only food of the children who, in turn, will themselves cook, milk the cows, and do the washing and gardening. The rest of the time, they will spin and weave for the house and the Indians who, I hope, we will have soon, first in small number, and for whom we will beg. I have already asked Mrs. de Rollin in my last letter to form a little society of parents and friends who could contribute something each year for this good work, which will have more success than with the whites. Already the Indian boys that the fathers have behave better in church than the local children, and one of them has more good spirit than anyone.

So, Reverend Mother, that is the only way that we can be useful in this country, where we must take on the customs: 1) of boarders at 100 *gourdes* who will always be few; 2) poor boarders at 30 or 36 *gourdes*, which is about 150 or 180 French F, and by whom we will be poorly paid; 3) free day students; 4) free Indian girls who will even cost us something, for example, with visits of the parents (who will need to eat). If afterwards we make a foundation in Saint Louis or New Orleans, we will need paying day students, because even in these cities, there will be few boarders. I think you will not oppose it, since you permitted it at Chambéry. The fathers had thought to do it in Washington, given the situation of the country, and their students succeeded as well as the boarding students at Georgetown, but the father general does not want them to continue to receive money from day students, and directed that the college was to close by Saint Ignatius' feast if they could not continue it gratis. I do not know the end of the affair, which seemed to worry father rector. When one knows the country, one counts little on foundations, benefactions, and contributions for maintenance of the professors.

I have told you that the Religious of the Visitation of Georgetown were obliged to separate. Their confessor, Father [de] Clorivière, tells me that an unexpected source of help is allowing them to stay, but he doubts that it will continue. The religious of the rue des Postes should help them. This priest asked me if I have the *Life of Father de Clorivière*, his uncle[191] because he wants it.

We have just lost, after a short visit, one of the great missionaries of America, Father Nerinckx,[192] a Fleming, founder of many churches in Kentucky and of the Daughters of the Cross, for whom he established at least ten houses. They are going to expand in this diocese where he himself had just settled, from there to move on with them to the Indians. Death took him as he was returning from visiting the Jesuits here, six of whom came from Europe with him on his last voyage, because he had gone there several times to beg for his foundations. Yesterday the Jesuits had a solemn service and funeral for him. It seems that this holy man came here only to breathe to his last breath for indigent people. He said that instructing them was the only means of introducing religion into the country, since the rich are too indifferent to it.

What is happening with the boarding school will also happen with the novitiate. I do not expect any more rich and educated young ladies, and father rector advised me to propose to you to accept poor girls and have them do the heavy work as do the daughters of Father Nerinckx. By this means, we would be able to live on a little land, with the labor of one man to cut the large pieces of wood and the work with the hay. But the garden and the cultivation of maize, with the weeding and cutting; that of cotton, potatoes, and flax could be done by the sisters who in winter will spin and weave, and we will have food and clothing. We

---

191 Father de Clorivière, confessor of the Visitandines, was the nephew of Father Picot de Clorivière, SJ (1735-1820), responsible for the reestablishment of the Society of Jesus in France.
192 See note 189 above.

are already built for it, and I hope that some alms will provide upkeep for the house. There will be studies only for a small number.

I think we must always keep the two ranks, even though already there is little difference. We have only two [coadjutrix] sisters, Sister Catherine and another, and they are the two weakest ones. Mother Octavie is better at hard work than they are. At the moment, she is weeding the nursery bed and enjoys all these abject tasks. Why must there be something light in her exterior and in her conduct, something I cannot pin down, that makes a number of people say, especially the bishop, that she is not suitable to be in command? But I do not believe it to the point of seeing with indifference that he prefers another, and this frustrates me because I do not know how to die without bringing on quite a few miseries. I hope I am wrong and that I am the worst offender.

Another one of my troubles is to see that our interests are completely contrary to those of the fathers. The church being so far away makes their situation more difficult. On work days the father says Mass three times at home and three times here; but on Sundays when he must come early for confession, all [the scholastics] must come here, and the heat of summer, the rain, the rigors of winter, and the streams that overflow, make the travel difficult, dangerous and sometimes impossible. Our house next to the church is really what would be good for them, but we, so poor, would lose all the fruit of so many efforts for our establishment and would have to begin again elsewhere, and I am too lazy!

In Saint Louis, success is uncertain, accommodations expensive, and we would not have the resources of our field, garden, poultry yard, and cows. They cost practically nothing here to maintain. They go alone into the common grazing land and come back by themselves. Wood is less expensive than in Saint Louis. I do not see anyone who would compensate us for so many sacrifices, and again, where would we be for spiritual help in Saint Louis? Nothing is clear. But it is sweet to live in the hands of Providence, awaiting his help each day for things spiritual and temporal. Who knows whether a letter may arrive from the Jesuit superiors prohibiting contact with us? Several times I have had reason to fear it, but since there was no way to ward off the blow, I abandon myself.

Although there are several priests, they will not want to lodge near the house, and if they stay where they are, the difficulty of travel is major. We are between two streams that have swollen so this year that our garden and our poultry yard just formed a lake. The little bridges and our fence have been taken away several times. In order to go or return, the father had to make his horse swim, while he crossed on a moving tree trunk. One day, we saw the horse arrive alone without its saddle. We looked in terror for fear that the father had stayed in the water. Finally he appeared, soaked up to his ears. His horse had thrown him. His saddle was found by a young man, who offered it to him in an insolent tone: "What will you give me to give it back to you?" These are the manners of the parishioners, their contribution and gratitude.

Please, Reverend Mother, answer us about all these issues. The work on the land might be an infringement of cloister. What shall we do?

Father rector asks again that you not purchase anything on his bill of exchange that I just sent you, if his sister does not pay for it. This one is to facilitate the passage of a father for America; he knows that several times lack of money has prevented departures. Would you please keep this one until it is asked for on his behalf? If his sister, to whom the bill is addressed, has died, which he fears might be the case, then address it to Father Bruson[193] of the Society at Ghent, or to *Mr. Bernard Poulman, rue Haute, in Ghent*. It is even doubtful whether he will obtain anything. His brother is against him. Do not put Father Bruson's name on it. He fears that it will cause the letter to be opened [by the police].[194]

[On the reverse:]
To Mother
Mother Superior of the Civil and Military Hospital
To deliver to Mother Barat
Superior General of the Religious of the Sacred Heart
Havre de Grace in France
Department of Lower Seine.
[Address changed by the superior of the hospital:]
Rue de Varenne, n° 41
Paris

---

193 Charles Bruson, SJ (1764-1838), was superior of the colleges of the Fathers of the Faith at Amiens and Belley before joining the Society of Jesus in Belgium.
194 The government of the king of the Low Countries [Holland and Belgium] was then hostile to Catholics, especially to the Jesuits.

Letter 246   L. 16 to Bishop Rosati

SS. C. J. et M.

[October 23, 1824][195]

Dear Bishop,

Father Dahmen just gave me the books you were so kind as to send. I am very grateful that in the midst of your many duties you thought of this little part of your family. We are now more persistent than ever in asking God to grant success to your labors. After the retreat the reverend father superior gave, I wanted our two novices to make their first vows of five years, even though they have not had the habit for two whole years. As this grace has often been given to those who merited it, I felt the desirability of restraining by these bonds the levity so common in this country. But the reverend father insisted on the exact observance of our rules, and I had failed to obtain the necessary permissions from you during your short visit.

We will never forget your wonderful visit, the graces it brought us and the proof of your interest, which is our happiness.

I am with profound veneration, Bishop, your Excellency's submissive and devoted daughter.

Philippine Duchesne, sup.

Saint Ferdinand, October 23, 1824

Letter 247   L. 63 to Mother Barat

SS. C. J. et M.

Saint Ferdinand, State of Missouri, November 22, 1824[196]
Rec to St Anthony of Padua
No. 54

---

[195] Original autograph, C-VII 2) c Writings Duchesne to Rosati, Box 6. On the reverse: "Oct. 23, 1824, Mother Duchesne, Florissant."

[196] Original autograph, C-VII 2) c Duchesne to Barat, Box 2. Copies, A-II 2) g Box 2, *Lettres intéressantes de la Société depuis 1816 N° 1*, pp. 408-410 ; C-III 1: USA Foundation Haute Louisiane, Box 1, *Lettres de la Haute Louisiane II 1823-1830*, pp. 226- 231. Cf. J. de Charry, II, 2, L. 191, pp. 292-296; Hogg, pp. 196-200.

Very Reverend Mother,

I have just received a short letter from you that presupposes one written before, to which it is a sequel. I am told there is a small packet waiting for me in Saint Louis. I hope it will contain that blessed letter, but I cannot wait for it before writing to you. The steamboats are not stopping much in Saint Louis, and ice will make communication rare.

My letter will not reach you before New Year's Day, but my wishes and those of my sisters will be ever welcomed by the most indulgent of mothers who, besides, knows this little portion of her family well, and that if it does not have other good qualities, it watches jealously so that no one will surpass it in appreciating its mother, desiring to please her by its fidelity and increasing her happiness by the continual prayers it addresses to God for her.

Your letter expresses the tenderness of your heart about the sad state in which Mother Octavie was last year at this time, but since we had the idea to ask you to write to the prince [de Hohenlohe], her healing began and it will soon be complete. I cannot call it a miracle, because treatment did not stop; but if it was one, I am tempted to attribute it to father rector, who asked to see this troublesome evil, and soon after, it was healed. If God makes use of remedies, it is the mercury that did the healing. It was used internally and externally for a long time. All that is left is a scar on the side of her mouth, which gives father the opportunity for her to make acts of humility. He makes her show it, then says: "Oh, how ugly!" He has worked on this soul with success. He leads her by renouncement, detachment, and humility.

We are all happy under such direction. For a long time, I feared that our good fortune would not last, partly because of the effect of poverty, and partly because of the rules of the Society of Jesus; but he has told me since that the father general let it go. He does not hold himself at a distance so much and even said to me that he might later build us a little house at Saint Charles, with a road between the two houses. When there are two priests, I think that one will reside there, with none still to the north of the Missouri, and crossing the rivers has been so dangerous this year that father rector sees the need. He has been very happy with our coadjutor Bishop Rosati, a Lazarist, who will soon be titular bishop. There has been reciprocal confidence and esteem. The good bishop spoke effusively of his love for the Society. He solemnly baptized a little Indian, to whom Mr. Mullanphy and one of his daughters were godfather and godmother. He gave minor orders to several of the young scholastics and finally Confirmation.

Since the departure of Bishop Rosati for the Barrens, where he resides in the seminary, father rector gave a retreat to his sons and then to his *daughters*; that is what he calls our sisters sometimes. Last year, they were only *Ladies*. This change of expression pleased our sisters very much, and they had a perfect retreat. He spoke to them six times a day, four meditations, a consideration and an instruction. The points for meditation were given in the evening and repeated in the morning. The good father was not stingy with his time in speaking with each one, even though he himself was in retreat with his companion. I remained out for the students and Sister Catherine for the orphans. She is the one who has had to walk straight for a while; she could communicate only on Sundays. Happily that did not endure, and it made me feel very sorry for her, because when one does not have external consolations, those of religion are really necessary. We do not have more than five boarding students, one of whom owes for the year, and there is no hope of getting it. One of them is the younger Miss Mullanphy, who has been admitted to First Communion. Father rector asked for it.

Bishop Dubourg does not write to us. You undoubtedly know that he does not want one of our foundations in New Orleans. He gives Mother Eugenie as the reasons the illnesses and the harm we would do to the Ursulines, who are in their new house. The old convent, given by them to the bishop, provides him with his own church,[197] his lodging, and his college confided to a secular priest. So far there are almost only day students.

Mother Eugenie, seeing our distress, is strongly in favor of an establishment on the river [at Saint Michael]. I have asked her to come here, since I cannot leave; it would be good to see each other, and she can take from here those who could help her. She says that there must be two houses in Lower Louisiana to sustain us if we have Indian girls and that she can bring one of your letters that allows it if we find favorable conditions...

I cannot answer your letters, dear Mother, since I haven't seen them, but waiting would delay my writing to you. I remind you not to forget to send the 600 F that Miss Mathevon has for the fathers. They await it impatiently.

If you have not yet gone the way of letters of exchange, Father Borgna will be a better commissioner, but you have to tell him to send it himself to the fathers or to us for them. How much more they need!

---

197 Bishop Dubourg lived in New Orleans from the beginning of the year 1824. He came to take possession of the house left by the Ursulines, since Father Antonio de Sedella was still occupying the cathedral.

The father told me they did not have enough to buy a single pig, and that serves half of life here. He has no altar. I received a few days ago an ugly piece of coarse material with a note pinned to it that read: "Please mend this; it is the frontispiece of our altar, *miserere nostri.*" It was soon replaced with something from dear France. Everything that you send is useful and precious to us.

The interest Father Barat takes in us is very dear to us. I have often wanted to write, but I am afraid of bothering him. The father here has his spirit and method. It is to make the most perfect picture after our heart's desire. I cannot conceive why Mother Eugenie advised us to leave this house. Although poor, I find it happier than hers. *The willing spirit* can keep it that way for a long time in the shadow of this good direction. I am at your feet, worthy Mother, your unworthy daughter.

Philippine

[On the reverse:]
To Mother
Mother Superior of the Civil and Military Hospital
To deliver to Mother Barat
Superior of the Religious of the Sacred Heart
Havre de Grace
Department of Lower Seine
France

Letter 248   **L. 17 to Bishop Rosati**

SS. C. J. et M.

[December 12, 1824][198]

Dear Bishop,

There is an opportunity for the Barrens; I hasten to take advantage of it as I believe it to be a surer means of reaching you than the post. Since Father Dahmen's visit, we have had only indirect news, and at most only a few words of the seminary, a place we like to think about. We see there the one whom God in his goodness has given us as a pastor and

---

198 Original autograph, C-VII 2) c Writings Duchesne to Rosati, Box 6. On the reverse: "Dec. 12, 1824, Mother Duchesne, Florissant."

for whom we thank God. We constantly recall the happy days of your visit. I love to see the same sentiment among our missionaries and hear them repeat, "We are blessed to have such a bishop." I am especially glad that I consulted you about my difficulty with our director. It has completely disappeared, a grace I attribute to your ministry.

We ask God daily to lighten your burdens with every consolation and success that may advance his glory. May he surround you with fervent and zealous ministers and dispose souls to profit by their help.

The Jesuits have received nothing from the government, and for my part I do not think they will. I regret this all the more since we cannot help them as we would like, but disappointments do not lessen our desire to work in the vineyard of the Lord. They are very satisfied with their little Indians.

Mrs. Fournier, Bishop Dubourg's sister, who wrote to tell me how happy she was on your nomination, asked me to send you her profound regards.

My sisters want me to ask your blessing and to unite with their unworthy mother in expressing sincere wishes for the prosperity of their bishop, his seminary and all his interests.

I am with profound veneration, Bishop, your Excellency's submissive daughter and humble servant.

Philippine Duchesne, sup.

December 12, 1824

[On the reverse:]
To His Excellency
Bishop Rosati
At the Barrens

Letter 249   L. 64 to Mother Barat

SS. C. J. et M.

Saint Ferdinand, January 6, 1825[199]
Rec. to St Anthony of Padua
No. 55

199 Original autograph, C-VII 2) c Duchesne to Barat, Box 2. Postmarks: St. Louis Mo., Jan. 12; Colonies by way of Le Havre; Paris, March 22, 1825. Cf. J. de Charry, II 2, L. 192, pp. 325-332; Hogg, pp. 216-222.

Dear Reverend Mother,

No doubt Mother Eugenie has told you that she has given her consent for a new foundation, thinking herself sufficiently authorized by one of your letters and by one of mine, in which I noted that she was in a better situation than I to understand and seize the opportunity. The bishop had written to her, saying that a foundation in New Orleans was not possible because of the illnesses that had reduced the Ursulines' boarding school to nothing; at the same time we would harm them by coming there. There was no longer any way to act against such an authority and such reasons. So, since answers here always take three months for the going and return of letters, she has given her word in writing to the pastor of Saint Michael, a parish twenty-five leagues from New Orleans, a wealthy parish on the river, that we will make an establishment there. She informs me that in eight days, she has been given 2,000 *piastres* in contributions. The rest of the price of the house will be provided by subscriptions from the parents who have children, who will be reimbursed little by little by reduction of their boarding fees. If this does not succeed, at least there will be no debts, which are terrible here.

I have asked Mother Eugenie to come to see us in order to take the two religious that we can give her. I do not want to go south, since my last voyage had so many difficulties. She is very happy to come, which makes me think that I have made a foolish mistake, because she already had the presumption to ask us, or at least me, to move down the river.[200] Apart from the fact that I am extremely against it, I see the very great advantage of staying in this region where we have in truth few boarders, but more vocations for us, and they are less indolent than in Louisiana where, with all her ability, Mother Eugenie has trained *only one* while we have had *six (crossed out, illegible)*.[201] Mother Lucile tried me out on who would go to Saint Michael; she had been told to get ready to go south, and I see very well that she was ready. I answered briefly that you had designated Mother Eugenie for New Orleans and that Saint Michael replaced it. And if you ask my opinion, only Mother Eugenie could be there. It needs her firmness, her tact, and her irreproachable conduct with the great prudence and stability that make her suitable to

---

200 Mother Barat had suggested to E. Audé to transfer the community of Florissant to Louisiana, including Philippine, leaving a small school with three or four religious, of whom Lucile Mathevon would be superior, but she nevertheless left the decision to Philippine.
201 Phrase struck out to make it illegible.

hold a position that is difficult because of climate, inhabitants, and the many relationships with clergy and people.

I was thinking of giving her the elder of our two Americans, Xavier Hamilton, who can teach in the two languages, is strong, sings well, has a pleasing appearance, is very stable, and full of esteem for Mother Eugenie, whose praises are always on her lips. She likes her more than Mother Octavie or even me, but without saying so. She said one day: "I would like to go down to Louisiana even if only to imitate my holy patron by passing by my family without stopping." I told her that it was possible that Mother Eugenie would ask for her. She did not say that that would make her happy, but I see it. She deserves to make her final vows for her attachment to the Society. It is almost two years since she made first vows, and she is twenty-two years old. Her companion would be a Creole [Judith Labruyère] who knows only French, but is capable in many ways and also of considerable progress in studies. The eighteen months after which you promised us some religious are about to expire. I hope you will give two to Mother Eugenie. She believes that Mother Anna [Xavier Murphy] is in a good position to take her place at Grand Coteau. She is well trained and attached to her, more than she was at the time of my trip there. If you also permit Sister Carmelite [Landry] to make her final vows, since she is sure in every way and is very able to cope with all the temporal matters and works, she would be assistant and would help with regularity in every way.

I see a disadvantage in sending Mother Lucile to the South: I do not think that she could sustain that trial, especially since the arrival of the fathers here; and, in spite of our poverty, she is very happy. After Mother Eugenie, she would be judged poorly by the parents who appreciate Mother Anna, and so do the children. Probably in a few years the fathers will be there as they are here. The superior [Father Van Quickenborne] asked me different questions that show that he is thinking in that direction when they have the personnel. He goes from time to time to Saint Charles, which is without another priest. He has been offered the purchase of the house where we were[202] as witness of the desire to have a permanent priest and one of our schools. In time that will be the right place for Mother Lucile, whom the father appreciates greatly.[203] She is the only one he would like to see as superior, even in Saint Louis, so greatly does he fear for others the unhealthy atmosphere

---

202 The Duquette house at Saint Charles, where the community lived from September 1818 to September 1819. In 1826, the Jesuits bought the property. Father Verhaegen was then charged with the foundation. The Religious of the Sacred Heart returned there in October 1828.
203 Lucile Mathevon would go to Saint Charles in 1828 with Mary Ann O'Connor.

there. I searched today among all your letters for those in which you tell me that she is destined to replace me. I cannot find any. I fear that I burned them because of certain expressions I did not want to be read after my death. It is true that I transcribed them in a collection, but then I also delete certain things that would prevent several people from having the consolation of reading and profiting from them. However, I may die and it is essential that we know whom you appoint for the leadership of this little house. The reverend father could be the one to keep the letter, or Mother Lucile, (Mother Eugenie).

You will be annoyed, dear Mother, that a third foundation is again being made outside the big towns, but you see the difficulties. The grandfather [Bishop Dubourg] does not want us in New Orleans. In Saint Louis, not a soul would help us. When a collection was being made for the fathers in Saint Louis, among other disobliging responses, one said: "The spirit of the city is against them; they will not find *a handkerchief.*" That is not quite true. To my knowledge, they have acquired 160 F, but that is nothing toward their needs. Without us, they would have lacked the really necessary things. I was astonished when, even in our lack, we have been able to help them. I have thought that I should not calculate, for fear of offending Divine Providence on which I still count for the coming year, since we have only five boarding students, one of whom has not paid for two years. Another is leaving on the 11th. The others are not sure. No one gives to the church; we cover all the expenses. Mother Eugenie furnishes the wine and candles made of whale fat, which are very beautiful. She is happy to have the means to sustain us. I have had a lot from her in money or supplies, more than 1500 F this year.

Believe me, dear Mother, that in this country where everything is changing, a city is soon a town and a country place a city. The reverend father told me that a city like Baltimore is nothing but a bad town. People and places change constantly. Our governor of last year has been replaced;[204] he lost everything to pay off his debts and is going to live among the Indians. The general[205] is in about the same state, etc., etc.

We have set the boarding fee at 100 *piastres* and announced the opening of a second boarding school in the school house at 36 *piastres*

---

204 The Lieutenant-governor William Henry Ashley (1778-1838), first governor of the State of Missouri from 1820 to 1824, was defeated in August 1824 by Frederick Bates (1777-1825), who died in office the following year.
205 Probably William Clark (1770-1838), who, after the famous exploration of the Midwest, received the rank of brigadier general and was governor of the Missouri Territory (1813-1819), then superintendent of Indian Affairs until his death.

per year. I think that even at this price we will have a hard time attracting students; there are only three out of twelve who have promised at that price, and the others give only food. But good is done in all this poverty. Sister Catherine is steady and delighted. Nothing costs her to stay here; she is much better about everything.

I beg you to let us know quickly whether you consent to the vows of the two sisters that I have proposed to you[206] and to dissuade Mother Eugenie from trying to get me to move south. I love our simplicity. I would like to die under our good direction. I do not please the bishop, and I fear to be in the way of the good wherever I would go. Besides, I have already said that Mother Eugenie is made to lead and to do it alone. Mother Bardot could perhaps be helpful to her, especially for house management and writing.

A priest from Saint Louis wanted to have us go there, but his terms could not offer any stability: no house, no protection, and doubtful spiritual resources. There was no hesitation about refusing. And he himself assisted at the solemn distribution of prizes at a Protestant school where all the younger sisters of the students we have had attended, and where the mothers say that a Protestant girl is *better off* with us. There, religion is on the side, and they do not know what to say when the priest's school has been given by him to a Protestant.

I have not been able to put the 600 F from Mrs. de la Grandville into land. It is impossible. Mr. Mullanphy surrounds us on three sides, and the fourth belongs to a legal minor. Land far from us with no protection would give us nothing, ten bushels or less per *arpent*, with a value of two and one half *piastres*. Please authorize me to wait still longer. The superior of the Jesuits, who sent you two bills of exchange on his sister in Ghent, asks you not to buy any sacred vessels. If you keep the money, could you not send those 600 F to Father Borgna for him, or send them through the Consul of France. He has great need of them. As for the 1700 F coming from Mrs. de Rollin and my brother, they are for you. We will need them, but it is better to pay what you advanced to us.

My humble greetings to Father Perreau, Father Barat, and the other fathers and mothers who surround you and who remember us.

Stir up the fathers, dear Mother, to help their brothers. What are they doing with their 600 students! While with 5 or 6, we find ways to help them sometimes.

---

206 Mathilde and Eulalie Hamilton had made their first vows March 19, 1823.

We do not have the formula of the document to be written when vows are made.

Do not worry about us in the least, dear Mother. We all love poverty and our situation. We are happy and we are doing well. It is true that I wrote in a lamentable tone to your dear brother, but it is because there are hard moments, especially when trials test our young people. If they are kept busy, they will be better.

I am at your feet your completely submissive and unworthy daughter.

Philippine

[On the reverse:]
To Mother
Mother Barat Superior General
of the houses of the Sacred Heart, rue de Varenne
Paris
By way of New York

Letter 250   **L. 65 to Mother Barat**

SS. C. J. et M.

February 28, 1825[207]
Rec. to St Anthony of Padua
No. 56

Dear Reverend Mother,

I have learned that Father *(name crossed out)* was returning or going to France. No doubt you will see him and *(line crossed out)* I wanted to write to you to assure you, but then I realized that this would be a thoughtless waste of time, since your prudence will know how to sort out what could come from the discontent of several persons who are discouraged, and what is the reality. It is a mistake to come to this country looking for good fortune, honor, and pleasure; but when one only wants the good pleasure of God, one lives in peace, even with lack of success, since God has not said that he requires that we be happy. All

---

[207] Original autograph, C-VII 2) c Duchesne to Barat, Box 2. Postmarks: Colonies by way of Le Havre; May 27, 1825. Copies, A-II 2) g Box 2, *Lettres intéressantes de la Société depuis 1816 N° 1*, pp 423-425; C-III 1: USA Foundation Haute Louisiane, Box 1, *Lettres de la Haute Louisiane II 1823-1830*, pp. 41-45. Cf. J. de Charry, II, 2, L. 194, pp. 338-342; De Charry-Hogg, pp. 224-227.

your daughters whom God has chosen for this house are happy with their lot and do not want to go elsewhere, even if it would place them at your feet, which would be the greatest temptation for them. The character of your family born in this hemisphere is more changeable; that is why it will always be good to have some Europeans, formed at the center of the family, who will lead according to its spirit.

I have much with which to reproach myself on this subject. You knew that even in France I was not considered to have good spirit, but every day I implore the Divine Spirit, Saint Regis, and especially the *Madonna del buon Consiglio* [Our Lady of Good Counsel]. I have often been preoccupied with death lately, but my soul is still strongly attached to my body. I would like someone else to repair my faults, and when I consider between Mothers Lucile and Octavie who will do better, I lean to one side and then to the other and end by seeing nothing clearly. But why should I want to see when it is for you to decide?

In my last letter, I spoke to you about the foundation of Saint Michael, for which there are already 75,000 F in contributions. Mother Eugenie, who has accepted it, will have given you all the details and says, as do I, that since we cannot go to New Orleans against the bishop's wishes, this house will do much good in Louisiana and will sustain the one in Missouri, which has three boarders. I expect Mother Eugenie this very month. She will come to take one of our community. She can hardly take anyone from Opelousas, where her absence will already leave an enormous gap. I still think that Mother Xavier Murphy, who is well formed and has confidence, is the best one to replace her.

The father superior of the Jesuits, with only the foundation of confidence in God, has bought the old house that we had in Saint Charles. He wants to be nearer to the church and has promised the inhabitants that we could have a school. I am very much inclined toward it, since there is so little to do here. Saint Charles has more people, and the canal ordered by the government and already finished from New York to the Lakes is supposed to open communication between the two oceans by way of the Missouri, which will make its banks more populated. It is the part assigned by the bishop to the Jesuits, who do not yet have anyone there because there are no priests. But when there will be one in Saint Charles, it seems to me that we cannot refuse to work in a place so destitute of help. Saint Louis is content with its Protestant schools; few want us there, and there is no man to drive. A boarding school for poor children, the only one that could be established in Saint Charles, would be well led by Mother Lucile, whom God blesses and who, I think, would not have the strength to go south and leave her fathers. Father superior appreciates her very much for virtue, peace, etc.

After having spoken of our abandonment to Providence, I cannot help admitting how impatient we are to see Father Borgna, who, I hope, will console us with recent news of you and some help for the fathers. We are waiting impatiently for what you, Reverend Mother, and Miss Mathevon have promised for them. They are in the greatest need. I am barely impressed by the contribution for Saint Michael when I see at the same time that such an interesting establishment is completely forgotten.

Our health is good, but we are pining for news from France.

On February 2, Miss Timon,[208] who has taken the name Aloysia, took the habit as a coadjutrix sister, even though her brother at the seminary of the Lazarists, full of virtue and talent, should soon be one of the most distinguished priests of the diocese.[209]

We have no postulants. Mr. Mullanphy has given his consent in advance to his fifth daughter who is here, but she has no vocation yet.[210] There will be few in this region. The primary education inhibits it.

I have written to my kind father, your brother, and I am hoping for a reply and that he prays for me.

My regards to dear Fathers Varin, Perreau, and Roger, and to my dear mothers who are near you.

I am in the name of all of us, in the beloved Heart of Jesus, your unworthy daughter.

Philippine

[On the reverse:]
To Mother
Mother Barat Superior General
of the houses of the Sacred Heart, rue de Varenne
Paris
France

---

208   Miss Timon did not stay in the Society.
209   John Timon, CM (1797-1867), born in Conewago Settlement, Pennsylvania, entered the Lazarist seminary at the Barrens in 1822, and was ordained in 1826 by Bishop Rosati. He was visitator of the American province from 1835 to 1847, then bishop of Buffalo, New York, where he died in 1867. Cf. Letters 518 and 523 to Father Tanon (Timon).
210   Mary Mullanphy would marry M. Harney.

Letter 251   **L. 18 to Bishop Rosati**

SS. C. J. et M.[211]

[February 28, 1825]

Dear Bishop,

I could not wish for more news of the Barrens, where our good wishes ceaselessly go, as to that place from where God sends us his most abundant blessings, pouring them out on us, his flock, through the worthy pastor who represents him and is so dear to us. Father Cellini surely was in St. Louis, but I knew of it only after his departure and learned that he left by the first steamboat.

We are expecting Mother Eugenie, superior of Opelousas, here this month, as she gave her consent in the name of our superior general to the foundation of Saint Michael in Father Delacroix's parish, a foundation Bishop Dubourg highly approved of. She is coming here for personnel before beginning the foundation. I beg you, Bishop, to give me the permission for these departures, in case Father Van Quickenborne still disapproves of them. I can have no stronger answer than your consent so that he will not repeat contrary opinions that it would be hard for me to resist, but I do not believe that I can refuse the persons Mother Eugenie so needs. Given the state of things here, I can do without them.

As we have only a few boarders, it is in our interest to do good elsewhere, if we can, and to support this house with help from another. At the same time, we shall be acting in accordance with the wishes of Bishop Dubourg and nearly all his clergy. St. Louis is still too ill-disposed to dream of going there for a while. If we return to St. Charles, as we have long been asked to do when they have another Jesuit priest, that will always be only a small school where we will need only a few people. We have never been able to get more than twenty or twenty-four free day scholars there because of the Protestant schools.

Would you be so kind, I beg you, Bishop, as to answer this letter, as I do not think Mother Eugenie can stay long. As to those who will be chosen, the selection can be made only when we are together.

A letter from Bishop Dubourg tells me that the Ursulines still owe $60,000 and that his income from the school has been used for several

---

211 Original autograph, C-VII 2) c Writings Duchesne to Rosati, Box 6. On the reverse: "February 28, 1825, Mother Duchesne, Florissant; received the 3rd; answered the 4th; departure approved."

years for repairs to the old convent. He seems to suffer with those who suffer. I believe that the only hope of the Jesuits is in the cross, carrying it with Jesus Christ. They are still opposed in their project of taking in the Indians, as help is not forthcoming.

All my sisters ask your blessing. At your feet, I am, Bishop, your Excellency's submissive and devoted daughter.

Philippine Duchesne, sup.

February 28, 1825
[On the reverse:]
To His Excellency
Bishop Rosati
Bishop of Tanagra
Barrens

Letter 252   **L. 66 to Mother Barat**

SS. C. J. et M.

[Saint Ferdinand], March 8, 1825[212]
No. 57

Dear Reverend Mother,

I have just received a letter from Bishop Dubourg [dated January 26] who tells me of the arrival of Father Borgna and Father Dusaussoy, and he adds that they have many letters from you, which they will send me when they come to the seminary, where Father Dusaussoy will join the Congregation of the Lazarists. I would have liked him to be in the Society that is nearer;[213] another priest is needed there.

The bishop adds that you have said to Father Borgna that I should go to Saint Michael and that he has therefore informed Mother Eugenie. I would have much preferred that he not be in such a hurry, thinking that I would wait for a direct and clear letter from you before making such an extraordinary change and one that I was not expecting. For

---

212 Copies, A-II 2) g Box 2, *Lettres intéressantes de la Société depuis 1816 N° 1*, pp. 413-415 ; C-III 1: USA Foundation Haute Louisiane, Box 1, *Lettres de la Haute Louisiane II 1823-1830*, pp. 45-48. Cf. J. de Charry, II, 2, L. 195, pp. 343-345; Hogg, pp.227-229.

213 The Society of Jesus (Jesuits) where he had already spent several years. He would later also leave the Lazarists.

a long time ago, you appointed Mother Eugenie for the foundation in New Orleans, which cannot be made since the bishop does not want it, and so Saint Michael replaces it. Mother Eugenie is favorably known in that part of the diocese. She will make the reputation of the house and is in a good situation to keep it going by her zeal, her prudence, and her talents with the children. I have given you all my thinking about this previously, especially in my last letter of February 28. Here, much more than in France, the elderly and the ugly are not given much standing. I am becoming more unsightly every day. Gray hair, no teeth, and horrible hands render me in no way suitable to function in such a fastidious country. I am all right in the town where, through friendship, they call me *poor devil*. With regard to spiritual aspects, there would be even more opposition. I always think that Mother Eugenie alone is right for Saint Michael and Mother Xavier Murphy the only one for Opelousas, where she is known and loved.

As for here, of the three, I profess that I should be the last. Nevertheless, father rector, with whom I have spoken about this, tells me that if this change were made, this house would be destroyed. It is true that it is poor and abject, but that is why it is dear to me, and it will never be in a position to be better sustained with regard to spiritual things. Father rector is now taking a true interest and, with time, we will set up the much-desired work with Indian girls.

It was even said to me that if Mother Octavie or another one whom he named were put in charge, neither he nor any of his men would have anything to do with the house. I am only telling you here what seems necessary; when one is vegetating in this country, one must be content. Other than food, we want for nothing; for clothing, we can get help from the South. If, according to our Rule, the poor should be preferred to the rich, we have nothing to envy Opelousas. We look after as many souls as they, and we will always have more novices. You see that Mother Eugenie has trained only one novice, and here ten have persevered; and this will increase with the coming of a neighboring establishment [of Jesuits] when the new direction will do away with old ideas. I wanted to write to you only when we had received your letters that are in New Orleans, but fearing that the bishop will press me for a decision, I ask you for it, keeping in mind my age awaiting death, my defects and incapacities.

I am at your feet, with profound veneration, Reverend Mother, your devoted daughter *in Corde Jesu*.

Philippine

Our health is fairly good. The fathers have finally received 50 *gourdes* from the government for the Indians.

Letter 253   **L. 67 to Mother Barat**

SS. C. J. et M.

Saint Ferdinand, April 23, 1825[214]
Rec. to St Anthony of Padua
No. 59

Dear Reverend Mother,

We wrote to you on April 5 when Father Niel, a priest of Saint Louis, departed. Since he delayed somewhat and visited the cities of the East instead of going through New Orleans, in hopes of obtaining some help to pay the church's debts, I think that this letter will arrive in France first. He is sure to beg for help in Paris; but if he does so in your house, he cannot be offended if you designate your contribution for the work with the Indians, boys as well as girls, and he will not be able to be annoyed about it, because when leaving, he showed our fathers a desire to obtain something for them, and it would be good, if you know what gifts were intended for us, that we get a list directly, so that we can claim whatever might be forgotten.

Although Mother Eugenie saw Father Borgna in New Orleans when coming here,[215] she was not able to collect everything that he had for us, since the notes were scattered on a great number of different papers, difficult to sort out, and the objects were so dispersed that several were still on the ship. So far I have only received the beautiful banner of the Blessed Virgin, the *Life of Aloysia*, the shortened versions of instructions, and some accounts, rosaries and pictures. The toys went to Opelousas. I am told that 500 F might still come to us, and the *Father Gallifet*.[216] The fathers have also received the amount of 600 F in gold. I think this was the amount promised us a long time ago by Mother Lucile's

---

214 Original autograph, C-VII 2) c Duchesne to Barat, Box 2. Postmarks: May 4; June 20, 1825. Partial copies, A-II 2) g Box 2, *Lettres intéressantes de la Société depuis 1816 N° 1,* pp. 415-419; C-III 1: USA Foundation Haute Louisiane, Box 1, *Lettres de la Haute Louisiane II 1823-1830,* pp. 231-233. Cf. J. de Charry, II, 2, L. 197, pp. 351-357; Hogg, pp. 233-238.
215 Before taking the steamboat in New Orleans for Saint Louis, Eugenie Audé encountered Father Borgna, who had just arrived, as well as Father Dusaussoy. She arrived in Florissant March 21.
216 Joseph Galliffet, SJ, *L'Excellence de la Dévotion au Cœur adorable de Notre-Seigneur Jésus-Christ,* Lyon, 1733.

sister, though through letters that we have had the pleasure to receive, it seems that it came from Father Barat. Since we cannot know exactly to whom we are indebted, please express our thanks.

Mother Eugenie, who arrived March 21, will probably leave again at the beginning of May with the young Mother Xavier Hamilton, who will be very helpful for her. Since a long time ago I asked your permission to shorten her five years, and I have received her cross from you, so I considered myself sufficiently authorized by that to have her make her final vows on Good Shepherd Sunday at the parish Mass. The father superior did the ceremony with an excellent discourse. Our other Sister Hamilton, for whom you have also sent the large cross, not yet being twenty-one years old, asks you, as soon as she has reached that age, to give her permission also, so that she can have the same happiness as her sister, who is our first professed of America and the first choir religious destined for a foundation. She will have as companions Sister Ignatius, a very good coadjutrix in first vows and Sister Aloysia [Timon], an American novice, also coadjutrix.

That makes three in all that Mother Eugenie is going to take and that is all we can give her, with all our divisions in three boarding schools, that of 500 F, that of 175 F, and that of the Indians, which is finally beginning and to which we have destined an Irish woman [Mary Ann O'Connor] who has made first vows on Good Shepherd Sunday. Her language, her age of about 40 years, and her solid virtue make her the most suitable for this work that keeps her separated from us for part of the day and all of the night. The Indian girls call her Mama, leap around her wherever she takes them, to the cows, the chickens, or the garden. We leave her the active tasks, since these children cannot stand a sedentary life.

We ask that the *dixième*[217] of the American houses, when they will be able to give it, be dedicated to the conversion and education of the Indians and to do it in such a way that it becomes law for the future, because there are superiors who think that it is best to keep it for their own house and who dream of superfluous things while others lack necessities.

Mother Eugenie has shown us the plan of the house at Saint Michael, which will be very comfortable and is located nicely. Everything indicates that this foundation, better situated than the first two, will prosper. It seems to us that the one in Opelousas will suffer too much from the change of superior to be able to take anyone else from there. So here

---

217 The tenth of the revenue that each house was supposed to contribute to the general treasury.

is how we propose to establish the government at Mother Eugenie's departure, which can happen at the end of October in order to open the boarding school on January 1, 1826:

1. Mother Xavier, superior, since she is well known in the area.

2. Sister Carmelite Landry, formed in this house, a Creole used to the area and an excellent religious, as assistant or sub-mistress of the coadjutrix novices, the only ones who will remain there. She is a completely formed religious with regard to age, evenness, virtue and to manage a house—what Mother Xavier lacks. She can also help in the boarding school with two aspirants, one American and the other French.

3. Sister Marguerite can do some surveillances, iron, and take care of the chapel. Two coadjutrices will be for the infirmary and the kitchen, but this kitchen so ruins health that it seems impossible to us not to have a Negro slave, whom we want to keep with us even outside her work time, in order to prevent dangerous means of recreation. Here they enter all the rooms of their mistresses, or with the children. An answer, please, about this issue.

If the boarding school at Opelousas remains, they will need a good French teacher, one at Saint Michael to help Mother Eugenie, and one here, especially if the foundation at Saint Charles goes through. The Jesuits want it very much; and it will be really necessary to establish religion in the north of Missouri, where there is no priest in place nor school, and no money to send the children away,[218] whereas on the same side of the river, not needing the crossings that are so expensive and often dangerous, they can pay school fees in kind.[219] That is how the fee of 175 F is paid and even made up for those who cannot pay it; nevertheless, the children lack nothing in food. The day school is impossible to establish in Louisiana because of the great heat, the Negroes who run around the country, the animals that roam without guardian, and the long distances. It seems better to have the children in one place day and night. We can manage on 250 F or 50 *gourdes* per year. The benefit will be more certain, the difficulty no greater, and these children can even help with the garden, the laundry, etc. Here they sleep either on furs or on coverings that they take up during the day. They can be 20 or 30 in a class, which is enough for the day students whom we would not have in so great a number.

---

218 To put the children in faraway boarding schools.
219 If they were established on the banks of the Missouri opposite Florissant, the students would not be exposed to the dangers of crossing the river, and without this expense, the parents could pay more easily in kind.

I hope that you will be moved by the amount of work there is to do, and that you will approve: 1) the foundation in Saint Charles; 2) that you will send us three middle-aged religious, but not Mothers Benoît Maujot and Bardot. I am too fearful about their mental health; 3) that you will permit the vows of Carmelite [Landry]; 4) the foundation of a secondary boarding school instead of a day school; 5) the admission of a married black woman for the kitchen; 6) that the novitiate for Lower Louisiana be at Saint Michael in the care of Mother Eugenie; it is the best situation for help of all sorts; 7) that you will name the superior and assistant for Opelousas; 8) the assistant here, whom you would like to be superior in my place in case of death, so that the house would not experience a change of governance if the assistant that you name became superior. All these answers are of singular importance to us. Please address them to the appropriate houses as soon as possible, by New York or Le Havre. If you prefer Mother Lucile or the one who is coming to succeed me, please name her assistant to avoid the bad effect of replacing Mother Octavie almost as soon as she took her place as assistant, which she would feel, and it would cause gossip. As for Mother Xavier, she has much improved, she is very zealous and much attached to the Society, and the bishop now holds to our rules. 9) It is impossible here to prevent Sunday visits, next to the church;[220] the parents, who come to town only that day from a distance of three or four leagues, would be irritated to be refused. 10) "Mutual education" is very much in style here in general opinion, even that of the priests. May we use something of it, at least for the reading and arithmetic of the poor?

Please, Reverend Mother, do not make us wait a long time for the answer to our ten questions. Pray for us all and for the mission. There are always setbacks, but in the midst of it one sees the finger of God who carries on his work, and we are happy to see it accomplished, happier still to leave this consolation to others, and keep only the Cross and abandonment to God in all things.

I am at your feet *in Corde Jesu,*

Philippine Duchesne Sup.
Eugenie Audé Sup.

---

[220] The house is next to the church, so it is normal that the parents, coming from Sunday church, want to see their daughters.

[On the reverse:]
Single
To Mother
Mother Barat Superior General
of the houses of the Sacred Heart
Rue de Varenne n° 41
Paris
France
By way of New York

Letter 254   **L. 19 to Bishop Rosati**

SS. C. J. et M.

[April 21, 1825] [221]

Dear Bishop,

The hasty departure of Father Timon leaves me only a moment to ask your blessing and give a report on our house. Father De Neckere has probably told you that he traveled with Mother Eugenie, who with Bishop Dubourg's permission has come here to consult about the proposed foundation at Saint Michael and to take two or three of our sisters.

Bishop Dubourg was asking for the two Hamilton sisters, but we can give up only the older one who can be very useful and who made her final vows in view of her departure. I had long asked our superior general to send her her cross [of profession] because of her solid vocation and her good conduct. The sacrifices she has made also warrant this dispensation. Bishop Dubourg gave the reverend father the power to examine subjects we present to him, and he presided joyfully at the ceremony on Good Shepherd Sunday. Sister Mary Ann O'Connor, an Irish woman, made her first vows the same day. The younger Sister Hamilton wanted to make her final vows with her sister, but this was impossible as she is not yet twenty-one.

Mother Eugenie will leave soon; besides Sister Hamilton she will take Sister Labruyère from Sainte Genevieve. Sister Tison wants to go with her also, but her uncertain vocation will probably not allow it.

---

221   Original autograph, C-VII 2) c Writings Duchesne to Rosati, Box 6. On the reverse: "April 25, 1825, Mother Duchesne, Saint-Ferdinand."

We have only four boarders at $100 and fifteen who give only their food or nothing at all. Besides the day pupils, we have *(number illegible)* little Indians we cherish as *(word illegible)* of the important work that drew us to America.

The reverend father asks for the holy oils. He is at *Côte Sans Dessein*.[222]

My sisters and I ask for your blessing. I am with profound veneration, Bishop, your Excellency's submissive and unworthy servant.

Philippine Duchesne

Saint Ferdinand, April 21, 1825

> [On the reverse:]
> To His Excellency
> Bishop Rosati
> *Barrens*

Letter 255   **L. 9 to Father Delacroix**

SS. C. J. et M.

May 1 [1824]
St. Anthony[223]

Reverend Father,

I am delayed in testifying to you my gratitude as much for the care you have lavished on us with such goodness, as for the inexpressible zeal with which you labor continually for our foundations.

I have avoided making a decision on a matter of this kind before knowing the wishes of our superior general. In her last letter, which assumes consent, she asked me if it would not be better for me to live near New Orleans. I answered her that I did not think so. Indeed this business could not be in better hands than those of Mother Eugenie, who is better known in the area and who has everything to make it succeed. If I am good for anything, this is not the moment for me to leave here, where it seems that perhaps our boarding school is going to be reborn from its ashes; several students have applied.

---

222   A French village on the Missouri about 115 miles from St. Louis.
223   Original autograph, C-VII 2) c Writings Duchesne to various Eccles., Box 8. On the reverse: "from Mother Duchesne, 1824, May 1. No. 6."

Since we have received a few Indian girls, the reason for our wishes to come to America, I would have great difficulty leaving them. Besides, these three divisions of classes require much work, and Mother Octavie, who is ever weak, cannot do everything.

I bless God that once again one of our houses will be under your care. This one is always well run by the father whom you know and who gathers confidence as you do—which does not at all mean that you are forgotten, either by our children or the parishioners, especially Mrs. Chambers and Mrs. Saint-Cyr.[224] Mrs. Greaux [Miss Catherine Mullanphy] has a son. Her sister has no children.

Before the house at Saint Michael begins, our mother general will make the final decision about its superior. But Mother Eugenie will certainly go to make the foundation with Mother Xavier whom I give with difficulty for us and with pleasure for such an interesting house. Two sisters go with her; that is all we can give.

Some will come from France, I hope, who are already preparing. Everything indicates that God will bless your labors, sustain our efforts, and draw from the work the glory of that Heart in whom I am with respect, your humble servant and devoted daughter.

Philippine Duchesne

My sisters send you their respects. Our compliments to Mr. Isidore.

[On the reverse:]
To Father
Father Delacroix
Pastor at Saint Michael
Acadian Coast

Letter 256   L. 53 to Mrs. Jouve in Lyon

Saint Ferdinand in Missouri, May 10, 1825[225]

My dearest Sister,

---

224 Mrs. Chambers is surely Jane Mullanphy Chambers, daughter of their great benefactor John Mullanphy. Mrs. Saint-Cyr is surely the mother of Emilie Josephine Saint-Cyr (1806-1882), student at Florissant, who later entered the Society of the Sacred Heart and devoted herself mainly in the Saint Louis area.

225 Copies: *Cahier, Lettres de la Mère Duchesne à sa famille*, pp. 114-117; *Lettres dactylographiées*. C-VII 2) c Duchesne to her family and lay people, Box 5.

I received your letter and that of Mrs. de Mauduit telling me of the death of our dear sister Lebrument,[226] but they reached me a year and two months after that sad event. My superior general had already told me earlier, presuming that I had received the details from my family, so I awaited them anxiously. In the midst of such deep heart-suffering, faith and devotion find great consolation in the heroic virtues of such a good mother, and in the touching resignation of her poor children and the husband who loved her dearly.

The distance does not permit me to say all that is in my heart. I beg you to send on to that afflicted family this little note that is only a feeble expression of my sentiments and my wishes for them.

Thank you for the details you gave me about your family and that of Mrs. de Mauduit. Please tell her of my condolences and also Melanie at Romans and my brother. How I regret not being able to write to them at this time; the departure earlier than I expected of four sisters whom I will probably never see again, who are destined for a third foundation of our Society in America,[227] takes from me all my free moments until tomorrow when we must be separated.

In spite of such painful moments, I cannot pass up the opportunity of the steamboat to answer you, and through you my sisters and your husband. I have already done so with regard to Mr. Pecoud. I enclose the note from the priest best informed about him. He says that they cannot bring suit against him because he has nothing and his associate is dead. I received some time ago the magnificent brocade material that he brought me as a gift from Mr. Jouve. The bishop was so envious that I gave it to him. It will certainly be more suitable on a bishop in New Orleans that in our poor village, and I really made use of it in the best way that gave me pleasure, for I enjoyed being able to present it as a gift to such a good bishop who has taken such interest in us.

I am all yours in the Heart of Jesus,

Philippine Duchesne

For Constance

My dearly beloved Friend,

I would like to write you a long letter urging you to imitate more and more closely your older sister, the memory of whose virtues consoles

---

226 Adelaide Duchesne (1779-1824), married to Henri Lebrument on May 1, 1798, died January 18, 1824, at Nantua (Ain).
227 The foundation of Saint Michael, November 30, 1825.

us, as well as her protection from heaven that helps us as we follow her footsteps. Try to deserve, as she did, the confidence and love of your good parents, and thus the special graces of God by your generous fidelity. Pray much for me and for your sister Josephine, to whom I cannot write, and ask your brothers, who are in boarding school with the fathers, to ask the same favor of them.

All yours *in Corde Jesu*,

Philippine

My regards to all the family.

Letter 257   L. 68 to Mother Barat

SS. C. J. et M.

Saint Ferdinand, June 8, 1825[228]
No. 60

Dear Reverend Mother,

My last letter, no. 59, dated April 23, was begun with Mother Eugenie, who left us on Ascension Day [May 12] with the three religious that we gave her, about whom I gave you the details.

That letter asked you to answer nine questions:
1. To appoint the superiors of the three houses, especially for this one in case I die suddenly, for my health varies quite a bit.
2. If we can use something of the educational method of mutual teaching, at least for the day students. This method is in general use here.
3. If we may admit a black woman into the house for the kitchen, which burdens everyone's health.
4. If you approve a second boarding school at either 175 F per year, or in exchange for food. This would bring the greater number here.
5. If you permit the final vows of Sister Regis here, whom I regard as the most essential religious for this house.
6. And those of Sister Carmelite, who could very well be assistant at Opelousas.
7. If a novitiate is necessary at Saint Michael.

---

[228] Copies, A-II 2) g Box 2, *Lettres intéressantes de la Société depuis 1816 N° 1*, pp. 411-413 ; C-III 1: USA Foundation Haute Louisiane, Box 1, *Lettres de la Haute Louisiane II 1823-1830*, pp. 48-52. Cf. J. de Charry, II, 2, L. 198, pp. 360-364; Hogg, pp. 239-242.

8. If you are not sending some religious.
9. That if Father Niel, pastor at Saint Louis, comes to you to beg, you would determine the destination for our fathers and for us, who have the work with the Indians. They now have ten boys, and we, six girls, about whom we are happy and who are doing well enough in everything. The government has appropriated a sum for the civilization of the Indians, under the care of the Secretary of War. I am now writing to him to ask for maintenance of four teachers and a subsidy to build them a house that will cost at least 3000 F.

The government plan is only to help and encourage associations that have the means to make foundations. So, supposing that he gives it to us, this would still be only the least part of our expenses. But we must count on Providence and not do less than the Protestants who have schools for Indians all over the States. Those who are with the Osage have little girls who already know Genesis by heart and know how to read.

Please have earnest prayer said for our work. We will still cry out: *money, money*, but you will not be displeased at this plea for the Indian girls, objects of all your prayers and for the love of whom you have sent us here.

The bishop had promised the fathers the alms that he was to receive from France for the work with the Indians. They have received nothing, and I think the bishop is the poorest priest of his diocese. This creates a little reciprocal unhappiness. So that it does not grow larger, when you could send something by the most direct way, that is always better; and since everybody knows everything in New Orleans, it would be better that it all came through New York, even at the risk of losing on the exchange.

I have heard nothing about the 1200 F for the fathers, nor the 300 for us, that you have been so kind as to tell us about in your last letter of January 10 this year. Father superior's sister told him that the 1200 F are coming from her, which you did not tell me.

My separation from Mother Eugenie was....[229] Her health is weakened and her nerves are often not well. It appears as an inclination to weep and to be sad, which, I see with difficulty, makes her less suitable for government. We must count on God alone and even on miracles in order to believe in a long existence for regular religious life in these lands.

---

229 Words replaced by suspension points.

In this region, we have only two priests, both in very bad health. Mine changes often, and I think some sudden attack will carry me off. I am so full of faults that the work would not suffer from this loss. The father superior told me to write to you to recall Mother Eugenie here, as the only one suitable to make the work with the Indians succeed. But I think she is more necessary in Lower Louisiana, since here a mediocre superior can avoid the pitfalls with the direction that we have. Down there, everything is dangerous; the climate alone turns people's heads.

I would very much have liked your nephew to be attached to one of our houses. But this one has so few resources, and when we have anything extra, it is so needed by the Jesuit Fathers, that it would destroy them to take it away. The bishop was willing to keep your nephew, and at Saint Michael they are too involved with the pastor [Father Delacroix] who runs the establishment. I hope that time will give us the possibility of a reconciliation, but at present it would just stir up too much. I do not repeat to you what I said in my preceding letters about Mothers Lucile and Octavie. The Spirit of God who lives in you can help you decide.

Please always write to me in such a way that the letter can be seen in case of death. How much do you not have to forgive now?

I fear consumptive disease in Sister Catherine. She is a Mother du Terrail with regard to zeal.[230]

I reckon with pleasure that my letter might arrive on July 22, your feast day. I unite myself to the holy joy of that day, which we will celebrate in absence, but in the most intimate union with our sisters and with the devotion I owe you *in Corde Jesu*.

Philippine

I implore Fathers Perreau, Varin, and Barat to pray much for us, and also our sisters.

Letter 258   L. 69 to Mother Barat

SS. C. J. et M.

[Saint Ferdinand], July 3, 1825[231]
No. 61

---

230 Marie du Terrail, RSCJ, was mistress general of the day school at Sainte-Marie d'En-Haut, in Grenoble.
231 Copy, C-III 1: USA Foundation Haute Louisiane, Box 1, *Lettres de la Haute Louisiane II 1823-1830*, pp. 53-57. Cf. J. de Charry, II, 2, L. 199, pp. 365-372; Hogg, pp. 242-247.

Dear Reverend Mother,

Tomorrow they celebrate the feast of *Independence* in these States.[232] There will be nothing but rejoicing in all classes and all religions. For the Catholics do not forget that on that day they obtained freedom for their own form of worship.[233] Until then, in Virginia anyone could kill a Catholic with no penalty; at least, that is what I was told. As for me, I cast my thoughts forward to the 22nd and celebrate in my heart, in advance and for always, the sweet and touching *dependence* that binds me to you. Yes, I will thank God for it to my last breath, and we unite our hearts to all the wishes that will be sent to you on the feast of Saint Madeleine.

Our last letters told you that my health had changed very much. I did not realize it myself. But the day of the feast of Saint Regis, without asking for anything or desiring anything, and I had been very weak the day before, I found myself in normal health. And so that I could not fail to recognize the hand that had touched me, everything then contributed to take my strength from me: heartrending thoughts, a painful future, a troubled conscience, poor success, difficulties in governing, long and painful waiting for news of our sisters who left on Ascension Day, oppressive heat...nothing is left to me but to make better use of the future. Nevertheless, since it is uncertain, I beg you to give me in advance your plans for our future government.

May the work with Indian girls that has begun at last touch your heart and make you decide to send us a good *head*, someone young enough to learn English. A very interesting account from Mother d'Avenas,[234] to whom I ask you to send my thanks as I await an opportunity to answer her, tells me about the extraordinary solemnity with which you celebrated the feast of the Sacred Heart last year. I think this year the feast would have been the same. Here it was quite different. I was not even able to receive Communion on the most solemn day for us,

---

232 The Declaration of Independence from Britain of the thirteen original English colonies in America on July 4, 1776, was later extended to all the new states on the day of their foundation.
233 American Catholics, many descended from English families who knew religious persecution, shared their compatriots' view about full religious freedom for all.
234 Aimée d'Avenas, RSCJ (1804-1871), born January 25, 1804, was then in the general novitiate in Paris, where she took the habit March 7, 1823, and made her first vows July 21, 1825. She made her profession December 25, 1830. An excellent educator, author of the *Plan of Studies of the Society of the Sacred Heart, 1852*, she was mistress general in Paris, then superior in Orleans, where she was especially appreciated by Father Dupanloup. She died August 12, 1871, in Brussels.

nor consequently to renew my vows publicly.[235] That had to be in the intimacy of my heart…low Mass, no sermon, nor the following Sunday, when the feast was in the church dedicated to the Sacred Heart. When we sang the Kyrie, we saw that the priest [Father Van Quickenborne] was ending the Gospel, feeling ill. So the rest was in silence.

If you can use your influence to bring another priest here, or so that the father general will give permission for the seminarians here to be ordained, it would be a great benefit for religion and for us. One priest cannot serve four parishes, two communities, and the sick at great distance. He is forever risking his life. Lately when he crossed the river to come here, the horse was swimming and threw him in the water. He held on to the mane until he could touch ground. On the way back, the water was even higher. On the horse, he had water up to his neck because of the horse's agitated movements.

The strictness of this holy priest displeases some, especially the French, who say that they do not like him and that they will go to another. But there is no other. We see only him. His charges are always in retreat. Father de Clorivière is not his equal in exactitude. I see that a second [priest] would calm their hearts far and near. One could not find a priest of greater merit, but sometimes weaknesses must be accommodated.

Since October, we have not had Ember Days. I asked the bishop for a dispensation for a while, so as not to begin with someone with whom we could not continue and who would have to be inconvenienced to do it well. When we realize the achievement of Mother Eugenie, we have to simply be happy with our lot and bless God for it. Nevertheless, since an abundance of spiritual benefits would do no harm, listen to my request, please, and weigh it without considering it to be about us. The idea of a report might be harmful to success.[236] It is enough to speak of the vast field offered by the Indians and the whites who are, in their distant homelands, just *like sheep without a shepherd*.[237] I intended to write to the Secretary of War to get help for the Indian girls. The superior, who is charged by the government for both sexes, as in the other

---

235   Though Philippine does not give the reason for this, the testimony of contemporaries preserved it: a few days before, she and Father Van Quickenborne had a disagreement over some small question of adornment in the sanctuary. In confession the day before the feast, he had refused her absolution and told her she was not to renew her vows. To avoid giving scandal, she pretended to be ill and stayed in bed during the feast day Mass. See Callan, p. 421 and n. 42, p. 775.
236   She invites Mother Barat to make known informally the situation of the American mission without making an official report and naming the sisters.
237   Matt 9:36; Mark 6:34.

seminaries of this kind, told me that we would cut off his chances.[238] So we must remain silent. He himself wrote on our behalf and to press the advantage of education separated by sex. I have little hope of success. The Presbyterians are watching carefully for their own advantage and will cry out against the novelty of the plan.

Today I heard that yellow fever has already arrived this year in New Orleans. I fear for your nephew unless, as I hope, the bishop sent him farther, perhaps to Opelousas to avoid the bad climate. He had written to me that if we were to go to the Indians, he would be our chaplain. Unfortunately this is a fanciful dream; the time has not come.

All the [Indian] nations live in such squalor that one cannot hope for anything regarding change of customs or safety for those who try it. They must be renewed by education at a distance from the parents. At home, they would never leave them alone long enough.

I conclude, Reverend Mother, by asking your pardon for having represented you so poorly. God is good to put up with me and to forgive me always.

My respects to our fathers and mothers. Our last novice [Therese Detchemendy] made her vows on the feast of Saint Aloysius Gonzaga [June 21] at the parish Mass.

I am at your feet asking your blessing in the name of the Sacred Heart. Your daughter,

Philippine

Letter 259   **L. 70 to Mother Barat**

SS. C. J. et M.

September 14, 1825[239]
Rec. to St Anthony of Padua
No. 62

Dear Reverend Mother,

---

238   Such an effort would risk ending subsidies for the college. On June 15, 1825, Father Van Quickenborne had asked for a subsidy of $800 from the Secretary of War for the Indian school, but it was in vain.

239   Original autograph, C-VII 2) c Duchesne to Barat, Box 2. Postmarks: St. Louis Mo., Sep. 21; Paris, 11 Nov. 1825. Partial copy, C-III 1: USA Foundation Haute Louisiane, Box 1, *Lettres de la Haute Louisiane II 1823-1830*, p. 58. Cf. J. de Charry, II, 2, Letter 202, pp. 383-390; Hogg, pp. 255-259.

This feast of the Cross reminds me of that day when our little girls in Grenoble enacted for you a little play about the love of crosses, which you had asked for yourself, and it gave us a few moments of recreation. Experience teaches that anytime and anywhere the scene of the crosses can be renewed. Personal crosses are light compared to those that have a bearing on our work; and I see many of these, which prevent me from being able to desire death, such a delightful sentiment when one is ready and when the work would not suffer from losing us. Without loving life but loving our establishments, I see that the least cross attached to them is necessary to sustain them.

Mother Eugenie has recently had difficulty with regard to two new persons who entered: one who was taken away violently in three minutes, and the other whose head is unsound, who thinks of nothing less than to jump over walls and seek freedom; she is young and pretty and far from her family. In addition to the small number of religious, your two poor daughters [Philippine and Eugenie], must put up with pride, the incurable malady of the country; no one ever wants to be of second rank [coadjutrix sister]. It will be so rare that one can count on it only occasionally. Here the most essential person in the house, our Sister Regis, must do all of the heavy and menial work because she is solidly virtuous and courageous, but then she cannot do the essential thing of taking her class, and she is the only one with good English pronunciation, something highly valued here. Everything else is nothing in comparison.

I tell you this detail, which is repeated in each house, to prove to you that, against the advice of Bishop Dubourg, good coadjutrix Sisters, strong, courageous, humble, and able to supervise the kitchen, would be at least as useful for us as the choir religious, giving the latter time to devote completely to the classes. Their duties do not demand knowledge of English, which the French rarely speak well. Mother Octavie, with all her ability, is not in a condition to speak it and write a good letter. She thought so, and I cannot judge; but some chance compliments taken too seriously had reassured us too much in this regard. The father superior, who saw her letters and translations, told me that we should not let them be seen for fear of losing the boarding school. Nevertheless, it seems to have risen from its ashes. From being reduced to four students for a while, we now have twelve; more are promised and I would like to have everything go in such a way that there are no complaints, since they will bring what is necessary for our stability, that of our neighbors who are always very poor, and the maintenance of the Indian girls.

Here are enough reasons, Reverend Mother, to convince you to join to the single religious whom you have destined for us in the company of your friend, two good sisters for service. This is not the advice of the father, who would prefer religious to govern, since he finds no one he likes for this; I am surely the first, but the two others lack a spirit of order and firmness, which renders many virtues useless on the outside. They say that Mother Eugenie came here to *restore order in the boarding school*. It is true that God has given her many means of pleasing the children and parents, without compromising in any way good order and regularity. My hope for the future here is in Sister Regis, but she is not twenty-one years old. She is so good that I have asked your permission for her final vows at the expiration of first vows.

Father's poor health is a great cross. He does not want to have priests ordained from among his scholastics. Meanwhile, we often miss Mass and many other things, and fear to lose everything with his life, because there is only one priest remaining in Saint Louis, as exhausted as he is. Besides this, the bishop expresses extreme discontent with him. Both say that the terms of their contract are not being kept by the other party. It seems true on the part of the bishop with regard to finances, since he promised help to those he received from Europe, and on the part of the Society [the Society of Jesus], which was to supply four priests for Missouri. But the general cannot give anyone and the father, by saying that he cannot yet have any ordained priests, has created an antagonistic situation that will last for a long time. The bishop accuses the [Jesuit] Society of *covering all its activities under an impenetrable veil*. I have had reason to fear that he might be removed from the area where we are. At this moment, another priest has arrived to spend a month here; he is an extraordinary man with regard to virtues and talents whose bad health made him desire our solitude. I would be very happy if he stayed and gave us the means to live the rule for religious exercises. But I perceived such discomfort in the father that I had to stand aside and let him after four days adroitly get rid of this man who came with a letter from the coadjutor bishop for at least a month, with no mention of afterwards.

I am aware that we are faced with the possibility of being completely lacking in resources, either by death or by the clouds I have seen beginning to form several times. But after having consulted our mothers and especially the Heart of Jesus, I saw that it was more to the glory of God to abandon ourselves than to harm by the least wrong action an establishment that is the only hope for religion here. The father thought that perhaps Father Dusaussoy performed a disservice to the bishop when he left the Society. I reassured him in that regard. I want as many students for them as for us, and we are the only house that can help them, far or near, by giving them what would be paid to a chaplain or whatever can be collected elsewhere. The father does not know where the 1200 F came from, about which you told me, and he has not yet touched them, even though the superior at Bordeaux addressed them to the bishop, who has acknowledged receipt. He assumed that the 1200 F from Bordeaux were not the same as those that his sister told him about from Flanders. I fear the opposite. The 300 F that you told me were attached have not come through either. Maybe you used them to free us from debt with regard to Mr. Mullanphy, a thorn that I am thankful to have removed and for which I owe you a great deal.

The Secretary of War has answered the father that he can give us nothing for the work with the Indian girls, since all the funds applied in that direction are already allocated.

Mother Octavie grows weaker without stopping her work. She is threatened by illnesses that circulate here in the month of September. Mother Lucile has a high fever, and Sister Catherine is often suffering. Mother Lucile has proved to me in the work of the storeroom that her head and her body cannot support either attention to many things or the fatigue of the work. *Fiat!* She does not hold her class well, and this has not escaped the all-seeing eyes of the father. What to do? Suffer, see things going poorly and be unable to improve them. I am much more incapable of the leadership that you assign to me. I bow my head, but I feel my incapacity. If only I were at the source of light of a Father Varin, of a Father Perreau, of a Father Barat, in a country less subject to change, to inconsistency, it would be bearable; but here, all ideas get mixed up when one wants to do good. The father himself told me: "I often do not know how things are going; I see nothing." It is a different thing for me, poor beast, old, without talents, without likeableness, without virtues.

So tell these three dear fathers already named to remember their brothers and sisters, white and Indian. God alone sees the end, but there are terrible hindrances to success. I want nothing except to spend my life in the greatest labor. I feel that rest is not for this life. One must have the body burdened and the heart pressed down. If I can serve in the least little work for the glory of the Sacred Heart, I consent to grow old here, without success, without recognition, for my lone immolation to the Heart in which I am your unworthy daughter.

Philippine

Please send some colored pictures for the Indians, especially the frightening ones of the death of sinners, hell, etc.

> [On the reverse:]
> To Mother
> Mother Barat, Superior General
> of the houses of the Sacred Heart
> Rue de Varenne
> *Paris*
> France
> *By way of New York*

Letter 260 **L. 29 to Bishop Rosati**

SS. C. J. et M.

[November 24, 1825][240]

Dear Bishop,

Added to our distress at having no news of you is our chagrin that you cannot visit us as you did last year. I hope that you can do so in a few months so that I can thank you personally for your kindness in thinking of us and writing to us when you are burdened with so many serious cares and worries.

Mother Eugenie will be as sorry as I am not to have seen you, and she will rejoice with me over the foundation of the religious from the Barrens in Assumption Parish. It can only be a consolation to the friends of religion to see it spread to all parts of the diocese. I would be most grateful if they would honor us with a letter of affiliation.[241]

We are still only seven and have no novices. A few persons have applied but are still hesitating or find obstacles in the way. The house is maintained through the generosity of my sisters who rest only by going from their duties with the children to their religious duties or to household work.

---

240 Original autograph, C-VII 2) c Writings Duchesne to Rosati, Box 6. On the reverse "Nov. 24, 1825, Mother Duchesne, Florissant."
241 On January 26, 1826, Bishop Rosati answered thus: "The religious of Bethlehem are sending you the letters of affiliation, in the hope that on your side you will not refuse them the same happiness." Letters of Bishop Rosati, manuscripts, 1815-1840. C-VII 2) c, Writings, Box 7.

Please bless them and believe me, with profound veneration *in Corde Jesu*, Bishop, your Excellency's submissive and humble daughter.

Philippine Duchesne, sup.

November 24, 1825

Letter 261   L. 21 to Bishop Rosati

SS. C. J. et M.

[December 15, 1825][242]

Dear Bishop,

I have already told you of our disappointment when you could not visit us upon your return from New Orleans. As I am not certain the letter reached you, I am taking advantage of this opportunity to again express our regrets and gratitude. Thank you for the news of Bishop Dubourg and of our house at Saint Michael that you so thoughtfully gave me. I am anxious for the new house of the religious from the Barrens to succeed so that together we can make our Lord loved in a place where he is not even known!

We have to go slowly toward this desirable goal because of the obstacle to our expansion created by the small number of our religious. We have only one postulant at present, and there are others who seem in no hurry to enter, although they need only good will to be received. If they do enter, please allow them to take the habit at the time prescribed by our Constitutions, after they have been examined by our confessor. I ask this as we shall not see you for several months according to your letters.

Our boarding school is having a re-birth after being reduced to five students; it has increased to sixteen. This number will be enough to support us along with the children we receive gratis.

Mr. McCay of New Madrid still owes us $30 board for one of his daughters. He has not answered any of my letters, but I think he would

---

242 Original autograph, C-VII 2) c Writings Duchesne to Rosati, Box 6. On the reverse "December 15, 1825, Mother Duchesne, Florissant; received the 18th; answered the 19th. She has to send me the dimensions, boundaries and location of the field, etc. Miss Eleonore Gray wants to become a religious at Florissant. The portraits of Prince Hohenlohe, etc."

pay his debt if someone from the Barrens would write to him. If so, please keep the $30 for the seminary, as I want to act only with prayer with this gentleman with whom I have always had cordial relations.

If it were possible for me to have the donation of the apple orchard that Bishop Dubourg asked you to give us, it would make it easier for us to get a field adjoining our own property, the only one in the country that is suitable.

I am embarrassed to bother you with these bits of business, but I believe I am writing to a father and a pastor who, like Our Lord, counts nothing as too little.

I am with profound respect, Bishop, your Excellency's submissive and devoted daughter in the Sacred Heart of Jesus.

Philippine Duchesne, sup.

December 15, 1824

[On the reverse:]
To His Excellency
Bishop Rosati
Bishop of Tanagra

Letter 262   L. 71 to Mother Barat

SS. C. J. et M.

Saint Ferdinand, December 27, 1825[243]
Rec. to St. Anthony of Padua
No. 64

Dear Reverend Mother,

We all transport ourselves in spirit to your feet to rejoice with our sisters at the happiness they have to offer you their good wishes. May we be your consolation by responding to your concern for us and working generously for the glory of him to whom all your works are directed. Nothing is of greater help to us than the letters of our mother, of the one who represents for us the will of our Spouse and whom he

---

243 Original autograph, C-VII 2) c Duchesne to Barat, Box 2. Post marks: St. Louis Mo., December 28; from the colonies by way of Le Havre; Paris, February 25, 1826. Cf. J. de Charry, II, 2, L. 203, pp. 390-397; Hogg, pp. 260-265.

animates with his spirit. I have received your dear letter of August 4 this year, which contained interesting details, and the paper with your decisions and permissions.

I find only too much latitude in your permissions, and I am so little faithful that I fear the blindness that might follow and the faults it might make me commit. I have already spoken to you with insistence about my replacement in case of death, and I told you in my last letter that the employment of supervision of supplies and an illness have shown up Mother Lucile's weakness of thinking, and I fear that a house would soon decline in her hands. She does not even keep order in her class, nor tranquility. She has no other conversation than about little nothings. She is completely unable to read in church any Latin except that of the Office of the Blessed Virgin. It would be impossible for this not to cause shock in a person in first position. She does not know a word of English, so that Mother Octavie would have to represent her in business affairs and have the confidence of others, and thus the superior would not have the ability to judge and follow up. It would be the same with Mother Maujot. So please keep Mother Octavie as assistant. A change would utterly destroy her, and she would attribute it to me. She already says she is afraid of me. She is getting on in age; her appearance shows it, and she has rather strict spiritual direction [from Father Van Quickenborne]. I think that with the help of divine Providence, she is at the moment the most capable of governing. Sister Regis will be some day, but she is only 20 years old. She does not yet know her happiness and will not know it until we can give her three months of retreat, as far as possible, before her final vows.

We have all been very happy about the merger with Mother Vincent. I formed the hope of having several religious from there. They have the kind that we need: good Sisters [coadjutrices], teachers who have good penmanship, who sing well and know how to spell. Mother Xavier in Opelousas needs a cook and a teacher of writing and French grammar, who could do the accounts of the French children and make clean copies in French. I will then ask again for the American cook, whom I am awaiting impatiently to put her with our Indians. She has all she needs for that class. Mother Eugenie also needs a good, strong Sister and a teacher. If Mother Maujot came at her age, she could not learn a word of English, and it does not go well when the superior speaks only through an interpreter. Mother Eugenie does not want it, nor do I very much, unless you do not at all want Mother Octavie in leadership. The age of Mother Maujot would put her ahead of the two mothers [Octavie Berthold and Lucile Mathevon], which would not be without consternation on the part of both of them. Human nature does not die here anymore than in France. I laugh when I hear people thinking we are good. I would rather weep at having received too many graces and, as you told me in Grenoble, still living according to nature.

I am delighted that the mothers will hold an assembly in spring. After the three or four religious that we want so badly, the most interesting thing to propose to them would be a small sum assured to each house, taken from the students' charity fund, to supply maintenance for one or two priests in Missouri. This opens a vast field for zeal. Several priests would devote themselves to this, but the superior who sends them cannot leave them to certain death through the misery and illness that follow. The father superior told me to ask you for something guaranteed for our boarding schools or those of the fathers, and then he would take steps to extend the mission. All those missionaries spread out in Paraguay and in California had 1000 F from the king of Spain that supported them, the churches, and the poor. Dear Mother, take this affair to heart; great good will result. The bishop promised alms and has not been able to deliver. He almost quarreled with the superior because he would not let his men be ordained. He answered: "They would have to have clothing and a horse for their travel, and I could not supply them."

I did not get into this discussion because I do not know the whole of it, but I see that all this good will cease if there is no help from Europe.

The policy of the government is to drive all the Indians out of the States. It buys their land and pushes them out to other uninhabited land. The chiefs say: "You are stronger. We have to yield to you," and they withdraw, not without suffering, because they no longer have room for hunting. The *Sac* nation by negotiation has reserved a large area of land to give it to a Frenchman and to the half breeds of their nation, to form a foundation that will be at the junction of the *Des Moines* River and the Mississippi, four days journey to our north. It is outside the United States,[244] and the chief of the establishment would happily welcome a priest, he says, but he has there only poor people who cannot support a priest. If this arrangement could come from Europe, the settlement of the half breeds, the Sac nation, and that of the *Fox*, which has had, they say, Jesuit martyrs, would soon be evangelized. The Osage and the Arkansas are farther away and more primitive, not having as much of an idea about religion as those nations closer to Canada. Take this affair to heart, dear Reverend Mother, and may it all work out directly. Several think that the Jesuits are rich, but it is quite the opposite, and

---

244   That area became Iowa Territory in 1838, and the State of Iowa in 1846.

no one thinks of helping them. What I want most for us is four large crosses [for the choir religious] and two little ones [for the coadjutrix Sisters], four cinctures, an Infant Jesus and a little Blessed Virgin for each house, a processional cross, some candelabra and braid for vestments, and some pictures, especially those likely to frighten sinners, large and in color, and several for each house, especially in red.

I forgot to tell you that in Saint Charles there will be almost all Americans, and how will Mother Maujot get along with them? I hope for three or four postulants who speak English, but will they persevere?

As long as there is no priest in Saint Charles, I do not think that it is good to go there. It will undoubtedly happen during the course of this year. I am always happy that you approve when the possibility arrives.

I hear nothing more from Grenoble. Sometimes I think God is asking me to cease all correspondence except to you, but I do not have the light to discern. I see both pro and contra. I am afraid of some of the opinions of the father [Van Quickenborne]. We do not always agree. I was not troubled at the Ember Days, because I discuss only temporal affairs with him.[245] This is necessary, however. We have 16 students, which is enough to sustain us. I beg only for our neighbors, which should give me a little merit.

Prayers for a happy death, that is what is best for me. I count very much for this on Father Perreau and Fathers Varin, Barat, Ronsin and Roger, to whom I offer my humble respects. Mother Xavier [Murphy] thinks that your nephew is already thinking about returning to France. It is astonishing how this country can discourage. This shows clearly that only one Society can be maintained and that it must be helped. Poor America! When one thinks that from us to Canada and to the West as far as the Pacific Ocean, there is not one church, no priest, and nevertheless up to 23,000 souls that have come this year from the East into this state of Missouri alone, besides the French and Irish settlements on all sides, nearly to the sources of the Missouri and Mississippi.

It is late and the opportunity leaves tomorrow morning. I cannot include here the accounts of the last six months because I forgot to enter them in the books.

I am at your feet, your unworthy but submissive daughter *in Corde Jesu.*

Philippine

My most loving greetings to our mothers and sisters.

---

245 She had another confessor during the Ember Days, the "extraordinary confessor."

[On the reverse:]
To Mother
Mother Barat Superior General
of the houses of the Sacred Heart
Rue de Varenne
Paris
France
By way of New York

Letter 263   **L. 22 to Bishop Rosati**

SS. C. J. et M.

[December 29, 1825][246]

Dear Bishop,

We were so sorry to hear of the loss your holy religious at the Barrens suffered from the fire. How happy we would be if we could help them with repairs; how quickly we would do it, but just now I am in debt and must use the little I have for food for the children.

God seems to work miracles for the Lovers of Jesus, for aside from the spiritual graces he pours out on them, he facilitates their foundations. Father Martial writes me from Bardstown that Father Chabrat,[247] their superior, is going to build them a two-story convent in brick, 125 feet long. It is paid for; he underlined the word paid. That seems all the more surprising to me since, in spite of much help from our superior general, we still owe Mr. Meynard for our building.

Father Martial tells me that Bishop Flaget is sending him to Rome, and he offers to do errands for us.

We shall be happy to receive, above all from you, the young Irish woman [Eleonore Gray][248] who is offering herself for our Society. The

---

246   Original autograph, C-VII 2) c Writings Duchesne to Rosati, Box 6. On the reverse: "December 29, 1825, Mother Duchesne, Florissant; received January 12, answered the 26th." Postmark: St. Louis Mo., January 7.
247   Guy Ignace Chabrat, born in Savoy in 1787, joined the Sulpicians and was ordained a priest in 1811, in Bardstown, by Bishop Flaget. Having become coadjutor bishop of Bardstown, in 1834, he resigned in 1847 and returned to France for reasons of health.
248   On December 19, 1825, Bishop Rosati proposed a postulant: "Among our boarders [of the Barrens] there is a young woman, 17 years of age, named Eleonore Gray; she was born in Ireland and came with her parents to America four years ago." *Lettres de Mgr Rosati,*

points that present the greatest difficulties are entire obedience and indifference to house and employments. It is on these articles that she must assess her strength and devotion.

I am delighted to learn of the course taken by Miss Patrocinia Canale, who was not only a boarder with us but a novice; even then she preferred the Lovers of Jesus. She left in spite of our objections, saying she had no vocation, in order to return to her family whom she loved more than the convent, where perhaps she had been a little overworked. She had, however, imprudently made the vow of chastity and returned to the dangers of the world without support for her piety. I thank God a thousand times for giving her shelter.

I am told that Miss Keeper, who with her sisters attended our free school, has gone as a boarder to the same holy house. We did not allow her to be with the boarders, as we do not admit day scholars among them. The sight of two [social] classes among our children offends many of the children of this country who threaten to go to the Barrens and would have you say, Bishop, that it is much better because there are no distinctions there. I have always thought that it was pride alone that wounded them, and I will never doubt your good will towards us. I could not admit the least doubt in my heart in this regard. It would be too destructive of our happiness because any coolness on your part would be due only to our fault and would thus merit our regrets.

I am enclosing here a note giving the boundaries of the land Bishop Dubourg gave us. Mr. Mullanphy drew it up and exchanged the land with the bishop.[249]

Our mother general at my request has given permission for Sister Eulalie Regis Hamilton to make her final vows when she comes of age, without waiting for the completion of the five years required by the rule. I ask your consent also to fulfill her desire and thus reward her virtues. She will be twenty-one this Lent.

Be pleased, Bishop, to bless our whole community, which places itself at your feet, asking your blessing through me and offering their best wishes for the New Year. May we procure for you some consolations and prove to you, I above all, the deep respect with which I am your Excellency's submissive and respectful daughter and servant.

manuscrits, 1815-1840, C-VII 2) c, Writings, Box 7. Eleonore (or Eleanor) Gray (1808-1862) entered at Florissant in 1827. Superior in Saint Louis in 1842, then in Buffalo in 1852 and in Saint Michael in 1855, she was part of the group that made the foundation in Saint John, New Brunswick (Canada) in 1854.

249 Bishop Rosati answered on January 28, 1826, "Here is the contract for the sale of the land, which Bishop Dubourg had given you and which I would have sent you through Rev. Father Van Quickenborne, if I had received your letter before his departure." *Idem.*

Philippine Duchesne, sup.

December 29, 1825

Commended to St. Anthony

[On the reverse:]
To His Excellency
Bishop Rosati
Bishop of Tanagra
Barrens

Letter 264   **L. 23 to Bishop Rosati**

SS. C. J. et M.

[January 16, 1826][250]

Dear Bishop,

I learned upon Father Van Quickenborne's return that you had not received my answer to the letter you sent me through Mr. Martin Lepère, in which you offered me a postulant and spoke of the great loss the religious of the Barrens had suffered. Doubtless my answer will come, but in case it is lost, I shall repeat its contents in a few words:

We can confidently accept the postulant you have offered and examined, provided she is predisposed to be indifferent to house and employment.

I expressed my regret that we cannot follow our desire to help the Friends of Mary, but I have no money after paying for our supply of salt. We consider ourselves fortunate when our books balance. I can take nothing from what is owed to our pupils. I see that God is protecting them especially and have been consoled to learn of their rapid growth in Louisiana.

Miss Canale is very fortunate to have found such a good home. She wanted to leave our house and return to the world after she had made a vow of perpetual chastity without advice; our arguments did not sway her. Without doubt God wants her where she is, for she still lacks sufficient light to see the dangers to which she has exposed herself.

---

250 Original autograph, C-VII 2) c Writings Duchesne to Rosati, Box 6. On the reverse: "January 16, 1826, Mother Duchesne; received the 21st; answered the 26th."

As to Miss Keeper who has left so suddenly, she never adjusted to our free school as did her sisters; she wanted to be among the boarders in the house where we do not admit day pupils. These distinctions in class displease many Americans who cannot afford to be boarders.

Our Sister Eulalie Regis Hamilton has our mother general's permission to make her final vows when she is twenty-one, although she has not completed the five years since first vows required by the Rule. I ask you to allow her to satisfy her ardent desires after she has been examined by our confessor, in whom I am sure you have every confidence and who, according to Bishop Dubourg's order, holds the place of ecclesiastical superior for us.

I am with profound veneration, Bishop, your Excellency's submissive servant and daughter.

Philippine Duchesne, sup.

Saint Ferdinand, January 16, 1826

[On the reverse:]
To His Excellency
Bishop Rosati
Bishop of Tanagra
Barrens

Letter 265   **L. 24 to Bishop Rosati**

SS. C. J. et M.[251]

[February 14, 1826]

Dear Bishop,

I received the deed of sale you sent me by our new priest and also the letter of affiliation you were good enough to procure for us from your holy daughters, the Friends of Mary. I am truly chagrined that my limited knowledge of English prevents me from expressing my joy and gratitude in a manner less cold. Their charity will excuse me. I was

---

251   Original autograph, C-VII 2) c Writings Duchesne to Rosati, Box 6. On the reverse: "February 14, 1826, Mother Duchesne, Florissant."

deeply moved also by the remembrance of Father Odin.[252] We do not forget to pray for the success of his apostolic labors.

Bishop Dubourg often told us of his desire to have two or three of our religious open schools in Saint Charles and Saint Louis. The same idea has been repeatedly suggested by the priests of these two cities, and I spoke to you about it when you were here. Things are ever the same, but since I expect religious from France this year, we could agree to open the houses if you will authorize them in advance. I do not want to make any definite commitments without your permission and that of our superior general, to whom I have spoken many times on this subject.

I am with profound veneration, your Excellency's submissive and humble servant and daughter.

Philippine Duchesne, sup.

February 14, 1826

Letter 266   L. 72 to Mother Barat

SS. C. J. et M.

Florissant, February 18, 1826[253]

Dear Reverend Mother,

I have written to you twice that the list of permissions asked for has been received. You have thought of everything that can make us more at ease and can make the enormous distance between us less painful to bear. There are only two articles that trouble us considerably. The first one concerns me: it is the duty of watching over three houses when I do so badly in one. More than ever my heart wants solitude, and I have neither silence nor solitude. I am growing old, my health diminishing. I would need to review many of my past years in tears, especially those of my religious life. I undertake the work as penance, but it makes me

---

252 Jean Marie Odin, born in France, arrived in America in 1822 and was ordained priest as a Vincentian in 1824 at St. Mary's of the Barrens, where he was when Philippine wrote. Named apostolic vicar of Texas in 1842, he was later the first bishop of Galveston in 1847 and second archbishop of New Orleans in 1861. He attended the opening of Vatican Council I in 1870 but had to leave because of illness and died in France.

253 Copy, C-III 1: USA Foundation Haute Louisiane, Box 1, *Lettres de la Haute Louisiane II 1823-1830*, pp. 241-242. Cf. J. de Charry, II, 2, L. 205, pp. 402-403; Hogg, pp. 268-269.

entirely lose the spirit of prayer. If you hear my plea, I will gladly obey whomever you give us to govern us.

The foundation at Saint Charles will not happen immediately. The reverend father says that he will not send a priest until the church is built; but the stone is still in the quarry. I think that if we follow the wishes of the pastor in Saint Louis to have a school directed by us in the city, this would be the only way to sustain us in the area permanently. This plan of being in Saint Louis attracts me, so much the more because you want it, wanting to leave only one school here. This could be the second level boarding school at 180 F per year. As for the better boarding school at 500 F, the important thing is finding a house for it; that will make the decision; or else it is better to drop it.

The bishop intends to give Saint Louis to the Jesuits. The father rector does not say so, but he suddenly decided to have two of his young deacons ordained [De Smet and Verhaegen], one of whom is a good preacher. I do not doubt that this project will happen. A new reason for us to make a foundation in Saint Louis.

Sister Regis thanks you wholeheartedly for the permission that you have given her to make her final profession. My regards to Fathers Perreau, Varin and Barat.

I am at your feet *in Corde Jesu* your most unworthy daughter,

Philippine Duchesne

Letter 267   **L. 73 to Mother Barat**

SS. C. J. et M.

May 2, 1826[254]
St. Ant.

Dear Reverend Mother,

I had written to you at the time that the bishop changed his residence, when he went down to New Orleans and had thus left us as poor orphans. By an unexpected good fortune, as he was planning a trip to France, he wanted to come through here to visit this part of his

---

254   Original autograph, C-VII 2) c Duchesne to Barat, Box 2. Partial copy, USA Foundation Haute Louisiane, Box 1, *Lettres de la Haute Louisiane II 1823-1830*, p. 243. Cf. J. de Charry, II, 2, L. 207 pp. 408-410; Hogg, pp. 272-274.

diocese and gave us the pleasure of several days of his company.[255] We rejoiced in his kindness; he himself wants to carry our commissions to the homeland. I cannot think of anything more urgent than our letters to you expressing once again our desire for the arrival of the sisters you have promised after the General Council.

I repeat that three choir religious seem indispensable: one for French classes in Opelousas, one or two to assist Mother Eugenie at Saint Michael, and one to replace me here. For you tell me in your last letter that we must not think of Mother Octavie for government. The bishop has no doubt about that; he told me that he *shuddered* in my absence. The reverend father says the same. Mother Eugenie, I your servant, and the teachers under her direction say the same. So many authorities and voices nullify what I said earlier, and besides, there are the illnesses without end that continue to create new obstacles. So if you think that Sister Benoît[256] can carry the office, I would be the first to want to obey her.

The bishop is the one best able to indicate the time for departure and arrival to avoid yellow fever and to provide a companion for the voyage, since there are several priests who are due to arrive this year.

The church at Saint Charles is finally being built, and our first house is being repaired to receive us a second time. You had designated Mother Lucile as superior, and she will only need with her persons who understand the other language, which is the more used. Although she is well qualified, it is agreed that she could not take on a heavier burden, I believe, especially that of the novitiate, for which Sister Regis could be assigned after her profession, which you have permitted, but her age has delayed until now. She is one of our best religious. She will receive our last large cross. We have no more for our two oldest aspirants and for a good Irishwoman without defects, about 40 years old [Mary Ann O'Connor]. She could assist, and if necessary replace, Mother Lucile at Saint Charles in any case. Therefore, three large crosses are urgently needed.

I will write to you by the post after the departure of the bishop, whom I am leaving alone just to write to you.

I am at your feet *in Corde Jesu* your daughter,

Philippine

---

255 Bishop Dubourg visited the religious houses of Saint Ferdinand, Saint Charles and Saint Louis for the last time before returning to Europe. On April 26, he arrived in Florissant; on the 30th, he baptized six Indian children (three girls from the Sacred Heart school and three boys from the Jesuit school) and gave Confirmation to fifty people.
256 Claudine Maujot, RSCJ, called Benoît.

[On the reverse:]
To Mother
Mother Barat Superior General
of the Religious of the Sacred Heart
Rue de Varenne
PARIS

Letter 268   **L. 18 to Mrs. de Rollin**

SS. C. J. et M.

May 2, 1826[257]

My very dear Friend,

Since the touching letter that you wrote to me telling me of the death of your husband, his good dispositions, and his generous remembrance of his childhood friend, of your friend for always, I have not heard anything directly from you. I know only that you left Paris, taking with you to Grenoble the remains of the one whom God took from you only for a time, and over whom I still see you shedding tears. I share the sadness because I know how sweet your union was, but it will be renewed forever. Let us not weep like those who are without hope; yours is too well established not to have its effect.

I will not give you details about my situation, which is still the same. Here we are with three establishments in these United States, and probably with a fourth one next year. That will make two in the South in the State of Louisiana, and two in the North in that of Missouri, at a distance of 300 leagues, but which can be covered by steamboat on the Mississippi in ten days to go up, and in five to descend when there are no setbacks from flooding or other obstacles.

Bishop Dubourg, our bishop, is with us now, and it is he who will carry this letter when he goes to Rome. He does for our houses much more than we could expect, but he himself is wanting for money. Please do not neglect to solicit the good will of charitable people for this mission. Everything is needed here: money, books, rosaries, crosses,

---

257 *Copies of letters of Philippine Duchesne to Mme de Rollin and a few others*, No. 17; *Cahier, Lettres à Mme de Rollin*, pp. 13-21. C-VII 2) c Duchesne to her family and lay people, Box 5. The extant copy bears the date 1824, but the situation of the houses described by Philippine is that of 1826.

pictures; everything has been of great use for us to begin and nourish devotion. A country in which all religions are permitted leaves few resources to the Catholics, whose liturgy requires ceremonies and a public solemnity that are costly to maintain. Our church is not finished, and another is being built on the other side of the Missouri, in a location very favorable for the Catholics on the other bank who do not yet have a permanent pastor, for lack of a church and financial means.

Do not forget me in your family and with my sisters, to whom I cannot write this time.

Believe in my tender affection that can only grow in the Heart of the good Master.

All yours,

Philippine Duchesne

Letter 269   L. 2 to Mother Deshayes

SS. C. J. M.

[May, 1826][258]

My very dear Mother,

Bishop Dubourg is going to France and is very willing to take our commissions. He leaves tomorrow, and I am robbing a few moments from sleep to write to my old and very dear mother. My heart has been waiting a long time for a chance to take this pleasure and seizes joyfully such a good opportunity.

I would have liked to write to all our mothers, especially to Mother [*] of Amiens, but the time is too short. The bishop is staying here and dined with us, so we had to converse with him after his long absence, which will be followed by another probably just as long. I beg you to fill in for me with my mothers and sisters and express to them my lively affection. Did Mother Girard receive my answer?

On Sunday the bishop baptized six Indians in our care or that of the fathers, and confirmed about 50 people of whom 22 were from our schools. It was a beautiful day. If there were alms to welcome other children with the fathers, they would revitalize the country in little time. Pray much for their work and for ours, and for the city of Sainte

---

258   Original autograph, C-VII 2) c Duchesne to RSCJ and Children, Box 4.

Genevieve, 30 leagues from here, where the inhabitants want to build us a house. I have to stop.

I am in the Divine Heart,

Philippine

[On the reverse:]
To Mother
Mother Deshayes
Religious of the Sacred Heart, rue de l'Oratoire
Amiens

Letter 270   L. 1 to Mother Ducis

SS. C. J. et M.

[1826][259]
Rec to St. Ant. of Padua

My very dear Mother,

Thank you for the registration forms that you sent me. I would not be able to fill them out completely for the two houses in Louisiana. I am going to write to Mothers Eugenie and Xavier so that each of them can send you her lists.

Would you kindly tell me whether it is necessary to send every year the list of the newly entered and of the vows or send a new list of the whole community?

I would very much like the boarding school rule with the latest changes; ours came from Amiens and still speaks of nankeen uniforms.[260]

I seem to have heard something about scheduling None, Vespers and Compline on Sunday, so that we say Sunday Vespers and None and Compline in private.

How I long also to have the questions that are going to be decided at the general council.

I am in the Sacred Heart, your devoted,

Philippine Duchesne

---

259 Original autograph, C-VII 2) c Duchesne to RSCJ and Children, Box 4. Postmark: Paris, Oct. 14, 1831.

260 From the foundation until 1822, the uniform of the boarders at the Sacred Heart in Amiens was made of nankeen (buff colored cotton). Each house of the Sacred Heart had a different uniform at that time. See *Album des uniformes*, F II, 2 d.

[On the reverse:]
To Mother
Mother Henriette Ducis
Convent of the Sacred Heart
Rue de Varenne
Paris

Letter 271 **L. 19 to Mrs. de Rollin**

SS. C. J. et M.

August 12 [1826][261]
Rec. to Saint Anthony

My very dear Cousin,

Have I been lacking in some duty of gratitude toward you; for since the letter in which you told me of your painful widowhood, I have heard no more news from you? What has reached me indirectly told me that you left Paris with the dear remains of your husband, and that a terrible accident has caused a considerable loss to two of your brothers. I shared in all these events, able to speak of them only to God; I have talked with him a great deal about you. I hope that he has not struck without later bringing relief; but if we do not understand his decrees in time, eternity will reveal them to us, and we will see that he has done everything to make us happy there.

Our three establishments in America keep going where faith is making progress; the creation of new dioceses and Catholic boarding schools will, I hope, extend it even further. We have more Protestants than Catholics in our little boarding school, and it is the same in several newly established convents.

Do not forget me with regard to all your family, who are very dear to me. Receive the expression of my deep affection *in Corde Jesu.*

Philippine

---

261 *Copies of letters of Philippine Duchesne to Mrs. de Rollin and a few others, No. 19; Cahier, Lettres à Mme de Rollin,* pp. 48-49. C-VII 2) c Duchesne to her family and lay people, Box 5. The extant copy bears the date of 1824, but the situation of the houses as described by Philippine is that of 1826.

I have answered all the letters and have not forgotten to mention the generous dispositions of Mr. de Rollin, with which we rejoice.

Letter 272　　　　**L. 74 to Mother Barat**

SS. C. J. M.

Florissant, June 15, 1826[262]

Dear Reverend Mother,

God seems to raise great obstacles against the instruction of the Indians. By buying their lands, the Government pushes them out of the Federation States. Closed into too small spaces and not having room to hunt, which is their only means of subsistence, these nations are herded together, make war, and destroy themselves without realizing it. This year they are no longer allowed to hunt in the State of Missouri, so the parents of several of our Indian children have come to take the boys away from the Jesuits and the girls from us, and we have no way to keep them here. All they say is that since they can no longer come to see their children, it is impossible to live so far away from them. I have been told that the Presbyterians, who are established near the Osage and are paid by their organization for the conversion of unbelievers, have not been able to retain any pure Indian child. They always escape, either because of their own inconstancy or that of their parents. Nevertheless, the fathers are not discouraged. They think that if establishments were made nearer to these banished nations, there would be hope of changing them or at least of gaining a few souls.

The church at Saint Charles is making progress; it has reached above the window level, and the masonry could be finished in a month. They have made an opening into the sanctuary for us, as we have here. They are waiting for us in that area with great eagerness, but unless we get some help, it will be difficult to come up with the necessary four religious, two for the French and two for the Americans, who will be more numerous and will need more attention.

262　Copy, USA Foundation Haute Louisiane, Box 1, *Lettres de la Haute Louisiane II 1823-1830*, pp. 244-246. Cf. J. de Charry, II, 2, L. 208, pp. 411-414; Hogg, pp. 274-276.

Mother Octavie is no better. Her body seems destined for suffering. After a strong bilious fever, vomiting continued for a long time. She has developed a squint and deafness. The blistering made her infirmities go away, but her legs are swollen, and now she is weak, with sweats and insomnia. She can only just do her class, and in doing that she renders a great service, because most of our students (who are 24) are new and with differing abilities. I could not do it all myself.

A week ago two streams flooded and carried away our fence and a bridge, destroyed our garden, etc. We have never seen the water rise so high. The children in the school had to sleep on the first floor (above the ground floor), since their classroom, where they ordinarily sleep, was flooded to a depth of three or four feet. We have had great anxiety about the school house that is made of wood, elevated on four posts, so that it has water not only under it but even inside; it could easily collapse. Our big house was dry but surrounded by water on all sides, as was the church. We were almost at the point of not being able to light a fire, for lack of wood, which the water made float around on every side.

I hope that you have already seen Bishop Dubourg. In Saint Louis they are expecting Bishop Flaget, bishop of Kentucky, and his coadjutor, Father David,[263] with Bishop Rosati, for the consecration of Father Portier, with whom we traveled when we came here and who has been named bishop of the Floridas and Alabama. We will see him.

The cost of postage, which we cannot avoid, holds me back from writing to our mothers; I am waiting for some opportunity to answer several letters. Meanwhile, please give my respects to Father Perreau, as well as Fathers Varin, Barat, and Roger. Their brothers have many trials, but they are always courageous. We have great need of their prayers and those of our sisters. I claim them with a large blessing from you.

Philippine Duchesne

Letter 273   L. 25 to Bishop Rosati

SS. C. J. et M.

[Saint Ferdinand, July 23, 1826][264]

---

263 Jean Baptiste David, PSS, arrived in America in 1792 with Benedict Joseph Flaget, whose coadjutor he became in Bardstown, Kentucky, in 1819.

264 Original autograph. C-VII 2) c Writings Duchesne to Rosati, Box 6. Postmark: St. Louis, Mo., Jul. 27. On the reverse: "July 23, 1826, Mother Duchesne, Florissant, received August 17."

Dear Bishop,

I received the letter with which you honored me and those enclosed. If you were pleased with our establishment at Saint Michael, all there speak of the happiness your visit brought them. Mother Eugenie fears that she did not express her gratitude sufficiently and asks me to do it for her. Her heart is filled with proofs of your paternal interest.

We have had a visit from Father De Neckere that moved me deeply. He is well liked in Saint Louis. Protestants flock to hear him speak, and it is difficult to find another to replace him when he is unable to speak.

The Jesuit fathers are in pretty good health, very busy with the church in Saint Charles, which is now fifteen feet above ground in sections. The expenses always exceed what was calculated, so it will be difficult to finish it. Father Verhaegen, who has settled there, has reaped much fruit in the section of the mission confided to his care, and he is generally loved by both Catholics and Protestants.

Our house has grown very little in personnel; we always have only two novices; but the boarding school has gone up to twenty-four students. These with the day pupils keep us very busy, especially since Mother Octavie has been ill for several months.

She sends you, as well as my other sisters, their profound respect, and we all ask for your fullest blessing.

I am with respectful veneration, your Excellency's devoted and humble servant.

Philippine Duchesne, sup.

Saint Ferdinand, July 23, 1826

[On the reverse:]
Right Rev. Joseph Rosati
Bishop of Tanagra
Barrens
Perry County

Letter 274   L. 3 to Mother Deshayes

SS. C. J. et M.

August 12, 1826
St. Ant.[265]

My very dear Mother,

I answered your letter, but I do not know if the expression of my sentiments reached you, which I want very much. I have not forgotten one of my first mothers, to whom I owe much restitution, and whose pain I feel more and more because of what I experience in my responsibility, which I am totally incapable of fulfilling. It is very shameful to be under qualified by talent and virtue, to feel that one prevents good instead of doing it, and to contribute nothing to the glory of God, who must be the only reason for our coming to this land so long desired. I count so much on your maternal affection that I hope you will pray much for me that I can make up for the past, and that if I do not have time to do this, God will cover up my infidelities with the blood that flowed from the Heart of Jesus. My life is moving on, and I need to be helped by the friends of Jesus in order to gain a favorable welcome.

You will hear news of our fathers, whose arrival here was marked by the protection of Saint Regis. They chose him as special protector of this mission, and I do not doubt that in the hidden and painful work like his, he will make them acquire great merit and will sustain their existence and their establishments by his prayers in heaven.

They are all united in a wooden house in our parish. The bishop has given them our church so that they will be freer, and all of northern Missouri, whose central point will be Saint Charles, our first home. They are building a stone church there, which is rising very slowly for lack of funds. If you could gather some alms to help this holy enterprise and the work with the Indians, it would be a good work. I do not doubt that Mother Prevost, who has shown us so much interest, will approve of your zeal and will help in many ways. I know that she has to expand the boarding school in order to accommodate the great number of your students, but I am convinced that there are enough of the treasures of the inexhaustible God for all.

---

265 Original autograph, C-VII 2) c Duchesne to RSCJ and Children, Box 4. Postmark: arrived October 14, 1826.

I think our dear Mother Barat will keep you up to date with our news, so I will say only a word. Mother Xavier [Murphy], your former novice, is fulfilling her office of superior perfectly at Opelousas and is loved by the 18 children who make up the boarding school and by her daughters as well, two of whom have been a burden: one, a novice, a *(torn word)* her departure; the other, an aspirant, who died suddenly.

Mother Eugenie is doing wonderfully in her new house at Saint Michael, on the river near New Orleans. Our coadjutor Bishop Rosati gave me perfect praise for that establishment, which he visited on his return from New Orleans. There are several very hopeful young vocations there; the children are very docile, and the sisters are very regular [in their spiritual exercises and work]. Our house here is doing a little better: from the 5 students to which we were reduced, we now have 22, born in different [Christian] communions, and for the most part true to who they are. All goes well for nearly all the children as long as they are here, but going out usually causes a terrible change.

Our greatest happiness is the proximity of the fathers who supply us with an abundance of resources: every Sunday, three excellent talks, perfect retreats every year, and very beautiful ceremonies for all the great feasts, when we sing the Mass and they do the Office with deacon, sub-deacon, etc.

Your voice is missed here. We are so poor that way that I help to sing Mass and Vespers with as much presumption as the fly that wanted to make the coach move.

Do not forget me with our fathers of Saint Acheul, with Mother Prevost, and Mother Girard. I do not know if I know the other sisters, but all are very dear to me, especially you to whom I am *in Corde Jesu*, a former daughter.

Philippine

[On the reverse:]
To Mother
Mother Deshayes
House of the Sacred Heart
Amiens
Dept. of the Somme
France

Letter 275   L. 26 to Bishop Rosati

SS. C. J. et M.

[18 August 1826][266]

Dear Bishop,

I answered the letter with which you honored me on your return from New Orleans and which filled me with consolation because of the proofs of your satisfaction with the house at Saint Michael. The superior [Eugenie Audé], who is still quite moved with the gratitude that your affection and benevolence have inspired, wishes me to express her thanks as well as I can. I confide my sentiments of gratitude to the divine Heart of Jesus, since it is impossible to convey, as I would like to, our feelings of appreciation to the best of pastors and fathers.

It is with great sorrow that we see Father De Neckere go away; he carries with him the esteem and regret of all Saint Louis.

Mother Octavie has been very ill again, but I hope she will recover quickly. The house has received no increase since my last letter. That of the Jesuit Fathers has grown by three brother postulants. The church in Saint Charles is not progressing; it seems that the contractor who undertook the church will not be able to continue; consequently our foundation there will be much delayed.

In the meantime, the Protestant schools are growing stronger and are spreading many books contrary to our holy religion. God, I hope, has indicated the moment when this evil will stop; and we do not feel that we have any possibility of remedying it, even if we were on the spot.

I am with respect your Excellency's submissive daughter and servant.
                                        Philippine Duchesne, sup.

Saint Ferdinand, August 18, 1826

> [On the reverse:]
> To his Excellency
> Bishop Rosati
> Bishop of Tanagra
> *Barrens*

266 Original autograph, C-VII 2) c Writings Duchesne to Rosati, Box 6. On the reverse: "August 28, 1826, Mother Duchesne, Florissant."

Letter 276   **L. 1 to Mother Prevost**

SS. C. J. et M.

Saint Ferdinand, State of Missouri, August 18, 1826[267]
St Ant.

My very dear Mother,

It has been a very long time since I have had one of your letters or taken the liberty to write to you, since there are few occasions for France now. The one from which I profit today was offered me by a Flemish priest, a man of great merit joined to great talents, hidden under the veil of humility, who is nearly removed from ministry because of his bad health; he will seek to recover in his native country. He has also asked us to help with his passage, which was very difficult for us.

A few days ago, a young lady who was leaving for Philadelphia also offered to take our letters to France by way of one of her family who was going. I took advantage of it to write to Mother Deshayes, and if she has not received the expression of my sentiments, please give them again, as well as to Mother Girard. I would not want to omit either one or the other, no more than my other sisters, your daughters, whether known to me or unknown.

I have not forgotten that you were dreaming of giving us some of them, and I expect from your zeal for this mission that you will press our mother to strengthen it with several good religious, who will make up for the mistakes I make and replace the old [sisters]. I will not be the last to pay tribute, and Mother Octavie is again close to leaving us; but at the moment that I despaired of her, the feast of the Assumption came, the day on which we had the consolation of seeing her in the chapel to receive Communion. I hope she will recover. Sister Catherine [Lamarre] becomes more infirm every day. You see that we have need of your help before God, as well as that of our fathers at Saint Acheul.

Their holy brothers, our neighbors, are always edifying and very courageous and always giving us their spiritual help with a holy generosity that fills us with gratitude to God.

Please excuse the hastiness with which I write. Give news of us to our mutual mother. The house offers nothing to tell her since my

---

267 Original autograph, C-VII 2) c Duchesne to RSCJ and Children, Box 4. Postmark: March 17, 1827.

last letter except the illness (raging fever) of Mother Octavie and her recovery.

Please have prayers offered for us to the divine Heart of Jesus, in which I am, dear Mother, all yours devotedly,

Philippine Duchesne

Bishop Dubourg, our venerable bishop, is now in Europe. We fear that he will not return, since here he had a very bitter cup to drink the whole time of his episcopate. He was the best of fathers for us, and we will suffer a great loss if he remains away permanently. You will know about his return and that of other priests who will make it known to our mother. Please take advantage of the opportunity to send us some rosaries and colored pictures.

[On the reverse:]
To Mother
Mother Prevost, superior
of the house of the Sacred Heart
Amiens
Department of the Somme
France

Letter 277   **L. 27 to Bishop Rosati**

SS. C. J. et M.

[October 3, 1826][268]

Dear Bishop,

I have received two letters from our superior in Opelousas [Xavier Murphy] telling me of her sorrow at the departure of Father Rosti.[269] With her and the inhabitants, from whom you must have received a letter, I too would have begged you to leave him in the position he holds to the satisfaction of all, with no slander touching him as it did his predecessors, if I had not thought that our reasons are not as weighty as yours

---

268   Original autograph, C-VII 2) c Writings Duchesne to Rosati, Box 6. On the reverse: "Oct. 3, 1826, Mother Duchesne, Florissant; received Oct. 19; answered the 20th."

269   Jean Rosti, C.M., was ordained priest by Bishop Dubourg, in 1821, and exercised pastoral ministry in Grand Coteau and in Missouri. He died at the Barrens in 1839.

and could not make you change your decision. If there were still time, I would join my prayers to theirs, asking you to leave with my sisters one who has their confidence and the approval of the whole parish.

The same superior tells me that an inhabitant wants to buy the part of the convent land that connects with the church property. I believe, however, that the deed of gift made by Bishop Dubourg requires the return of the entire property in the event that the establishment should fail, thus rendering all sale impossible.

There is much sickness in our house at Saint Michael. Our sisters have been so disabled that the children had to be given a vacation. This beginning would be unfortunate if we did not know that God wanted it so.

Father Niel, who was in Paris in June, convinced our mother general that a house of ours in Saint Louis would be very successful; and she writes me that she believes it necessary for us, telling me to foresee the means of making it succeed. Bishop Dubourg had often spoken to us of a school for this city, and on his last visit he intended to give us the land. It was found to have been sold; and Father Van Quickenborne, to whom I spoke about my letter, does not approve of the project. Our mother insists, however, and I foresee that our house here may not be large enough for the children who are applying. We can accommodate only thirty, and it is possible that we will reach that number in a few months. Many Americans want to send us their daughters to learn French. I would like to know your wishes in this matter; besides, there are many children in Saint Louis who are not able to pay board but who could be day pupils.

The church in Saint Charles is not progressing. The fathers have had many mishaps, which do not help the temporal situation, but they know how to profit from it for Heaven.

I had offered to be security for Father De Neckere for $100 as well as for the small sum of $25, which has been paid. Now I am told that it was Father Desmaillé's. I should like to know if this is so.

We hope to see you with Bishop Portier and to receive your blessing. Meanwhile, I beg you to send it to us and to believe me with profound respect, Bishop, your Excellency's submissive servant and daughter.

Philippine Duchesne, sup.

Saint Ferdinand, October 3, 1826

[On the reverse:]
To His Excellency
Bishop Rosati
Bishop of Tanagra
Barrens

Letter 278 **L. 75 to Mother Barat**

SS. C. J. M.

Saint Ferdinand, October 6, 1826[270]
Rec. to Saint Anthony
No. 72

Dear Reverend Mother,

I was waiting for your letter with great impatience. You had told me that the General Council would be held in June and July, and I had calculated that I could have heard the results with many details about the dear Society, all the representatives of which you had brought together. Your letter for the feast of Saint Regis [June 16] took three months to get here and told me of the delay of the Council. As regards the religious that you are preparing to send to us, I only want the ones you choose. Your choice will undoubtedly be the best. I add only about Sister Boisson that, if God gives her health, she would be very useful here, since we have so much sewing to do for the fathers' house. She could also teach our children needlework. But she would have to take either fifth or sixth class, because each of our houses needs a class mistress.

The same day that you told me about Father Niel and his project for Saint Louis, I received a letter from Father Anduze, who is at Natchitoches with Father Dusaussoy, where there is a house all ready for us in a wonderful location near the lake, in a region that is populated, wealthy and more French than English. In his first letter, he said that Father Dusaussoy was sure that you would not hesitate to accept right away. In this letter, he says that he is not happy there, *but that he never is*, which makes me think that the location is not as advantageous as

---

270 Original autograph, C-VII 2) c Duchesne to Barat, Box 2. Postmarks: St. Louis Mo. Oct. 9; from the colonies via Le Havre; Paris, November 27, 1826. Partial copy, USA Foundation Haute Louisiane, Box 1, *Lettres de la Haute Louisiane II 1823-1830*, pp. 248-249. Cf. J. de Charry, II, 2, Letter 213, pp. 432-438; Hogg, pp. 289-293.

Father Anduze says, and that is the opinion of Mother Eugenie. Besides, we would have to give him each year free board for two children, for an indefinite period, to help him pay for this property that he has acquired, at a very good price, however.

If one could be sure that he did not exercise too great a control over the house and that he did not visit too often, that establishment would offer more advantages than that of Saint Louis. I think that Father Niel was delirious when he talked of a property for 12 to 15 thousand F; such a sum would not be needed to make a foundation there. The land is too poor to be cultivated and enclosed and is a burden rather than an advantage because of taxes to be paid and the damage done by all the wandering herds. As for building, how can Father Niel help us when he has always had debts? He says that his fundraising has not gone well and that he cannot prevent the imminent sale of the little college that he had built along with the presbytery, for the payment of the debts of the church, because the creditors have obtained authorization from the State to do it.

I am not in favor of building anywhere; here it is never possible to pay off the debts. In spite of all your help, we still owe nearly 2000 F for this house. Happily it has been agreed that we will pay it off in boarding fees, and we have a boarder who is free for this reason. Mother Eugenie, with her subscription of 4500 F, is in debt for several thousand F. The house in Opelousas goes surely but slowly, and it would be the same in Saint Charles or Natchitoches. The little house at Saint Charles with a beautiful orchard and a large garden and woods only cost the reverend father 3500 F, which I told him we would pay back if we went there. But there is still the church; maybe there will be an agreement with the workers, and how can we go there without a priest? The father might well put one there now; I do not know why he does not want it.

Far from refusing Saint Louis, however, I want it very much, seeing so many children who could not be boarders but would be day students. The difficulty is that it is not according to our institute to receive money from day students, and it would probably be the only resource for survival in Saint Louis, in Saint Charles, and partially in Natchitoches. I would really like to know what your wish is with regard to payment for day students. The bishop thinks that the same parents who give us their children here would let them be only day students in Saint Louis and that they would always be there to criticize everything. The Americans want to see everything for themselves. The climate there is not as good as it is here. But I do not completely believe that. This is what I think: that sooner or later, Mr. Mullanphy, who owns half of Saint Louis, or his son who is very devout, could give us a house already built, on condition that we take some orphans. He had projected this for some others, and it could happen that others will have similar views. It could also happen that we will find a good deal from people who are forced to sell, and to find a house at a quarter of the price it would cost to build. Mother Eugenie will not give up the 6000 F; she needs it too much for several years, and the only resource will be what is brought from you by the little colony that is awaited with great impatience.

I have spoken about your project for Saint Louis with the reverend father, and he is not of that opinion. But without doing anything, I wrote about this to Bishop Rosati so that, if there is a favorable opportunity, we could seize it under ecclesiastical authority, and I think it would be better, if possible, to begin before the arrival of Father Niel. He is not at all good for religious. The bishop named him our extraordinary confessor, which he never stops repeating, but I have told the bishop about the general dislike of him and he has left us free to choose. This would be the same problem at Natchitoches. Father Dusaussoy would be better for the house, and we would fear to be at odds with the parish priest if we set him aside.

We have great need of religious to advance Catholic instruction. Mother Octavie goes continually from one illness to another, though at this moment, she has a class with eleven students. One novice is very ill, and another is about to leave because of the caprice of her parents, while two or three postulants have been rebuffed before entering.

I would like very much to have the examples of the acts of profession and death; also permission to suppress the school reports that give offence for a single *bad note*.[271] The children are idols who must be adored and glorified by their parents.

Thirdly, would you allow us to admit the postulants to first table, while keeping them away from time to time so that we can be free? This is because of our small numbers and the lack of enclosure from which we could profit. The reverend father also thinks that it would discourage them a great deal from coming [to be absent from community meals].

Please tell me exactly what you want with regard to the principal articles of my letter: 1) what to do regarding Saint Louis; 2) the response to give to Father Anduze, pastor of Natchitoches, near New Orleans; 3) if in the new establishments we can accept money from day students; 4) if we can suppress the school reports; 5) what is the formula for the

---

271 The parents object to the evaluation of "Poor" in a school report, so Philippine thinks it better to omit the reports.

act of entrance of a postulant, her first vows, profession, and death; 6) when we must say None on Sunday.

We have here a newspaper from Paris that says Bishop Dubourg has resigned. This will be a great loss for this ungrateful diocese that has made him suffer so much.

Mother Octavie has recovered, but she has a kind of growth near her neck. Mother Lucile is weak. Mother Regis has been less well for several months. I hope that will change; she has been sorely tested. I hope that God permitted it to give her experience. She will need it, as she has all the confidence of the children, especially the Americans who love only those of their own nation.

My regards to our good fathers, to our mothers, and please bless us and treat me as your poorest servant.

Philippine

[On the reverse:]
To Mother
Mother Barat, Superior General
of the Houses of the Sacred Heart
Rue de Varenne
PARIS, FRANCE
By way of New York

Letter 279   **L. 28 to Bishop Rosati**

SS. C. J. et M.

[November 3, 1826][272]

Dear Bishop,

We are impatiently awaiting the happy moment of your arrival with Bishop Portier. We are hoping too that Father Dahmen, who has long promised us a visit, will take advantage of so holy an opportunity to come to Saint Louis. I have asked one of our good Catholics if he could give hospitality to some members of your suite. He has accepted with great pleasure. We are afraid that after the visit you promised us we

---

272 Original autograph, C-VII 2) c Writings Duchesne to Rosati, Box 6. On the reverse: "Nov. 3, 1826, Mother Duchesne, Florissant."

shall not be able to find room for those who will be with you, having only our little sacristies, where I hope you and Bishop Portier will stay. We have all the necessary room for meals, and I hope you will honor our house with the presence of our fervent missionaries.

I am with profound veneration your Excellency's submissive and unworthy daughter.

Philippine Duchesne

November 3, 1826

Letter 280   L. 29 to Bishop Rosati

SS. C. J. et M.

[November 11, 1826][273]

Dear Bishop,

We have just received news that I am unable to keep from the best of fathers, knowing the joy he takes in all the joys of his family; it is the approbation of our Society by the Holy See. Our superior general promises to send me a copy of the Brief from his Holiness. Bishop Dubourg was expected the next day in Paris; in Bordeaux they found him much changed and very sad.

Our mother repeats the expression of her desires on the subject of a house in Saint Louis. And Father Niel, who also writes, wants an affirmative answer. It would seem that he is ready to ask religious of other orders to fulfill the proposed mission if we should refuse.

Mother Eugenie, who is ill at the moment, saw Father De Neckere at Saint Michael; his vessel was aground for three weeks on a sand bank.

Rachel,[274] our Negress, says she spoke to you, and she knows now that she does not belong to us. I think this is a story she has made up out of her own head. We bought her from Bishop Dubourg and paid

---

273   Original autograph, C-VII 2) c Writings Duchesne to Rosati, Box 6. On the reverse: "Nov. 11, 1826, Mother Duchesne, Florissant."

274   Rachel was an enslaved Negro woman, acquired from Bishop Dubourg, who worked at Florissant and City House during the 1820s. The information about ownership here and in the following letter is contradictory, unless "bought" and "paid for" here refers to a lease. In January 1829 she is better (Letter 331), but in May of the same year she was sold (JSA).

for her. He asked for her back from Father Saulnier;[275] he wished to sell her to his nephew if we had not kept her. I thought Bishop Dubourg had told you so himself.

I am with profound veneration your Excellency's submissive and devoted daughter.

Philippine Duchesne, sup.

November 11, 1826

Letter 281   **L. 76 to Mother Barat**

SS. C. J. et M.

November 25, 1826[276]
Rec. to St Anthony of Padua
No. 73

My venerable Mother,

Your letter of September 2, 1826, has given us the purest joy that I can have here below, after the experience of union with Jesus Christ in the Blessed Sacrament. We had a foretaste of the beautiful day of our approbation when Pope Pius VII favored us with his personal blessing through the mediation of three of his cardinals, and also when the present Holy Father sent us his blessing through the kindness of one of our missionaries [Father Borgna]. But what a happy event is this blessing that we almost despaired of obtaining! How it commits us to perfection! And how it makes me blush when I see what I am, after so many graces showered on us that have not made me less unworthy of the blessed body to which I have the happiness of belonging! I will never forget the one who admitted me, good Father Varin who determined our union, all the fathers and all the mothers who have striven to make it firm by showing us the way that leads to the Heart of Jesus.

---

275   Edmond Saulnier, born in France, was ordained a priest by Bishop Dubourg in 1822. He taught in the college in Saint Louis and was pastor of several parishes in the area before being named chancellor of the diocese in 1850. He died in 1864. In 1827, Philippine complained to Bishop Rosati at seeing Father Saulnier interfere in the affairs of the community.

276   Original autograph, C-VII 2) c Duchesne to Barat, Box 2. Cf. J. de Charry, II, L. 215, pp. 441-446; Hogg, pp.295-301.

All my sisters have shared the communal joy of the Society, but the father superior has especially shown us a personal interest on this occasion. He has repeated several times that no news would make him happier. He wanted to announce it himself to our sisters and then to the children. The next day, Sunday, he celebrated a sung Mass of thanksgiving with deacon and sub-deacon. He had each of his priests say three Masses for the same intention, and the brothers, three rosaries. He would have allowed as many Communions as we wanted. This is how on great occasions the interests of the glory of God are shown by the saints. Since that about which I spoke to you, there have been no more reproaches; but he does not favor the establishment in Saint Louis, saying that first we must train superiors. I answered him that shut in in such a little town, we are practically unknown and that far from finding superiors, we are only able to accept mediocre candidates and not often.

Strengthened by your authority and that of Bishop Rosati, episcopal administrator of this diocese, I was preparing the way while waiting anxiously for the arrival of some sisters, who will need a little rest and time to get used to the customs of this country. I think we cannot wait for Father Niel if we can get a house before that. We could take advantage of the public sales that are held often or those of people who leave the country, for to build is to get mired in debts from which one cannot escape. Mother Eugenie, with a subscription of 50,000 F for the building, of which 40,000 are already paid, is very constrained, since her house went up to 60,000 F, plus furniture, etc. We will get nothing from the residents of Saint Louis, nor will Father Niel, who will have enough trouble keeping himself afloat.

In that blessed letter in which you told me of the good news from the Holy See, I found the letter of Mrs. de Rollin with its news of a gift of 1000 F. I will use it as you wish, with the strong hope that God will grant success to the new establishment. The church building at Saint Charles has been halted, so that frees us for the moment on that side.[277] Nevertheless, that place will bring the advantage of gaining members. Many families come there from the Eastern States and from Ireland and Germany, attracted by the excellent farmland, and they settle along the Missouri and the rivers that flow into it. Saint Charles will offer the only Catholic school where there are none yet. Those scattered families keep innocent ways better than those in the towns; and when they take to

---

277 The return to Saint Charles happened in October 1828, when the construction of the church was finished.

religion, they do so solidly. The Creoles, otherwise good people, are very changeable and idolized by their parents.

Father Niel is asking me for an answer. Please read it and send it to him, though I do not know where he is. I am going to write to my dear cousin to thank her. I think she is in Grenoble, from where I have heard nothing more. I wrote twice to Bordeaux to Bishop Dubourg, especially to tell him of our very real regrets. Perhaps I will be obliged to ask him for a receipt for the black woman whom he sold us and for whom I must pay the rest of the price to the reverend father, which has been done. She is not so good anymore, and says that she does not belong to us and will not stay. If you see him, please speak to him about this, because the reverend father has his power of attorney for something else but says he can do nothing about this.[278]

Another great hindrance is that at Saint Louis, we will have almost only day students. Can we have them pay? How else can we keep going?

The consecration of a new bishop [Bishop Michel Portier] happened in Saint Louis on the Sunday in the octave of All Saints. He has a strange title and will be appointed vicar apostolic of the State of Alabama, in the south, a state with high population that borders on Florida, for which he also has the responsibility and where there are only three priests in all.

We are much happier here because of the establishment of our fathers and of the Lazarists, who have no less interest in us. One of them told me recently, as he offered us two boarders and a postulant, that never a day goes by that he does not pray for the houses of the Sacred Heart. The bishop just consecrated and the bishop who consecrated him came to our house and to that of the fathers. The news of Bishop Dubourg's resignation, which his coadjutor learned the previous day by a Brief appointing him administrator of the diocese, made him very sad and thoughtful.[279] Someone told me today that they had written to Rome that the father superior here is the only one who could take charge of the part of the diocese that will be taken from Bishop Rosati.[280] Father Fenwick is already in charge in Boston and Bishop Dubois, a Sulpician, in New York, where there are more than thirty thousand Catholics.[281]

---

278   Philippine needs to obtain from Bishop Dubourg the right kind of receipt, without which Rachel could contest the sale and claim her liberty.
279   Bishop Rosati became apostolic administrator of both dioceses. The Brief of March 20, 1827, named him bishop of Saint Louis and kept him as administrator of New Orleans.
280   Alabama and the Floridas, of which Bishop Portier became apostolic vicar.
281   Benedict Fenwick, SJ (1782-1847), uncle of the Hamilton sisters, was from Maryland. As rector of Georgetown College, he negotiated with Bishop Dubourg in 1823 the transfer of the Jesuit novitiate from White Marsh to Florissant. In 1824, he succeeded Bishop de Cheverus in Boston. Jean Dubois, PSS (1764-1842), was born in Paris, ordained a priest in

Mother Octavie's health is restored. All the others go on as usual, especially I who am no better.

I send my regards to Fathers Perreau, Varin and Barat who keep a rigorous silence. I no longer have a reason to motivate them to break it.

I am with deep devotion in the Sacred Heart, dear Mother, your bad daughter.

Philippine Duchesne

I beg Mother Bigeu to write to us at length and I send her my regards.

[On the reverse:]
To Mother
Mother Barat Superior General
of the houses of the Sacred Heart,
Rue de Varenne
Paris
France
By way of New York

Letter 282   L. to Mr. Leduc[282]

SS. C. J. et M.

[Saint Ferdinand, December 11, 1826][283]

Sir,

I have no doubt at all of the kindness with which you are willing to advise us in finding a house in Saint Louis. I know that it is not easy, because I believe that it would be more harmful than useful to have one that does not suit us, either because of distance or the small size of the property.

1787, arrived in the United States in 1791, became a Sulpician in 1809, and exercised his ministry in Maryland and Pennsylvania. He was consecrated bishop of New York in 1826 and remained there until his death.

282 Original autograph, C-VII 2) c Duchesne to her family and lay people, Box 5. Philippe Marie Leduc was a notary and judge in Saint Louis, and had been an official translator for the last Spanish governor of Upper Louisiana.

283 Original autograph, C-VII 2) c Duchesne to her family and lay people, Box 5.

At first, I strongly resisted Father Niel's opinion that we should buy a property and build. He suggested procuring land indirectly from Mr. Lucas (because apparently he believes him unwilling to aid in our establishment). I was very much afraid to plunge us into debt. But I am told that building in St. Louis is very quick and not costly; that while obtaining delays, it would not be imprudent to undertake this; that Mr. Mullanphy knows better than anyone and that he would tell us exactly how much it would cost to build a house on a suitable property.

Before deciding anything, I thought about writing to him; maybe among all his houses he would have something less expensive to let us have. I ask you to tell the bearer of the letter, Mr. Lepère, if that would be your advice; if so he will take my letter to him [Mr. Mullanphy].

I have nothing to recommend myself to you except the purity of my intentions and the desire to serve the cause of religion; you are too devoted to the same cause for me to be shy with you. That is why I have come to ask your help again. Begging you to accept my deepest respect, Sir, I am your humble servant,

Philippine Duchesne, sup.

Saint Ferdinand, 11 December 1826

[On the reverse:]
To Mister
Mr. Leduc
in Saint Louis

Letter 283   L. 30 to Bishop Rosati

SS. C. J. et M.[284]

[December 30, 1826]

Dear Bishop,

Your whole family at Saint Ferdinand offers you its wishes for a holy New Year. She who has the privilege of writing in the name of all feels more than any other the esteem for her first pastor who is always

---

[284] Original autograph, C-VII 2) c Writings Duchesne to Rosati, Box 6. On the reverse: "Dec. 30, 1826, Mother Duchesne, Florissant; received February 22; answered March 2."

busy about her before God, thanking him for his gift and begging him to keep this father with us.

I had the pleasure of a letter from Father De Neckere on December 1, which enlightened me concerning what I had the privilege of asking you. He seemed distressed at having waited for you in vain in New Orleans. As for me, I am relieved that your health was not endangered by this bad weather.

Bishop Portier arrived with his relative.

There have been no more details about our approbation. Four of our religious ought to have left there, however, destined for our three houses. They will be full of the stories that are so interesting to us.

The brother of the postulant whom you promised us came to see about conditions here on his way to the mines. His sister's journey has been postponed until spring.

I have heard nothing of the young women of whom Father Odin spoke. As compensation we must ask God to make us worthy daughters of the Church, which has given us recognition through his vicar.

I am with veneration and respect your Excellency's submissive and devoted daughter.

Philippine Duchesne, sup.

December 30, 1826

[Philippine continues on a second sheet:]

Dear Bishop,

I have already taken some steps toward the foundation in Saint Louis, which will be extremely difficult in view of the lack of interest in the city for such works and our own lack of funds, as we are never able to put anything aside. I do not doubt, however, that it will succeed one day.

What troubles me greatly and for which I need your decision is concerning some difficulties in connection with the vow of poverty, which I made while keeping some property; I obtained permission from my superiors to dispose of what remained to me and to make the vow of poverty as earlier, no longer having the freedom to receive, to possess or to make a will. I did not have this obligation in mind when Bishop Dubourg, without informing me beforehand, gave me the land where our house is and told me to make a will in favor of two of our nuns. I explained the situation to him, and he gave me the necessary dispensations. Now I shall have to do the same thing for new foundations. Our mother general, not wishing to lift my burden, desires rather that I be charged in some way with all the houses of the Society in this country. Would you please, I beg you, indicate what I must do in conscience while safeguarding the property of our houses.

I ask you to excuse my bad handwriting because of the extreme cold and the disorderly letter. You are a father; this gives me confidence.

[On the reverse:]
To His Excellency
Bishop Rosati
Bishop of Tanagra
Barrens
By way of Sainte Geneviève

Letter 284   **L. 20 to Mrs. de Rollin**

SS. C. J. et M.

January 1, 1827[285]

It has been some time, dear and beloved Cousin, since I received your letter of August 30, in which you tell me of a new gift of 1000 F, which fills me with gratitude. I do not know how to express it to you; I can only ask the Heart of Jesus, so good and generous, to give back to you a hundredfold what you do for us. Everything already shows us your benefaction: our chapel is decorated, and when we are there, we cannot forget you or your husband, or my aunt or everyone who belongs to you.

I learned from my brother about the terrible accident that happened to Vizille.[286] Please tell Augustin [Perier] and my cousin how I sympathize with them, but still more in the loss of their beloved daughter.[287] Mrs. Teisseire and her husband also have many claims on my gratitude, and

---

285   *Copies of letters of Philippine Duchesne to Mme de Rollin and a few others, N° 22; Cahier, Lettres à Mme de Rollin*, pp. 51-54. C-VII 2) c Duchesne to her family and lay people, Box 5. The copy of this letter bears the date 1824, but the situation of the houses as described by Philippine is that of 1826 or 1827.

286   In 1825, a fire destroyed a major part of the castle of Vizille (furniture, decoration, the eighteenth century wooden structure, and the tapestries). Augustin reconstructed the whole building according to the original.

287   Their daughter Fanny, born in 1800, married Count Charles de Résumat. She died in 1826.

the loss of Marie is also shared, as it must be.[288] One of my companions who knew her at Sainte-Marie speaks of her as a model of perfection.

When you see Father Rambaud, give him my respectful greetings and tell him that I will never forget all the hardships he endured for me, and that those he continues to have with so much kindness stir up still more gratitude in me.

If death has not removed Fathers de Jonc, Luc, Bernard and de La Grée, please commend me to their prayers, as well as our converts who are so exposed to apostasy in this land, for change of religion is done as easily as a change of clothing. The work with the Indians is uncertain in outcome. To carry it on demands the miracle of miracles, to change their nature that is completely corrupt from their earliest years. One needs to be in their midst. So far no women have dared to go there! And the priests, far from finding even the poorest level of existence there, are obliged to give them help because every year many perish from misery or as a result of drunkenness. The American nation has had a policy of buying their lands that are located in the States in order to assure public peace, on condition that they move into more distant territory. This is the last year that the Indians have been able to hunt and even to cross the State of Missouri. Having been gathered into restricted areas, they no longer have sufficient land for hunting, and this makes them most miserable. Some have done what they could to take care of their children, but they give them up for a short time and then take them back. The children are worse then than before, because when they take up again a life of licentiousness, they are acting with more awareness.

Some Presbyterians, paid by a society in New York, have been established among the Osage, but they complained mightily about the conditions. They were not able to keep the Indian children. They have only half-breeds, neither white nor Indian. It is rumored that they will give up their mission. Some Lazarist priests, who journeyed along the Arkansas River that is more than 500 leagues long and flows near the borders of Missouri, were begged by the inhabitants of the region that is being settled to come among them, since they were disgusted with the Methodist ministers who swarm around these regions from all sides, never offering anything but the Bible. But there is no way to support the Catholic missionaries, while those of the abominable sects that even deny the divinity of Jesus Christ are sustained either by the government or by different societies. Here is a reason for great zeal on our part.

---

288 Marie-Josephine Teisseire, born November 19, 1804, in Grenoble, married Baron Chretien Louis de Hell December 2, 1823, and died January 1, 1827.

Please excuse my illegible writing, but we are having such severe cold now that the ink freezes at the end of the quill, beside the fire.

Since you always take an interest in our Society, I will tell you that our two houses in the State of Louisiana, one at one day's journey and the other at four or five from New Orleans, are doing well. Especially the last one, begun a year ago, already has more novices and boarders than we do, of whom several are excellent and from very good Creole families. We have less success with the Americans, with whom education is organized by quarters: 3 months to learn French, 3 months for music, 3 for art, etc. After that, education is supposed to be finished. Recently four children left us, each having been here for 3 months. The Protestant parents fear too that they will become Catholics, as they all want to do. The parents say that they are free, but there is always some reason why they are not.

Goodbye, dear Friend, let us remain so in time and hope that our union will be still stronger in eternity *in Corde Jesu,*

Philippine

Letter 285 **L. 77 to Mother Barat**

SS. C. J. et M.

March 1, 1827
Rec. to St Anthony of Padua[289]
No. 76

Dear Reverend Mother,

I have not written to you since December 25, 1826,[290] when I sent you the six month statement, crossing the wide ocean in spirit so as to find myself at your feet with my dear sisters, offering you with them all our New Year's wishes. It would be hard to wish you a happier year than the last one, which gave us what we wanted most on earth [the approbation of the Constitutions]. I have received Mother Bigeu's interesting

---

289 Original autograph, C-VII 2) c Duchesne to Barat, Box 2. Postmark: Paris, May 5, 1827. Copies: USA Foundation Haute Louisiane, Box 1, *Lettres de la Haute Louisiane II 1823-1830,* pp. 60-63; C-III 1: USA Foundation Haute Louisiane, Box 3, *Lettres de la Louisiane I,* p. 292. Cf. J. de Charry, II, 3, L. 217, pp. 1-5; Sweetman et al, pp. 1-6.
290 We do not have this letter.

account and am thanking her on the note that I enclose here.[291] The little word that you wrote at the bottom [of a letter of November 5, 1826] suggests some doubt about the near departure of our sisters who are awaited every day in New Orleans.[292] With this hope, I advanced the business of our house in Saint Louis, seeing many difficulties if we wait for Father Niel [pastor in Saint Louis], of whom many are saying that he will not return [from France] and has not succeeded in raising the money he went there to seek.

At least 30,000 F given in advance would be needed to have a town house like ours here, and I realize that I could count neither on Father Niel nor on the sum advanced to Mother Eugenie that she says could not make a return for several years, nor even on what you told me about in a previous letter (6000 F),[293] since in your last letter, you mention only the 1000 F from Mrs de Rollin. So I wrote to Mr. Mullanphy, asking him if among the great number of houses that he has, he would be willing to let us have one under favorable conditions, given our intention to have a free school for the poor.

He answered me by asking how many orphans we would take under the following conditions:

1. that he would give us a brick house built seven years ago, situated a quarter of an hour from the Catholic church, with 24 arpents of land around it, uncultivated except for the garden. The house has 12 rather large rooms, and is overall smaller than ours here.
2. that he would give, either he or his heirs, to each orphan upon entrance the sum of 50 F for bed, etc.; and in addition, 25 F each year for clothing.[294]
3. that he would give 5000 F in cash for the first expenses.

I answered that I would accept on these conditions 15 to 20 orphans. He wanted 20, presented by him or by his older daughters.

I have been to see this house, whose location is less attractive and poorer than that of Sainte-Marie d'En-Haut but somewhat similar: on a height, isolated, in healthy air, overlooking the Mississippi and with a view of the town on one side. It seems to me that we would be going

---

291 The note has been lost.
292 Their arrival was expected on August 6, 1826.
293 These 6000 F correspond to the sum advanced by Mother Barat to E. Audé.
294 This reference to the amounts in francs allows a calculation of the exchange rate into American dollars at this period: 5 F to the dollar. The contract with Mr. Mullanphy specifies $10 at entry and $5 annually for maintenance.

against our interests to refuse this offer. It is true that we are taking a great responsibility and have a relationship of dependence; but the alternative is 20 or 30 thousand pounds of debt, or our confinement in a village where we are surrounded by 6 feet of water up to our door five or six times a year, and that suddenly, so that it washes away the bridge that leads to us, tears down all our fences, and destroys all our garden that has yielded nothing for two years because everything was ruined by the water. In addition, there is the very real possibility that if we do not take the initiative, others will forestall us and crush us by depriving us of the means of subsistence. Are these not considerations that deserve to be weighed?

The advisors whom you gave me have been of the opinion to accept.[295] The reverend father, at first opposed, later came round to the idea, nevertheless without applauding it. Perhaps he would have preferred Saint Charles, but the church is not finished and he does not want to place a priest there permanently; and no other will go, since it is an area assigned [by Bishop Dubourg] to their personal mission. He even said that I was going against every divine and human law in burdening the Society without your opinion given on the conditions spelled out [by Mr. Mullanphy]. Without responding to that, I told him that you had always regretted our being in the country, that you found an establishment in Saint Louis really necessary, and that you told me to prepare for it and to make one there before any other. The other father [Theodore de Theux],[296] the one who comes for confession four times a year, was completely in favor of the foundation. I accepted and everything is beginning before the deed of gift has been signed. Mr. Mullanphy, very experienced in the matter of repairs, will have these done at his expense, because it was necessary to add a kitchen and a room for a man [employed in the service of the convent], to repair the ceilings, etc. Everything will be ready by Easter and we will be able to begin the establishment if the desired help comes. It was not possible to wait for your response; several buyers were ready to take the house, and how could I even set a time for your response with the maritime dangers and delays?

---

295 The Jesuit priests in Florissant.
296 Theodore de Theux, SJ, born in Belgium in 1789, was ordained priest in 1812, and was professor at the seminary in Liège. He came to America in 1816, entered the Jesuits in Maryland and came to Missouri in 1825. In 1836, he was superior of the Jesuit mission in Missouri, but later returned to teaching. He died in Saint Charles in 1846.

I regret that you are not sending a good superior; I had hoped that Mrs. Baker[297] from New York, who is known favorably here, would have done marvels in Saint Louis, where people would have appreciated an American for language and character, since this nation more than any other holds itself in high esteem. If I am deceived in my hopes at this time, the youth of our sisters gives grounds for expecting that, more than we, they will learn the language and the customs of the country. In the meantime, I think that I should go to Saint Louis at the beginning. The place would be dangerous for some: we should not be too amiable; that would mean risking great dangers in our relations with outside, and many people have a quite high level of education. Mother Lucile [Mathevon] would not be able to do it. It is often said of her: not much ability, but a good person. I think Mother Octavie, who still sees more of the children's parents than I do and whom they love, could continue her office without taking on any new title before we hear from you. Being less free, she may also be more prudent. She is reliable, educated, and zealous. It is tact or prudence that is lacking. I have great confidence that under the protection of Saint Joseph and Saint Regis, the two works will succeed here and in Saint Louis. One will be the support of the other, one for temporal matters, the other for the spiritual. They will come here to make retreat, to recover health, etc. One can come and go in one day.

An Irish postulant has arrived, about whom we will need to inquire from the Abbot of La Trappe.[298] She spent six months at Bellefontaine, where she saw the father prior, and two years in England. She left for health reasons.

I would be very glad to have understood your intentions and to have that assurance. In a country with no resources for young people, must we draw back because of the orphans? We have a separate building to house them, but we are connecting ourselves to the most powerful family in the region. Mr. Mullanphy still intends to build two rooms reserved for his granddaughters, as boarders in the school or as lady residents.[299] If we keep the boarding school here, the one in Saint Louis will grow slowly, and the house will need to be enlarged. So the promised money will be quite necessary. We will have many day students and, if you approve, we could take the money from the rich

---

297 An American lady who had begun her novitiate in Paris.
298 Dom Augustin de Lestrange. The postulant is probably Eleonore Gray. The Abbey of La Trappe de Bellefontaine is situated in the department of Maine-et-Loire, near Angers.
299 Lady pensioners, as was the custom to receive in convents. But the General Council of 1826-1827 prohibited this practice in houses of the Sacred Heart.

to sustain the orphans and their teachers. Their work will be very little at the beginning.

I am with profound respect *in Corde Jesu* your devoted and very unworthy daughter.

Philippine

[On the reverse:]
To Mother
Mother Barat, Superior General
of the Religious of the Sacred Heart
Rue de Varenne
PARIS

Letter 286   **L. 31 to Bishop Rosati**

SS. C. J. et M.

[March 8, 1827][300]

Dear Bishop,

I had the honor of writing to you two months ago about our establishment in St. Louis. Having had no response, I wonder if my letter reached you. In the meantime the project is moving forward, as I am relying on the answer you had given me earlier *that you would see it with pleasure* and on the explicit wish of our superior general.

Mr. Mullanphy is giving us a house and fourteen acres of land situated about fifteen minutes' distance from the church. We are to maintain twenty orphans to whom he is giving $10 upon entrance and $5 per year for their upkeep. He will present the children and his oldest daughters after him. We have agreed to these conditions, and the matter was closed, but Father Van Quickenborne seemed to disapprove. If he were more experienced in business matters, I would consider this an obstacle; but his hesitant character leaves me no doubt that this is a shadow that will disappear, all the more since he has signed as a witness, which seems extraordinary. If I had been able to get in touch with you, I would have given you all the details moment by moment;

---

300   Original autograph, C-VII 2) c Writings Duchesne to Rosati, Box 6. On the reverse: "March 8, 1827, Mother Duchesne, Florissant; received 22nd; answered 23rd."

but the distance that separates me from my superiors is my greatest cross, and it must be borne.

Now that the preparations have begun at Mr. Mullanphy's expense, the whole city knows about it and proofs of satisfaction reach us from all sides. It seems to me that it would be really lacking in trust in these promises if this charitable work were even delayed.

Be so kind, your Excellency, as to send me your full consent immediately to relieve me of my anxiety and to comfort me by repeating your approval.[301] We have promised to begin work on the first of May. Until the registration, Mr. Mullanphy wants to act on the conditions agreed upon between us.

I have learned with sorrow that our Sister Xavier Hamilton is very weak. I asked that she come back here if she can stand the trip. The air agrees with her here, for she was perfectly well here. I would like to save her at any cost.

I am with respectful veneration your Excellency's submissive and obedient daughter.

Philippine Duchesne, sup.

Saint-Ferdinand, March 8, 1827

[On the reverse:]
To Bishop
Bishop Rosati, Bishop of Tanagra
Entrusted to the care of
Father Jeanjean
New Orleans

Letter 287 L. 32 to Bishop Rosati

SS. C. J. et M.

[May 10, 1827][302]

Dear Bishop,

---

301 On March 24, 1827, Bishop Rosati sent her his full consent, accompanied by an official approbation. *Lettres de Mgr. Rosati, manuscrits*, 1815-1840, C-VII 2) c, Writings, Box 6.

302 Original autograph, C-VII 2) c Writings Duchesne to Rosati, Box 6. On the reverse: "May 10, 18270, Mother Duchesne, St. Louis; received June 25th; answered 30th."

I would not be able to thank you enough for your kindness in answering me, giving me such peace by your approval of the foundation with which I am involved, to everyone's satisfaction.

Here I am in Saint Louis with only one companion and three orphans. I asked that the rest wait until the plastering is finished.

I had believed that since there are two priests in Saint Louis one of them would say Sunday Mass for us, but Father Saulnier told me that he was already saying two Masses and that Father Lutz[303] was going to a mission. However he promised to say Mass for us every fortnight before leaving for Vuidepoche.

In the meantime Father Richard is asking to be our chaplain, having heard that there is to be a house in Saint Louis; he wants only lodging and meals, a convenience for a new house that has so many expenses. Besides Father Richard is a member of a community and therefore very suitable for our houses. There remain only your consent and some way of not inconveniencing the Ursulines who however have never liked Father Richard as we do.

I shall speak with no one while awaiting your decision; besides, as we are so few, I am troubled at having a priest come just for us.

There is hope that you will visit us *(...)*[304] but if not, please be good enough to give me your decision regarding a chaplain and tell me whether Father Richard would be free.

The postulant you had the kindness to send us is at Florissant and we are very satisfied with her.

I am with respect your Excellency's submissive daughter.

Philippine Duchesne, sup.

Saint Louis, May 10, 1827

> [On the reverse:]
> To Bishop
> Bishop Rosati
> Bishop of Tanagra
> Sainte Geneviève

---

303 Joseph Antoine Lutz, born in Germany in 1801, came to Saint Louis as a diocesan priest in 1827. He was then Father Saulnier's vicar. Later he was a missionary in what is now eastern Kansas and contributed to the increase in number of Catholics in Saint Louis.

304 Words torn out in opening the letter.

Letter 288 **L. 78 to Mother Barat**

Saint Louis, May 13, 1827[305]
Rec. to St. Anthony
No. 77

Dear Reverend Mother,

The date of my letter will tell you that we are at last in the place that you consider most suitable for our houses. Since you told me what you wanted after Father Niel's visit, I began to cast my nets, to sound out the terrain, and to engage the interest of certain persons. I found nothing but opposition, coldness and indifference on every side. Finally, I appealed directly to Mr. Mullanphy, asking him if among his many houses he could give us one at a low price for a good work. He soon offered me one in a pleasant situation, a little apart from the roads, a quarter hour from the church, nearly new, made of brick, in the middle of 24 *arpents* of land. He offered it to us free, on condition of keeping 20 orphan girls for whom he or his heirs would provide the maintenance. Besides that, he would give 5000 F for the initial costs of the establishment. I wrote to you that the father superior did not like it, and even after he had signed the agreement with us, he wanted a delay in order to legalize it by the consent of the bishop, who was then in New Orleans. Fortunately, a steamboat departed that brought my request in a few days, and it brought back his answer. Besides his letter, he sent a certificate of approval that I attach here:

> Joseph Rosati, by divine mercy and the authority of the apostolic Holy See Bishop of Tanagra and administrator of the diocese of Saint Louis and that of New Orleans,
>
> To Mother Philippine Duchesne, superior of the Religious of the Sacred Heart of Jesus, greetings and blessings in Our Lord Jesus Christ.
>
> Having been informed that Mr. Mullanphy of Florissant, full of zeal for the spread of our holy religion, and believing that the best way to do this is by the instruction of youth, has made a gift and complete cession of a house and portion of land in the city of Saint Louis, State of Missouri, with the conditions specified in the deed of donation, we give our full and

---

305 Original autograph, C-VII 2) c Duchesne to Barat, Box 2. Postmark: Paris, June 22, 1827. Copies: USA Foundation Haute Louisiane, Box 1, *Lettres de la Haute Louisiane II 1823-1830*, pp. 64-68; C-III 1: USA Foundation Haute Louisiane, Box 3, *Lettres de la Louisiane I*, pp. 297-299. Cf. J. de Charry, II, 3, L. 219, pp. 10-14; Sweetman et al, pp. 10-16.

entire approval to the new foundation that the said Mother Duchesne is going to make in Saint Louis, persuaded as we are that this will result in very great profit for religion and that it cannot help but add new lustre to the brilliant success enjoyed by the Society of the Sacred Heart in Europe and in the United States.

Given at New Orleans, March 24, 1827
Joseph, Bishop of Tanagra

This authentic approval under the seal of the bishop and your often expressed desires give me the consolation that I am where God wants me and that Saint Joseph has helped a great deal; he is the special patron of the house. The 5000 F have already been used for the addition of a cellar, a kitchen built of brick, and a room above that is very suitable for a priest, and for floors, ceilings and shutters. I had promised to go for May 1; the circumstances of my feast, of the distribution of prizes, a new class division to be made and a new teacher installed, all of this delayed my departure from Florissant to May 2 (Wednesday), still with none of the rooms finished. We have had Mass only on Sunday; and without expecting it, I had great joy when, following the ritual of the diocese, the priest said the Mass of Saint Joseph.

The pastor already says two Masses on Sundays, and his vicar alternates in two parishes that are pretty distant from each other, one of them across the river. In this difficult situation, the father superior offered me Mass at three o'clock. After saying the first at Saint Ferdinand and preaching a High Mass, he still has 5 leagues to travel. I told him I did not think I was obliged to have Mass at such a price. Nevertheless, he came today, but at noon; and the vicar told me yesterday that in the future he could come to say Mass early in the morning and then go to the parishes. That is an advantage for the moment, but since he is not strong, and that will be too difficult for him in bad weather, divine Providence offers us another resource: Father Richard, our first chaplain at Saint Charles, a great friend of the Jesuits—with whom he has just once more been refused, for he had asked to end his days with them—he has offered to be our chaplain in Saint Louis, asking only food and lodging. He will for this purpose leave the religious in New Orleans who were giving him 1500 F per year, beautiful lodging and good food. But his desire has always been to end his life attached to a house of the Sacred Heart. I accepted his offer, but I do not know if the bishop will agree.

This foundation has presented many difficulties. Our sisters can only just manage in Florissant, where there are more than thirty boarders, orphans and Indian girls, in three separate groups. Mother Octavie is in charge as assistant, treasurer and mistress general. Mother Lucile is mistress general of the orphans and day students, mistress of choir and assistant treasurer for the management of the house. Mother Regis [Hamilton] is mistress of the American class, of needlework and of health and supplies. Mother Aloysia McKay[306] is mistress of class including English: she made her first vows on April 16. Mother Stanislaus Shannon is mistress of the Indians: she also made her first vows on April 16. Mother Therese Detchemendy is teacher, surveillante and in charge of the vestry. Sister Catherine takes charge of the day students. Miss Eleonore [Gray], an Irish postulant, who wants to be called Josephine, is portress, and is responsible to get the French students to read in English. I took with me only Sister Mary Ann O'Connor, an Irish aspirant, who will have responsibility for the orphans, since she is not suitable for the boarding school.

We are waiting to admit other children until our sisters arrive from France. Remember, dear Reverend Mother, that you promised two more if the establishment in Saint Louis happened. While waiting, I have requests to accept children from the highest-level families. But how can we say yes to everything? The father says that if we have a boarding school here, we will ruin the one in Florissant, and I am afraid of this, too. Meanwhile, I say that we can have only a few students here because of the orphans, so we reserve the places for children who are to study with [secular] masters. I hope that you will permit us to have paying day students. That will be the main work, then the poor. I think that the thought of snatching students away from the Protestant schools where boys and girls are mixed will be enough to make you agree. The best thing of all is to be able to offer a refuge where those who have been converted will have the means and the resources to practice their religion.

Up to now death has not entered among us, but this morning it took one of the girls in the Indian school. I have also learned that Mother Lucile is not well. I have only three orphans from Saint Ferdinand here, of whom two are paid for by Mr. Mullanphy. The third is very useful to us, since we do not have as at Saint Ferdinand a competent Negress for the kitchen, etc.

---

306   Susannah (Aloysia) McKay, RSCJ (1802-1860), was born in New York in 1802 (according to the vow register of Florissant, and not in Ireland). She entered in Saint Louis in 1825 and made her final vows in 1830. She died in Saint Charles in 1860.

They are sending me the necessities in food from all sides here. I lack nothing. I wish you would write to Mr. Mullanphy to thank him. Maybe he will help us for a church; he could do it without difficulty, but he wants to do things himself. He does not want to be pushed! He is a man who is powerful in both wealth and ability. He could govern a kingdom. His daughters all think well of us. Miss Octavie [Mullanphy][307] whom he placed with us has just left to assist her mother in France, who has lost her oldest daughter, a person of great merit. If she comes to you to pay a visit, please extend friendship to her. She needs some connections. She is very attached to us and very virtuous.

Mother Eugenie has been very upset, as I have, by the painful death of Mother Xavier Hamilton,[308] an irreparable loss (she was the only one who could have translated our Constitutions). She has 45 boarders, and there are 34 at Opelousas, with 10 refused because of lack of teachers. It seems that Mother Xavier [Murphy] steers her ship quite well and that she has a wonderful reputation in the area.

My regards to good Fathers Varin, Barat and Perreau. We hope to see the father provincial.[309] The fathers are going to have with them the son of the chief of the Osage, and the father superior will go to that nation composed of 22,000 people. The government is having a beautiful house built in their village for the trapper[310] who will receive one of the fathers and maintain him.

I am at your feet,

Philippine

---

307 Octavia Mullanphy (1808-1876) married Denis Delaney in Saint Louis in 1836 and had two children. After the death of her husband, she married Henry Boyce in 1848; he died in 1873. She died three years later in Paris.

308 Mathilde Hamilton died on May 1, 1827. She had the positions of assistant and mistress of novices at Saint Michael.

309 Francis Dzierożyński (1779-1850), a Polish Jesuit, was born January 3, 1779 at Orsza, now Belorussia, entered the novitiate August 13, 1794, and was ordained December 24, 1806. After having taught Humanities at Saint Petersburg (1803-1806), he was professor of Philosophy and Mathematics at Mogilev (1810-1811), now Belorussia, and of Dogmatic Theology in the Jesuit faculty of Polotsk (1814-1820), where he was rector. After the expulsion of the Jesuits from Russia in 1820, his superior general, Aloysius Fortis, sent him to North America as provincial of the Jesuit mission (1823-1830), at which time he visited the house in Florissant in 1827, then of Maryland (1840-1843); he was also master of novices at Frederick (1834-1840). At the same time he was professor of Philosophy (1821-1825) and of Theology (1825-1838) at Georgetown University, where he fought against slavery. He visited Florissant in July-August 1827, mainly to inspect the seminary and examine those preparing for ordination. In 1829, he directed the opening of the Jesuit college in Saint Louis, then of Holy Cross College in Worcester, Massachusetts. He is considered as the one who laid the foundations for Jesuit education in the United States. Everyone venerated him as a spiritual director. He died September 22, 1850, at Frederick, Maryland. http://pl.wikipedia.org/wiki/Franciszek_Dziero%C5%BCy%C5%84ski .

310 A hunter of European origin settled in Indian Territory. The whites installed more and more of them in lands that in principle belonged to autonomous tribes.

[On the reverse:]
To Mother
Mother Barat, Superior General
of the Religious of the Sacred Heart
Rue de Varenne
Faubourg Saint Germain
Paris
France
By way of New York

**Letter 289   L. 1 to Mr. Auguste Chouteau
and Response**

[1827][311]

Sir,

When there was question of the establishment that we are beginning here, Mr. Mullanphy assured me that you would place no obstacle to our having a foot bridge across your creek; he added since I have been here that you had given your formal consent and that you had promised to put it in writing when the time came.

I come now, Sir, to thank you for your kindly feelings in our regard; I would not have imagined having the work begun without informing you and asking again for your permission in writing.

I beg you kindly to honor me with an answer and believe me, Sir, with deep respect,

Your devoted servant,

Philippine Duchesne sup.

[The letter is accompanied by the following response:]

Madame,

A few days ago I received your respectable letter concerning the promise I made to Mr. Mullanphy to allow the building of a bridge on my creek in front of your establishment and for its use.

---

311   Original autograph, Mill. Coll. Auguste Chouteau Papers. 1827, Archives USC Province, Series XII. C. Callan, Box 7 packet 1, Letters to lay people.

I repeat, Madame, that I place no obstacle whatever and, according to Mr. Mullanphy's request, I formally permit you to build a foot bridge across this creek for the use of your establishment; and I consent for myself and my household that it remain as long as it does me no harm or causes no prejudice.

I have the honor, Madame, to be with deep respect your very humble and obedient servant.

Aug. Chouteau

Saint Louis, June 4, 1827

Madame Philippine Duchesne Sup.

Letter 290   L. 33 to Bishop Rosati

SS. C. J. et M.

[July 1, 1827][312]

Dear Bishop,

I received your letter and whatever pleasure it afforded me, that of seeing you would have been much greater. I have been looking forward to a visit from you for a long time. It is impossible for me to thank you in writing for the official approbation you have given our foundation in Saint Louis. I showed it right away to the reverend father, and it put an end immediately to the sort of opposition he had hitherto shown.

I am told now that he is displeased that I have engaged Mr. Martin Lepère, who worked for us in Florissant, to come and settle near us here in Saint Louis, where I have real need of him to oversee our work. He alone knows our limitations and can do the work for which knowledge of the two languages is necessary. The father superior objected that he is lazy; but since he is not paid, it seems to me it is simply up to him to act freely, and any honest person can take his place, which is not enough for me here. As I could not get in touch with you quickly enough, Bishop, and as Mr. Martin Lepère was willing to make the

---

312   Original autograph, C-VII 2) c Writings Duchesne to Rosati, Box 6. On the reverse: "July 1, 1827, Mother Duchesne, St. Louis."

change, I have not retreated from my position in spite of the protest, and I shall carry the matter through, unless you should wish otherwise.

Judging that a letter could not reach you in New Orleans, I asked Father Dahmen to deliver one to you on your arrival asking for Father Richard who has offered to be our chaplain. Now that I have had no answer from him, and you tell me of the departure of Father Delacroix, I am afraid he is lost to us. Father Saulnier is already saying two Masses on Sunday. Father Lutz is unable to come to us either when he goes to Cahos [Cahokia]. The reverend father offered to come to us that day, but it is after he has preached at Saint Ferdinand. Last Sunday he arrived here at two o'clock very exhausted. I asked him if he would like to build the school on our property since he lost his own land; he refused. I am hopeful, however, that if Father Richard cannot come, and if you use Father Lutz as he hopes you will, that you will decide that the father superior should send us one of his priests, Father Smith [Smedts?], for example, who will not trouble anyone and who is not strong enough for the life of a missionary.

Miss Eleonore Gray, whom you sent us as a postulant, took the habit last Sunday; she is here with me. Miss McGuire replaced her in spite of her poor health.

I have asked Father Odin to get us a suitable Negro woman. Dare I ask you to have him answer? We are told that in Kentucky the choice is better and the price more reasonable.

I am with respect your Excellency's most devoted servant.

Philippine Duchesne, sup.

July 1, 1827

[On the reverse:]
To Bishop
Bishop Rosati
Bishop of Tanagra
Barrens
Sainte Genevieve County
Missouri

[Additional sheet:]

Convent of the Sacred Heart of Jesus in Florissant[313]

The community numbers seven: four professed and three religious in first vows, plus a postulant.

The boarding school numbers thirty young ladies

The purpose of their education consists of 1) religion, which holds the first place; 2) reading in English and French; 3) English and French grammar; 4) elements of literature; 5) arithmetic; 6) ancient and modern history; 7) geography; 8) various kinds of manual work; 9) household management, etc.

Free day school

The children in this school number 51. They receive instruction in religion, English and French, reading, writing, fundamentals of arithmetic and manual work such as sewing, spinning, etc.

Indian School, numbering twelve

The pupils in this school board. The religious care for their meals, their sleeping quarters, and their clothes. They have the same instruction as the pupils of the free school. As their scholastic aptitude is not great, at least in some, we try to make up for this by encouraging a love of work. However, in the two and a half years since the Religious of the Sacred Heart have taken up this work, they have often had the satisfaction of seeing these children learn and become fairly skillful in knitting, sewing, carding, spinning, weaving, etc.

Letter 291 **L. 79 to Mother Barat**

SS. C. J. et M.

July 9, 1827
Rec. to St Anthony of Padua[314]

---

313 This prospectus, in another handwriting, dated July 28, 1827, was added to the letter.
314 Original autograph, C-VII 2) c Duchesne to Barat, Box 2. Postmark: Paris, 2 September 1827. Copy, USA Foundation Haute Louisiane, Box 1, *Lettres de la Haute Louisiane II 1823-1830*, p. 251-252. Copie partielle, C-III 1: USA Foundation Haute Louisiane, Box 3, *Lettres de la Louisiane I*, p. 302-304. J. de Charry, II 3, L. 222, p. 20-23; Sweetman et al, pp. 23-27.

Dear Reverend Mother,

I have just received your letter sent in March, in which you were kind enough to excuse the faults in my way of exercising authority, which I see as well as others do. I see, too, by this letter, that you did not yet know about my foundation in Saint Louis, where I have been since May 2, with the two Irish choir religious, an aspirant and another novice. The first one [Mary Layton] has been here as long as I have and is now working with the Indian girls.

This distance from the center has been bad for her; I have found her here much inferior to what I had thought, and I am no longer of the opinion of advancing her final vows. The second is a new novice, called Eleonore Gray, who took the habit on the Sunday after the feast of the Sacred Heart [June 26] and along with it, the name Josephine, as I had promised to that saint, patron of the new foundation. She needs a great deal of formation. In all our houses, we are waiting impatiently for help from France. Mother Eugenie [Audé] has a fever every night. Mother Xavier [Murphy] had a very bad fever, and her community, who are only four, are exhausted. I was obliged to refuse students here. The Irish sister is for the orphans; the novice can only get the children to read English. The day students of the first [social] class will be the main source of income, because unless we build, we can house only 15 boarders along with the orphans. I have already spoken to you about being authorized to receive payment from them.[315] You had given this permission for Saint Ferdinand where, from the moment that Saint Louis began, we no longer accepted day students, and this gave us hardly 40 F a year.

To shorten the way to the town, we have built two bridges, one for pedestrians and the other for carriages. On another side, we installed a well, since the former one was in ruins, and there is plastering and carpentry needed. This is beyond the 5000 F given by Mr. Mullanphy, which had been spent on essentials before my arrival. It remains to enclose ourselves with planks and poles, which will be a great expense, with a stable and a house for the domestic, necessary because of our isolation from other houses, something that is desirable because no one can get too close to us. We will leave a part of our 24 *arpents* in woods, and it will give us wild grapes, which are often quite good, nuts, strawberries and especially mulberries in abundance. But we will

---

315 According to the Constitutions (no. 142), the day school should be free if it accepted children from poor families, but this is not the case here, since the day students belonged to rich or comfortable families.

still have plenty of space inside the enclosure for a garden, an apple orchard, woods to take a walk; and it contains a very good spring that never fails. Finally, a plot for corn and potatoes still has to be cleared.

I have been helped to stay alive by several ladies who sent me some garden produce, as much as we could eat. The mother of two of our children has put her carriages and servants at our disposition for all the times that I will need to go to Florissant. I took advantage of it twice for necessary business. I was forced to take on three boarders here that Florissant could not take. This has been a great blessing, to get the increase in money at a time when money was so necessary. If our religious had been here taking advantage of the moment, our two houses would have been full at the same time.

But I am beginning to be a storyteller speaking about their coming arrival. I am especially ashamed with Mr. Mullanphy. I think Miss Octavie, his daughter, will have visited you. Her attachment to us will, I hope, prompt you to give her a great welcome.

Good Father Richard, our chaplain in Saint Charles, who shared only our privations there, is nevertheless so taken by love of the Sacred Heart that when he learned of our foundation in Saint Louis, he wrote to me offering to be our chaplain for free because, he says, "since the beautiful days in Saint Charles, I have always wanted to die at the Sacred Heart." He will give up the 1500 F given him by the Ursuline Sisters, a beautiful lodging, special food, etc. The house at Opelousas and this one would like to have him as the one necessary, but neither will get him, because the bishop, whom I asked, refused it cold, saying that he cannot leave without a priest a house of 150 persons to whom the bishop owes his lodging and his existence[316] and who is obligated by contract to give it to them, which is difficult given all the departures that disappoint him. This good Father Richard still thinks that he will come, and he sent me in the meantime a beautiful missal, a ciborium and other objects.

Since the positive approbation of the bishop, the father superior of our fathers is no longer against the establishment; he even told me that he was "more than ever able to help us," but he told me yesterday not to count either on him or on the fathers, because they were going to make their tertianship.[317] At this I shed bitter tears *(line crossed out, making it illegible)*. I hope for a little from the visit of the father provincial, who

---

316 The Ursulines of New Orleans had given their convent to the diocese when they moved to the outskirts at the end of 1824.

317 The six scholastics, ordained priests by Bishop Rosati, were about to begin their "third year," which would last until July 31, 1828.

is expected this month. Meanwhile, we must live in privation. We have had no octave of the Blessed Sacrament nor of the Sacred Heart.[318] Often four Communions are lost during a novena. Those are fast days for me, because it is impossible for me to eat, hoping that some stroke of Providence will bring a priest by for Communion. I beg our sisters to receive Communion for me, and Our Lord will be more glorified by it.

Mother Octavie steers her boat very well. There is only her illness that causes me grief. She is already very weak in the chest, and she has been stung by a spider that kept her in bed and made her suffer greatly. They say the poison is as bad as a snake bite. Her boarding school is going well since the expulsion of one student and the departure of another who was unsuitable. The sisters also seem happy. Mother Lucile would not have been able to replace her *(words crossed out to make them illegible)*. Fortunately she is better.

My expense account does not tally with that of Saint Ferdinand concerning the money I received from there, because I added the value of various things that I brought here. We are in good shape for the sacristy. Since the fathers have received help from Flanders, we do not have to furnish everything for Saint Ferdinand. I do not have the time to put into francs the financial statement from Saint Ferdinand. Mother Octavie forgot (you just have to multiply the amounts by 5). Father Boccardo nearly lost his mind when he arrived in New Orleans. He wrote to me that he lost 10,000 F that fell in the water along with many letters for us.[319] There may have been money for us. I have spent Mrs. de Rollin's gift. Since then I have been given credit.

I am at your feet in the Sacred Heart, your unworthy
Philippine Duchesne

I am very disturbed by the illness of Mother de Gramont. Is Father Rambaud dead?[320]
My respects to your good brother and to Fathers Varin and Perreau.

---

318 Exposition of the Blessed Sacrament was prescribed during the octaves of the two feasts according to the ceremonial of the Society of the Sacred Heart of Jesus.
319 Angelo Boccardo, an Italian Lazarist, was greatly desired by Bishop Rosati, who had the intention of naming him master of novices. But he was so upset by this terrible accident that he returned immediately to Italy. Several years later, he tried to return to America but was not allowed by his superiors.
320 Former chaplain at Sainte-Marie d'En-Haut in Grenoble.

[On the reverse:]
To Mother
Mother Barat, Superior General
of the Religious of the Sacred Heart
Rue de Varenne
Paris
France
By way of New York

Letter 292   **L. 34 to Bishop Rosati**

SS. C. J. et M.

[15 July 1827][321]

Dear Bishop,

I had no intention whatever of withdrawing Father Richard from his station, but ever since his stay at Saint Charles he has not stopped expressing his wish to die near us and has been even more insistent since he heard about the new foundation (…).[322] He wrote me that because of the heat in Louisiana he had given notice to the Ursulines that he was going to leave them and that he would offer to be our chaplain free of charge asking only for lodging and food.

However advantageous this offer was, I did not answer immediately, thinking, in any event, that the Saint Louis priests or the Jesuits who are planning to build a school here, would supply our needs. However, when both laid their difficulties before me, I then answered Father Richard that if his transfer were agreeable to you, we would be glad to have him. I also wrote you about it, Bishop, and sent the letter with Father Dahmen, because I did not think my letter would reach you in New Orleans. Moreover, I knew the Ursulines were not at all attached to Father Richard, for they told me so themselves; and no one, or very few, went to confession to him when I saw them. They offer great advantages to a priest, so they can easily provide for themselves; but at this moment when we have nothing but expenses, what can we

---

321 Original autograph, C-VII 2) c Writings Duchesne to Rosati, Box 6. On the reverse: "July 15, 1827, Mother Duchesne, St. Louis; received the 29th."
322 Words torn out in unsealing the letter.

offer a priest, above all with our desperate need of a servant. We would make promises that we could not keep.

I do not know whether you spoke about us to the father superior who was here on Sunday and to whom I gave your letter. He was very sick and said he could no longer continue such tiring trips. He says his priests are going to make their tertianship, that they are very busy for the moment and that he has not permitted anyone to come; this I can well believe for he alone did the work of four men. Insisting would have done no good, and if the father provincial, who is supposed to come, does not decide something we shall still be in uncertainty. Father Saulnier cannot leave on Sunday. Father Lutz, with whom I can make no arrangement without word from you and until I know about Father Richard, is continually sick. He thinks he is able to go to the Indians, but the three-minute horseback ride from here to the presbytery often leaves him exhausted. I told the father superior that there have been saints who became holy without Mass and that I was ready to make the sacrifice in view of future good, but I already perceive the discouragement of my helpers. I would not know whom to send to accompany the children to church, especially three or four boarders. I foresee the trouble that would inevitably result. I should prefer them to miss Mass if you should so decide. It is in the midst of these thoughts that I begin to think I can beg for Father Richard, should he ask me again. It was the father superior who was annoyed that I took Mr. Martin [Lepère] for Saint Louis. I spoke to him about it, and he said nothing but showed his displeasure to others. Since then he has calmed down. I talked nothing over with him, and as Mr. Martin desired the change, I accepted before receiving your reply, judging that the difficulty was removed by the change of superior.

He told me, as did Father Saulnier, that we are sure of keeping you. I cannot adequately express our joy. It is a great blessing from God, for which we will never cease thanking him.

In several of our houses in France the bishop is withdrawing us from dependence on the parish priest and is putting us under his own special jurisdiction, naming someone to represent him for the house if he is too far away. I should very much like to have the same privilege for Saint Louis, for it is not always easy to go to confession to the priest who deals with external matters and with whom one is sometimes in conflict concerning business affairs. I do not know if I make myself clear, but I have experienced several situations of this kind in Florissant.

Father Loiseul[323] will have given you the distressing details from Father Borgna about Father Boccardo.[324] If we are going to lose money, I shall be that much more in debt, for I have spent what I was counting on. *Fiat.*

I am with profound veneration your Excellency's submissive and devoted daughter.

Philippine Duchesne, sup.

July 15, 1827

[On the reverse:]
To the Bishop
Bishop Rosati
Bishop of Saint Louis
Barrens
Missouri
Sainte Geneviève County

Letter 293   **L. 35 to Bishop Rosati**

SS. C. J. et M.

[July 29, 1827][325]

I have just received a letter from Father Van Quickenborne who is displeased because of a note that Mother Octavie wrote for the Charlestown newspaper, with which I had nothing to do. The priest who transcribed the article about the Indian girls is hurt by it, because in the eyes of the government they are part of his school. I find the article badly organized, and I beg you to suppress if it there is still time.

I strongly dislike seeing us in the newspapers, and if you say a few words, I would like them to be as short as possible.

Bishop, I do not know if you have received my last letter enclosing one from Father Richard that would show you his own desire and also

---

323 John Francis Loiseul, born in Saint Louis in 1805 and ordained in 1828, exercised his ministry in many parishes and Indian missions. He died of yellow fever in 1841.
324 Angelo Boccardo, CM, the Italian priest, to whom some documents and a large sum of money had been entrusted; he dropped them into the Mississippi.
325 Original autograph, C-VII 2) c Writings Duchesne to Rosati, Box 6. On the reverse: "July 29, 1827, Mother Duchesne, St. Louis."

that we had no intention of removing him. I cannot help seeing every day more and more how valuable a man like him would be for one of our houses. The father provincial arrived, but I could not make him decide anything in our favor for Saint Louis.

Please, I beg you, let me know if we have no Mass on a Sunday, whether our children may be dispensed from going to church. I should very much like it.

I am with profound veneration your Excellency's submissive and devoted daughter and humble servant.

Philippine Duchesne, sup.

July 29, 1827

Letter 294   **L. 80 to Mother Barat**

SS. C. J. et M.

Saint Louis, August 18, 1827
St. Anthony[326]

Dear Reverend Mother,

You have never put me through a worse trial than by delaying the arrival of our sisters. Father Boccardo, entrusted with letters for us, let them fall into the Mississippi, with the result that I am in complete ignorance about their voyage. Each letter from our houses makes me tremble, and I am always afraid that she who keeps it all going may have died and that the work will perish.

Sometimes I live in the hope that you will double the help, knowing that the foundation in Saint Louis has begun. You promised it to me that way. We hope that Father Delacroix,[327] who tells me to write to him at your address, will bring us a second reinforcement. I count on having the American lady [Mrs. Baker] in the first group. She is known and thought well of by our fathers, and they agree that she will do

---

326 Original autograph, C-VII 2) c Duchesne to Barat, Box 2. Copy, USA Foundation Haute Louisiane, Box 1, *Lettres de la Haute Louisiane II 1823-1830*, pp. 251-252. Cf. J. de Charry, II, 3, L. 224, pp. 26-27.

327 Father Charles Delacroix, a secular Belgian priest, had been pastor in Florissant from 1820 to 1823. He left for Louisiana when the Jesuits arrived in Missouri, and was pastor at Saint Michael when the Religious of the Sacred Heart came there in 1825. In 1827, he was in Ghent, in Belgium.

much good here. I beg you to leave her with us for some time. The father provincial of Georgetown, who is doing his rounds here and has made several changes, told me that she was destined for Washington, and that it was a very suitable place for a foundation, but that her husband is still living there, so it would be better to wait. If she were to spend this delay here, I would be very happy. I have a real need to be replaced by someone who has the art of creating relationships and bringing about change. Everything will stagnate under me. As for the two religious whom you have promised me besides, great talent is not necessary. I need a good needlework teacher and one for handwriting who could also teach English. If these could also bring knowledge of music, especially piano, that would be wonderful.

As for education, the best qualification here is to speak English well. I cannot expect this from France, unless you have a second Mother Xavier [Murphy], who does wonders where she is. Some Protestant families, who cannot even hear the name Catholic said without spite and anger, are now saying: "We like Mother Xavier's religion."

I am always worried that you do not approve the contract with Mr. Mullanphy. At least your desires are partly fulfilled. Bishop Rosati, who has definitely been named for Saint Louis, writes to me that he will reside there for part of the year. This will bring us more spiritual help. For a long time I can no longer hope for this from the Jesuits in Saint Louis. The father provincial has been impervious to all my requests. We will only have flying visits from them. Father Richard has also been refused to us.

Worthy Mother, I am devotedly *in Corde Jesu* your unworthy daughter.

Philippine

[On the reverse:]
To Mother
Mother Barat, Superior General
of the Religious of the Sacred Heart
Rue de Varenne
Paris
France

Letter 295   **L. 10 to Father Delacroix**

SS. C. J. M.

St. Anthony
August 18, 1827, Saint Louis[328]

Reverend Father,

I received your letter from New York, which continues to prove to me your attachment to our Society. I hope it will bring you back to Saint Michael, a house that should be even dearer because it has cost you more. Saint Ferdinand never forgets you, and Mr. Mullanphy and his family are still attached to you. I really wish that it would be part of your plan to return from the north by descending the Ohio and paying us a visit on your way back.

Our mother general promised me that if a foundation in Saint Louis is made, she will send me two more religious. I would hope that she would confide them to you. We are very much upset by the delay of the first group, promised so long ago. The first three houses rest on persons who are at the end of their strength. Father Caretta,[329] who came back up north with the bishop and who is here now, tells me that Mother Eugenie is absolutely killing herself, and that she listens to no one about her health. To try her, they say to her that Mother Aloysia [Hardey] is too perfect, that she cannot survive. Imagine what this house would become if these two went missing!

Mother Octavie's health continues to decline.

I lost your address in Ghent and am delighted to be able to respond through the intermediation of our mother.

You are so good to ask me if I have any commissions. I would have a thousand if I did not hope for many things to arrive from our sisters. Knowing that in France as here, one must limit one's desires, I do not dare ask for anything until I know what they are having the goodness to bring us.

You could find out if with our mother there is a censer and a little ostensorium. Those are the most essential things we lack, along with two books of Roman chant for Mass and Vespers; 24 grammars of

---

328 Original autograph, C-VII 2) c Writings Letters to M-S. Barat, Box 2. Letter attached to one addressed to Mother Barat.
329 Father Jean Caretta, C.M., was confessor of the Sisters of the Cross at La Fourche.

Lhomond,[330] 24 sacred histories, 24 chronologies, and two copies of the history course of Father Loriquet.[331]

I will try to give you advances, if it is possible for you to do this as quickly as possible.

Our house is already too small. If we get help, we would need a chapel or little church, a dormitory and a classroom for the day students.

We are building a house for Mr. Lepère,[332] which will adjoin our house. His family is already here. He has raised his price, but since he has so much to do with the workers and nearly all in English, I need a faithful interpreter. Mr. Mullanphy has told me several times: "You need that man, you will find no one like him." One of the Maille family, a holy young married man, is replacing him at Saint Ferdinand. Father Saulnier[333] is well.

I am with respect, good Father, your devoted servant.

Philippine Duchesne

Letter 296   L. 81 to Mother Barat

SS. C. J. et M.

Saint Louis, September 11, 1827[334]

Very dear and good Mother,

As I receive more benefits from you, how much I feel my gratitude increasing! I want to express it as well as I can at the arrival of our dear sisters [Helene Dutour and Xavier Van Damme].[335] Once more it is the Blessed Virgin who has brought them. I was a bit discouraged when I saw that all the novenas to the Sacred Heart, to Saint Regis and to Saint Ignatius produced nothing, and that the Blessed Virgin, in the season of

---

330 Father Charles-François Lhomond, French priest and grammarian (1724-1794).
331 Jean Nicolas Loriquet, SJ (1767-1845), was author of most of the student manuals used in the Jesuit schools and the Sacred Heart boarding schools.
332 M. Martin Lepère, Bishop Dubourg's farmer at Florissant, worked in collaboration with Father Delacroix.
333 He replaced Father Niel as pastor in Saint Louis.
334 Copies, USA Foundation Haute Louisiane, Box 1, *Lettres de la Haute Louisiane II 1823-1830*, pp. 252-254; C-III 1: USA Foundation Haute Louisiane, Box 3, *Lettres de la Louisiane I*, pp. 304-306. J. de Charry, II, 3, L. 227, pp. 32-33; Sweetman et al. pp. 36-38.
335 They arrived in Saint Louis on September 9. Xavier Van Damme, RSCJ (1794-1833), was born in Belgium, entered the Society of the Sacred Heart in 1825, went to America in 1827, and died at Saint Michael in 1833.

the Assumption and her Immaculate Heart, seemed to have no effect; but I heard in the depth of my heart, as I complained to her on the morning of the feast of her Name, these consoling words: "My protection will never fail you." I set aside the thought as illusory, but after Mass, the words returned to me, and an hour later, the parish sacristan came hurrying to tell me that our sisters had arrived at the presbytery and would be at the 10:30 Mass, so that we saw them only at dinnertime.

After Vespers, I went with them to Florissant, where joy overflowed. On Monday, we took advantage of the meeting to distribute prizes, done by Father de Theux, accompanied by another father, since Father Van Quickenborne was with the Osage. This good father had united himself to our novena and had said Mass the same day for this intention. I returned in the evening to Saint Louis with Mother Dutour, since Mother Xavier Van Damme wanted to stay a few days at Saint Ferdinand to make a retreat. Nevertheless, I got her to return here, persuading her that because of her age and her facility in speaking English, it would be for the greater glory of God.

[Obliged to interrupt her letter, Philippine resumed it on September 29.]

Bishop Rosati came to see us today, and he is pleased with our location, which he finds very agreeable. He made me a proposition that needs a quick response from you. Knowing that you want us to limit ourselves to our four houses, I cannot accept a fifth one without your consent. The Daughters of the Cross,[336] very widespread in Kentucky, have a house in this diocese at La Fourche, near Mother Eugenie. Father Bigeschi, a holy priest who has returned to France and whom you must have met, got them to build a house and gave them land, furniture, etc.; but since they are all Americans who speak only English, they cannot hold out at La Fourche, where all the customs are French as well as the language. They find themselves unable to train their novices and to teach their students, since only one of them speaks French passably well and teaches it, so they want to join us. The bishop and the clergy of the area also want this. The bishop has spoken to them about the differences of rank. It is all agreed upon, and only lacks your consent.

Will you refuse it to a thickly populated part of the country, when all that is lacking is someone to be superior? This person, in my opinion, could be Mother Carmelite, who was Mother Xavier's [Murphy] assistant,

---

336 The Congregation of the "Friends of Mary at the Foot of the Cross," founded by Father Charles Nerinckx; also known as the Sisters of Loretto.

but since the arrival of Mother Dorival,[337] she is far less necessary at Grand Coteau. She seems to have been made for that house of La Fourche, known positively by the inhabitants and completely on their level. We could take some of these good sisters for our other houses that need English teachers and put French sisters in their place. By these exchanges and without need of any new vocations, we could build up there a very worthwhile establishment. Mother Eugenie could send there children whom she cannot accept at Saint Michael for lack of space and even look after this house and help it in so many ways. Please, Reverend Mother, give me an answer right away. I have asked Bishop Rosati for a four-month delay, hoping to receive your answer, which I hope will be favorable. I ask it of God through the intercession of Our Lady of the Seven Sorrows, especially honored in this place. She told me that her protection would never fail us....[338]

Letter 297   L. 36 to Bishop Rosati

SS. C. J. et M.

[October 3, 1827][339]

Dear Bishop,

You always show such great kindness that I am taking the liberty of stealing a few moments to consult you on some matters that could slip my mind should you be good enough to visit us, or that cannot be said in the presence of a third person.

1. We have had several children baptized secretly in our house at Saint Ferdinand. Many of them have already gone back to their homes, and some have returned to their erroneous ways. Would it be better, in order to ensure their perseverance, to have them profess their faith openly? Many would not have the courage to do so; others would expose themselves to violent persecution. Moreover, several who do

---

337   Louise Dorival, RSCJ (1795-1832), born in 1795 in Paris, had first tried two other religious congregations before entering the novitiate of the Sacred Heart in Paris in 1820. She made her profession in Bordeaux in 1823 and arrived in America in 1827. She was the first French missionary to die in the New World, at Grand Coteau in 1832.
338   The copy ends this way.
339   Original autograph, C-VII 2) c Writings Duchesne to Rosati, Box 6. On the reverse: "1827 Oct. 3, Mother Duchesne, St. Louis."

not profess their belief and who attend Protestant sermons are greatly endangering their faith.

2. I must have your consent if we are going to build. Our greatest needs are a suitable chapel and a dormitory. At the moment we are able to accommodate only twelve boarders, which is insufficient for the upkeep of the house. Of course, we cannot even consider two buildings; but if I could get payment in advance from the parents, I believe we could erect one building. In this case could the dormitory be above the chapel or at least up to the sanctuary?

3. According to the decrees of the last [General] Council, our sisters may no longer be visited by their relatives in the infirmary; and the children's infirmary must be so situated that fathers and mothers do not enter the cloistered part of the house. The only place where we can put our sick now is precisely on the side of the chapel where any noise made there can be heard. Do you think a thick tapestry would be sufficient to intercept the noise?

4. I do not know whether I should have given you our Constitutions, which are to be printed. The manuscript has already undergone several additions or changes that make it hard to read, but I have the new ceremonial and the summary of the Constitutions translated into English by one of our religious.

5. If you are willing, Bishop, when you next send an extra priest to Saint Louis, if he is not too young and if you judge him capable of directing religious women, would you please assign him to be our confessor? Father Lutz speaks no English, and Father Saulnier knows so little of both tongues, French and English, that our nuns have a hard time getting used to him; this would prove a great hindrance to the perseverance of several in this house. I myself have two things against him: the first is that he rarely gives me absolution, and the second is that he does not like at all to give Communion outside of Mass. This means a loss of Communion when all cannot be present at Mass and when it is necessary to go out with sick children or for strangers. Our religious [newly] arrived tell me to ask for a Jesuit, but neither the father provincial nor the superior was willing to promise me anything. I even encountered the opposite frame of mind. Moreover, if we are under direct obedience to the superior, it might interfere with our work as, for instance, when he opposed our foundation here.

6. May I beg you once more, Bishop, to tell Mr. Lepère that it is his duty to finish one of his rooms as soon as possible because of the

unseemliness of his living so close. He is often obliged to have men at his place. Would you be kind enough to tell him too that he will have to be content to finish without the plaster, since he is not able to carry so many expenses at one time.

7. There is a lady who is to arrive with our nuns who has permission from her husband to be a nun and who also has official permission from our Holy Father the Pope, which has been ratified by the archbishop of Baltimore. In spite of this, my sisters tell me that the archbishop of Paris refused permission to give her the religious habit, saying that such permissions were valid only in foreign countries. Our mother tells me to keep her here, to give her the habit and to see that she does not go back to France. What shall I do if she still insists on asking for the habit?

8. Our mother did not have Mother Xavier make her final vows, from which now one can be released only by the Holy See; but if she allows it and you were to be in New Orleans, would she be able to make them?

Please be so good, Bishop, as to give me a word in response either on the letter itself or however you wish. Please believe in the profound respect and submission with which I am in the Sacred Heart of Jesus, your humble daughter and servant.

Philippine Duchesne, sup.
Religious of the S.C.

Saint Louis, October 3, 1827

[On the reverse:]
To Bishop
Bishop Rosati
Bishop of Saint Louis
Saint Louis

Letter 298   L. 8 to Mother Bigeu

SS. C. J. M.

[October 3, 1827]
St Anthony[340]

My very dear and respected Mother,

I have received your precious letter, and I keenly appreciate this little sheet as a token of your remembrance reminding me of all your goodness to me.

Our religious arrived on the feast of the Holy Name of Mary, when we had just ended a novena to the Blessed Virgin for this intention, and a Jesuit father took it on himself to say Mass for this same intention.

The smallness of our house, the number of mothers and our poverty astonish and discourage Mother Xavier [Van Damme], but her virtue seems to have overcome. As for Mother Dutour, she was at home right away.

To the pleasure of seeing them, God adds the very dear hope for me that you will come to America to found a house in one of the large cities of the East. What you have told me several times, your courage, even your health, which improves with travel, seem to have brought to reality for me what is not visible to me now but will be in the future, and I am happy in advance.

I hope that you will come by way of New Orleans, that you will visit first the two houses in Louisiana and then come up the river to Saint Louis and visit the two in Missouri. From here, it is not easy to go to the cities of the East. What a joy it would be to see you again! What good you would do for all!

You will not doubt the unspeakable pleasure it gave me to read the Briefs and all the details about our dear Society. I learn that you are in Lille,[341] working again for the glory of the Sacred Heart.

---

340 Original autograph, C-VII 2) c Duchesne to RSCJ and Children, Box 4. Copies: C-III 1: USA Foundation Haute Louisiane, Box 1, *Lettres de la Louisiane I 1818-1823*, pp. 312-313; C-III 1: USA Foundation Haute Louisiane, Box 1, *Lettres de la Haute Louisiane II 1823-1830*, pp. 255-256.

341 In January 1827, Mother Bigeu accompanied Mother Barat to Lille, where a new foundation was projected. There she met the Countess of Grandville, one of the first students at the house of Amiens. She could not return there in October because the state of her health had become alarming. She was replaced as superior by Reverend Mother de Peñaranda.

Bishop Rosati, who is now in Saint Louis and blessed our house yesterday, offers us a merger with the Daughters of the Cross, established near Saint Michael, one of the parishes of La Fourche, on the other side of the river. Three American sisters were the first stones, but in an area that is all French and with French novices, they can neither form them nor have children [boarding students]. It would be only a question of giving them a French superior from our Society, to which they wish to unite themselves. I have thought of Mother Carmelite, assistant at Opelousas, who has a great zeal for foundations and who could be replaced there by someone else since the arrival of Mother Dorival.

I wrote to our mother about it. I do not know if she received the letter. Please get me a prompt answer. The bishop, who came this morning to baptize one of our students 16 years old, would like to send word at once. I said that I cannot without permission.

I am with respect, my very dear Mother, your entirely devoted daughter and servant,

Philippine Duchesne
Religious of the S. Heart

Saint Louis, October 3, 1827

[On the reverse:]
To Mother
Mother Bigeu
Superior of the Religious of the Sacred Heart
Lille

Letter 299   **L. 82 to Mother Barat**

SS. C. J. M.

Saint Louis, October 7, 1827[342]
Rec. to St. Anthony of Padua

Dear Reverend Mother,

---

342 Original autograph, C-VII 2) c Duchesne to Barat, Box 2. Postmarks: Liverpool, November 27, 1827; Paris, December 13, 1827. Copy, USA Foundation Haute Louisiane, Box 1, *Lettres de la Haute Louisiane II 1823-1830*, pp. 64-68. Cf. J. de Charry, II, 3, L. 228, pp. 34-37; Sweetman et al pp. 38-43.

I have already written you since the arrival of our sisters on September 9, feast of the Holy Name of Mary. Mother [Helene] Dutour adapted at once. Mother Xavier [Van Damme] has had strong temptations to return. Everything repulsed her, but by the grace of God, she is now calmed down. She will need plenty to do, and at the moment there is not as much work, in contrast to the beginning when nothing was ready, and the need came from all sides. Little by little we will take up the studies again.

I found it difficult to know whether I should leave Mother Dutour in charge here and return to Saint Ferdinand; but on rereading your letters attentively, since I devour them at first reading, I have seen that you are leaving me free to decide about her. Mother Octavie pleases everyone at Florissant; and I think she should stay there, since she is used to dealing with the parents. Mother Hamilton is a very good assistant. It is Mother Lucile who is least satisfactory. She is not very regular. My absence does not worry her; she does better following her own style. She has long been accustomed to meddle in many things and to be always on the move. She is very weak with the children. We have left the house at Saint Ferdinand as it was, giving them only the American postulant [Margaret Short] sent by the Bishop [Fenwick] of Cincinnati; she seems good and is talented.[343] I am staying in Saint Louis, and following your permission, here is the distribution of charges: Mother Dutour, assistant, councilor, mistress general, admonitrix, teacher of the youngest class, in which no child knows how to read, and first *vestiaire*. Mother Xavier, councilor, secretary, in charge of the parlor, of the reading, of singing, and the English class. Sister Mary Ann, Irish, in charge of the orphan boarders and the day students, and *dépensière*.[344] Sister Josephine Gray, novice, portress, second *vestiaire*, teacher of English classes and help with the orphans. Vacation will end on October 8, delayed by Confirmation [given by Bishop Rosati on September 30].

The bishop has often visited us, encouraged us, and seems happy with this establishment. He blessed the house [on October 2], preached at the ceremony, and the next day preached again a second time for the solemn baptism of one of our day students.[345] He left today. He spoke to me again about our union with the Sisters of the Cross. When I gave

---

343 Margaret Mary (Madeleine) Short, RSCJ, born in 1807 in New York, made her first vows in 1830 in Saint Louis and her profession in 1842 at Saint Michael. She died at Kenwood, Albany, in 1870.
344 The person in charge of supplies and meals.
345 On October 3, Bishop Rosati solemnly baptized Miss Elisabeth Dodge. Helene Dutour was her godmother.

him the same answer, that I needed to follow your orders, he seemed to think that they could not wait until then, and that one of the French novices had already left. So I suggested sending them to Saint Michael. That did not seem to enter into his views, because far from consolidating the establishment at La Fourche that way, this measure would take away vocations that perhaps would not return if you refuse the union of the two houses [Saint Michael and La Fourche], which, if you consent, could continue with a single superior; that is what they are asking for.

Mother Octavie is always ailing, though she is on her feet nearly every day and is faithful to her work. I am so used to seeing her constantly ill, and yet recovering from the most dangerous states, that it makes me hope that she will last a long time yet; but if she fails, tell me if you would appoint Mother Dutour as superior there. I do not think she would succeed in Saint Louis because of her physical limitations and the fact that she does not understand English. Even more, if she were at Florissant, the novitiate could stay there until a place and especially spiritual resources could be found in Saint Louis, where the novices would be too distracted. That is why we left the new postulant [Margaret Short] there, who looks hopeful. The novice [Eleonore Gray] spent some time there and is absolutely necessary for us here. We are only five in all, with the help of three adult orphans, mulattos or Creoles, to help with the service.

Several times I have repeated to our newly arrived sisters the permissions that you gave with regard to the decrees of the General Council. Everything cannot be done at once, and the children need to be more carefully handled than in France. They arrive never having known obedience. To exact it too strictly would empty the school at the end of a trimester. Mother Dutour went after them too much the first days. The result was an uproar. Many said they wanted to leave, etc., etc. I hope that experience will adjust everything.

The small number of children who apply will leave us enough room for this winter, but if we get help it would be absolutely necessary to have a larger dormitory and another chapel. I have spoken about it to the bishop, who agrees if we have the means, and I ask your permission for this. Otherwise, the small number of students cannot sustain the house.

I was and am still chagrined by my precipitation in accepting this establishment, seeing in the decrees that one cannot do so in a case like this without explicit consent on your part. The article in the contract where Mr. Mullanphy reserves the right to build a room for his daughters or granddaughters, which would, of course, conform to the order of the house, is also prohibited by the decrees of the council that do not permit something like this except for a founder. Mother Dutour says about this that you have admitted Miss de Cassini[346] into your house, but that does not remove the difficulty.

During the illness of Mother Octavie, I had asked Mother Eugenie for a religious who speaks English to replace her. Mother [Xavier] Hamilton was still alive, and her house would not have suffered. But she resisted greatly, wrote to you, and had someone write to the bishop, not only to keep that religious but to prevent others from going. She wrote to me herself in a high-handed way and continues to treat me with coldness. I answered her first letters saying that Mother Therese [Maillucheau] had refused you Aloysia Jouve and God took her himself, so she should be on guard lest the same thing happen to her. The premature death of Mother Xavier Hamilton only fulfilled what I had said unintentionally; and on seeing this loss, I took care not to repeat the request. Nevertheless, her letters are still cold. She is afraid even to name her daughters. I am not eager to communicate with her. I sympathize a great deal with her difficulties, since she has no one old enough to represent her when necessary and does not receive any help from Mother Piveteau,[347] who has haughtily announced that she will not stay, and perhaps that is for the best. Mother Eugenie does much good and is very well esteemed in the area, but she is one of those people who need to act alone. Given her state of health, and if I might add, her nerves, I think that every contradiction would harm her and that she has more need of encouragement than admonition. Nevertheless, she listens to no one about her health and follows no advice. It seems that there is also some coolness toward Grand Coteau. Mother Xavier Murphy, on the contrary, shares everything and helps us here as much as she can.

I hope that God will bless the name of Xavier and that Mother Van Damme will guide this house well when you think opportune. She is better suited than Mother Dutour, who will do better at Saint Ferdinand or even at La Fourche, a French region that is well populated.

I am at your feet *in Corde Jesu* your unworthy daughter.

Philippine r.S.C.

---

346 Cecile de Cassini (1777-1867), for whom an exception had been made to the decree of the General Council of 1826-1827, had been one of the first members of the community of Amiens.
347 Laure Bernardine Piveteau, RSCJ, was born November 27, 1784, in Santo Domingo. She went to Amiens, entered the novitiate in Paris on August 9, 1820, and made her first vows July 31, 1822. She left for America before final profession, on June 11, 1827, with L. Dorival, H. Dutour and X. Van Damme. She went to Saint Ferdinand September 9, left for Saint Michael, but returned the next year to Saint Ferdinand, where she stayed until her death in 1838.

[On the reverse:]
To Mother
Mother Barat Superior General
of the Religious of the Sacred Heart
Rue de Varenne
At Paris
France
By way of New York

Letter 300   **Letter to Several Religious**

SS. C. J. et M.

Rec. to St Anthony of Padua
Saint Louis, October 7, 1827, feast of the Holy Rosary[348]

My very dear Mothers and Sisters,

Our dear Mother Dutour and Sister Xavier Van Damme, who arrived in Saint Louis on the feast of the Holy Name of Mary, have given us news of you, which we were awaiting impatiently. They told us that almost all the houses had contributed to the expense of their voyage or to the gifts that are coming to us; but since the gifts took a different route from that of the religious, they have not yet arrived. But whatever they are and to whatever house they are addressed, they stir up my lively gratitude, and they are precious to us in every way. We have never received anything that has not been useful in some way; and coming from our houses, these gifts have a special value because they are the measure of the holy and lasting union that unites us in Jesus Christ.

When we receive your letters and when something comes to us from France, we no longer think about the great ocean that separates us. We think we are in France, witnesses of your benefactions, of your labors, and learning from your virtues.

We are not aware of our situation except when, by the small buildings, the poor beginnings, the small number of vocations, the difficulty brought by other religions, the different languages, and the customs of the country, we encounter obstacles in establishing order in the

---

348 Original autograph, C-VII 2) c Duchesne to RSCJ and Children, Box 4. Copies: A-II 2) g Box 2, *Lettres intéressantes de la Société depuis 1816 N° 1*, pp. 444-447 ; C-III 1: USA Foundation Haute Louisiane, Box 1, *Lettres de la Haute-Louisiane II 1823-1830*, pp. 91-95.

community and the classes: an order that is so necessary and to which now we can only tend with all our heart.

I cannot continue this letter without thanking the Heart of Jesus with you for our approbation, without telling you of the pure joy that it caused us, and that it gives us the courage to suffer in order to maintain, if it is possible from our labor, a work that God himself conducts, and to which he has admitted us with a totally free bounty.

Each new establishment brings us new happiness because it extends the glory of the Heart of Jesus and procures for him his spouses. The one in Saint Louis is one of the last in all respects. But it is to Saint Louis that we were destined at first; it is in Saint Louis that our mother general thought we would be best located, and from where the repeated wishes of pastors have called us. Mr. Mullanphy, one of the leading citizens of this city, when I asked him for a house at a good price, offered us one in the part of Saint Louis that is not yet built up, situated in the center of 24 *arpents* of land that he offered with the brick house, on condition that we would have twenty orphans for whom he and his heirs would supply bed and clothing.

This abandoned and deteriorating house was thought to be haunted, so it was sought after at a low price by several people just at the moment when he wanted to give it to us. I regarded that as a ruse of the devil, who wanted to prevent our entry into Saint Louis. I confided myself to the protection of Saint Joseph for what followed, because he was invoked constantly during the negotiations, and I did not see any other possibility for us to be established in the city. I was aware of the serious disadvantages of our isolated location, so I accepted Mr. Mullanphy's condition and promised Saint Joseph that he would be the patron of the house, and that the first novice and an orphan would bear his name. However, I was going against any assurance of success, since Mother Octavie was ill, Mother Eugenie refused me any of her religious, and I had a bad leg that seemed as if it would make me useless; and before May 1, the day when we were to begin, God called to himself our young mother, the first professed in America, Mother Xavier Hamilton, a rare vocation for us, who had the gift of teaching perfectly in the two languages and was my only hope for a perfect translation of our Constitutions. So I had to go alone to Saint Louis, with only an Irish postulant; at that time the house was not ready, the teachers were lacking, and there was a crowd of children who escaped from us, now that we would have been able to receive them.

Our greatest trial is the uncertainty about spiritual resources: the distance from the Jesuits and the "third year" that they will make results in the fact that they rarely devote themselves to giving us these resources; and the two priests of Saint Louis have two parishes and are obliged to be occupied there. Ask God to soften this privation by one of those strokes of Providence that cost him nothing.

I saw with great joy that cloister is tightened. To go along with the desire of the pastor, we had the procession of the Blessed Sacrament on our property on the feast of the Sacred Heart, only for the members of the confraternity.[349] But the singing, the order, the repository, and the sense of recollection were carried out poorly in my opinion, so I am delighted to be able to decline a new request because of a prohibition of the [General] Council. We are still deprived of exposition because we do not have an ostensorium or a censer and enough people for adoration; I hope it will be possible after the arrival of the trunks and the religious. But our chapel is not very appropriate for the divine majesty; it is the former kitchen, half underground, what they call a basement here. You can touch the ceiling with your hand, and the chimney has deteriorated. I have killed several toads there and other hideous animals and big spiders that sang like a little bird in the evenings when I was alone in the chapel. These are, along with a big feral cat resident in the attic, the only ghosts we have seen, and frankly, I feared them less than live men at the beginning.

This poor chapel and the disadvantage, because of the orphans, of not being able to lodge more than 12 boarders—who are not enough to maintain the house—make us resolve to undertake, if our mother consents, a building that would contain a chapel on the ground floor and be built according to the rule and with a dormitory. Money is what wages war with us, for the house at Saint Michael is not out of debt; Saint Ferdinand and Opelousas do not have debt, but the former is heavily drained because I have taken so much for Saint Louis and for the maintenance of the poor Indians and orphans who are there. Fortunately, we are able to clothe them from gifts from the boarding school at Opelousas, whose boarders weep when their clothes are not given to the poor. This house is blessed under the leadership of Mother Xavier Murphy who, by her zeal along with her rare talent of speaking and writing English, charms the Protestant parents, of whom several

---

349 The parish in Saint Louis, therefore, has a Confraternity of the Sacred Heart. These lay associations, constituted on the model of older societies of devotion and charity, were erected by ecclesiastical authority in the churches of religious, cathedrals and parishes, and filled with indulgences. They multiplied under the influence of the revelations of Paray-le-Monial from the end of the seventeenth century and spread to mission countries. The confraternities met on certain days in a chapel specially dedicated to the Sacred Heart. Cf. J. de Charry, *History of the Constitutions*, part 1, pp. 16-20.

have consented to let their children become Catholics. The establishment of Saint Michael is very much appreciated in the region, and Mother Eugenie is highly esteemed.

That of Saint Ferdinand abounds in spiritual graces, perfect retreats each year, confessions as often as one wants, and instructions of all kinds in the two languages. Nothing is lacking, neither Mass, nor Benediction, nor exposition. All the children there are becoming Catholic, but most of them secretly. Eight Jesuit priests are at the parish, now in retreat; in a year, they will be spread out in different places, one of which will be close to the Indians.

Bishop Rosati has just ordained 4 of these good priests.[350] He solemnly blessed the house in Saint Louis, baptized a student 14 years old, preached at two ceremonies, and finally, today, Sunday, after Mass, he left us with the hope that he will reside in our city.[351]

There is space left only to offer you our wishes for a good year, to commend me to your prayers, and to say that I am all yours in the Sacred Heart,

Philippine Duchesne r. S. C.

Letter 301   L. 37 to Bishop Rosati

SS. C. J. et M.

[Saint Louis, October 24, 1827][352]

Dear Bishop,

I just this moment received this letter addressed to you, which Father Borgna tells me is urgent. I am sending it by post for lack of a messenger.

For several days, I have been thinking about writing to you, anxious though I am not to interrupt your important work; however I do need enlightenment on a difficulty I am having with the father superior. He is

---

350   Fathers De Smet, Verreydt, Van Assche and Elet were ordained by Bishop Rosati in the church at Florissant: sub-deacons on September 21, 1827, deacons on September 22, and priests on the 23. Cf. *JSA*.

351   At the time, Bishop Rosati was apostolic administrator of the dioceses of Saint Louis and of New Orleans, recently created by the division of the diocese of Louisiana. Named bishop of Saint Louis in 1828, he took up residence in his diocese only in 1830, after the arrival of Bishop Leo De Neckere in New Orleans.

352   Original autograph, C-VII 2) c Writings Duchesne to Rosati, Box 6. On the reverse: "Oct. 24, 1827, Mother Duchesne, St. Louis; received Nov. 2; answered 4th."

giving me qualms about assigning novices in small employments, saying that if they do not persevere, I shall be in part responsible. I am still using our only novice and our one postulant, although our rule says they shall be employed only in their own religious instruction and manual work. My reasons are: first, that I look upon myself here as making a beginning for the Society, and there are no older religious to relieve the young; second, that this was done in all the foundations in France; finally, because I am sure that the newcomers will become accustomed to religious life sooner by varying their work a little. Otherwise they would be very lonely, for they have no companions with whom to relax and recreate together.

I avoid going to confession to the father because should he say the same thing to me in confession, I would be in even greater difficulty. I content myself with the one whom Providence has given us, always an opportunity to sacrifice for others. Father Lutz was sick all last week. The Jesuits also have many fever-stricken, and the reverend father has not yet recovered from his last trip to the Osage. This winter will be one of privation for us, for Mr. Lepère's house could not be finished; I was obliged, therefore, in order to take back our kitchen, to give him the only room that has a private entrance, one that I optimistically hoped would be a shelter for priests who would be kind enough to visit us.

I hope that in time you will be able to give us that great consolation.

I am with respect and veneration in the Sacred Heart, Bishop, your very humble and devoted daughter and servant.

Philippine Duchesne, sup.

Saint Louis, October 24, 1827

[On the reverse:]
V R D Rosati
Bishop of Saint Louis
Barrens Perry Country
Missouri

Letter 302   **L. 83 to Mother Barat**

SS. C. J. M.

Saint Louis, January 3, 1828
Rec. to St. Anthony of Padua
Confidential[353]

Very Reverend Mother,

As fond as I am of this new world, where we see the spread of the loving devotion that unites us in the dear Society, still I would very much like to cross the distances and be able again to find myself really at your feet, where I am so often in spirit. How I need to open my soul to you and be strengthened by your advice. I remember the happy days on the mountain [Sainte-Marie d'En-Haut, in Grenoble], and I deeply regret that I did not profit better from them.

You must have seen from the letter from the father superior that I sent you how matters stand between us with regard to the foundation in Saint Charles. He continues to be displeased and tells my sisters that I am the reason that he does not want to come here. He told me himself that I am an opinionated person who will do bad things for our houses; that the brothers and the fathers were all unhappy. When I inquired, I found that it was just the opposite. They are very annoyed that there is not a foundation in Saint Charles and do not want other religious; but they realize full well that I can do nothing without your consent, which they want. But the father thinks it is I who am putting up obstacles; and he practically wants me to submit your letters to him, because he wants to know if, when you say not to multiply foundations, you explicitly named Saint Charles, and that a permission given cannot be taken away. The others want to help us, but they cannot approach us.

We are here thanks to the charity of the pastor and of a missionary who has two parishes. He says Mass for us several times a week, and the former on Sundays when he can. But God permitted for our trial that he was ill for several months. Now he comes as usual, but a little late. The pastor hears the confessions of the whole house. He himself has been to confession with good Father Barat and keeps one of his letters as a remembrance. Father Dusaussoy also taught him a class in

---

353 Original autograph, C-VII 2) c Duchesne to Barat, Box 2. Postmarks: Le Havre, July 3, 1828; Paris, July 5, 1828. Cf. J. de Charry, II, 3, L. 233, pp. 49-53; De Charry-Sweetman et al, pp. 55-60.

Bordeaux. His name is Father Saulnier. His unselfishness helps us a great deal, for where would we find 1000 F, which would be the least that a chaplain would cost us, besides food and lodging? We still do not have any appropriate apartment. The only room that could possibly be given is now occupied by a domestic servant until the house is finished, and it gives onto a passage used constantly by our sisters and the children, and that would not do for a priest.

So many drawbacks together make me think that it is best for now to take advantage of the good will of the priests of Saint Louis. Since we are so few, regularity would suffer from having a resident priest, because of the work involved. It is also a good idea to be sparing now in order to enlarge the house: our chapel, half underground, is humid and not appropriate. It would become a classroom, and when we build a chapel we would also do a good dormitory, which is necessary to maintain the house; in its present state it can only house 12 children.

Mother Dutour seems happy and says so. Mother Xavier [Van Damme], with so many ways to succeed here, is not happy and even less at Saint Ferdinand. Her state of health might be a contributing factor; she has had some abscesses that have caused her much suffering until they broke open. She is now a little better and went to the retreat at Saint Ferdinand given by the father superior. After three days, she was in bed with a severe attack of erysipelas in the head, and a nervous crisis *(illegible word)*. Today she is in bed with fever. She disdains our little establishments and the simplicity of the sisters and is very ready to pass judgment. She thinks everyone has *temptations*, etc.

Father Eccleston,[354] traveling companion of our mothers, wrote to them that the bishop of Baltimore had entrusted to him correspondence with you about an establishment in his city and sees it as important. Our mothers believe that you will send the necessary people there in the spring time. Mother Eugenie thinks that she will be in charge of negotiations. I do not think she knows enough English to do business in this country. She is about to begin an establishment for orphans and thinks she has your permission. The house at Opelousas, which is overwhelmed, has been asking for an assistant. Sister Marguerite is moving into a childish state. I assure you that two of those religious, of which you have enough in certain houses, would be very useful here and just as many teachers, since they would replace the latter for the

---

[354] Samuel Eccleston, PSS, organized the voyage of the religious on the boat from New York to New Orleans, watched over them, and saw to their baggage at his expense. Once in Baltimore, he tried to persuade Bishop Marechal to open a house of the Sacred Heart, but it did not happen. He succeeded Bishop Marechal as archbishop of Baltimore in 1828.

material work. For example, Sister [Benoîte] Boisson[355] would do well at La Fourche, if you accept the union with the Sisters of the Cross, and their travel would cost much less than the purchase of a single Negress. Mother Xavier [Murphy] tells me that if she purchases one, she will not be able to send anything, and I counted on her for our buildings. Besides other advantages of having only sisters, a single Negress will cost 2000 F, and the travel of two sisters 1000 or 1500 F. A trousseau is not necessary; here we clothe ourselves with very little.

A postulant sent here from Washington by the father provincial of the Jesuits and the pastor of the city says that Mrs. Baker has not left her husband's house since her return, and that people have stopped blaming her because she is believed to have taken up the care of her family again, and that one of her daughters in her absence was preserved from danger by a Protestant gentleman and did not want to see her mother when she returned. None of her daughters has a vocation. She says that her husband's permission was: "Let her go to the devil!" I cannot believe it because the Holy Father would not have made a decision without adequate documentation.[356] But in the East they are in agreement that her presence there would do harm to one of our establishments. She says that this land and even more, Louisiana, are good places to die. We think she will not come. I have sent her your decision about Saint Michael.

This postulant [Mary Noyer] took the habit at Saint Ferdinand on the feast of Saint John, with the name Ignatius. She is fully formed in virtue, but she has deplorable health and is already tempted to leave. When I learned this, I wrote to stop her from receiving the habit. The father superior led her to decide to do it, and Mother Octavie consented. The one from Cincinnati [Margaret Short] took the habit on November 21 and wants the name Magdalene. She has much talent, but is not very solid. There are 3 Sister postulants [coadjutrices] of 16 and 17 years of age. Please grant that they not have to wait until 18. Here they are more mature than in France. *All* the girls marry quite young. Later on, none of them would want to come. I do not ask much but these three things: reception of the habit at 16 years, permission to go to Saint Charles as soon as possible, and the union with the sisters of La Fourche.

The expense account done by Mother Octavie has not been converted.[357] I am sending it anyway because my letter has waited several days,

---

355 She wanted very much to come to the American mission.
356 The pope had given Mrs. Baker the exceptional permission to enter the convent even though she was married.
357 The expense account of Florissant is in dollars and has not been converted into francs.

and I want your answer very much. You only have to multiply the totals by 5 to have the result for ten months in francs. The entry "contribution" refers mainly to the house at Saint Louis and for the church of Saint Ferdinand.

I am ever in your hands, wanting to be forgotten and retired, but totally devoted to the work in every way, if you say so. I am *in Corde Jesu*, Reverend Mother, your unworthy daughter.

Philippine r. S. C.

My respects to our good fathers.

[On the reverse:]
To Mother
To Mother Barat, Superior General
of the Religious of the Sacred Heart
Rue de Varenne
Paris
France
By way of New York
Overseas by way of Le Havre

Letter 303   **L. 38 to Bishop Rosati**

SS. C. J. M.

[January 6, 1828][358]

Dear Bishop,

It was with justifiable consternation that I received the news of the different mishaps of your journey. Fortunately for us, divine Providence saw fit to save you, I hope this loving Providence will give you length of days for our own happiness and let success crown all that your zeal prompts you to undertake for the glory of God. These are always our wishes, but I offer them to you in particular now at the beginning of this New Year.

---

358   Original autograph, C-VII 2) c Writings Duchesne to Rosati, Box 6. On the reverse: "January, 6, 1828, Mother Duchesne, St. Louis; received March 9; answered the 12th."

I have as yet received no answer from our mother general regarding our uniting with the Sisters of the Cross. It seems that this was proposed to Mother Eugenie at Saint Michael even before you spoke of it to me, and there was question of it openly in Opelousas when she went there. Mother Eugenie is afraid that a foundation of ours so close to hers might hinder the progress of Saint Michael. Mother Xavier, the superior in Opelousas, thinks that Sister Carmelite Landry is absolutely indispensable to her, while at the same time she admits that she would make an excellent superior for the proposed house. All these difficulties will disappear if our mother gives her consent, and I have urged her to do so.

I am meeting with new obstacles here. The father superior of the Jesuits, whom we had promised to go to Saint Charles, came to ask me if we would not fulfill our obligations. I told him we could not without a new permission from our superior general who, after our foundation here, had told me to stop and to strengthen our four houses. He insisted on having a *yes* or a *no*, saying he needed an answer. I was unable to say *yes*, and I thought *no* would satisfy him since he wanted something that was impossible at the moment. So I gave him *no* as an answer, and he seemed satisfied. That made me feel sure that he had other plans and wanted to get out of the situation if possible. However, contrary to my expectations, he became very angry and said that he had announced at Saint Charles that there would be a convent, and hence the townspeople were ready for whatever he proposed and that our refusal would do much harm. My excuses did not mitigate his indignation. He is extremely put out with me and added that my highhandedness was causing great trouble in our houses. If you know anything about this, Bishop, please be good enough to tell me; believe in my utter submission. I am in the position I hold only by obedience. I have always cherished the last place and longed with all my soul for peace and solitude.

I asked our mother again to do the utmost[359] so that we can make a foundation in Saint Charles. Answers take so long in coming that many things happen before receiving them. We have two novices and two postulants whose vocations are not very sure.

Father Odin paid us a visit and consoled us very much with the news of the seminary and the parish. Without him we should have missed Sunday Mass. Father Lutz is still sick. He does what he can for us with great kindness, as does Father Saulnier. However the hour of Mass, when we have it, is irregular. Nothing better can be done given

---

359 Philippine uses the colloquial expression, *Nous mettre en quatre,* meaning to try one's best.

the lack of lodging and resources. Our religious who have just arrived find the going hard, and the one who seemed the strongest is nearly always ill. We have ten boarders. Please excuse this long letter, Bishop. Please bless me and all my sisters and believe me in the Sacred Heart of Jesus your Excellency's submissive and devoted daughter.

Philippine Duchesne, supr. of the S. Heart

January 6, 1828

> [On the reverse:]
> To Bishop
> Bishop Rosati
> Bishop of Saint Louis
> *New Orleans*

Letter 304   **L. 21 to Mrs. de Rollin**

SS. C. J. et M.

January 14 [1828][360]
Rec. to Saint Anthony

My very dear Cousin,

I last received news about you from Mother Barat, who had the pleasure of seeing you at Sainte-Marie, a house that has new responsibility toward you and consequently toward me. I have expressed my gratitude, but since the mail can be unreliable, I am telling you again, as much for your protection of the refuge of my happiness and for your gift of 500 F that I received complete in September.

Please also thank my cousin Augustin [Perier] for his obliging response dated from Paris, which held so many interesting details about the whole family.

Our houses in Louisiana are growing, and those of Missouri are still small. It is my lot and I cherish it. But the need to lock up more securely, since we were robbed, makes me recall again that you have had the charity to ask in one of your last letters if I had any needs, if

---

360 *Copies of letters of Philippine Duchesne to Mme de Rollin and a few others, No. 21; Cahier, Lettres à Mme de Rollin*, pp. 50-51. C-VII 2) c Duchesne to her family and lay people, Box 5. The existing copy bears the date of 1825, but the situation of the houses corresponds to the year 1828.

you could do something this year. I hope not to have to make a similar request again, and nevertheless, do not be upset if you have to say no.

Goodbye, dear Friend, many good wishes to our good relations,

Philippine

Letter 305   L. 39 to Bishop Rosati

SS. C. J. M.

[January 24, 1828][361]

Dear Bishop,

I have heard with deep concern of the accidents that occurred on your trip, and we are redoubling our prayers for your safekeeping and for the continuation of your work in the happy diocese of which God has given you charge and to which we have the joy of belonging.

Our superior general has just written me telling of the death of a very precious religious; another, the one who worked in Rome to obtain our approbation is in danger of death [Joséphine Bigeu]. She tells me to postpone indefinitely a foundation in the East; she is being urged to make one in either New York or Baltimore. The difficulty of finding personnel and funds for such an enterprise has put an end to her plans. I have all the more hope that she will agree to our uniting with the Sisters of the Cross, which can take place without cost and with only one or two persons.

However, Mother Eugenie will pose obstacles to us in this, and possibly she has written to our mother general to the contrary.

1. She says this establishment will harm hers.
2. She wants Mother Carmelite herself.
3. She counters that our mother said not to make another foundation in Louisiana.
4. Without contradicting her opinion, which would be useless, since our mother's answer is inconclusive, I shall answer:
5. That since we want to open an orphanage, it would be far better located at La Fourche in a ready-made building than at Saint Michael

---

361 Original autograph, C-VII 2) c Writings Duchesne to Rosati, Box 6. On the reverse: "January 24, 1828, Mother Duchesne, St. Louis; received at Donaldsonville, March 10; answered the 12th."

where there is already an overwhelming amount of work and where we should have to build and incur debt again.
6. That Mother Xavier, superior in Opelousas, can give up Carmelite only in the extreme need of finding a superior, because she looks after the material needs of the house with which Mother Xavier is not familiar; neither is Mother Dorival, who has just arrived from France; the others are untrained. I should then have to replace her, not an easy task.
7. In truth, our mother did advise not extending ourselves further for a while, but that is because she was afraid we would ask for money and personnel, both of which she wants to save for the East, which she is giving up for now.

I am surprised at Mother Eugenie's displeasure, of which she has told me to inform you. Our mother has given me charge of all the houses in this country in spite of me. Mother Eugenie does not wish to give any religious for the foundation and has already kept a Sister from here whom I needed; I have given in. Now her community numbers seventeen, and she wants to take a necessary person from Opelousas where they are only five. Is there justice in that?

Because I told her she was exceeding her powers, she has taken offense. I cannot say that something wrong is right. And I have been telling her for a long time that rather than get herself into even greater debt by expansion, it would be better to limit herself to the number of children that can be actually cared for; otherwise there is danger of decline.

Not only did I write our mother about La Fourche but also again about a foundation in Saint Charles, and I need both these answers. The father superior came one day to ask me when we would be in Saint Charles. I told him it was impossible for the moment, that we had to get settled first in Saint Louis and that our mother wants us to stop making foundations for the present. He insisted, saying he had to have an answer, *yes* or *no*. I could not say *yes*, so I said *no*. He became very embittered and said he would never come back, etc., etc. He accused me of being the sole cause of the refusal. Alas! I have rather too much eagerness for our expansion.

I represented this to our mother, saying I would much prefer to go alone to Saint Charles than to have this rift. If I should receive her answer by spring, that you still approve the union with La Fourche, I plan to accompany one of our nuns to Opelousas where I am much needed. It is the return trip alone that will be difficult. Father Richard is still speaking to me about coming here. If you would release him at this time, it would be most advantageous for us. However all is still indefinite. Health is very poor here.

All I pray is that yours is still good and that you will return to us soon.

I am with respectful veneration your Excellency's submissive daughter and servant.

Philippine Duchesne, sup.
r. of the S. Heart

January 24, 1828

[On the reverse:]
To Bishop
Bishop Rosati
Bishop of Saint Louis
New Orleans

Letter 306   L. 84 to Mother Barat

Saint Louis, March 23, 1828[362]

Dear Reverend Mother,

I have just received your two letters at the same time, the first from November 25 and the second from December 13, both telling me of the death of Mother Bigeu. Although we were warned from what you wrote in September, we were very distressed. The void that she leaves for you, as well as that of Mother Camille, and the painful wound it has made to your heart are what touch me the most. As for her, her lot is to be envied. When she was in Grenoble, I was practically the one who saw her least, since I could not attend her instructions in the novitiate, which were shared by the whole community.[363] All the rest

---

362 Copy, USA Foundation Haute Louisiane, Box 1, *Lettres de la Haute Louisiane II 1823-1830*, pp. 82- 86; Partial copy, C-III 1: USA Foundation Haute Louisiane, Box 3, *Lettres de la Louisiane I*, pp. 345-347. J. de Charry, II, 3, L. 234, pp. 54-55; Sweetman et al, pp.60-62.

363 Josephine Bigeu was superior in Grenoble from September 25, 1813, to October 26, 1815, and Philippine was her assistant. They left Sainte-Marie d'En-Haut to go to the General Council that opened in Paris on November 1, 1815. They then lived in the generalate, Josephine as assistant general and mistress of novices, Philippine as secretary general until her departure for Louisiana.

of her life is better known to you than to me, and all I could say would only be repetition.

I have learned through a letter from Mother Eugenie that Bishop Rosati has already sent her six novices from the Sisters of the Cross, and that she has already sent away two who are unsuited for the Society. I do not know whether those who have made their vows still want to join us, or to return to their former house. They have to decide one way or the other, since they cannot keep their boarding school in a country where only French is spoken, a language that only one of them knows....[364]

I come once more to ask you, Reverend Mother, to approve the establishment in Saint Charles. Father rector is continually asking for it with insistence. Saint Regis, patron of the mission, will work a miracle for this area under the care of the Jesuits, and Saint Joseph, who filled us with devotion on his feast day, will sustain that of Saint Louis, which increased its day school during his novena and that of Saint Xavier.[365] We now have 12 boarders, 10 orphans, 10 paying day students, and 30 free. Besides this, on Sunday we have a school for mulatto girls, after the parish service, to instruct them in their religion. So there are more than 60 children to whom we have the happiness of making known the Sacred Heart. If the labor involved surpasses the temporal profit, isn't it for the sake of heaven, an added benefit, and I rejoice in it.

The father superior is leaving today to go to the Osage, where he will stay for a month. He has formally given me the house in Saint Charles.[366] On the feast of Saint Joseph, he preached for us and said Holy Mass.

I am at your feet, reverend and very dear Mother, your daughter,

Philippine Duchesne

---

364 Eugenie Audé did not wait for the agreement of the superior general, considering it given. On December 27, she offered to Bishop Rosati to receive the five novices of the sisters of La Fourche at Saint Michael. They arrived on January 21, 1828, and three of them took the habit on March 25: Louise Aucoin and Marie Rose Girouard as coadjutrices, and Eulalie Guillot as choir religious. Bishop Rosati then envisioned the merger of the house of La Fourche with the Society of the Sacred Heart, which suggested that the two professed should stay there.

365 This is the "novena of grace," held from March 4 to 12, in honor of Saint Francis Xavier. It coincided partially with the novena preceding the feast of Saint Joseph, March 19.

366 Father Van Quickenborne forced Philippine to accept the donation of the Duquette house in order to found a school of the Sacred Heart there.

Letter 307   L. to Mother Quatrebarbes[367]

SS. C. J. M.

[March 22, 1828][368]

My dear Sister,

Only yesterday I received your letter of November 10. It came to me by way of the house at Saint Michael where it was undoubtedly sent.

Everything that comes to us from France is very dear, but if we were to distinguish the most precious letters, they are those that come directly from the center of the Society, and from this novitiate that is its consolation and hope. Since you have been willing to be its interpreter for us, please convey for us the witness of gratitude that we owe for this dear remembrance. Keep showing us the same signs of affection in Our Lord by keeping us up to date in news about the two Societies. It is our happiness to learn about their progress, and the afflictions that God bestows on them teach us how we should bear ours.

You cannot doubt how the foundations in Rome and Perpignan excited us, not out of envy, because we cherish the place God has marked out for us, but of gratitude towards God, who testifies that he does not disdain the services of the daughters of his Heart.

The sister who compiled the narrative about your feast of the Sacred Heart did not add her name, but you undoubtedly know it; and I hope you will tell her for us how interesting it was. Our houses of Louisiana are not in a hurry to send their copies, which joined to mine, will put together three for our three houses in Missouri.

You do not yet know that we are no longer here in what was previously called *Louisiana* or *Illinois*. The state closest to the mouth of the Mississippi is the only one to have kept the name of *Louisiana*. We are separated by the large territory of *Arkansas*, and our State of *Missouri* extends only from New Madrid. The State of Illinois is on the left bank of the Mississippi, pretty much along the same extent as ours.

The houses of Saint Michael, La Fourche, and Opelousas are the only ones in the State of *Louisiana*. At least three hundred leagues separate them from the State of Missouri, where are the three other houses of

---

367 Virginie de Quatrebarbes, RSCJ, was born January 6, 1817, and took the habit in Paris, July 31, 1827, so she is presumably a novice at the time of writing. She made her profession May 4, 1832, and died April 25, 1865.
368 Original autograph, C-VII 2) c Duchesne to RSCJ and Children, Box 4.

the Sacred Heart in America: Saint Louis, Saint Ferdinand, and Saint Charles. I am happy that you will find there nothing but saints' names, in a country that you would think is completely infidel or barbarian.

I can assure you that it is more difficult here than in Paris about the outer appearances of education, table manners, attire and pleasures. There are faithful souls everywhere; ask that we be such and that we will not shame the Society, our mother.

I am *in Corde Jesu*, all yours,

Philippine

March 22

[On the reverse:]
To Mother
Mother de Quatrebarbes
House of the Sacred Heart, Rue de Varenne
Paris[369]

Letter 308   L. 22 to Mrs. de Rollin

SS. C. J. M.

April 10, 1828[370]
St Anthony

My very dear Cousin,

It has been a very long time since I have heard news of you, and it is dear to me to remember her whom the bonds of relationship, friendship, and gratitude unite in the same way. I could add even better, those of religion. Indeed, it is your zeal for our holy faith that has overwhelmed me with your gifts and that has helped me in the establishment begun in the city of Saint Louis itself since last May. Though we lack accommodations and personnel, we are giving instruction to more than 70 children, both boarders and day students, of whom 10 are orphans in our care. Saint Louis is our 4th establishment. The two in Louisiana have only boarders; the two in Missouri are a mixture of boarders and

---

369   The address was changed; the letter was sent to Poitiers.
370   *Copies of letters of Philippine Duchesne to Mme de Rollin and a few others, No. 23*; *Cahier, Lettres à Mme de Rollin*, pp. 55-56. C-VII 2) c Duchesne to her family and lay people, Box 5.

day students, which makes much more work. Two other houses are in preparation: one near here in Saint Charles, our first house, and the other again in Louisiana.

The health of my traveling companions has changed very much; mine is better for the past year. I am concerned about yours, since I have had no news of you, and when I consider how many death has harvested in our family since 1818, the year of our separation, I dread with each letter to learn of more blows.

As for you, good Friend, I will see you again! God did not bring us together only for the brief instants of this life; after this move from one to the other hemisphere, we will be reunited quickly to keep an eternal union. How beautiful and consoling religion is when, in exchange for light labors, it gives us in return all the enjoyments that ensure happiness.

Do not forget to convey my sentiments to Mrs. Perier, Teisseire, to my sisters, and to my brother, whose health worries me; to your brothers to whom I owe so much, to my sisters at Sainte-Marie d'En-Haut, from whom I hear almost nothing, to their good pastor, Father Rambaud whom I cannot forget, and to Father Dumolard; I forget if he is still near Grenoble.

Bishop Dubourg's return to France has caused the departure of many ecclesiastics, but others are being formed in the seminary who will replace them, and the Catholic religion is doing well in the United States. The Protestants generally hold Catholic institutions in esteem and gladly send their children there.

We will be happy if, at the price of many sacrifices, we will have made God known and loved by one more soul.

I am all yours in the Heart of Jesus,

Philippine Duchesne
r. S. C.

Letter 309   L. 40 to Bishop Rosati

SS. C. J. M.

[April 24, 1828][371]

Dear Bishop,

---

371   Original autograph. L. 40 to Bishop Rosati. C-VII 2) c Writings Duchesne to Rosati, Box 6. On the reverse: "April 24, 1828, Mother Duchesne, St. Louis."

Mother Xavier Miles[372] arrived yesterday morning and gave me the letter with which you honored me. I was pleasantly surprised to learn that she is the superior of the Sisters of the Cross. I had no suitable room to give her, and as the novices are at Florissant under the direction of the reverend father, she went there. She was worn out from her journey, and I recommended that all possible care be given her.

Mother Eugenie has said nothing to me about who is to be superior at Assumption, and she cannot supply one. Mother Carmelite was recommended to our mother general on condition that you approve of this choice. She is well able to manage a house, which ought not to be as large as Saint Michael. Otherwise it would be detrimental to the latter.

In his last letter Father Richard said nothing more about coming here. This is all the harder now that Father Saulnier finds the burden too heavy. Moreover, there will never be regularity in the house until the time of Mass is fixed. However, we have much work: fifty day pupils in the free school, eighteen paying day pupils, twelve boarders, ten orphans; these ninety children are much more difficult to manage than if they were all together. Here we are beginning to build our chapel.

I am with veneration *in Corde Jesu*, your Excellency's devoted and submissive servant.

Philippine Duchesne

April 24

[On the reverse:]
To Bishop
Bishop Rosati
Bishop of Saint Louis
New Orleans

---

372 Joanna (Xavier) Miles (1800-1868), discouraged by the circumstances in which she found herself (debts, lack of an approved Rule, ambiguity about merger with the Society of the Sacred Heart, and departure of the novices for Saint Michael), left her community at the end of January 1828. After a time in New Orleans, she presented herself to Philippine Duchesne on April 25, supplied with a letter from Bishop Rosati dated April 9; he had advised her to go to the novitiate at Saint Ferdinand. She left with two other postulants on June 24, the day of a visit by Bishop Rosati, to return to the motherhouse at Loretto. She then left her congregation and in 1831 married Richard Maddock, with whom she had four children. Widowed, she ended her life at the Barrens.

Letter 310   **L. 41 to Bishop Rosati**

SS. C. J. M.

[May 1, 1828][373]

Dear Bishop,

I have just received the letter you were kind enough to write to me on April 15, which contains so many interesting details. It seems that you did not receive the one I wrote you. In it I spoke of some complaints Father Saulnier wished to make to you about me. I would be happy if I were not the cause of them, but I am forced to face the truth.

I added a word about Father Loiseul, who after being ill for three months, then away, had been replaced here by Father Lutz. On his return I did not ask him to come back because he was still sick and does not like the climate of Saint Louis, which he believes is not good for him. I hoped to avoid continual changes of plan, and I even feared it would offend Father Lutz who has been so good to us. Father Dusaussoy has gone back to France and the father superior to Washington. There is rumor of his being gravely ill.

Our mother general had told me to ask your permission to visit the houses in Louisiana and together with the superiors to draw up a report for her of what could best contribute to establishing uniformity and regularity, as well as an account of expenses in this country. An indisposition that was making the trip difficult for me and conditions in this house prevented me from leaving. I found it easier for Mothers Eugenie and Xavier to make the visitation, for they have enough people. Doubtless, they will have said a word about this and asked your advice.

Our superior general has been insisting in her last letters that Mother Dutour not enlarge her establishment. The letters she writes our mother show that she is not willing to maintain simplicity; she asks for marks of distinction that not even our largest boarding schools have. She complains that she has only *three histories of France*. That is to say that Mother Dutour wants to give the same education with simpler dress and moderate fees and consequently bring to her school what goes on in the others. Our mother gave her consent to the foundation at La Fourche only on condition that it would be different. I have proof that

---

373 Original autograph, C-VII 2) c Writings Duchesne to Rosati, Box 6. On the reverse: "May 1, 1828, Mother Duchesne, St. Louis; received the 30th."

Mother Dutour, upon going there, before she had seen anything, had already planned to bring it up to the level of our other schools. She has exceeded her authority by making some who should be coadjutrix sisters into choir religious; she wanted to train her own novices, contrary to our rules, which require that they all be in the same house. Our mother wants me to prevent Sisters who do not have the necessary qualifications from becoming choir religious.

What can I do when all this is done without even consulting me? She does not write. Mother Dutour's independence is really blameworthy. We do not contradict her announcements, which are published in the newspapers, in order to avoid scandal. But our mother does not want her to raise the level of the studies to the highest classes. If she is caring for thirty children, she has enough to occupy her staff, and we cannot send her any teachers. It would be better to go at a moderate pace than to fill the house, then see it fail. How happy we would be if the number of thirty pupils were self-supporting everywhere.

I am with veneration your Excellency's submissive daughter.

Philippine Duchesne
rel. Sacred Heart

May 1, 1828

[On the reverse:]
To Bishop
Bishop Rosati
Bishop of Saint Louis
New Orleans
Louisiana

Letter 311   Letter to William Carr Lane[374]

Evening of 3rd May 1828

Sir,

I have recourse to your authority for the redress of an abuse, which I look upon as very much against the welfare of our establishment.

You know, Sir, that our young ladies, day scholars, in order to reach our house have to pass the creek that runs all round our house.

---

[374] Original autograph. Series XII, C. Callan Box 7 packet 2, *Letters to lay people*. Mr. William Carr Lane was at the time mayor of Saint Louis. This is the only extant letter of Philippine written in English.

The warm weather invites a number of men and boys to swimming in the creek, and every day our young ladies meet with that disagreeable sight, both in coming and leaving the house; and as I understood that some regulation of Court forbids swimming in public places, I suppose that it is merely by some negligence of the Sheriffs in the discharge of their duty that it takes place.

As you are, Sir, the father of an amiable family, I need not say how much that rudeness is against that delicacy of sentiments we strive to endow our young ladies with, and I am convinced you will be so good as to use your power to remove that obstacle.

I offer you beforehand my thanks and beg you to believe me with deep respect, Sir, your most obedient servant.

Philippine Duchesne
Sup.

Letter 312   **L. 42 to Bishop Rosati**

SS. C. J. M.

[May 12, 1828][375]

Dear Bishop,

My first letter missed the [steamboat] *Oregon*, which was to have taken it, and I preferred to wait for the *Jubilee*, which arrived a little afterwards, than to take the long way of the post. Your invitation to me to go down was a tempting one, but since I had told my sisters, who were expecting me, that I could not leave and I had asked Mother Eugenie to go herself, I hesitated to reconsider. We are so far apart that I feared coming to cross purposes [without reaching a meeting of the minds]. What kept me back more than anything else was the oft repeated discontent of Sister Xavier Van Damme, which made me fear strongly that she could not replace me, especially since she has not won the children.

When I received word from our superior general, I stopped trying to keep her here against her will. There is question of either changing her to another house or of sending her back to France. I have reason to

---

375 Original autograph, C-VII 2) c Writings Duchesne to Rosati, Box 6. On the reverse: "May 12, 1828, Mother Duchesne, St. Louis; received May 30."

hope she will be happy at Saint Michael, where everything is as it is in France and better equipped. She is eager to renew herself in the Society and to persevere therein. I judged that I had enough authority under the direction of our superior general and the advice of our confessor. I could not wait for your permission to reach me from so far away because Father Tichitoli[376] told me that Mother Dutour needed one more person. Aware that her lungs cannot long withstand the work she has to do, I am sending her Sister Therese Detchemendy, whom she seemed to like in Florissant. This sister herself once asked me if she might go to Louisiana in order to be more French, although she reads and speaks English when she wants to.

I have just received a letter from Bishop Dubourg, who is delighted with our two new foundations and especially with that of the Sisters of Charity in Saint Louis. He says that he will die satisfied when he hears that the college is founded here and that you are living here.

I am with veneration in the Heart of Jesus, your Excellency's submissive and devoted daughter.

Philippine Duchesne
r. du S. C.

Saint-Louis, May 12, 1828

[On the reverse:]
To Bishop
Bishop Rosati
Bishop of Saint Louis
New Orleans

Letter 313**L. 43 to Bishop Rosati**

SS. C. J. M.

[May 31, 1828][377]

---

376 Joseph Tichitoli, CM, was ordained sub-deacon before arriving in Baltimore in 1816 with Father Rosati and his companions. He was sent to Missouri, but his health did not permit him to stay there. He left for Louisiana in 1819 and was parish priest in Donaldsonville, where he died in 1833.

377 Original autograph, C-VII 2) c Writings Duchesne to Rosati, Box 6. On the reverse: "May 31, 1828, Mother Duchesne, St. Louis."

The letters you had the kindness to write me during March reached me only after the one telling me of your happy arrival at the Barrens. We were hoping to see you from day to day, and I did not want to bother you with an answer, when the speedy return of Father Borgna from his visit with you made me decide to write to you of Mother Xavier Miles' deep dislike of our Society and of her explicit wish to return to La Fourche. If it seems wise to you, I shall be happy to allow her to do so, for we certainly cannot do better than she. Besides, it is impossible to accede to Mother Eugenie's desire to put Mother Regis Hamilton there as superior. It would ruin her health and possibly upset her spiritually. The sudden death of her sister[378] was a great shock, and she has been seriously ill several times since then.

Finally, Bishop and true Father, if Mother Xavier Miles can wait until you come to Saint Louis, we will be able to say more for and against this solution in fifteen minutes than in many letters. Meanwhile we are looking after her to the best of our ability. Father Borgna, who will have seen her, will give you his opinion.

I am with profound veneration *in Corde Jesu*, your Excellency's devoted daughter and servant.

Philippine Duchesne sup.
Rel. S. Heart

Saint Louis, May 31, 1828

Letter 314   L. 54 to Mrs. Jouve at Lyon and Mrs. de Mauduit

Saint Louis, June 3, 1828[379]

My dear Sisters,

For a long time I have heard no news of you. Though Aloysia is in Paris, she is scarcely reliable about giving me any. It is also a long time since I have written to you; it is the sacrifice that my new vocation and the distance that separates us demand. I have heard of so many deaths in our family since I have been in America, and deaths of those younger than we, that I no longer know if I can count among the living

---

378 Mathilde Xavier Hamilton, born in 1802, died March 1, 1827, at St. Michael.
379 Copies: *Cahier, Lettres de la Mère Duchesne à sa famille*, pp. 120-123; *Lettres dactylographiées.* C-VII 2) c Duchesne to her family and lay people, Box 5.

all our childhood friends. We said goodbye to one another in this life; now we have only to maintain by good works the sweet hope of being reunited forever in the next.

I am addressing my letter to Mrs. Jouve because I have more certainty of finding her at home. I still do not know if the solitude of Mrs. de Mauduit will have made her decide to leave Grâne, in spite of the precious legacy there of our dear mother and her children, but all these remnants will be collected, revivified, and will have an immortal existence that will bring us to forget all separations in time.

Your friendship expects information about a sister who always loves you. After having lived in Saint Charles on the Missouri as a foothold, and Saint Ferdinand at 7 leagues from here, as our first establishment; after having obtained two in *Louisiana*, a different state from *Missouri*, I have now been in the episcopal city of Saint Louis for a year, in our establishment that is in its infancy but that promises more than the others because of its location in a city that is becoming a clearinghouse of everything that goes to Indian country and to the different settlements on the Missouri and the Mississippi for the trade in pelts and the development of the rich lead mines. I have not yet lost any of my companions from France, but we are divided in the four houses. There are two more planned, but the great difficulty is our small number.

Our holy religion is making much progress in this country through the zeal of the missionaries; and in spite of the return to France of Bishop Dubourg and many priests, God has not left his vineyard without workers. The seminary that was established has already given some good vocations and promises more to come. If it is possible for you to procure a Mass at Notre Dame de Fourvière and one at La Louvesc, you would do a great favor for me.

Please remember me to your husbands, your children, to the Lebrument family, and to our aunts at the Visitation in Romans; I have been told that Melanie is now at Valence.

I wrote the last letter to Mrs. de Rollin; I am afraid that this dear friend whose feelings have been so assaulted by such terrible trials will have quite diminished health.

If Mrs. Jouve is in contact with Mothers Geoffroy and Prevost, superiors of our houses in Lyon, please recommend me to their devoted memory *in Corde Jesu* in whom I am yours,

Philippine

Letter 315 **L. 11 to Father Delacroix**

SS. C. J. M.

St. Anthony
[June 18, 1828][380]

Father,

I do not want to let Mr. Audiament leave without entrusting to him a letter for you. I am late in expressing to you again our gratitude, but for a long time I did not know where you were. Someone said in Ghent, in the Beguinage. This country has suffered some severe losses, but the hope of knowing you are happy and that your days will be prolonged brings consolation to religion and to those who will always be called your daughters.

The houses of Louisiana prosper with the cross, that is, health is poor there, and the children who come for instruction are numerous. At Saint Michael there are more than 70 boarders, 40 at Opelousas. We are being asked for a merger of our Society with the Sisters of the Cross at La Fourche; three of their novices have already taken the habit at Saint Michael; but the professed are more indecisive, and this house does not suit us, so it is possible that it will not go through. The bishop, who should arrive today, will decide it.

The Jesuits, who now have eight priests, also want us at Saint Charles in our former house, on the property where they are building the church, which is not yet complete for lack of money.

The house at Saint Ferdinand holds its own with Mother Octavie, whose health is always bad. I am in Saint Louis, where it was already necessary to build to enlarge the house in which we could lodge only twelve boarders, which was constraining for us; but we have many day students. Still no chaplain. The bishop is going to place another priest here, which will be helpful for us, because we often lack Mass.

I have for companions: Mother Dutour, a Savoyard; Mother Van Damme, Flemish; Mother McKay and Mother [Mary Ann] O'Connor, two Irish; Sister Catherine [Lamarre], and Sister Mary Layton, who has returned from Opelousas.

---

380 Original autograph, C-VII 2) c Writings Duchesne to various Eccles., Box 8. On the reverse: "Mother Duchesne, 1828. No. 8."

Father Saulnier is well but has a great deal to do. He is full of goodness to us, as is Father Lutz who serves Le Cahot and Vuidepoche.[381]

I am with respect in the Heart of Jesus, Father, yours devotedly,

Philippine Duchesne
r.S.C.

June 18, 1828

> [On the reverse:]
> To Father
> Father Delacroix
> Chaplain of the Great Beguinage
> *Ghent, Flanders*

Letter 316   L. 44 to Bishop Rosati

SS. C. J. M.

[June 23, 1828][382]

Dear Bishop,

The mother of one of our children, Mrs. Chouteau, who is lending us her carriage, wants to know what day you are to confer Confirmation. Please be good enough to tell Mr. Lepère.

We had expected a visit from you during Ember Week and had not made our extraordinary confession, which is set for this time, in the hope that you would hear us yourself. I was unable to express this wish to you when you arrived, and now I understand that you are to be away all week. I hope you will give us a few moments sooner or later. I am most anxious for you to know the condition of the house so that you can tell me the truth afterwards.

I have only one difficulty in getting to Saint Ferdinand, and it is that you will need Mr. Lepère to drive you.

I am with respect your devoted daughter and servant.

---

381 The location of Le Cahot is unknown. Vuidepoche is another name for Carondelet, six miles south of Saint Louis.
382 Original autograph, C-VII 2) c Writings Duchesne to Rosati, Box 6. On the reverse: "June 23, 1828 Mother Duchesne."

Philippine Duchesne

June 23

Letter 317   **L. 85 to Mother Barat**

Saint Louis, July 3, 1828[383]

The last two letters I received from Paris were not from you. Instead of the happiness of reading your writing, I learned that you were ill. But good Mother de Charbonnel told me that your fever was nothing to cause anxiety. I have answered dear Mother Ducis,[384] who told me the good news of our foundations in Rome, which redoubles our gratitude to the divine Heart of Jesus. I think that Mother Bigeu, who can draw from this divine source of graces from close up, must have done her part in obtaining such a signal favor. Her circular, sent to us by Mother Eugenie, was full of interest for us.

The reverend father superior was very pleased with your decision for Saint Charles and has asked me to thank you. The bishop is also pleased with your decision for La Fourche. I am sorry that Mother Carmelite cannot be superior there. The bishop, having seen Mother Dutour, asked for her; I refused, but she herself told me in the evening that she could not get rid of the thought that she would go to La Fourche, and I saw that she would be very glad to do so. Everything seemed to come together for this choice, and since a sentence in Mother de Charbonnel's letter showed me that you were leaving me free in the choice of Mother Dutour, I felt empowered to act. I am obliged to withdraw Mother Regis [Hamilton] from Saint Ferdinand, even though she is very useful to Mother Octavie; but I absolutely need her to bring round the children to our house; many do not like it for reasons that you know.

Mother Octavie and I are very busy with our three classes of children, even four here: boarders, orphans, paying day students, and free day students, about 100 children; and we are only eight, including two sisters. Sister Catherine does the French class and is very happy, even though it is difficult for her; she renders us many other services.

---

383 Copy, USA Foundation Haute Louisiane, Box 1, *Lettres de la Haute Louisiane II 1823-1830*, pp. 271-274. J. de Charry, II, 3, L. 238, pp. 63-65; Sweetman et al, pp. 70-72.
384 Catherine de Charbonnel was then assistant and general treasurer; Henriette Ducis, secretary general.

The superior of the Sisters of the Cross at La Fourche,[385] who had come to Florissant presumably to make her novitiate, could not persevere there. The bishop was not happy at this turn of events and does not want her to return to La Fourche. He sent her back to her motherhouse, which shows that it will be better for her two companions [Agnes Cloney[386] and Elizabeth Elder[387]] to make their novitiate elsewhere than at La Fourche, where they might disturb the new order of things. It seems from Bishop Dubourg's letter that he thought all the Sisters of the Cross wanted to join us; but it is only those of La Fourche, who cannot succeed there because they do not know French.

The bishop arrived here on the feast of Saint Aloysius Gonzaga [June 21]. I went with him to Saint Ferdinand on the feast of Saint John [the Baptist, June 24], and the next day to Saint Charles, to see the church and our future house. In Saint Louis, he performed a solemn ordination on the feast of Saint Peter, and gave Confirmation to our children on July 1. He departed on the 2nd, after hearing our confessions and saying Holy Mass in our chapel. He will return in two months. He is taken up with building to enlarge the seminary. Four ecclesiastics have come to him from Paris.

I think Mother Lucile will be for Saint Charles; she expects it and wants it. The Jesuit fathers think highly of her. It would be better to have an American there, but where to find one? We have two or three lovely postulants in the house, and several still in the world who are only 16 years old and who are waiting impatiently for your answer for the dispensation from having to wait until they are 18.

This month of July tells me of your approaching feast, with the happy times when I offered you my wishes from near at hand. While wanting to see my reverend mother, I have never wavered in my vocation, nor have my four traveling companions. We combine this attraction for our mission with an incomparable love for the whole Society and

---

385 Mother Xavier Miles. See note 372.
386 Alice Agnes (Regina) Cloney and Elizabeth (Rose) Elder came from the Barrens; they were only 23 years old. Alice Agnes (Regina) Cloney, RSCJ, was born in Baltimore in 1804 and was a member of the Daughters of the Cross at La Fourche. She joined the Society of the Sacred Heart in 1828, made her first vows in 1830, and her profession on February 23, 1835, at Grand Coteau. She died a few months later.
387 Elizabeth Elder, RSCJ, was born June 15, 1804 (or later), of a family originally from Emmitsburg, Maryland, who settled in Kentucky. She took the name Rose and made her perpetual vows with the Daughters of the Cross on February 21, 1818 (again, an unlikely date). She participated in the foundation of La Fourche in 1825, and was the second sister of this congregation to transfer to the Society of the Sacred Heart, making vows in 1830. She died September 21, 1836, at Grand Coteau.

for its revered mother, before whom I am on my knees *in Corde Jesu* the humblest daughter.

Philippine Duchesne

Letter 318   L. 45 to Bishop Rosati

SS. C. J. M.

[July 14, 1828][388]

Dear Bishop,

I heard with deep sorrow that you are suffering from the same disease that Father De Neckere had. We are praying most fervently for your return to good health, which can be used so advantageously for the glory of God, and for you to be with us permanently. How greatly all who love religion long for this moment!

Dare I ask you, Bishop, to assign a Saint Louis priest to say Holy Mass for us? The responsibility is too great to be overlooked. Fathers Saulnier and Lutz have spent their charity on us in a way that we shall never be able to repay sufficiently; but devoted as they are to their parishioners who absorb their attention, they will leave it to others to say Mass for us. If this matter could be settled, everything could be done more regularly. I tried to get an answer from Father Saulnier, but he said only, "You will have either one or the other sometime." I suggested that he give the youngest children's confessions to Father Loiseul. He disapproved, saying that there are many confessions here, adding that it is a trial for him and that when he comes, he calls that his purgatory. I do not know how to relieve him of them at the moment, for changes are not much use; and I long for the time you have given us reason to hope for. Meanwhile I must be wanting neither in gratitude nor in zeal for the welfare of this house. I will have done everything possible when I have submitted it all to you. Would you add to your touching kindness to us that of settling everything yourself without my seeming to have asked you? Father Richard's arrival would solve everything, but God has his reasons since he is still keeping him.

---

388   Original autograph, C-VII 2) c Writings Duchesne to Rosati, Box 6. On the reverse: "July 14, 1828, Mother Duchesne, St. Louis; received 17th; answered 22nd."

I am with profound veneration in the Heart of Jesus your Excellency's submissive and unworthy servant.

Philippine Duchesne sup.
r. of the Sacred Heart

July 14, 1828

[On the reverse:]
To Bishop
Bishop Rosati
Bishop of Saint-Louis
Barrens

Letter 319   L. 46 to Bishop Rosati

SS. C. J. M.

[July 22, 1828][389]

Dear Bishop,

Mother Xavier Murphy is once more being urged by the citizens to move her establishment into the city of Opelousas or close by. They even went so far as to ask that, in case Mrs. Smith wants take back her donation, we should be ready to give it up.

Mother Xavier strongly urged me to do down. The departure of Mother Dutour on the *North America* gave me a favorable opportunity. As I was not able to have recourse to you, Bishop, I sought the advice of the father superior, who thinks there is no great hurry and that we should wait for permission from our mother general. As to the permission, I am quite sure of it because she has always regretted our founding in small places; several times she has urged me to move the house in Saint Ferdinand either to Saint Louis or to New Orleans.

I came to the conclusion that, as I was unable to act without consulting you again and as it was impossible to have your permission before the departure of the steamboat, it was necessary to forego a trip on which no decision could be reached and which would have many

---

[389] Original autograph, C-VII 2) c Writings Duchesne to Rosati, Box 6. On the reverse: "July 22, 1828, Mother Duchesne, St. Louis. Answered."

disadvantages regarding what I should have to leave behind, as Mother Dutour is leaving a big vacancy here.

It even seems useless to me. If you would have the kindness, please write to Mother Xavier as soon as your work allows, letting her know your wishes in the matter, and at the same time sound out Mrs. Smith without indicating your intention. She wants to return to Opelousas and maybe would be delighted to have the opportunity of having her house back.

If on the other hand, the townspeople are making an equivalent offering, what can we lose? It is a fact of experience in France that convents fare badly in small places and that during the Revolution [of 1789] almost all of them dissolved.

Please use some of your benevolence towards us to guide in this instance your inexperienced daughters who want only the good of religion and who desire only to know your wishes in order to conform to them.

I am with respect your Excellency's obedient daughter.

Philippine Duchesne sup.
r. S. Heart

Saint-Louis, July 22, 1828

[On the reverse:]
To Bishop
Bishop Rosati
Bishop of Saint-Louis
Barrens

Letter 320   **L. 86 to Mother Barat**

Saint Louis, July 22, 1828[390]

Dear Reverend Mother,

The desire to get letters off quickly caused me to make a mistake in sending the accounts of the houses on July 1 with my last letter.[391] I

---

390 Copy, USA Foundation Haute Louisiane, Box 1, *Lettres de la Haute Louisiane II 1823-1830*, pp. 112-113. Cf. J. de Charry, II, 3, L. 240, pp. 68-69; Sweetman et al, pp. 75-77.
391 The house accounts were compiled on January 1 and July 1 and sent to the motherhouse. In her letter of July 3, Philippine forgot that of Florissant and includes it here.

will be more exact in January. I thought that the reading of these two letters from the very hand of the bishop[392] would give you more pleasure. Our mothers advised me to have them copied. Mother Dorival writes to me that you have allowed Saint Michael to invite parents to the distributions of prizes and plays, and that Opelousas was to obtain the same favor. I have a natural aversion to great displays; and having heard nothing about your permission, and on the contrary heard it said that Saint Michael seemed to want to be on different footing from that of the other houses, I replied that I would be astonished, now that cloister has been tightened, if they wanted to do what I have never seen done, either in Grenoble, or in Paris: invitation to the prizes given to seculars, and that in a dissolute land, where there would be major disadvantages in making a spectacle of the young religious.

Mother Octavie is in a pitiful state of suffering with angelic resignation, patience, and courage. It would have been a mortal blow to send her to Opelousas. I think she will not live long, but we need her so much. I have confided her to Saint Regis by the promise of a novena of Masses at La Louvesc, which cost only 9 F. Would you be so kind as to do this for us? This letter will depart tomorrow with Mother Dutour.

I told you in my last letter how Carmelite, by general agreement, was considered unsuitable for the house at La Fourche. The bishop asked for Mother Dutour; I refused her until she said: "I cannot get rid of the thought that it is I who will go to La Fourche." I regarded that inspiration as a sign of the will of God, since at the same time, you had told me to separate her from Mother Xavier [Van Damme], and the children, at least the older ones, could not endure her. Please name her superior. She is leaving with a kind of eagerness. But I think that Mother Eugenie will form the novices better and that they should be left with her.[393] The former [Mother Dutour] is not the type who suits the Americans.

Mother Octavie has sent me her letter open, so I can add mine.

I am at your feet, etc.

Philippine Duchesne

I received with great joy your April letter containing the translation of the Brief. The reverend father [Van Quickenborne] was delighted with it.

---

392 Philippine is sending her two original letters of Bishop Rosati.
393 The novices from La Fourche had been at Saint Michael since January 21.

Letter 321   **L. 87 to Mother Barat**

Saint Louis, July 24, 1828[394]
Rec. to St. Ant. of Padua

Dear Reverend Mother,

Here is my third letter this month. The first contained the account of the expenses of the last six months; the second was enclosed in the one that contained the financial statement of Saint Ferdinand. That second letter went by New Orleans on the same steamboat that took Mother Dutour to go there to establish the house at La Fourche, for which, by common agreement, it was decided that Mother Carmelite would not do. I will not repeat what I said in previous letters, since I have had the experience that under the protection of Saint Anthony, our dear friend, they will all arrive.

We spent your feast day on the cross, without Mass that day, with only one priest in Saint Louis, who was not willing to neglect the parish because of your feast. He came to give us Benediction and Holy Communion; and since on that day we had all the day students, and Mother Dutour was to leave the next day, recreation was put off until today, Thursday. I was very taken up with the idea that I should also go down, since Mother Xavier [Murphy] was urging me strongly to do so because of the pressure she was under from the inhabitants of the town of Opelousas to transfer the school there. When I first heard of it, I spoke to the bishop and he did not approve. Having no possibility to have his answer before the departure of the steamboat, I consulted the reverend father by a night express letter. His answer was that he did not see this journey to be useful; I was very glad for this decision.

I wrote to Mother Xavier that she could begin the subscription for the building, which should be carried out in such a way as to honor the neighborhood; that they should see where she says it will be, without pledging herself to anything as long as she does not have the permission of her superiors and until she actually receives it. Since my answer from France may be long in coming, it is a matter of neither suppressing nor making a new establishment,[395] but only of situating it in the midst of a larger population, with greater advantages for spiritual and material help.

---

394 Copy, USA Foundation Haute Louisiane, Box 1, *Lettres de la Haute Louisiane II 1823-1830*, pp. 121-123. Cf. J. de Charry, II, 3, L. 241, pp. 70-72; Sweetman et al, pp. 77-80.
395 Since this is not a new foundation or the suppression of a house, she could act without the explicit permission of the superior general.

I also wrote to the bishop to please give his opinion to Mother Xavier directly and that I was certain of your permission, since you always regret seeing us in small towns or open countryside, like Grand Coteau.

The subscribers hope to profit by the sale of the house and lands given by Mrs. Smith. But since she is still alive and she regrets having left Opelousas, I feel certain that if we leave the house, she will take it back for herself. The reverend father told me that we had made an agreement with her, but that her donation was to the bishop, and the bishop gave it to us. Nothing could be better arranged than by him, and you will see by the two letters that I sent you previously, how favorably disposed he is toward us. He has also written to Rome to have Jesuits to locate on the other part of the land given to the church, which also includes the church and the presbytery, which however is too small for a school. So I said to the father superior: "If you agree to go to that parish, there would be fewer difficulties if you were to go into our house that cost so much to make it suitable for a boarding school." He did not want to give any response. Perhaps there will be a more favorable one from Rome. I am telling you here what I did, hoping at the same time that Mother Xavier wrote before me, and that it is possible that she had your permission before they began or refused the project of the transfer. Mother Dutour has left a large hole here, so that it would have been difficult for me to get away.

The Brief has filled us with consolation, as does your recovery. Please, dear and revered Mother, name the superiors of La Fourche, Saint Ferdinand, and Saint Charles. I think for this last, it is Mother Lucile. She is rather expecting it.

Mother Octavie has been very distressed by the loss of Mother Regis, though we had decided on this at our last meeting.[396] Fortunately, besides Mother Lucile, she has an excellent novice, very talented, who is making the reputation of the house by her beautiful voice and her piano playing, for which she can give lessons, something eagerly desired in Opelousas.

I am at your feet and in the sorrowful Heart of Jesus, your unworthy daughter.

Philippine Duchesne

---

396   Eulalie Hamilton, called Regis, whom Philippine had moved from Florissant to Saint Louis.

Letter 322   **L. 47 to Bishop Rosati**

SS. C. J. M.

[August 25, 1828][397]

Dear Bishop,

I have just received a letter from our superior general, to whom I had given an account of our new building and the debts it caused. Our mother spoke of it to one of the priests in the royal chaplaincy who influenced the Commission of the Propagation of the Faith to give us some help, and it has set aside the sum of $2,000, possibly three, for us. We must, however, receive the money from you, and it ought to have been sent to you at the same time as my letter or shortly afterwards. Our mother tells me also that the fathers have not been forgotten, without being more specific. Doubtless everything will be sent to you as the head and father of the Mission.

You will see, Bishop, in the papers I am enclosing that Mother Xavier asked me to send you, that the fathers of the families who want the transfer of the establishment have opened the subscription. She had received neither your answer nor Father Jeanjean's nor mine, which worried her greatly.

I have found the reasons for the change explained in a very winning manner, and if you had the goodness to make it agreeable to Mrs. Smith in order to avoid any complaint, it seems to me that it should be done, unless your letters and letters to me that arrive later put an end to the matter. Once the fire of desire dies out, it cannot be relighted; and if some mishap should occur in that lonely place, we should have to blame ourselves for not profiting from the generous dispositions of some inhabitants. It seems good to me also that Mrs. Smith thinks it is only a proposal. And actually there is nothing definite. I continue to believe that our superior [general] will agree to the change if it has your approval.

Father Loiseul is very good to us and very punctual. Father Dusaussoy seems cold and unhappy. I think he expected more attentiveness on our part since he is related to our mother. I am moving forward the

---

397   Original autograph, C-VII 2) c Writings Duchesne to Rosati, Box 6. On the reverse: "August 25, 1828, Mother Duchesne, St. Louis; received 27th; answered 28th."

arrangements with Father Richard, who writes me that he still wishes to die in our house.

I am with deep respect your Excellency's most devoted daughter and servant.

Philippine Duchesne sup.
r. S. Heart

Saint Louis, August 25, 1828

[On the reverse:]
To Bishop
Bishop Rosati
Bishop of Saint-Louis
Barrens

Letter 323 **L. 88 to Mother Barat**

SS. C. J. M.

Saint Louis, August 25, 1828[398]
St. Ant.

Reverend and dear Mother,

I have just received your letter of June 6, which gives me even greater proof of your maternal concern for us and tells me of the help of 2 or 3 thousand F from the Society for the Propagation of the Faith, another source of hope for our fathers. I have written to the bishop according to your intention to tell him what he was to receive for us. At the same time, I sent him two pages of the Louisiana newspaper about the transfer of the establishment of Grand Coteau to the town of Opelousas. He did not approve of it, but Mother Xavier [Murphy] asked me to send it to him. They are really fascinating because of their tactful praises of the establishment and the advantages that the change of location will bring to the town, for parents and for children. For to what dangers could an establishment not be exposed in a solitary location? When she weighs

---

[398] Original autograph, C-VII 2) c Duchesne to Barat, Box 2. Postmarks: Le Havre, April 4, 1829; Paris, April 5, 1829. Partial copy, USA Foundation Haute Louisiane, Box 1, *Lettres de la Haute Louisiane II 1823-1830,* pp. 125- 128. J. de Charry, II, 3, L. 242, pp. 73-76; Sweetman et al, pp. 80-84.

these advantages, Mother Xavier suffers from not having a decision from her superiors. The editor of the newspaper himself subscribed for 2500 F, a senator for 1500, and others just as much; and they think that the Louisiana Legislature will contribute. They think the house, if it is built as it should be, will cost 80,000 F.

On the other hand, there is the unhappiness of the foundress of Grand Coteau, the cost of moving, furniture, etc., because the house would be given up with no return, although it would remain in the town if we left. I advised Mother Xavier to let the subscription run, so that while waiting, we could hope for your response. But since I also told her that I was strongly convinced of your approval, perhaps the fear of losing the enthusiasm that could not be reestablished later may well have led her to begin the move. We need two months for an answer, the same for the bishop, because letters going through the post take a month or more to go and just as long to come. There are great drawbacks or rather great inconveniences to always be obliged to go 5 leagues for a doctor, for meat, etc.

Mother Octavie's health is still deplorable. Now she has two sores, one on her neck bone and the other on her shoulder, which make every movement painful. Far from being able to go to Opelousas, at least 300 leagues away, she could not go 5 leagues in a good carriage to come here. God has called her from such a distance that I still hope to keep her. She teaches her classes with great courage and clearly is growing in every virtue, but perhaps that is because her time is coming. And after what you told me about having her change place with Mother Dorival, which is impossible, here is what I have to propose to you if God takes her: 1) to put Mother Xavier Van Damme *(words crossed out, illegible)* with Mother Xavier [Murphy] in Opelousas, which has only children of good background; 2) to put Mother Dorival at Saint Michael to free up Eugenie from that house *(illegible words)*, and Eugenie in Saint Louis. The two latest arrivals [Helen Dutour and Xavier Van Damme] have not succeeded here, either with the parents or with the children: I received the compliment that at the beginning we gave a better education. That was attributed to Mother Eugenie. She would set the tone in this house, which is important to demonstrate. She can deal with English and French parents *(words crossed out, illegible)*. And I would return to Saint Ferdinand, Mother Lucile at Saint Charles, and Mother Dutour at La Fourche. She will not succeed here in a large house. Mother Eugenie promised two religious to replace the one she asked for to be superior at La Fourche [Helene Dutour]. The steamboat returned with no one, no letter, and without news of Mother Dutour, which upsets me very much. There is the same silence with Opelousas, where they are complaining about it.

This delay in sending religious is going to hamper the establishment at Saint Charles, which is so desired. Mother Benoît [Claudine Maujot] could not be superior there, since she does not understand a word of English. She would be better at La Fourche, where there are more French than Americans. There are also her age and her health; we would have more need of teachers of needlework and writing who are young enough to learn English. There were several with Mother Vincent [at Bordeaux] who would do very well as assistants.

Mrs. Smith is complaining of a failure to keep promises. If we only had three sisters, we could keep up a little boarding school there helped by the big one [that would be in the town of Opelousas]. There is no need for a trousseau here; with three of each, one is supplied;[399] we wash every week. If persecution breaks out [in France], wouldn't you be glad to keep land and a house worth 80,000 F that cost more than that? If you want to have two houses in Opelousas, Mother Benoît would do well at Grand Coteau, in the French section.

As for the vestments that you were so kind to promise me, we have enough now, because at Saint Ferdinand and at Saint Charles, the fathers' sacristy suffices; they have been well supplied from Flanders. What we lack are cinctures, and medium-size white and yellow braid to use with the beautiful dresses brought by our sisters to make vestments. They are cheaper in Lyon; and text books: Gospels, Sacred History, Lhomond's Grammar, mythology, and science summaries. Arithmetic and geography have to be taught in English. We really need [the *Treatise on Christian Perfection* of] Rodriguez in that language. It will have to come from England or Ireland. There are none in America. Besides all this, money is the most necessary thing when one is founding a house. Saint Charles will cost us at least 3000 F.

Father Dusaussoy is coming here *(illegible words)*. They are keeping him for the college, but doing the simple abc's frightens and disgusts him.

Several times the bishop has offered to the fathers the church, presbytery, and lands around Grand Coteau; those who are here have refused it. He has written to Europe. Why do they not put down a foot in this place where it would be easy to establish a college and, if our sisters leave their house nearby, it would be adequate for that? There is also plenty to do there for missionaries. They are near Mexico, another

---

399 It suffices to have every part of the trousseau in triplicate.

liberal country where the clergy are corrupt. They publically admit women in certain quarters.

I am finding my paper short, and the quick moments when I am at your feet. I call myself your unworthy daughter in the Sacred Heart.

Philippine Duchesne r. S. Heart

[On the reverse:]
To Mother
Mother superior of the Civil and Military Hospital
To deliver to
Mother Barat superior of the Sacred Heart
Rue de Varenne in Paris
By way of Le Havre
Department of the Seine

Letter 324   **L. 89 to Mother Barat**

SS. C. J. M.

Saint Louis, September 11, 1828[400]
St. Ant.

Dear Reverend Mother,

I wrote to you less than a month ago by way of New Orleans, and since there are fewer ships leaving for France from that city, I fear that my letter was delayed. I am sending this by New York, hoping it will come more speedily. It appears that the inhabitants of Opelousas have not waited for the responses that Mother Xavier wanted before undertaking the transport of her establishment to their town. They present it in the newspaper in glowing colors. I am too far away to follow their plans. I shared the page of the newspaper with the bishop, who agrees to the change and has written to the foundress of Grand Coteau.

Since this affair, Mother Xavier [Murphy] has been ill, and I think her illness is due to the state of anxiety in which she found herself, not having the answers that would authorize her to act sure of not failing in

---

400 Original autograph, C-VII 2) c Duchesne to Barat, Box 2. Postmarks: Le Havre, October 28, 1828; Paris, October 30, 1828. This letter arrived at its destination before that of August 25, which arrived April 5, 1829. Certain passages covered in ink have not been able to be reconstituted. Cf. J. de Charry, II, 3, L. 243, pp. 77-80; Sweetman et al, pp. 85-89.

her duty. She complains, as do I, of the silence of Mother Eugenie. I do not understand it, and I fear lest too much adulation where she is will weaken the bonds of our union and harm it. After having considered all sides, I am repeating my proposal to put Mother Van Damme [if she is willing] in Opelousas, where a French person is indispensable, Mother Dorival at Saint Michael, Mother Eugenie in Saint Louis and *the old lady*[401] at Saint Ferdinand, where poor Mother Octavie is going, to our great regret. Two wounds on her chest and a slow fever leave little ground for hope; but the more her heart weakens, the more her sensitive and grateful soul clings to her spouse and sacrifices herself as he did on her bed of suffering.

If these changes are approved, they will give rise to many protests, which could be forestalled if our common mother would indicate her place to each one with that art that sweetens everything. I do not have this gift. I was quite sure that having given Mother Dutour to La Fourche, I would receive the two promised replacements for our house. I have not failed to insist on having them; but not only did the steamboat make a special stop at our request and bring no one, but neither the boat nor the post has brought any letter to us since that time to explain the behavior of Mother Eugenie. I have the one from Mother Dutour, who has already borrowed 4000 F on the Bank of Louisiana to carry on. It will be very difficult for her to recoup it with boarding fees, and from what I have seen, I do not think she is a good business manager. And she plans to give the same education there.[402]

I wrote to the bishop to speak with him about the 2,000 pounds of which he knew nothing, and he says he had nothing from the same fund last year except travel funds for some of his people. Things have gotten a little murky here between him and my brothers [of Florissant].[403] The establishment of a college planned by the two sides is the cause. May God take it in hand, and the dear home country, too. I do not hear much news, but what I hear is distressing. Mother Xavier convinces herself that the misfortunes of one country will *bring blessings* for hers, and that she will obtain what has often been wanted in her neighborhood,

---

401 Philippine speaks of herself here.
402 H. Dutour wanted to give the same level of education as at Saint Michael and Grand Coteau, but at La Fourche, the students were from more modest backgrounds and not very wealthy. The expenses thus exceeded the resources.
403 The episcopal college (secondary level) of Saint Louis was founded in 1818 by Bishop Dubourg and confided to the cathedral clergy, whose parish tasks were too heavy to assume this role. Closed in 1827, it was redeemed after difficult negotiations by Father Van Quickenborne, who had pursued it since 1824. It was reopened by Peter Verhaegen on November 7, 1829, and grew into Saint Louis University.

but where sometimes impressions that are opposed to her happiness are propagated in people's minds by different articles in the newspapers, etc.[404]

The person whose letter I sent you [Father Van Quickenborne] is now very happy with us; but the weak condition of Mother Octavie, which makes the help of Mother Lucile necessary, is delaying Saint Charles, for which house he thinks her completely unsuitable, and that she should never be in charge. This is because of the imagination that makes her always think that *everything is going well* and makes her a little independent and too confident in herself, too little aware of the need of supervision. The worst thing is that she is planning to go there and to do quite well. What a good thing it is to know oneself! To regard oneself below what one really is. Given all these things, confirmed by Sister Hamilton, who has the confidence of everyone at Saint Ferdinand and so is better able than anyone to know how things stand, Mother Benoît would be necessary at Saint Charles. Sister Hamilton says that Saint Ferdinand is languishing, that people do not have confidence in Mother Octavie, that the children do not like her, that she is very sad, which depresses those around her, that she does not dare to say anything to Mother Lucile, who manages everything and not very economically, and that the children say they can do whatever they want with the latter, etc.

The house that the village of Opelousas wants to build by subscription will be able to accommodate 80 children and employees. It will be given in perpetuity unless we leave the region, and one child in ten will be accepted free. Nothing was concluded, but the desire is so lively that they did not wait for consent to advertise in the newspaper and open a subscription. The first one promised 2500 F, the second, a senator, 1500. The children who are there belong to those in the Legislature of Louisiana, who are invited in the article to contribute.

If Mrs. Smith, the foundress, does not take back her donation, she would be a great help, if she consents, for the brothers whom we want, or for placing two or three of ours who would be recruited little by little.[405] If you send several of those whom you call supernumerary, they would be very useful; it would be better to borrow here for the journey.

---

404 If the French Jesuits were expelled by the revolution, which appeared imminent then, Louisiana would be able to receive them. But the American newspapers repeated the calumnies that circulated about them in France.
405 Philippine proposes in the case of a transfer to Opelousas to leave a few religious at Grand Coteau to continue a school, or to offer the house to the Jesuits to begin a college.

Here we are suffering persecution for justice' sake: the apostasy of several of our children makes them and their families our enemies, and then what is not said about us? Mother Eugenie is the best one to reestablish confidence. If you put her in Saint Charles, I beg you not to say that I suggested it.

I am writing to my dear Father Perreau by way of New Orleans, remind him, please…*(sentence left in suspense)*.

I am with profound respect *in Corde Jesu*,

Ph. Duchesne r.S.C.

My respect to Fathers Joseph [Varin] and Louis [Barat], please.

[On the reverse:]\
To Mother\
Mother Barat Superior General\
of the houses of the Sacred Heart\
Rue de Varenne\
Paris\
By way of New York

Letter 325   **L. 90 to Mother Barat**

SS. C. J. M.

Saint Louis, October 21, 1828[406]

Dear Reverend Mother,

I have just received the letters confided to Father Martial,[407] two small ones from you and several from your holy brother, with six notebooks, of which the one about Rome greatly interested us. How many proofs of God's providence for us! How could we not trust it? I hope that all

---

406 Manuscript copy of Mother Ducis, C-VII 2) c Duchesne to Barat, Box 2. Some passages have been deleted, replaced by suspension points. Another copy, CVII-2) c) Duchesne: Letters to RSCJ and children, Box 4. Letter written soon after Philippine's return from Saint Charles, where the consecration of the new parish church and the reopening of the Sacred Heart school in the Duquette house next to the church took place. Cf. J. de Charry, II, 3, L. 245, pp. 85-88; Sweetman et al, pp. 94-98.

407 Bertrand Martial, former vicar general of Bishop Dubourg, had separated from him because of disagreements and returned to Europe in June 1826. This means that he later returned to America.

your difficulties will be mitigated and will result in glory for the Heart of Jesus. Among all the things that Mother De Coppens[408] told us were coming, there was mention of a cope and a statue of Our Lady given by Miss de Cassini; but these have not arrived, and we would be very sorry if they were lost. The reverend fathers have put into their new church [of Saint Charles] all their best vases and vestments, and there are enough, but the altar is absolutely bare. We have given the frontal made from the beautiful pink dress, along with flowers, altar cloths, etc. But we have only lent the beautiful candlesticks given by Mother de Marbeuf, which provide the only adornment for our church at Saint Ferdinand. They would like to keep them at Saint Charles, but it was impossible to leave them there. If Mother De Coppens had the means to get us some that are a little taller, for the church requires this, she would fill Mother Lucile with joy as well as the one who gave the church.

We saw again at Saint Ferdinand several of our former students, for whom all our care has not been lost. Several have died fervently, and those who remain are more civilized than most and are faithful for the most part. We had to put in an appearance, especially Octavie for the English speakers. Mother Lucile and the Irish woman [Mary Ann O'Connor] were complete strangers in this part of the country. The bishop wanted all our sisters to be present at the ceremony,[409] but I represented to him our stricter cloister, our work, and the expense, all of which would be a great obstacle.

For several days, I got together several coins of 25 *sols* for the baker, stopping all other expenditures, and I did not see any way to be able to give something to Mother Lucile for Saint Charles except by borrowing. Finally, the day before, Mother Dutour sent me 25 F that will suffice for the first needs. They have food for now, and then the children will come, nearly all day students; and it will be necessary for a time, if you permit, for them to pay in order to give support and for the upkeep of the church. They have stopped taking day students at Saint Ferdinand since we have taken some at Saint Louis, thinking that the permission is only for one house. If you agree, it will now be for two [Florissant and Saint Charles] until we can pay the debts about which I am somewhat constrained.... The chapel and the dormitory cost 6000 F more than

---

408 Anne De Coppens, RSCJ (1797-1837), was born in Ghent, entered the Sacred Heart in 1820, then left briefly for reasons of health. In 1828, professed at Paris, she asked to go to America. She arrived in Saint Louis with Henriette de Kersaint on August 24, 1831. She had a difficult and unstable character, and went from Missouri to Louisiana from 1831 to 1835. She returned to France in August 1836 and died in Amiens the next year.

409 Octavie returned to Florissant and Philippine to Saint Louis, leaving Lucile Mathevon and Mary Ann O'Connor at Saint Charles to begin the school.

we thought. The fact is that I had counted on 10,000 F promised on one hand and 2000 F on the other that cannot be given to us now, and the bishop has not received the 2000 F that you told me were coming from Father Perreau.

We have only seven boarders [in Saint Louis], and among them are three whose fees are paid a year in advance. You see that with 5000 F of debt for the chapel, 3000 F promised in reimbursement for the house, garden and beautiful orchard in Saint Charles, and some other debts of about 1000 F, we could not survive without the payment from day students. We will do it all for free as soon as possible, and even now, except for our orphans, we have some free day students. Those who have paid want nothing better than to leave us for the winter. If 15 remain, we will have to be satisfied; and in spite of our lack of money and vocations, we had to go to Saint Charles to keep our promises.

The house at Opelousas is going very well. La Fourche is doing well, too. They wrote to the bishop that Mother Dutour has 22 children and is charming all the inhabitants. As for Mother Eugenie, she could not be more highly esteemed and successful!... Sister Maria Lévêque,[410] whom Mother Eugenie sent me, made her first vows here yesterday. If your "flower" is for Rome, would you not have a few green leaves for Saint Charles and for us? To read, write, and work are the essentials after virtue....

I am at your feet, Reverend Mother, your respectful daughter,

Philippine Duchesne r. S. C.

[The copyist, Mother Ducis, wrote these few words on the address of the superior to whom she sent this letter]:

What can I add, dear Mother, to such edifying things? When reading these letters, one absorbs the trace of such rare virtue, one is full of admiration. May not we, after the example of these so perfect mothers, so zealous for the glory of the Sacred Heart, respond more than ever to the graces of which he is for us the inexhaustible source. (....)

It is from the Heart of Jesus that we await all our consolation, and it is also in him that I renew the assurance of the sentiments with which I am,

Ducis, Secretary

---

410 Maria Lévêque, RSCJ (1793-1833), was the eldest of six sisters who entered the novitiate at Saint Michael between 1825 and 1830. Born in New Orleans, she entered at Saint Michael on December 26, 1825, took the habit April 6, 1826, and arrived in Saint Louis September 23, 1828, with Eulalie Guillot, a novice who came from La Fourche (these were the two sisters sent by Eugenie Audé in exchange for Helene Dutour). She made first vows on October 20, 1828, in Saint Louis. As her health could not stand the Missouri climate, she returned to Louisiana on November 7, 1829, accompanying Philippine Duchesne. Sent to Saint Michael in 1832, she died of cholera in 1833.

Letter 326   **L. 48 to Bishop Rosati**

SS. C. J. M.

[October 1828][411]

Dear Bishop,

I cannot tell you how sorry I am not to be able to give you a larger offering for the great number of good works that you have to look after. I hope it will not always be this way.

I am sending you all I have for the moment for Father Loiseul; if he could wait, I would replace this small amount later; but in our present straitened circumstances, I do not think I can give him more than $35 per quarter. The reason I am asking him to wait is that I would like today's $25 to go toward your priests' traveling expenses, for the glory of God.

I am with respect your Excellency's submissive and devoted daughter.

Philippine Duchesne
r. S. Heart

[October 1828]

If Father Dusaussoy continues to come, it is impossible to pay twice.

Letter 327   **L. 1 to Bishop Dubourg**[412]

[October 21, 1828]

Dear Bishop,

I have not had the honor of a reply to the letter I had the honor of addressing to you at the time of the foundation of our convent in Saint Louis. I am not the only one who complains of your silence and is pained by it. Each time I ask news of you I am told that you do not write. The same is true of Father Niel. Can you have forgotten the land you watered with your sweat and tears or the people who were subject to you and who often recall the one to whom they owe so much? They may have

---

411 Original autograph, C-VII 2) c Writings Duchesne to Rosati, Box 6. On the reverse: "October 1828, Mother Duchesne, St. Louis; answered in person."
412 Copies, C-VII 2) c Writings Duchesne to various Eccles., Box 8; A-II 2) g, Box 2, *Lettres intéressantes de la Société, N° 2*, pp. 20-22.

rebelled at the orders of their pastor,[413] but they are not ungrateful and your name is never spoken by them without respect.

You not only gave me permission to write to you; you even recommended out of love for your children, that I give you news of them at times, and I have never had a better opportunity than this to do so. On October 12, the day indicated by you for honoring the Holy Angels, I assisted for the first time in my life at the consecration of a church. It was that of Saint Charles, built at the cost of the Jesuits, who have put into it all the money they have received for their support and even for that of their Indian pupils, who are now greatly reduced in numbers. The church faces the Missouri River, standing on what had been our garden, at the very place where you lent an episcopal hand in uprooting a little tree. It is made of stone, very pretty, and is completely finished except for the sacristy.

Bishop Rosati, who officiated at the ceremony, was assisted by all the Jesuits, by two Vincentians, and by several young men from his seminary. While he was making the first circuits of the building, Father De Theux preached in English, then Father Dusaussoy in French, to the crowd assembled before the door of the church. These people had never seen so magnificent a ceremony. Your beautiful dalmatics were used. Next day the bishop gave Confirmation to sixty-six people, among them Mrs. Spincer of Dardenne, a convert from Protestantism like all her family. That very day she and her husband brought us their daughter, also a convert, who desires to become a religious. I left soon after this with Mother Octavie, whom the bishop had wanted me to bring to this ceremony in spite of her infirmities, which keep us in constant dread of losing her. The bishop and the clergy remained to bless the new cemetery. A sermon he preached on that occasion made a deep impression. We also left behind in our former house, Mothers Lucile and Mary Ann, Irish, to begin our sixth house in Louisiana. The house is so run down, without windows, so that I had to serve breakfast to the bishop with the shutters closed. I put a copious helping of salt in his coffee, not being able to distinguish it from the local sugar.

As I said our sixth convent, you may ask where the fifth one is. It is at La Fourche in the very house used by the Sisters of the Cross who united with us, all except the superior, who is really quite ill. She came to Florissant but could not remain with us and so returned to her motherhouse. Afterwards, only two stayed with us. The convent at

---

413 Bishop Dubourg resigned as bishop of Louisiana and Florida as a result of conflicts with the "lay trustees" who were the proprietors of the churches' property. Arriving in France in November 1826, he was named bishop of Montauban.

Saint Michael has eighty boarding students and in no way harms that of the Ursuline religious, who have more than one hundred. There are forty at Opelousas, and after two months La Fourche should have thirty. Everywhere there has been the need to enlarge or to repair the buildings. As a result, there is no more ready money in the convents in Louisiana than there is in Missouri, though Florissant has only twelve boarding students and here we have only eight, with about eighty day students, most of them in the free school. I have been obliged to borrow in order to erect a chapel. Bishop Rosati blessed it yesterday, the twentieth, and received the first vows of Sister Maria Lévêque, who had the happiness of being one of the first to receive the first *(word missing)* from your hands at Saint Michael.

Now there are eighteen at Saint Michael, counting the novices. Father Lutz is on a mission among the Indians. The Feves River[414] is a district that is being rapidly settled because of the lead mines, and the people there are asking earnestly for a priest, but they have not obtained one yet. There are two Jesuit fathers and a brother at Saint Charles carrying on a ministry and a free school. They are taking up a subscription in Saint Louis in order to offer the same advantage there, and they are putting their best men to it. Meanwhile they have some boys from Saint Louis at Florissant where Father De Theux is pastor. The father superior's health is very poor, but he oversees all that is done. Father Saulnier continues to take good care of his flock; he is helped by Father Loiseul, a Creole priest.

In sending this letter, I must certainly count on your indulgence, Bishop, for it has taken me a long time to write it, and if I put it aside now, I do not know when I shall take it up again. There are so few of us, and there is so much work to be done.

I am with the greatest respect, Bishop, your lordship's obedient and devoted daughter.

Philippine Duchesne
Religious of the S.H.

P.S. We expect in a few days four Sisters of Charity for a hospital. Mr. Mullanphy is giving more than 30,000 F for that.

---

414 The Fèves (Beans) River took its name from the large quantity of wild beans that grew along its banks. It crosses Wisconsin and Illinois to empty into the Mississippi. Today it is called the Galena River after the name of a mining town founded in 1826.

Letter 328   L. 49 to Bishop Rosati

SS. C. J. M.

[November 7, 1828][415]

Dear Bishop,

You already know of the arrival of the four Sisters of Charity, of the superior's illness and that they are staying with us at Mr. Mullanphy's request. Therefore I will not go into detail.

The reason for my letter is the subject of one I received from Mother Eugenie enclosing a copy of a clipping from the newspaper giving the prospectus of Mother Dutour's school, a thing contrary to our customs. But what Mother Eugenie is complaining about is that all the subjects we teach are offered with board at a lower price, which will necessarily take children away from Saint Michael and possibly prevent her from paying her debts. She adds that there is a movement in La Fourche to cause Saint Michael to fall in favor of La Fourche.

I find too that Mother Dutour has taken no notice whatever of the things that had been decided for her establishment:

1. She has borrowed money that was not entirely necessary.

2. She has said that the same education would be given in her house as at Saint Michael.

3. On her own authority she has given Sister Rose the rank of choir religious, not being the superior; it is only the mother general who can name her so. I have told her all this, but I do not expect that it will have any effect in preventing what Mother Eugenie fears, especially if the school in La Fourche is enlarged.

I beg you, therefore, Bishop, to insist:

1. That the house not be enlarged at all without your express permission;

2. That the children not number more than thirty;

3. That no other history except Bible history be taught; that neither *globes, mythology,* nor *literary verse* shall be taught and only the four operations of *arithmetic*; and explain all this to these gentlemen who are giving to this establishment, because it is not good to judge by first impressions.

---

415   Original autograph, C-VII 2) c Writings Duchesne to Rosati, Box 6. On the reverse: "Nov. 7, 1828, Mother Duchesne, St. Louis; received Dec. 10; answered in person."

Mother Dutour has few religious and is in poor health, and if she does too much after having done harm to Saint Michael, which has debts to pay, she would then see her own house closed. It is better to go slowly and carefully.... She will not have paid her debts if the number of children is reduced. There are already fewer in Opelousas and very few here.

Forgive me, Bishop, for taking your attention for our business, but I know I am speaking to a father who encourages full confidence in her who is very happy to be able to call herself your most devoted servant and daughter.

Philippine Duchesne
r. S. C.

November 7, 1828

Letter 329   **L. 91 to Mother Barat**

Saint Louis, November 28, 1828[416]

Dear Reverend Mother,

The last news I had of Europe came to me through Mother Eugenie. It was an account by Mother Armande de Causans of her visit to the Holy Father. I have always thought that you would go to visit her new and interesting foundation, and that my letters would not be able to find you in Paris; so as a result, a little after my last letter to your address, I sent one to Mother Ducis' address, since I was charged by the bishop, in his travel during the month of October, to remind Father Perreau of his request for his diocese, because he received no direct reply.

In his last visit this month, the object of which was the establishment of the Sisters of Charity of Maryland for the hospital,[417] he told me the good news that he had at last received a satisfactory response from Father Petit in Lyon. He told him he has 1) 25,000 F for him, of which about 9000 is to pay off debts; 2) 6000 F for the fathers; 3) 6000 F applicable

---

416   Copies, C-III 1: USA Foundation Haute Louisiane, Box 3, *Lettres, Relations de voyages, Louisiane,* pp. 7-8; USA Foundation Haute Louisiane, Box 1, *Lettres de la Haute Louisiane II 1823-1830,* pp. 147- 150. Cf. J. de Charry, II, 3, L. 246, pp. 89-90; Sweetman et al, pp. 99-100.

417   The Sisters of Charity of Saint Joseph, founded in 1809 at Emmitsburg, near Baltimore, Maryland, by Saint Elizabeth Seton, née Bayley (1774-1821). Mother Xavier Love and three companions arrived in Saint Louis on November 1, 1828, to organize the hospital founded by Mr. Mullanphy, lodged at the Sacred Heart for the first three weeks.

for other debts for travel of missionaries and printing of books for the mission. That leaves 4000 F, from which he told him to give something to the Religious of the Sacred Heart if they need it. The most that the bishop proposed to give was 1000 F, and I assure you that with the detail with which he told me of his tight situation, I would not have had the courage to take it. I would prefer to keep going. So what you told me was coming will be reduced to nothing here. With the reputation for opulence that our houses have, no one will take much pity on us; and I myself sense that as much as possible, we should give of our temporal goods to the pastors. What is a bishop without revenue? A seminary where he has to furnish everything for the young people out of funds supplied by Providence?

I have to tell you that with regard to Opelousas, the change of house is still undecided. Mother Xavier [Murphy], under the pretext that she cannot express herself well in French, begs me to ask you for two religious, for whom she will pay traveling expenses and trousseau. The essential for them would be knowledge of the French language and if possible, piano and drawing; note that the two artists need not have great strength.

I am at your feet *in Corde Jesu* your unworthy daughter,

Philippine Duchesne

Letter 330   **L. 1 to Mother Boilvin**[418]

SS. C. J. M.

[December 31, 1828]

My dear Adeline,

It is with great pleasure that I will see you bearing the name of a saint of whom I hope you will live the characteristics. So choose among *Louise*, *Louisia* or *Gonzaga*, because *Aloysia* is already taken.

I hope that Mother Octavie's illness, far from harming the regularity of the novitiate, will draw down many graces. Your good hearts will be happy to obtain for her the deepest satisfaction in the midst of her sufferings: that of seeing you labor courageously to merit the title of spouses of the most perfect and most tender of bridegrooms.

---

418   Julie Adeline Boilvin, RSCJ (1813-1848), entered at Florissant in 1828, made her vows in 1831 in Saint Louis, and her profession at Florissant in 1838. She was one of Philippine's most beloved novices, a novice at the time of this letter. She died in Canada.

You more than any other can contribute to this fervor; the yoke of the Lord that you have carried with joy from your youth makes you more fit for religious virtue and to march under the standard of the Heart of Jesus, upon which one sees written only *littleness, simplicity, recollection, obedience, regularity, silence, sacrifice.*

May they be able to say of you what they said of the patron you have chosen, of Berchmans and of several religious I have known, that you have never on your own neglected the practice of a single observance. This is the happiness that I wish you as I call myself all devotedly yours in the Sacred Heart,

Philippine Duchesne
r.S.C.

December 31 [1828]

Say something for me to each of your companions.

[On the reverse:]
To Mother
Mother Boilvin
Novice of the Sacred Heart
At Saint Ferdinand

www.ingramcontent.com/pod-product-compliance
Lightning Source LLC
Chambersburg PA
CBHW070516010526
44118CB00012B/1023